The

# 100-YEAR WAR

Between

# MONOPOLY POWER

and

# DEMOCRACY

# GOLIATH

## MATT STOLLER

*Simon & Schuster*
New York   London   Toronto   Sydney   New Delhi

Simon & Schuster
1230 Avenue of the Americas
New York, NY 10020

First Simon & Schuster hardcover edition October 2019

SIMON & SCHUSTER and colophon are registered
trademarks of Simon & Schuster, Inc.

For information about special discounts for bulk purchases,
please contact Simon & Schuster Special Sales at 1-866-506-1949
or business@simonandschuster.com.

The Simon & Schuster Speakers Bureau can bring authors to
your live event. For more information or to book an event, contact
the Simon & Schuster Speakers Bureau at 1-866-248-3049 or
visit our website at www.simonspeakers.com.

Interior design by Lewelin Polanco

Manufactured in the United States of America

1  3  5  7  9  10  8  6  4  2

Library of Congress Cataloging-in-Publication Data has been applied for.

ISBN 978-1-5011-8308-9
ISBN 978-1-5011-8309-6 (ebook)

# CONTENTS

# PREFACE

"Power always thinks it has a great Soul, and vast Views, beyond the Comprehension of the Weak, and that it is doing God's Service, when it is violating all his Laws."

**—John Adams**[1]

. . . . . . . . . . . . .

M ary Russell of *The Washington Post* called them the "Red Guard of the Revolution."[2]

In January of 1975, a giant crop of angry and newly elected Democrats—nicknamed "Watergate Babies"—came to Washington, D.C. They were long-haired, young, aggressive, and progressive, determined to clean up government and stop the war in Vietnam and they flooded into Congress. The raw number of pickups understated the change to the Democratic Party itself. Due to retirements, there were seventy-five new Democrats in the House of Representatives alone, many young, eager, and disdainful of the party hierarchy. More than 40 percent of all Democrats in the House had served for less than six years.[3] The white whale of liberals, Richard Nixon, had resigned a few months earlier, but these newcomers hadn't just campaigned against the Republicans. They were after the Democratic establishment as well. "We were a conquering army," said George Miller, the twenty-nine-year-old congressman from California. "We came here to take the Bastille."[4]

One of the first people this group targeted was an old man from rural Texas, a former tenant cotton farmer named Wright Patman, the head of the House Banking and Currency Committee who had first been elected to Congress in 1928. Antiwar liberals saw that the key to power in the House was through committees, with the flow of legislation controlled by committee chairmen picked based on length of service. Old men—often southern reactionaries—had used this seniority system to do terrible things, such as bottle up civil rights legislation. So existing liberals in office, with votes from the new radicals, demanded that the full Democratic Caucus get a say on who ran what committee.

Ironically, Patman had a lot in common with the incoming class. He was, for instance, the very first Democrat to investigate Watergate. But he was vulnerable to the new liberals he had helped elect. They were young, he was old. They were vehemently opposed to the war in Vietnam, he had voted for it. They were a TV generation, and knew affluence and campus politics. He was rural, southern, without a college degree, and had gone through the crucible of the 1930s. By contrast, as Watergate Baby Paul Tsongas observed, "Our generation did not know the Depression."

And yet, something else was going on. Liberals were the face of the coup, but bankers were quietly organizing the rebellion from behind the scenes. For forty-five years, Patman had fought concentrated financial power and monopolies, part of a politics that stretched back to the founding of the country. He was the living embodiment of an American tradition, the last populist. And it was a tradition the financiers sought to kill.

The Watergate Babies didn't understand they were being manipulated. They were antiwar, not anti-bank. Some had even been bankers. "His economic ideas were not in pace with modern concepts," said liberal congressman Pete Stark. Stark had been elected just two years before, becoming famous by putting a giant peace sign on his bank. Enemies of Patman told the newcomers that to be important, they had to make a mark. Nothing would do that like getting rid of the genial old man. Toby Moffett, another young congressman, bought into this. He called Patman "a terrific fighter," but, he said, "it seemed time to move on." Patman's politics, which focused on financial and monopoly power, was irrelevant.

The Texas delegation rose up in defense of the old man. Barbara Jordan, the star of the impeachment against Nixon and one of the few black women in Congress, supported Patman. His defenders were led by powerful Texas Democrat Jim Wright, who pleaded with the new members not to "depose the one man who has been our most inveterate, most persistent, most consistent and most outspoken foe of monopoly, exorbitant interest rates, and special privileges of all sorts." In what one young member called the greatest political speech he had ever heard, Wright asked, must we commit "patricide"?[5]

When it came time for the vote, Patman's loss was a foregone conclusion. He was crushed. It was indeed, as *The Washington Post* put it, "a revolution."

A short time later, Patman died of pneumonia. His body was flown back to Texarkana in a United States Air Force transport plane, and his body taken through the district, stopping at a catfish restaurant in the African American section of town he frequented when he returned to the district. As the hearse passed, his constituents, whom he had called the "plain people," lined the streets several deep. More than a thousand people packed the church at his funeral.

Jim Wright, later Speaker of the House, eulogized Patman's life. "He often comforted the afflicted and afflicted the comfortable," talking of Patman's fights against big business, banks, and the Klan. "Well done."[6]

For two hundred years, Americans had fought concentrated power, relying on leaders like Patman. But now there was no one left to carry on the tradition. The new generation had, unwittingly, committed patricide.

Almost immediately, the liberal-led Congress was confronted with a mess of incomprehensible economic problems. The American economic engine was supposed to produce an endless surfeit of goods, services, and jobs, automatically. But now it was sputtering, with inflation, oil shocks, corporation bankruptcies, deep recession.

Without guidance, the new generation panicked. Rudderless and afraid, they turned to a group of scholars who promised them efficiency, progress, and freedom. All they had to do was undo the chains on concentrated power that men like Patman had spent their lives securing.

And so they did. They released the beast of monopoly upon the land. The revolution was here.

■ ■

During the most recent financial crisis, in 2009–2010, I was a congressional staffer working for a member of Congress on the Financial Services Committee, what I would learn was Patman's old stomping grounds. I kept getting calls from constituents in foreclosure, in crisis, and nothing that my government and my party offered could help them, or was designed to help them. In aggregate, from 2008 to 2012, during the crisis, the American middle class lost roughly $6 trillion. The assets of the powerful recovered value quickly, those of the middle class did not. Meanwhile, political leaders rewarded the so-called Too Big to Fail banks with bailout money, and bank executives, far from being punished, would be rewarded with large bonuses.[7] All over the world, the story was pretty much the same. Bonuses for bankers, little for the rest of us.

It was in that period that I began to ask myself a question, a question that turned into this book. The question was as follows. Our leaders responded to a financial collapse caused by a concentration of wealth and power by pushing even more wealth and power into the hands of the same people that caused it. Why?

Answering that question—why did our leaders help confiscate the basis of American stability—was surprisingly difficult. Was it purely protecting the rich? That seemed unlikely; there were ways to make sure the rich did well while not undermining everyone else. Was it corruption? I didn't think so. There were some payoffs, but from what I saw, bribery really did not drive policy. Was it poor strategy or partisanship? I doubted it. There were political fights and recriminations, but both parties came to agree on the need to seize the wealth of the middle class and protect a concentrated financial apparatus. Was it personal immorality? No. Many of our political leaders felt they had a moral obligation to do what they did, that it might be sad, but it was necessary and inevitable. The concentration of wealth and power that I saw, with terrible consequences, occurred largely due to the actions of well-meaning technocrats who did not understand what they were doing.

The more I thought about the question, the more difficult it became to answer. The policy choices around the financial crisis were odd because they were destabilizing. Making sure people owned homes has been a core way to stabilize our society since the 1930s. The original modern housing finance system was designed with political goals in mind. In the words of William Levitt, the founder of the first postwar suburb, "No man who owns his own house and lot can be a Communist. He has too much to do."[8] This was a literal statement. People with a stake in society—a bit of property—do not rebel. People with no stake have nothing to lose. It seemed clear to many of us during the bailouts that the public would turn vehemently against the political establishment for taking their property, their stake in America, and so it has.

After years of research, I came to believe that the answer to the question is ideology, and in particular, turning our back decades ago on an old populist way of organizing our culture. But in 2009, I didn't know this older tradition had existed. The first hint it was there was when an economist, Jane D'Arista, told me how and why the financial system was blowing up, almost in real time. At the time, no one else, not the bankers or lobbyists or government officials, had any idea what the system they had constructed was doing. But she did, and pointed me to old papers she had written on why the system would blow up.

Her ability to see clearly when everyone else was panicking seemed a bit like magic, so I asked her how she knew all about these problems before anyone else did. D'Arista told me that she learned how the system worked when she was a staffer for a congressman named Wright Patman in the 1970s, a congressman who had helped structure parts of the New Deal. I had never heard of Patman, but D'Arista told me about how he had tried to impeach Andrew Mellon in 1932 and had in turn been overthrown in 1975. A few years later, I read a book by a journalist named Barry Lynn, the founder of what was becoming a new antimonopoly movement. In that book, Lynn wrote about the Robinson-Patman Act, a law written by Patman designed to constrain chain stores in the 1930s. Somehow, one man had been involved in dealing with the giant threats of his day, banks and chain stores, that paralleled the threats of our day, banks and Walmart. And I had no idea who he was. Patman's role in the twentieth century was the key to answering the question.

To understand what was in the mind of policymakers from 2008 to 2010, I had to see how they learned to think about the world. There was an entirely different set of stories and traditions in the heads of policymakers before the 1970s than there was after the 1970s. And it was these differing approaches to power that explains why we took such dissimilar approaches during the New Deal and the Obama era.

Barack Obama and his generation had learned their politics from the Watergate Babies, a generation born in rebellion against Patman's populism. Policymakers in 2009 didn't understand this at the time; few of them had ever heard of Patman, and few were aware of the origins of their own intellectual traditions. They believed, proudly, that they were nonideological and pragmatic. But most of these officials had a visceral reaction toward populism. They wore the armor of Ivy League degrees, believing that being an economist or having some sort of widely respected credential offered them the divine right to rule. Voters might have formal mechanisms of democracy, but real decisions should be made by experts in opaque institutions like the Federal Reserve, the courts, the Congressional Budget Office, the Office of Information and Regulatory Affairs, and so forth.

Toward the end of the Obama administration, a left-wing type of criticism emerged, an argument that the financial crisis and the response to it was all just an inevitable unspooling of capitalism with booms and busts and rampant inequality, a simple fact of life under a free market system. This critique, though appearing to present a radical challenge to the status quo, actually bore the same logic of the officials in charge during the financial crisis. It had an elitism of its own, a naïveté similar to that of the Watergate Baby generation, an unwillingness to think hard about commerce and markets. Inevitabilism, whether oriented around the sin of capitalism or the glory of it, reflects a refusal to entertain free will.

For much of this time, I felt alone, frustrated, angry. The financial crisis of 2008 was not a technocratic problem that happened in the banking system. It was a political crisis that happened everywhere. It was not a result of a few bad actors, it was a broad sweeping restructuring of our culture, the result of forty years of political choices, the same misfiring of institutions that led to the second war in Iraq, and an endless series of gruesome social consequences. The men in suits told us Saddam Hussein had weapons of mass destruction, just as they told us taxpayer-funded bank bonuses were essential to the economy.

Even political leaders I respected did not seem to understand how to make democracy work. But still, I believed that we could have done better. Our political leaders, and we ourselves, can and do make choices. I was not naive, but I looked around and saw tremendous hard-earned wisdom, inculcated in our science, our arts and songs, our bridges, our technology, our medicines, our societies. We didn't always organize our world around the ideas of highly educated technocrats with bad judgment. We once could do greatness in our politics. So where was a tradition I could honor?

And then I found Wright Patman, and I saw through his eyes.

Going through hearings, archives, letters, he helped teach me about the vitality, the energy, the love, the beauty, the fear of what it means to live in a democracy. I saw the coldness of Andrew Mellon, the vibrancy and error of the Watergate Baby class, the intensity of Citibank leader Walter Wriston, the tragedy and racism of Woodrow Wilson, the narcissism and violence of Teddy Roosevelt, the elitist cunning of Aaron Director, the genius and spirituality of Louis Brandeis. This was the tradition I had missed, a battle that took place over how our banks and corporations would be run, a battle over America and the world. This is the tradition that finally made sense. This is the tradition that, if we had known about it in 2008, would have helped us restore our democracy, or at least given us a shot to do so.

Once I learned of this ideological battle, one that Americans before the 1970s understood, my time in politics began to make sense. Toward the end of the Obama administration, the musical *Hamilton,* based on a book written by journalist Ron Chernow, offered a capstone to the era of the Watergate Baby generation. The musical celebrated a telling of history in which Alexander Hamilton, the founding father Democrats had traditionally associated with the banker-friendly Republican Party and a self-proclaimed elitist who created Wall Street and distrusted democracy, had somehow become an icon of progressive thinking and national greatness. He had become a left-wing political hero, instead of the traditional enemy of democracy that historians—and members of the Democratic Party—understood him as for two hundred years.

The musical provided something of an answer to my question. In the 1930s, Franklin Delano Roosevelt publicly blamed Wall Street and monopolies for ruining the economy, and used the political power he acquired with that criticism to decentralize and democratize the corporate sector in what became known as the New Deal. But in the Obama era, political party elites from both sides and cultural taste-makers engaged in a moral celebration of Wall Street. Barack Obama said that enjoying *Hamilton* was the only thing he and Republican Dick Cheney—the former vice president—agreed on. The musical reflected an ideological takeover, not left or right, but a joint attack on populism by the left and the right by people who, for their own reasons, distrusted the messiness and vibrancy of democracy. Those who organized our response to the financial crisis loved *Hamilton* because it celebrated their moral approval of rule by elite technocrats. And in this love, I saw, in its totality, the grand vision that had led to the crisis, and to the response. The bailouts from 2008 to 2010 were not intended to stop a depression, they were intended to stop a New Deal. And so they did.

■ ■

Our world looks very different than it did in the mid-1970s, and not just because of technological advances. There's a sameness to everything. In 1974, we often shopped at a local store. Today we live in a world dominated by chain stores, not just in the U.S., and in many cases with a sameness of experience in most major cities in the world.

Take a look around. You probably have a phone made by one of two companies. You likely bank at one of four giant banks, and fly on one of four big airlines. You connect with friends with either Facebook, WhatsApp, or Instagram, all of which are owned by one company. You get your internet through Comcast or AT&T. Data about your thoughts goes into a database owned by Google, what you buy into Amazon or Walmart, and what you owe into Experian or Equifax. You live in a world structured by concentrated corporate power.

This goes far beyond consumer brands. Our increasingly concentrated and corrupted medical system is literally killing us. As one analyst put it, "due to medical errors and other forms of harmful care, contact with the American health-care system is now the third leading cause of death in the United States."[9] That's 10 percent of all U.S.

deaths.[10] This too can be traced, in part, to monopolization. Because of a wave of mergers, 40 percent of hospital stays occur in markets where one entity controls all hospitals, and these hospitals, like all monopolies, no longer have a strong incentive to deliver quality care at a reasonable price.[11] Instead, they sometimes over-treat, and kill, their patients.

There's also the ghastly opioid crisis. In 2017, 130 people in America died every day of overdoses by heroin-like medicines, peddled by doctors paid by pharmaceutical companies based on how much they prescribe.[12] The monopolization is grotesque; one of the billionaires who helped create the most important opioid, OxyContin, Richard Sackler, recently received a patent for addiction treatment.[13] And the Sackler family name, as of 2019, graced facilities at Harvard and Yale. Even the drug used by police and EMTs to treat overdoses, naloxone, is monopolized by Amphastar Pharmaceuticals, tripling in price since 2012 and stretching the budgets of those tasked with saving the lives of overdose victims.[14]

Monopolization opens back doors for bad actors to undermine our democracies. Facebook, for instance, accidentally allowed Russian meddling in elections across the West. But that's just the most high-profile problem. Three voting machine companies, down from eight in 2002—Election Systems & Software (ES&S), Dominion Voting Systems, and Hart InterCivic—control 92 percent of voting machines in the United States, and have a high global market share. Concentration in the industry leads to lower security standards and more easily hackable elections.[15]

Our chains of production are concentrated and globalized. Virtually all vitamin C production—a key food preservative—is controlled by a cartel in China. Most saline solution, a key medical supply, is made in hurricane-prone Puerto Rico. Hospitals are facing shortages of cancer drugs because of supply chain problems. After Hurricane Sandy, few noticed that the lean "just in time" food supply lines organized by corporate giants like Sysco nearly failed, with some warning New York City was "nine meals from anarchy."[16]

We hear blips of this occasionally, tweets from an angry president, or a Democratic politician complaining about airlines. Occasionally someone will mention the financial crisis brought to us by Too Big to Fail banks.

But largely, we are a sullen people, frustrated at unseen forces we cannot describe, squabbling among ourselves. Those of us who demand some sense of control over our economic lives are marginalized as emotional, or racist, or ignorant, whatever stereotype is most useful.

In the meantime, old problems have returned. Wage stagnation and economic inequality is back with a vengeance, as is regional inequality, with a few gilded cities full of capital and opportunity, and vast swaths of impoverished rural areas beset with addiction and depression. Civic leaders, who used to run local stores, churches, small businesses, local law firms, and farms, have been washed away by a wave of Walmarts and Targets and Amazons. This is not just true in America, but globally.

In the commercial realm, more and more of us work for really big companies. Farmers must sell grain, buy seeds, potash, and chemicals, and sell chicken and beef through a small group of giant companies. Every small business is at the beck and call of a credit card and payments cartel. Concentrated power is in every nook and cranny of commerce. Peanut butter. Poultry. Supermarkets. Movie theaters. Vaccines. Drugstores. Advertising.

Increasingly, the systems on which we rely, such as airlines, seem to be falling apart. Software failures knock out thousands of flight schedules at once, and random fees frustrate passengers as much as bad scheduling software frustrates flight attendants and pilots. Prices for health care seem insane and unrelated to anything rational. A massive policy celebrated as bringing us universal health care exists side by side with untold Americans putting up GoFundMe accounts online to beg their fellow citizens for money to buy medicine.

Even the wonders of new technology, like the open internet, have been subverted to allow meddling in elections worldwide and induce ethnic conflict. Somehow, we took the greatest communication platform ever created and used it to manufacture a new generation of Nazis.

Then there's politics, the specter of disillusionment and demagogues all over the world. It's a regular part of discourse now to hear fears of autocratic forms of politics, and the potential end of democracy itself. Former secretary of state Madeleine Albright wrote a book titled *Fascism: A Warning.* Proto-fascist gangs appealing to disillusioned young men, with names like Proud Boys, organize across continents.

There are many arguments for what is at the root cause of our current social dysfunction. Various explanations include the prevalence of racism, automation, the rise of China, inadequate education or training, the spread of the internet, Donald Trump, the collapse of political norms, or globalization. Many of these explanations have merit.

But there's another much simpler explanation of what is going on. Our systems are operating the way that they were designed to. In the 1970s, we decided as a society that it would be a good idea to allow private financiers and monopolists to organize our world. As a result, what is around us is a matrix of monopolies, controlling our lives and manipulating our communities and our politics. This is not just happenstance. It was created. The constructs shaping our world were formed as ideas, put into law, and now they are our economic and social reality. Our reality is formed not just of monopolized supply chains and brands, but an entire language that precludes us from even noticing, from discussing the concentrated power all around us.

The baby boom generation did not mean to build the world that they did. They wanted a world based on justice and equality, and responded to the problems they saw based on what they knew. They were simply never taught to understand corporate power. There was in essence something of a cultural transmission problem, where lessons going back hundreds of years—lessons Patman carried forward—just didn't get passed down. In attempting to bring us liberation as they understood it, baby boom leaders accidentally forsook their own liberties.

In many ways, the baby boomers are still organizing our society, controlling much of the wealth and decision-making authority in our political and cultural institutions. Many of the Watergate Babies stayed in Congress for decades. Both the Affordable Care Act and the Dodd-Frank financial reform legislation—the main Democratic response to the bailouts—were written by congressional committees chaired by politicians elected in 1974. Three presidents, Bill Clinton, George W. Bush, and Donald Trump, are old baby boomers, and Barack Obama is a young boomer. But even as newer generations rise, the transmission problem won't be fixed. Younger generations never learned our earlier tradition either.

And yet, as hopeless as this situation might sound, we have been here before. There have been periods in history fraught with petty tyrants in the commercial realm, regional inequality, slowing wages, and even hints of fascism, and ideological systems justifying all of it as natural law. Previous generations have been able to recover our republic.

We can learn from our forebears, going back hundreds of years, who knew something about concentrated corporate power and tensions with liberty. Learning from our forebears, however, is a strange and difficult undertaking. Just as those who sought racial tolerance in the 1970s accidentally invited the specter of monopoly into our midst, there have been slave owners or people considered paranoid cranks railing about bankers who nonetheless had useful things to say about the problem of liberty and monopoly.

A generation ago, there was a revolution. It was not a left-wing or right-wing revolution. It was a revolution of ideas. That revolution was so powerful and dominant that it stole from us not just our liberties but even the words that helped us describe our world. Words like "liberty" and "markets" and "competition" and "monopoly" and "citizen" have been perverted, taken by technocrats who hide the levers of power from most of us. Popular debates are stuck in the 1970s. We attack or praise capitalism, or socialism, or the free market. All of this misses the point. The fight has always been about whether monopolists run our world, or whether we the people do. That is the fight hidden from us by the revolution of the 1970s. This book is a story of this revolution, why it happened, and just what the revolutionaries were overthrowing.

This book will bring you back through these debates and show you the world as Wright Patman and millions of Americans like him saw it. It will teach you that language. It will help you see our world both in a new way and through the traditions that our ancestors learned through blood, sweat, and struggle. If we relearn the language of antimonopoly, then perhaps, together, we can regain our liberties.

## CHAPTER ONE

# 1912

"I take my stand absolutely, where every progressive ought to take his stand, on the proposition that private monopoly is indefensible and intolerable. And there I will fight my battle. And I know how to fight it."
—**Woodrow Wilson**[1]

■ ■ ■ ■ ■ ■ ■ ■ ■ ■ ■ ■ ■

It was August 31, 1910, and men were flocking into the town of Osawatomie from all over Kansas. The state had been drenched in rain, but still, farmers trudged miles through the mud, some riding as far as two hundred miles, all through the night. They were coming to be on time for the speech, to listen, or for those too far away, to get a peek at the energetic man with the squeaky voice and love of self-dramatization.[2] Speaking was the figure who once again promised to transform decades of agitation and organizing into a new society, a society that would not be dominated by these new giant corporations, by corruption, by greed.

The speech was set out on soil rich with historical drama. Little more than a decade earlier, in this flat state, populism had flourished, a tradition of farmer politics based on a call for justice against eastern banks, monopolies, and railroads. Five decades before that, Kansas, and Osawatomie, had been the seat of ferment against slavery, the flash point of the Civil War. Attending this speech, for a Kansan, might be the political thrill of a lifetime.

Even Kansans who couldn't go were excited. As the special train carrying their hero passed through the little towns on the flat Kansas prairies, contingents of men whooped cheers, standing in the downpour just to get "the chance to yell at the train as it flew by," even as they knew they wouldn't be able to see their idol. Wherever the train stopped, even as early as 6 a.m., howls went up, demands to see the person inside.

When their hero finally stepped out just to offer a wave to the crowd at the Osawatomie platform, great cheers broke out, jubilation.[3] Teddy Roosevelt was, as Mark Twain put it, "the most popular human being that has ever existed in the United States."[4] He was a warrior, against greed and dishonor, and for an America bristling with industrial muscle.

By 1910, Roosevelt had had a deep relationship with the American people for a decade, having been president for nearly two terms. While president, he suppressed a rebellion against American military rule in the Philippines and became the first great conservationist. He formalized America as a key diplomatic power when he won the Nobel Peace Prize in 1906 for settling a war between Russia and Japan. He was the most controversial, bold, brilliant, and beloved man in American politics, a man whose lust for attention and publicity infused the office of the presidency with immense power.

But he did more than build a new model of national leadership. While president, he had done what no political leader in America had yet managed. He had taken on the great trusts, the corporations and railroads, the powerful plutocrat J. P. Morgan. And he had won. "Of all forms of tyranny," Roosevelt argued, "the least attractive and the most vulgar is the tyranny of mere wealth, the tyranny of plutocracy."[5] The people loved him, and he in turn loved their adulation.

And yet, Teddy Roosevelt had a dark side. A lust for power. A belief in aristocracy, a distrust of, as he put it, "the mob," and an understanding that the important skill of a leader in a democracy was that of "political manipulation."[6] He venerated war and violence; manhood meant proving oneself in combat. "A Quaker may be quite as undesirable a citizen as is a duelist," he wrote.[7] Roosevelt loathed one of the founders of the country, Thomas Jefferson, because he saw in Jefferson's statement that his "passion is peace" were the words of an effete weakling pacifist. Above all, there was his need for attention. "My father," said Alice Roosevelt Longworth, "always wanted to be the corpse at every funeral, the bride at every wedding and the baby at every christening."[8] Now, Roosevelt would attempt to use his popularity in ways both novel and frightening.

There had always been a great conflict, coursing throughout American history, a fight between monopoly and democracy. The struggle over the control of trade was a political and philosophical debate in America, between two different political systems. There was the system, promoted by Alexander Hamilton, of concentrating power in the hands of an elite, in banks, in monopoly corporations, in a better, more educated sort. And there was the rival system of Thomas Jefferson, who sought to place power through elections in the hands of the farmer, the worker, the small businessman. Roosevelt, in this speech, was to openly take the side of monopoly.

Roosevelt saw himself as a great champion of the people, but he was also, like his hero Hamilton, America's first treasury secretary and a powerful proponent of plutocracy and monopoly, a believer in the importance of the upper class. And, in spite of his reputation for fighting J. P. Morgan, Roosevelt also had a quiet, if tacit, alliance with the great banker and monopolist, a man these Kansas farmers feared and hated. Despite Roosevelt's words against plutocracy, Roosevelt had as his main political financier for this 1912 presidential campaign Morgan partner George Perkins, the man who put together the great steel trust U.S. Steel. He was to come as close as any major American presidential candidate ever would to openly fusing the power of the state with the power of big business.[9]

At Osawatomie, the reason for the event was the dedication of a state park on land where pro-slavery raiders battled abolitionists, led by antislavery martyr John Brown, fifty-four years earlier. Brown had become a symbol for the Union, in its march against the Confederacy, and a world-renowned hero. In 1910, there were seats for five hundred at the new park, but thousands attended, even though the roads were nothing more than impassable tracks in deep black mud. It was "the greatest John Brown celebration this John Brown town ever saw."[10]

And Roosevelt was the man leading America to address what he called its third great national crisis. A new force was extending across the land, the "special interests" known as corporations. While president from 1901 to 1909, Roosevelt had struck at these great private powers.

But now he pledged to tame them, once and for all. This was a crusade. "We stand at Armageddon," Roosevelt would later say, "and we battle for the Lord."[11]

The time was ripe. A financial collapse, the "Bankers' Panic of 1907," induced, as one congressman observed, a "broad national awakening and widespread agitation for relief, especially monetary, economic, and social."[12] Two years later, 259 workers, including young boys, died in the Cherry Mine Disaster. In 1910, twenty-one people died when a bomb went off during a strike at the *Los Angeles Times*. The Triangle Shirtwaist Fire of 1911 killed hundreds, illustrating the lack of safety provisions and poor treatment of workers.[13] Radicalism even invaded the middle class, as grisly train accidents produced hundreds of mangled bodies every year due to bad management of the rail lines.

The barons of industry were unapologetic, almost gleeful. "One human being is killed every hour and one injured every ten minutes," said W. L. Park, general superintendent of the Union Pacific Railroad. "There is a steady grinding and crunching of human flesh and bone under the juggernaut of modern car wheels. It is the price we pay for progress, for the great industrial conquest of the country."[14] And there was endless corruption, corporate payoffs to politicians, newspapers, and academic experts, city bosses, everyone.

The result was political chaos. Union organizers, like "Big Bill" Haywood, led strikes, increasingly marked by violence. Just three weeks before Roosevelt's Osawatomie speech, the mayor of New York was shot in the throat by a deranged former city employee.[15] Milwaukee elected a socialist mayor in 1910, followed by cities in Montana, New York, and California.[16]

Ten years earlier, as one magazine writer put it, the attitude of most Americans was one of cynicism and apathy, a "let us alone" sentiment. But now, the country was electrified with excitement and radical ideas.[17] In Kansas, Roosevelt was in the midst of a speaking tour, the beginnings of a presidential campaign, and he would carry his crusade into Missouri the following day. In his speeches, and in his coming campaign, Roosevelt would attack both corporations and what he called "mob rule."

He was battling for control of the conservative Republican Party. And while the people loved Roosevelt, his foes, the "stand-patter" conservatives, did not. William Barnes, the Republican boss of Albany, New York, and the leader of the old guard, responded to the speech with warnings. Be wary of the "hysteria" running "riot throughout the country," Barnes said. "All thoughtful men" should see a "frightful danger" in Roosevelt's ascendancy.[18]

The stakes were high. If reform did not come at the ballot box, it might come, as it had less than fifty years earlier, through civil strife. The rise of industrial power challenged political systems all over the world. The telegraph and railroad broadened knowledge and sped people and goods across the land at breakneck speeds. But they also extended the reach of any financial or political leader, in ways that posed entirely new challenges to existing political institutions. Many countries failed to control this power. The result, in coming years, would be fascism if private actors took over the state, or communism, when groups used the state to take over the private sector. As Roosevelt himself predicted, Russia might soon "experience a red terror which will make the French Revolution pale."[19] Other nations would seek to adapt their democracies to control this power. In 1912, the contours of this world were still inchoate, born but not animate.

In Kansas, Roosevelt gave his philosophy a name: the New Nationalism. This was a call for courage in a great and violent drama. Americans must face the need for reform, even risk "temporary disaster," he told the farmers, rather than give in to those with swollen fortunes pushing America toward a "sordid and selfish materialism."[20]

Celebrating antislavery hero John Brown while discussing the rise of corporations, great wealth, and radicalism made sense to the farmers in the crowd. There were Civil War veterans in the audience, the greatest generation of the era. But alluding to history was more than just a sop to the veterans. Debates over the founding, and the Civil War, regularly framed discussions of justice and corporate power.

"There have been two great crises in our country's history," Roosevelt told the crowd. The first was the American Revolution, which was not just a break with the British, but with a whole system of aristocracy, and the construction of a new nation. The resolution of that first crisis sowed the seeds for the second, which came from the rising political power of slaveowners. The founders had constructed a solid national body, with slavery as its deeply immoral flaw.[21]

The people at Osawatomie knew that the Civil War was not just a war against slavery, but also against a plutocracy of planters, in some ways similar to the men who controlled the great corporations they now faced. By the time of that war, cotton planters had concentrated ownership of land and slaves. In 1860, an oligarchy of eight thousand men ruled over millions of enslaved blacks, and poor whites, in the South.[22] The wealthiest men in the country were cotton kings; half the millionaires in 1850 lived in one town in Mississippi.[23] Slave cotton was at the center of a global financial and trading system, one stretching from Mississippi to Wall Street to the looms in Manchester across the sea. The greed of the planters at the heart of the system, their need to expand and dominate, caused a political crisis kicked off in Kansas, in which, as Roosevelt put it, "the special interests of cotton and slavery threatened our political integrity." [24]

Roosevelt quoted Abraham Lincoln, noting Lincoln argued that "labor is the superior of capital, and deserves much the higher consideration." These farmers knew that Lincoln went further than defeating the Slave Power. He passed the National Banking Act, to regulate banks and the money supply; the Homestead Act, to distribute land; and the Morrill Act to found universities in every state.[25] His party passed the Telegraph Act of 1866, which encouraged competition in the telegraph industry. The Civil War, to Roosevelt, and to Kansans, was a second American Revolution, not just abolishing slavery, but striking at plutocracy as well.

Now the third crisis, of corporate power, was upon the land. This crisis was, to Roosevelt, "exactly" like the crisis of slavery, only instead of cotton barons this time, he noted it was that "great special business interests too often control and corrupt the men and methods of government for their own profit." [26]

Like slavery, this third crisis was a long time coming. It had its roots in commerce, in progress, in science. The steamship, the telegraph, and the railroad were nothing short of astonishing. No technology had ever allowed humans to move over land faster than a horse, or communicate instantly at a distance. These technologies were matched with equally important legal innovations. Railroad managers created the modern multidivisional corporation and new accounting methods. They even standardized time itself, creating time zones to synchronize scheduling.[27]

The new railroad corporations expanded radically during the war, eventually settling the West and eliminating all Native American control in the continent. In 1862, Congress passed the Pacific Railway Act to authorize the first transcontinental railroad. From the 1860s onward, the federal government subsidized the growth of railroads with money, land, and military support. The federal land grant to just one railroad, the Union Pacific, was about the size of New Hampshire and New Jersey combined, much of which was occupied by Native Americans. As historian, railroad regulator, and railroad executive Charles Francis Adams put it, "the Pacific railroads have settled the Indian question."[28] Railroads were followed by new giant industrial corporations of the 1880s and 1890s, steel and oil, as well as chartered public utility corporations for telegraph, telephone, gas, water, and electric networks. Behind all of these lay Wall Street, where bankers and lawyers arranged the legal forms and credit arrangements that governed it all.

Industrial barons were a new group of would-be aristocrats, and they innovated many ways of concentrating power and wealth. Key to this concentration of wealth was political corruption. Perhaps the most famous example was the Union Pacific–Crédit Mobilier railroad scandal of the late 1860s. The Speaker of the House, the treasury secretary, the vice president, and a future president were all on the payroll of the railroad. This was what Mark Twain called the Gilded Age.[29]

In 1860, the Republican Party of Abraham Lincoln had as its ideological grounding a phrase coined by his Treasury Secretary Salmon Chase, "Free Soil, Free Labor, Free Men," an ode to Jefferson's argument in favor of "yeoman farmers." But by the 1890s, the leading Republican Party boss, Mark Hanna, raised, at modern prices, $3 billion for William McKinley's 1896 presidential campaign, saying, "There are two things that are important in politics. The first is money, and I can't remember the second."[30]

In 1877, mass unrest erupted in Maryland, Pennsylvania, Illinois, and Missouri in response to a series of railroad wage cuts. Striking workers from multiple industries, as well as business owners tired of being under the thumb of railroads, protested as revolutionaries had done years before. Railroad barons put down the protesters. The head of the Pennsylvania Railroad said that strikers should get "a rifle diet for a few days and see how they like that kind of bread." In Pittsburgh, riots destroyed 39 buildings, 104 locomotives, and 1,245 freight and passenger cars. Dozens were killed.[31]

Until the 1880s, vast new industrial power was regulated at a state level through restrictive corporate chartering. For instance, state corporate charters did not allow one corporation to buy stock in another. But in 1882, an oil refiner named John D. Rockefeller helped invent a centralizing legal tool to capture industries across state borders. He placed all stock from various oil properties into one legal structure called a "trust." Known as the Standard Oil Trust, Rockefeller's oil companies might look independent legally, but the trust's board of directors set policy for the combined group. With this new legal tool, Rockefeller built the largest and most powerful monopoly of the era.[32] In 1887, the whiskey and the sugar trusts formed, with many more on the horizon.

A trust became a legal mechanism to enable and accelerate the concentration of financial power that started with the railroad. Endemic corruption in the industry induced a backlash from working people and businessmen. Distrust of railroads and associated network industries like oil went beyond workers. Virtually the entire commercial order of late-nineteenth-century America was oriented around small and midsized proprietorships, from independent farmers to drugmakers, pharmacists, printers, stationers, booksellers, manufacturers, specialty producers of brand-name foodstuffs, grocers, and distillers. All distrusted railroads. Journalists took the lead in formulating an antimonopoly critique. In 1884, Henry Demarest Lloyd, a leading antimonopolist journalist, wrote, "Monopoly and anti-monopoly, odious as these words have become to the literary ear, represent the two great tendencies of our time: monopoly, the tendency to combination; anti-monopoly, the demand for social control of it."[33]

It was not size they feared; the post office was a vast organization, but as it was an open-access network run by a democratic government, it did not pose the same odious threat as private monopolistic institutions. They also did not seek untrammeled competition. Unregulated competition in networked industries like railroads, which had high fixed costs, could be catastrophic. To win business from rival roads, railroad executives might slash prices below what they could reasonably afford, and begin to bleed cash. They would then cut wages and defer maintenance. This so-called "ruinous competition" caused horrific accidents, bankruptcies, and violent strikes. If enough railroads raised too much capital and built too many tracks, price wars would eventually bankrupt railroads en masse and ensure widespread bond defaults. In 1873 and 1893, widespread defaults turned into financial crises and then economic depressions.

The people organized for their rights against these new private centralizing corporations and an unstable political economy. Small business owners and farmers organized cooperatives and professional associations to create standardized production and pricing policies to retain their independence in the midst of centralizing forces.[34] Farmers and merchants organized the Granger, Greenback, and other populist movements to demand state regulation over railroads and associated technologies, like grain elevators. In John Brown country, farmers had been angry at corporate power for decades.

By 1887, Congress had established the Interstate Commerce Commission (ICC), the first federal regulatory commission, to oversee the railroads. In 1890, Congress passed the Sherman Antitrust Act, to rein in industrial trusts such as Standard Oil. This law prohibited "monopolization" and "restraints of trade." Senator John Sherman had intended the law to destroy the trusts, but how to do so was a new and difficult problem for the government. Congress cut much of his original language, and the Sherman Act ended up largely as a statement of principles, with courts and conservative judges able to interpret the meaning of the terms.[35]

The attempts at reform weren't enough. The ICC was supposed to bar price discrimination and secret rebates by railroads, but it was defanged by the Supreme Court. And throughout the 1890s, courts used an interpretation of the Sherman Act to rule that price-fixing among competitors tended to be illegal, but mergers were not.[36] This inverted the meaning of the antitrust laws and ended up *encouraging* mergers. This made it illegal for competitors to fix prices as separate entities, but if competitors combined and fixed prices as a single giant corporation, the law offered sanction. This inversion created a central tension in antitrust law that remains to this day. Cartels were often illegal, but monopolies or trusts—including those achieved through massive combination—might not be.

In 1892, another event, the Homestead strike, further highlighted the danger of industrial power. This conflict took place near Pittsburgh, in the rough-and-tumble world of rail, steel, and oil that grew out of the rich coal lands of western Pennsylvania. Strikers, like their rebel forebears, targeted Carnegie Steel, the high-tech corporation of the 1890s.

The strike pitted emerging tycoons against iron and steelworkers. The tycoons were led by a slender, ruthless, Hamilton-admiring coal baron named Henry Clay Frick, who was running Carnegie Steel at the time. Frick hired mercenaries known as the Pinkerton detectives and built walls around the Homestead mill with apertures for guns. In a ferocious battle between guards and strikers, sixteen people died. Frick had more than a hundred strikers arrested, some for murder, and the union ran out of money. Carnegie Steel, with tens of millions of dollars of capitalization, held out until the union was destroyed.[37]

The next year, one of Frick's allies, a banker named J. P. Morgan, began consolidating control over the American industrial commons. Morgan had been attempting to solve the problem of "ruinous competition" in the railroad industry for years. In 1885, on his yacht, the *Corsair,* Morgan settled a price war between two major railroads, the aristocratic Pennsylvania Railroad and the New York Central. The railroad men agreed to stop competing, at least temporarily, and respect their separate spheres of influence.[38] Morgan was attempting to settle the same problem that Congress sought to address through public regulation with the ICC in 1887. But voluntary agreements could only go so far.

Morgan, along with a few financial titans, was finally able to seize control of the railroads after the Panic of 1893, a financial crash caused in part by railroad overbuilding. A third of American railroads went bankrupt, fifteen thousand commercial firms failed, and labor violence erupted across the country.[39] In the wreckage of the downturn, with railroad and industrial assets lying fallow in bankruptcy, the railroads would be regulated at last. But this regulation would come in the boardroom, not through public agencies. Wall Street never liked competition, but its preference was for bankers to set the rules and govern, rather than the public.

In the downturn, J. P. Morgan, the trusted agent of British investors, stepped forward as the leader of the American political economy.[40] When a Morgan banker took control of a bankrupt line, he would "Morganize" it, firing (often corrupt) management, restructuring the debt, buying competitors to eliminate rate wars, and creating a monopoly that could service the new credit arrangements. Morgan became so powerful and so wealthy that—during the Panic of 1907—the government turned to him to organize a mass bailout to stop the run on the financial system.

As Morgan centralized power, farmers continued to suffer at the hands of the railroads and the bankers. These farmers swept from the South and the West into a new political party, the People's Party, to translate their desire for liberty in an industrial age into a political program. They called themselves populists, and drew upon the ideas of Alexander Hamilton's great foe Thomas Jefferson, who had disdained "aristocratic corporations." They sought an active federal government as a means to discipline the centralizing power of national corporations. In 1896, a young Nebraska politician-cum-preacher, William Jennings Bryan, took this program into the Democratic Party as its nominee that year.

Bryan, known as the "Great Commoner," faced the candidate of J. P. Morgan and the plutocrats, William McKinley. Bryan saw the election as a "struggle between the idle holders of idle capital and the struggling masses who produce the wealth and pay the taxes of the country." Bryan referenced the founder of the Democratic Party, Thomas Jefferson, and attacked the moneyed aristocracy Jefferson had fought. "The banks," said Bryan, "should go out of the governing business."[41]

Bankers poured money into the McKinley campaign, because McKinley pledged to "preserve the financial honor of the government." Bryan lost. Bryan tried again in 1900, when the Democratic

platform called the giant corporations known as trusts "the most efficient means yet devised for appropriating the fruits of industry to the
benefit of the few at the expense of the many, and unless their insatiate
greed is checked, all wealth will be aggregated in a few hands and the
Republic destroyed."[42] But McKinley triumphed again, this time with
a young vice president on the ticket, a former governor of New York.
This was Teddy Roosevelt's entrance into national office.

Morgan continued with his great centralizing project. In a merger
wave that ran from 1894 to 1904, Morgan centralized business into
modern corporate America, structuring companies such as General
Electric and International Harvester. Consolidation followed consolidation. American Tobacco rolled up 250 firms into one. At least
seventy-two consolidations led to a situation in which one entity controlled at least 40 percent of an industry, and forty-two consolidations
created situations where one entity controlled upward of 70 percent
of an industry.[43] Many newspapers cheered Morgan, lauding him as a
heroic commander of the economy.

In 1901, Morgan had his greatest triumph of financial engineering,
the creation of U.S. Steel, which was a final combination of two hundred companies in 127 cities. A Morgan partner noted, upon signing
the last paper necessary for the merger, this "signature is the last one
necessary to put the Steel industry, on a large scale, into the hands of
men who do not know anything about it."[44]

In the industrial era, these centralizing forces had escaped control
of democracy. The people tried to fight the plutocrats but they had
lost. But on September 6, 1901, an assassin named Leon Czolgosz shot
President William McKinley on the grounds of the Pan-American
Exposition at the Temple of Music in Buffalo, New York. And this
brought Teddy Roosevelt to power.

Roosevelt grew up a wealthy, sickly aristocrat at a time when old-
money Republicans did not make a career out of politics. Roosevelt
broke the mold. In the 1880s, he won election to the New York Assembly in a safe silk stocking Republican seat, and attacked corruption
so theatrically that he got the nickname the "cyclone Assemblyman."
His animus toward corruption was paired with disdain for farmer populists, who he felt threatened the natural ruling order.

Roosevelt desired to build a great American empire through combat. "The clamor of the peace faction," he said in the 1890s before the American war with Spain, "has convinced me that this country needs a war."[45] During that conflict, he led a group of volunteer cowboys, nicknamed the "Rough Riders," to battle in Cuba. The publicity-seeking worked, and his popularity helped him into the governor's mansion in New York. Republican bosses then gave him the vice presidency, a symbolic but powerless position.

At first, even after the assassin had pumped two bullets into McKinley's stomach, it didn't look like Roosevelt would become president. Doctors told the nation, and Roosevelt, that McKinley was recovering. But he wasn't. Gangrene had set in, and within a week the nation grieved McKinley's death. Now, "that madman," as one Republican Party boss called Roosevelt, was in charge. Roosevelt pledged to maintain "absolutely unbroken, the policy of President McKinley for the peace and prosperity and the honor of our beloved country."[46]

His presidency began with an aggressive settlement of a coal strike. For decades, the only authority any American president had seemed to show in addressing labor conflict was to use troops to put down strikers. Roosevelt broke with precedent. Faced with a massive dispute in the mines, Roosevelt publicly mediated a dispute between coal miners and the mine owners. Roosevelt continued his attempt to hold business aristocrats to a code of honor, establishing the Bureau of Corporations to investigate and publicize corporate practices.

Most importantly, he took on J. P. Morgan.

In 1902, Roosevelt filed a lawsuit under the Sherman Antitrust Act, designed to break up Morgan's Northern Securities railroad company, which had formed the previous year. This company was no mere railroad. The great oligarchs in America, the oilmen and the steel men, the bankers and the railroad barons, had had a bitter fight over control of the northwestern rail territory. The resolution was Northern Securities, a collective agreement to build a giant transportation system of steamships and railroads wrapping from Japan to Chicago, a $400 million empire.[47]

The oligarchs behind Northern Securities had never had to pay attention to the vagaries of politicians. William Vanderbilt, son of the first tycoon, once explained the attitude of the great centralizers with the unofficial slogan of the railroads, when he said "the public be damned." But Roosevelt was a different kind of politician. Roosevelt told Morgan no, and he meant it. In 1904, the Supreme Court validated Roosevelt, and broke up the railroad holding company, earning Roosevelt the title "trustbuster."

But in truth, while Roosevelt did invest the antitrust laws with real power, he generally did not want to break up monopolies. Roosevelt's hunger for authority, his desire to centralize commercial and political authority, his aristocratic bearing, were inconsistent with decentralizing power. Roosevelt respected Morgan as a fellow aristocrat, more so than rabble farmers. His view was that Morgan had erred, not in the merger, but in presuming to act as the nation's boss. That job was for the president—Roosevelt. Roosevelt needed a stick to make that clear, and, in this instance, the Sherman Act was that stick.

After the Northern Securities suit, Roosevelt and Morgan reached a secret alliance. Roosevelt came to a "gentleman's agreement" with Morgan's U.S. Steel. The company's president, Elbert Gary, cooperated with Roosevelt's newly founded agency, the Bureau of Corporations, in return for an acceptance of Gary's role as the head of the steel industry. Gary hosted what became known as "Gary dinners," where steel company heads shared pricing information with each other. From then on, Roosevelt would file suits against large corporations, but not those belonging to Morgan.

In 1904, Morgan bundled $150,000 for Roosevelt's reelection campaign.[48] Their alliance tightened. When Roosevelt's attorney general moved to sue another Morgan enterprise, International Harvester, Roosevelt ordered him to cease. In 1907, during a financial panic, Roosevelt's administration gave J. P. Morgan tens of millions in government deposits, allowing the financier to choose who would get loans. Roosevelt also secretly promised Morgan that he would not use the Sherman Act to stop U.S. Steel from buying a rival, Tennessee Coal and Iron. In 1906, Roosevelt forced Congress to pass the Hepburn Act, allowing the ICC to finally regulate the railroads at a federal level. The Bureau of Corporations, the Gary dinners, and Roosevelt's deal with Morgan were part of a broader institutional reshaping of the federal government, an attempt to turn it increasingly into a partner of big business.

After two terms as president, Roosevelt left politics for a year-long safari in Africa, his trip financed by a steel baron. It had seemed to the public that Roosevelt had addressed the problem of the trusts, when in fact Roosevelt had done more to secretly enhance the power of Morgan. But Roosevelt's successor, conservative William Howard Taft, began antitrust proceedings against Morgan enterprises. Roosevelt's deal with U.S. Steel was exposed.

The crisis of monopoly, contained under Roosevelt, worsened under Taft. In 1911, the Supreme Court broke up Rockefeller's Standard Oil into thirty-five separate companies, but in a pyrrhic victory for antimonopolists, the court simultaneously gutted antitrust law. The Sherman Act prohibited all restraints of trade, but the court ruled that the federal government could only halt "unreasonable" restraints of trade.

In the case of Standard Oil, the court ruled that the company's behavior was "unreasonable," and the bonds between the various subsidiaries of Standard Oil were dissolved. But judges, the court asserted, would now organize antitrust law. To challenge a monopoly, the government would now have to prove not only that there was a restraint of trade involved, but also that such a restraint was unreasonable. Judges elevated themselves above Congress and the executive branch, deciding what constituted a reasonable versus an unreasonable restraint.

In addition, the court also allowed John D. Rockefeller to keep his stakes garnered from the monopolistic practices. He had gotten away with what Democrats thought was a billion-dollar crime.

William Jennings Bryan cried out, "The Trusts have won."[49]

## THE ELECTION OF 1912: WILSON VERSUS ROOSEVELT

By 1910, new rhetoric had exploded into American politics. A series of left-wing pro-monopoly thinkers—Herbert Croly, Thorstein Veblen, Walter Lippmann, and Walter Weyl—put together theories on how to address the trusts. These men imported German scholarship of the nineteenth century, which emphasized an inevitability to the progress of events, known as "scientific history."[50]

These thinkers viewed the issue in much the same way Roosevelt did during his Kansas speech. Croly, who became Teddy Roosevelt's key advisor, was also an ardent admirer of Alexander Hamilton, and saw this moment as another founding, a moment of radicalism. Through Roosevelt's candidacy, Croly would seek to mimic Hamilton and attempt not to break this corporate power, but to co-opt it. Roosevelt wanted to place control of all large corporations in his own hands, and run them on behalf of the muddy Kansas farmers shouting his name. As one prominent academic of the time characterized it, the goal of the centralizer progressives was "concentration, cooperation, and control."[51]

Roosevelt and Hamilton were in many ways similar. They both had biases toward aristocracy, toward rule by a better sort. Roosevelt saw the power of the trusts, and sought to centralize their power in public hands, rather than to decentralize it. Similarly, Hamilton believed the American Revolution was the chance not to break from the British empire, but to emulate it.

Hamilton prioritized cooperation between military and financial elites so that the vulnerable colonies would not be easy prey to the Spanish or French empires, or to internal corruption. Roosevelt felt if America mistreated its monopolies, foreign competitors would win, preventing the creation of an American empire. In an era when none but aristocratic societies had ever existed, Hamilton feared self-government. To Hamilton, and many of his allies, democracy was a "disease."[52]

Roosevelt excused Hamilton's disdain for democracy. After all, this was not uncommon for the founding generation who men like Roosevelt revered. Children in colonial America understood the difference between gentlemen and commoners before they learned the difference between right and left.[53] If Roosevelt saw a failure in Hamilton, it was not from disrespecting the moral right of the people to rule, but that Hamilton's party, in spite of containing nearly every man of "talent" and "good sense" in the country, had failed to develop the "ability for political manipulation" to govern in a democracy.[54]

Roosevelt and Hamilton shared an admiration for centralized corporate power. Corporations existed in Hamilton's era. Chartered corporations, like the British East India Company, were monopolies licensed by the king to organize trade, such as the tea trade that fomented the Boston Tea Party that kicked off the Revolution.

Hamilton's goal was to protect the new nation by ensuring that it had the necessary strength to defend itself from external foes and internal insurrection. To do this, he sought to place domestic lords in charge of commerce in the new American state, so that they could mass the necessary men and capital to build a strong industrial base and a powerful military. This idea was similar, though less developed, to what industrial barons of the late nineteenth century believed. Men might vote, but they would be the better sort, ensconced in government-chartered private banks and corporations, who would do the governing. Hamilton even led an attack on a rebellion against the forebears of the farmers at Osawatomie, the rebels in the so-called "Whiskey Rebellion," who opposed Hamilton's schemes to concentrate power over farming and industry.[55]

Hamilton's centralizing ideas were ultimately defeated by the founder of the Democratic Party, Thomas Jefferson, a man Teddy Roosevelt loathed as weak and incompetent. Jefferson opposed corporate power, seeing in moneyed corporations the return of aristocratic privilege. Jefferson's writing framed much of the democratic language in use in the election of 1912. Even the name of this new party, then called the Democratic-Republican Party, was an attack on aristocracy. Thomas Jefferson became president, in what he called the "revolution of 1800," the first peaceful transition of power in America from one elected political party to another. "Sometimes it is said that man cannot be trusted with the government of himself," Jefferson said in his first inaugural. "Can he then be trusted with the government of others? Or have we found angels, in the form of kings, to govern him?"[56]

Just over one hundred years later, Croly updated Hamilton's theories, with scientific experts replacing wealthy merchants as the arbiters of the public good. He argued "huge corporations" induced efficiency and cooperation, and "all civilized societies" should seek such values when possible.[57] Roosevelt was to be the Alexander Hamilton of the corporate era, and bring his centralizing theory into the election of 1912.

As a Hamiltonian, Roosevelt believed the problem with the trusts was that they just had to recognize who was boss. Roosevelt needed "complete power to regulate and control all the great industrial concerns engaged in interstate business," power he would vest in scientific experts, appointed by him. His proposal was to nullify the antitrust laws for monopolies that agreed to obey government orders.[58] He attacked the judiciary, which stood athwart his crusade. Unlike Hamilton, Roosevelt loved elections, loved the practice of political manipulation, but like Hamilton, his goal was to place power among the responsible upper class, men who adhered to a moral code of imperial greatness. Roosevelt's vision terrified his opponents. President William Howard Taft called Roosevelt a "dictator who, once he received a third term, would cling like a leech to the White House and never leave it until death removed him."[59]

Roosevelt had used his self-righteous drive to become the youngest president in history. But soon, Roosevelt would face a real opponent as brilliant as he, a man named Woodrow Wilson, who was the Democratic Party nominee. Wilson, unlike anyone Roosevelt had ever had to defeat, saw through the crowd-friendly politician, the attention seeking, to the would-be demagogue underneath. Wilson would block Roosevelt's great, and frightening, plan, to combine the forces of all corporate monopolies under the control of a powerful, imperial president.

There were two other major presidential candidates running for president in 1912. William Howard Taft carried the mantle of the conservative Republicans. Taft was a "stand-patter" who largely wanted to continue the status quo of corporate dominance, but without embracing monopoly. Eugene Debs, a socialist who saw monopoly as inevitable and efficient, sought not to break up trusts, but to nationalize them.[60] But the contest was really between Roosevelt, campaigning under the aegis of the Progressive Party (aka the "Bull Moose" Party), and Wilson, with two very different visions of reform.

Like Roosevelt, Wilson was an intellectual, and a progressive reformer. Though proposing big ideas, he was no hothead, being a former head of Princeton University, and an acquaintance of the titans of business and finance—John D. Rockefeller, Andrew Carnegie, J.P. Morgan—from whom he had once solicited funds as college president. At Princeton, Wilson had been a Democrat, but had criticized both Bryan and Roosevelt as excessively radical.

Wilson had illustrated strong anticorruption progressive instincts, as well as the toxic racism of the Jim Crow era. He had fought a high-profile battle against the exclusive, fraternity-style eating clubs that dominated the campus, and transformed Princeton from a provincial college for the wealthy into a world-class university, while still ensuring that it would remain an all-white institution. Then, as governor, Wilson had proved he was no puppet for big money. He got his start through the political machine, but once in office, Wilson enthralled progressives. He pushed election reform, the direct election of New Jersey senators, and a public utilities commission that could effectively prevent monopolists from getting around pricing rules. Yet Wilson, like Roosevelt, did not intend the American promise to extend to African Americans.[61]

By 1912, Wilson was thinking big. "All the people are radical," he said. They wanted "proper control of their own affairs."[62] But Wilson didn't want government control of monopoly; he feared Roosevelt's vision, the union of centralized political power married to centralized government power. Wilson sought political liberty for citizens, against the trusts. Just twenty years earlier, Wilson noted, men used to work for themselves. Now, great corporations had become "our masters." But breaking up monopolies was dangerous. Unregulated competition, as railroads experienced in the 1870s, was disastrous. The great practical question was, what to do? If there was not to be a public master in the form of government control, or a private master in the form of monopoly control, then . . . what?

Wilson received an answer in a three-hour conversation the August before the election. Louis Brandeis, nicknamed "the people's lawyer" because of his longtime battles with "corporation lawyers," had come to the governor's seaside cottage to discuss what progress, as he put it, was being made "toward industrial freedom."[63] Brandeis had been thinking, for decades, about how to update traditional Jeffersonian democracy for the industrial age. He would show Wilson a practical way to break monopolies, to decentralize power the way Jefferson had. Brandeis had a program, which Wilson would call "The New Freedom." Brandeis would formalize the populist social sentiment of the late nineteenth century into a rigorous set of legally actionable ideas, becoming a founding figure of twentieth-century Constitutional thinking. America, well into the twentieth century, would be a nation of entrepreneurs because of Brandeis.

Born in the late 1850s like Roosevelt and Wilson, Brandeis had seen the conflict between the old and new worlds throughout his career. He had started as a brilliant corporate lawyer out of Harvard Law, but from the 1890s onward, he led a famous fight against J. P. Morgan's railroad consolidation, which framed his vision of political economy.

In this fight, Brandeis faced a $200 million Morgan-controlled corporation called the New Haven Railroad, which sought to monopolize all transportation in New England, including railroads, trolleys, steamships, and inner-urban rail lines. It was an ugly fight, with the Morgan men bribing politicians, journalists, and academics to allow the company to buy up its competitors. The company spent lavishly, according to regulators, "in 'educating public opinion'" and in "payoffs to newspaper writers."[64] Roosevelt, as part of his deal with Morgan, had refused to use antitrust law against the company.[65]

Brandeis beat the Morgan syndicate by proving that the company had been lying about its financial condition. At first, his allegations that this railroad was losing money subjected Brandeis to scorn and ridicule; the company paid a reliable dividend, and legends like William Rockefeller and J. P. Morgan were on the board. How could a simple lawyer question great men with names like that?

But Brandeis was right. The New Haven was grossly mismanaged. It invested little in safety equipment, and its board of directors comprised financiers so busy they paid no attention to the company. Soon, grisly accidents led to dozens of deaths on a regular basis. After one particularly deadly accident in Wallingford, Connecticut, "a disastrous wreck even in the history of that disastrous road," a reporter tried to ask J. P. Morgan's son, who inherited the firm from his famous father, what could be done. "Mr. Morgan cannot see you," said his butler. "He says he can do nothing about it and does not care to be annoyed."[66] By 1912, the press had turned on Morgan and the New Haven. The railroad was, as the Interstate Commerce Commission later called it, "one of the most glaring instances of maladministration revealed in all the history of American railroading."[67]

With his exposure of the corruption of the New Haven Railroad, Brandeis fully earned the title "the people's lawyer." But this did not make him antibusiness. Brandeis respected business, and saw how market structures that supported farmers and workers, as well as corporate structures like cooperatives, could develop citizens.[68] Like Jefferson, Brandeis loved science and gadgets. He helped found the American Fair Trade League, a business association that included specialty producers and retailers in medicine, brand-name foods, printing, electronics, machine tools, and tobacco companies.

Brandeis's goal was to achieve what he called "industrial liberty." Trusts, he felt, took away the ability of Americans to have control over their commerce. Economic and financial combinations had become so big that they could not be controlled. Regulation of giants was often futile; even trusts couldn't control what was happening inside themselves. "Man's works have outgrown man. Man has remained the same," Brandeis said.[69] He contrasted American politics, where men were free to vote, and American commerce, where they were under the thumb of petty tyrants. These two systems were in conflict, a contrast "between our political liberty and industrial absolutism."[70]

Before meeting Brandeis, Wilson had believed that the way to address trusts was to punish the guilty individuals behind them. Brandeis argued that it was the system itself and the legal context, not any specific individual, that created a commercial system oriented toward cheating and monopolization. The solution was not to regulate monopoly or just punish wrongdoers. The government should both break up concentrations of power, and then regulate markets so monopolies didn't return. He envisioned a system of regulated competition.[71]

On Labor Day of 1912, Wilson used Brandeis's framework to attack Roosevelt. "Once the government regulates the monopoly," Wilson told a rally in Buffalo, "then monopoly will see to it that it regulates the government."[72] Wilson pledged to break up monopolies, and attacked Roosevelt's plan of putting together a board of experts to govern monopolies. "What I fear," said the Princeton professor, "is a government of experts."[73]

Four days later, in North Dakota, Roosevelt struck back. Antitrust, he argued, had failed, as would Wilson's "vague, puzzled, and hopeless purpose feebly to continue the present policy."[74] Wilson was a fraud, pretending to attack monopoly while actually just supporting the status quo. One could not undo the trusts, or, as J. P. Morgan put it, "unscramble the eggs in an omelet." Attempting to do so was nostalgic and foolhardy.

For most of the month of September, the two men offered two different visions to American voters over the shape of corporate America. It was Jefferson versus Hamilton over the nature of liberty, only this time in the industrial era. Two schools battled, both of whom saw themselves as progressive. There were Wilsonian progressives, influenced by rural populists, who thought breaking up concentrations of power would bring forth liberty. And there were those who stood with Teddy Roosevelt, seeking not to smash concentrations of power, but to have progressive experts use the power of trusts and monopolies to deliver a better world. This philosophical split would remain, cascading through the next century.

Wilson won the election, and would work to smash Morgan's power. Finally, the industrial age would become democratic. Intellectuals, businessmen, politicians, and social reformers rallied to the cause of the new president. The chairman of the Banking and Currency Committee, Arsène Paulin Pujo of Louisiana, began a large-scale investigation of the "money trust," with a focus on J. P. Morgan, National City Bank, Kuhn Loeb, Kidder Peabody, and First National Bank. Over the next year, Pujo showed how a small group of financiers in New York had come to dominate many of the "great industrial and railroad corporations of the country," and wielded "despotic" power over the business and commerce of the nation.[75]

To break the industrial corporations, Wilson would invigorate antitrust. The Wilson Justice Department restructured the New Haven Railroad conglomerate, with the former president of the railroad indicted criminally for monopolization.[76] He reorganized America's communications system by breaking up the "telephone trust," or AT&T. The phone and telegraph giant spun off its Western Union telegraph subsidiary, and was required to allow independent phone companies to interconnect with its system so all Americans could have access to reasonable phone service.[77]

To take on the banks and the money trust, Wilson created the

Federal Reserve system, a central bank designed to move power over the economy from Wall Street to the people. He passed the first federal aid to farmers, the income tax, the first federal child labor law, the first law mandating an eight-hour workday for industrial workers, and a major tariff revision.[78] He would create the Federal Trade Commission, a regulatory body set up both to help structure fair trade rules for small and medium-size businesses and end monopolization. He passed the Clayton Act, to protect labor, stop big mergers, and end the practice of price discrimination.

The goal of Wilson's New Freedom was to change how Americans saw the world, by equipping them with a public set of institutions to reduce the power of the private government. Private banks would become less important because the Federal Reserve system would now govern the financial system. The ability of trusts to set the terms of trade would now be challenged by the Federal Trade Commission, a public body that would structure markets for the people. The Clayton Act set rules to protect workers and stop predatory pricing by trusts, and lower tariffs that limited the ability of manufacturing monopolies to ward off competition from abroad. This structure would be undergirded by a political coalition of farmers and labor unions, who would form the backbone of the Democratic Party. The ideological revolution of the New Freedom lived inside these new public institutions, and a revamped party of the people.

The elder J. P. Morgan died in March of 1913, just as the new rules he hated were enacted. In January of 1914, Morgan partners resigned from the boards of thirty powerful corporations and a dozen railroads.[79] The money trust was being broken apart.

In 1916, Wilson nominated Brandeis to the Supreme Court. Wilson was proposing that the Supreme Court, the most sacred temple of business probity, now have as a member a radical, an activist, an attorney who had dared call into question the structure of the giant corporation. "When Brandeis's nomination came in," a Washington correspondent wrote, "the Senate simply gasped." This maneuver, too, was a fight. Seven former presidents of the American Bar Association, including William Howard Taft, called Brandeis "unfit" for the court. But Wilson's mastery of the political process conquered the emerging network of big law firms and Wall Street. After a brutal confirmation process, Brandeis took his seat. "I can never live up to my Brandeis appointment," Wilson said. "There is nobody else who represents the greatest technical ability and professional success with complete devotion to the people's interest."[80]

In 1910, Roosevelt had put forth the idea that America was confronting its third great Constitutional crisis. Wilson agreed with the diagnosis, but not the cure. Wilson would smash monopoly power, not co-opt it. And now, the democratization of industry that Brandeis and so many reformers since the advent of big business had envisioned seemed to be here. The corporation could once again become a means for citizens to cooperate in industry and self-government, using techniques like arbitration boards, credit unions, cooperatives, and worker ownership.

But a new kind of war in Europe interrupted Wilson's great experiment. In World War I, Americans watched as sclerotic aristocratic political leaders used their industrial power to send millions of people to their graves with poison gas, machine guns, and artillery. Yet the war, though horrific, forced a global debate over liberty, imperialism, and trade. Far from stopping Wilson's great crusade, perhaps it might be possible to use the war's ghastliness to stop tyranny everywhere.

With the Great War, the question became, could Wilson match the moment?

Indeed, when Wilson finally took America into the war, he didn't retract his grand promises, but instead elevated them. He no longer sought to remake America, but the world. The idealism of 1912, the democratic rebellion from the 1890s onward, soared around the globe. In May 1919, from peace talks in France, Wilson cabled Congress and called for a "genuine democratization of industry."[81]

America would not just sign a peace treaty, but create a new form of global society, a League of Nations, a global government, to make war itself illegal. Wilson would bring peace and justice, everlasting, everywhere. By 1919, after the crusades of Teddy Roosevelt, the election of Wilson, the battles of Brandeis, and a horrific world war, the stage was set to eject the moneychangers from the temple, not just in America, but in the Old World as well. The people seemed to demand nothing less.

## CHAPTER TWO

# MELLONISM

"The poor have occasionally objected to being governed badly. The rich have always objected to being governed at all."

—G. K. Chesterton[1]

■ ■ ■ ■ ■ ■ ■ ■ ■ ■ ■ ■ ■

Inauguration day, March 4, 1921, was cold and clear. A new president, Warren Harding, stood outside the Capitol in a velvet collar and a dark coat, flanked by approving wealthy men in silk hats. This was their president, their guy. Finally. After twenty years of absurd reform and fights over "progressivism," first from the odious egomaniac Teddy Roosevelt, and then the catastrophic Woodrow Wilson, the people had come to their senses and returned power to society's natural rulers.

The theme of the campaign Harding had run to devastating effect was "a return to normalcy," which he conveyed in his very persona. Harding was not particularly competent, and he knew it. He once described himself as "a man of limited talents from a small town."[2] For his inaugural address, the new president gave a stilted speech illustrative of his commitment to mediocrity. His ruddy complexion was the picture of health, in contrast to the broken man he succeeded.

Eight years earlier, Woodrow Wilson had carried the hopes of a nation. Now he lay prostrate, a figure no longer of dignity but, as one reporter put it, "a living ghost." A year and a half before his second term ended, Wilson had suffered a stroke, rendering him partially paralyzed and largely bedridden. His voice was reduced to an almost robotic gurgle. He was "a broken, ruined old man, shuffling along, his left arm inert, the fingers drawn up like a claw, the left side of his face sagging frightfully."[3]

Harding helped Wilson into an open-topped car for the ceremonial drive to the inauguration at the Capitol. This was the first time Wilson had been in public since his stroke, and the people lined up on Pennsylvania Avenue to watch the now "pathetic picture," and his successor. Upon arrival, Harding helped Wilson out of the car, and then bounded up the stairs.

Before Edward D. White, the conservative chief justice of the Supreme Court, Harding put his hand on the Bible used in George Washington's inaugural and swore an oath to protect the Constitution. Later that day, Harding presented his new cabinet to the Senate. The real power of Harding's administration would lie here. Andrew Mellon, the heir to J. P. Morgan as the ruler of American finance, would take his oath as the secretary of the treasury in the office of Philander Knox, the Pennsylvania senator and former lawyer to the most powerful members of the money trust.

Wilson was put in a wheelchair and wheeled away.[4]

## WILSON'S DOWNFALL

The election of 1912 had held such promise, with Wilson's pledge to bring forth what he called a New Freedom to liberate Americans from the railroads and the trusts. His White House was, according to Brandeis, "the only time in recent American history when rich men had not had an undue influence with an administration."[5] In his first eighteen months, Wilson passed more legislation than any president in the industrial era. He settled long-standing political questions, like the century-long dispute over whether the United States would have a central bank. America almost had a peaceful economic revolution.

How did it all go so wrong?

It was true that not all parts of Wilson's New Freedom had gone smoothly. The Federal Reserve, designed to break the money trust, had no clear center of authority, with both its public federal headquarters and its banker-dominated regional branches vying for control. The Federal Trade Commission, with its broad mandate, was hamstrung by bad appointments, men with, according to Brandeis, "no grasp of the real problem."[6] But Wilson's new institutions would eventually serve as the foundation for what Democrats would later achieve in the 1930s. And on the immediate question—the money trust—they were having a huge effect. In mid-July 1914, the ICC recommended criminal prosecution of the board of directors of the New Haven Railroad. The Morgan men were reeling.

But just two weeks after the ICC's report on the Morgan-Rockefeller control of the New Haven, war broke out in Europe. Everything but the war became irrelevant. Because when the guns of August 1914 boomed, panic struck. Foreigners dumped American stock to raise money for the war, and the stock market crashed. Bankers huddled at the offices of banker J. P. Morgan; the governors of the New York Stock Exchange shut the stock market down for six months. One hundred thousand Americans were stuck in a now-warring Europe.

And yet the war, while awful for the millions who died, would become a boon for the United States economy. American businesses and farmers profited. The U.S. shipped weapons, food, and raw materials to England and France, and American banks extended credit to their governments. America, at least at first, had commercial, not military, objectives.

But such a delicate attempt to profit off war could only last so long. The German government, unable to buy much from America due to an effective British blockade, saw the U.S. profiting in supplying Germany's enemies as a significant strategic problem. In response, the Germans engaged in submarine warfare, often against neutral shipping.

Wilson was caught, trying to balance a commitment to neutrality with the profit afforded American farmers and manufacturers by selling war supplies to the Allies. By 1917, unrestricted German submarine warfare drew American ire. A little over a month after the British revealed that Germany had secretly proposed a military alliance with Mexico against the United States, Wilson finally took the country to war.

Wilson understood the stakes. He feared that entering the conflict might cause the loss of every reform he had implemented. War would require cooperation with big business, which might again rule the government. Wilson entered into the morass anyway, ruing to a cabinet member that "neither you nor I will live to see government returned to the people. More than that—Free Speech and the other rights will be endangered. War is autocratic."[7] He was right.

World War I transformed the global order. "It was in World War I," wrote John Kenneth Galbraith, "that the age-old certainties were lost. Until then aristocrats and capitalists felt secure in their position, and even socialists felt certain in their faith. It was never to be so again."[8] A new utopian communist experiment in Russia drew admirers all over the world, terrifying the old order.

One result was to transform America into an economic and military superpower. American businesses were no longer dependent on European investors for capital. Prior to the war, it was American corporations who borrowed from the Europeans. They were the ones who financed the American railroad system. But during the war, this financial relationship was reversed. France and England bought billions in American supplies, and went deeply into debt. Europeans were now the economic vassals. Culturally, too, America led, in everything from armaments production and high technology to the film industry.

Another result was to unleash ideological chaos, and challenge both aristocracy and democracy. A world of European empires run by monarchs gave way to a world where communism and nascent fascism existed alongside democracies and de-colonizers. The British empire was wracked with independence movements. Within just three years, Portugal, Spain, Italy, Greece, Turkey, Russia, Poland, Czechoslovakia, and Belgium "endured" dictators. A little more than a decade after the war, Austria, Hungary, Germany, and Yugoslavia became dictatorships as well.[9]

Domestically, a sustained popular and scholarly attack challenged the idea of democracy in America. To organize the war effort, the Wilson administration had centralized power to an astonishing degree, implementing a military draft, a censorship regime, and an unparalleled propaganda effort. The ability to control large swaths of the public through hyper-nationalistic messaging and censorship shook progressives hard. In 1922, Walter Lippmann, who had advised Wilson before the Treaty of Versailles, expressed despair in his book *Public Opinion,* noting that man was easily manipulated by symbols; in 1925, he published *The Phantom Public,* concluding democracy was unworkable.

This became a common view in magazines and in popular novels. A 1928 U.S. Army Training Manual even concluded that democracy resulted in "demogogism, license, agitation, discontent, anarchy."[10]

The loss of faith in democracy penetrated academic institutions. Out of the war came standardized testing, which had been used to screen soldiers, and professionalized public relations, perfected by Wilson's censorship board, the Committee on Public Information. These helped structure the new field of "political science," which professionalized within a rapidly growing university system. The social sciences, focusing on knowledge, efficiency, and an aesthetic of scientific objectivity, replaced prewar reform movements oriented around popular democracy. Scholars began focusing on propaganda and the inherent irrational motivations of human beings, as well as emphasizing the racial pseudoscience of eugenics. Antidemocratic and racist ideas were popularized by writers like H. L Mencken, but they represented an increasing consensus of the intelligentsia.[11]

The postwar decade was, for those who believed in democracy, an era of despair. The autocrats were not only winning, but perhaps, better at governing than the progressives had been. As a *Christian Century* editorial put it, "The hope of democracy will revive when it learns how to do the things that need to be done as efficiently as autocracy does them."[12]

A final result of the war was to unleash monopolists at home, much the way the Civil War had done fifty years earlier. Despite significant government efforts to avoid it, financial and industrial power concentrated once again.[13] The war induced so much demand for steel, coal, oil, explosives, aluminum, and credit that big business came out stronger at the end than the beginning. Explosives maker DuPont earned $82 million in profits in 1916, ten times its average earnings before the war. The company paid out large dividends and salaries, and had enough left over to buy 25 percent of General Motors. U.S. Steel earned $272 million in 1916, twelve times its profit from two years earlier. J. P. Morgan earned $30 million in fees and leverage over the economy as the purchasing agent for America's allies.[14]

After the war, Wilson went to Paris for months to negotiate the Treaty of Versailles. Wilson aimed to rebuild the European economies, promote stable democracies, and construct a global order based on equality of trade among nations, what would be called the League of Nations. Wilson sought a commitment that all countries, including the United States, would be willing to protect each other from aggression, with differences resolved peacefully. Wilson was committing American power and wealth to stabilizing a world order. Without a means to ensure collective security, he believed, there would be another world war, with weapons that made those of the first Great War seem like toys.

Domestically, two unseen forces were at work undermining Wilson's peace plan. The first was concentrated capital. In 1919, Andrew Mellon and Henry Clay Frick provided funds for a group of opponents to the treaty known as "irreconcilables," including a barnstorming tour across the country by isolationist senators. Frick and Mellon believed that America should use its power solely to enhance American financial interests, not to engage in some scheme for world peace.

The two men saw opposition to the treaty as a way to discredit the Democrats and drive them from power. After the Senate voted against the treaty, Wilson decided to go over their heads, to the voters, on a grand national speaking tour of his own in favor of ratification. He would force the Senate to do his bidding. Just a few years later, it might have worked. Brandeis observed, "If Wilson had had the radio, so that he could have reached a larger part of the population, he might have won."[15] But radio would only become popular in the 1920s.

The second unseen force was Wilson's health.

This created a power vacuum, one made worse by the Federal Reserve, Wilson's great creation. The Fed badly mishandled the financing of the war and the period of demobilization. The war transformed the Fed and the government into the key global actors in the world of finance. To finance the guns and supplies for the fight, federal debt increased tenfold to $25 billion after the war.[16]

The war destabilized the American economy. During the war and immediate postwar era, America experienced, according to the Fed, the "greatest expansion of business ever known," what the central bank called "a period of intense business activity, expansion, speculation, and extravagance, the like of which has never before been seen in this country or in the world."[17] The problem, at first, was inflation, as too much money chased too few goods. In a very complex series of maneuvers, regional Federal Reserve branches essentially engineered a massive inflation to protect commercial bank profits. Demobilization, including the end of credit restrictions, accelerated the boom as people rushed to buy consumer goods.

Inflation created political chaos, which Wilson ignored. "The citizens of the United States want you home to help reduce the high cost of living, which we consider far more important than the League of Nations," wrote one group of Massachusetts Democrats to Wilson while he was in Europe.[18] One of the largest strike waves in history ensued, with five million workers in 3,600 separate actions. In late 1919 and early 1920, inflation was running at 25 percent annually. Companies like GE and U.S. Steel seized this moment to go on the offensive. In the most significant episode, U.S. Steel's Elbert Gary refused to recognize a labor union, and 365,000 workers went on strike. To contain them, the company used 25,000 private security guards in Pennsylvania alone, with martial law in the steel town of Gary, Indiana. Twenty people died in the strike.[19]

Coal miners walked off the job, calling for the nationalization of the mines, while businessmen supported the brutal crushing of strikes launched by "long-haired Slavs and unwashed East-Side Jews."[20] In early 1920, despite the White House pleading with the company, U.S. Steel prevailed totally, and talk of industrial democracy in the steel industry ended forever. Race riots, as whites attacked blacks—especially soldiers returning from war—took place across dozens of cities.

Finally, in a dramatic reversal, the Fed stepped in to cut the speculation, radically increasing the cost of borrowing money. In eight months starting in November 1919, the New York Fed raised its discount rate from 4 percent to 7 percent. Said one Treasury official, "If a panic in New York should break out, he would be glad of it." The economy cracked. In May 1920, commodities prices across the board dropped spectacularly as general prices fell at the fastest rate ever measured. Unemployment went from 4 percent in 1920 to 12 percent in 1921, industrial production dropped by nearly a quarter, and over five hundred banks failed.[21] Hyperinflation of the first half of 1920 turned to deflation, as prices in the second half of the year dropped by a severe rate of 15 percent.[22] This savaged the Farm Belt in particular; cotton prices fell by 93 percent, as the agricultural producers of Europe were coming back online after the war.[23]

In this "trying emergency," as the Fed put it, the central bank's engineered decline went out of control into a full crash. The banking system, which it had sought to protect, nearly collapsed, with the number of bank failures larger than in any year since 1893.[24] Because America had become the key financial actor in the global economy, the period of inflation and deflation, organized by the Fed, went worldwide. So did social instability. Fascism rose in Italy, communism in Russia. In Germany would come Hitler's attempted coup at a beer hall.

The Republicans used this episode they called "the crime of 1920" to bludgeon the Democrats in the 1920 elections. The boom and bust shattered the electoral coalition of farmers and workers that Wilson had sought to organize as the Democratic Party coalition.[25]

The agrarian crisis led to a revival of the Ku Klux Klan, as a Wilson official alleged that low commodity prices were due to Wall Street conspiracies. The Klan was reborn in 1916 with a few hundred members. But by the early 1920s, the Klan had four million members, and this time it wasn't centered in the South but stretched across the country: the mayor of Portland, Oregon, and the mayor of Portland, Maine, were both Klansmen. Texas, Alabama, and Indiana sent Klansmen to the Senate in 1923.

With war had come fears of subversion and a wave of xenophobia. These did not disappear when the troops came home; on the contrary, they often grew worse. Congress passed racist immigration policies. "The dregs of Europe" and elsewhere, cried one politician, had "Orientalized, Europeanized, Africanized, and mongrelized" America.[26]

Wilson, so energetic at the beginning of his term, could do nothing by the end of his tenure except lie in bed as his administration jailed thousands of innocents, and as the plutocrats swiftly subverted the new order he had imposed just a few years earlier. Wilson's presidency became, as one observer put it in a best-selling book ten years later, "an era of lawless and disorderly defense of law and order, of unconstitutional defense of the Constitution, of suspicion and civil conflict—in a very literal sense, a reign of terror."[27] So much for the New Freedom.

The Democratic Party's pro-monopoly conservative wing also returned in force. In 1924, the party nominated as its presidential candidate a powerful corporate lawyer named John W. Davis. By 1928, the party was being run by a DuPont executive, John Jakob Raskob, who in 1929 was peddling a high-risk get-rich-quick scheme for small investors under the slogan "Everybody Ought to Be Rich." The Democrats fought over the prohibition of alcohol and the KKK, the social issues of the decade, but shied from finance and monopoly.

The people "are docile, and they will not recover from being so for many years," observed leading progressive Hiram Johnson.[28] The country had been aroused by idealism, but now, even Democratic Party leaders had given up on the New Freedom. In this decade, one of cynicism and fear, people turned to those who promised them distraction, or anger, or get-rich-quick prosperity and nothing more.

## THREE PRESIDENTS AND THEIR BOSS ANDREW MELLON

The new president was a plodding, corrupt mediocrity picked by rich party bosses. Harding had no use for phrases such as Brandeis's "industrial liberty," Wilson's New Freedom, or Roosevelt's New Nationalism, or anything with the word "new" in it. The promises in his inaugural address were packaged in ugly, clunky phrases. "Lightened tax burdens." "The omission of unnecessary interference of Government with business." "An end to Government experiment." And above all, "normalcy." Experimentation and reform were over.[29]

But at his inauguration, the wealthy backers of the new president clapped at his financier-friendly phrases as if it were poetry. Harding was their dream, a candidate whose very lack of talent had appealed to a nation looking for calm.

The triumph over progressives was total. Harding had restored the old coalition of 1896, winning sixteen million votes to the Democratic nominee's nine million, 60.3 percent to 34.1 percent. The GOP even penetrated the Confederate South, taking Tennessee, and safe

Democratic states such as Arizona and Oklahoma. Not a single Democrat won a Senate or governor seat anywhere outside the South. In 1912, Wilson had started with House and Senate majorities; now the Republicans would have a super-majority of 303–121 in the House, and 70–26 in the Senate.

After his inaugural speech, Harding introduced the man who was to run the Treasury Department, a man who would become far more important than the president who hired him. Andrew Mellon had a quiet demeanor, rail-thin bearing, and beautifully manicured hands. His habit of taking long vacations, his age, his manners, and his soft-spoken shyness might have been mistaken for weakness and frailty in someone else. Mellon may have been born rich, but he was not soft. He was a hard man, a banker, an emperor of money, an owner of several companies later included in the *Fortune* 500. He would help lead the restoration of rule by private financiers.

President Warren G. Harding formally appointed Mellon under the pretense that a plutocrat like Mellon was so rich he couldn't be bought.[30] The real reason was that a Mellon Bank had lent $1.5 million to Harding's campaign in 1920. Mellon had become bored with being a mere tycoon. As one of his enemies put it, "Mellon needed a change, and the Grand Old Party needed the cash."[31]

Mellon's appointment was probably illegal. A statute from 1789 prohibits the treasury secretary from engaging in commerce or trade, an absurd expectation for a man with such industrial power.[32] The founders had also written a law blocking the treasury secretary from holding bank stocks, another absurdity. Mellon overcame these legal restrictions by pretending to sell his assets to his brother. The rules existed for good reason: a man clothed in public power should not use that power for private ends, though Mellon did exactly that throughout the 1920s. Mellon explained the need to raise tariffs to protect domestic industrial monopolies to Harding even before the election. Harding dutifully mentioned tariffs in his inaugural address.

Mellon left even the other millionaire politicians shocked at the scale of his reach. In one cabinet meeting, the discussion turned to whether the government should shut down a government war plant, or refurbish it with additional investment. Mellon observed he owned a similar plant, which cost $12 million, roughly the same value as the one the government was considering closing. He had the same dilemma, to spend money maintaining an unprofitable but valuable plant. "I scrapped mine," he said.

In another, someone brought up the Chinese Eastern Railway. The president whispered to his attorney general, "Now we've got him. Surely he wasn't in on this." Harding asked if Mellon had any interest in the railroad. "Oh yes," came the casual answer. "We had a million or a million and a half of the bonds."

"He's the ubiquitous financier of the universe," marveled Harding.[33]

Harding, so healthy at his inauguration, became consumed by corruption scandals, and ended up dying within three years of taking office. Mellon, by contrast, would remain treasury secretary for eleven years, under three presidents. Or, as progressive senator George Norris put it in a common joke of the era, "three presidents served under him."[34] The decade might have started with Warren Harding's presidential victory, but the political economy of the 1920s would be structured by Andrew Mellon.

## MELLON'S MILLIONS

When Harding hired Mellon, he was installing the most powerful private banker in the country into the most powerful public office in the country.

Mellon was the perfect symbol of an administration hoping to return to the pre-1900 era. Mellon's life and career bridged the conservative robber baron politics of the nineteenth century with increasingly large federal government structures of the twentieth. He was born just before the Civil War to a wealthy, austere father, Thomas Mellon, a judge and real estate developer. His gloomy Pittsburgh mansion was in the tony East End of Pittsburgh, a town so smoggy from pollution that someone described it as "Hell with the lid off."

Judge Mellon was deeply suspicious of democratic politics and lower classes asserting power. During the Civil War, he held no strong views on slavery, but the imposition of high taxes on the wealthy during the war enraged him. Public schools drew his ire; he believed children would study harder if they had to pay. Labor unrest among lower classes, he believed, needed to be met with violence, and may even "require blood to purify."[35]

Judge Mellon imparted this ideology to his son. In the Mellon household, "the air was heavy with the imperative to acquire." According to one in-law, "they had absolutely no fun. . . . It was work, work, all the time. The one thing they understood, the end of all their efforts, was money."[36] Judge Mellon insisted that his children learn accounting, at a private school he had set up for them. Judge Mellon also helped launch his son in his career. Judge Mellon was the first lender to a young man on the make, Henry Clay Frick. Frick in turn became a best friend and mentor to Andrew.

Andrew, the smartest of the boys, inherited his father's empire in his twenties. For most of his life, he had a solitary routine. Rising early, he took the train to work, spent the day at the bank, lunched at a private club, and then brought documents home at night for study, "after a silent supper with his parents." He read little, enjoyed little music or plays, and did no sports.[37] Mellon grew to become neurotic, secretive, and soft-spoken, suspicious of taxes and the press.

Judge Mellon was just a banker, but Andrew Mellon became a mini–J. P. Morgan, from whom he learned investment banking. He would take stakes in promising companies, lend to them, and fit them into the "Mellon system" as buyers or suppliers. He had a cadre of loyal associates to move about his various enterprises, as management consultants would a hundred years later. "Mellon men" were tough, loyal, and competent. Most were Scotch-Irish Presbyterians (no blacks, Jews, or Catholics allowed), and would, if they met Mellon's standards, become wealthy too. If not, they would be marginalized ("cut their throat" is one description).[38] "When I send for a man," Mellon would say, "I want him to come."[39]

Unlike other tycoons, he did not specialize in one area. At one point, five *Fortune* 500 companies owed their lineage directly to Mellon: Alcoa, Gulf Oil, Mellon Bank, Carborundum, and Koppers. He controlled a network of ninety-nine banks. He had interests in coal, steel, chemicals, oil, sleeping cars, railroads, building construction, utilities, magnesium, and airplanes.

Mellon even commandeered the use of an entire element of earth—aluminum—through his control of the monopoly aluminum producer Alcoa. This power gave him control not just over aluminum, but over sectors of the economy that depended on it, such as the increasingly vital aerospace industry. The technology to create aluminum emerged too late for the first generation of financiers, but Mellon, who learned from the earlier generation, used all their tricks, and then some. No one firm had ever dominated a metal industry as Alcoa had aluminum for so long a period, from the 1890s until the 1940s.[40]

Beyond commercial control of an element of the earth, and all that went with it, Mellon's empire was unavoidable for ordinary Americans in myriad other ways. The Mellon system was a set of industrial and financial enterprises that aided each other and had interlocking boards of directors and even personnel. Coal unearthed on Mellon lands would find its way into Mellon steel mills, which would help build Mellon ships to carry Mellon oil, all financed by Mellon banks. Being a part of the Mellon system meant customers, credit, financing, and prosperity, but also control. Being outside of it meant a constant battle with the Mellon interests.

If you lived in Pittsburgh, Milwaukee, or Minnesota, you bought Mellon coal; in Philadelphia or New England, you purchased Mellon coke; in Boston or Brooklyn it was Mellon natural gas. Mellon's Union Trust bank financed utilities all over the country; his Koppers company with its expertise in gas and coke ovens helped organize them. The combination of Koppers and Alcoa gave Mellon a strategic advantage in controlling much of the private electric utility industry. Koppers and Alcoa, together, dominated utilities in Texas, Kansas, Iowa, Nebraska, Missouri, Illinois, Indiana, Ohio, West Virginia, Wisconsin, Oklahoma, and throughout New England.[41]

The South was the most exploited region. The "richest deposits of the iron, coal, and limestone that form the basis for the steel industry" in the South were organized by Mellon and his business colleagues. As a result, Birmingham was subordinated to Pittsburgh based on an artificial mechanism for pricing steel. Rich deposits of bauxite, the critical ingredient for aluminum, were concentrated in the South, and they became owned or controlled by Alcoa.[42] With Mellon interests came the Frick model of labor relations, which used ethnic divisions to strip workers of power. One of the worst race riots in American history, in East St. Louis in 1917, started outside an aluminum facility, as white workers on strike faced 470 black strikebreakers recruited from the South. The local authorities stood aside as white mobs murdered over two hundred African Americans.[43]

Mellon held stakes in steel, plate, glass, paint, and iron ore. Mellon men sat directly on the boards of railway lines such as the Northwestern, the Omaha, the Norfolk and Western, and the Pittsburgh & Lake Erie. American Locomotive and Standard Steel Car, which both made cars for railroads, were Mellon companies. Air brakes made by Westinghouse, owned partly by Mellon, stopped these trains. Timber for railroad ties, bridges, and canal locks were built by Mellon-controlled McClintic-Marshall, fired by coal from Mellon's Pittsburgh Coal Company. Mellon's industrial empire sold inputs to the automobile industry, from aluminum to nonshatter glass through Pittsburgh Plate Glass.

Mellon was also an important player in the oil industry. To enter it, Mellon had battled the wealthiest man alive, John D. Rockefeller. Oil brought Mellon interests deep into the heart of Texas, and eventually Mexico and Colombia. Mellon became a proprietor of Gulf Oil, the largest oil company outside of Standard Oil.

World War I generated massive demand for not only aluminum and oil, but chemicals to use in warfare—which were made by Mellon companies. Toluol, naphtha, benzoyl, and ammonia, as well as ships made by the Mellons' New York Shipbuilding Company, and armor made by Bethlehem Steel, sent rivers of cash back to the Mellon empire. By the end of the war, Andrew Mellon was an officer or director of more than sixty companies.

Mellon was also the "financial angel" of the Pennsylvania Republican Party, so powerful that when his ill-considered marriage fell apart in a scandalous split, he had the state legislature pass a law giving judges the right to deny women a trial by jury in divorce cases.[44] Local newspapers, afraid or in thrall to the Mellon family, reported little on the matter.

Fifty years of industrial politics, dominated by men of finance, co-incided exactly with Andrew Mellon's adult life. Mellon had known most of the great robber barons. He played a regular card game with Frick, the Carnegie brothers, and George Westinghouse. He sold oil interests to the Rockefellers. And his home base, Pittsburgh, was a center of American industry.

By 1921, the early generation of robber barons—Frick, Carnegie, Westinghouse, Henry Heinz, and Morgan—had died (though Morgan's son, Jack, was still alive). Mellon had inherited the mantle, the leader of American finance.

## KING ANDREW

Mellon never had as much control over the private financial system and industry as the elder Morgan did. However, after his appointment as treasury secretary, Mellon did have one source of power Morgan did not: a large administrative state, and in that difference lay his power. Mellon, more than Morgan, would fuse government and business to make the world safe for monopolists. Throughout the 1920s, Mellon ran the Treasury Department, set tax and government debt policy, and sat as the chairman of the Federal Reserve.

Many of Woodrow Wilson's achievements offended Mellon, but Wilson's most rank achievement was the income tax on the wealthy. For the eleven years he was at the Treasury, Mellon sought to reduce that tax any way he could. He pestered Congress to lower the top individual rates, to lower rates for corporations, and to end that most odious of taxes, the one on inheritances. That tax would have blocked Mellon's father from bequeathing Andrew the beginnings of an empire. Mellon won substantial reductions in the Republican Congress, but a combination of progressive Republicans and southern Democrats blocked him from a full victory.

When he couldn't win through Congress, he could win through administration, and through his control of the Bureau of Internal Revenue, the forerunner of the Internal Revenue Service. Under Mellon,

the Bureau of Internal Revenue changed the way it calculated tax liabilities incurred during World War I. As a result, billions of dollars of refunds, some to Mellon companies, flowed back to corporate America.
The bureau was especially malleable in these years, because it had just
started collecting income and corporate taxes. In 1916, Americans filed
roughly 450,000 income tax returns. By 1921 the number had jumped
to eight million. This surge allowed Mellon to decide a host of policy
questions around accounting, as corporations demobilized factories
and a suite of nationalized industries returned to private ownership. He
would even set up a special tax court to interpret and make tax law.[45]

Virtually every large corporation in the country received large
rebates, including forty Mellon-affiliated companies or people. Mellon
personally received a $400,000 tax refund, the largest awarded to a
single individual. Gulf Oil got $3 million. Mellon even had men from
the bureau preparing his own returns. These refunds achieved more
than just cash in Mellon's pocket. William Randolph Hearst, whose
newspapers had decried Morgan's spiderlike control years earlier, received $1.7 million of tax refunds. The Hearst papers were so grateful
for Mellon's financial wizardry that they talked up Mellon for the 1928
Republican nomination.[46]

Mellon was a savvy bureaucratic infighter. In perhaps his most
bitter feud of the era, with Republican senator James Couzens, the
wealthiest member of the Senate, Mellon had the Bureau of Internal
Revenue investigate Couzens and leak information about his tax returns. Few Democratic senators dared support Couzens because of the
structure of the developing system for taxing corporate and personal
income. Senators often had to ask the Bureau of Internal Revenue for
decisions on technical questions, on behalf of constituents or corporations. As reporter Frank Kent put it, "not one of them knows when
he will be forced to go there and ask for more. Almost any question
can be decided by the bureau in three or four different ways—all legal.
One of these ways saves a man or a firm a lot of money, and the other
doesn't." Couzens later said, "Give me the control of the Internal Revenue Bureau and I will run the whole darned country. . . . The Commissioner of the Bureau has the power to perpetuate a political party
in power indefinitely. . . . It is a power that no man should be allowed

to exercise in secret." And yet, Mellon did. There was, Kent wrote, no longer a Democratic or Republican Party, but instead, "a Mellon party and a small non-Mellon party."[47]

Mellon could also see to it that his industrial empire flourished in the era through other mechanisms. He blocked antitrust action against Alcoa. The FTC didn't bother to look into Gulf Oil, or any of Mellon's other vast holdings. Mellon didn't just ward off attacks, but negotiated with foreign leaders for oil concessions for his own oil company, both in Colombia and in Kuwait.[48] And the great tax reductions he pushed through Congress, which slashed his own tax bill, ended up slashing into the stock market, pushing up the value of the stocks he held.

Mellon could even hold up the entire political system to serve his own interests. In 1930, Democrats attacked the merits of the high protective tariff on aluminum imports, attempting to reduce the duty from five cents to two cents a pound on crude aluminum. The bill narrowly passed the Senate. Suddenly, New York Democratic senator Royal Copeland made a plea to reverse course and go back to the five cents a pound rate; the jobs of ten thousand workers in New York were at stake. If the tariff dropped to two cents a pound, Alcoa would move production to Canada.

Progressive senator George Norris noted that Copeland "frankly admits that it is on account of fear of the power of this corporation to bring distress, poverty, and unemployment to the American toiling masses" that he supported the Mellon monopoly tariff. Copeland replied that the "people of this country are at the mercy of this monster monopoly, no matter what we do." The higher tariff held.[49]

This might be unfair, but fairness didn't matter. Treasury Secretary Mellon told voters that there were immutable economic laws that could not be evaded. "Just as labor cannot be forced to work against its will, so it can be taken for granted that capital will not work unless the return is worth while."[50] Great wealth not only shouldn't be curtailed through government policy, in fact it couldn't be.

Mellon promoted his philosophy in a 1924 best-selling book called *Taxation: The People's Business*. Anything that taxed the wealthy was full of "menace for the future," threatening the very stability of society. He went further. "Our civilization," he wrote, "is based on accumulated capital, and that capital is no less vital to our prosperity than is the extraordinary energy which has built up in this country the greatest material civilization the world has ever seen."[51]

The question during the election of 1912 was how to fit industrialization into the democratic system. Wilson, and Brandeis, had argued that the failure to constrain the power of trusts would mean monopolies and financiers would be our "masters." In the 1920s, this was becoming a reality, as Mellon helped create a new political order, not quite a democracy, not quite corporatism, but a mix.

## THE ROARING TWENTIES

In 1925, President Calvin Coolidge coined the slogan of the 1920s, telling assembled newspaper editors that the "business of the American people is business." The rich were now heroic. "Men with large resources," he said, "use their power to serve, not themselves and their own families, but the public."[52] *The New Republic* stamped Coolidge's theory on Mellon, arguing sarcastically in 1926 "a fortune of that size raises its owner out of the class of private citizens and stamps him willy-nilly as a human public utility."[53]

In this decade, Mellon, DuPont, and Morgan were names that meant more than wealth, they referred to an informal system of governance. Inventors and scientists were bringing an unending stream of inventions and improvements to daily life. But it was the financiers, not the inventors, who governed this system, choosing how these inventions were unleashed and ensuring that it would be centralized powerful corporations that controlled them.

Placing power in the hands of business seemed to work. After a brutal recession of the early 1920s, economic growth soared. The unemployment rate for 1925 dropped to 4 percent, on its way to a peacetime century low of 1.9 percent in 1926.[54] A giant financial bubble was undergirding economic growth, but it was easy to overlook that in the haze of prosperity and the continued spread of next-generation industrialization technologies.

New technologies made even the old ones prosperous. The automobile industry boomed, energizing basic sectors of the economy—steel, machine tools, petroleum, rubber, roads, and chemicals.[55] By 1930, 68 percent of households had electricity, and more than 70 percent of industry was electrified. In 1928, a Ford Model T rolled off the assembly line every ten seconds. In 1920, Americans bought radios for the first time, and Hollywood professionalized into studios.[56]

Validation for financial leaders embedded itself in the culture, a national pride in great fortunes, the faith in the new nation-spanning sinews of transportation and energy. "Our industrial and financial growth has broken all records in the history of progress," said one official. America had just twenty-five years prior been looked at with "supercilious disdain," but was now "the mightiest, strongest, and richest nation of the globe—the balance wheel of the world." It produced more coal than the entire world had just a quarter century before, twice as much pig iron, and three times as much steel. The combined resources of the banks of Europe and Japan were just one half of the national banks in the United States.[57]

At first little known, the Republican-dominated press gradually gave Mellon more and more credit for the boom times, especially after the horrific economic experience of 1919–1920. Millions of Americans soon revered him. He was commonly known as the best secretary of the treasury "since Alexander Hamilton."[58] Indeed, it was Mellon who placed Hamilton, America's original proponent of monopoly, on the $10 bill.

"Never before, here or anywhere else," wrote *The Wall Street Journal,* "has a government been so completely fused with business."[59] The Federal Trade Commission, created by Wilson, was in the Mellon years led by W. E. Humphrey, a man who proudly announced it would no longer serve as a "publicity bureau to spread socialist propaganda."

In 1926, the Supreme Court limited the FTC's authority to block mergers.[60] This decision may not have mattered in any case, as the FTC in the 1920s largely confined itself to bringing businessmen together to set informal codes over their industries. As business consultant Charles Stevenson later told the National Association of Cost Accountants, "practically, under the Harding, Coolidge, and Hoover administrations, industry enjoyed, to all intents and purposes, a moratorium from the Sherman Act, and, through the more or less effective trade associations which were developed in most of our industries, competition was, to a very considerable extent, controlled."[61] The 1920s saw an antitrust regime based on public relations, not enforcement of the law.[62]

Lax antitrust enforcement induced a giant merger wave. Bethlehem Steel and Republic Steel merged, and Allied Chemical and Dye formed out of five separate chemical companies. Auto giants bought up parts suppliers, with DuPont's General Motors introducing large-scale consumer credit to foster car buying.

These changes went far beyond heavy industry. Food giants such as National Dairy Products, Standard Brands, and General Foods came to rule the food industry.[63] A 1911 Supreme Court decision allowed stores to sell below cost and drive their competitors out of business.[64] Retailers with access to capital, known as chain stores, could now destroy those who didn't. This legal change, plus the spread of the automobile, which let Americans shop around more easily, began replacing local retailers with chains. Chain stores exploded, led by the Great Atlantic & Pacific Tea Company, known as the A&P. In 1914, A&P had $31 million in revenue and fewer than five hundred stores. Ten years later, it had $440 million and fourteen thousand stores.[65]

Chain stores became part of the increasingly consumer-oriented American experience, growing their share of the grocery market from 4 percent to 19.2 percent from 1921 to 1929.[66] The A&P was the largest retailer in the world at that time, a billion-dollar seller by 1930. Safeway, Kroger, Walgreens, and A&P expanded rapidly, both through internal investment and by buying out rivals.

Legal devices for centralizing power multiplied. Holding companies permeated the utility and transportation fields. Banks such as Goldman Sachs and J. P. Morgan began setting up financial holding companies to let financiers borrow money and control enormous utility empires with very little of their own money at risk. The government had allowed banks and investment companies to merge in 1911.[67] The big got bigger.

It seemed like an endless sea of prosperity. Just not for everyone.

## MELLONISM

"I have just returned from a visit 'Hell-in-Pennsylvania,'" wrote New York *Daily News* reporter Lowell Limpus, about a strike in coal country. "I have seen horrible things there; things which I almost hesitate to enumerate and describe." It was a far cry from anything he had ever witnessed. "We saw thousands of women and children literally starving to death. We found hundreds of destitute families living in crudely constructed bare-board shacks. They had been evicted from their homes by the coal companies."

This was not just a story of desperation, a story of political absolutism within a supposedly free country. "We unearthed a system of despotic tyranny reminiscent of Czar-ridden Siberia at its worst. We found police brutality and industrial slavery." And referring to the odd set of judicial decisions against unions, such as those banning singing of hymns by miners, he wrote, "We discovered the weirdest flock of injunctions that ever emanated from American temples of justice."[68]

In the Roaring Twenties, steelworkers and coal miners in Appalachia faced "coal and iron" police who wielded the power of the state but who were paid by private interests. "Workers born in Tsarist Russia were not surprised to see mounted troopers riding into their very homes," wrote one observer. "The state troopers were dubbed 'Cossacks' by strikers who had felt the impact of mace on skull." As a Labor Department official later described the coal mines of the 1920s, there was "an order in that industry which is not without its resemblance to the Fascist order."[69]

In 1921, a *New York Post* reporter said it simply: "West Virginia is today in a state of civil war."[70] The war was over the right of miners to form a union. While the financiers could organize together, the miners could not. As one lawyer put it, a miner makes an "individual contract with the agent of the United States Steel Corporation, or with the agent of the Norfolk and Western Railway Company, controlled by the Pennsylvania Railroad Company—in short, he makes this contract with the associated financiers of the Nation."[71]

Local mine owners were no more independent of the great

financiers than the miners they employed. Large buyers of coal, such as the DuPont-controlled General Motors, threatened to stop buying coal from mine owners who wouldn't crush unions. Railroads controlled by Morgan or Mellon interests would refuse to ship coal from mine owners who didn't cooperate. Banks threatened to call in loans. The "Mellon banking interests," said one mine owner, would "ruin me" if he recognized the union.[72] Mellon didn't just provide symbolism for the era, but was one of the key leaders who could control thousands of companies, and millions of lives. When Wilson and Brandeis and their allies talked of "autocracy" in business, this is what they meant.[73]

This autocratic machinery, vast and laden with capital, was connected to the White House itself. It was even connected with actual weaponry. In 1928, Mellon's brother Richard had let slip in a congressional hearing that his management model required machine guns. "You could not run a mine without them," he said.[74]

Life in the mines was only the most brutal manifestation of the other market of the Mellon decade, with inequality driven by low wages among workers and farmers. Crop prices were low throughout the decade, and Mellon and the Republicans blocked relief and farm supports. "Farmers have never made money," said Calvin Coolidge to the Farm Loan Board. "I don't believe there is much we can do about it."[75] A series of court decisions weakened the ability of workers to strike, and employers across the country sought to eliminate unions. The American Federation of Labor fell from 5 million to 3.6 million members from 1920 to 1923 and continued falling through the decade. Productivity jumped by 30 percent, but wages were up by just 8 percent in the decade. As one foreign visitor to the United States remarked in 1928, "America is an employer's paradise."[76]

There was also stark regional inequality. Most assets, such as 90 percent of money-producing patents and over 90 percent of all dividends and interest payments, were held in the North, starving the South and the West of capital. Of the top 200 corporations, 9 were in the South, 11 in the West, and 180 in the North. Chain stores, insurance companies, banks, railroads, oil companies, industrial outfits—all owned and used the resources and markets of the South and West, and then shipped the profits north.

No region suffered more than the South. Since the end of the Civil War, the South was commonly known as the nation's chief economic problem. The richest state in the South ranked lower in per capita income than the poorest state outside the region. Farmers, half of whom were tenant farmers, had the smallest farms in the nation. They couldn't afford crop rotation, so the land eroded. Sixty-one percent of all the land damaged by erosion was in the South, with 22 million acres of fertile soil in South Carolina alone washed away.

The South put its tax burden on the poorest through the sales tax, and "the vigorous opposition of interests outside the region which control much of the South's wealth" beat back efforts to oppose it.[77] Outsiders exploited the natural resources of the region, leaving little for the people themselves. Mellon's empire extended into the region. He built Gulf Oil off the profits of the legendary Spindletop oil strike in Texas that created the term "gusher."

Roughly 10 percent of the children in the South worked, accounting for three fourths of all child labor in the entire country. The most productive workers of the region simply left the region. By 1928, 30 percent of households in the South were headed by women past middle age. Fifteen percent of South Carolinians were illiterate, and 1,500 school centers in Mississippi lacked school buildings.[78]

There was also a perpetual health crisis. Two million people a year were infected by malaria, which cut industrial output by a third; railroads throughout the region listed malaria as a business challenge, and utility companies "had full-time mosquito-fighting crews at work during the year."[79] That same study noted that 1,467 coal miners and 1,232 ore miners died every year from tuberculosis. Prosperity, marbled with poverty.

## MELLON AND MUSSOLINI

Far from an anomaly, Mellonism was not just the way of the mining economy. It was increasingly the way of the world. The 1920s began with a sharp turn to reaction and radicalism, with fascist leader Benito Mussolini defeating socialists in Italy, the Soviet Union consolidating power in Russia, and weak democracies retaining power in England and

France. In the early 1920s in Germany, the postwar republic withstood a failed coup attempt by young war veteran Adolf Hitler. Hitler was jailed, but even so, the German Weimar Republic allowed a wave of mergers and the re-creation of a corporatist state with centralized commercial power. Within ten years after being jailed, Hitler led the Nazi Party to control of this centralized corporatized state.

In the 1920s, many American business leaders appreciated how Mussolini imposed law and order, seemingly balanced the budget, paid off war debts, and restored the gold standard and Italian credit. They admired his alliance with employers through industrial councils. Most importantly, they liked how he beat back the Bolshevism that seemed to threaten a worldwide revolution after World War I. Mussolini spoke their language, presenting his proposals on borrowing American money as a business proposal. "I am just as much an American in that respect," he told the U.S. ambassador.[80]

U.S. Steel chairman Judge Elbert Gary encouraged Americans to "learn something by the movement which has taken place in Italy." Investment banker Otto Kahn lauded the "courageous, wise, and skillful financial statesmanship" of Mussolini. The president of the U.S. Chamber of Commerce Julian Barnes called the rise of Mussolini "the beginning of a new era in Italy."[81] And the American Legion, a conservative association of war veterans, compared themselves to Italian gangs who had helped defeat socialists in Italy, gangs known as "fascisti."[82] Corporatist progressives, such as Herbert Croly, argued that "the Fascist route has its significant and even promising aspects," substituting "movement for stagnation, purposive behavior for drifting and visions of a great future for collective pettiness and discouragement."[83]

In the late 1920s fascism was not yet, as it later became, defined by the Holocaust, or the other extreme outrages of the Nazi regime. Fascism was centered in Italy, where Mussolini ran an anticommunist government with big business support. Mussolini was happy to take American investments and participate in loan syndications floated by American investment banks. Some of Mussolini's ideas, like industrial councils where business leaders could exercise direct political power in their own realms, were not that different from the 1920s trade association movement in the U.S. known as "Associationalism," and had some resemblance to Teddy Roosevelt's New Nationalism. It was what Brandeis feared when he observed "industrial absolutism," mastery over people in the commercial sector, tipping into the political realm and fusing business and government. In the 1920s, this fusion of business and government was a worldwide intellectual and political trend. Italy's version was simply the most extreme.

Pro-Mussolini sentiment came from the top. In a 1924 campaign speech, Mellon lauded Mussolini as an exemplar of laissez-faire economics and a key bulwark against Bolshevism, attacking socialists in Italy. Mellon's admiration fortified Mussolini in American financial circles.[84] Mellon continued the praise. "We have watched, " said Mellon, "Italy emerge from the chaos of war, straighten out her industrial troubles, cut her expenditures, and put her budget in equilibrium, all under the direction of one strong man with sound ideas and the force to make those ideas effective." He continued, "We in America appreciate constructive action."[85] Mellon pushed for substantial American aid in rebuilding Italy, noting that the "sound policies under the forceful direction [of] Premier Mussolini have radically reduced governmental expenditures." Mellon offered fascist Italy the best postwar financial terms available to any nation in Europe.[86]

In 1926, Mellon even visited Mussolini during Mellon's summer vacation, traveling through Europe to buy art for his collection. After the meeting, the newspapers ran a photo: Mellon, standing prominently beside Count Volpi, Italy's finance minister, and Mussolini himself. Next to the thin, lonely, wraithlike symbol of American financial supremacy, Mussolini seemed to smile and strut.

A week later, Mellon gave an interview. He had "gained much information as a result of informal talks" with Mussolini and Volpi. And what did he think of the dictator? "He is one of the most remarkable of men, and his grasp of world affairs is most comprehensive. If he carries out his program, in which the whole world is vitally interested, he will have accomplished a miracle and ensure himself a conspicuous place in history." Mussolini responded by saying that "I am happy to have earned the flattering commendation of this great American."[87]

Mellon found it useful to promote a certain image of Mussolini, and Mussolini needed American capital. But the affinity made sense.

Great industrial establishments built under Mussolini in Italy reminded
Mellon of America's own mighty industrial factories, run out of Pittsburgh and New York by similar, harsh men. "Modern capitalists are
great captains of industry, great organizers of men, who must have in
high degree a sense of their civic, economic responsibility," said Mussolini in a speech that Mellon kept in his files. They were "men on
whom depend the salaries, well-being, and fate of scores of workers."
Mellon was particularly happy with Mussolini's decision to relax the
Italian inheritance tax, but Mellon appreciated Mussolini's industrial
structures as well.[88]

The two differed in their political rhetoric. Mussolini didn't have
any use for the vote, and Mellon was willing to ask for the support of
his countrymen. Mussolini used murder as an instrument of politics,
and Mellon did not. But they agreed that assets in a moral society
should remain in the hands of a worthy few, those men best equipped
to manage them. Mellon believed Mussolini was bringing an economic renaissance to his country, just as Mellon was presiding over
prosperity in America.

Mellon even used the fascist example on the campaign trail in 1928
to elect Republicans. In the final week of the election, Mellon gave a
radio address to promote Herbert Hoover, the GOP nominee. "Russia is
an example of what happens when credit values are destroyed," he said,
attacking the new communist state and linking it with the policy ideas
of the Democrats. In the Soviet Union, the standard of living had collapsed, and "large corporations" had "ceased to operate." By contrast, he
said, in Italy "the Bolshevik menace was met and vanquished." Mussolini
had not only rescued "Italy from any possible danger of economic and
social collapse," but had "improved the well-being of the people of the
country." The Italian government, unlike the Soviet one, "operated in
accordance with established economic laws."[89]

For misery, voters could elect Democrats. For prosperity, they
should place their faith in big business leadership. In the boom times
of the 1920s, many Americans had become docile, placid, increasingly
tolerant of living under big business masters, less and less interested in
high ideals.

An insidious form of corporatism was gaining power over not only

America's industrial sinews but the heart of the people. Many leaders attacked the corruption, the machine guns in the mines, the poverty in the South, the links to fascism both implicit and overt, Prohibition, deals with fascists, and the monopolization of essential goods and industries. But many other Americans, intellectuals weaned on the centralization of the war and its aftermath, were losing faith in traditional democratic balances. Nearly a generation had passed since the heyday of populism, and millions of Americans had known only centralized control, by the state during the world war, and by the monopolists since. After decades of antimonopoly crusading by aggressive politicians, pledging to stand up to big money, and failing spectacularly, this was the aftermath. The monopolists were in control.

The last presidential election of the decade was similar to the first one, ending with a smashing Republican victory. Republican nominee Herbert Hoover took forty states, in a third straight GOP landslide. Two days after the election, a reporter asked Mellon if prosperity would continue. "There is no reason why," he said, "a steady improvement in our standard of living . . . should not continue indefinitely," if, he continued, "conservative and well-tried economic principles continue to be followed."[90]

Wilson's ambitions had been great, and almost had matched the moment, as gargantuan as the Great War had been. Almost. But not quite. The Roaring Twenties, a dangerous, desperate time, under the thin sheen of prosperity, was the price of Wilson's failure.

## CHAPTER THREE

# THE IMPEACHMENT OF THE OLD ORDER

"The people of the United States are now confronted with an emergency more serious than war."

—**Louis Brandeis**[1]

"Mr. Mellon has the consolation of knowing that he has violated more laws and that his policies have caused more suicides, undernourished children, and human suffering, and he has illegally acquired more property and done the most damage to the general welfare of the people than any other person on earth without fear of punishment, and with the sanction and approval of three Chief Executives of a civilized nation."

—**Wright Patman**[2]

■ ■ ■ ■ ■ ■ ■ ■ ■ ■ ■ ■ ■

It was raining outside, a heavy, soaking rain, matching the gloom in the air. Congressmen crowded the well in the U.S. House of Representatives. There had just been a quorum call, a legislative maneuver designed to get members of Congress into the room, basically the party leadership taking attendance. Congressmen chatted, hanging off the old desks, about baseball, families, elections, the Hoover administration, women. But the economic crisis, the political crisis, was on everyone's mind.

A man stood and addressed the chamber. "On my own responsibility as a member of this House," said Congressman Wright Patman, "I impeach Andrew W. Mellon, Secretary of the Treasury of the United States, for high crimes and misdemeanors."[3] With these words, on January 6, 1932, five and a half years after Andrew Mellon's summer meeting with Mussolini, Patman began the next great campaign to destroy monopoly power in America.

Patman represented Texas's First Congressional District, Texarkana, one of the poorest areas in the country. The district bordered Oklahoma, Louisiana, and Arkansas, a suffering cotton district, hit by the commodity crash and the general poverty of the South. Though America prospered in the 1920s, the First District did not. The value of agricultural land had fallen throughout the decade. It was a feudal area, with tenant farmers outnumbering landowners. Few farms had telephones, and just one percent of the farms in the district had indoor plumbing. Only seven out of ten school-age children attended school. It was also a radical area where the Farmers' Alliance, one of the main organizations behind the populist movement, had been strong.[4]

Patman had been threatening impeachment of Mellon for the past year, but few believed him. Now he spoke for an hour, laying out his case in crisp terms that revealed his training and experience as a county prosecutor. Members of Congress scrambled to understand the charges, and the peculiar process of an impeachment, with "page boys moving like shadows about the chamber, rushing for law and reference books."[5]

He unveiled the charges, one by one. He started with an old anti-corruption statute prohibiting the secretary of the treasury from being involved with commerce or seagoing vessels. The charges grew more incendiary. Mellon had, as treasury secretary and thus boss of the Bureau of Internal Revenue, given his own companies tax refunds. He held bank stocks while serving as chair of the Federal Reserve. He also owned a massive distillery while enforcing Prohibition, and illegally traded with the Soviet Union. Patman even noted that Mellon had had the Treasury Department launch a magazine dedicated to the use of aluminum in architecture, while controlling the Alcoa aluminum monopoly. The basic accusation was self-dealing; Mellon had been transacting his own business at the Treasury Department, and had retained control, if not formal ownership, in over three hundred corporations engaged in global commerce.[6]

Most of the accusations against Mellon weren't new. The charges, and many others, had floated around Mellon since 1921, when Harding first appointed him secretary of the treasury. His brother, Richard King Mellon, had always been his junior partner, a director of almost every company from which Mellon had claimed he had divested. The feigning of disinterest was absurd.

In May of 1929, four progressive senators fulminated that Mellon "control[s] some of the most gigantic financial operations in the world," that "most of the products of these corporations are protected by our tariff laws, and Mr. Mellon has direct charge of the enforcement of these laws." He should be disqualified from holding his office, they wrote, because of the law against the treasury secretary having an interest in the business of trade or commerce. "It would perhaps be impossible to find in the United States a single citizen who has a greater interest in the business of trade or commerce."[7] But in the boom days, these arguments hadn't worked.

The crash revealed the true cost of cynicism and self-dealing. Not only were Patman's fellow congressmen now ready to take his impeachment charges seriously, senators in a nearby committee room were examining Mellon's use of his office to extract oil concessions from the Colombian government for an oil syndicate put together by J. P. Morgan and his own company, Gulf Oil. Perhaps more important, outside the Capitol Dome, fifteen thousand unemployed people were demanding action.[8] Theirs would not be the last large-scale protest of the economic emergency. Mellon's political shield, a vibrant prosperous economy, had been shattered.

This time, it was Mellon's opponents who had an army. This time, Mellon, and the entire apparatus he represented, his entire globe-spanning machinery of business, finance, and politics, was in trouble. The moneychangers system of rule over the economy had failed.

## THE GREAT CRASH

The truth was, the foundation of the 1920s economy over which Mellon had presided, and which shielded him politically, was rotten.

The high technology of the 1920s—automobiles, electric utilities, chemicals, airplanes, radio—generated massive wealth. But this wealth wasn't really paid out to workers in the form of higher wages. Machine guns in the mines, and a legal framework biased against unions, made sure of that. Profits didn't go to farmers, who were at the mercy of commodities prices in the Midwest and landowning masters in the South. And the Mellon tax cuts took away the last mechanism for democratic forces to structure the political economy; the profits of the decade did not pass into government hands.

By 1928, the top one percent of the population received nearly a quarter of all income.[9] This excess income flooded into the stock market, and into speculation. At the same time, the Federal Reserve, created by Wilson to give the public control over banking, was instead controlled by shortsighted private bankers who could not or would not stop speculative bubbles. It was a dangerously unstable system.

Indeed, weakness in the banking system had almost caused a depression in 1920, during the postwar readjustment. The boom of the war turned to bust during the "crime of 1920" the Republicans had used to get elected, similar in some ways to the crash ten years later. Yet, far from seeing the 1920 downturn as a problem, policymakers in some ways welcomed it. Warren Harding pledged "intelligent and courageous deflation" at his GOP acceptance speech. The Federal Reserve had actually engineered the downturn, and even increased interest rates as the economy swooned. The economy was only saved after policymakers relented. The Fed finally lowered interest rates, and the federal government extended loans to farmers and passed emergency legislation to spend money on highways.[10] The economy began recovering in 1921, with a Great Depression–like scenario of a total bank collapse avoided not by prudent policies like deposit insurance and regulation, but essentially by luck.

Unfortunately, the lessons of the crash of 1920–1921 went unheeded by those in power. Instead, the "abounding confidence engendered by Coolidge prosperity" created a get-rich-quick fervor.[11] Profits began flowing into speculation, land, and the stock market, into "brokers' loans," and a thousand different devices to capture industrial power in financial structures, an endless variety of holding companies. The ever-present stock ticker became the symbol of the decade.

In what would become an American tradition, real estate in Florida soon proved an irresistible speculative lure. This was not for any good reason. In 1920, Miami had just thirty thousand people. But prospectors put the word out. S. Davies Warfield, president of the Seaboard Air Line Railway, predicted a million people in Miami within a decade. In 1923 buying in mosquito-infested Florida seemed lunacy, but two years later, according to a book by a best-seller social observer of the time, speculators "were buying anything, anywhere, so long as it was in Florida." An ad offered luxurious estates near the "fast-growing city of Nettie," which had the unfortunate problem of not existing.[12]

Uncontrolled financial exuberance and banker control was familiar to farmer populists, and those from areas with populist traditions. Though no longer a formal political party, the populist tradition was still powerful among politicians from the South, as well as Brandeisian lawyers. These people understood how destabilizing speculative flows could be. In 1925, a Boston judge named George Anderson warned Tennessee Democratic senator Cordell Hull about the financial frenzy. Anderson was a bankruptcy judge, which meant he oversaw what happened after fraudulent schemes came unmasked and creditors came calling. "The amount of money now seeking investment is so great as to be a menace to common honesty, sound principles of finance, and wholesome business development," he wrote in urging Hull to oppose the Mellon tax cuts. Investment bankers "do not intend to offer unsound or essentially fraudulent securities to their customers." But they did, without even knowing it.

Anderson got an early preview of the problem, in his bankruptcy court. "Schemers are buying up the common stock of the utility companies," he wrote, "putting them into a holding company, and offering stocks and bonds grounded merely on thin or non-existent equity. These schemes mean either that the investing public will be robbed, or that the rate payer in the utilities thus controlled will be robbed." Hull, a prominent opponent of the Republicans, agreed. But Mellon had the votes. There was nothing Hull could do until the get-rich-quick "period of psychology" had passed.[13]

The Florida bubble popped in the middle of the decade. Several hurricanes hit the Sunshine State, and the Florida fever collapsed into a tangle of lawsuits. But rather than end the national euphoria, the Florida collapse only proved a prelude. Speculative fever shifted to

Wall Street. In 1927, in a complex gambit to hold together weak European economies buffeted by unpayable war debts and American tariffs, the Federal Reserve pushed more money into the financial sector. Stocks boomed. The American banking sector began concentrating a good portion of its lending into what were called "brokers' loans," lending to speculators to buy stocks at high rates. It was fantastically profitable . . . as long as stocks went up. In 1928, a memo circulated inside J. P. Morgan, stating the following: "The market is boiling."[14]

Meanwhile, financial leaders were piling more and more assets into opaque holding companies, complex financial structures no one could decipher. John Jakob Raskob, the head of the Democratic National Committee, was setting up plans to run a highly leveraged stock market fund to let ordinary people get rich at a price of just $15 a month.

Herbert Hoover won the presidency in a year when the stock market started to swerve. The mythology of Hoover—he had grown up a poor orphan only to become a millionaire business leader and an administrative genius—made him one of the most admired men in the world. In his career, he had run mines, made millions, and then turned to public service. When the war broke out, Hoover organized to get Americans out of Europe. After the war, Hoover organized relief programs that saved millions in Europe.

Hoover seemed to be the best of America. Not a politician, but a successful businessman, a progressive forward-looking leader. He was the Great Engineer, the Great Humanitarian, the Great Idealist, the Great Administrator. And now he was president, with seemingly limitless potential. And yet behind the image, Hoover was deeply conservative, skeptical of federal action, paralyzed by his own brilliance, and a mean-spirited micromanager. It would be hard to find a worse leader for a crisis.

In June and again in December of 1928 the market dropped, but came back, prompted by positive comments from the president. Just before the crash, economist Irving Fisher argued that stocks had reached a "permanently higher plateau." The Fed gingerly tried to pull back credit from speculators, but the head of the large National City Bank (now Citigroup) offered, over the Fed's objection, loans to speculators at lower interest rates to buy stocks. The market soared again.

Speculators learned their lesson: never be out of the market.[15] Yet the underlying economy was sputtering; residential construction was dropping, consumer spending was slowing, and commodities prices kept falling.

On October 2, 1929, brokers' loans reached $6.8 billion, a new record. The market began to wobble, but bravado continued, with a lead banker saying, "The industrial condition of the United States is absolutely sound and our credit situation is in no way critical."[16] Hoover reassured the public by announcing that Mellon would be staying on as treasury secretary for three more years.[17] And then, toward the end of the month, the market cracked. Torrents of selling, with no buyers.

The stock ticker itself was hours behind the actual trading business, so far behind that no one could tell what actual stock prices were. The most prestigious stocks—GM, U.S. Steel, AT&T—were collapsing. The top businessmen in the country—Thomas Lamont of J. P. Morgan, George Baker of First National Bank, and Albert Wiggin of Chase—tried to organize a bankers' pool to instill confidence. John D. Rockefeller announced he was buying stock. For a few days, the market stabilized, as the men who had ensured prosperity for nearly fifty years seemed to have a plan to save the day. But the credit crunch was too severe. The market collapsed on October 29.

Despite the severity of the crash, the fall in the stock market didn't thrust the economy into depression immediately. Political leaders had seen booms and busts before, and they didn't panic. Mellon told the president that the speculators "deserved it." The economy, he announced, would recover by the spring of 1930 and that "during the coming year the country will make steady progress."[18] This made sense, as that's how the depression ten years earlier had gone.

Policymakers were intellectually unprepared for what happened next. The president, Mellon, and prominent Democrats had assured the public that all was well. This was a common view; the Harvard Economic Society predicted that a downturn wasn't a problem; the Fed would step in to "ease the money market" and prevent harm to industry.[19] But cracks that had been apparent since 1920 widened. The crash spread from the stock market into the banking system. Banks had lent heavily to stock market speculators and were taking losses. And then in 1931, bank defaults in Europe led to a wave of bank collapses in the U.S.

The problem increasingly became one of deflation, or a collapse in prices and wages. When a bank went bust, that bank would stop lending and deposits would be frozen. This meant credit would contract, and money would be taken out of circulation. People and businesses would in turn have less purchasing power to buy goods and services, and to service their debts. So they would buy less, hire fewer people, pay less in taxes as well as default on loans. Prices and wages would go down. Farmers, having borrowed on the assumption that the corn or cotton they grew would sell at a certain price, would find their crops selling at half or a quarter of what they thought they'd be able to get. As farm mortgage defaults spiked, more banks would in turn go bankrupt. Politicians, in thrall to the notion the government had to balance the budget, would often raise taxes as tax revenue fell, making the problem worse.

As the depression worsened, a group of what were known as "inflationists" began arguing that the government should step in and raise the purchasing power of farmers and workers. Inflationists were drawn from the South and the West, from the populists who had helped pressure Wilson to create the Federal Reserve. Their solution was to have the government get more currency into circulation through government spending so prices would go back up. But having the government print money and interfere deeply in the affairs of private bankers was anathema to the orthodox thinking of the time. Mellon, for instance, blocked federal relief action, because he believed that deflationary periods were natural and helpful moments. When prices were low, prudent financiers were rewarded and could buy up industrial assets cheap.

Mellon's orthodox thinking dominated. In 1929, the unemployment rate was 3.2 percent. A year later, it rose to 8.7 percent. Still, President Hoover argued the country's economy was on a sound and prosperous basis. In 1931, unemployment spiraled up to 15.9 percent. By 1932, it hit 24.9 percent. Congress held hearings on the collapse. "The leading industrialists and bankers testified. They hadn't the foggiest notion," said one commenter. The transcripts of these hearings "make the finest comic reading."[20] Most key financial leaders still encouraged balanced budgets and sound money, more orthodoxy to meet the crisis, more belt-tightening to meet the economic famine.[21] The old order did not know what to do. The depression wasn't just an industrial or credit shock, but a political crisis.

## DESPERATION

By 1932, when Patman filed his impeachment charges, Americans were desperate.

"People are ready to commit suicide because of their inability to get a job and inability to live....They are blue. They are depressed. They do not know where to turn," noted the National Catholic Welfare Council. Charities had no more to give in the face of deep hunger. Up to 250,000 people in Philadelphia were facing actual starvation after a relief committee headed by a leading city banker ran out of funds. In Toledo, 60,000 people out of a total population of 300,000 stood in a breadline every day. In Detroit, municipal employees had their salaries cut by 20 percent to pay for relief supplies, which quickly ran out.

A physician named Sidney Goldstein testified before the Senate that men and women in New York who had been out of work and were desperate for relief could not even find the right office in which to apply. The Home and Relief Work Bureau set up by the city had been closed the preceding April, overwhelmed by the need. People were moving into basement tenements that had been condemned twenty-five years before, whose only inhabitants for decades had been rats. Almost eleven million jobless Americans roamed the streets, according to a conservative estimate.

Business too was dying. In New York state, factory payrolls fell 10 percent in just one month, down to 45 percent of what they had been in 1929. Steel production in Pittsburgh was at 15 percent of capacity. Pig farm products were selling at 64.8 percent of 1915 prices, and going down. Cotton was at its lowest price in two hundred years. Building permits were off 73 percent from May 1931 for 215 leading cities in the country. Even the John D. Rockefeller Consolidated Coal Company, named for the richest man in the country, entered receivership.[22]

"Vagrancy," a slur for homelessness, became the most common cause of arrest during the 1930s. It was an era of national humiliation. "Brother, Can You Spare a Dime?" was the most popular, and dangerous, song of the early depression. The song was a story of a man, a country, which built skyscrapers to the sky, railroads to race time, fought in the hellish mud, who is now reduced to waiting in lines for bread. "Once I built a railroad, now it's done, brother, can you spare a dime?" The Republicans tried to have the song banned from the radio.

National Association for the Advancement of Colored People official Roy Wilkins testified that the Communist Party, which had nominated a black man for vice president, was making inroads among blacks. Part of the reason, he said, was blacks were not getting their share of relief. Racism made the problem much worse. Blacks had difficulty getting emergency assistance across the South. In the "good city of New Orleans," for instance, he noted, "they have ruled that only 33 percent of the relief expenses may go to negroes, no matter what the unemployment among negroes is."[23]

Children were competing with rats for food. Thousands were dying of dysentery. Hungry girls as young as thirteen were selling their bodies for loaves of bread. In West Virginia, coal mining families lived under cliffs. Workers in Passaic County, New Jersey, were told "frankly and brutally" that legislators could do nothing about starvation; the workers warned they might try to "solve it in their own way," meaning rebellion. In the mill areas of the South, local Red Cross chapters were explicitly using the threat of withholding food to force workers to accept wage cuts.[24] Union leaders warned Congress that no talk of "Americanism or our Constitution" would stand against empty bellies.

At a municipal and state level, officials acted, but the problem was that the banking system had collapsed, so there was no currency, no credit, and little means of payment local officials could use. Bankers were afraid to lend money to cities; as a labor leader in Philadelphia put it, "The city itself is bogged down financially so badly that the mayor feels constrained to declare in public that no one is starving in order to bolster the courage of the bankers who so reluctantly and slowly take municipal bonds when these are offered." The situation was catastrophic. "We are running our local governments in Pennsylvania," he said, "on the principle that it is more important to reelect Mr. Hoover than it is to face the facts about unemployment and starvation."[25]

A march of a few hundred communists in Philadelphia ended with bloody beatings. In Dearborn, Michigan, municipal police, outside the giant and famous River Rouge Ford factory, opened fire along with private Ford company police with guns and tear gas, killing four unemployed protesters and wounding dozens more.[26] It was starvation or revolt, according to John Edelman of the Pennsylvania Federation of Labor.[27]

Hoover worked eighteen-hour days but could not shake his deep-seated belief that the crisis was simply one of confidence, not problems in the banking system run by those he felt should rule. Even as reporters he knew were going broke and pleading for help, every evening Hoover sat down to a black-tie dinner and had a complete seven-course meal. Hoover knew this seemed callous, but he feared that not indulging would signal a lack of belief on his part in the imminent return of prosperity. Toward the end of 1930, an apple wholesaler disposed of an apple surplus by selling them on credit to the unemployed, who would resell them for a nickel each, leading briefly to "shivering apple sellers" everywhere. Hoover responded to a question about these men by saying, "Many people have left their job for the more profitable one of selling apples."[28]

Reactionaries prepared, not to aid the people, but in fear of them. In 1933, former Republican presidential candidate and current president of Columbia University Nicholas Murray Butler told his freshmen class that totalitarian dictatorships were putting forward "men of far greater intelligence, far stronger character, and far more courage than the system of elections."[29] The military put together a scenario called "Plan White" to put down an internal rebellion, modeling it on German tactics used against communists after World War I.[30]

Hoover was afraid of the increasing social chaos and the potential for mass rebellion. The government was cutting spending on everything it could to deal with the depression, except Army personnel. Such a cut would "lessen our means of maintaining domestic peace and order." When Congress sought a 10 percent government-wide cut in pay, the president secretly requested that the Senate exempt soldiers to prevent mutiny in the ranks.[31] The Secret Service established new procedures for defending Hoover, as assassination threats reached an all-time high. No person with a package was allowed to approach Hoover.[32]

A labor leader finally told Congress, "I want to assure you gentlemen that if the Congress of the United States and this administration does not do something to meet this situation adequately, next winter it will not be a cry to save the hungry but it will be a cry to save the government."[33]

## THE LAST POPULIST IN HIS FIRST CRUSADE

Into this moment stepped Wright Patman. This thirty-nine-year-old radical had an owlish face, an accountant's glasses, and a scrupulously polite demeanor. Yet in picking a fight with Mellon, he put into the crosshairs the entire old order of finance-friendly politics that had organized American politics during most of the years since the 1870s. This conflict would set the stage for a forty-six-year career in Congress working to constrain the money lords.

His influence in the Democratic Party was profound. Much of mid-century banking law bears his stamp, and he used his perch to launch investigations against banks, foundations, and corrupt government agencies. Sam Ealy Johnson, Lyndon Johnson's father, told LBJ that when he went to Washington, D.C., as a congressman, if he was ever unsure of how to vote on a bill, he should follow Patman's lead, as Patman was for the people.

Born in 1893 to a cotton-farming father in a hardscrabble area of Texas, Patman was always fascinated with politics. As a high schooler, his hobby was reading the *Congressional Record*, and he would do so even while plowing fields. "It will stack up like cordwood if you don't use it right," he said. "But you can use it right, and you'll get an education out of it."[34] While a teenager, he was imbibing the monetary debates of the early 1900s, the years of Teddy Roosevelt fighting his first major antitrust case with J. P. Morgan over Northern Securities, the monetary collapse of 1907 leading to the founding of the Federal Reserve, and the third presidential campaign of William Jennings Bryan.

Patman never attended college. Ever studious, he put himself through Cumberland Law School in Tennessee by paying with bales of cotton. He served in the military during the war, was elected to the Texas House of Representatives in 1920, and then appointed to be a district attorney in 1924.

Patman was a self-described "proud Hillbilly" and righteous Baptist. Throughout his life, his unyielding focus on the immorality of extreme wealth led to mockery. Patman had enemies, and they feared him. They charged him with being "Wild as a March Hare," a "funny money man," and a vain and obsessive publicity hound. He genially pushed forward regardless of his critics. "The man who keeps a stiff back and a stiff moral code can defeat the forces of evil," he would tell people throughout his life.[35] He always remembered the high interest rates charged by bankers that had kept his father and his community impoverished. Sam Rayburn, his good friend, would much later gently mock Patman by saying that "if he got shipwrecked on a lonely island with Liz Taylor, Liz in the nude, he'd say, 'Ms. Taylor, do you know the workings of the Federal Reserve Board?' "[36] In the Texas state legislature, he exposed that the wealthy did not pay much in taxes, and he supported free high schools (though he himself had paid tuition).[37] As a local prosecutor, he went after powerful local interests. In his campaign for Congress, he pledged to be "against monopolies, trusts, branch banking, and discriminatory freight rates."[38] This was not a simple political ascension, but an overthrow of the local establishment candidate. Patman defeated a popular rival within the Democratic Party in a primary to win his seat, out-organizing and out-working a much more established member.

The northeast corner of Texas, bordering Oklahoma, Arkansas, and Louisiana, oil-drenched, cotton-growing, rural—that was his home. Patman's district was peopled by those who had come from the Deep South, Mississippi, Alabama, Georgia, Arkansas, and Louisiana.[39] It was radical territory, the seat of the farmer revolts of the 1890s. In 1914, in Oklahoma, "the Socialist Party candidate for governor, Fred W. Holt, received over 20 percent of the vote statewide. In Marshall and Roger Mills counties, where the Socialist Party was strongest, Holt captured 41 and 35 percent of the vote, respectively." These counties were not far from Patman's Texas district.[40]

Patman was not a socialist, but he came from the same soil and the same economic circumstances of rural poverty as the Oklahoma socialists. He was a populist antimonopolist, and he believed that eastern bankers, centered in New York City, were colonial in their approach to farmers, small businesses, and even industrial enterprises. The disparity in wealth among regions came from what he argued was "the unholy operation of monopolistic interest of the North in a most thorough sapping of the commercial and industrial strength of the South and West. . . . In the broad sense, the North is the American money mart that is fed by the monetary streams of trade and commerce originating in the South and the West."[41]

This area was seething with not just regional resentment of the North but racial resentment based on the establishment of Jim Crow in the 1890s. Patman's complex racial politics reflected this dynamic. In the 1920s, he joined Sam Johnson in attempting to roll back the power of the Ku Klux Klan, and had to carry a pistol to protect himself from death threats. Patman treated black constituents on economic matters as he did white constituents, and pushed for economic opportunities regardless of race. He also helped put the first black governor of the Federal Reserve in office in the 1960s.[42] Throughout his career, he was challenged by arch-segregationists in primaries.

Yet Patman's key local political booster in 1928 was James "Cyclone" Davis, a People's Party organizer in the 1890s who became a KKK member in the 1920s. And Patman was a supporter of segregation in the 1950s and 1960s and signed the Southern Manifesto in opposition to civil rights legislation because, he argued late in his career, he would have lost his seat had he not supported it. He was no racial demagogue, and his focus was economic equality regardless of race. But neither was he willing to challenge his white constituents on their racism and lose his political office. It was a cynical deal his constituents, white and black, understood. After blacks got the right to vote, they tended to vote for Patman.[43]

Patman took his seat in the U.S. House of Representatives for the first time in 1929. Though much of America was prosperous, in Texarkana there was already a deep recession born of low commodity prices. In the 1920s, even as the rest of the country prospered, his district's population fell from 271,472 to 255,452, and the value of land and buildings fell by $93 million (versus $103 million for the entirety of Texas).[44]

Most freshmen members of Congress are quiet, seeking to gain favor with their more senior colleagues. Not Patman. "He is of that fearless sort that believes in getting what he goes after," wrote the *Calhoun County News*. "He went to Congress in 1928 and since his election has kept himself in a conspicuous light because of his lack of deference for hide-bound rules and regulations pertaining to the assembled Congress."[45] Patman was persistent, dogged, and, while polite, he didn't let up, even on small matters. He sought a seat on the House Banking Committee, but was blocked by his own delegation, angry that he had dethroned a fellow Democrat in a primary. He received minor committee assignments, including the Committee on the District of Columbia and the Committee on Coinage, Weights, and Measures.

From the moment he entered the House, Patman began his crusade against the banking interest, against monopoly, and for the "plain people." At one hearing, on real estate licensing in the District of Columbia, he proceeded to press a far more senior member, Clarence McLeod, showing that McLeod's bill, framed as a consumer protection measure, would in fact aid the local real estate industry in fixing prices.[46]

His first congressional crusade was against a cottonseed oil conspiracy organized by Swift & Co., Armour & Co., and Procter & Gamble that was depriving farmers in his district of income.[47] Cottonseed grown in his district was used to create cooking oil, but he argued food processors were monopolizing the trade and pushing down the price paid to farmers. Patman accused the FTC of working to organize the cottonseed processing monopoly in the first place. He laid out the case to the FTC and the Department of Justice but was unable to persuade the Hoover administration to act.

Yet within his arguments one can see how he connected the power of monopolists in an individual market with the functioning of the economy at large. "Some manufacturers are grumbling about not being able to sell their goods in the South," he said. "Why? It is because the purchasing power of the southern farmer has gone down $50,000,000 to $100,000,000; it went down that much last fall, and it was due to one thing. That is the organization and the existence of an unlawful trust."[48] To Patman, monopolies weren't just harmful to individuals or companies deprived of unfair opportunities to participate in a real and open market—their extractive ways wreaked destruction throughout the whole economy. A corporate monopoly, a chain store, and a powerful banker were organized around the same goal, stripping the purchasing power from the small businessman and farmer.

Patman targeted the Federal Trade Commission, the commission created by Wilson that had failed to enforce fair trade in the marketplace. "Representative Wright Patman, Dem, Texas, has attacked the Federal Trade Commission," wrote *The Pittsburgh Press*, "for alleged lack of speed in conducting its inquiries and declared this delay made the investigations doubtful value from a legislative viewpoint. Patman pointed to the power trust, chain store, and cotton seed inquiries."[49]

But Patman had eyed a much bigger target. "The day he took his oath of office," said a colleague, "he took after Andy Mellon."[50] Patman attacked Mellon's ownership of Alcoa by pressuring the government to act against the company's aluminum monopoly. Three years later, at a hearing attacking Mellon, Patman explained that "there was a complaint filed before the FTC, in which it was alleged that the Aluminum Co. of America owned 95 percent of the aluminum industry of the country, and that they were setting prices and compelling small dealers to refrain from using any products that might be manufactured in the other 5 percent of the industry, and otherwise violating the antitrust laws. And the FTC did nothing about it for years and years and it was not until after I got after them, about three years ago, that the FTC concluded to do anything; and then, when they took the matter up, it exonerated the Aluminum Co. of America, without any written opinion being handed to the press; and I have not been able to get any written opinion from them. The matter was just dismissed."[51]

As the downturn worsened, Patman would give speeches on the floor attacking Mellon, and the entire philosophy of the Republican Party. "We can no longer depend upon prosperity coming from the billionaire class," he would say. "It fails to percolate through on down to the masses."[52] In Mellon, Patman saw the personification of the old money trust. Prices of the crops farmers grew and sold had dropped dramatically. This meant that a debt burden grew heavier over time, even if the number of dollars owed stayed the same, because the amount of, say, wheat necessary to earn the same number of dollars had gone up. "Deflation cheats the man who is in debt just as much as undue inflation cheats the creditor," Patman told his fellow congressmen. If these financiers like Mellon continued to use falling prices to distort the purchasing power of the farmer, the worker, and the businessman, "this country faces," Patman said in a floor speech, "some sort of revolution."[53]

Patman fixed on Mellon as his great villain. Mellon had made a fatal political error that would only become apparent in the 1930s; he had fought an accelerated pension payment for the millions of veterans who had fought in the world war. These men would become Patman's allies. In 1929, Patman introduced an aggressive piece of legislation, a bill that would establish how the American political system would respond to the Great Depression: the Bonus Bill. This bill was not important legislation in 1929, but four years later the context of veteran politics, like everything else, had changed radically.

After the Great War, no one knew how veteran politics would play out. But smart politicians knew that veterans would be one of the major forces in America for at least a generation. Nearly a quarter of the adult male population between the ages of eighteen and thirty-one in the United States served in the military during World War I, half of them abroad in the American Expeditionary Forces.[54] In this "War to End All Wars," 116,516 Americans died, and millions came home to jobs that had disappeared or that had been occupied by other men while they were away at war. The number of dead was fifty times higher than the number in the Spanish-American War, which had happened just fifteen years earlier. This war experience shaped the culture, ideas, and lifestyle of a generation.

At first, those who risked life and limb were treated the same as those who risked property. The 1914 War Risk Insurance Act protected the property of corporations running American ships to Europe. When millions of American soldiers were sent to Europe, they were given "war-risk" life insurance. The insurance assumed that a soldier who lived through the war without injury needed no pension, because he was able-bodied, was paid for his service in the war, and could get a job.[55] Such a veteran would be the equivalent of a ship that had undertaken a dangerous mission and come through unscathed. One's labor and the property of a corporation were thus considered equivalent, a point of tension that would become the focal point for political conflict for decades.

After the war, property, it seemed, was more important than veterans. In 1919, Congress passed the Dent Act, authorizing the secretary of war to give more money to corporations that had become military contractors.[56] This bonus for corporations enraged veterans, who had been systematically underpaid for their service. Many Americans had volunteered for service and gone abroad at the pay of a dollar a day. Those who remained at home saw their pay double or triple, while many of those who served came back to joblessness.

A veterans lobby began agitating for redress, to pay in one payment the difference between what a soldier would have earned as a civilian and what he earned as a soldier. The key group was the American Legion, an organization formed for world war veterans by wealthy Americans who sought to ensure that veteran politics would not be tempted by the communism to which they had been exposed in Europe. Ogden Mills, Mellon's subordinate, was one of the founders and financiers of the group.[57] These men, known in the organization as "the kingmakers," made sure the American Legion had ample funds, and it became the largest veterans group. It did have a smaller competitor, the Veterans of Foreign Wars, composed of working-class veterans.

In the 1920s, most veterans sought roughly a thousand dollars apiece to make up the pay differential during the war. Both parties opposed the payment of what they called the adjusted compensation certificate, but what became known as a soldier's "bonus." Wilson's secretary of the treasury, David Houston, said that floating a bond issue of the size required would result in "disaster," and Mellon picked up this mantle and ghost-wrote several presidential vetoes of the Bonus payment.[58] Harding even came to the Senate to lobby against the Bonus.[59] The National Industrial Conference Board, an industrial organization composed of big banks and corporations, published a special pamphlet in 1923 opposing the payment; even Thomas Edison argued the nation could not afford it.[60] In 1924, Mellon placed the Bonus in opposition to his tax cuts; the country could not have both. Should fourteen million taxpayers get a tax cut, or four million selfish veterans a bonus?

Big business opposition to payment of the soldier's Bonus enraged veterans. After all, war was good for business. Major General Smedley Butler, an iconoclastic military celebrity, wrote a book titled *War Is a Racket* in which he pointed out that war delivered high corporate profits. He reported, for instance, that war contractors sold twenty million mosquito nets, and not one made it to France for use. A billion dollars was spent on airplane engines that "never left the ground." The war cost $52 billion, he wrote, while total profits from the war were $16 billion. Losses to possible profits, he noted, were structured to be limited by contract, but "there is nothing in this scheme, apparently, that says not more than 12 per cent of a regiment shall be wounded in battle, or that not more than 7 per cent in a division shall be killed." The government, he noted, "cannot be bothered with such trifling matters."[61]

It was not just big business, however, that opposed the payment of a soldier's Bonus. Progressives like Senator William Borah opposed the payment. "A nation whose citizenship has been drugged and debauched by subsidies and gratuities and bonuses," he said, "has taken the road over which no nation has ever yet been able to effect a successful retreat."[62] *The New Republic* and *The Nation* considered the notion of a payment for veterans a corrupt special interest bribe.

In the 1920s, opposition to a bonus did not suggest callousness toward veterans. President Harding, when lobbying the Senate, listed the already extensive benefits, the compensation and insurance claims offered to over 800,000 veterans costing a half a billion dollars, as well as "vocational training and rehabilitation for disabled soldiers, which cost $65 million annually."[63] Veterans already got a substantial amount from the government, more than any other class of citizens. When Herbert Hoover took office, 18 percent of the federal budget was dedicated to veterans, and Hoover himself created the cabinet-level Department of Veterans Affairs.[64]

To buttress their fiscal, moral, and political arguments, business leaders also evoked racial hatred. In 1920, the U.S. Chamber of Commerce argued that if the Bonus were paid out, "the half million

Negroes in the South, who probably would receive $500 or $600 each, would immediately quit work until the money was spent." This was, according to the African American newspaper the *Cleveland Advocate,* "an insult to the race, and a most reprehensible injustice to the white world war veteran."[65]

In an era of prosperity, President Harding had no trouble defeating the Bonus. He died in 1923, and Calvin Coolidge became president. In 1924, parades and petitions by veterans again caused Congress to take up the legislation. Coolidge angered veterans, including veterans serving in Congress that might otherwise be opposed to the bill, by arguing that those who sought money for service were not patriotic. Congress passed a bonus over Coolidge's veto.

But there was a hitch. Veterans would get their payment, but they would be paid with a classic budgetary gimmick. Congress authorized special certificates for veterans, redeemable in 1945. Because of this long period, and the number of veterans dying young, it became known as "The Tombstone Bonus."[66]

This was a manageable problem in the 1920s, a time of prosperity. But veteran politics changed with the depression. When Wright Patman was elected, in 1928, few noticed the man who called himself a "Missionary Baptist," as he was a Democrat in a Congress run by Republicans.[67] Few noticed the Bonus Bill when Patman introduced it in May of 1929. The premise of the bill was simple. It would have the government print money and grant veterans of the war an accelerated pension payment for their service in the war. They could redeem their bonus, immediately, just like any bank could trade an asset for cash at the Federal Reserve. But why would anyone notice such a bill in 1929? Unemployment was at 3.5 percent, and the stock market was still on its way up.

But as the jobless lines lengthened, Patman's bill began looking more enticing. It would provide ready cash in a country starving for lack of it. "We should not start putting out money at the top with the hope that the money will percolate down to the needy and the poor," Patman argued, "but we should start at the bottom." To do this, he argued, Congress had to "carry out the constitutional mandate" to print money. His bill would place that money in the hands of veterans, from every corner of the country, every region, and of "every class, race, and creed."[68] Money in the hands of the "plain people," as Patman called them, would cure the endless deflation of the depression. Patman's Bonus Bill hadn't changed, but the country had.

The argument began working. Patman encouraged Democrats to use the Bonus as an election issue, which helped the Democrats take Congress after the midterm election of 1930.[69] He organized an internal House caucus of members supporting the Bonus Bill. The war was increasingly seen as a cynical endeavor, and a new generation of politicians, media entrepreneurs, and organizers began seeing political opportunity. Veterans had been aligned with Republicans. Now veterans were increasingly aligned, not just with Democrats, but with populist Democrats.

The Bonus Bill even became a focal point for intellectual combat over the nature of money. Patman became a leader of a group of members—southerners mostly, and including Fred Vinson, who later served as treasury secretary under Harry Truman and then as Supreme Court chief justice. They sought to combat falling prices by having the federal government print money and distribute it until prices started going up again. Inflationists wanted to put money in the hands of the plain people—the farmers in bankruptcy, the girls prostituting themselves for food, the homeless. Inflation during a depression would restore 1929 prices. Farmers had borrowed in 1929 prices; shouldn't they be able to sell their commodities at 1929 prices so they could service those debts?

At the start of the congressional session in 1931, Patman reintroduced his bill, which would have required a $2.2 billion payout. But forty-seven other bonus-related proposals—twenty-eight from Democrats, eighteen from Republicans, and one from a Farm-Labor member—were also introduced. A thousand VFW members marched in January in front of the Capitol to deliver petitions for the Patman bill, and 124 members of Congress accepted them. The American Legion National Executive Committee recommended supporting payment, angering its financial backers. Hoover persuaded the membership at the next convention to reverse the decision. Mellon argued that if the Bonus passed, "we can expect a business depression and a period of acute human suffering the like of which this country has never known."[70] Veterans began dropping out of the American Legion, and joining the more aggressive VFW.

Patman had found his army, and his villain. In 1931, Patman started telling people that he was going to impeach Mellon. "I really have the goods on Uncle Andy," he wrote constituents. "I really believe we will 'get his scalp.'"[71] He began his investigation by combing old hearings, reading old Mellon company investor documents, and pestering agencies for information about Mellon. He went to the chief of the Navy and asked about lubricating oil sales by Gulf Oil, got reports from the Legislative Reference Service on the federal government's use of aluminum, and read hearings from the Select Committee to Investigate the Destruction of Government Bonds on how the Treasury handled government debt in the 1920s.

Patman also went to the Hoover administration directly. He asked Secretary of State Henry Stimson, and the Library of Congress, for information about Mellon's chemical company Koppers and its $200 million contract with the Soviet Union. Congress's research department sent him a list of Mellon's companies that was twenty-six pages long. He read investigations and speeches from senators in the 1920s, on Mellon's administration of the antidumping act of 1921 in a complex scheme to help Soviet producers sell manganese—an input into steel—to his own steel interests at a lower cost than domestic producers. From the Joint Committee on Revenue Taxation, he asked for information on tax refunds from the five biggest Mellon companies.[72] He badgered the FTC about their suit on Alcoa and collusion among oil giants that included Mellon's Gulf Oil.

Tips began to pour in, many from small businessmen and veterans, but some from disaffected enemies of Mellon. A hotelier in Iowa argued the Treasury was maintaining an office in his hotel to market Alcoa's aluminum. A Mr. Jalonick of the Republic Insurance Company of Texas wrote to tell Patman that the post office was forcing employees to buy gas not from local gas stations but Gulf Oil gas stations.[73] A New Jersey businessman detailed the links between "Uncle Andy," J. P. Morgan, and the way they organized a Pullman rail car monopoly. A former tax auditor, Douglas Van Horne, wrote Patman to tell him he had found that Eastern Oregon Light and Power hadn't paid its full income taxes. The company tried to bribe him to keep quiet, but he wouldn't accept the bribe. Upon returning to his headquarters, he was fired. Van Horne found out later that the company was 51 percent owned by Andrew Mellon, and he blamed Mellon for his firing. He also noted that Mellon was his second cousin.[74] A former *New York Times* reporter, J. A. Truesdell, relayed a story of corruption among bank regulators to favor Mellon. The Office of the Comptroller of the Currency used its power to injure Mellon's competitors in nonbanking businesses. The OCC barred non-Mellon banks from supporting a rival oil company to Mellon's, but allowed Mellon banks to buy the company's stocks and bonds. The company was eventually merged out of existence.[75]

And he got tips on Mellon as secretary of the treasury making a deal with the Colombian president Enrique Olaya. Colombia was in financial trouble and needed American loans to balance its budget. Patman heard Mellon offered to exchange a set of American loans for an oil-rich concession in Colombia for Mellon's Gulf Oil and an oil consortium led by the firm J. P. Morgan.[76] A Colombian socialist and labor organizer, Carlos Melguizo, wrote Patman, noting that the president of Colombia had attended a party in Washington, where Mellon as treasury secretary offered the deal. Patman wrote Secretary of State Henry Stimson and demanded answers.[77] Mellon denied the story, saying that, though he had met with Olaya, he had never mentioned the Barco concession.

As the case against Mellon solidified, fellow members of Congress lent Patman support, if fearfully. Influential Missouri congressman Clarence Cannon offered "every possible service to you in the matter," but asked his name be kept out of any public discussions.[78] Then-congressman and eventual New York mayor Fiorello La Guardia joined Patman, and the two began plotting. Constituents, both in his own district and nationally, were behind him. Said one voter, "We have just got Al Capone. Now let's get some of the others."[79]

Through this campaign, Patman and his allies were learning how power in government and banking worked. His investigation of Mellon led him to see how the government administered taxes, organized its debt, managed the money supply, enforced trade relationships and foreign affairs, regulated banks, and related to monopolies. New Deal policies on progressive taxation, securities regulation, and antitrust would be debated, in germ form, in this investigation. Patman attacked the FTC during the investigation. He told the Texas attorney general, James Allred, that he had managed to cut the FTC's budget by $300,000, and that eventually "we will finally abolish that useless Commission altogether."[80] By the mid-1930s, the threat from Congress to abolish the commission forced the FTC to reorganize into a much closer version of what Brandeis had envisioned originally.

As Patman's investigation picked up steam, the Veterans of Foreign Wars began a publicity campaign for the Bonus. It sent out twenty-three million "ballots" asking veterans to "vote" on whether they supported the Bonus. Roughly a quarter of a million said yes, around five hundred said no. Patman and VFW commander James Van Zandt started a national speaking tour. In January, Patman and Van Zandt went on NBC. Patman made the case for the Bonus, while Van Zandt conducted the organization's induction ceremony's oath over the radio. Twenty-one thousand new members joined, a 15 percent boost in membership overnight.[81]

The Bonus Bill was a flashpoint of political controversy, and Patman encouraged Democratic House candidates to use it in their campaigns to get votes. Famous veterans, like Joseph Angelo, testified on behalf of the bill. Angelo had in World War I saved the life of military icon George Patton by dragging a wounded Patton to safety under machine gun fire. Mellon, meanwhile, admitted in 1931 that he had sabotaged the ability of the government to pay out the Bonus. He had paid down $3 billion of the national debt prematurely, so there wouldn't be any cash for the veterans.[82] Democrats nearly captured control of the House of Representatives in 1930, and would continue to gain. They eventually won the majority later that year after winning a special election held to replace a Republican member from Texas who died.

In December 1931, communists launched a "hunger march" in D.C., in an attempt to incite violence from the authorities so as to generate sympathy. D.C. police chief Pelham Glassford, who had been a young general in the war, met them with soup, not guns, trying to defuse the situation instead of creating martyrs.[83] The marchers were less communist than they were hungry; they ate. Later that month, Philadelphia's John Alferi, a veteran, told Glassford he would bring a group of veterans to march in D.C. There were fewer than fifty marchers, but it was the first rumblings of something bigger.

Father James Cox of Pittsburgh worried about the communist-inspired marches. So he held his own march. On January 6, 1932, Cox brought ten thousand men to Washington to demand jobs. "Our president is still trying to give money to the bankers, but none to the people," he said. "If I had my way, it would go to the people, who need it badly. There is plenty of money in this country, but try and get it. I do think that our mission to Washington will have its effect. The government sent Al Capone to jail for cheating it out of $100,000, yet John D. Rockefeller is giving $4,000,000 to his son to escape the inheritance tax."[84]

And that is the day that Patman stood, and offered his impeachment resolution against Mellon.[85] His charges against Mellon were that Mellon had willfully broken the law as treasury secretary to benefit his own business empire. It was not unusual for a member to seek attention, but normally such attempts failed. But Patman was persuasive. When he finished speaking, "House members were stunned, as if having just heard that some great man had died."[86] The resolution was sent to the Judiciary Committee, where Patman's ally La Guardia would sit.

The Republicans waged a counterattack. During Patman's investigation of the Mellon empire, the FBI, the White House, and the Treasury Department would send security officers to break into Patman's congressional office and destroy papers relating to the investigation. After the impeachment, his phone was tapped and "his offices were ransacked; Capitol police were ordered to patrol the hallways outside his office." Mellon defenders throughout the press portrayed Patman in cartoons as a fool and inept, and editorials criticized him for wasting time and "Mellon-baiting" and scapegoating someone for an economic downturn no one could have prevented.[87]

A week after Patman's initial statement, the Judiciary Committee began hearings.[88] Many members of Congress agreed with Patman quietly, but would not take on the power of Mellon. Why throw away their careers, as Patman had obviously just done? "It has been said that it is hard to convict a million dollars in the criminal courts," said Patman. "It can also be said that it will be hard to impeach a billion dollars."[89]

But in the Judiciary Committee—the closest forum to a trial the Democrats could muster without control of the executive branch—Patman drew blood. Mellon was forced to admit that when he had sold his bank stocks to gain eligibility for the Treasury position, he had sold the stock to his brother.[90] Mellon was represented by a former solicitor for the Bureau of Internal Revenue, and a high-powered Pittsburgh attorney. But they were no match for the populist from Cumberland Law School, who had been obsessed with Mellon for years.

Mellon claimed that he had terminated all connection with his businesses "as completely as if I had died." This statement was a lie.[91] Mellon's lawyer argued that Mellon had little to do with Alcoa, aside from his family relationship with his brother and former partner Richard, a key official in the company. But in 1924, there had been a merger between Alcoa and a company with substantial hydropower assets in Canada, which both aided Alcoa in producing more aluminum and blocked the entrance of a potential competitor. The head of Alcoa had brought Mellon into the negotiations because of his prestige as a financier and the treasury secretary.[92] The negotiations took place in a private railroad car. Mellon's lawyer admitted that Mellon had been in the private car with all of the key negotiators. But, he said, Mellon looked out the window the whole time and didn't take part or pay attention to any conversations.[93] Suddenly, impeachment seemed plausible.

At the same time as the impeachment hearing, on the other side of the Capitol, California Republican senator Hiram Johnson picked up on the Barco concession scandal. Johnson spent two hours cross-examining Victor Schoepperle, National City's vice president responsible for Latin America loans, the man in charge of loans made to Colombia after the government had granted the oil concession to Mellon's Gulf Oil. Schoepperle denied it. "I don't give a damn about the Barco concession," Schoepperle said. Two hours later, after lunch, Schoepperle mysteriously changed his story. It turned out the State

Department had encouraged the bank to make the loan, mentioning the concession as a key reason.[94] Two days later, Johnson put into the record information Patman had gotten from Colombia, including a newspaper interview where Olaya relayed a conversation with Mellon about the country's fiscal crisis. Mellon, Olaya said, told him to "settle your pending questions on petroleum" and implied loans might be forthcoming.[95]

The explosive news about the Barco concession and the impeachment hearings destroyed Mellon's reputation and finally spurred the administration into action to address the economic downturn. Three days after the end of the Judiciary Committee hearing, Hoover established the Reconstruction Finance Corporation, a government bank that could lend to failing railroads and banks. The public interpreted this as a corporate bailout. Comedian Will Rogers mocked Hoover, noting "you can't get a room in Washington. . . . Every hotel is jammed to the doors with bankers from all over America to get their 'hand out' from the Reconstruction Finance Corporation." The bankers, it seemed to Rogers, had "the honor of being the first group to go on the 'dole' in America."[96]

On February 4, 1932, less than a month after Patman filed his articles of impeachment, Mellon resigned. Hoover appointed him ambassador to England, where he would attempt to work out loans accrued during the war. Patman called this a presidential pardon. As he "goes to England with his bag of gold that has been wrenched from his innocent victims in America," said Patman, "our people may enjoy a sigh of relief and turn their thoughts to rebuilding our Nation for the benefit of the plain people—the ones who build our country in time of peace and who save our country in time of war."[97]

As Mellon's reputation sank, Patman became a national figure. "Patman may congratulate himself that his campaign which he and his committee have waged has brought a satisfactory result," wrote newspapers as far as Maine, like *The Saco News.* "He has driven his man from his office, even driven him out of the country."[98] Voters wrote in from all over the country, one man writing, "England is too close get him sent to China."[99]

The fight wasn't over. While Mellon had gone, the Hoover

administration would not relent on the Bonus Bill. Over 2.5 million veterans signed a petition for the Bonus. A policy impasse developed until mid-March, when a Portland, Oregon, veteran named Walter Waters suggested a veterans march to D.C. Hoover doubled down on his opposition, blaming the "agitation of the bonus" for the down economy.[100] The House Ways and Means Committee shelved a version of Patman's bill, and on May 11, 250 veterans unfurled a banner reading "Portland Bonus March—On to Washington" and caught an empty boxcar to D.C. If the bank lobbyists were going to make demands from their government, the veterans would as well. In late May, the first marchers entered the city. The police chief Pelham Glassford described them as "a bedraggled group of seventy-five or one hundred men marching cheerily along, singing and waving at the passing traffic." As they passed him, one protester handed him a leaflet titled "Don't Let the Bankers Fool You."[101]

Over the next few months, thousands of veterans would follow. The march riveted the nation, not just the demands but even the way that marchers would get to the capital. In every town, on every rail line, it was a conflict between the railroad employees to help the Bonus Marchers, and the management, which tried to kick them off the cars. Said one marcher, "The conductor'd want to find out how many guys were in the yard, so he would know how many empty boxcars to put onto the train. Of course, the railroad companies didn't know this, but these conductors, out of their sympathy, would put two or three empty boxcars in the train, so these bonus marchers could crawl into them and ride comfortable into Washington. Even the railroad detectives were very generous."[102]

From May until July, these Bonus Marchers, or the "Bonus Expeditionary Force" (BEF) as they called themselves, camped out throughout Washington, D.C., in unoccupied federal buildings, and in tents in Anacostia Flats. Dwight Eisenhower, then just a major, observed that "the veterans were ragged, ill-fed, and felt themselves badly abused."[103] Police nervously patrolled the camps, which became the biggest shantytown in the land of what were increasingly known as "Hoovervilles." Hoover thought them ex-convicts and communists, not veterans.

A quarter of them, in Jim Crow America, were black, but there was no discrimination in the camps.[104] Black and white joined together in hunger, though white newspapers avoided reporting the multiracial nature of the protest.

Throughout that congressional session, they marched and lobbied; their camps became a local tourist attraction. In June, the Bonus Bill passed the House, but it failed in the Senate. On July 28, Washington police tried to force veterans to evacuate unoccupied buildings; two veterans died and eight policemen were injured. A spokesman from the White House blamed it on those who were "entirely of the communist element."[105] President Hoover, determined that the government should not be "coerced by mob rule," ordered General Douglas MacArthur, then Army chief of staff, to drive the veterans from the city.[106] Troops from the Third Cavalry, led down Pennsylvania Avenue by George Patton himself, wielded naked sabers, followed by a machine gun detachment, bayonet-equipped infantrymen, and six tanks tearing up the street's asphalt.

At first the veterans waved at the soldiers, believing it a parade of active-duty troops saluting war veterans. Soldiers charged, led by Patton and on the orders of Chief of Staff MacArthur, in full formal uniform with boots polished to a glass shine. The soldiers didn't distinguish between spectator and protester. A tear gas canister landed at the foot of a United States senator.[107] The soldiers burned the shacks of the marchers so they couldn't return.[108] Before MacArthur fought in the Pacific and Patton waged tank warfare in Europe against Nazis, they rooted out defenseless American veterans in D.C.

Until Hoover drove them out of the city, the Bonus Marchers' claim had been controversial, a case of special pleading. But when Hoover set the Army on the marchers, that dynamic changed. La Guardia wired an angry message to Hoover: "Soup is cheaper than tear gas bombs."[109] These "ragged and hungry people have as much right to petition Congress as those who arrive in Washington on special trains," said Patman. "Has the president adopted the policy of using the Army to drive lobbyists from Washington?" he asked. "The people are going to get the truth one of these days and when they do, there will be some changes in our economic system." The Bonus Army, and his Bonus Bill, would show that the power to control money could be, and should be, placed in the hands of the people. "The issuance of money by private interests and the abuse of Government credit," Patman said, "has become the world's greatest racket."[110]

This moment was a climax of the old order. It colored politics for decades, including ensuring that these protests wouldn't be repeated after World War II with educational, housing, and medical subsidies for veterans.

The depression led to an overwhelming victory for Franklin Delano Roosevelt in 1932. But at this moment, Roosevelt was not the leader of the opposition to Herbert Hoover, and he did not structure the populist anger against Herbert Hoover and Wall Street. He was not the nation's leader when the Bonus Marchers were setting up camp in the southeast corner of Washington, D.C. He was the governor of New York, something of a political cipher angling for the Democratic nomination.

In the dance of politics, a dance between the great mass of ordinary citizens, righteous activists, and opinion leaders organizing protest movements, and practical politicians taking advantage of this energy to build power and a new system of political economy, it was not Roosevelt, but Patman, a young Democrat from rural Texas, who stepped into the void.

This march, and Patman's crusade, set the stage for Roosevelt, who would become president. Patman would never become a New Deal insider; he continued to prod Roosevelt and his advisors, publicly pushing, teaching, inspiring and annoying not just Roosevelt, but every president, until the 1970s. He played a role in organizing the New Deal, ensuring that the voice of the "little guy" would be heard, respected, even feared.

Even after Roosevelt was elected, he did not support the Bonus Bill. The first piece of legislation Roosevelt passed, the Economy Act, cut services to veterans. In response, veterans set up a second protest, in May of 1933. Eleanor Roosevelt greeted the protesters with hot coffee, and the administration arranged for jobs for 25,000 of them in the Civilian Conservation Corps. One veteran commented, "Hoover sent the army, Roosevelt sent his wife."

But Patman didn't relent. Bankers set up shadow political groups, such as the National Economy League, to attack proponents of the Bonus. Patman responded by accusing the group of using anonymous donors as the KKK used the "hood and the sheet," and called these groups "hooded" and "outlaw" organizations. "Some of the members of that group," he claimed, "only believe in law and order when they can make the law and give the order."[111]

Democrats picked up more seats in the midterms of 1934. Patman released two books on the Bonus, including one titled *Bankerteering, Bonuseering, Melloneering*. He also forced a vote in the House on the Bonus. And, said one observer, "when the battle shifted from the South to the North wing of the Capitol, the bonus generalissimo from the Lone Star State marched over and commandeered a rear desk in the Senate as his 'field headquarters.'" Patman buttonholed senators, working with Louisiana senator Huey Long to get around Roosevelt's opposition. In January, both chambers of Congress passed the bill. The president vetoed it, delivering a message to Congress on fiscal responsibility. On January 27, there was enough support for the bill that Congress overrode Roosevelt's veto. The bill became law.[112]

Billions of dollars would now be handed out to veterans. None of the downsides warned of by opponents came true. There was no economic collapse. In 2013, an economist analyzed the effect of the Bonus Bill, using data gathered by the American Legion on what veterans spent the money on. They bought cars and houses, and the Bonus added "2.5 to 3 percentage points to 1936 GDP growth."[113] That year, the U.S. economy grew by 13 percent, the biggest peacetime expansion in history. Roosevelt won a smashing reelection victory on the back of this growth, and Democrats took seventy-six Senate seats for their biggest majority of all time.

There were many protest movements during the depression, but the Bonus Marchers and their legislative leaders represented the forces of democracy removing the power of monopoly, Andrew Mellon, from government. They had fought to support a country. It was now time for that country to fight for them. That the democratic forces had a substantial role to play in structuring the financial system in 1932 seemed a radical proposition. The Bonus Army took the flag, took patriotism, and essentially said otherwise. Monopolists and financiers would no longer rule America.

Indeed, Martin Luther King Jr., in his final protest campaign in 1968, cited the Bonus Army as a model for his struggle for economic rights. It had, he said, an impact of "earthquake proportions."[114] These marchers, and Patman, projected a long, but now mostly forgotten, shadow over America. It is forgotten because those who wrote the history of this period focus on the personality of Franklin Delano Roosevelt. They are not wrong to do so. FDR and the establishment he formed organized the New Deal. But Patman was not a White House insider; he was not trusted by the New Dealers. Patman was an agitator. And in 1932, that is what democracy needed.

Patman brought forward what the farmers of the 1890s demanded of their society, a democracy with an egalitarian system of free enterprise, where small business had the same shot as Andrew Mellon to compete. He stood up to Mellon. He stood for the plain people, and the veterans. And in doing so, he destroyed the legitimacy of the plutocrats that dominated America.

## CHAPTER FOUR

# POPULISTS TAKE POWER

"Mellon was a ruthless hard man. I would not want to be at his mercy. His code was a hard code which left no place for weak men. To let live was not in his code as to others."
**—Robert Jackson**[1]

■ ■ ■ ■ ■ ■ ■ ■ ■ ■ ■ ■ ■

Brandeis had crafted an ideology of industrial liberty, meant to free the farmer, the worker, and the businessman from the banker and the monopolist. Patman and the Bonus Army had then used that ideology to eject Mellon from office, shocking the political establishment. But to restore democracy required far more. Not only Mellon, but the entire old order, had to be exposed and toppled. The antimonopolists would have to take power within the Democratic Party, defeat Herbert Hoover, and then wield power, all while ignoring the lure of powerful financiers whispering in their ears.

It would fall in 1932 to Franklin Delano Roosevelt, known as FDR, the governor of New York and a distant relative of Teddy, to carry the antimonopoly crusade forward. But he didn't side with Teddy; Franklin learned his politics under Wilson's New Freedom. He had been an upstate New York politician, served under Wilson as assistant secretary of the navy during the Great War, and then was the vice presidential candidate in the fruitless 1920 Democratic campaign to succeed the Wilson administration. The great event in his personal life was the loss of the use of his legs from polio, occurring in the early 1920s after he had become a national political figure. When he finally reentered politics, he hid his handicap with metal braces and help from reporters, and captured the New York governor's seat in 1928. It was a shocking upset, a Democrat winning an election in a big state during the Hoover landslide.

Roosevelt had been an enemy of Mellon for years. In the 1920s, when Mellon was at the height of his popularity, FDR attacked Mellon's political funding of the Republicans, saying, "Calvin Coolidge would like to have God on his side, but he must have Andrew Mellon." Mellon was "a master mind" of the "malefactors of great wealth" who didn't see a problem in using millions to corrupt politics, only "in . . . getting caught at it."

Roosevelt also attacked Alcoa. "Mr. Mellon's aluminum trust," he said, "which every housewife in the country unduly enriches, is but one of the tariff-created monopolies sold for political and monetary support." And he criticized Mellon's management of European war debts, saying Mellon operated as a "tight-lipped, steely-eyed, tight-fisted 'financial wizard' who thinks only in dollars and cents and whose answer to a discouraged and bewildered borrower is 'Well, you hired the money, didn't you?'"[2]

When he became the governor of New York, Roosevelt tangled with the power barons, a practical training in how to constrain monopoly. He attacked both the House of Morgan, which was financing and controlling much of the new electric utility industry, and Mellon, who used his control of Alcoa and financial muscle to share in the spoils. Alcoa and Morgan bankers together had tried to control the hydroelectric resources of the St. Lawrence River in New York.

In 1929, Roosevelt ordered an investigation into a merger of a series of upstate power utilities spanning the area from Buffalo to the Hudson Valley and Niagara Falls. Many of the smaller electrical utilities in New York had fallen, Roosevelt told New Yorkers, under the control of a small group of oligarchs composed of both Alcoa and a Morgan cartel.[3] The Morgan, DuPont, and Mellon interests, along with General Electric, combined forces to control power in New York state.[4]

Roosevelt had to pay constant attention to voters, because New York had two-year terms for governor. He made the main theme of his 1930 gubernatorial reelection campaign the issue of public utilities and electric power.[5] In 1930, after seeing the consolidation of power in New York, he sought aggressive regulation to reduce the "unfair rates" charged to small householders and small businesses. He told the people of New York that electricity companies were, he argued, public utilities, and not "merely a general private business on the same footing with, let us say, a department store or a steel mill or an automobile factory."

Like Wilson, Roosevelt attacked the corruption of experts. There was, he said, a "deliberate and definite attempt on the part of some of the power companies' publicity agents to make the average citizen think that the electrical industry is so vast and so complicated that nobody but highly trained experts in the employ of the private companies can possibly carry it on."[6]

By 1932, as the Great Depression turned the country against Hoover and Mellon, Roosevelt became the most popular Democrat in the country. He had shown his political mettle by winning the governor's office in a heavily Republican year in 1928. But he also had something to say about the depression. "Not since the dark days" of the Civil War, he said, "have the people faced problems as grave, situations as difficult, suffering as severe." He attacked banks, the concentration of wealth and power, and argued that policymakers should implement new rules to restrain financial power immediately. "The public has burned its fingers in the flame of wild speculation and has learned to fear the fire. While it still fears the fire is the time for us to act."[7]

Despite Roosevelt's popularity in the South and the West, the presidential campaign was not an easy fight. Despite moments of concern, many Democrats assumed they would win the upcoming election. As publisher Clark Howell put it, Democrats would win if the party did not "make a fool of itself."[8] But this did not mean the money trust would lose.

An unseen force, the "heavy financial contributors to Democratic campaigns, who usually keep in the background and hold no party or official position," sought to undermine Roosevelt.[9] A Nebraska congressman and former assistant to William Jennings Bryan accused international bankers and the "power trust" of electric utility men of attempting to defeat Roosevelt, though "nine of ten men in nine of ten States are for Roosevelt."[10]

As they had been since Wilson's collapse, in 1932 Democrats remained split between populist voters who hated monopolies and establishment insiders who supported it. It was a battle of people versus money.

At first, the pro-monopoly forces had control. After Democrats won seats in the midterm election of 1930, seven key Democratic leaders pledged cooperation with Herbert Hoover. The signers of the pledge included James Cox, John Davis, and Al Smith, former Democratic nominees for president in the 1920s. John Nance Garner, leader of House Democrats; Joseph Robinson, leader of Senate Democrats; as well as John Jakob Raskob and Jouett Shouse, the executive heads of the Democratic National Committee, also signed on. "No rash policies," they said, would be part of the Democratic program. Democrats could be trusted to protect industrial interests.

The bankers and utility men who funded the party wanted Democrats to continue this strategy in 1932. They encouraged leading candidates to run on social issues, specifically whether to repeal the unpopular ban on liquor, or Prohibition. The liquor question split the country along ethnic lines, but didn't offend business interests. The DuPont and Rockefeller interests supported repeal; legal liquor taxes could serve as a way to reduce taxes on the wealthy. As one newspaper reader put it, "sound, intelligent men claim that if prohibition were repealed, at once the wheels of business would start purring immediately."[11]

Populists understood what was happening. One of Patman's allies, the former governor of Oklahoma, Charles N. Haskell, told Democrats that financiers "are grasping upon prohibition as an issue to excite and bring about election results which monopoly desires."[12] Cordell Hull, the key intellectual opponent of Mellon's tax cuts and tariffs in the 1920s, called any focus on "extraneous issues like prohibition" a form of "sham fighting." Like Patman, Hull had attended the one-year Cumberland Law program rather than an elite school. The populist and cerebral Tennessee senator had foreseen the attempt to subvert the Democratic Party agenda with an undue focus on Prohibition. "Basically," he wrote, "I wanted the Democratic fight in 1932 to be waged on economic issues."[13]

The field was thick with Democratic aspirants, with many acceptable to the anti-Roosevelt moneymen. There was Albert Ritchie, governor of Maryland, adored by throngs, who attacked government involvement in the economy as no different than the "Communism, socialism, sovietism, Hitlerism, black shirts, red shirts, and all the other new theories and isms running amuck in Europe."[14] He sought enlightened leadership by industry. We should rely "less on politics, less on laws, and less on government." Andrew Mellon couldn't have said it any better.[15]

There was General Electric chairman Owen Young; corporate lawyer and former Wilson secretary of war Newton Baker; right-wing John Nance Garner of Texas, known as "Cactus Jack" Garner (supporter of a regressive sales tax to balance the budget); segregationist Virginia political leader Harry Byrd; and Oklahoma governor William "Alfalfa Bill" Murray, a power-hungry reactionary who, faced with a drought, once announced crops would grow best if planted when the moon was right and ran against the "Three C's"—Corporations, Carpetbaggers, and Coons."[16]

But the real front-runner challenging FDR was Al Smith, the former governor of New York and the Democratic presidential candidate in 1928. Smith was a self-taught child of urban machine politics, an Irish "Bowery mick" born within a few blocks of many of the worst parts of the Lower East Side of Manhattan. He had grown up poor, and become a reformer, implementing wage and hour restrictions, building state parks, and improving education in New York.

In many ways, Smith trod the same political path that Teddy Roosevelt had in 1912, seeking to unite progressive social reforms like better labor conditions with overall support for big business. While governor of New York, Smith began taking money from wealthy patrons, including thousands of shares of the Pennsylvania Railroad and hundreds of thousands of dollars in cash.[17] Smith ended up on the payroll of John Jakob Raskob, a millionaire who was part of the DuPont faction that had, along with the Morgans, the Mellons, and the Rockefellers, what FDR later called an informal "economic government of the United States."[18] Smith repaid Raskob for his support by making him the leader of his presidential run in 1928, and then appointing him to run the Democratic National Committee to set up the 1932 campaign. Not only did Smith support monopoly power, he had been corrupted by it.

Raskob knew Roosevelt was popular, so he had to win in the back rooms, rather than among voters. Raskob made a power grab, calling for a DNC meeting at the Mayflower Hotel in D.C. on March 5, 1931, the day after Congress adjourned.[19] At the meeting, Raskob expected to force through a motion committing the Democrats to repealing Prohibition. This would focus the election on the social question of liquor rather than the depression. He also sought to end the party's traditional support for antitrust laws.[20] Ideally, Raskob would want to see Smith be the party nominee, but he would approve any candidate that was not Roosevelt. Democratic National Committee members deeply respected Raskob because he had bankrolled the party for years; now the big-business forces in the Democratic Party were ready to leverage this respect to set the party agenda.

But Hull was ready to parry the attack. For years before Raskob struck, Hull had been meeting with almost every Democratic National Committee member who came to Washington. He lobbied for his perspective. He wrote letters. He gave speeches. He made public statements.

On March 3, two days before Raskob's DNC meeting, Hull received a surprise call from Roosevelt, whom he knew only vaguely. Roosevelt wanted to work together, and the New York governor had been able to peel away some of Raskob's support.[21] Hull realized that, despite his money, Raskob was politically weak and could be beaten.

Hull's pitch to committee members was not just electoral, but a warning of fascism globally that he saw in both Mellonism and abroad. The Democratic Party, he said, had a broader moral mandate in a world sinking into chaos. He pointed to the "condition of autocracy that is springing up in South America and throughout Europe, and even in the Orient," a great worldwide ideological conflict between "despotism and democracies." It was up to the Democratic Party to create "a revival" of the "civilized nations of the world, back to a keener realization of what government really means."[22] The Democratic Party, Hull believed, had to stand against corporatism and fascism.

When Raskob unveiled his plan, he met a chorus of boos. The sergeant-at-arms had to intervene so one senator could finish a speech, and the meeting nearly ended in a riot. Joseph Robinson, the Democratic leader in the Senate and the vice presidential candidate in 1928, blamed Raskob. "Someone has said that Herbert Hoover has given more assistance to the Democratic Party during the two years of his Administration than any other agency," he asserted. "And now I fear our beloved chairman has paid him back by giving similar aid to the Republican Party. The only way the Republican Party can hope for victory is to rely on the lack of leadership in the Democratic Party." Cries of "yes, yes" were heard throughout the hall.[23] Roosevelt became the front-runner for the nomination.

Hull's concerns over the rise of fascism were increasingly common. Six days after the DNC meeting, George Norris, a Republican progressive from Nebraska, said at a convention that the preservation of "our civilization" demanded that the "power of wealth be curbed." Robert Scripps of the Scripps-Howard papers argued for a "much more wide distribution of wealth," and noted "the alternative is the goose step, one way or another, and Lenin or Mussolini makes mighty little difference."[24] Roosevelt was gaining supporters among Republican progressives, for the same reason Hull was now fighting for him.

Meanwhile, Hoover and the Republicans expressed political exhaustion. At their convention in mid-June, the Republicans adopted a platform endorsing Hoover's actions to stem the depression. Reporter H. L. Mencken wrote, "I have seen many conventions but this one is the worst. It is both the stupidest and the most dishonest."[25]

Two weeks later, the Democrats filled the hotels and convention hall of Chicago for their own convention. The presidential candidate was going to be picked by delegates. In 1932, voters had relatively little say; there weren't modern primary elections. Instead, delegates chosen through byzantine processes came to a national convention to debate the best choice. Delegates were free to change their minds, and sometimes deadlocks occurred. In 1924, for instance, it took over one hundred ballots before Democrats picked a nominee.

This convention was something of a youth wave; the Democrats were younger, more stylish, and more fun than the Republicans. A majority of delegates, though not the required two thirds, supported Roosevelt. The anti-Roosevelt forces believed they could block his nomination for several votes, which would cause the convention to turn to a compromise nominee, probably Newton Baker, who had been a cabinet member under Wilson.

The three candidates with large numbers of pledged delegates were Roosevelt, Smith, and the conservative Democratic Speaker of the House, John Nance Garner. Garner had won California because of the large number of Texas transplants in the state, and because of the support of publishing magnate and Democratic power broker William Randolph Hearst. Garner arrived first, coming out for repeal of Prohibition, pledging a one third cut in government spending, and saying that the nation's greatest threat was "the constantly increasing tendency towards socialism and communism." Raskob arrived next, claiming Prohibition to be the key economic and social question, to which Hull responded by saying that it would be "a damnable outrage bordering on treason" if the Democrats didn't engage in some "serious thought or mention of the unprecedented panic." Smith came to town the next day in a blue suit and a white straw hat, jauntily saying, "I am here to get myself nominated."

The anti-Roosevelt forces split. Despite Roosevelt's majority hold on delegates, there was no consensus for a nominee. He had majority support, but also bitter enmity from opponents. Roosevelt's forces simply couldn't detach enough delegates from any other candidates to get to the required two thirds.

On the third day, an all-night session resulted in another deadlock, with the convention adjourning at 9:15 a.m. so delegates could rest. The atmosphere was deeply unpleasant. It was hot, and rowdy political operatives had left behind mounds of rotting trash in the arena. Cleaning crews had to use seventy-five gallons of disinfectant on the floor. Without a deal soon, Democrats might turn to Baker out of fatigue.[26]

In a last-ditch effort for the Roosevelt forces, one of Roosevelt's biggest donors, an Irish American business leader named Joseph P. Kennedy, called Hearst, and asked him to get Garner to throw his delegates to Roosevelt. Kennedy warned Hearst that the convention would turn to Baker or Smith, both anathema to the publishing magnate. Hearst was an isolationist, and the conservative internationalist Baker was his least favorite pick. At this point, Hoover weighed in for Roosevelt, thinking that Roosevelt would be his weakest possible opponent. Hoover contacted MGM boss Louis B. Mayer and had him work on behalf of Roosevelt; it would be Roosevelt or Baker, he said.[27] Hearst also relented, and he and Garner threw the nomination to Roosevelt.

Roosevelt centered his acceptance speech on growing political instability. As he spoke, he noted the desire for radicalism, and with autocracy rising throughout the globe, the subtext was clear. Americans had not succumbed to this worldwide madness, and he complimented the public on the "orderly and hopeful spirit" that prevented "disorderly manifestations that too often attend upon" times of depression. But, he warned, to fail to act "is not only to betray their hopes but to misunderstand their patience." Meeting the threat of radicalism with "reaction," rather than a "workable program of reconstruction," meant American political and business leaders were inviting disaster.[28]

A little less than four weeks after Roosevelt accepted the Democratic nomination, Herbert Hoover and the U.S. Army had the Bonus Marchers violently evicted from Washington. The next morning, Roosevelt spread out newspapers of the account and pointed at the pictures of burning shacks and fleeing protesters. Hoover's actions were not just inhumane, but politically damaging. Movie theaters would show footage of the camps being burned down, horrifying voters all over the country. Roosevelt never again doubted he would win the election.[29]

Garner encouraged Roosevelt to remain quiet, and just win the election by default.[30] But Roosevelt loved campaigning, and more than that, he believed in campaigning, in telling stories to the American voter and conveying his ideas. Roosevelt had been a Wilsonian who looked up to Brandeis. Like Wilson, his goal was not just to win an election, but to defeat the oligarchy in control of the United States that had destabilized politics globally. He sought, as he put it in a speech in Salt Lake City, to find a corrective in the "present unhappy tendency to look for dictators."[31]

Roosevelt's campaign was building a constituency for the laws Congress would pass. More importantly, he was publicly naming the enemy, financiers who had concentrated private power. Roosevelt went on a speaking tour to criticize these domestic oligarchs, and their methods of concentration. He saw these men and this centralization as a rival governing system. "We find two-thirds of American industry concentrated in a few hundred corporations," he said, "and actually managed by not more than five human individuals." Power was concentrated, which was the opposite of the individualism that Hoover promised. "I believe that the individual should have full liberty of action to make the most of himself," Roosevelt said, "but I do not believe that in the name of that sacred word a few powerful interests should be permitted to make industrial cannon-fodder of the lives of half the population of the United States."[32]

Senator Hiram Johnson attacked Hoover's philosophy as "the divine right of big business and of the international bankers and of great corporations to maintain operate and conduct our government." James Cox warned of radicalism and a loss of faith in American democracy, and blamed it on the Republican system put in place by big business. Betting houses were taking odds of 5:1 or 6:1 against Hoover. Clothing stores advertised "landslide" sales on furniture and coats.[33]

Roosevelt won 57.4 percent of the vote, to Hoover's 39.7 percent, and became the first Democrat since the Civil War to win the presidential election with a majority of the popular vote.

## THE WINTER OF DESPAIR

And yet, in a holdover from the days of horseback, the election was held in November, but the inauguration would be in March. This was a long period with confused authority. In those four months, a long winter between November and March, Herbert Hoover would still be president. And in this time, the old order, declining rapidly, would collapse. The banking system, the heart of the system, would simply stop functioning. This banking crisis seized up the arteries of commerce the day before the inauguration. All eyes would be on the new, vigorous president-elect.

This lame-duck period was terrifying, a giant sustained banking panic to cap the Hoover administration's record of mismanagement. When Hoover was elected, the nation had twenty-four thousand banks. By 1933, it had dropped to fourteen thousand. Every bank failure was a nightmare to the affected depositor. One's life savings might disappear, or your employer might lose the money meant to go to your wages. Businesses had to hold large sums of cash.[34]

Rumors of banking weakness would draw mobs of panicked

savers, seeking to withdraw their savings before the bank ran out of cash. Bank runs could cause otherwise healthy banks to fail. And even healthy banks might try to call in loans early out of fear, which could cause otherwise healthy borrowers to default. Panic fed on itself and accelerated the deflationary spiral.

The bank failures that crashed the country into the Great Depression started in late 1930; in December, the wave began hitting New York City. A large bank called the Bank of the United States closed, locking up the savings of more than 400,000 people. A brief pause, and then another wave of failures in 1931 and early 1932. Even the Anti-Saloon League, the force behind Prohibition, was on the verge of collapse, and not just because Prohibition was unpopular. The group held its deposits in the Bank of Westerville, which had failed.[35]

In areas with no banking system, cash became king. Crime and theft were no longer simple hazards, but a threat to survival. Entire communities had no cash, nothing with which to transact, no means to procure much at all. Banks continued to fail, in greater and greater numbers as loans soured. Between 1929 and 1933, over 9,000 banks failed, with $7 billion of deposits frozen.[36]

The banking collapse accelerated. In early 1933, the banking system in Michigan, the heart of the automobile industry, froze up. The state closed down its banking system; nearly all other states would follow. A scrip movement spread across the country, with cities from Urbana to Philadelphia printing their own currency, and merchants having to decide whether to accept it. Local stores usually did while chain stores did not. In Los Angeles, during the bank closures, armed police guarded stores laden with cash.[37]

In late January, the governor of Iowa asked for a halt on all foreclosures.[38] In Storm Lake, Iowa, farmers stopped a lawyer about to conduct a foreclosure with the persuasive argument that they might hang him if he went through with it. In Pleasanton, Kansas, someone discovered the corpse of a man who had succeeded in foreclosing on a farm. As historian Arthur Schlesinger Jr. wrote, "In one bankruptcy proceeding after another, friends of the debtor, using unspoken intimidation to cut off other bids, bought back the property for a few cents and restored it to its owner."[39]

Americans had voted for new leadership, but these four months were governed by the feckless Hoover. The old order still had no answers. Hoover refused to act. The bankers had fled their positions of responsibility, but in this lame-duck period, no one was in charge. Americans hungered for new leadership, for an end to the fear. In early December, the Tammany administration in New York yielded to the bankers yet again, and cut the pay of city employees. A week later, railroads demanded a 10 percent cut in pay.[40]

Abroad, the situation was much worse. Just a few days after the U.S. election, eight people were killed in a gun battle between police and socialists in Switzerland.[41] Britain was begging the American government for debt forgiveness, with a heavy payment hanging over the broken country in the summer. Just a few weeks later, President Paul von Hindenburg of Germany offered Adolf Hitler the chance to form a cabinet in Germany, as long as Hitler adhered to certain conditions. Hitler refused.[42] As Roosevelt came closer to his goal of the presidency, Hitler would come closer to his goal of dictatorship.

The big business world was in its own moment of panic. The $160 million Paramount-Publix movie studio and distribution company collapsed. Albert Wiggin, the cynical head of Chase National Bank, retired. Chase, known as the Rockefeller bank because of the large stake that the Standard Oil interests owned in it, was taken over by a reformer named Winthrop Aldrich. Aldrich would divest Chase's securities affiliate, in a prelude to the Glass-Steagall Act breaking up the rest of the banking industry.[43]

The utilities, whose financial model had collapsed in an orgy of corruption, adopted a code of conduct. They got rid of their old trade association, the National Electric Light Association, and replaced it with the Edison Electric Institute. Americans still respected Thomas Edison, even if they didn't respect the men who profited from his light bulb. One of the leading utility magnates, Samuel Insull, was on the run from American authorities. The Greek court had refused the American extradition request, and the State Department canceled his passport. Insull would turn to England for asylum.

American intellectuals and businessmen began embracing increasingly autocratic ideas. A movement called "technocracy" became a fad;

technocrats sought to replace elected politicians with engineers and scientists who could plan without the need to respond to voters. *Liberty* magazine published an essay, "Does America Need a Dictator?" written by Wilson advisor Colonel Edward House. Unless economic circumstances improved, House wrote, "we are almost certain to have trouble." House wrote that "there is to be found considerable sentiment favorable to a Mussolini sort of dictatorship in conservative circles in America." And this, he argued, might be the optimistic scenario, with the alternative being Russia in 1917.[44] On the first day of 1933, the President's Research Committee on Social Trends, assembled by Hoover and financed by Rockefeller, came out with the dour prediction that without national planning, there could be no assurance against a violent revolution.[45]

Roosevelt told advisor Rexford Tugwell that "there was latent . . . not far below the surface of our disrupted society, an impulse among a good many 'strong' men, men used to having their way, mostly industrialists who directed affairs without being questioned, a feeling that democracy had run its course and that the totalitarians had grasped the necessities of the time. People wanted strong leadership; they were sick of uncertainty, anxious for security, and willing to trade liberty for it."[46]

Roosevelt told Tugwell he was picking up "talk of this kind," as "it had been passing around in clubs and business gatherings for some time as the depression ran on and as disorder threatened." Americans would be willing to turn to dictatorship if they found a military demagogue to follow. It was happening in German and Italy as legislatures in those countries "were even now voting themselves out of office." One man who could bring this about in the U.S., a man "endowed with charm, tradition, and majestic appearance" was, Roosevelt told Tugwell, Douglas MacArthur. The "Nazi-minded among American leaders recalled with approval" how MacArthur had dispersed "with tanks and tear gas" the "unemployed veterans," during the Bonus Army episode, in what became known as "the Battle of Anacostia Flats."[47]

Three days before the inauguration, California, Alabama, Oklahoma, and Louisiana closed their banks; Mississippi restricted withdrawals. The next day, eight states in the West did the same. Then came

New York state, closing its banks for two days. This precipitated the closure of the New York Stock Exchange. In April, the Minnesota Farmer-Labor governor threatened martial law and seizure of property if the legislature did nothing to provide help to the people.

All the while, Roosevelt was preparing for the presidency. During the transition, Hoover and Roosevelt had a complex and embittering series of passive-aggressive encounters. The two men had been somewhat friendly in 1920, though Hoover never respected Roosevelt. The campaign soured their relationship, which continued to deteriorate during the lame-duck session. By 1932, Hoover thought of Roosevelt as a cripple who was not up to the job of the presidency, and who represented the forces of Bolshevism. Roosevelt found Hoover priggish, condescending, brittle, and stubborn.

Hoover continually tried to entice Roosevelt into repudiating his campaign promises—to abandon, as Hoover wrote a senator, "ninety percent of the so-called new deal."[48] Roosevelt refused, telling Hoover that he would not change his policy ideas in return for cooperation from Hoover. Despite his crushing loss, Hoover still did not take Roosevelt seriously, and was planning to run against him in 1936. Hoover taunted Roosevelt publicly and privately, and blamed Roosevelt for the banking crisis. It was uncertainty from Roosevelt's radical proposals, Hoover said, that was panicking business leaders and causing the final collapse of the banking system. Roosevelt pronounced one of Hoover's letters "cheeky." By inauguration day, the two men were barely on speaking terms.[49]

Roosevelt sensed the hunger of the country. Two weeks after the election, two thousand people in Washington, D.C., greeted his arriving train at Union Station. Two days later, at Warm Springs in Georgia, 1,500 people showed up to cheer. This was FDR's country, for now.

Roosevelt put together his cabinet, assuring a Democratic colleague that it would be a "radical" cabinet, that "there will be no one in it who knows the way to 23 Wall Street" (the address of J. P. Morgan) and "no one who is linked in any way with the power trust or with the international bankers." He said he would inflate the currency. In February, Roosevelt picked populist Cordell Hull for the most prestigious slot, secretary of state. He chose Frances Perkins, the first female cabinet member, to be secretary of labor, against the wishes of AFL president William Green. Harold Ickes, a progressive Republican, would run the Interior Department. Henry Wallace, later to become a dreaded inflationist, would head the Agriculture Department.

William Woodin, a businessman and friend of Roosevelt, would take the reins at the Treasury. The Republicans mocked Roosevelt for being unable to bring in the big brains of the party, the heavies. "Where are Young, Baruch, Smith, and Baker?" they jeered, mocking FDR for failing to attract what they perceived as the most prominent corporate leaders on the Democratic side of the aisle (Owen Young, Bernard Baruch, Al Smith, and Newton Baker). Republican operatives were of course missing the point.

Just after the 1932 election, powerful Morgan banker Thomas Lamont offered ideas to policymakers. He sought to expand bailout powers, and to enable banks to expand their business by opening branches. Lamont too was disappointed. By January, "Washington observers began to note that liberals making the pilgrimage" to Roosevelt "returned more cheerful than conservatives."[50]

For much of the rest of 1933 and well into 1934, rather than dictating policy, as they had long been accustomed to do, Wall Street bankers instead were exposed to their own winter of despair. They found themselves called before an increasingly unfriendly Congress.

## A POPULIST PECORA

For Wall Street and the banking industry, the winter of despair was terrifying, and not just because of the bank runs. What framed the winter for the bankers, and paralleled the bitter and public back-and-forth between Hoover and Roosevelt, was the most far-reaching public investigation of the financial sector ever undertaken, originating from the United States Senate.

The investigation started in 1932, when Hoover encouraged the Senate Banking Committee to investigate the banking sector. But under the Republicans, in thrall to Hoover, it had been ineffective. Two general counsels had been fired, another quit.

Pressure was building for a real inquiry. Over the previous four years,

Americans, and the increasingly populist Congress, had become hungry for credible information on what was happening. Populists in particular were embittered by the lack of any real oversight over the collapse, frustrated by the ineffectiveness of the existing government agencies that had been set up by Brandeis and Wilson, but subverted by Mellon and Hoover. Samuel Untermyer, who had conducted the Pujo hearings in 1912–1913, demanded a new investigation of the money trust.

For years, the Federal Trade Commission had been looking into the byzantine structure of the utility industry, composed of a complex network of holding companies, most of which collapsed. Wright Patman found the agency so ineffective that in early February he tried to defund it. The investigation, he said, "has cost this Government more than a million dollars . . . a good prosecuting attorney," he said, "could have gone before a grand jury and disclosed that information in less than 30 days."[51] Democratic members of Congress applauded.

Brandeis, sitting on the Supreme Court, had his book, *Other People's Money*, reissued as an inexpensive paperback; it became popular among incoming members of the new liberal Congress. Populists in Congress angrily claimed that institutions meant to address the depression, such as the bailout fund Hoover created called the Reconstruction Finance Corporation, were only helping politically connected Republican bankers.[52] They wanted answers.

In January of 1933, the outgoing Republican chairman of the Senate Banking Committee hired a pugnacious lawyer, an Italian American named Ferdinand Pecora, as the new general counsel for the committee's inquiry. A progressive Republican with working-class roots, Pecora had been an effective prosecutor of small-time financial crooks. As the banking collapse accelerated and Democrats took over the committee, Pecora began looking into the key organizers of the financial system. He was so effective that the investigation eventually became known as the "Pecora Commission."

Pecora's goal was simple—to assign blame for the crisis to the men who caused the crisis. There was immense pride, a haughtiness among aristocratic American financiers. New York Stock Exchange president Richard Whitney said the stock exchange was a "perfect institution," and that America had been "built by speculation."[53] During much of the first part of the depression, the public still believed banks were, as Pecora put it, "captained by men of unimpeachable integrity, possessing almost mythical business genius and foresight."[54] But Pecora was not intimidated by Wall Street bankers, the aristocrats of American commerce, who could with an arched eyebrow cut off credit to large companies in distress, or even nations in distress. He sought to strip away their veil of respectability, and instead treat them as a seasoned prosecutor would address common crooks.

In January, new hearings began with the spectacular story of Ivar Kreuger, the match monopolist who raised $760 million over fourteen years through American banking syndicates, stole much of it, and then committed suicide.[55] The hearings then exposed the Insull empire, the complex set of holding companies allowing famed entrepreneur turned fugitive Samuel Insull to control much of the American electric utility field with borrowed money.[56]

But the key hearings would start in late February. Eleven days before the inauguration of Roosevelt, Pecora would begin his evisceration of the business practices, and leadership, of the giant commercial bank National City (the basis of today's Citibank), which he called "the superbank."

Forceful, persuasive, and self-confident, National City's president, Charles Mitchell, took the stand in front of the Senate Banking Committee. The fifty-five-year old Mitchell presided over one of the largest banks in the world, a bank so big it had global operations and over eleven thousand miles of "private wire" between its various offices.[57] By 1929, National City wasn't just one of the largest American commercial banks, but also one of the biggest investment houses, issuing $20 billion of securities over the previous decade to a public that had believed in its gold-plated reputation.

Pecora showed, as the banking system collapsed, that National City had ceased to be a bank to service the payment needs of the nation. Using its banking arm, it captured control of the savings of American workers and businessmen. National City had used its gilded reputation to trick people into buying stocks and bonds that it issued and in which it had an interest. One "shorn lamb," Edgar Brown of Pottsville, Pennsylvania, testified to the Senate that he lost his fortune of

$225,000 through National City's scams. He had run a chain of theaters, but after contracting tuberculosis, he sold his business interests and left to California while entrusting the money to National City. He asked that they put his money into bonds and safe investments. Nevertheless, his City broker instead used Brown's savings to buy Peruvian bonds, Anaconda copper, and even the stock of National City itself. National City had interests in all of these. Brown ended up in poverty.

National City, rather than operating as a bank entrusted with the care of the nation's money, was an unseemly marketing organization, using the savings of the American worker and businessman to purchase unreliable securities its own assembly line generated. In 1924, National City floated $15 million of bonds for the Cuban Dominican Sugar Company, even though the Cuban sugar industry had fallen apart just a few years before. It did the same with $32 million of bonds for the Chilean nitrate industry. The company made "only an honest mistake" when it offered $90 million of Peruvian bonds in 1927 and 1928, even when told by its own overseas manager that the Peruvian government wasn't a credible borrower. National City customers often ended up with these worthless bonds in their portfolios.

And Mitchell himself was revealed to be deeply unethical, no better morally than a common petty crook. He profited handsomely in 1927, 1928, and 1929, with an aggregate bonus of $3.5 million. He also avoided income taxes in 1929 by selling stock at a loss to his wife, then buying it back for an artificial loss. The day after these were revealed, progressive Montana senator Burton Wheeler gave a speech on the floor of the Senate demanding that Mitchell be treated as a tax avoider, just like Al Capone.[58] The Department of Justice began an inquiry.[59]

The National City hearings lasted just nine days, but as Pecora put it, "in those nine days a whole era of American financial life passed away." Roosevelt was busy putting together his cabinet, but he saw the benefit of having an ally attacking financiers on the front page of the newspaper every day. Pecora was giving the incoming Roosevelt administration power and momentum. Roosevelt encouraged Democrats on the Senate Banking Committee to continue the hearings. Even after Roosevelt was inaugurated, Pecora didn't stop. He exposed that sacred institution, the center of Wall Street, the firm of J. P.

Morgan. "The problems raised by such an institution go far beyond banking regulation in any narrow sense," said Pecora. "It might be a formidable rival to government itself."[60]

Pecora's crusade met resistance. As he penetrated deeper into Wall Street, Carter Glass, the conservative senator considered the preeminent financial authority in the Democratic Party, tried to close down the investigation. Glass voted to keep information secret.[61] He protested requests by Pecora that he perceived as outside the scope of the inquiry. Glass and Pecora bickered during one cross-examination, with the banker being questioned allowing a half smile to crack his lips as he watched the disarray of his opponents.[62] Roosevelt intervened multiple times, asking that the committee widen its investigation.

The House of Morgan was so famous everyone knew its address: 23 Wall Street. But its tricks were no different than anyone else's: holding companies, insider trading, tax loss avoidance strategies, and organizing the control of corporate assets with large amounts of borrowing.

The deposits of much of corporate America sat on J. P. Morgan's books, ready for use at any time. The bank, as newspapers reported, touched virtually every American.[63] Its power extended everywhere from asphalt beds in the Caribbean island of Trinidad to copper mines in the Arctic Circle, to U.S. and Mexican railroads, mail order goods, farm implements, steel, oil, and automobiles. Morgan men controlled companies like General Motors, AT&T, Standard Brands, the United Company, U.S. Steel, General Electric, Montgomery Ward, ITT, Johns-Manville, and American Radiator.

Like National City's Mitchell, J. P. Morgan Jr. himself, son of the deceased J. P. Morgan, hadn't paid taxes in years. Neither had Thomas Lamont, and many other Morgan partners. Nonpayment of taxes generated rage and mockery. In West Virginia, a legislator offered a bitterly sarcastic "expression of sympathy" to the wealthy Morgan, "because he has not enough money to pay his income tax." The West Virginia House of Delegates passed it unanimously.[64]

Pecora also uncovered the extensive system of bribery by which the Morgan firm paid off political, military, and financial elites through the stock market, a system known as the "preferred list." The preferred list was a list of people from whom the company sought to keep in their graces, and to whom it would offer below-cost stock that could be resold immediately at a profit. This trick hid bribery in the swirling eddies of financial markets.

George Whitney (brother of Richard) defended the preferred list, saying it wasn't a gift. After all, these men took the risk in buying a stock. Pecora produced a letter from Raskob, in which Raskob expressed thanks for being included on the list, and offered a hope he could "reciprocate" in the future.[65] The Senate Banking Committee voted 7–4 to make J. P. Morgan's preferred list public (with the rumor that Pecora threatened to resign if they refused).[66] The list of names was explosive. It included the establishment in both parties. Democratic Party chair John Raskob, Democratic presidential candidate John Davis, Democratic financier Bernard Baruch, and Democratic presidential hopefuls Owen Young and Newton Baker were on the list, as was former Wilson cabinet member and now senator William Gibbs McAdoo. So too was ex-President Calvin Coolidge, Supreme Court Justice Owen J. Roberts, prominent Republican officials, and Mellon family members.

World War I legend General John Pershing, and celebrity Charles Lindbergh were on the list. Silas Strawn, ex-president of the U.S. Chamber of Commerce and the American Bar Association. The heads of National City Bank, Chase National Bank, First National Bank, the New York Stock Exchange, General Electric, U.S. Steel, Standard Oil of New Jersey, Postal Telegraph, AT&T, ITT, MetLife, Electric Bond and Share.

This was the network of men running the country, from the giant corporations like Standard Oil of New Jersey to the private bank J. P. Morgan to judges, party leaders, a major general, even a president and a Supreme Court justice. These men were bound by financial relationships, in which the borders of business, banks, and personal accounts were murky.

Pecora also found that, at the height of the stock market boom in 1929, large corporations were lending tens of billions of dollars in "call loans" to encourage speculation.[67] Standard Oil of New Jersey alone lent an aggregate of $17 billion in twenty thousand separate loans; the oil company was making so much cash it had nowhere else to invest it other than the stock market. The head of the company, naturally, was also on J. P. Morgan's preferred list.

The old order was being named. Pecora brought this network, this private government, out of the shadows, issued subpoenas, revealed their plots publicly, and embarrassed them. He smashed their credibility, allowing not only the space for policymakers to act, but prompting immediate changes within the institutions themselves. Top bankers resigned and reformers took over. Boards fell apart. Once in power, Roosevelt ordered investigations and prosecutions.

As the investigation went on, Congress debated reform of the stock market, utilities law, the tax code, and holding companies. In 1933, Congress passed the Securities Act, which made lying about stocks and bonds on offer illegal. This was passed unanimously by the House and with only quiet grumbling by the now discredited bankers.

The investigation would last until 1934, when Congress set up a regulatory agency, the Securities and Exchange Commission (SEC), to police the practices Pecora had uncovered, and Roosevelt named Pecora to the SEC. "Never before in the history of the United States," said Pecora, "had so much wealth and power been required to render a public accounting."[68]

## THE FIRST HUNDRED DAYS

Two days after Pecora finished his hearings on National City, President Franklin Delano Roosevelt swore the oath of office. The timing of the hearings to coincide with the inauguration was intentional. Financiers who once whispered calming words in the ears of a new president and a new Congress were terrified and embarrassed, squabbling among themselves.

The new president went on the rhetorical attack immediately. "Practices of the unscrupulous money changers stand indicted in the court of public opinion, rejected by the hearts and minds of men," Roosevelt said in his inaugural address. "The money changers have fled from their high seats in the temple of our civilization."[69]

The banking system Pecora had been investigating was frozen.

Hotels in D.C. the day of the inauguration were refusing to take checks from out-of-state banks. Governors had closed the banks in the financial strongholds of Chicago and New York, meaning financial markets were closed as well. Americans waited, afraid, hopeful, anxious. As Hitler took power in Germany, Americans had more local concerns. What would happen to their local bank? Their local savings accounts? The value of the dollar itself?

Roosevelt's first act was to declare a bank holiday, to shut the system down, and in effect end the gold standard. Roosevelt called Congress into an emergency session, and a banking bill passed that allowed the Reconstruction Finance Corporation to inject money into large and small banks, and restructure them. Roosevelt then spoke to the nation through the radio, to explain what he was doing, in what became known as a "fireside chat."

"Some of our bankers had shown themselves either incompetent or dishonest in their handling of the people's funds," he said, leading to a loss of confidence in the banking system as a whole. The government's job was to "straighten out this situation and do it as quickly as possible. And the job is being performed." The government would reopen the banks gradually, he explained. Any bank that opened, he told the public, was sound, backed by the government and new authority the government had to offer enough currency to honor all deposits. Federal examiners would keep insolvent banks closed, and work out with depositors a way to minimize losses.

Roosevelt asked for confidence. This fireside chat wasn't the first time Americans had heard how the balm of confidence could fix their problems; Hoover had said that as well. But Roosevelt had acted, with new authority, and acknowledged the dishonesty of the bankers. The day the banks began reopening, Americans rushed to the banks. But they did not withdraw money; they deposited cash they had stuffed in their mattresses. They believed. The stock market had its greatest gain in history, up 15 percent in one day.[70]

The president's immediate success in restoring the banking system empowered the Democrats to organize the New Deal. In the first hundred days of the new administration, Congress and the president passed fifteen key pieces of legislation. This legislation included measures to end the gold standard, cut expenditures, regulate the stock market, build out public power to compete with the private utilities through the Tennessee Valley Authority, guarantee bank deposits, put Americans to work through the Civilian Conservation Corps, and offer relief in the agricultural sector.

In these first hundred days, Pecora, Roosevelt, and populists in Congress exposed that the political economy of Wall Street and big business was a top-down concentrated system of corruption and lawlessness. The public responded by rejecting the old order with protests. For instance, banker Charles Dawes had won the Nobel Peace Prize in 1925 and served as vice president under Calvin Coolidge. He had been a financial and political icon, but in this new era, his reputation had turned to mud. His Chicago bank had received a $90 million bailout from the government, yet he was refusing to lend money to the city of Chicago so that the city could meet payroll. A month after FDR's inauguration, five thousand teachers with armbands, unpaid for months, stormed banks in Chicago, yelling "We want Dawes," demanding an audience. Dawes came out to speak with the teachers, before testily snapping "to hell with troublemakers."[71]

Americans were angry at Wall Street.

The election, and the months after the inauguration, also inspired hope and self-confidence. "The first days of the Roosevelt Administration charged the air with the snap and the zigzag of electricity," said Brooklyn congressman Emanuel Celler. "What before had been black or white sprang alive with color. The messages to Congress, the legislation; even the reports on the legislation took on the briskness of authority."[72] White House advisor Rexford Tugwell remarked in June of 1933 that it was not through violence, but at the ballot box that the people brought about "a revolution accomplished in a particularly American way."[73]

But it was only a beginning. The war over the "economic government of the United States," and the actual government of the United States, would be fought not just at the ballot box, not just through protests, not just in the court of public opinion. It would take more than just a series of elections, and a new president, and a hundred days, to take apart a system underpinning politics, the business world, and Wall Street for the bulk of the previous fifty years.

## FALL OF THE HOUSE OF MELLON

Almost immediately, Roosevelt signaled he would hold the bankers accountable. Roosevelt asked the new attorney general, Homer Cummings, to "vigorously prosecute any violations of the law" that emerged from the investigations. Administration officials told *The New York Times* that "if the people become convinced that the big violations are to be punished it will be helpful in restoring confidence."[74]

Just a few weeks after taking office, his Department of Justice indicted National City's Charles Mitchell for tax evasion. Mitchell was known as the best bond salesman in the country, "Sunshine Charlie," whose salary was more than $1 million in 1928 and 1929, whom the press lauded as "brilliant," "dynamic," and eagerly sought his comments on current events. He had been brought low by Pecora, exposed as a charlatan who admitted he had avoided taxes and cheated his own customers. As two Citibank officials later wrote, "If Mitchell were convicted, then all banks would stand guilty."[75]

Mitchell was acquitted of criminal charges in June, because he persuaded the jury that he had acted on advice of counsel. The administration chose to continue the case with a civil charge. Mitchell was eventually fined over $1 million for tax fraud in a case that ended up at the Supreme Court.[76]

Mitchell wasn't the only "bankster" on the hook. Samuel Insull was eventually prosecuted, and though acquitted, he died penniless and in disgrace. Richard Whitney was later jailed for embezzlement. And as the investigations wore on, the new administration and state attorneys general cracked down. The nephew of robber baron Edward Harriman, J. W. Harriman, was indicted for bank fraud. He tried to escape the charge by faking his own death and stabbing himself in the chest while out on bail.[77]

In the hothouse environment of the Pecora hearings, which placed blame for the banking freeze at the feet of the great banking houses, Mellon was finally vulnerable. In January 1933, "confidential information was filed with the Bureau of Internal Revenue by an official long in the service" who gave a tip that Mellon was evading taxes.[78] The Republican appointee running the tax bureau, refusing to take a position, passed the case on to his successor. The Department of Justice began an investigation in April.[79]

In June, as the first hundred days of the New Deal concluded, progressives in the Senate began encouraging Pecora to probe the House of Mellon, including Andrew, his brother Richard, and the "mighty corporations" they controlled, just as he had the House of Morgan. The Department of Justice and individual senators looked into the Mellons' income tax returns.[80]

After Mitchell's acquittal, Cummings reorganized the Department of Justice to create a specialized tax division, and declared a war on tax avoidance. In March 10, 1934, Cummings offered four simultaneous criminal complaints against powerful political figures for tax fraud: James Walker, a corrupt former mayor of New York City; the House of Morgan's Thomas Lamont; and Thomas Sidio, a law partner of former Democratic presidential hopeful Newton Baker. But the fourth, and most important target, was Andrew Mellon.[81] To underscore the point, Cummings, who had represented a company in a private antitrust suit against Alcoa, also said there would be an inquiry into Alcoa.[82]

The day of the public announcement, Mellon, already angry at the Roosevelt administration over the implementation of New Deal banking laws, pronounced the accusation and the proceedings "impertinent, scandalous, and improper."[83] The basis of the criminal case was similar to that of Mitchell. Mellon had fraudulently claimed that he lost money selling stock, as a way to avoid paying income tax. He hadn't sold the stock, but had placed it with family members or with companies he controlled, selling stock to himself, in essence, so he could pretend not to have income.

As with Mitchell's case, Mellon was acquitted at first. He never even got to trial, as the grand jury convened in Mellon's hometown of Pittsburgh, which was still friendly to "Uncle Andy." The entire case was presented and dismissed in just five hours. Mellon declared victory, pronouncing the decision "proof of the good sense and fairness of the American people." Mellon's friends and allies were elated; Henry

Stimson was "greatly gratified" that the appalling miscarriage of justice had been averted, and Herbert Hoover said he found "tremendous satisfaction in the result." Some Democrats agreed. Walter Lippmann accused Roosevelt of a "low and inept political maneuver," and pronounced it inconceivable that a man with a multimillion-dollar income would bother to cheat the government. This was "one of those stunts that politicians stoop to every now and then."[84]

Mellon was right to take the matter personally. His entire edifice of monopoly control was falling apart. Industries were being liberated from financial overlords. New laws broke apart Mellon banks, forced Mellon companies to disclose financial details, raised inheritance taxes, and closed tax loopholes.[85] That same year, the airline industry, in which Mellon was invested, was subjected to investigation for corruption. Airline holding companies were dissolved, breaking apart the airline manufacturers from the airlines themselves, and reorganizing mail contracts that had allowed larger airlines to take over independent airlines with government subsidies. Among companies hit by the cancellation of mail contracts was the Pittsburgh Aviation Company, the last company that Mellon and his brother had put together.[86]

In debates in Congress over New Deal policy, members of Congress would use Mellon as a rhetorical punching bag and a chief example of plutocracy.[87]

Mellon's victory over his criminal complaint was short-lived. The Department of Justice had to drop out, but the Bureau of Internal Revenue, the tax department, could act. And the ultimate boss of the Bureau of Internal Revenue was Henry Morgenthau Jr., a close friend of Roosevelt and one who believed that tax fraud by the very wealthy was a direct threat to democracy. In late March, the Bureau of Internal Revenue sent Mellon a letter demanding $1.3 million in back taxes, along with a 50 percent penalty fee. Mellon hit back. Not only did he refuse to pay, but he claimed his taxes had been miscalculated, and demanded a refund. The bureau upped its demand to $3 million. Mellon decided to appeal to the Board of Tax Appeals to hear the case, a board he had set up in 1924 to allow taxpayers to dispute unjust claims.[88] Mellon would put the Roosevelt administration on trial.

Because of the failure of the criminal indictment, the administration

was vulnerable to the charge of political vindictiveness. "Many enemies of the President are interested in maintaining" the system, wrote
Robert Jackson, the man to represent the Roosevelt administration in
the eventual case. This made the case, Jackson noted, "one of importance to the entire administration."[89] It became essential to win some
sort of payment of back taxes. Yet it would be a tough, high-profile
case. Mellon was a ruthless and savvy old man, with access to the
most expensive tax attorneys. His finances were endlessly complex,
and the tax laws seemed vague, especially as they applied in an unusual
economic situation like the depression. In the trial, there would be
forty-seven witnesses, roughly ten thousand pages of testimony, and
847 exhibits in evidence.[90]

Robert Jackson, a tall and husky forty-three-year-old with a smile
that "crinkles his eyes" was the man to prepare the case for the government. Before coming to D.C. to work on the New Deal, Jackson had
a thriving law practice as a small-town lawyer in western New York.
Jackson was brilliant, and like Patman, a throwback to an earlier era; he
had attended but not graduated from Albany Law School, earning his
entrance to the bar by apprenticing to a practicing attorney. Despite his
lack of formal credentials, he was an exceptional attorney. His courtroom gestures, "timed with the precision of an acrobat," contrasted
with his leisurely style and his dry wit.[91] While shy and cautious in
politics, Jackson was an aggressive trial lawyer.

The charges centered on Mellon using his control of banks and
corporations to lie about his income. But the most spectacular charge
was that Mellon had been claiming tax deductions for the money he
spent on his art collection, perhaps the most valuable group of classic
European paintings in the world.

In 1931, Mellon, while secretary of the treasury, claimed only
$1.93 million in taxable income. While he had made $10.89 million that
year, he claimed he had suffered investment losses of $7.28 million. The
government disallowed most of the losses, determining that Mellon's
income had been understated by $5 million due to a miscalculation on
the gains of the sale of one of his companies. Jackson felt Mellon had
contempt for paying taxes. Mellon's initial return, Jackson said, did not
even name the stocks upon "which the losses had been suffered."[92]

Jackson alleged the losses were faked, that Mellon had not sold shares of two companies, but had only pretended to sell the shares at artificially low prices to his own family members, or to trusts and holding companies that he controlled. Jackson also sought to show that Mellon understated his income; a large steel company Mellon owned, McClintic-Marshall, had been bought that year by Bethlehem Steel, using a complicated series of dividend transactions upon which Mellon hadn't paid taxes.

From the beginning, the trial was difficult for Jackson. "When we came here nobody took the Government's case seriously," he told Treasury official Herman Oliphant. "The press was either hostile or openly skeptical."[93] The earlier failed criminal indictment hurt, but more than that, the administration was putting a $200 million fortune on trial, and the perception of political motivation was strong. Moreover, the Board of Tax Appeals had been set up by Mellon himself, in 1924, in a system of corporate tax enforcement largely designed under Mellon at the Treasury. In 1934, the Board of Tax Appeals had fourteen members appointed by Mellon, and just two by the new administration.[94] The man presiding over the hearings, Ernest H. Van Fossan, was an Ohio Republican.[95] One of the few Democrats on the board, Charles Trammell, "mysteriously resigned" toward the end of the trial to represent the DuPont family before the very Board of Tax Appeals on which he had recently sat.[96]

The board often seemed to act as Mellon partisans, refusing to allow anything more than narrow subpoenas of business records by Jackson's team while allowing subpoenas for the Treasury and attorney general's office with broad direction, hindering the efforts of the prosecution. Mellon's lawyer even attempted to subpoena the confidential reports of Jackson's investigators.[97] The lack of ability to get records, in a case involving complex and extremely boring questions of nested trusts and corporate shells, would have been a challenge for any legal team.

Jackson also faced a skilled opponent, Frank Hogan, later the president of the American Bar Association. Hogan had cleared oil tycoon Edward Doheny in a major Harding-era political corruption scandal known as "Teapot Dome," receiving a reported $1 million fee. He had, as his proponents noted, "the burning zeal of a defender" and "the

delicacy of a poet." A lover of Byron and Shakespeare, he took frequent
long trips to Europe, and carried a copy of *Hamlet* in his pocket. He
was brilliant, elitist, and sarcastic; he liked to joke that "an ideal client
is a very rich man, easily scared."[98]

Most of the corporate records needed by Jackson to prove his case
were held by Mellon companies, and there had not been much precedent in going after these kinds of large-scale corporate tax evaders. The
income tax had only been imposed in 1913, and for much of that time,
Mellon had been the one organizing the enforcement machinery.

Mellon also had substantial influence, and in some cases, control
over the press. He was obsessed with his own image and reputation,
even having to be talked down from a libel lawsuit against the author
of a critical book.[99] Mellon made personal requests for better coverage.[100] Many newspaper publishers were Republican, and most would
endorse Roosevelt's opponent in 1936. Beyond that, Mellon had influence over advertising revenue. Mellon made requests to his fellow
Pittsburgh corporate executives, such as those who ran Heinz, on their
advertising choices, and newspapermen knew it.[101]

The trial was awash in interest from the beginning. Charles
Schwab, the chairman of Bethlehem Steel; Eugene Grace, the president of Bethlehem Steel; and James Farrell, the former president of
U.S. Steel, all testified on behalf of Mellon, and to help answer a series
of technical questions on how much Mellon profited from the sale of
one of his companies.[102] Jackson's team worked the press, who had initially been hostile, but "at the end of our week of waiting, the boys on
the press had gotten acquainted with us." While reporters still thought
there was nothing to the case, they were willing to treat the government's side fairly.[103]

Hogan, despite his myriad advantages, was overconfident, and
frittered away some of the goodwill the press had toward Mellon's
side. He dubbed Jackson a "country lawyer," an unsophisticate, which
ended up endearing Jackson to the press. At one point, Jackson asked
Hogan if he was going to ask a technical set of questions on tax law
toward a witness, and Hogan made fun of him for being unfamiliar
with the intricacies of tax law. A moment later, a technical piece of

a tax return in turn confused Hogan. "Do you want to borrow a tax attorney?" asked Jackson. Hogan reddened.[104]

The main strategy of the Mellon legal team was to portray the dispute as a technical difference in the interpretation of tax laws, pursued only because of political vindictiveness. Roosevelt sought to punish an innocent old man who wanted to donate his fortune to charity. Mellon was a loving family man carrying on the honorable tradition of the Mellon name, a builder of key industries, and a patriotic citizen who only came to public office, reluctantly, because he was asked by the president-elect in 1921 to serve his country.[105]

Hogan spoke of Mellon's charitable donations, donations to educational foreign exchange programs, medical research, and relief for the unemployed.[106] For such a generous man, wasn't it more likely that technical questions involving confusing matters of cost bases were just good faith disagreement? And then Hogan announced that Mellon would be donating his personal collection to the public in a museum. "It has been the plan of Mr. Mellon . . . to establish in the capital of the nation a Great Temple of Art," said Hogan. There is no reason why, he continued, "Washington should not overtake, if indeed not surpass, Paris, and London, as an art center," though humbly noting that "perhaps no one dreams of ever surpassing Rome, and Florence, in that respect." Not only had Mellon been planning this museum for years, asserted Hogan, but the museum would not even have his name attached to it. What humility! What magnificence! What vision! The defendant was "a persecuted man who was on the verge of giving America its greatest art institute."[107]

With his opening statement, Hogan had been aiming for favorable publicity for Mellon, and he got it. The front page of *The New York Times* contained the headline "Mellon Planned Gift of $19,000,000 in Art to Nation" on February 19, with portrayals of the stunning works, such as a triptych of *The Crucifixion* by Perugino, Raphael's *Alba Madonna,* and *Adoration of the Magi* by Botticelli. All had been purchased by Mellon from the Soviet government from the czar's Hermitage collection.[108] The government responded to Hogan by showing that Mellon's transactions had no economic rationale except for tax avoidance, that they were meant to deceive, and that they were "carefully planned and skillfully executed."[109]

Within just a few days, Hogan's case fell apart. Mellon's financial secretary, Howard Johnson, revealed on the stand that Mellon was betting against stocks in 1931 as secretary of the treasury. More damning, Mellon employed a former Bureau of Internal Revenue employee, D. D. Sheppard, as a tax attorney, and Sheppard, though not a government employee, had an office in the Treasury building with "ready access to Mr. Mellon's office as long as the latter was Secretary."[110] Mellon had requested a memo from the Bureau on tax avoidance by the wealthy. The commissioner who wrote the memo then recommended Sheppard to Mellon as a bright young Bureau official who could help Mellon with his income taxes, and Mellon used several of the strategies recommended in the memo.[111] Mellon had not even signed his 1931 tax return, an embarrassing if petty revelation.

Johnson also revealed that Mellon had given millions in stock to charity and his children, but Mellon himself was receiving dividends from the stock and retaining control of the companies. He also revealed that Mellon was always in control of his employees, running his businesses regardless of government position.[112] Mellon's arguments that he had set aside his management of his financial empire so he could serve dispassionately in public service seemed like obvious, and increasingly ridiculous, lies.

Jackson was privately jubilant over the prospects for the case. His team was not only working to perfect their argument, but trying to "give the newspaper boys a sensation a day."[113] This approach annoyed Hogan so much that he said to the press, "I regret that Mr. Jackson still finds it impossible to refrain from trying this case in the newspapers."[114] But the approach was working, and Hogan knew it.

Hogan's initial strategy to get favorable coverage for Mellon's art donations backfired. "It is now a joke around here that every time we bring out a bad point, Hogan brings out a picture," Jackson told his superiors. "I think their supply of art is about gone." The opening day had been rough, but since then, it had gone the government's way. To improve his odds in the trial, Jackson joked, Mellon "may give away another art gallery."[115]

On February 26, Jackson still had Johnson on the stand. He tried to show that Mellon had access to J. P. Morgan's infamous preferred list, and could use it as a means of bribery and favoritism toward his own favored few. The presiding member of the Board of Tax Appeals stopped Jackson from revealing the extent of the dealings, as it was not relevant to the tax trial. But it garnered headlines nonetheless, linking Mellon with the Pecora hearings and the House of Morgan.[116]

In April, Mellon testified, with Jackson letting him speak with few questions or interruptions. Mellon spoke fluently, and in doing so, made several key points for the prosecution. He admitted he had made no commitment to build an art gallery anywhere, and the paintings for which he had taken tax deductions were hanging on his wall.[117] This testimony was consistent with evidence Jackson had produced. Hogan attempted to show that Mellon was planning a museum by revealing that the 1935 insurance policy on the paintings was written in the name of Andrew Mellon's charitable trust. A member of Jackson's legal team asked for prior-year policies, which were only written in Andrew Mellon's name, and did not mention the trust.[118]

As truck drivers and auto workers went on strike, and as big businessmen with the U.S. Chamber of Commerce ripped the New Deal, the Board of Tax Appeals—set up by Mellon—took sides as well. The government asked for internal confidential documents relating to the McClintic-Marshall merger with Bethlehem Steel; Hogan responded by calling the government lawyer who made the request a "contemptible libeler," and the Board agreed with Hogan, calling the documents of "little use" and suggesting the request was "ill-tempered." Jackson, offended at the insult to his team's professional integrity, offered his resignation, but Morgenthau sent a telegram rejecting his resignation and asking Jackson to continue the case with "no abatement in vigor."[119]

As the trial dragged on, it became clear that Mellon was trying to refight the 1932 election, to prove to the whole country that the New Deal was madness. Mellon assailed "tactics pursued by high Government circles," accusing Secretary Morgenthau of using the trial to attack an important political opponent. Morgenthau publicly said the trial was about finding the "simple truth" and "common business honesty," infuriating Hogan and Mellon.[120]

Mellon thought the request from Morgenthau to vigorously pursue the case revealed how the trial was simply born of political vindictiveness and nothing more. Hogan portrayed the government as engaged in "personalities of the pettiest sort." Jackson responded by noting that while "it is Mr. Mellon's creed that $200,000,000 can do no wrong, our offense consists in doubting it."[121]

This trial, as with Charles Mitchell, was about principle, not just money. Mellon could afford $3 million in tax payments, and the government didn't need the money. It was true that many tax trials would hinge on precedents set during this one, as many wealthy men would avail themselves of Mellon's methods had he escaped penalty.[122] John Jakob Raskob and Pierre du Pont would both be put on trial in 1937.[123]

But this trial was also political. It was a proxy war between the barons of industry and a new political system that populists had been trying to organize. It was, as Morgenthau put it, democracy on trial. Jackson felt the trial, and its attendant publicity, were key to undermining the undemocratic habits of the "old order, which many of the enemies of the President are interested in maintaining."[124] The revelations of how Mellon had done business as treasury secretary prompted revulsion, and reform.[125]

In May, the case venue was moved to Washington, D.C., and the trial wrapped by June. More New Dealers were put on the Board of Tax Appeals, and more briefs were filed in 1936.[126] In the meantime, Mellon sailed to Europe, continued to buy art, and participated in politics. Jackson became more prominent, speaking out against inequality and for the Roosevelt reelection campaign. He went to Europe, including Germany, to investigate the Kreuger safety match monopoly, where he saw up close the growing power of the Nazi state. This experience influenced Jackson's increasingly vocal political advocacy, and his writings against fascism and its relationship to the concentration of wealth and power.[127]

In the 1936 election, Andrew Mellon responded to his tax trial by attempting to defeat Roosevelt politically. He gave $20,000 to the Republican Party, with Richard K. Mellon giving another $20,000. The entire old order fought back against the various insults of the New Deal. The DuPont family donated $144,430 and J. P. Morgan kicked in

$50,000.[128] Much larger sums went to the Liberty League, an independent group opposed to the New Deal. Meanwhile, the Mellon family, and the Mellon name, became a useful political prop for Democratic political officials.[129] The trial, with its charges and countercharges, paralleled the vicious political fighting, through the courts, within businesses, and for the hearts of voters.

On the eve of the 1936 election, Roosevelt gave a famous speech at Madison Square Garden. The mandate of 1932, he told the voters, was "a restoration of American democracy." He continued, "I should like to have it said of my first Administration that in it the forces of selfishness and of lust for power met their match. I should like to have it said of my second Administration that in it these forces met their master."[130]

The crushing victory for Roosevelt, and the overwhelming number of Democrats in the House and Senate, made the Republican Party irrelevant. Finally, business leaders acknowledged defeat. After the election, the National Association of Manufacturers had a conference at the Waldorf-Astoria, broadcast over NBC radio, to discuss the social responsibilities of business. E. T. Weir, chairman of the National Steel Corporation, called for a redistribution of wealth. Colby Chester, the chairman of General Foods, called for business to "stand foursquare against monopoly." *The New York Times* headlined it "Industry Gives Up Fight on New Deal." Leaders of most major corporations, including DuPont and Mellon companies like Gulf Oil, were in the room. The titans of industry, disingenuous or no, shell-shocked by the election or no, had heard the anger of the American people.[131]

In the aftermath of the election, Mellon publicly and prominently offered his art and money in the construction of a new museum, to be titled the National Gallery. He and Roosevelt exchanged public letters, with Roosevelt pronouncing himself "happy" at Mellon's offer.[132] This exchange shocked and annoyed Jackson, who noted that it would in all likelihood give the Board of Tax Appeals the impression that Mellon had the informal sanction of the administration.[133] Wright Patman too was angry, exchanging letters with Fiorello La Guardia, by now the mayor of New York City. La Guardia encouraged him to let the matter go, which Patman did.[134] Roosevelt would not turn down this gift of priceless art.

Jackson's fear was partially realized. The board did dismiss the fraud charge. But importantly, it also required the payment of back taxes. Eight members, all but one who had been appointed by Mellon, voted to require a payment of half a million dollars. Seven others dissented, accusing the board of unfairly aiding Mellon.[135] Andrew Mellon died in August 1937, and the Mellon estate settled related tax charges on favorable terms to the government to avoid more publicity.[136] But Mellon had been forced to pay something, a concession there had been wrongdoing instead of political prosecution. Jackson, Patman, and La Guardia all believed that the verdict had not been harsh enough, that the museum donation by Mellon had been the real settlement.

The Revenue Act of 1937 closed loopholes used, as Roosevelt put it to Congress, in "clever little schemes" of certain large taxpayers peddled by "lawyers of high standing at the Bar."[137] The Interstate Commerce Commission opened an investigation of Mellon Railroads in connection with Pittsburgh Coal, one of the main companies at issue in the trial (and one of the largest coal producers in the world).[138] The Department of Justice filed antitrust charges against Mellon's Gulf Oil, seventeen other major oil companies, forty-six individuals, and three trade publications for fixing gasoline prices. It was the largest oil case since Standard Oil had been broken up. And at Mellon's Alcoa, Alcoa executives were forced to negotiate with newly formed unions, which had power over pay, job security, health and safety, discipline, and even output.[139]

Andrew Mellon was never jailed, but he would be the last of the great robber barons. His son, Paul, would have the aristocratic life of a wealthy gentleman of leisure and a patron of the arts, but would run no corporate empire. The Mellon family kept their money, but not their power. Not even a life of leisure was safe from democratic forces. Andrew's nephew, Richard, had to contend with a strike by the farmhands at the farm where he relaxed with his foxhunts. True to the family tradition, Richard shut down the farm rather than giving in. Meanwhile, there was a sit-down strike in the potato cellar of Mellon ally Charles Schwab's summer estate.[140] Even foxhunting and potato cellars on summer estates were no longer safe for plutocrats.

In 1937, Congress ratified Roosevelt's acceptance of Mellon's gift, chartering a museum to be on the National Mall between the White House and the Capitol, the site of monuments and symbols of national unity. The museum opened in 1941. The National Gallery became, for a time, the largest marble structure in the world. The dedication by Roosevelt was a jovial affair. Roosevelt nicknamed the National Gallery "Bob's Museum," after Robert Jackson.[141] Decades later, in taxi rides to the Federal Reserve, Patman would point to the National Gallery and say to accompanying staff, "That's Uncle Andy's mausoleum, and I helped build that."[142]

# TRUSTBUSTERS AGAINST HITLER

"History proves that dictatorships do not grow out of strong and successful governments, but out of weak and helpless ones."

**—Franklin Delano Roosevelt, 1938**[1]

"Bear in mind that it was the steel monopoly, in conjunction with other combinations, which finally placed Hitler on the throne."

**—William Borah**[2]

"There never was a monopoly as tight and as agile as Alcoa."

**—Arthur Goldschmidt**[3]

■ ■ ■ ■ ■ ■ ■ ■ ■ ■ ■ ■ ■

Robert Jackson was afraid. It was early 1935, and he had been looking into Andrew Mellon's taxes for months. He had to investigate the interlinked corporate structures of the Mellon system and the Pittsburgh economy, but what he was finding went way beyond the tax avoidance covered in the case. In a memo, he offered to the treasury secretary a picture showing the scope of Mellon's power. What Mellon had done to cement this power was so audacious that it may be of interest, Jackson noted, "to the President."

"Pittsburgh, so far as defense in war time, and basic heavy industry in peace time," Jackson told his superiors, "is the heart of America." The area, with its strategic placement in coal country and with three rivers—the Allegheny, the Monongahela, and the Ohio—all running nearby, had been a center of American industry for a hundred years.

The industrial productive capacity of this region determined America's prosperity in peacetime, and even more importantly, whether America could build enough weaponry to equip and defend itself during a world war. And Mellon was in charge of it.

"The effect of the depression," Jackson reported, had reduced the dollar value of Mellon's properties. But relatively speaking, the proportion of what he owned in "America's heart," and his "relative control of its credit and industry," had increased. Even more than he had before, Mellon controlled "the wages and living standards" of the people of western Pennsylvania.[4] Jackson found out Mellon had cemented this control during the banking crisis, using his treasury secretary position not to arrest the crisis, but to take advantage of it.

In September of 1931, banks all over the country were shutting their doors because they were either insolvent or caught without enough cash on hand for panicked depositors. One troubled bank was the 121-year-old Bank of Pittsburgh, a bank nearly as old as the city itself and one of the key non-Mellon banks. Its $46,921,065 of deposits were now frozen.[5]

For years Andrew Mellon had tried to gain control of the bank. In 1931, when it closed its doors, the bank was solvent, with over $53 million of assets to cover its $47 million of deposits. The closing was voluntary, and done to ward off a panic. The banking community in Pittsburgh wanted to save the bank, since bank runs are contagious. Moreover, the Bank of Pittsburgh was a banker's bank; it held only five thousand deposits, but many were large deposits from other banks.[6] If it closed its doors, other banks would as well. Even President Hoover was encouraging a private rescue of the bank.

Even Richard Mellon wanted to save the Bank of Pittsburgh. But not Andrew, who demanded majority voting shares in the Bank of Pittsburgh in return for participating in the rescue. The directors refused, assuming they would have other options to avoid insolvency besides Mellon's ruthless offer.

They would not. The next day, on September 21, 1931, the Bank of England went off the gold standard, inducing a much broader financial panic. Stock exchanges in London, Berlin, Vienna, Brussels, Oslo, Stockholm, Amsterdam, Johannesburg, and Calcutta closed.[7] "It is believed," Jackson told both Morgenthau and the president, that "A.W. Mellon knew England's plan at that time."

The squeeze on the Pittsburgh banking system was on, and Mellon had prepared his banks to take advantage by loading them with funds. Meanwhile, many non-Mellon banks began failing. Highland Bank and the Franklin Savings and Trust Company shut their doors, as did the Pittsburgh-American Bank and Trust, and the Merchant Savings and Trust Company.

This was the national banking crisis, now localized in Pittsburgh.[8] Only this time, the man profiting was the treasury secretary, who was supposed to be looking out not for his own banking interests, of which he had pretended to disclaim ownership, but the public at large. Instead, Mellon sought to use confidential information acquired via his position as a government official to capture either the Bank of Pittsburgh, or by keeping it shut, its business. He was gaining not just more profit, but power and control.

This banking consolidation into the hands of the House of Mellon, as Jackson noted, had other consequences. Non-Mellon companies who had kept their deposits in non-Mellon banks couldn't access their money. Failures of business enterprises led to the "acquisition of many properties by the Mellon interest which had advantages in access to credit." The proportion of Pittsburgh industry "under the Mellon thumb . . . has vastly increased."[9]

Ruthless behavior by a banker didn't surprise Jackson. What was surprising was the seamless linking of public and private power; in this case that it was "the Secretary of the Treasury, with access to accurate, current, and confidential information from banks and industry" that "was the guiding hand."[10]

Later that year, Jackson went to Germany to investigate a safety match cartel. He saw the Nazi storm troopers and the Hitler surveillance state up close.[11] Germany had once again created an air force, and Hitler's aggression was becoming more and more obvious. Meanwhile, Mellon, out of office and on trial, still had a choke hold over a vital region necessary to building a modern military, a choke hold stronger than he had held in the 1920s. If America attempted to build an arsenal of democracy, Mellon could stand in the way.

"Today there is only one force in the world big enough to cope with the Mellons in Pittsburgh," Jackson wrote. "That is the Federal government and I sometimes doubt whether it, bound by a myriad of technicalities and limitations, can effectively . . . restore economic freedom." Jackson was not alone. Inside the Department of Justice, debates raged over the right way to handle monopoly power. Attorney General Cummings peered at Germany's cartelized industrial structure, and its now fascist government, with apprehension.[12]

One of Jackson's fears was that financial control of the American industrial heartland meant that production of key materials, like aluminum, would be held back to suit the needs of financiers rather than national defense. He also feared that the financiers would dominate America. "Modern European history," Jackson said, "teaches us that free enterprise cannot exist alongside of monopolies and cartels." He noted "there is no practical way on earth to regulate the economic oligarchy of autocratic, self-constituted and self-perpetuating groups," which were a "menace" to political as well as economic freedom. Democracy could not stand against "interlocking directors, interlocking bankers, and interlocking lawyers," with power to hire and fire thousands, to dictate to business suppliers, and to donate campaign cash.[13]

From the early years of the New Deal into World War II, populist leaders would use antimonopoly policy not only to address what Brandeis called industrial absolutism, but as a means to return control of national security to the people.

## THE ROOSEVELT RECESSION

New Dealers feared corporatism at home, and fascism abroad. Cordell Hull had pointed out that the forces of autocracy were rising globally as early as 1932, during the bitter debate over who would capture the Democratic nomination. Hull believed, as Wilson and Brandeis had about Teddy Roosevelt's vision of "regulated monopoly," that the fusion of corporate and state power was a fundamental threat to democracy. If government attempted to oversee instead of break up monopolies, soon Americans would find monopolies overseeing the state. This was why Hull fought to nominate Roosevelt years earlier.

But the nominating contest didn't end the ideological conflict. Roosevelt didn't reject the planners, but incorporated them into his administration, side by side with the antimonopolists. Until the late 1930s, Roosevelt was torn between "the Theodore Roosevelt theory of regulated business and the Wilsonian-Brandeis theory of free competition and retention of the smaller units."[14] Once again, the progressive world split, between corporatists who sought to deliver a better world by working with monopolies, and those who thought the path to a better world lay in breaking them up.

This was apparent in the early part of the New Deal; even as the administration and Congress waged a Brandeis-influenced attack on Wall Street with new securities laws, the planners sought, unsuccessfully, to centralize industrial power. In 1933, Congress passed the National Industrial Recovery Act, a bill putting together a central group of experts in a body called the National Recovery Administration to run the corporate state in a partnership between government and industry. The bill emerged from an obsession with planning by both big business, including the U.S. Chamber of Commerce, and progressive corporatists, such as Adolf Berle and Rexford Tugwell.

Brandeis believed that fair trade rules for smaller businesses, such as loose coalitions, protections of smaller brands, and sharing of certain kinds of production information, would allow them to compete with larger industrial concerns. Cooperation among the small would allow fair competition amongst everyone. Corporatists, by contrast, took the rhetoric of fair trade and cooperation, but used it to allow larger capitalists to monopolize and price-fix.[15] Within the National Industrial Recovery Act, however, government regulators, often deferring to industry trade associations, wrote "codes" for every industry, to determine pricing, output, and wages.

The National Recovery Administration's regulations were a disaster, with price-fixing inducing high consumer prices and unworkable instructions for many businesses. Separate codes, for instance, dealt with hauling coal, sand, and gravel, all of which were handled by the same company. One of the original drafters of the law retracted his support, musing that the law was "fascistic."[16] In 1935, the law was finally struck down by the Supreme Court. "This is the end of this business of centralization," Justice Brandeis told an aide to Roosevelt. "And I want you to go back and tell the President that we're not going to let this government centralize everything."[17]

In 1937–1938, the New Deal again began to falter. Roosevelt, after a smashing reelection, decided to once again return to orthodoxy, and balance the budget, throwing the economy into a downturn. The so-called "Roosevelt Recession" began. FDR expressed fear of gains fascists would make both abroad and inside the United States if he failed to halt the slump.[18] For a brief time, in the face of this recession, FDR was afraid, listless, without a program to combat the slump. He received conflicting advice. Statist liberal Adolf Berle attempted to bring together industrialists, such as Owen Young of GE and Thomas Lamont of J. P. Morgan, along with labor leader John Lewis, to persuade FDR to work out a "grand truce" between government and big business. This arrangement would result in a planned economy of cartels, similar to failed experiments earlier in the decade.[19] Once again, the debate between the corporatist planners and the antimonopolists flared.

Fascist gains abroad heavily weighed on New Dealers. Fears of another war, and foreign fascist gains, were long-standing. Fiorello La Guardia, in a 1931 congressional speech, noted how American financial policy of impoverishing Europe was helping the thuggish Hitler gain power. American troops would, he predicted, return to Europe.[20] By 1935, Hitler's rearmament program was obvious, in open violation of the Treasury of Versailles. Nazi storm troopers paraded around German cities, saying, "Today Germany belongs to us; tomorrow the whole world!" Hitler was eyeing territories to the east and the south as new "colonies" for Germany.[21]

In 1937, Bernard Baruch, the man in charge of industrial production during World War I for Wilson, returned from abroad concerned. The whole world is a "tinderbox," he said.[22] The Nazi military was sleek and modern, France's and England's capabilities were a joke. American air specialist Charles Lindbergh reported in the fall of 1938 that German planes were so much better than those of Russia, England, and France that Germany could destroy any structure it chose in France.[23] In the Pacific, the extremist militarists running Japan were "vigorously invading China."[24]

In late 1937, several New Deal officials, including Jackson, began speaking out publicly. The recession had opened the door for a loose coalition of conservative Democrats and Republicans to, as Jackson put it, "destroy the work of this administration." New Dealers seemed to be retreating. Jackson's speeches were aggressive, and he proudly noted, "Instead of asking what they can do to the New Deal, 'big business' is now asking what the New Deal is going to do to them."[25] For five years, New Dealers had attempted to reduce the danger to democracy from big business, and Jackson wasn't going to give up on that fight.

Harold Ickes, the secretary of the interior, was even more explicit than Jackson. In late December, Ickes denounced big business's latest attack on the New Deal, saying that "if the American people yield to this bluff, then the America that is to be will be a big-business fascist America, an enslaved America."[26] All of this rhetoric was in preparation for a message that Roosevelt would be giving on monopoly, which Jackson had suggested to Roosevelt a few months earlier.[27]

In April of 1938, Roosevelt made this clear in a fireside chat over the radio. "Democracy has disappeared in several other great nations," he said. "Not because the people of those nations disliked democracy, but because they had grown tired of unemployment and insecurity, of seeing their children hungry while they sat helpless in the face of government confusion and government weakness through lack of leadership in government. Finally, in desperation, they chose to sacrifice liberty in the hope of getting something to eat."[28] The government had to act.

Later that month, Roosevelt sent a message to Congress on monopolies, linking the external and internal fascist threats. "Unhappy events abroad have retaught us two simple truths about the liberty of a democratic people," he argued. He continued, "The first truth is that the liberty of a democracy is not safe if the people tolerate the growth of private power to a point where it becomes stronger than their democratic state itself. That, in its essence, is fascism—ownership of government by an individual, by a group, or by any other controlling private power."[29]

Roosevelt's message was no mere rhetoric flourish. Hitler was using corporate law and trading power to undermine Western democracies. In 1938, Nazi Germany threatened the tax haven of Liechtenstein, which had no army. There was no rationale behind this threat, except that Liechtenstein held the charters of many holding companies that, according to one senator, "[controlled] the commerce and industry of the Northern Hemisphere." These were not just European concerns. "Some corporations, the principal sphere of activity of which is in the United States, were created by the government of diminutive Liechtenstein."[30]

Hitler also began dominating, even before his physical invasions, the trading flows of Europe. In the Munich Agreement of 1938, the British traded away Czechoslovakia to Hitler in return for a promise of peace. Negotiations of a different Munich-style agreement were underway in the industrial sphere. The next year, British industries pledged cooperation with German cartels, with French industrialists working to collaborate as well.[31] In these cartel agreements, non-German companies would cut their output, while German companies would not. German companies used patent agreements to manipulate American companies, like Standard Oil, over vital materials like synthetic rubber.[32]

It was apparent to antimonopolists that the fascists in Europe were doing this work in America as well. "The distinction between bombing a vital plant out of existence from an airplane and preventing that plant from coming into existence in the first place, is largely a difference in the amount of noise involved," said one assistant U.S. attorney general to the Indiana State Bar Association in 1941.[33] Hitler was using industrial power and cartel arrangements to make unwitting allies of American monopolists, as he had done with British and French cartels. Such was the fascist threat.

## A WAR OF PRODUCTION

The coming war would be a war won not just on the battlefield, but by production. And the lesson of World War I, for Americans, was a frightening one.

Despite two and a half years of warning, the U.S. entered the First World War unprepared. By 1918, the American field army numbered five million men but still relied on British and French allies for artillery and other equipment. "The country which had invented the airplane," wrote one New Deal defense official, "had been unable to put a single fighting plane of its own manufacture into combat."[34] America started late, and tried to "bait" its manufacturers into expanding plants with lucrative contracts. American soldiers had to use British and French weapons.

The America of the late 1930s was now in the same situation. On the eve of Germany's invasion of Poland in 1939, 85 percent of U.S. factory machinery dated from the 1920s or earlier. Some predated the Civil War.[35] Hitler had used new technologies, such as the dive-bomber, to wage a new kind of war, "Blitzkrieg," or "lightning war." Unlike the slow and bloody trench warfare of World War I, Blitzkrieg combined air and mechanized forces to overwhelm the enemy with speed, requiring a powerful air force. After the invasion of Poland, Americans didn't necessarily want to intervene in Europe, but preparedness and support for military spending began to increase. Roosevelt asked for larger Army and Navy budgets. But to build that larger Army and Navy, massive supplies of steel, aluminum, copper, and every other material would be necessary. The control of the monopolists, who wanted to restrict supplies of these metals, would have to be broken.

The war against Hitler would require conflict within each country almost as much as it did between countries. Would democracies survive this challenge? Or would Hitler, who was a symbol of angry rebellion against the failure of democracies to tame their worst impulses, succeed?

These were the stakes when Hull organized for Roosevelt in 1932, when Jackson put Mellon on trial for tax fraud, and when New Deal foundered on the rock of a recession in 1937–1938. War was coming. It wasn't always obvious how it would come, or when, or who would bring it. But for years, decades, even, farsighted people saw a new war on the horizon, one that centered on different visions of how to run industrial power—based on top-down control or broad freedom.[36]

## DESTROYING THE ECONOMIC ROYALISTS

Mellon's tax trial would end in 1937 with the creation of the National Gallery and some back payments. But this would not be enough, not nearly enough. Andrew Mellon was a cold and ruthless banker, but it was the system over which he lorded, not him personally, that was dangerous. "Mellon is but a fading symbol of an age and system," Jackson believed. "But Mellonism goes on."[37]

What Roosevelt called in 1932 the "unofficial . . . economic Government of the United States" had to be dismantled, and replaced with democratic means of wielding power.[38] The system that Morgan and Mellon put together did not just wield power over government; it was a government in and of itself.

This government of the monopolists had two separate layers of power. There were individual monopolies. Alcoa, for instance, was not only an aluminum producer, but the regulator of the aluminum trade itself. It controlled pricing, output, wages, and the buying of key inputs, such as electric power. As Morgan, and then Mellon, took a set of businesses and turned them into monopolies, power passed from the engineers, workers, and communities who created, invented, and produced, to financiers, salesmen, and lawyers who controlled, restrained, and manipulated.

The second layer was how these monopolies related to one another. An individual monopoly controlled just a single branch of trade. It became a political system when its power, the power of one boss, was combined with other monopolies, the power of many bosses. And this system, of big business bosses monopolizing the key channels of trade and commerce, still lived on Wall Street. Wall Street was where financiers moved resources around through lending or borrowing money, and combined or split up companies. This is why Morgan, and then Mellon, sat arrayed in the clothing of finance, because finance was the tool by which they exercised political power.

The task for the White House and the populists in Congress was to take this private government apart, and construct a democratic one. That meant breaking up the industrial monopolies that ruled specific industries, and replacing rule by banker with competitive regulated markets, with protections for workers and producers. It meant recapturing the ability to print money and control the economy. It meant breaking apart and replacing Wall Street with public channels of financing, so that corporations were free from financial masters. This did not mean undermining business, but liberating it from monopoly and financial power.

In 1938, renowned British economist John Maynard Keynes wrote a private letter to Roosevelt about how to handle business leaders, saying, "You could do anything you liked with them if you would treat them (even the big ones), not as wolves or tigers, but as domestic animals by nature, even though they have been badly brought up and not trained as you would wish."[39] Roosevelt would seek to domesticate big business.

Robert Jackson would again lead the way. Jackson had been a favorite of Roosevelt since the Mellon tax trial. He had done stints at the Securities and Exchange Commission, the Department of Justice, and the Bureau of Internal Revenue, and defended New Deal programs to a hostile Supreme Court. He was FDR's legal ace. As he had shown with his high-stakes Mellon trial, Jackson loved litigating, he was good at it, and he could take on some of the tougher and more complex cases.

In 1937, FDR assigned Jackson the task of reviving a moribund corner of the government, the Department of Justice's Antitrust Division, which the corporatist planners of the New Deal had effectively shut down for years. With limited resources, Jackson decided to focus only on the "most flagrant cases" of monopolization in the country, and the one in which the "greatest public interest is involved."[40]

On April 23, 1937, the government filed suit, seeking dissolution of the Aluminum Company of America. Andrew Mellon and his children were all named individual defendants. When Homer Cummings presented the case to the president, he said, "You might get another art gallery out of it."[41]

## THE ALCOA DANGER

"Aluminum is Mellon's metal," blared *The Milwaukee Journal* on the front page in 1937, explaining to its readers why the Department of Justice was launching an antitrust suit against the Aluminum Corporation of America.[42] "Of the 93 chemical elements that compose the earth, 92 are the common property of all mankind. The remaining element—aluminum—which may be as vital to the future of civilization as gold, lead, or iron, is in the hands of one man, Andrew W. Mellon."

In the age of aviation, aluminum was a strategically important metal. Lighter than steel, it is durable and never rusts, making it ideal for airplanes. It has two key inputs. The first is the clay bauxite, which is the best source for alumina, the substance from which the metal is drawn. At the time, known high-quality bauxite deposits existed mostly in British and Dutch Guiana, in Alabama, and in a small corner of Arkansas. The second input is electricity. Processing aluminum required enormous quantities of electricity, so making aluminum meant being near cheap water power.[43]

World War II would require enormous quantities of most raw materials, from steel to chrome to tungsten to petroleum to cotton. The government needed not just machine guns and tanks, but the machine tool parts to manufacture those machine guns and tanks.[44] The government would acquire and finance almost everything, because private industry just didn't have the money to do it. The Metals Reserve Corporation, a government company, for instance, bought five million carats of diamonds as a strategic stockpile.[45] But in terms of pure military necessity, aluminum—controlled by Alcoa—was at the top.[46]

In no other industrial field was there one supplier. Steel, oil, coal, sugar, packaged foods—all had multiple producers, even if those producers tacitly or overtly colluded. Alcoa was unique. It had 100 percent of the market. Mellon had made sure of it, from the beginning.

Aluminum is difficult to produce. Today it is cheap and disposable, used to wrap sandwiches and cigarettes. But in the 1800s, it was twice as valuable as gold. Though aluminum is 8 percent of the earth's crust, the smelting process for commercializing its production was not discovered until the 1880s. In the mid-nineteenth century, aluminum was more fashionable than gold or silver, and more expensive.[47] Napoleon III once reserved utensils made from aluminum at a formal dinner party for the best guests, with gold and silver utensils for his less important dinner companions.[48]

The potential for this metal was widely understood, but no one had managed to craft a cheap production method. In the early 1880s, a professor at Oberlin College told his students how to get rich. Find a way to commercialize the tantalizing metal aluminum, which was strong, lightweight, and versatile. Twenty-two-year-old student Charles Hall said, "I'm going for that metal." Hall tinkered endlessly, and eventually created a small aluminum company with some Pittsburgh steel men.[49] Mellon put $25,000 into the venture, in return for roughly 40 percent of what would eventually become Alcoa.

The new company sought to capture the market. It acquired patents, bought up raw inputs, domestic and then worldwide, of the bauxite deposit sources suitable for commercial production. It used political influence to gain access to hydropower sources that could deliver the electricity it needed, such as generation facilities near Niagara Falls. Alcoa even sought to corner the market in reusable aluminum scrap metal. A friendly senator established a tariff to protect domestic markets.[50]

And Mellon used finance to block competition. In the 1910s, a French businessman tried to start a competitor to Alcoa, but couldn't get the money to do so. He "made the rounds of Wall Street—J. P. Morgan, GE, Lee, Higginson, First National—and even appealed to International Nickel and Henry Ford. All declined." Eventually he was forced to turn to Mellon's Union Trust, the financial guardian of the industry. Alcoa picked up the assets of the French company cheap.[51]

Alcoa was profitable, but not an industrial giant until the First World War. And then its profits exploded. "Ninety percent of its production," wrote one journalist, "was dedicated to aid the efforts of the civilized nations to annihilate each other." Alcoa aluminum was used in the wings of the 1918 Curtiss Jenny aircraft, in gas tanks, seat backs, and other frame parts for aircraft, and canteens, field mess kits, and dog tags for the U.S. military. A major source of demand was aluminum powder to be mixed with ammonium nitrate for explosives.[52]

The Wilson administration forced Alcoa to modernize. Germany had better aluminum technology, and the random tinkering within the company wasn't sufficient to catch up. The government stepped in. The Navy and the National Bureau of Standards both made aluminum alloy breakthroughs to rival German technology and forced the company to set up a professional research lab.[53] The company also went global. By the end of the war, Alcoa was importing bauxite from South America.[54]

After the war, Alcoa moved to protect its market power. Mellon protected Alcoa's domestic market from foreign competition by encouraging Harding to raise tariffs. The company returned to prioritizing control above production; faced with a shortage of production, in the mid-1920s the company even imported raw aluminum from Europe and sold it under the Alcoa name.[55] It became a global powerhouse, buying European aluminum producers and technology. Through its Canadian affiliate, Alcoa participated in a global aluminum cartel to divide up markets by nation.

In the 1920s, Alcoa prospered, seen as a high-tech darling powered by Mellon's monopoly money. As a Mellon critic put it, "To the future belonged Mellon-metal; aluminum planes, ships, railway cars, automobiles will speed through air, water, or along earth's crust."[56] Mellon pistons were in every automobile in America, "Mellon wings" in every plane, and "Mellon sheet" covered "every streamlined train." Housewives that used Mellon utensils and developers who used aluminum fixtures or decorations had to pay the Mellon aluminum toll. "Radios, refrigerators, building beams, paints, furniture, machine gun bullets, and war helmets" were all made with "Mellon's metal."[57]

Alcoa was a giant operation, and the executives were proud of the hundreds of millions of pounds of metal they produced, and the technical and business processes they had developed to do so. In October of 1933, the chairman of the company, Arthur Davis, led a cheerleading session to build corporate morale. Davis asked questions of a roomful of Alcoa executives. "Do we own that company?" he asked, and a chorus of executives would respond, "Yes!" He asked how much virgin aluminum his company controlled, and the chorused response was "100 percent!"[58] Their monopoly, in their minds, was clearly a deserved monopoly, a flexible and benevolent monopoly that existed because the company was innovative and efficient, that it used its monopoly profits on behalf of social good.

In the 1930s, Alcoa was so powerful that it could raise the price of aluminum ingots from 19 cents to 20 cents a pound, with no economic

rationale. The cost of pots, pans, airplanes, radios, trains, bullets, and refrigerators went up. Senators joked, when the U.S. went off the gold
standard, that the country should adopt the aluminum standard. Without competition, the only check on the power of Alcoa to change the
price of aluminum was the "despair of industrialists like Henry Ford"
who would use nickel or steel or another substitute, or as *The Milwaukee Journal* put it, "some other one of the 92 free elements which are
mankind's common property."[59]

It took four years before the Roosevelt administration brought a case.
This is not because the administration didn't notice the problem of the
Alcoa monopoly. Key figures understood the danger. Alcoa was a part of
Patman's impeachment campaign. Cordell Hull saw Mellon's control of
the tariff policy, which protected Alcoa, as an international danger. Roosevelt had fought with Alcoa in New York state, and Jackson had seen
Alcoa's power through work with New York utilities and in the Mellon
tax trial.[60] The attorney general, Homer Cummings, had in private practice represented a company in an antitrust lawsuit with Alcoa. But the
government was weak. Cummings believed FBI agents and DOJ investigators were patsies for the company.[61] He even wanted the investigation
called off, to allow aggressive private lawsuits to continue unbothered.

The reason it took so long to bring a suit was policy. The National
Industrial Recovery Act, written by the Bull Moose planners early in
the New Deal, was the law Roosevelt initially used to organize big
business. The act suspended the antitrust laws, and in their place created an agency called the National Recovery Administration to write
codes organizing pricing, production, wage guidelines, and standards
for most industries.

Throughout this first part of the New Deal, Alcoa's monopoly
would remain untouched. It would be codes written by the National
Industrial Recovery Administration in collaboration with the company that would structure the aluminum industry.

In 1935, the Supreme Court unanimously struck down the increasingly unpopular National Industrial Recovery Act. Roosevelt got rid
of the corporatist planners, and put authority over the industrial sector
in the hands of the antimonopolists. In 1937, Jackson, by now one of
Roosevelt's favorite lawyers, was sent to restore the antitrust division.

## THE ALCOA CASE

In April of 1937, Robert Jackson brought the suit in what was often called "the largest proceeding in the history of Anglo-American law."[62] Alcoa, argued the government, was a domestic monopolist in the production of the basic metal. The government also argued the company dominated every part of the global aluminum business, alleging Alcoa ran an international conspiracy to control a vital trade, "one of the most complete and far-reaching monopolies which has ever developed in a major industry of this country."[63]

Prosecutors accused the company of monopolizing bauxite supplies, alumina, virgin aluminum production, hard alloys, extruded and structural shapes, wire, cable, bars, rods, aluminum pistons, and tubing, as well as controlling the aluminum castings, foil, bronze powder, and cooking utensil industries. Alcoa had restrictive contracts for hydroelectric power, to block potential competitors. The government provided evidence that the company owned subsidiaries in Canada and throughout Europe, for which it was willing to pay above-market value to sustain its monopoly. The conspiracy was global; what Alcoa didn't own or couldn't co-opt, it threatened to drive out of business with below-market prices for its own products.[64]

No one was fooled that this was an ordinary antitrust suit. Alcoa was Mellon's company, and the suit a continued battle between the New Dealers and the old order. The attack on the Alcoa monopoly, like the tax suit against Mellon, was front-page news. Newspaper cartoons linked the antitrust suit to the Mellon gift of the National Gallery.[65]

Jackson felt the sting of Alcoa's political power. Before the filing, Jackson and Cummings met with Alcoa chairman Davis to inform him they were going to attempt to break up his company. After the meeting, the price of aluminum mysteriously began dropping. When the suit was filed, an Alcoa-friendly member of Congress filed a resolution calling for an investigation of the Department of Justice attorneys. The allegation was that these were crooked cops, using their antitrust suit to make money in speculation.

House Democratic majority leader Sam Rayburn called Jackson to ask what he should do with the resolution. Jackson suggested Rayburn have Congress investigate not only Department of Justice officials, but Alcoa company officials. According to SEC sources, Alcoa executives had unloaded blocks of shares prior to the suit being made public. After Rayburn made his suggestion to expand the investigation, the proposal for an investigation was buried.[66]

That was just the first of many political hurdles for antitrust enforcers. Alcoa's influence reached into the military establishment and the nascent air force, as well as into elite academic institutions like Harvard Business School. After the case was filed, a secretary in a planning office in the Army offered a tip to the Department of Justice. She was sympathetic to Roosevelt, and had heard chatter from the Army officers she worked for about a plan to conceal and destroy military records relating to Alcoa.

Alcoa and the Army had a long working relationship. In 1920, the War Department created the Army Industrial College (AIC), so that its officers could learn the industrial arts necessary for economic mobilization. Many also received business degrees from Harvard Business School, in a joint program between the business school and the War Department.[67]

The secretary told the DOJ investigator, Walter Rice, that one of her bosses, an Army colonel, was trying to destroy a report on Alcoa's capacity to "furnish aluminum for war needs" because the report had implications about the company's monopoly power. Rice learned the colonel had taken a two-year course at Harvard Business School and done a study with the company's help. The report contained data about the company's capacity to produce aluminum during the war, its plant capacity, and its bauxite deposits, all of which would be useful during the case. The document was, according to one Army officer, "so hot" that "the contents of the report would convict the Aluminum Company of the pending monopoly charges."

Alcoa-friendly officers in the planning division sought to hide the records. One colonel got rid of the report by mailing it back to the company under the "innocuous" pretense he wanted the company to update it with new information "whenever necessary at your earliest convenience." That very day, he handed the report back to an Alcoa representative.

When Rice began asking questions about the report, the officers feigned ignorance. After Rice left, the secretary told him that one of the officers had contacted Harvard Business School and asked for all remaining copies to be destroyed.

The military officers and Rice played a cat-and-mouse game over copies of the report, until the attorney general simply asked the secretary of war for any remaining copies. With the conflict at the cabinet level, the secretary of war said no, the report had been returned to Alcoa for updating and he had to protect the company's confidential information. Unwilling to name their informant and show that the Army officers had deliberately destroyed evidence, the DOJ couldn't move the military.[68]

And there was another force, much more important to the prosecutors than the military, that stood in the way of the suit. Judges.

In the 1930s, American judges were by and large old men who didn't like the New Deal, labor unions, liberal young lawyers, or the president. When the Roosevelt administration entered office in 1933, three quarters of the federal judiciary were conservative Republicans; the average lower court judge was sixty years old and had gone to law school in the McKinley administration.[69] In the summer of 1935, "more than 100 district court judges held Acts of Congress unconstitutional; federal courts issued more than 1,600 injunctions blocking enforcement of New Deal laws."[70]

Judges believed in a Constitutional system known as "Lochnerism," in which it was simply unconstitutional for the state to write laws protecting workers or otherwise interfering with private business. The name Lochner comes from the 1905 Supreme Court case *Lochner v. State of New York,* in which the court struck down a New York state law saying bakers couldn't be forced to work more than sixty hours a week. The New Deal restructuring of political economy didn't fit in this Constitutional framework. The courts were so conservative, and so willing to strike down New Deal legislation, that the president proposed restructuring the Supreme Court. Finally, the Supreme Court caved, and began to validate most New Deal laws as Constitutional.

In Alcoa's case, the problem wasn't just the conservative nature of the judiciary, but judicial corruption. Just six days after the suit was filed, District Judge Robert Gibson, from Mellon's hometown of Pittsburgh, claimed jurisdiction over the case even though it had been filed in New York. He argued that an old 1912 complaint and consent decree with Alcoa and the current case were "substantially identical," and so the case must be held in his courtroom. Gibson then barred Jackson, Cummings, and all other government attorneys from proceeding with the suit.

The Department of Justice appealed Gibson's injunction. The old case had been minor, and twenty-five years old. Just one of the sixty-three defendants in 1937 had been involved. The aluminum industry was different, and Jackson sought to dissolve the company. And not coincidentally, Gibson had been appointed in the 1920s, upon the recommendation of Mellon himself.[71]

Roosevelt attacked the decision, saying that this was an example of "reform" being delayed by an out-of-control judiciary. Homer Cummings then recommended legislation to the president blocking judges from being able to issue restraining orders or injunctions in antitrust suits.[72]

The move also sparked uproar in Congress. Wright Patman spoke with House Judiciary Committee chairman Hatton Sumners, who demanded to know if there was anything "crooked" involved in the judge's decision.[73] There was. An Alcoa lawyer was married to Gibson's niece, Gibson's daughter was employed by Mellon's Koppers company, and his son was with the law firm employed by another Mellon concern, the Pittsburgh Coal Company.[74] The judge's nephew-in-law, who worked at a law firm employed by Alcoa, had even paid traveling expenses for the clerk to serve subpoenas in Washington on each Department of Justice official, with the goal of preventing further action by the government.[75]

Sumners began musing impeachment proceedings against Gibson, with several members of his committee incensed at the judge.[76] He had introduced a resolution authorizing an investigation of the judiciary, but wanted the Gibson matter kept quiet until it was adopted because, as he put it, "those people have long arms" in Congress.[77] Even so, the House passed a different bill Sumners authorized, to create a way to remove a district judge without having to go through a cumbersome impeachment trial. It would allow a panel of three judges to remove a lower court judge for simply not engaging in "good behavior," as opposed to the much higher standard required for an impeachment.[78]

Sumners later appointed a subcommittee to look into Gibson, as multiple members of his committee were "highly incensed" and considering issuing a subpoena to have the judge testify. Seven months later, the Supreme Court defused the situation by setting aside Gibson's decision. In June of 1938, the trial began. It would become the longest antitrust trial up to that point. It would take four years to complete and comprise some 58,000 pages of testimony. Jackson was promoted to the number two slot in the Department of Justice, the solicitor general position, and hired in his stead an iconoclastic Yale professor from Wyoming named Thurman Arnold, who took over the case.

The antitrust case was difficult for two reasons. First, the DOJ was pursuing a novel legal theory, that mere possession of a monopoly was illegal. Since the passage of the Sherman Act, it had not been clear whether being a monopoly was illegal. In 1920, the Supreme Court struck down a suit against U.S. Steel on the grounds that size itself was no offense. It was abusive behavior, not the holding of a monopoly, that courts had held as illegal. The second difficulty was that Alcoa withheld documents. The company believed the threat was existential, that competition in aluminum would destroy the industry, and Alcoa's general counsel was not about to help the DOJ do that.[79]

The division did have advantages. Cordell Hull's State Department worked with the Department of Justice to investigate Alcoa's role throughout Europe.[80] And the president, members of the cabinet like Ickes, and New Deal officials working on power resources provided strong support. And by the time the case was resolved, the courts would look very different. But in 1938, the judiciary continued to stand in the way of antimonopolists. Judge Francis Caffey, a conservative appointed to his position by Herbert Hoover at the height of the stock market in 1929, presided over the case.

Alcoa's lawyers didn't dispute the company's monopoly. They simply argued that being a monopoly wasn't illegal, and that the company was a socially beneficial, rather than predatory, monopoly. There was value, they pointed out, in having just one entity focused on a process of continuous innovation around a vital strategic metal. Ex-military engineers agreed, testifying on the importance of this fount of metal-lurgic knowledge. One former naval liaison and MIT aerospace professor claimed that Alcoa's R&D had done what otherwise would have been impossible, creating alloys that aided the U.S. airline industry.[81] It was hard for the government to rebut this claim with its own experts as nearly everyone with expertise in aluminum worked for Alcoa.[82]

Arthur Davis's description of Alcoa's technology impressed Caffey, and he didn't like New Deal lawyers.[83] After more than three years, at the beginning of October 1941, he finally ruled on the antitrust suit. Over nine days, he read his opinion from the bench, dismissing every single claim by the government. Caffey attacked the government's witnesses, referring to their "bias" and "wishful thinking," while praising Davis, who according to the judge began his career as "a laborer . . . not infrequently forced to whistle for his pay" but who had with wisdom built "Alcoa [into] what it is today." The company, Judge Caffey noted, had a "great number" of "competitors as well as customers who have completely exculpated Alcoa from blame and have praised its fairness as well as its helpfulness in the aluminum industry." Caffey, like Alcoa men themselves, believed that the company deserved its monopoly.[84]

Arnold, now in charge of the division, appealed the decision, and took the battle to Congress and the press, noting Alcoa's monopolistic behavior. Alcoa's counsel responded to Congress that Arnold was "destroying the morale of this country and of key men in defense production."[85] Secretary of War Henry Stimson echoed this critique, aggravated by Arnold's posture while a mobilization was on. But after America entered the war, Alcoa began losing credibility. Davis had promised that Alcoa could easily meet any aluminum needs for the war. As soon became apparent, it could not. And Arnold would publicly wrap Alcoa in the Nazi flag as punishment.

## THE BREAKING OF THE BANKERS

Big business leaders organized to defeat FDR in the 1936 reelection. "If I find any of my executives voting again for Roosevelt, I'm going to fire them," one of them said. They "are just too stupid to be of any use to me."[86] Some went further. At the 1935 conference of the American Bankers Association, Utah banker and eventual ABA president Orval Adams urged his colleagues to destroy the New Deal. "Since the [Federal government] cannot spend without using the bankable funds of the nation, it is up to us to declare an embargo," he said. This would happen if the banks refused to buy government bonds.

"We must decline to make further purchases," he exhorted. "We must declare that we will not finance further spending by the government until a genuine, honest, and sincere effort is made by the Federal government to restore a balanced budget. . . . The Bankers of America should resume negotiations with the Federal Government only under a régime of rigid economy, a balanced budget, and a sane tax program."[87]

The economy was in better shape in 1935 than it had been in 1933, but as Adams fretted about a balanced budget, more than ten million Americans were still unemployed. It wasn't Jackson, but a different reformer, who stood up to rebut Adams. This man was no young New Dealer, eager to try new theories of social planning. This was a hard-bitten millionaire banker from Utah named Marriner Eccles. Government spending and the hated Roosevelt, said Eccles, had saved capitalism. In the same period Jackson began attacking Alcoa and industrial monopolies, a new group of economists, led by Eccles, restructured how the business cycle itself flowed. Eccles asserted that it was the sovereign right of government to print money, to run deficits, to organize whether the economy would boom or ebb. There would be no more talk of natural boom and bust cycles due to greed and fear, or needless deflation. If there was a lack of money in the economy, the government could provide more of it.[88]

Eccles had come to this theory by an unusual path. He had inherited from his father a banking empire in Utah. He ran it well, and became even richer. But in the early 1930s, after stopping several severe bank runs, he began to rethink his orthodox views of finance and spending. In the transition period between Hoover and Roosevelt, Senator Pat Harrison invited representatives of industry, agriculture, and labor to present their views on how to cure the depression.

Harrison invited two hundred men, but only forty-seven appeared. Sixty presented their views in writing, as they were afraid to be away from their businesses in the midst of a liquidity crisis.[89]

The solutions were mostly orthodox, similar to what Al Smith and John Jakob Raskob would have offered. Balanced budgets. More efficiency in government. Charity. Both the head of the Chamber of Commerce, Henry Harriman, and the head of the American Federation of Labor recommended Roosevelt slash federal spending sharply.

Eccles alone broke from the crowd of somber business and labor leaders, and endorsed the kind of thinking that had previously only been put forward by inflationists and populists. He declared, "I am a capitalist." He then offered a different way to think about money and government, one much more in sync with Patman and populists in Congress who wanted to circulate cash throughout the economy with the Bonus Bill.[90] Balanced budgets were foolish, he said; the federal government needed to create and distribute money across the land.

"We shall either adopt a plan which will meet this situation under capitalism," Marriner Eccles told the Senate, "or a plan will be adopted of us which will operate without capitalism."[91] Where Mellon dithered in the face of the crisis, the iconoclastic Eccles would govern. His economic blasphemy went further; he sought federal aid to states, deposit insurance, government action to stop foreclosures and create a mortgage market, farm supports, and cancellation of inter-Allied debts. All of these became policy, and ultimately, laid the basis for the New Deal. Before John Maynard Keynes would formalize the economics of deficit spending, Eccles recommended it as policy.

The White House eventually noticed this millionaire banker advocating for radical solutions, and hired him as a deputy in the Treasury Department. Eccles then persuaded FDR to restructure the Federal Reserve, taking control from the private bankers in New York and centralizing control in the hands of democratically elected officials in Washington. In the Banking Act of 1935, FDR had restructured the Fed to make that happen. This law had moved power from privately owned Fed branches to the presidentially appointed board in Washington, D.C. It transformed the Federal Reserve into a public entity, ensconcing power over the economy in the hands of a publicly run central bank. Roosevelt appointed Eccles as chairman of the Fed, to take the position Andrew Mellon had held for eleven years.

Two years later, in the 1937 "Roosevelt Recession" induced by lower net government spending, Eccles was prepared. The recession sparked a debate between planners and antimonopolists. But a third group, led by Eccles and aligned with the antimonopolists, joined the fight. Eccles believed the recession was caused by insufficient government spending, and he pressed FDR to reverse his position on budget balancing and spend once again.

Eccles took sides in the debate over the political power of big business. Like Jackson, Eccles had antimonopolist sympathies. He just saw the problem from the perspective of a central banker. Monopolies could interfere with the broader economy and the price system itself, leading to the pooling up of risk and the lack of sufficient production. Before the recession, Eccles had warned speculation was being caused by "monopolistic practices" leading to price hikes. He was telling Roosevelt that steelmakers were raising prices far more quickly than they were raising wages, and this led to unused resources in terms of both unemployment and inflation. When the speculative bubble about which he warned popped and the economy slid rapidly, he fell in with antimonopolists. Pointing to the steel industry, he said that "those industries that have maintained prices and curtailed output should seek the restoration of profits through increased rather than restricted output."[92]

Eccles also questioned the political judgment of the planners. The attempt to conciliate big business bore "no fruit either in dollar terms or in goodwill." Indeed, "big business is utilizing the opportunity to drive for repeal and inaction." The old order had to be defeated. "The greatest threat to democracy today," he told FDR, "lies in the growing conviction that it cannot work." Only by bold "democratic leadership" to make the system function "can the growing threat of Fascism be overcome."[93] Eccles wanted Roosevelt to go on a government spending binge, to have big government counteract the slump in spending from the private sector.

Though Roosevelt inflated the currency in the early part of the

New Deal, he also had instincts toward fiscal conservativism, and had generally bought into the need to balance the budget. But in 1937, Roosevelt accepted Eccles's arguments. Eccles persuaded Roosevelt to jump-start spending with government support for the Federal Housing Administration. This would expand fixed rate mortgages and induce a pick-up in the residential construction industry. He also pushed for investment in low cost housing, a national health program, and a revitalization of railroads.

During the war, the Fed was there to print as much money as the government would need, rendering banker threats powerless. Under Eccles, the Fed was not independent of politics, but subject to the policy choices of the elected president. During the war, the federal government ran budget deficits as high as 26 percent of GDP, but the Fed offered as much money as needed, at low fixed interest rates set by the Fed. Eccles oversaw the most successful experiment in central banking history, bringing unemployment down to one percent, financing World War II, and rebuilding the banking system and the savings of the middle class. This war would be a New Deal war; it would be financed not by tycoons such as Mellon, but by the public.

Every part of the economy began growing again, save Wall Street. In 1940, Wall Street had 200,000 fewer workers than it had before the crash. Trading volumes were anemic, and there was more vacant office space in and around Wall Street in 1939 than at the beginning of the decade. In 1935, financiers were still openly and angrily flouting the idea that democratic forces could constrain private bankers. By 1940, J. P. Morgan Jr. sold his seat on the New York Stock Exchange for $40,000, a seat that had been selling eleven years earlier at $625,000. There was no Morgan sitting in the stock market for the first time since 1871.[94]

## A DEMOCRATIC GOVERNMENT REPLACES THE BANKERS

In the summer of 1939, an official from a French aluminum company, Philippe Levelle, visited an American business executive, Richard Reynolds, in Virginia. Reynolds was president of Reynolds Metals, which bought aluminum from Alcoa and fabricated it into aluminum foil.

Reynolds had heard that the Germans were buying large amounts of bauxite from France. He wondered if this was being used for armaments. Levelle wasn't worried, and said that the Germans were short of brass and were using aluminum for window frames and door knobs. Germany had become the largest aluminum producer in the world by 1938. Within a few months, as Reynolds put it, "French bauxite was being returned to France in the shape of German planes."[95]

When the war started, Germany seemed unstoppable. Poland's army collapsed immediately in 1939. In April of 1940, Germany conquered Denmark and Norway, and in early May, Hitler's forces invaded France. Americans had expected a long stalemate similar to the First World War, and the ample time that would afford America to ramp up if necessary. France had a powerful military and was considered one of the most important major military powers in the world. But faced with Germany's awesome new weapons, wielded through Blitzkreig tactics, France surrendered within six weeks.

England stood alone. The Germans began bombing Britain from the air. Even so, the defense buildup in the U.S. was agonizingly slow. When France surrendered, the Army Air Corps had 2,755 planes, and most of these were old or used for training purposes.[96] Hitler was receiving more material from French factories he had taken over than Britain was receiving from the United States. "Prime Minister Churchill said of the Royal Air Force that never in history did so many owe so much to so few," wrote investigative journalist I. F. Stone. "It might be said of us," wrote Stone, about American monopolies, "that never did a people do so little with so much."[97] Churchill was talking about the Battle of Britain, where a few RAF pilots saved England from the German air force's constant bombing barrages over London. Stone was comparing this courage to Alcoa, and its habit of withholding desperately needed aluminum production—for planes and other war-related industrial parts—to preserve the price of the metal.

To Stone, American financial masters were colluding with the fascist powers. And there was proof, in the cartel deals that Standard Oil of New Jersey and Alcoa, among others, had with German chemical and metal companies.

In May of 1940, Roosevelt, with what looked to be an absurdly fantastical goal, sought to direct America's industrial might in building every kind of weapon imaginable, as well as inventing new ones, and churning out the foodstuffs, metals, medicines, and raw materials necessary to equip a ten-million-person army. He publicly said that the nation would need to build fifty thousand planes a year, which was equivalent to the total number the military had bought between 1909 and 1940.[98] To build much of this, especially an air force, it would need aluminum.

Shortly after Roosevelt called for fifty thousand planes a year, Reynolds went to see Arthur Davis of Alcoa. To Reynolds, Davis seemed as complacent about America's aluminum supply as Levelle had been about French needs. Germany would soon be able to make much more aluminum than the U.S., noted Reynolds. Perhaps Davis should ask the government to finance the buildup of capacity, to match the billion-pound-a-year capacity of the Nazis. Davis, who felt it a burden to accept funds from the government, said Reynolds was "unnecessarily alarmed." There would be no shortage.[99]

Davis's prediction proved laughable. In November of 1940, the Northrop Aircraft Company cut hours by 20 percent due to a metal shortage. By May 1941, work on bombers by one of the more promising American aerospace companies, Boeing, had ceased because of inadequate aluminum supplies.[100] Congress reacted angrily. Senator Joseph O'Mahoney attacked Alcoa for delaying the manufacture of warplanes by "keeping supplies down in order to keep prices up," while adding that the chemical, iron and steel, metal, electric, and shipping cartels had "all played their part in the growth of Hitler's power." Whether the ongoing antitrust suit was decided for or against Alcoa, he said, "it is clear that the manufacture of American airplanes needed to fill our own and British orders has been seriously delayed because parts manufacturers have been unable to get a sufficient amount of aluminum to fill their orders."[101]

In August of 1940, after a conversation with and encouragement from Alabama senator Lister Hill, Reynolds decided to enter the aluminum manufacturing business himself and compete with Alcoa, if the government would lend him the money to do so. Fortunately for Reynolds, a low-key antimonopolist in government named Clifford Durr had realized that the American government would have to become the major banker in the war. Durr was a corporate lawyer from a wealthy family in Montgomery, Alabama; he moved to Washington, D.C., in the early 1930s on the recommendation of his brother-in-law, Hugo Black. Durr took a job rescuing banks and railroads at the Reconstruction Finance Corporation, the bailout fund created by Herbert Hoover that Roosevelt repurposed to finance various parts of the New Deal.

In the 1930s, Durr became concerned over the Nazi threat to liberal values. "Our immediate problem," he believed, "was one of productive capacity for military supplies—particularly airplanes." America didn't have much of an air force. Roosevelt's goal of fifty thousand planes a year was 100 times what the industry had produced in the late 1930s. The U.S. hit that target by 1942, and doubled it by 1944.[102]

Durr saw that the government would have to finance an armaments buildup, and lobbied Congress to charter a large public bank to lend money to build factories. It was controversial. One congressman asserted that a bill to let the RFC deploy private capital "would grant such broad powers to the executive branch of the Government as to make it possible to establish a Fascist state in the United States." Arthur Krock of *The New York Times* said the bill was "totalitarian" and "an alarming measure."[103] The head of the Investment Bankers Association declared that "government financing for private capital was 'a short cut to national socialism.'" Yet Durr succeeded in getting Congress to charter what would be called the Defense Plant Corporation and to begin the rapid buildup of the U.S. armaments industry.[104]

Over the course of the war, the Defense Plant Corporation financed the construction of roughly a third of the new facilities needed to fight the Axis powers, with the Army and Navy supplying much of the rest. It would be a war financed by government bankers, not private financiers.[105] Because of the power this financing brought, anti-monopolists ensured that government owned the plants it financed, and hired businesses leaders and engineers to run them. After the war, the government could then use its disposal of plants to create less concentrated markets.

In 1940, Reynolds would be the beneficiary of this strategy. Alcoa was still obstinate, refusing to take government money to expand facilities unless the company also received tax advantages, even as the country desperately needed aluminum. Meanwhile, Reynolds mortgaged his own assets, and received a $15.8 million loan from the government to begin producing aluminum.

Alcoa, which sold Reynolds aluminum ingots for the company to fabricate, sought to punish him by cutting his supply.[106] It was too late, because Reynolds was now itself making aluminum. Alcoa had competition in the manufacturing of aluminum for the first time since the 1880s. Reynolds would be followed by Henry Kaiser, another New Deal businessman who sought to build commercial entities within the democratic system that antimonopolists had set up.

Meanwhile, the antitrust suit against Alcoa was still going on. In January of 1942, Alcoa's lawyers attacked antitrust chief Thurman Arnold for destroying the morale of the key men in production. In March, at a House Military Affairs Subcommittee hearing, Thurman Arnold took his revenge. He told congressmen that there was Nazi influence over American industry, but that he had the situation in hand. "We had an industry dominated by cartels before the war," he said, cartels that worked with Nazi companies. "Indictments must go out to make that sort of thing hazardous."[107]

Arnold was an excellent lawyer but an even better press hound. He noted that none of these companies lacked patriotism; it just so happened that their behavior helped the Nazis. "It is obvious that this kind of practice on an extended scale throughout industry has been one of the causes why we are short of basic materials," he would say.[108] Men were dying and prices were going up. But don't worry, the companies meant well.

Senator Harry Truman, a Brandeis disciple, used the word "treason" to hit the Rockefeller concern.[109] Standard Oil of New Jersey couldn't jump fast enough. Professing innocence about a deal with Nazi dye maker I. G. Farben to withhold production of synthetic rubber, Standard Oil paid a fine and released its patents for all to use. Across the economy, American firms rushed to break the cartel agreements they had with German firms.

Arnold, in this particular hearing, let slip the name of one pernicious outfit. Arnold told the congressmen that Alcoa had been withholding the production of aluminum metal, thus preventing the development of an American air force. Senator Robert La Follette Jr.

later attacked the company as a Nazi collaborator, accusing it of having "intimate and dangerous ties" with the Nazis.[110]

Antitrust enforcement would wax and wane during the war, depending on the military's ability to block the DOJ Antitrust Division. But regardless of the division's power, congressional investigations played a key role in preventing industrialists from withholding production. Senator Harry Truman, Senator Homer Bone, and Senator Harley Kilgore all ran committees during the war investigating cartels and war profiteering. Attorneys for the Department of Justice and the Federal Trade Commission later told Congress that these senators were critical to the war effort.[111]

Eventually, the military blocked the Antitrust Division from prosecuting more suits; they could bring suits, but had to suspend them until the war was over. So the division started attacking international cartel arrangements. The DOJ went after optical goods (Bausch & Lomb's tie-up with the German Zeiss corporation), tungsten-carbide (GE and Krupp), electric lamps (GE and AEG in Germany), electric light glass bulbs (Corning Glass and Phillips), potash and nitrogen (DuPont and Allied Chemical), chemicals and pharmaceuticals (Sterling Chemical and I. G. Farben, Schering Corporation and the Schering Corporation of Berlin), dye stuffs and photographic supplies (General Aniline and I. G. Farben), synthetic rubber, toluol (used to make TNT), and magnesium (Aluminum Corporation of America, Dow Chemical and I. G. Farben).[112]

Cabinet members, Department of Justice lawyers, and midlevel procurement officials battled to ensure that the war would not repeat the mistake of the First World War in creating a new class of "mushroom millionaires" and monopolists. The Army, Navy, Defense Plant Corporation, and the Department of Justice structured markets. And when stymied, the congressional committees served as places where the fear of bad press could intimidate monopolists.

## A NEW DEMOCRACY

Antimonopolists had sought to change business culture, and by the late 1930s they had done so. The "Old Dealers" in business had dominated labor, resisted government, ignored consumers, and acted ruthlessly toward small business. But they had lost. New leaders in step with new democratic norms took over America's industries. The old plutocrats had become as irrelevant as Herbert Hoover.[113]

Meanwhile, Arnold's campaign extended far beyond Alcoa and had shifted American business culture at large. As Congress publicly exposed how monopolies acted in the economy, Arnold didn't even have to prosecute cases. A lawyer for U.S. Steel, who later became an antitrust enforcement official, recalled that businessmen would line up outside of Arnold's office; "they come in and say, 'Show us a consent decree and we'll sign it.'"[114]

Arnold spent five years in office. In that time, he brought a little fewer than half of all antitrust cases that had been brought in the first fifty-three years of the Sherman Act. He overhauled the automobile, motion picture, dairy, housing, construction, tire, newsprint, steel, potash, sulfur, retail, fertilizer, tobacco, shoe, and parts of agricultural industries. Just a year after he took the job, he had 1,375 complaints in 213 cases in 40 different industries. There were 185 investigations ongoing, and just launching an investigation dropped prices by 18–33 percent.[115] Arnold was so aggressive that Roosevelt ordered him at one point to drop an indictment against prominent railroad shareholder Averell Harriman for price-fixing. "We can't indict our ambassador to Great Britain," said Roosevelt.[116]

In March 1945, Alcoa lost its antitrust suit on appeal in federal court, and it was forced to license its patents on a royalty-free basis to competitors. Alcoa was so important, and had had so many investigations for so long, that four Supreme Court justices—now including Justice Robert Jackson—had recused themselves. Congress created a special lower court to hear the case. Judge Learned Hand wrote the decision, setting aside Caffey's dismissal of the case, and held that Alcoa's monopoly power itself, and not any intent to misuse its power in anticompetitive ways, was the crux of the matter. In doing so, the Alcoa decision settled an important debate in antitrust law. Being an industrial monopoly was now illegal.[117]

Alcoa was never split apart. By the time of the decision, the government had created competition through financing and military purchases that resulted in the emergence of Reynolds and Kaiser as aluminum powers. Roosevelt had instructed his administration to use its ownership of plants to ensure that Alcoa wouldn't dominate the industry after the war.[118] And Alcoa was forced to share its patents, its industrial know-how, and supplies of bauxite with these new competitors, thus preventing the company from reconcentrating power in the industry.

The government restructured the market by selling off competitive aluminum plants. In the disposal of the government plants to industry, Surplus Property Administrator Stuart Symington worked with Joseph O'Mahoney and the DOJ Antitrust Division to combat Alcoa's attempt to recapture its "benevolent monopoly." Instead, aluminum plant ownership was dispersed, leading to a more competitive market structure.[119]

This occurred in industries far beyond aluminum. By the end of the war, the government "held title to 90 percent or more of the synthetic rubber, aircraft, and magnesium industries, owned 55 percent of the nation's aluminum capacity and the bulk of the nation's machine tools, and had significant ownership in a variety of other industries."[120] In restructuring production, the government restructured the economy.[121]

The government financed a new generation of entrepreneurs in fields like aluminum and aerospace. These business leaders wanted to, in the words of one executive, "get busy and build airplanes."[122] It set up competitive public finance against Wall Street directly as a competitor in bond sales, so that the Federal Reserve would control swings in the economy. And it served as a banker and buyer to finance factories to produce materials, such as aluminum and synthetic rubber. Overseeing this restructuring was an aggressive Congress.

And people remembered the change, and knew it. In April of 1937, after the smashing election of 1936, the Supreme Court handed down a decision that ten steelworkers from the Jones and Laughlin Company steelworks in Aliquippa, Pennsylvania, had been improperly dismissed because they were union members. Aliquippa mills, nicknamed "Little Siberia," were horrific in terms of working conditions. When the court ruled, a steelworker echoed Roosevelt: "I say good,

now Aliquippa becomes part of the United States."[123] After the passage
of the Wagner Act in 1935, the government and strikers unionized
some of the most powerful firms in the economy, the "Big Boys." This
included not just Alcoa but Carnegie-Illinois, Inland Steel, Republic Steel, Swift, Standard Oil, Shell Oil, Western Union, Consolidated
Edison, Montgomery Ward, Consolidated Aircraft, Douglas Aircraft,
Goodyear, the Associated Press, Chevrolet, Ford, Remington Rand,
and United Fruit.[124]

By the time of Truman's ascension to the presidency after Roosevelt's death in 1945, a different American order was dawning. Large
and innovative aerospace companies, along with their communications
and electronics suppliers, emerged in this period. These were firms
such as Hughes, McDonnell-Douglas, Rockwell, Grumman, General Dynamics, United Technologies, TRW, Litton, and Lear Siegler.[125]
These companies created new industries and a new industrial geog-
raphy of America, helping to build out the electronics and airplane
industry that would undergird American prosperity. A scientific establishment emerged, free from control by monopolists, linked to the
military and academic worlds.

And there was the memory, the deep memory, of how monopoly
and fascists were intertwined. In 1944, a Senate subcommittee reported
that "Germany under the Nazi set-up built up a great series of industrial monopolies in steel, rubber, coal and other materials. The monopolies soon got control of Germany, brought Hitler to power and forced
virtually the whole world into war."[126] Roosevelt, in 1944, wrote to
Secretary of State Cordell Hull that destruction of Nazi armies had to
be followed by the "eradication of these cartel weapons of economic
warfare."[127] In October of 1945, Dwight Eisenhower was publicly advocating smashing the German I. G. Farben monopoly as essential to
preventing a recurrence of the Nazi war machine.[128]

## THE POSTWAR ORDER

New Dealers took their domestic system of controls on financial
power global. A trading system based on eroding barriers to trade,
both formal tariffs and private cartels, came to fruition as both a means

to spread democracy among allies and a mechanism to block the expansion of Soviet influence. U.S. policymakers, stung by the failure of Wilson after the First World War, sought to bind the Europeans together into one economic unit, so as to block a resurgence of nationalism. They helped the Europeans, and the Japanese, break up the cartels that had led to the war.[129]

In the postwar era, antitrust lawyers trained by Arnold joined a State Department in Cordell Hull's shadow. They went abroad, and engaged in campaigns to break up monopolistic German and Japanese industrial structures. The United Nations, the International Monetary Fund, and reciprocal trade agreements were designed to restrain the commercial institutions behind toxic nationalism, notably international cartels and monopolies. Senator La Follette, in 1944, demanded an end to the cartel-based control of world trade, which "will condemn millions of people to an unconscionably low standard of living. . . . The domestic monopoly is a menace to free enterprise and the economic welfare of the nation. An international monopoly . . . is a breeder of wars."[130]

Attorney General Francis Biddle noted, in a prelude to the reconstruction of Europe, "We have good reason to dread the reconstruction in Europe, after this war, of a strong centralized economic empire run on totalitarian lines." It would be the policy of the American government to oppose cartelization and what Biddle noted would follow, totalitarianism.[131] Said one State Department official just a few years later, "it is, therefore, an important part of U.S. economic foreign policy to press for the elimination of cartel arrangements which block the expansion of multilateral, competitive, international trade."[132]

The massive investments by the government, the entrepreneurship of men like Reynolds, combined with Arnold's work, and Truman's oversight smashed big business's control over the U.S. defense industrial base. There were other, remarkable benefits in the creation of this new industrial system. The Defense Plant Corporation could now direct investment into the South, which had been neglected since the Civil War.[133]

The military sought to have new war plants moved out of any concentrated geographic area. Some would be placed in the Deep

South, because, as wartime planner and later famous economist John Kenneth Galbraith argued in 1940, there were large groups of unemployed poor blacks and whites, and putting plants there would raise the region out of poverty.[134] As Mississippi congressman Frank Smith put it, "Willingly and knowingly or not, the South is finally entering the mainstream of American life." Patman himself had a steel factory put in his Texas district.

Alcoa prospered in the aftermath of the war, though it did so under younger leadership, with a unionized workforce, and with much less political power. Competition spurred expansion, as well as innovation and new product development, like monumental architecture and aerospace alloys. The company's research budget tripled, and it expanded its efforts to work with newer commercial metals such as magnesium, beryllium, gallium, and titanium.[135]

Workers too benefited from the massive demand for their labor, and from the variety of choices they had in employment as well as increased organizing rights. In 1940, Jackson ruled that any defense contractor violating the Wagner Act in contravention to the rights of labor might be prohibited from getting government contracts. Congress and defense officials pushed back and forced Jackson to walk back the ruling, but the wave of unionization was unstoppable.[136]

Many black Americans and Hispanics found better jobs, with blacks seeing the beginnings of the rate of income growth double that of whites, a trend that lasted for thirty years. In 1940, poverty in America was endemic; nearly a third of homes had no running water or indoor toilets. Many lacked bathtubs, and 60 percent had no central heating. The war, and the postwar economy, lifted huge numbers out of poverty and offered a better life than millions had ever had.[137]

World War I had allowed a whole class of "mushroom millionaire" war profiteers to exploit shortages of materials and contracting opportunities. In World War II, New Dealers made sure that this experience wouldn't be repeated. Instead, the mobilization of society for war not only helped defeat the Axis powers, but vastly enlarged the American middle class and set the stage for postwar global prosperity.

## CHAPTER SIX

# A DEMOCRACY OF SMALL BUSINESSES

"Now we do not ask paternalistic privilege for the farmer, but we do demand that the hand of privilege shall be taken out of the farmers' pockets and off the farmers' throats."

**—Claude Bowers, keynote speaker at the 1928 Democratic convention**[1]

■ ■ ■ ■ ■ ■ ■ ■ ■ ■ ■ ■ ■

The New Deal did not just restructure industrial power, but also reorganized two fundamental economic units over which Americans had fought since the founding: farming and shopkeeping. America had always been a nation of merchants and farmers, and a wide dispersal of property had been fundamental to the American political system and its political debates. Americans understood concentrated land ownership and control over commerce as an aristocratic system, turning citizens into dependents, and thus eroding democracy. Liberty meant being free from domination, by autocrats of both politics and trade. The rise of big business, and the collapse of the economy in the 1930s, was a new challenge to this self-conception.

New Dealers and their opponents saw the debate over industrialization in terms of updating the founding principles of the nation—between what they perceived of as Hamilton the Wall Street aristocrat and Jefferson the founder of the American democratic tradition. "The issues," said Roosevelt's favorite historian, Claude Bowers, at the Democratic convention of 1928, "are as fundamental as they were when Jefferson and Hamilton crossed swords more than a century ago."[2] Just as Mellon Republicans put Alexander Hamilton on the $10 bill in the

1920s, it was during the New Deal that Democrats constructed the Jefferson Memorial.

The project to restructure an individual yeomanry had two parts. First, New Dealers attacked the most desperate part of the depressed economy in 1933 by ensuring that land, the basic unit of American power, remained widely dispersed. These efforts were a speeding up and widening of earlier attempts to protect small capital and independent farmers. They had their roots with Jefferson, who argued family farmers were the "cultivators of the earth" and "the most valuable citizens" in the republic. By the 1930s, it was not just farmers, but grocers, pharmacists, small manufacturers, and industrial workers who formed this yeomanry. It was in land and farming that New Deal populists like Roosevelt and Patman first focused attention.

The New Dealers also drew upon the Civil War, the last great moment of national crisis. During that war, northern armies did not just enforce emancipation of slaves. The Union freed poor southern whites from plutocracy through broad dispersion of land. With the Homestead Act of 1862 and the Southern Homestead Act of 1866, the Union handed out small plots of land to hundreds of thousands of white farmers, roughly 10 percent of all the land in the U.S.[3] Ugly racism played its part; with the Dawes Act in 1887, the U.S. government seized tens of millions of acres of Native American land and transferred it to homesteaders.[4] The Homestead Act and emancipation were together the most radical redistributionist policy in American history. A quarter of all U.S. adults alive in 2000 were descendants of Homestead recipients.[5] The Homestead Act was the New Deal of that era, a bounty and economic independence awarded to citizens (with the definition of *citizen* hewing to white supremacy).

By the 1880s, that bounty was under assault from plutocrats. Railroads, banks, and trusts controlled farm implements and the sale of crops and livestock, and had begun rolling up the land once again and turning Americans into tenant farmers on large estates. In response to this attack on their political independence, farmers organized into Greenbacker and populist antimonopoly movements. They blocked discrimination by railroads for carrying crops and farming commodities. They worked with merchants on antimonopoly laws and supported the third-party movement of the People's Party to re-structure credit arrangements.

By 1912, this populist thinking—designed to protect the Civil War–era deal of broad land ownership for citizens—was embedded in the Democratic Party. Louis Brandeis lauded "the courage, the energy and the resourcefulness of small men" in farming, retail, and technology.[6] The protection of the family farm as a modern Democratic agenda item was in parallel to industrial democracy and the independent businessman and shopkeeper.

Wilson shared this vision of a political economy of small land holders. In the 1910s, the Wilson administration investigated the concentrated meatpacking industry, the small group of men who had used refrigerated railroad cars to consolidate power over hog farmers and cattlemen through their control of large slaughterhouses. This led, in 1921, to the passage of the Packers and Stockyards Act, which gradually eroded the power of the packers.

It also included the democratization of credit. Money, along with land, labor, and seeds or fertilizer, is the key input into farming. Credit to farmers had been controlled by eastern bankers. Wilson sought to loosen this with federal aid in the form of federal land banks and cheaper mortgages. There was the Federal Reserve, designed to smooth out fluctuations in the money supply due to seasonal needs of farmers.

But during World War I, farmers had put large amounts of land into production to feed the armies during the war, and had borrowed to do so. In the 1920s, commodities prices collapsed. Price drops led to farmers producing even more, to make up for the shortfall in revenue, which led to even lower prices. It was similar to the ruinous competition among railroads as rival roads cut prices against each other, except railroads could collaborate to raise prices since there were so few of them, while millions of farmers couldn't coordinate and began going into bankruptcy en masse.

At the depths of the depression, with crop prices having fallen far below what it took to buy the inputs and pay back the loans needed to grow crops, the prospect of consolidating land into giant corporate farms reemerged. Farmers sought to protect their independence by asking the government to regulate the overproduction of crops. "We do not want a mass-production, corporate agriculture," said Patman in arguing for regulating credit to farmers to preserve family farms.

Two of the first key proposals by the new Congress and Roosevelt targeted this problem. One was a law allowing farmers to refinance farm mortgages at lower rates of interest, helping to reduce payments to banks and cut foreclosures. This kept farmers on the land.

The second was called the Agricultural Adjustment Act, passed as part of the first hundred days of the FDR administration. This addressed the problem of purchasing power for farmers. Prices for farm goods—wheat, cotton, corn, hogs, rice, tobacco, milk—had fallen much further than those for industrial products.[7] This made it much harder for farmers to buy things from the rest of the economy, and harder to repay loans borrowed earlier when prices were higher. Using this new law, the secretary of agriculture imposed processing taxes on basic farm commodities and paid that money to farmers who agreed to cut overproduction. This system—known as "domestic allotment" or "supply management"—not only helped preserve family farming, but was also a way to protect topsoil and the farming environment.[8]

New Deal rhetoric of liberty, like Jefferson's, retained deep inequities. Land and property ownership in the South was concentrated among whites. Even into the 1940s, just one out of eight blacks owned their own land; most blacks worked as sharecroppers.[9] Orienting aid to farmers solely through those who owned land retained the structural racism of the American order, often driving black sharecroppers off their land.[10] FDR argued this was "political expediency."[11] Roosevelt's New Deal was a political coalition incorporating both African Americans and southern racist political machines based on a shared economic agenda of regional equity, but diverging on the rights of black Americans within those regions.[12] In the southern farming regions hit by crop price declines, this tension grew particularly difficult to manage. The idealized yeoman farmer as citizen largely, though not entirely, excluded black Americans and women.

Still, by the middle of the century, across the countryside, the American farm continued to be independent and family-owned, while a few national enterprises provided the farmer with advanced machinery and scientifically advanced crops and fertilizers. On America's main streets, independent, locally owned businesses dominated, while a smattering of chain stores served regional markets. The Jeffersonian ideal was restored; albeit refitted for the industrial era, and rooted in a segregated, though equalizing, culture.

But farming was only part of the new yeomanry. In many respects, the fight to protect the shopkeeper proved one of the most difficult of the period. The chain store had long served Wall Street financiers as one of their most effective tools for capturing control not only over buyers but also over producers. The fight took place in every state and town from coast to coast. But for many observers, the central story was the twenty-five-year conflict between the populists and the most powerful chain store America had faced since the East India Company: the Great Atlantic & Pacific Tea Company, or the A&P.

The battle came to a head soon after the end of the war.

On December 1, 1949, Americans all over the country picked up their local newspaper to find the following announcement from the A&P supermarket chain: "Don't Let Anybody Fool You! These Things Will Happen if the Anti-Trust Lawyers Have Their Way." It was a brutal multimillion-dollar public relations campaign, masterminded by a savvy lobbyist working for the A&P.

"Your Food Will Cost More." "Others Will Be Hurt." A threat to the "welfare and standard of living" of ordinary Americans. Other ads confronted Americans. "Isn't America a Wonderful Country!" blared one, with notes from A&P competitors asking the government to back off the suit. "Here in America we have learned to live together in friendship."[13]

The target of these advertisements was the Truman administration's antitrust suit against the A&P. The public relations campaign was meant to scare the government into settling, by ginning up anger among consumers toward the Department of Justice. But it didn't work. The president during this suit, Harry Truman, had been a farmer and an independent businessman. He understood the dangers of chain stores and monopolies.

Truman spent his career advocating for small business, both as a small businessman who had lost his clothing store in the vicious recession after the First World War, and then as a senator who uprooted corruption in the defense industry during the Second. He was friendly with Brandeis, who served as his mentor; the two bonded over their shared obsession with railroad corruption. In the Senate, he helped author the bill creating the Civil Aeronautics Board, which regulated airlines. The committee Senator Truman led on war profiteering exposed the links between some of the most powerful companies in the world and the Nazi empire. As president, Truman would not be intimidated by a large chain store's campaign against his administration.

In the middle of the twentieth century, A&P sat atop the corporate kingdom, second in size only to General Motors. The company was, as a reporter put it in 2010, "Walmart before Walmart," as well known "as McDonald's or Google is today." And like McDonald's and Google, it too paid the maestros of Madison Avenue to depict it as neighborly, benign, and a symbol of American prosperity. John Updike wrote a short story in 1961 titled simply "A&P," and a popular love song was published by Alexander Mueller and Company that ended with the line, "Sweetheart, can you picture where our home will be? Just around the corner from an A&P."[14]

In the 1940s, A&P had over 4,500 stores across the country. There was the A&P radio hour and the company's multimillion-circulation *Woman's Day* magazine. A&P had the best-selling coffee brand in the world, selling four million pounds of beans a week. The chain alone accounted for 15 percent of all coffee imports from South America.

A&P kept prices low by buying in bulk. Where it could not bludgeon suppliers, it produced its own private-label brands. A&P had a massive wholesaling division—the Atlantic Commission Company—to buy fruits and vegetables from farmers. This division did not just service A&P stores, but served A&P's competitors. It owned dozens of industrial bakeries, six canneries in Alaska, and its Quaker Maid division made catsup, candy, pasta, evaporated milk, jams, preserves, cereal, baked beans, and peanut butter. One high-level executive's entire job was sourcing sugar.[15] A&P's own branded products sat conspicuously next to those of its suppliers. The company spread the supermarket format, and bought and shipped so much it could even dictate lower shipping prices to the railroads.[16]

And now it was under attack by the Truman Antitrust Division.

This suit was the culmination of a decades-long fight against the behemoth. "I would rather have thieves and gangsters than chain stores in Louisiana," said populist Louisiana senator Huey Long, an ally of Wright Patman in the 1930s. It wasn't just populists; "If a man undertakes to go into the grocery business, there is hovering above him the shadow of the Great A&P," said rabid anticommunist and segregationist Martin Dies of Texas. These politicians were responding to complaints from wholesalers, jobbers, retailers, and workers, but also from shoppers. In 1937, Americans, while many shopped for some of their groceries at a chain, also sought restrictions on chains to protect their community stores.[17]

At the turn of the century, A&P was still a small operation, with 198 stores doing $5.6 million in sales.[18] A&P wasn't the only chain. Kroger, Safeway, and Woolworth's would eventually become major players. There were also mail order companies, like Sears and Montgomery Ward, who later moved into retail. But A&P would become the biggest. By 1904, it had added coffee, spices, canned milk, soup, soap, and packaged products to its stores, and had essentially become a grocer. The company hired salesmen to take market shares from peddlers, the traditional traders who sold such supplies door-to-door. Competitors in the grocery business noticed, with "Stealing from the Grocer" blaring from *The American Grocer* publication, chortling over the arrest of an A&P salesman in Armstrong, Iowa, for violating a town ordinance against peddling.[19] Still, A&P, though an ostentatious medium-size chain, was no behemoth.

But in 1911, the Supreme Court engaged in a series of conservative rulings. One was *Dr. Miles Medical Co. v. John D. Park & Sons Co.* The court found that a maker of branded patent medicines had to let retailers set the price of the product, even if the retailer sold it below cost and it undermined the brand value. Preventing price-cutting among discounters had been a common practice since the rise of mass production and retailing in the nineteenth century. Effectively, the Supreme Court crippled the traditional mechanism with which businesses had protected themselves and consumers.[20]

Dr. Miles made medicine, and pricing schedules were common in the medical industry. They were common among the makers of many specialty goods. Ingersoll, a company that made watches, could, say, require end retailers, no matter the size, not to sell an Ingersoll watch for less than a dollar. Retailers could sell other watches at other prices, but were prohibited from discounting Ingersoll watches below the minimum price Ingersoll set.

No one was required to sell their products with this kind of arrangement with retailers and distributors, but many did. In the twentieth century, Sunbeam, Champion Spark Plug, General Electric, Samsonite, Corning Glass, Hart Schaffner & Marx, Parker Pen, Eli Lilly, Bissell, and others used resale price maintenance as a means of concentrating on quality, and on building out sound networks of independent distributors and retailers who knew their product lines and could service and support them.[21] Independent pharmacists, small liquor sellers, small businesses, and newspapers all supported these laws.

More importantly, fair trade practices helped block the ability of concentrated capital to monopolize and dominate retailing and manufacturing by a) predatory pricing aimed to drive rivals out of business, and b) manipulation of pricing that interfered with the ability of producers to control their own businesses. The court, however, found that letting small producers set a price of his or her own product violated the Sherman Act.

Populists and small businessmen viewed the court's decision as radical and dangerous. Justice Oliver Wendell Holmes issued a stinging dissent, writing, "I cannot believe that in the long run the public will profit by this course, permitting knaves to cut reasonable prices for mere ulterior purposes of their own."[22] Brandeis, meanwhile, warned that "Americans should be under no illusions as to the value or effect of price-cutting. It has been the most potent weapon of monopoly—a means of killing the small rival to which the great trusts have resorted most frequently."

After the *Dr. Miles* decision, chains could specifically pick well-known branded goods to discount at a loss to drive competitors out of business, and then use their purchasing volume to demand lower prices, and thus lower quality, from the maker. The court had removed power from the small producer, and placed power in the hands of the financial middlemen who controlled the chain stores.

The year after the *Dr. Miles* decision, John Hartford, a co-owner of A&P, built the first low-cost store format. He believed the huge A&P storefront, with its ornate front, delivery wagons, offers of credit to customers, and elaborate system of prizes for frequent shopping were inefficient. His family scoffed. Nevertheless, in the fall of 1912, he presented them with a plan for the "economy" grocery store format.

This store would have no frills, just low prices. It had no telephone for orders, and not even a sign; just a storefront piled high with groceries that operated on a pure cash basis. He piloted one around the corner from one of A&P's larger operations in Jersey City. Within six months, the high-price store went out of business. A&P rolled out the "economy" grocery store format nationwide, ushering in the modern era of food retailing.[23]

A&P's growth exploded, aided by a large infusion of capital from Wall Street. From 1907 to 1914, the company's revenue jumped from $15 million to $31.3 million. By 1914, there were 100 stores in Boston alone. In 1915, A&P had just under two thousand stores. Just a year later, the company's revenue hit $76.4 million. In 1920, it surpassed Sears as the biggest retailer in the country, at $235 million in sales.[24] But efficiency was not the only source of A&P's explosive success. Much of the business operation was based on power.

Increasingly, the corporation was able to exploit a "buying monopoly" (or in economic literature "monopsony"). Because A&P controlled so much of America's food market, it was able to demand that food suppliers give the company better prices, which it could then use to further undercut rivals. It also forced suppliers to pay kickbacks to stock their products. These bribes took the form of "advertising allowances," or payments by manufacturers for A&P to advertise its products. The chain would then use this special pricing advantage to underprice its retail competitors, and acquire yet more power to extract concessions from suppliers.

The business model of A&P was based on both widely spreading innovative formats, like the economy store and then the supermarket, and using threats, bribery, and extortion to destroy competition and control suppliers.[25] In 1915, A&P was first declared a monopoly by a judge, when Cream of Wheat refused to sell to the company and its thousand stores after A&P demanded to be able to sell the cereal at a lower cost than rivals.[26] It would encounter legal trouble around misuse of its power for forty more years.

The Hartford family, unlike the Carnegie or Rockefeller or Morgan families, kept a low profile. They did not go to fancy summer holiday spots.[27] The company did not issue public stock, to avoid being an objective of the speculative fervor of that decade. A&P is typically not ranked as an all-time powerhouse in big business, and its monopolistic power is understated. Moreover, A&P's monopoly wasn't oriented toward charging consumers high prices, as electric utilities were, but the opposite. It charged, as the East India Company had, low prices. It used its power to bully farmers, workers, and suppliers.

But in Mellon's decade, the company began dominating American food retailing. In the 1910s and 1920s, mass-buying monopolies were growing quickly, using the freedom allowed by permissive pricing laws and anti-union open shop rules to bully farmers, manufacturers, small retailers, and workers. By 1925, A&P had 14,000 stores and $440 million in sales.[28] A&P began a manufacturing arm and started a bakery division so it could have its own branded products. The company didn't just limit aggressive tactics to suppliers and farmers. In the early 1920s, the company began scuffling with organized labor; in 1923, A&P hired private detectives to beat up strikers in Newark, with the police arresting one of the company's security guards. John Hartford blamed the union.[29]

Socialists and statist planners saw the growth of chains as a sign of progress. Walter Lippmann, in his influential 1914 book *Drift and Mastery,* wrote of the "dingy little butcher-shops, little businesses with the family living in the back room, the odor of cooking to greet you as you enter the door, fly-specks on the goods—walk through any city and marvel at the anarchy of retail business. Well, the large department store, organized markets, the chain of stores, the mail order business, are changing the situation radically for the purchaser."[30] And a new consumer movement, born in the 1920s, had less allegiance to small businesses. In 1926, *The New Republic* called for both the elimination of small bakers and antitrust policy, preferring instead "enforcing complete monopoly with price control . . . or by public or consumer ownership."[31] Independent merchants, workers, farmers, and manufacturers were less favorable to chain stores.

The growth of chain stores generated a political backlash. States began to pass state laws legalizing fair trade practices. Fair trade laws allowed manufacturers to set the price at which retailers had to sell their products. These protected producers of goods from the chain store's ability to pick out popular items and discount them to drive competitors out of business. New Jersey led the way in 1916.

In 1928, A&P became the first retail store with $1 billion in sales. North Carolina, South Carolina, and Georgia levied chain store taxes, which were challenged in court. The FTC launched an investigation.

But the depression accelerated the popular movement against chain stores. The collapse in commodities prices in 1930 served to offer even more power to A&P's buying hulk. By the summer, John Hartford announced the company had cut prices by an average of 6 percent.[32] In the 1920s, such an announcement would have incurred eagerness to shop; now it stoked fear among helpless producers. The company's power over pricing of basic goods served as a potent symbol of the depression, as symbolic in many communities as Rockefeller, Mellon, and Morgan.

In the 1930s, politicians aimed special antimonopoly laws and taxes at A&P, pressured by smaller stores and distributors. During the first part of the depression, the National Industrial Recovery Act incorporated fair pricing rules into the retailing sector. When the Supreme Court struck down the law in 1935, the discounters began price cuts yet again.

Meanwhile, the FTC found that large chain stores threatened manufacturers to secure kickbacks unavailable to smaller stores.[33] Small retailers and wholesalers turned to Patman for help, because of his fame in the impeachment fight against Mellon. Congress and Patman responded, with the House authorizing Patman to lead a special select committee to investigate the American Retail Federation, the lobbying arm of the chain store movement. This investigation uncovered the use of "killing prices" designed by chain stores to destroy independent stores when they opened.[34] Patman argued A&P was a dictatorship of the grocery business in America.

In 1936, in what was called the "March of the Little Men" in Washington, D.C., 1,500 small businessmen came to the capital, lobbying President Roosevelt to support an anti-predatory-pricing law.[35] Congress passed a criminal and civil statute, called the Robinson-Patman Act, nicknamed the "anti-A&P Act." The law barred the use of discriminatory pricing to gain monopoly power. "The expressed purpose of the Act is to protect the independent merchant," Patman wrote, "and the manufacturer from whom he buys."[36] The law essentially outlawed the whole kickback system that chain stores and supermarkets had been using to extract special bulk discounts in the form of advertising allowances from producers.

Small merchants and politicians designed this pricing law not to protect the slothful or inefficient, but simply to ensure that the playing field was level. An individual shopkeeper still had to do a good job of stocking the shelves, of keeping the store clean, and of providing courteous service, lest some better-run independent down the street drive him out of business. Chain stores used price cuts, the lure of discounts to create powerful buying monopolies, a Wall Street–powered winner-take-all monopolization. Legislators sought to distinguish between the accomplishments of A&P in terms of building a better food distribution system, and the brute use of coercion to run rivals out of business. Better distribution would force independent retailers to improve their service (which they did through, among other means, forming cooperatives to gain bulk-purchasing efficiencies), but policymakers sought to discourage the use of market power to destroy competition.

The year after Robinson-Patman passed, the FTC brought a suit against A&P for violations of the law. The chain store founders understood the threat. A&P refused to comply, and attempted unsuccessfully to have the law thrown out as unconstitutional.

As it turned out, despite the claims of A&P and chain store proponents, the investigation revealed that it was mostly the corporation's raw market power, and not better stores or smarter practices, that gave the chain its advantage. Between 1935 and 1937, manufacturers complied with the law, and stopped paying advertising kickbacks to A&P. This decision cost $4.5 million, a quarter of the firm's annual profit.[37] From the time the Robinson-Patman Act was introduced in

Congress in 1935 until the end of 1937, grocery chain stocks collapsed by 58 percent, even as the broader stock market went up by about 8 percent. Before Robinson-Patman, A&P always had profit margins of at least 2 percent of sales. Afterward, it would never have profits of more than 2 percent of sales.[38]

It didn't stop at Robinson-Patman. Another set of laws legalized fair trade laws allowing producers to set prices for their own products. In 1937, Congress passed the Miller-Tydings Act, which partially reversed the *Dr. Miles* decision by letting states legalize fair trade contracts within their own borders. Most states eventually passed fair trade laws.

These laws were politically potent, particularly in the South, which had far less wealth than the rest of the country, and whose residents perceived chain stores as controlled by non-local interests. In 1934, populist Democrat James Allred had won the Texas governorship on a platform of chain store taxes.[39] Between 1933 and 1935, fifteen states imposed chain store taxes. In just one year, in 1937, Georgia, Montana, South Dakota, and Tennessee adopted them. That was the year Texas congressman and eventual House Speaker Sam Rayburn convinced Roosevelt to support Miller-Tydings, the federal act legalizing state fair trade laws.

During the depression, the new policy architecture helped rebuild small grocers, who could now compete based on quality and service. Over the course of the 1930s, smaller retailers began gaining back market share, with grocery stores taking 44.1 percent of sales in 1933 and 36.7 percent in 1939.[40] The number of family-owned retail stores increased from 1.4 million to 1.6 million from 1929 to 1939, and independent grocers kept roughly two thirds of the market throughout the decade.[41] A&P still competed, but based on its effectiveness as a grocer. Chain stores and independent retailers were in a stable coexistence.

By 1951, forty-five of forty-eight states had fair trade laws. Thousands of dealers and retailers found protection in the fair trade laws, "involving billions of dollars of goods covering a wide variety of products, such as liquor, drugs, proprietaries, food, cosmetics, and consumer durables."[42] In 1951, once again the Supreme Court attacked fair trade practices. It ruled that producers, who had been able to control minimum prices for their products, could only do so against sellers who contractually agreed. A retailer who didn't sign a contract with the producer could break fair trade prices. Once again, Congress overrode the court with a law called the McGuire Act.[43]

Still, Robinson-Patman and fair trade laws hadn't satisfied the opponents of chain stores. In 1940, Patman overreached, asserting on NBC radio, "We, the American people, want no part of monopolistic dictatorship in either our American government or in our American business. . . . Think of Hitler. Think of Stalin. Think of Mussolini. Let's keep Hitler's methods of government and business in Europe."[44]

States continued to pass chain store taxes, and Patman introduced a chain store tax bill in Congress, H.R. 1, with rates so high that it was nicknamed the "death sentence bill."[45] If the bill had been in effect in 1938, A&P would have had to pay $472 million in taxes on profits of $9 million. For A&P, the chain tax bill was an existential crisis. It had to be stopped.[46]

In 1936, the company, along with a host of other chain stores, funded a trade association to attack chain store taxes. Chain stores set up educational tours for housewives and had store managers join local civic groups to show they were involved in their communities. The next year, the company hired Carl Byoir, a wealthy public relations expert and lobbyist who had relationships with political leaders in both parties, including Hoover and Roosevelt. Byoir was ruthless, having worked in the early 1930s for the German tourist ministry to promote visits to Nazi Germany, but also hosting successful fundraisers for Roosevelt's Warm Springs charity.[47]

Byoir contacted hundreds of consumer, farm, and labor groups; editors of farm magazines and small-town newspapers; economics professors; and union leaders. Liberally sprinkling A&P money, Byoir welded together a potent political coalition. In the spring of 1938, A&P began aggressively funding consumer groups. Byoir persuaded the American Farm Bureau Federation and the National Grange to support A&P's case, noting that the chain had helped them sell surplus produce.

Byoir used fake front groups secretly financed with A&P money, such as the National Drainage, Levee, and Irrigation Association, and

Business Property Owners Inc., to lobby against the bill. He created the National Consumers Tax Commission, and financed a staff of seventy-two to create discussion groups on women's issues, framed as supporting "average American housewives" who wanted to be involved in civic affairs. The Emergency Tax Council of New Jersey was another false front group. Ultimately Byoir used $1.6 million of fees and expenses paid by A&P to fight chain store laws, often by setting up groups that pretended to have mass membership, but were controlled by the company.[48]

A&P also used political kickbacks to promote its ends. Federal investigators argued that A&P rewarded a milk producer with orders for milk in return for help fighting a specific bill.[49] Chain stores dangled jobs in front of James Farley, a key Roosevelt advisor, and John Hartford lent $200,000 to Elliott Roosevelt, the president's son, for a radio venture.[50]

By 1938, the corporation was so desperate that it cut a deal with organized labor, after years of viciously opposing the unionization of its stores and warehouses. Just four years earlier, A&P and organized labor were mortal enemies. In 1934, labor struck at A&P shops in Cleveland. The chain was unpopular there because it had, unlike local stores, refused to accept local scrip during the depths of the depression. In October, Teamsters stopped hauling goods for the chain, and labor began picketing.

Instead of negotiating with the union, John Hartford decided to greet the unrest with full-page ads announcing it was, sadly, closing its business after fifty years in the city. A&P closed all 293 of its Cleveland stores and laid off 2,200 workers. Hartford, angry at the mayor of the city and the unions, said that this would "make a lot of these people do some real thinking."[51] Only after an all-night negotiating session called by Roosevelt himself did Hartford agree to reopen the stores, but A&P did not recognize the unions who called the strike. A&P had, as the Amalgamated Meat Cutters put it, a "bitter anti-union policy."[52]

But in 1938, Hartford needed labor allies to fight the chain store tax. "I'm a union man myself at heart," John Hartford said in a convenient turnaround. "Whatever labor got, it had to get with a gun."[53] After Byoir's political deal with labor, A&P and five unions signed contracts covering employees in Washington and Chicago, spreading from there. "The past few weeks has witnessed one of the largest increases in membership in the Association that has been experienced for some time," the *Retail Clerks International Advocate* proclaimed.[54] The company had all its printing done in union shops, and placed chain-friendly articles in labor bulletins (with a secret $80,000 payoff to a labor public relations specialist).

The quid pro quo? That the American Federation of Labor defend the now unionized chain. And indeed, representatives from the Amalgamated Meat Cutters and the Retail Clerks Association now praised chain stores. One union representative attacked the "unsanitary and uninviting" small stores. Consumer groups like the American Home Economics Association and the American Association of University Women, and farmers groups like the National Council of Farmer Cooperatives, joined sides with A&P, as did left-wing agriculture secretary Henry Wallace.

In 1942, the Department of Justice brought a criminal antitrust suit against A&P in Texas; the judge was hostile to the government, so the DOJ refiled it in Illinois in 1944. In the trial, which began in 1945, the Department of Justice showed that the company cut prices below cost in areas with competition to drive out competitors, and made that money up with higher prices in stores in noncompetitive areas. In 1939, the company decided to gain shares in New England and the Atlantic division, marking up prices in its other five divisions. Meanwhile, Byoir's deceptive publicity campaigns and his direction of the company's policy led him to be named as a defendant in the antitrust suit. Byoir and the A&P were found guilty.[55] In 1949, the company faced another Department of Justice suit in which the antitrust division attempted to break up the retailing company into seven parts and force it to spin off its distribution and manufacturing arms.

In the 1930s, A&P nearly destroyed itself by bullying farmers, workers, and local communities. But by engaging not just in a public relations and legal campaign but forgoing its power to extract bribes and then incorporating a whole set of new stakeholders in its organizational structure, the company blunted the anti-chain-store movement sufficiently to save itself.

Because of this, the company was able to portray the suit as an attack, an attempt to break up this jewel of corporate America, this machine of distribution and commerce. The company used iconic imagery; one ad featured a photo of the Empire State Building with the caption "It's Far Too Big. It Ought to be Seven Buildings."[56] In Henry Luce's *Time* magazine, A&P leader John Hartford extolled bigness, saying, "I don't know any grocer or anybody else who wants to stay small." The whole country was growing, "our cities, schools, labor unions, everything."[57] Luce's other magazine, *Fortune,* published an article titled "The Great A&P Muddle." The article asserted there was a "disturbing lack of competence on the part of a government agency to do its job." Arthur Krock of *The New York Times* criticized the confusing antimonopoly Robinson-Patman law.[58]

But A&P had a formidable political coalition to protect its remnants. The nation's labor leaders deluged the Truman administration, voicing opposition to the antitrust suit. Butchers, meat cutters, clerks, warehousemen, truck drivers, all sent telegrams of support to the company's headquarters.[59] By the end of the decade, two-thirds of voters had heard of the A&P case.[60]

Still, it was an expensive argument to make. In 1949, the company spent $5 million just on advertisements criticizing the government's suit, one-seventh its annual profits. Seven hundred-plus newspapers and commentators took the side of the company, perhaps not coincidentally because of A&P's large advertising budget.[61]

The suit was in many ways anticlimactic. The company had already been forced to allow other stakeholders to share power, from organized labor to farmers to manufacturers to smaller competitors who could now bring private suits under Robinson-Patman. Before it was reined in, A&P, like the Mellon empire, was a frightening force. But the structure of bribery that dominated food distribution had been dismantled.

A&P had been tamed, so Americans were no longer afraid. Over the course of the New Deal, A&P's power had been submerged, in a truce with the workers, food processors, farmers, small retailers, and suppliers it had previously bullied. A&P had become an aging boxer who had lost his punch.

Though the company won the public relations battle, it lost the lawsuit and agreed to end its practice of bullying suppliers and dismantle its large middleman fruit and vegetable wholesale operation. The suit was also a test case; two other chains, Kroger and Safeway, were indicted for similar practices. A&P's dominance, and the dominance of the old guard in distribution, would pass.

Into the 1960s, with such antitrust suits as *United States v. Von's Grocery*, the Antitrust Division still viewed increases of chain store power as a threat to democracy and an independent citizenry. The independent businessperson and small businesses would have a place in the postwar era.

## CHAPTER SEVEN

# THE NEW DEAL CONSTITUTION

"The realm of science and its application to technology is expanding at a startling pace, and its limits are beyond calculation. The advances of the future can be made to serve the common welfare by affording opportunities for initiative and enterprise. Or they can contribute increasingly to the growth of private monopoly."

**—Leon Keyserling, Council of Economic Advisors Vice Chair under President Harry Truman**[1]

■ ■ ■ ■ ■ ■ ■ ■ ■ ■ ■ ■ ■

"M r. President, my name is Mrs. Mary Lanuti." It was 1956, and the first Republican president in twenty years, Dwight Eisenhower, was taking questions on CBS from women voters just before the upcoming election. Eisenhower could be confident in his reelection. The American economy was doing well and he was a beloved political leader. But voters were nervous. The scars of the Great Depression ran deep.

Lanuti was from a small mining community. "We are very, very prosperous, and due to your Administration, Mr. President, we feel very secure; we think it's a very good, sound government," Mrs. Lanuti said. But she had a concern. "My husband is affiliated with the union; he's a laborer, and there is talk going around about a depression. That's what I would like to know, Mr. President: Is there any truth in that?"[2]

"All of the economic factors," responded Eisenhower, "point towards a continuation of good times . . ." But, he went on to assure her, that if there were signs of a recession or depression, he would not act like the last Republican president, Herbert Hoover. "Everything the Government can do, every single force and influence it has to bring to bear, will be brought in timely fashion and not after any such catastrophe occurs." This Republican president then praised Social Security and unemployment insurance. Even twenty years later, memories of Hoover and Mellon were political poison.

The next question came from a beauty shop owner from Cleveland. "I come in contact with a lot of ... women ... who have small businesses," she said. "Some ... say that the wealth in this country wants to do away with small business. Can you give me your thoughts on this subject?"

Eisenhower answered by talking about trustbusting. In 1955, "we instituted 54 suits for antitrust action to keep these big businesses from getting in such a dominant position that they can squeeze out the little fellow," he said. "Now it is true, we want many of the things that big business give us," like cars and TVs. But, he said, "we do try to keep those people from getting that influence over our economy that can override the little fellow no matter what the size of his business or what type it is."[3]

These questions, and Eisenhower's answers, sound canned, like propaganda. But after more than twenty years of monopoly busting and populist programs, Americans did believe in their government. In 1958, 73 percent of Americans trusted the federal government most or some of the time, most thought government was run for the benefit of all instead of a few big interests, and less than a quarter of the public thought government officials were crooked. In 1952, 63 percent of Americans thought that public officials cared what they thought and 68 percent believed they had a say in government.[4]

The war generated massive broad-based income growth, but the postwar years were even better. From 1940 to 1970, economic growth was strong. Income growth increased faster for the bottom fifth of the country than the wealthy, and for blacks much faster than whites.[5] In 1945, more than 40 percent of the country still lived below the poverty line. By 1970, this numbered a little over 10 percent. A third of American workers were unionized, getting access to homeownership, paid vacations, health care insurance, pensions, and holidays. Blue-collar workers had discretionary income they could spend, and by 1970, there were as many private cars as families in America. It was an age of prosperity.[6]

Eisenhower was telling the truth about his administration, and his Antitrust Division. In 1959, the Eisenhower administration brought more suits than had been brought since the days of the New Deal, suing auto giants and TV producers, and many of the other giants of American business, including RCA and AT&T.[7]

The American political system had changed. The question put forward in the 1880s, when the great centralizing force of the railroads and the financiers first emerged, was what to do about the robber barons. It was asked again in 1912, when Wilson sought to organize industrial democracy, but failed.

Finally, after the second great war of the century, democracy had taken hold in the commercial sphere. Business leaders, workers, politicians, citizens, judges, and lawyers had created a much more equal society and business world, with far less monopoly power, and free from private financiers and from what Franklin Delano Roosevelt had called an informal group amounting to an economic government of the United States.[8] By the 1950s antimonopoly policy was integrated into the governing fabric of society.

No longer would American society produce super-wealthy men and women. There were still a few families, such as the Mellons, the Rockefellers, and the DuPonts, but that would be it. As Walter Lippmann put it about John D. Rockefeller, "Before he started his enterprises, it was not possible to make so much money; before he died, it had become the settled policy of this country that no man would be permitted to make so much money. He lived long enough to see the methods by which such a fortune can be accumulated, outlawed by public opinion, forbidden by statute, and prevented by the tax laws."[9] Paul Mellon could ride his horses, and the Rockefeller children could be diplomats and bankers, but there would not be another Andrew Mellon, J. P. Morgan, or John D. Rockefeller.

And the culture of business was different. Keynes had told Roosevelt that business leaders were not tigers or wolves, but "domestic animals" badly brought up. By the 1950s, they had been trained. The Great Depression and a world war had reorganized every facet of

American society. Whereas the old order had protected monopolistic enterprises controlled by Wall Street, the new one emphasized good jobs, high-technology production, and political liberty. It was as close as America, and the West, would come to Brandeis's vision of industrial democracy.

## THE NEW DEAL IN BANKING

The two pieces of the Morgan-Mellon government system had been Wall Street, which exerted power over corporate America, and individual corporate monopolies, which ruled specific markets. By the postwar era, New Dealers had cleaned up the broken balance sheets of the American banking system, while also obliterating the centralized power of Wall Street finance. In the 1930s, Roosevelt and Congress put in place a set of controls on the banking system, and these controls held throughout the war.

New Dealers would not allow a repeat of the experience of the First World War, when bankers used the need for centralized mobilization to take control over the economy, and then used the chaos of demobilization to gain political power. During this second great war, New Dealers ensured the banking business was simple and boring. Banks took in deposits, and then turned around and lent those deposits to the government by buying bonds. New Dealers strengthened the separation between banking and industry, which had been a feature of the American system since the Civil War, with a powerful regulatory and legal apparatus.

Savings bond drives diverted income away from purchases of consumer goods, and toward goods needed by the military, while new rules by the Fed killed consumer borrowing. There were mandatory and voluntary credit controls that limited both mortgage lending and certain types of business loans. Government told bankers who they could lend to and what they could pay for deposits. Loans to defense contractors had priority. Sometimes the government stepped in directly to finance entire industries, as it did when it funded the new aluminum plants of Kaiser and Reynolds that helped break the Mellon aluminum monopoly.

With budget deficits of roughly 30 percent of GDP, there were plenty of bonds to sell.[10] By 1946, 57 percent of all financial assets were government securities.[11] If there were banks that had fragile balance sheets in 1941, those balance sheets had been cleaned up by 1946.

Even after the war, the government for a period retained control over minor credit choices to prevent a repeat of the chaos that happened after World War I. In 1946, for instance, the Fed imposed restrictions on borrowing to buy fridges, dishwashers, stoves, and washing machines, while reducing regulations on borrowing for automobile batteries and tires. Americans could borrow to repair their cars so they could get to work, but not for home improvements.[12] The Fed had a detailed understanding of how to make sure that credit flowed according to both social priorities laid out by Congress and to avoid production bottlenecks that caused inflation.

This period of central management in the wartime and postwar period was brief. By the late 1940s, banking was regulated far more assertively than any time in American history. The war had changed the culture of finance.[13] "Banks offer an opportunity to an educated, personable, but uncourageous young man for a pleasant, interesting, dignified life," wrote a Chicago banker in 1950.[14] Depression-scarred Americans wouldn't allow bankers anywhere near power, preferring their bankers inoffensive, white, male, Protestant, and dull. A would-be striver went to work for GM or DuPont for a high salary, not National City.[15]

The idiot son of a local elite was stashed at the local bank. As one businessman put it, when encountering a Yale grad at a bank, one needed to speak "very slowly." Banking was, as a later CEO of Citibank, put it, "kind of a nice club."[16] One old banker, asked of the most important innovation in finance, responded "air-conditioning."

Audits were routine, and if a bank officer cashed a bad check, the loss was often taken out of his salary.[17] The conservatism of the bankers was evident in whom they hired. Jews and Catholics couldn't hope to get a job, while blacks worked only as porters. College-educated women could get secretarial work. Divorce was grounds for termination. An image of almost reactionary probity was important to senior bankers who a generation earlier had seen their institutions wrecked by sales, promotion, greed, and fraud.

Talk of efficiency or creativity was discouraged. Any sign of intelligence in the banking business meant that the men displaying the unfortunate trait might be tempted to larceny. Even into the 1960s, National City officials were still finding bad debts that Charles Mitchell had hidden in various overseas branches decades earlier. And even if there were such men seeking to enter the money game, no one was hiring. From 1929 to 1950, the New York Stock Exchange hired a total of eight floor traders. There was an entire "missing generation" in banking and Wall Street, multiple decades where few entered the profession. The power to create money, the power to dominate commerce and eventually politics, was submerged in the simple, carefully governed routines of third-rate dunces, old men, and the children of the well-to-do.[18]

"The Money Trust has disappeared, and Wall Street is a symbol only to students and those with long memories," wrote Harvard antitrust economist Carl Kaysen in 1954. Corporations no longer needed Wall Street, because every large business, Kaysen wrote, "is its own banker."[19] Big companies could use their own profits to invest in more factories or output. Wall Street had in many ways been reduced to a utility, with financiers as supplicants to businesses, attempting to get their deposits and borrowing business. The flow of power between businesses and banks had been reversed; bankers sometimes sat on the boards of industrial firms, but more often industrialists were on the boards of banks.[20]

The machinery to assemble and concentrate industrial power had fallen into disrepair. Organizing mergers was difficult. There were of course restrictive antitrust rules, and not only those from the turn of the century. The Celler-Kefauver Act of 1950 barred anticompetitive mergers, and the Supreme Court interpreted it strictly. Between 1948 and 1952, industrial corporations devoted almost all their investment dollars to building new factories and buying new equipment, spending less than 3 percent of the total on acquiring other corporations.[21]

Beyond explicit legal barriers, the financial industry powering mergers in corporate America had been shattered. Prior to the 1930s, mergers had been handled within large financial institutions combining investment banks with lending facilities. Commercial banking and investment banking had been separated in the 1930s. And banks were more decentralized, so pulling together large sums of money was harder. Just finding the relevant bankers who could put together a syndicated loan was no longer as easy as lunching at a private club in New York, Pittsburgh, or Chicago.

The legal chops for acquisitions had disappeared. Acquirers needed lawyers to prepare the papers and the legal strategies to get around potential legal or regulatory problems. Barriers were different in every industry; a railroad company couldn't, say, buy an airline, and the Supreme Court was casting suspicious glances throughout American commerce. But lawyers who had gotten their training within a New Deal legal and court system dominated antitrust and regulatory law, so the legal establishment was less inclined to offer creative pro-merger strategies.

The stock market was also less centralized. The set of 1930s reforms that centered on the creation of the Securities and Exchange Commission had aimed mainly to promote and protect the interests of the small investor. And by the 1950s they had worked remarkably well, and corporate stocks were now in the hands of a large number of small investors who rarely sold. Getting the permission of the stockholders took more work. It was hard to buy the stock in small lots without driving up the price in an era without significant institutional block trading of shares.

Within the corporate world, industries were fragmented, so a merger attempt could call down a more unified opposition of ordinarily antagonistic suppliers or customers. And managers in the era had been focused on organizing production, not organizing acquisitions. It was possible for creative and driven individuals to overcome these problems, and some did, but it wasn't common.[22]

As the founding theorist of central banking, Walter Bagehot, once put it, "Money will not manage itself."[23] Someone is always in charge. In the postwar era, public officials structured markets, and private banks operated within those markets. Finance was run out of Washington, D.C., and state capitals. Democratic forces, through Congress and regulatory institutions, didn't raise rates to slow the economy, they simply told private financial institutions where they could operate, or built public financial channels to do it. They had a complex set of spigots of credit they could turn off and on, and did so.

Banks became essentially public utilities, unconcerned even with profit. Public control of finance in the U.S. by the 1940s was organized consistent with the scale of the collapse in the 1930s. Banks were also tightly restricted from branching or seeking any financing for loans aside from gathering deposits wherever they happened to be located, becoming dependent on the wealth of their local communities.[24]

Government became a key player in structuring financial markets in ways that distributed power, and supported independent business, family farms, and home owning. The government structured the Federal Reserve, the Federal Deposit Insurance Corporation, Federal Home Loan Bank System, the Federal Housing Administration, and Fannie Mae to insure and regulate bank accounts, oversee the stability of the system, and ensure a steady flow of credit into the housing sector. The Reconstruction Finance Corporation, and then the Small Business Administration, pushed credit into the small business sector, disaster relief, bankrupt railroads, rural electrification, military mobilization, and municipalities.

The centerpiece of the entire system was a powerful regulation, one that blocked both speculation with hot money by banks, and forced decentralization in banking, moving lending decisions from New York and Chicago back to thousands of local bankers across the country. In the Banking Act of 1933, Congress sought to stop the ability of New York banks to centralize power over the flow of credit, which these banks—led by Morgan—used to lend in a reckless orgy of speculation that brought down the entire financial system. The law authorized the Federal Reserve to control flows of deposits within the banking system, which the Fed did with a rule it issued called Regulation Q.[25]

The law blocked banks from paying interest on checking deposits, and Regulation Q imposed a cap on what banks could pay for savings deposits. Broadly, it stopped banks from competing with each other to acquire bank deposits, or from acquiring "bought money" (also known as "hot money"). Bank deposits are the rocket fuel for lending and credit. They are what Brandeis called "the quick capital" of the country. Since the Civil War, banks in New York City and Chicago—known as "money center banks"—had bought up deposits from all over the nation and lent them to speculative endeavors.

Control of this flow of money had allowed J. P. Morgan and the money trust to dominate corporate America. There were tens of thousands of banks in the 1920s, but unregulated deposits ended up centralizing power over finance into the hands of a few. Credit in farm areas dried up, instead flowing into an already frothy unregulated stock market.

Regulation Q was a response to the way that the stock market crash reverberated through the banking system and then into the economy. The more you could pay for hot money, the more loans you could make. Regulation Q inverted the power dynamic. Now money center banks couldn't buy deposits from small country and regional banks, so they needed to gather deposits from local areas and from corporate customers. Bankers had to beg from corporations, instead of being able to tell corporations what to do.

Regulation Q was also designed to impose a set of speed bumps to both deter speculation and prevent financial shocks from imperiling activity in the real economy. The Fed regulated deposits, the basic input into credit. This regulation stopped the bidding war for hot money that had destabilized the economy. It also decentralized financial power; now that money center banks couldn't bid for deposits, local banks simply held on to money and made loans in local areas as the war induced factories and payrolls to spring up in the Southwest, South, and West Coast.[26] Regulation Q also made it easy for the government to move economic activity from or toward housing, consumer goods, business lending, speculation, military procurement, or anything else. It became the "balance wheel" of the banking system.[27]

Millions had placed their incomes into war bonds instead of chasing scarce wartime consumer goods. In 1945, a tremendous amount of financial spending power had accumulated in the hands of workers and returning soldiers. A large national debt was not, as Mellon believed, destructive. It was a safe storehouse for financial wealth. After the war, rather than a feared return to depression, savings accounts around the country helped people to start businesses and buy homes, cars, and every conceivable new consumer product.

## THE NEW DEAL IN INDUSTRY

This new financial system also freed the American businessperson from the banker. Corporations could finance their own expansion and build valuable assets like research divisions. They were safe from bankers attempting to buy the company through the stock market and seize the assets. Large businesses would be organized by a range of stakeholders, from their CEOs to workers to smaller suppliers and innovative competitors to the national defense sector.

American industry had three tiers. In network industries, where monopolies were sometimes unavoidable, like electricity, telephone, railroad, and airline service, government regulation prevented concentrations of power. They were sometimes kept relatively small; electric utilities, because of the memory of men like Insull revealed by the Pecora hearings, couldn't cross state lines to do business. Sometimes the government placed these technologies in the hands of the community through rural cooperatives for electricity.

Airlines, trucks, and railroads—which had network properties but were not fully monopolistic—were regulated to ensure universal service and reasonable rates. The government prevented AT&T from expanding outside of the telephone space. It also forced the company's internal know-how, including technical knowledge and patents, to be licensed for use by smaller firms.[28]

For industrial corporations requiring the use of science and technology in scale production, the government aimed to ensure that at least three or four firms competed to make the same basic industrial products. Alcoa could stay big, but it couldn't remain a monopoly. By 1956, Alcoa made 43 percent of primary virgin aluminum, Kaiser had 27 percent, Reynolds had 26 percent, and Anaconda had 4 percent. Production was eight times larger than 1940. Eventually there were seven aluminum companies in the North American market.[29]

In areas of the economy that did not require substantial amounts of capital, fair trade rules and farm price supports retained family-owned and decentralized production. This included areas of the economy such as retailing, banking, farming, pharmacies, small-scale manufacturing, printing, and restaurants. The campaign to dismantle A&P had long-lasting effects. Chain stores were constrained; the A&P case cast a long shadow.[30] For instance, in 1966 the Supreme Court blocked a merger between two grocery chains that had just 7.5 percent of the Los Angeles market.

Branch banking restrictions and credit unions kept credit in the hands of local communities. The government also lent money to small business directly. Local farms were protected with localized control over livestock and grain markets, and with a complex set of financial structures to protect farmers from wild swings in commodities prices.[31] In the automobile industry, local dealers meant communities had some power over distant Detroit-headquartered goliaths. America became, once again, a nation of tradespeople. In this newly decentralized economy, an astonishing 49.7 percent of returning veterans from World War II eventually started businesses.[32]

Finally, the government took responsibility for pulling the country out of downturns, instead of letting recessions and depressions run their course. Farm supports, as well as government backing of suburban construction and the mortgage market, allowed the Federal Reserve to expand or withdraw credit to housing, becoming the "transmission belt" from the banking sector to the construction industry and underlying commercial activity.[33] No longer would a downturn drag on and allow the roll-up of land or industrial assets into the hands of plutocrats.

This new political arrangement was tested early after the war. In 1948, the president told Congress that "a sharp break in grain prices spread concern throughout the economy."[34] A speculative boom had broken, and the market collapsed. But this did not crush the economy.[35] The banking system stayed strong, and farm price support programs stopped this collapse from impoverishing farmers or spilling over into the rest of the economy.

The boom and bust cycle had tended to concentrate power in the hands of the powerful. Social Security payments, unemployment insurance, farm subsidies, and a strong Federal Reserve stopped this dynamic. The government even held stocks of metals, to ensure that companies like Alcoa could continue operating at capacity in downturns and that commodities prices would not swing the way they had before the 1930s.[36]

## A NEW POLITICAL CULTURE

When World War II ended, Americans feared that the country would revert back to a depression, or that the chaos in the aftermath of the First World War would happen again. New Dealers were determined to make sure neither occurred. Wright Patman authored and helped pass the Employment Act of 1946, a bill setting up the machinery to make it the government's role to maximize employment, production, and purchasing power, and "to foster and promote free and competitive enterprise and the general welfare."

At the core of this vision lay two new responsibilities for the government. First, the government would use competition policy to make sure no financial or corporate entity became too powerful or dominated unchecked in any critical market. Two, it would use its central banking, taxing, and government spending power to make sure that everyone could have a job.

The Truman administration and later the Eisenhower administration saw these goals—full employment and regulated competition—as compatible and mutually reinforcing. Competition could provide a flexible system where prices could rise and fall consistent with changing conditions and changing movements of cost, price, and production.

This bill set up new public administrative machinery. It established a White House Council of Economic Advisors (CEA) to advise the president on the economy as a whole, providing an advisory council that could counter the traditional bank-friendly role that the treasury secretary had played as presidential advisor. It also established a Joint Economic Committee (JEC) in Congress, where members of the House and Senate could have a forum to deliberate broad economic strategy. Congress now had an official place to think about the future of the economy.

The bitter conflicts of the 1930s, between the Mellon system and

New Dealers, had also trained a generation of policymakers. The first president of the postwar order, Harry Truman, remembered the robber barons and hated both monopoly power and corruption.

"I was a member of the committee that investigated the utility scandal and recommended the holding company death sentence," he told the Missouri House and Senate as a senator. "It was my duty to sit day after day and listen to railroad woes and to learn how so-called great bankers, financiers, and rail management had ruined great transportation systems."[37] Every monopoly, he believed, had a "smug, public-be-damned attitude," which needed to be corrected with government action. During the war, he expressed excitement at breaking the Alcoa control over aluminum through government financing of the development of magnesium as a substitute, noting that "our shortage will be solved and a cutthroat monopoly broken up."[38]

Truman associated corruption with financial power. "To me, morality in government means more than a mere absence of wrongdoing," he told Democrats in 1952. "It means a government that is fair to all. I think it is just as immoral for the Congress to enact special tax favors into law as it is for a tax official to connive in a crooked tax return. It is just as immoral to use the lawmaking power of the Government to enrich the few at the expense of the many, as it is to steal money from the public treasury." This was a direct strike at Mellon. "All of us know, of course, about the scandals and corruption of the Republican officeholders in the 1920s," he continued. "But to my mind the Veterans' Administration scandals, in those days, and the Teapot Dome steal, were no worse—no more immoral—than the tax laws of Andrew Mellon.... Legislation that favored the greed of monopoly and the trickery of Wall Street was a form of corruption that did the country four times as much harm as Teapot Dome ever did."[39]

In 1949, Truman wrote Congressman Emanuel Celler, who had convened a special congressional subcommittee to study monopoly power, pledging his full support. "Since the end of the war, other matters, both foreign and domestic, have at times appeared to overshadow the monopoly problem, or at least have been the subject of greater public pre-occupation," Truman wrote. "But it is my conviction that year in and year out, there is no more serious problem affecting our country and its free institutions than the distortions and abuses of our economic system which result when unenlightened free enterprise turns to monopoly."[40] This wasn't just rhetoric; FTC and DOJ staff members routinely attended planning meetings for Celler's subcommittee.[41]

Wright Patman and Emanuel Celler in the House, and Estes Kefauver in the Senate, reinforced the ethics of this new Constitutional system with a constant barrage of oversight hearings, reports, and speeches. Through the Small Business Committee, Patman investigated concentration in banking and interlocking directorates. Celler debated the CEO of DuPont over his groundbreaking anti-merger law, passed in 1950, the Celler-Kefauver Act, which Eisenhower used to stop the Bethlehem Steel merger with Youngstown Steel (with positive economic effects).[42]

Antitrust enforcers and public officials thought of themselves as instruments of democratic power. Many had been influenced by Thurman Arnold, and fought in World War II. They learned a will to power, a respect for commercial systems, and skepticism toward bankers and would-be robber barons. They were backed up by members of Congress like Patman, who argued that "the way to defeat crooks is not to join them but to fight them relentlessly, to fight them without mercy or quarter."[43]

Truman's antitrust chief, Graham Morison, launched key suits against IBM and AT&T, both of which were essential to the formation of the electronics and computer industries. When he brought the AT&T suit, he had to fight against the Defense Department, which sought to have the government drop the case over national security concerns.[44] Morison then launched an investigation of the politically powerful Radio Corporation of America (RCA). Into the next administration there was sufficient integrity in the division that important suits moved forward without him. And Senator Estes Kefauver watched the entire process, with the implicit threat of oversight.[45]

Eisenhower, like Truman, had small-town roots; his father had owned a general store in Kansas. After World War II, Eisenhower made sure that the occupying authorities in Germany took apart the German goliath I. G. Farben.[46] Despite being friendly with many of the most powerful leaders in big business, Eisenhower would pursue a strong antimonopoly political framework when president.

The Eisenhower administration had an antitrust attorney named Robert Bicks, a rock-ribbed conservative who sought to assertively enforce the law. Bicks believed, as Eisenhower did, that if businessmen had done something wrong, they should be prosecuted. Bicks sued General Motors even though three of its executives served in Eisenhower's cabinet. He filed suits against General Electric, Westinghouse, RCA, Allied Chemical, U.S. Steel, and DuPont, even as the DuPont family gave $248,423 to Eisenhower in 1956. He went after Kennecott Copper, Bethlehem Steel, Firestone Rubber, Alcoa, and National Steel. Harvey Firestone was a good friend of Eisenhower's, former Eisenhower secretary of the treasury George Humphrey was the chairman of National Steel, and the Mellon family had given the GOP $106,000 in 1952.

When Eisenhower nominated Bicks to take over the Antitrust Division, it became clear how much opposition Bicks had generated. The opposition came from arch-segregationist Democratic senator "Big Jim" Eastland, who chaired the Judiciary Committee. Bicks had tried to prevent a beer merger between Pabst Blue Ribbon and Blatz. Eastland wanted it to go through, and tried to prevent the Senate from confirming Bicks as revenge.[47]

New Deal antitrust culture, built by Jackson and Arnold, and nurtured by Truman and Eisenhower, was so entrenched that in the late 1960s, Attorney General Ramsey Clark complained to Lyndon Johnson that he and his Antitrust Division head, Donald Turner, couldn't control his Antitrust Division, that they were a bunch of "wild horses."[48] Senators, high-level officials, and businessmen lobbied Morison, but the system was solid enough to withstand political meddling.

The private antitrust bar expanded dramatically. Private antitrust suits exploded. Individual lawyers could bring suits on behalf of competitors and suppliers and not rely on the government. In the first half-century of the Sherman Act, there were just 175 private antitrust suits, and plaintiffs rarely won. Over two thousand suits were filed in the 1950s.[49]

There was more competition, and increasing competition, in the economy at large. In 1940, there were 3,906 American corporations per million individuals. That number jumped to 4,367 in 1950, to 6,211 in 1960, and 7,936 by 1968.[50]

The most influential organization for business in Washington was no longer the hard-line U.S. Chamber of Commerce, but the Committee for Economic Development, a moderate group that sought to accommodate business to the New Deal and had supported the Employment Act of 1946. In 1946, the head of the U.S. Chamber of Commerce even said, "Labor unions are woven into our economic pattern of American life, and collective bargaining is a part of the democratic process. I say recognize this fact not only with our lips but with our hearts."[51]

The corporate CEO was still a powerful and influential actor both within the corporation and in the wider society. But his boss was no longer the investment banker. He had to look out for a mix of stakeholders: organized labor, antitrust enforcers, national security officials, regulators, shareholders, congressional leaders, suppliers, and customers. There was competition, but attempts to merge or collude with competitors could be met with a swift antitrust suit.

## A WORKER DEMOCRACY

In the 1930s and 1940s, America became a much more equal society, and into the 1960s, wage gains spread evenly across income brackets. Workers also participated in this new industrial structure. "The all-powerful tyrannic employer is all but gone," wrote David Lilienthal, a New Dealer celebrating the postwar economy of the 1950s. The Frick system, with workers enduring long hours, unsafe conditions, and no unions, was of concern to "only historians." Gone, he continued, were the "abuses of company stores, child labor, and 'yellow dog contracts.'" Though he was overstating the point, and ignoring the plight of millions of blacks in a segregated society, as well as poor Appalachian whites, Lilienthal wasn't wrong that most Americans had seen tremendous gains.[52]

By the 1950s, Americans were able to reminisce about the bad old days. Coal miners told stories of what it was like before the New

Deal. They talked of dragging out dead co-workers, of poor safety and ventilation. But another detail stuck out, of not being paid in dollars but in company scrip. One miner said, "We saved $20 in the office. They laid us off two weeks till we traded that $20 in the store. We had to trade it out in the store, or we didn't get to work no more. It was a company store. What we made, we had to go next evening and trade it off. If we didn't, they'd lay us off. They didn't let you draw no money at all. It was scrip."

That was in 1932. By the 1950s, "it was a lot different. They had the union there and we worked just seven hours and fifteen minutes. We didn't work as hard as when the Depression was on. . . . We made some good money, me and my dad, both." And when there were strikes, the police were on the side of the miners, confiscating the guns that the company had bought for its private police force.[53]

And on the farms? "I wanted to be at my parents' house when electricity came. It was in 1940. We'd all go around flipping the switch, to make sure it hadn't come on yet. We didn't want to miss it. When they finally came on, the lights just barely glowed. I remember my mother smiling. When they came on full, tears started to run down her cheeks. After a while, she said: 'Oh, if we only had it when you children were growing up.' We had lots of illness. Anyone who's never been in a family without electricity—with illness—can't imagine the difference."[54]

The shifts in the American order were unimaginably big for those who lived through them. Malaria and polio were vanquished, and antibiotics revolutionized treatment of infection. The South industrialized and broke free of its reliance on northern capital. A Supreme Court stacked with New Deal appointees from Roosevelt (including Robert Jackson) began to strike down the heart of Jim Crow. Clifford Durr, after various roles in government, wound up as the lawyer for Rosa Parks.

In his second inaugural address, Roosevelt had noted, "I see one-third of a nation ill-housed, ill-clad, ill-nourished. But it is not in despair that I paint you that picture. I paint it for you in hope—because the nation, seeing and understanding the injustice in it, proposes to paint it out."[55] And paint it out this new political order did. In 1940,

35 percent of Americans did not have flush toilets, including over 80 percent of residents in Mississippi and more than 70 percent of people in North Dakota. By 1970, nearly all Americans did. Less than half of households had washing machines or refrigerators in 1940. By 1970, more than 90 percent did.[56]

Harry Truman tried, and failed, to achieve universal health care. But health care coverage expanded through an employer-sponsored model. From 1950 to 1965, the percentage of Americans with surgical coverage jumped from 36 percent to 72 percent. Historian Alan Derickson said around this time, "Health insecurity became the exception rather than the rule."[57]

As millions of soldiers came home from World War II, policy-makers prepared the largest set of benefits for Americans since the Homestead Act in the form of the GI Bill. This was a direct result of Wright Patman's work in the 1930s, the Bonus Army, and the memory of what one congressman called the "stark tragedy of Anacostia Flats" and the bayonets and tear gas. "The long hard fight of the veterans of World War I for decent treatment," said Congressman Chet Holi-field, "has formed the foundation of this piece of veterans' legislation." These included low interest loans for farms, homes, and businesses, access to college and vocational training, and unemployment insurance. Veterans used these eagerly, with 49 percent taking advantage of the educational opportunities. By 1947 half of college students were veterans. Millions got loans and education, and these benefits helped spur the suburbanization of the country through home mortgages.[58]

Along with this material prosperity came increasing political liberalization. The New Deal framework allowed social movements to chip away at the inequities of race, gender, and sexual orientation. This started as early as 1932, when improved economic circumstances were far more compelling than what Hoover had to offer. African American voters began to move into the Democratic Party in 1932, flooding into the party by 1936.[59] While the early New Deal model loosened white supremacist control of American culture, this was not the explicit goal. Political leaders from the 1930s to the 1960s oversaw a massive improvement in race relations and economic rights over the KKK-infused 1920s, what one historian called a "second Reconstruction."[60]

New Deal government programs of the 1930s usually did not re-mediate racial inequality, nor did they end the fascist structure of the Jim Crow South. But for decades after 1940, wage gains for blacks were far higher than wage gains for whites. And the New Deal fight against monopoly did protect black-owned businesses throughout the country that were organizing platforms for racial equality.[61]

The New Deal not only elevated the economic rights of all Americans but created a platform by which people without access to political and social rights could petition for them. The civil rights movement used as key organizing platforms independent black-owned funeral parlors and grocers across the South. In the 1970s, gay rights leader Harvey Milk used his camera store as a political organizing base, a store protected as it was by the Robinson–Patman Act and fair trade laws. The civil rights, gay rights, and women's rights movements were built on top of the New Deal.

## THE ADVANCES OF THE FUTURE

In the 1950s, there was another wave of innovation born of wartime technologies. The railroad era had given birth to the first generation of robber barons, and every significant technological wave had opened up an opportunity for financiers to capture control of markets. The television and the computer could have as easily been captured as well.

But in the 1930s, Roosevelt, the New Deal Congress, and enforcers embarked on an aggressive set of attempts to decentralize the American communications apparatus. The Federal Communications Commission (FCC), set up in 1934 to oversee the telephone trust AT&T, as well as radio, wire, and eventually television, was a key actor in these fights. In the 1940s, the FCC and the Department of Justice's Antitrust Division split up RCA, which owned two national broadcasters, the National Broadcasting Company (NBC) and the Blue Network. The Blue Network was spun off, and renamed the American Broadcasting Company (ABC). The FCC and DOJ also blocked these national broadcasters from controlling local radio affiliates.[62]

The Antitrust Division also broke up the Hollywood boss system, whereby five large studios and three small ones controlled distribution of movies through ownership or coercive deals with theaters. Taking apart this system allowed independent filmmakers and artists to create and sell their work, and broke the ability of movie moguls to control the careers of actors. New Dealers sought to ensure that communications technology, whether in film, TV, radio, or over the phone, would not be controlled by a monopolistic or coercive business model.

Then in 1952, Graham Morison, the head of the Truman Antitrust Division, set out to democratize access to the technologies themselves, in ways that would allow the people themselves to determine the technological future of the nation. He did so through a suit against IBM. The company was the most important name in technology. It produced, serviced, and rented the tabular punch card business machines that powered the analytical capabilities of most large organizations, including much of the military apparatus. This rudimentary data processing had become indispensable to logistics. During the war, at Bletchley Park, where Alan Turing would help break the German codes, two million punch cards were used per week.

In World War II, a series of scientists and engineers worked out the basic architecture and model for a fully electronic computer, which threatened to make IBM's business obsolete. One of the first functional digital computers was known as the Electronic Numerical Integrator and Computer, or ENIAC, and was being constructed during the war. The men who invented it, J. Presper Eckert and John W. Mauchly, signed a contract with the U.S. Census Bureau in 1946 to replace the bureau's millions of tabular punch cards with their new device. Savvy strategists understood IBM's punch card business would eventually be replaced by the electronic computer.

Thomas Watson Sr. was not ignorant of these technological advances. He just didn't think that electronic computers were a good business. Watson believed IBM's business lay with its legacy punch card tabulators; electronic computers were unreliable and would not be profitable.

His son, however, saw the future. In 1952, Thomas Watson Jr. was ready to take over the company. He realized that electronic computers would require a strategic transformation in the business. But Thomas

Watson Sr. dominated the company, his big personality infusing it, making dissenting viewpoints, even from his son, difficult.

Morison, however, had no problems telling Watson Sr. to invest in the future rather than hold on to the past with monopolistic tactics. Morison was filing a lawsuit against IBM for attempting to control the tabular punch card industry. The company had been sued already for doing this, in 1936. "You have suppressed competition," said Morison, proceeding to list the various anticompetitive tactics IBM used to retain control over the punch card business. Morison even said he was being lenient. "IBM really deserves a criminal suit, but I've only filed a civil suit against your company."[63]

But he also said something with which the younger Watson agreed. "I believe, Mr. Watson, that in time, if you would go in right now and accept the decree, don't litigate, this will save your company. The technology of electronics, which is fast emerging, from all I can gather from the Bureau of Standards, and it is going to pass you by and you will be an antiquated company in the major business of your company."

Watson Sr. did not want to accept this reality, and in another era he would not have had to do so. He was a remarkable and remarkably cynical political operator. He had, for instance, found a way to sell punch card machines to both Nazi Germany and the United States during the war. He had put his political influence to work on Morison. Watson had had friends of Morison call and plead IBM's case, lobbying, as Morison recalled, with lines like, "Don't bring this suit against IBM. Mr. Watson is an aged man, it will kill him." Pat McCarran, a Nevada senator, threatened to have Morison's "hide" if he didn't drop the suit. But Morison pressed on. Watson had been a "robber baron," in Morison's words, "violating the antitrust laws and getting away with it for years."[64]

Morison wasn't just a courageous public servant. He was also pursuing administration policy. Truman's chief economic advisor, Leon Keyserling, encouraged Truman to consider the relationship of monopoly and technology. "The realm of science and its application to technology is expanding at a startling pace," he wrote. "And its limits are beyond calculation. The advances of the future can be made to serve the common welfare by affording opportunities for initiative and enterprise. Or they can contribute increasingly to the growth of private monopoly."[65] Morison would ensure that the electronic century would serve the common welfare.

IBM fought the suit for years, but it also moved into the electronic computer industry. This growth was spurred by the suit, but also by the market in analytical machines. IBM, under the leadership of Thomas Watson's son, made the IBM 650, the "Model T" of computers, in the middle of the twentieth century, and led the computer business. The company ramped up hiring engineers, and helped invent some of the early computer programming languages.

Years later, after IBM led the industry, Thomas Watson Jr. saw Morison at a Roper Conference. His father had died, and he was now head of IBM. "I've never forgotten what you told my father," he said. "I know you did it gently, and he, of course, was emotionally upset, but you are absolutely right. And as his son, I couldn't say it, but we were going to be passed by and just the pressure of this decree, because he dominated the company, was the only thing that saved us."[66]

Antitrust was a key fulcrum of policy. But there were others. Through government contracts, the Truman administration pushed IBM toward creating a computer business, while also forcing openness in the entire electronics industry. IBM built the SAGE Air Defense system in conjunction with the Massachusetts Institute of Technology, and did work for Los Alamos Laboratories of the Atomic Energy Commission and the National Security Agency.

This Eisenhower administration continued this policy. The Antitrust Division pushed to have knowledge developed inside the big corporation shared broadly, by forcing IBM to license its patents. AT&T and RCA encountered similar suits as part of government policy "to open up the electronics field." AT&T's Bell Labs invented the transistor. Because of the antitrust suit, however, the company had to allow anyone to use its knowledge, and a whole set of companies emerged to build electronic transistors. These three suits opened up the data processing, consumer electronics, and telecommunications fields to both

American and foreign competitors, and shaped the evolution of the computer.

Herbert Brownell, the attorney general in the Eisenhower administration, continued Morison's crusade. He called 1955 "the antitrust year."[67] And upon announcing the final settlement with IBM in 1956, he announced the underlying policy goal. "The recent developments of the revolutionary electronic machines" meant that antitrust action to open up the electronics business would "have far-reaching effects upon major segments of the business world."[68] In 1967, a threat of yet another antitrust suit against IBM spurred the company to unbundle its software business, leading to the creation of the modern software industry.

The new technologies of the postwar electronics era would not be controlled by robber barons. Astonishing technologies, from mainframe computers to networking, microprocessors, printing, computer memory systems, telecommunications equipment, audio and video equipment, copying technologies, and even the building blocks of the internet in the 1960s came forth in the "electronic century." Middle-level antitrust enforcers, trained in the New Deal tradition, served as what the great business historian Alfred Chandler called the "gods" of creation to bring forth the global information revolution.

## CHAPTER EIGHT

# CORPORATISTS STRIKE BACK

"To have failed to solve the problem of producing goods would have been to continue man in his oldest and most grievous misfortune. But to fail to see that we have solved it, and to fail to proceed thence to the next tasks, would be fully as tragic."

**—John Kenneth Galbraith**[1]

"I don't even believe students are dangerous or that all professors are subversive. Eggheads of the world, arise— you have nothing to lose but your yolks."

**—Adlai Stevenson, 1956**[2]

▪ ▪ ▪ ▪ ▪ ▪ ▪ ▪ ▪ ▪ ▪ ▪ ▪

In 1944, Wright Patman faced a rocky reelection. He had two opponents, both backed by big money. Abe Mays, a former legislator and Atlanta merchant, was merciless about the congressman's career. Patman, said Mays, was corrupt. He had gone to Washington and didn't spend time in the district. He was a "handler of the yes-man bill" creating wartime price limits, and a "trained seal . . . for the bureaucrats."[3] And he was helping the communists "learn how to control the United States." Yet another candidate, Harold Beck, accused Patman of being insufficiently violent in protecting "states' rights," which was code for racial segregation. Oil money was pouring in against Patman, and his allies.[4]

It didn't work. There was a war on, a war America was winning, in which it was fighting alongside the Soviet Union. The people of Texarkana loved Wright Patman; he was handily reelected. The attack on Patman was the start of a newly assertive vitriolic right-wing movement, organized by plutocrats. This movement would flower into the second "Red Scare" in the late 1940s, eventually whipped into hysteria by FBI director J. Edgar Hoover, turning into unhinged anticommunist attacks by Wisconsin senator Joseph McCarthy in the early 1950s.

At the end of World War I, reactionaries had grabbed control of the American political order. Now, after World War II, they were trying to do it again.

Patman's foe in 1944 was no longer Mellon, the plutocrat from the Northeast who had along with Frick destroyed Wilson's New Freedom after World War I. The paranoid right-wing organizers of the Red Scare came mostly from a new set of plutocrats who lived in Patman's home state of Texas.

These men were called the "Big Rich," a small set of ultraconservative oil tycoons, grown wealthy, ironically, from the war and from New Deal policies of the 1930s.[5] In 1944, they created the Texas Regulars, an anti-labor, anti-government, anti-Roosevelt group. The Regulars were Democrats, but on the far right of the American political spectrum, calling explicitly for the "restoration of the supremacy of the white race" and seeking, along with national conservative groups, to pass a Constitutional amendment essentially overturning the federal income tax. Aside from the 1944 challenge to Patman, the Regulars also ran lavishly funded unsuccessful campaigns against Sam Rayburn and Lyndon Johnson. They tried, and failed, to keep Texas's electoral votes from going to Roosevelt. "All they do," said Rayburn, "is hate."[6]

In 1944, these new plutocrats failed. But an environment for a campaign of fear was ripening. In 1945, Americans celebrated victory over Japan. The celebration was short-lived, because of the fear induced by the reality of atomic weapons. Later that year, over a quarter of Americans came to believe the world would be destroyed in a series of atomic explosions. In early 1946, once-ally Joseph Stalin seemed to confirm this fear with a pugilistic speech about the superiority of the Soviet system, as the Red Army remained in Eastern Europe while the American Army mostly came home, leaving Western Europe seemingly defenseless.[7] Domestically, inflation and the largest wave of strikes in American history broke out.

An anticommunist campaign of fear enveloped the nation. In 1946, a young California conservative named Richard Nixon won a seat in Congress by calling his opponent's voting record "more Social-istic and Communistic than Democratic." The head of the Republican National Committee said voters faced a choice "between Commu-nism and Americanism," as the Democrats were intent on "sovietizing" the country.[8] Nixon not only won his seat in Congress that year, but Republicans won control of the U.S. House of Representatives for the first time since 1930. Fear worked. Fear of communism. Fear of strikes. Fear of anticommunist witch hunts. And in the late 1940s, the A&P fought its battles, and as the postwar intellectual order coalesced, the FBI, wealthy Texas conservatives, and their allies in Congress helped organize a wave of terror throughout American culture. One designed in no small part to grease the return of the monopolists.

Anticommunist crusades swept through American culture, orga-nized by FBI director J. Edgar Hoover and promoted by Senator Jo-seph McCarthy (both on the payroll of the Texas oil barons). More than a fifth of American jobholders had to go through a security or loyalty program.[9]

The House Un-American Activities Committee scoured aca-demia and Hollywood, not just for foreign agents, but those sym-pathetic toward organized labor and the New Deal. Antimonopolists found themselves targets. Clifford Durr, who had set up the Defense Plant Corporation to build the arsenal of democracy against the Nazis, breaking Mellon's aluminum empire in the process, had gone on to become an official with the FCC. Durr resigned his position in gov-ernment rather than submit to loyalty oaths.[10] Many who had been sympathetic to communism in the late 1930s, so-called "parlor pinks," and those actively in the campaign against racial segregation, were swept up into a cultural dragnet.

Patman tried to ward off the anticommunist hysteria with a good attack. Just before the 1946 election, he told a radio host, "the same Fascism that was fabricated in Italy and finished in Germany is now being peddled in America." He named prominent Republican media tycoons and lobbyists, and said they would "attack, defame and destroy, and especially destroy labor and fool the farmers," using fear of com-munism as a weapon.[11]

The next year, the Library of Congress produced a book at Patman's request, titled *Fascism in Action,* a look at the economy, culture, government, and labor relations of fascist countries. The book warned that fascism could happen in America, that it was rooted in ancient ideas and institutions of privilege. But by 1947, the environment was so hostile that Patman had to engage in a fight on the House floor just to have his book published.[12] Meanwhile, the Library of Congress, at the behest of a faction of right-wing members, had the year before published a similar book, *Communism in Action.* Congress printed hundreds of thousands of copies, at government expense.[13]

The Red Scare was particularly brutal for academics. One important target was Robert Oppenheimer, the liberal who spearheaded the development of the atomic bomb, who had his security clearance stripped. The newly professionalizing field of economics, increasingly ensconced in the academies and using anti-plutocratic Keynesian economic theories, was vulnerable to the anticommunist charges. In 1951, oil heir William F. Buckley published a best-seller, *God and Man at Yale,* which attacked Keynesian ideas as illustrative of liberal moral laxity and communistic leanings.

Conservatives sent letters to the trustees of universities that used the first textbook on Keynesian economics, destroying the career of its author, a Canadian student of Keynes, Lorie Tarshis. Tarshis's book was well written and had sold well initially. In it, Tarshis bluntly discussed the relationship between democracy and the economy.[14] His approach to Keynesian ideas about the role of government opened him up to attack, and sales fell off as the conservative attack intensified. Economists such as Paul Samuelson got the message. Samuelson wrote a foundational textbook on economics in 1948, marketed as incorporating Keynesian insights. But in it he avoided the more controversial arguments by Keynes, such as observations about the perils introduced by instability on Wall Street. Samuelson was aware of the "virulence of the attack on Tarshis," so he prepared his text "carefully and lawyer like."[15]

But the two differed on more than just Keynesian assumptions about investment. Samuelson, unlike Tarshis, tried to avoid talking plainly about power. In Tarshis's textbook, Tarshis singled out aluminum as a monopolistic industry and included a chapter on the need to fight monopoly. Samuelson, however, differed subtly. In his discussion of monopoly, he argued that, though Americans might prefer small-scale competitors over large monopolistic corporations, in reality they had little choice but to devise "ways to improve the social and economic performance of large corporate aggregates."[16]

In time, the Red Scare impacted the nature of the economic debate. Economists retreated into mathematized technical jargon to disguise political leanings. The impact of the turn away from plain, popularly accessible language on political economy and toward passive-sounding depictions of social and economic structures would play out over decades; in 1951, *The American Economic Review* "contained a mathematical expression without an empirical use" on just 2 percent of its pages. In 1981, nearly half of the pages in the journal did.[17]

When antimonopolists did speak out, they faced an assertive backlash. In 1949, Congressman Emanuel Celler held hearings on monopoly power to prepare to pass his anti-merger bill. "From the opening day," he wrote, "I was the subject of cartoons and editorials, copy for columnists, and for feature article writers. Celler was destroying the American heritage. Celler was going to chop down all big business into tiny segments and scatter the pieces. Celler was tinkering with the economic machinery and throwing a monkey wrench in the works."[18] Celler could and did stand against this backlash, and his bill, one of the most important antitrust bills of the twentieth century, passed. But economists largely did not stand against the red-baiting tide.

Three things were happening simultaneously. First, Brandeisian antimonopolism was being fully embraced by the Eisenhower administration, normalizing the institutional thinking and practices perfected by the New Dealers. At the same time, a wing of the Republicans was using anticommunism against exposed Democrats. They couldn't really train their firepower on the Eisenhower White House, so they targeted the left.

But there was another, and in some ways more subversive, attack hidden in the hysteria. In the midst of this wave of fear, a group of former New Dealers and corporate leaders responded to anticommunist attacks by beginning to develop the basis for taking down populism. The red-baiting and paranoid corporate right had gone after their enemies. At the same time, and much more quietly, the corporate left, those who had lost the battle during the New Deal to Brandeis over central planning and monopoly, found the Red Scare equally convenient to do the same thing.

There was, in other words, a complex double assault on Brandeisian populism, from both the paranoid red-baiting corporate right, and from the corporate left, who began to frame their reformist corporatist thinking as "the vital center."

## THE CORPORATIST COMEBACK

In 1941, at age eighty-four, Louis Brandeis died of a heart attack. He had remained active until the end of his life, helping Patman with chain store legislation after his retirement from the court. But he left no clear intellectual heir. His legacy would be carried on by practical politicians, small business leaders, trained regulators, law professors, and populists who supported FDR on most issues, but split with him by opposing chain stores and supporting the Veterans Bonus.

The anticommunist environment of the 1940s and early 1950s threw the New Deal coalition into disarray. No longer could administration officials taking on big business count on being protected by FDR or Congress. A corporate lawyer and Roosevelt advisor, Adolf Berle, along with a social circle of New Dealers, took advantage of this moment to centralize control over liberalism.[19] Berle was part of the Americans for Democratic Action, a group that sought to eject communists and assertive leftists from the Democratic Party. ADA members, and Berle in particular, built strong alliances with progressive big business leaders.

Coming out of the war was a powerful network of corporate executives who were happy to work with this new corporatist left. Many big business executives had developed personal relationships with corporatist liberals in the administration, coming to see a shared interest with the nascent anti-populist liberal elite in structuring a postwar order. They were willing, in some cases even eager, to accept a strong reformist state, but in return wanted to work with progressive planners who didn't mind entrenching corporate power, versus populists, who sought to diminish it.[20]

Moderate business leaders coalesced around the Committee for Economic Development, rather than the more reactionary U.S.

Chamber of Commerce. Berle's intellectual partner from the early New Deal era, Gardiner Means, served as economist for the CED. Joining this project in constructing a new American liberalism was Henry Luce, whose burgeoning publishing empire included *Fortune* and *Time,* and who had framed this period as "The American Century." The corporate left in academia, progressive big business leaders, and the Luce empire would restructure what it meant to be a liberal.

Berle was deeply elitist, and brought his elitism into his thinking about corporate power. He was one of Roosevelt's original "Brain Trust" advisors, the group that lost power after the fiasco of the National Industrial Recovery Act. Berle was also a foe of Brandeis, and believed large businesses were more efficient, and that pushing for small-scale enterprise was hopelessly backward. In 1912, Berle was so aligned with big business that he had supported William Howard Taft.[21]

By the 1930s, Berle had become part of the Republican progressive faction that had come into the Democratic Party, supportive of state control over monopolies. A brilliant student graduating from high school at thirteen, Berle came from moralistic Calvinist stock, building a successful practice as a corporate lawyer in the 1920s. In 1932, Berle and Means wrote *The Modern Corporation and Private Property,* which became one of the most cited legal texts on corporate law of all time.

Berle was deeply anti-populist, a Bull Moose progressive planner. Throughout the New Deal, Berle was relentless in his attempt to soften Roosevelt's approach to big business. In the 1938 recession, he attempted to organize a "grand truce" between J. P. Morgan, General Electric, and the CIO labor union. His populist opponents were never far; *The Milwaukee Journal* called this attempt "fascist."[22]

Berle was also deeply ideological, with a dream of becoming the "American Karl Marx." And he transformed the meaning of the word "liberal" into something meaning top-down elitist planning, subtly recrafting the New Deal into something it hadn't been.

"Liberalism" had been a word Roosevelt used to organize his political movement. In 1932, a reporter asked Roosevelt to describe his political philosophy. Roosevelt called himself "a liberal." This did not mean, as classical liberalism had meant in much of the previous era, protecting the rights of industrial barons using the rhetoric of self-sufficiency. It meant moral leadership, the willingness to address a civilizational crisis by updating the machinery of governance. A liberal, Roosevelt said, broke from the past, but not too quickly to provoke violence.[23]

After the war, Berle would again redefine the term "liberal," slowly changing it to mean a form of soft corporatism. He did this by using the Red Scare to centralize power over postwar policy development into a small network of planners and Ivy League intellectuals, what conservatives derisively called "eggheads." Over the next twenty-five years, liberalism would come to mean a gentle form of elitism. And since Roosevelt had called himself a liberal, this became what Democratics increasingly believed the New Deal had been.

After the war, Berle based his intellectual work out of the Twentieth Century Fund, a New York–based think tank respected by progressives for its studies on stock market regulation and Social Security. The fund adopted a quasi-scientific approach to social questions, appointing a mix of experts to study specific issues. It explicitly based its strategy around intermingling corporate and government officials with academics, much in the way Brookings had done in Washington.[24]

With Berle as chairman, the Twentieth Century Fund sought to assert intellectual leadership over liberalism. It developed relationships with nascent television stations, as well as newspapers, large corporations, civil society institutes, and political officials. Everything from the problem of inflation to tariffs to technological progress to urban planning to economic foreign policy was covered by its network of scholars, labor allies, and business leaders. The results of the think tank's studies were blasted out over the air, and written about in newspapers, magazines, and among columnists.

The environment was conducive to new kinds of thinking, and not just because of the atomic bomb. After the war, the depression, contrary to expectations, did not return, both because fragile balance sheets had been cleaned up by wartime finance, and because policymakers ensured it would not with new policy tools. Instead there was seemingly endless bounty; Americans were rich and getting richer.[25]

While this new generation of business leaders found planning and government spending eminently reasonable, and even accommodated unions, antimonopolism was a different matter. After the war, Truman almost immediately decided to allow the resurrection of antitrust suits that had been suspended during the conflict.[26] In 1948, Truman won reelection, partially on the strength of his campaign against monopoly.[27]

Several other events alarmed business leaders. In 1950, Emanuel Celler passed the landmark anti-merger Celler-Kefauver Act, and ran a special subcommittee investigating monopoly practices. Then in 1953, the Eisenhower administration made clear it intended to continue with aggressive enforcement. The Truman and Eisenhower continuation of assertive antitrust enforcement was, to some business leaders, like A&P, an existential threat.

For this generation of enforcers, the final great antitrust battle against A&P was a crucial learning experience. While the Department of Justice and the Federal Trade Commission restructured the company, A&P's sophisticated attacks on the antitrust laws took their toll. Two-thirds of Americans supported the chain over the government.[28]

A&P wasn't the only company seeking to reorganize how Americans understood big business. The Truman administration attempted to sever DuPont's control of General Motors, in one of the most ambitious antitrust suits of the era. DuPont embarked on a public relations campaign, even going so far as to have its president, Crawford Greenewalt, debate Celler in *Reader's Digest*.[29] General Motors spent $50,000 on survey research just to find out what Americans thought of big business.[30] AT&T fought against its antitrust suit with arguments about national security, noting its capable stewardship of the nation's atomic arsenal.[31] Toward the end of the decade, a Bell publicist also began a long-term campaign to reshape the study of academic history.[32]

During the Red Scare, this fierce reaction against antitrust enforcement had an effect. Both corporate leaders and corporatist planners were able to push aside traditional liberal antimonopoly thinking. In the 1940s, the Twentieth Century Fund commissioned a series of studies expressing the conventional wisdom of liberal antimonopolism, overseen by the well-respected New Deal official James Landis. There were reports on cartels in 1946 and 1948, and a volume on monopolies published in 1951.[33] The study on monopoly power received enormous pushback from General Electric and Westinghouse. "This was the only study in the Fund's history," said a confidential internal memo by a fund official, "in which all our releases, review summary, etc., were gone over by a lawyer." The next study on monopoly should, it said, portray "a business firm as hero, hampered by public misunderstanding and stupid, inflexible laws" because "that kind of story would be welcomed in business circles and publications with open arms."[34] When the next study came out, it endorsed certain forms of monopolies. The author of the study soon became the chief economist of the Federal Trade Commission.[35]

Growing numbers of intellectuals embraced bigness and monopoly, circling in and out of the various networks of academia, foundations, corporations, and Luce's media empire. A wave of books made the case that the new prosperity was a function of cooperation among big labor, big business, and big government. These books were written by intellectuals on the left, like C. Wright Mills, nascent big business progressives like Peter Drucker, former New Dealer turned investment banker David Lilienthal, famous historian Richard Hofstadter, and popular economist John Kenneth Galbraith.[36]

While there was much disagreement among these writers, the common theme was a general approval of bigness and central planning. And what unified these thinkers with big business progressives was their disdain for the attack on A&P, a case that represented an attack on their whole model of political economy. These men respected expert planning, not small-town yeoman citizenry. These writers looked at the world the way A&P executives did; Americans, in their view, were not citizens, but consumers.

David Lilienthal, who had once been a Brandeis disciple and run the Tennessee Valley Authority under Roosevelt, turned vehemently against the Jeffersonian ideal of yeoman citizenry. The centralization of power by chain stores like A&P, he said, represented "the most spectacular change in the face of everyday American life." Lilienthal argued that "bigness . . . served the consumer's interest," not only improving food quality and hygiene, but even helping Americans achieve "democratic aspirations."[37]

The anticapitalist Mills, who popularized the term "New Left" to describe the emerging young counterculture generation, mocked labor leaders for failing to fight for the nationalization of industry. He lauded "more efficient and cheaper" chain stores and approvingly quoted a New Deal agricultural economist turned Kraft Foods executive demanding we simply accept them due to the "ineptitude of the average person." Mills reserved special venom for small businessmen, such as those who ran groceries and small stores competing with A&P. These were the "lumpen-bourgeoisie," petty, aggressive, repressed, patriarchal, and dull.[38] Mills denounced the idea that small businesspeople, or anyone, understood their own self-interest, believing such an assumption to be a "fetish of democracy."[39] Americans were consumers, and should get used to it.

The most important scholars in this movement to transform the American from a citizen to a consumer were historian Richard Hofstadter and economist John Kenneth Galbraith. Both men were part of this postwar corporatist network, hired as consultants and promoted by Berle's Twentieth Century Fund.[40] Both were spectacular writers, using popular prose that overwhelmed millions of readers with beauty, originality, and wit. They would create a new language to displace the antimonopolist tradition.

Hofstadter would shape a new vision of history, while Galbraith would create a popularized version of technocracy on the left. They would win prizes and accolades, and shape the minds of Americans, who, now living in a world free of robber barons, were soon told, gently, and over and over, that robber barons had never really existed. They would—in time—displace Brandeis's creed.

## RICHARD HOFSTADTER: CONSENSUS HISTORY AND STATUS ANXIETY

When Republican presidential candidate Dwight D. Eisenhower defeated the more cerebral Democratic candidate Adlai Stevenson in 1952, the thirty-six-year-old historian Richard Hofstadter panicked. Hofstadter agreed with Stevenson, that the election of Eisenhower was a replacement of "the New Dealers by the car dealers." A rising star in the elite liberal firmament, Hofstadter believed he was witnessing an "apocalypse for intellectuals in public life."[41]

For Hofstadter, Harry Truman had been bad enough. Truman was no intellectual. He was a populist from Missouri and had not graduated from college; for Hofstadter, Truman's "impassioned rhetoric, with its occasional thrusts at 'Wall Street,' seemed passé and rather embarrassing."[42]

By contrast, the Democratic nominee in 1952 and 1956, Adlai Stevenson, was a beloved intellectual who surrounded himself with Ivy League men. Stevenson stood up to the anticommunists, but not the plutocrats; in between presidential runs, he defended the powerful communications company RCA against Eisenhower's Antitrust Division.[43] Stevenson opposed public funding for housing, union power, "socialized medicine," civil rights for blacks, agricultural stabilization policies, and deficit spending.[44] But Stevenson was eloquent and beautifully spoken, and earned Hofstadter's ardent support.

The Red Scare had terrified Hofstadter; Eisenhower's victory even more so. So he did what he could to fight back, combining his skills as a historian and polemicist. He began to study right-wing extremism, and created a social language to root it in American history. He used new tools, tools developed by sociologists, iconoclasts such as Thorstein Veblen and Sigmund Freud, especially Freudian arguments about "status anxiety." He began to imply, though not state outright, that conservative politics was a mental disease, a condition called the "Authoritarian Personality."[45] Angry and increasingly elitist liberals, in thrall to the pull of corporatism, loved it.

Richard Hofstadter would go on to be one of the most important historians of the middle of the twentieth century, inventing new techniques through which to study history, and rewriting the American tradition with a series of beautifully sculpted books and essays. One, *The Paranoid Style in American Politics,* is resurrected every election cycle to explain fringe and extreme attacks. Another of his essays, "What Happened to the Antitrust Movement," was perhaps the most influential work written on monopoly politics since Brandeis's *Other People's Money.* Hofstadter was, as one scholar put it, "*the* historian of the [postwar] generation."[46]

And fear would be his touchstone. Like many of the planners who later aligned with big business, Hofstadter grounded his intellectual foundation in the crucible of the depression, leading him to join the Communist Party and become a "parlor pink," a lightly committed hobbyist in radical politics rather than a hard-core organizer. He didn't last long in the party, feeling that intellectual freedom was not a value embedded in autocratic communism. He turned elitist, coming to believe there was no place for intellectuals among the working class. In 1940, he confided to a friend that he feared striking American autoworkers were more likely to adopt fascism than socialism. Were those workers to gain power, he believed they would target intellectuals like himself.

During World War II, Hofstadter lived in Washington, D.C., teaching at the University of Maryland. He became friendly with a group of left-wing scholars who lunched together and bonded over what Hofstadter's biographer called "the group's common hostility for Roosevelt, the war, capitalism, and southerners."[47] Unlike most men of his age and in his era, Hofstadter sought to avoid service in World War II, a decision that nagged at his conscience. He had appealed to the draft board, arguing that teaching soldiers made him an essential civilian employee. He later claimed allergies and digestive trouble, but confessed to his son that that he wouldn't have had the courage for war.[48]

While in person Hofstadter could be engaging and friendly, his charm masked a fear that his half-Jewish heritage would inhibit his career.[49] This was not an unreasonable concern; his ascension in the immediate postwar generation of scholars was precisely when Jewish academics such as Paul Samuelson and Milton Friedman struggled to get tenure at top universities.

Hofstadter soon wrote a series of powerful books. In 1948, with *The American Political Tradition and the Men Who Made It,* he developed a new historical narrative that reinforced what the postwar big business progressives were organizing. Hofstadter argued that these traditions were not ideological but cultural, founded upon the nefarious force of Anglo-Saxon puritanism of the Midwest and southern "heartland." Historians had traditionally seen mass movements of the Midwest and South, such as the farmers' revolts of the nineteenth century, as populist; Hofstadter recast them as oppressive cultural reactions to modernization. He contrasted Anglo-Saxonism with polyglot, tolerant, and forward-looking immigrant cultures of eastern cities.[50]

This narrative would come to be called "consensus history," and with it, Hofstadter began the process of erasing the key intellectual and political struggle of the New Deal and the entire Jeffersonian tradition. Consensus history rested on two assumptions about the American past. The first was, according to Hofstadter, an "absence of deep, persistent, and consistent class conflict" throughout American history. The second was that nearly all Americans of any political importance shared "common, bourgeois, entrepreneurial assumptions" about the value of capitalism.[51] In Hofstadter's telling, as one contemporary critic noted, Americans had no real ideological disagreements over political economy.[52] Hofstadter did not like capitalism, which he associated with the small businessman and farmer. He liked bigness; it was the scientist and technocrat who was the hero, the bringer of the future.

This narrative, however, created a problem. It was impossible to ignore the many mass movements and American figures who stood outside such a consensus, such as the populists of the nineteenth century or independent retailers opposed to A&P's power. Hofstadter solved this problem by recasting such factions not as ideological rivals to concentrated capital, but as groups of nostalgia-driven Anglo-Saxon white men irrationally adhering to an "American mythology," seeking to return to a time when their racial group was the most important part of the social order and struggling with modernity and cosmopolitanism.

In Hofstadter's hands, Thomas Jefferson's rhetoric about agrarian democracy and against monopolies and financial power became utterly cynical, hypocritical, and backward-looking. Hofstadter pronounced nineteenth-century populists as "equally cynical in design" for attempting to regulate railroad power and for passing the Sherman Antitrust Act. The populists of the 1890s were not so much against monopolies, he implied in his next book, *The Age of Reform,* as they were nascent fascists.[53] It was a book written for frightened elitist liberals in the McCarthy era, and in 1956 Hofstadter won the Pulitzer Prize for history.

Hofstadter even scorned Roosevelt, calling him identical to Hoover in everything but temperament. Both, after all, believed in an Anglo-Saxon form of capitalism. "When Hoover bumbled that it was necessary only to restore confidence, the nation laughed bitterly," Hofstadter argued. "When Roosevelt said: 'The only thing we have to fear is fear itself,' essentially the same threadbare half-true idea, the nation was thrilled. Hoover had lacked motion; Roosevelt lacked direction."[54]

Several contemporary historians considered Hofstadter's writing "highly manipulative," and his work was not based in actual historical primary source evidence.[55] Nevertheless, with his succinct writing style, his placement within powerful Democratic networks, and keen sense of what kinds of ideas could sell, his work would prove to become essential to dampening the American intellectual suspicion toward concentrated financial power.

Hofstadter's development of consensus history paralleled the overall move that postwar planners and companies like A&P were attempting to organize, a consensus among big business, big labor, and big government. It was perhaps not surprising then that Hofstadter was hired as a consultant not only to examine business ideology by the Twentieth Century Fund, but also by the Fund for the Republic (a spin-off the Ford Foundation), to examine extremist groups on the right and left.[56]

In time, Hofstadter's work would help to all but erase the American historical tradition—tracing to the Revolution itself—that held that the great ideological conflict was between democracy and monopoly. "Americans may not have quarreled over profound ideological matters," he wrote early in his career, "as these are formulated in the history of political thought, but they quarreled consistently enough over issues that had real pith and moment." *Pith and moment* was a beautiful phrase, but what Hofstadter meant was that there were no conflicts in America in political economy, only social anxiety. It was too scary for Hofstadter to concede that democratic movements were anything but a rabid mob.[57]

## JOHN KENNETH GALBRAITH: THE POLITICS OF AFFLUENCE

Thanks to Louis Brandeis, and Senator John Sherman before him, Democrats had found a way to structure commerce around the concept of industrial liberty. Whether farmers, manufacturers, shopkeepers, or workers, this kind of competition policy centered on engineering maximum liberty for the producer as opposed to the financier or monopolist.

In 1958, a new concept replaced industrial liberty: affluence. That year, John Kenneth Galbraith, already one of the most famous economists in America, published the best-selling book *The Affluent Society,* plucking the word "affluence" from the realm of the esoteric and turning it into a household phrase. For millions of Americans, Galbraith helped explain the exceptional increases in wealth they had experienced since the dark days of the depression. He explained it not as a triumph of policy, but as an inevitability of the munificent monopolies around them.

Galbraith's writing had immense charm and style, both simple to understand and seeming to let the reader into a world of power and secrets. He created, for instance, the phrase "the conventional wisdom," a subversive way of characterizing commonly held opinions. He pandered to his readers, naming the large group of young college-educated Americans as part of what he called "the New Class," and telling them they were the most essential people in society.

Galbraith's argument was simple: America was rich. Modern institutions, meaning big government, big business, and big labor, had evolved to produce more and more over time, using the fabulous technology that came from the corporate research labs and new universities. Yet, politics was still rooted in questions of scarcity, poverty, and class conflict. "These—productivity, inequality and insecurity—were the ancient preoccupations of economics," he wrote. No longer.[58]

Not only had the large corporation and modern technology solved the problem of production, but the structure of big corporations, big labor unions, and big government had emerged to distribute wealth relatively equally among workers and executives. Old ideas, such as antimonopolism, what Galbraith dubbed "the conventional wisdom," dominated political debates. The key, he almost whispered to his readers, as if discussing a kindly but doddering old man sitting across the room, was that these old ideas did not matter. The wealthy of the 1950s were neither powerful nor important. Wall Street was irrelevant. The state was firmly in control of the ship, guiding a course toward ever sunnier climes.

Both political parties embraced the concept of affluence. John F. Kennedy in a 1962 speech at Yale said, "What is at stake in our economic decisions today is not some grand warfare of rival ideologies . . . but the practical management of a modern economy."[59] Nixon's view in his first inaugural in 1969 was indistinguishable: "We have learned at last to manage a modern economy to assure its continued growth."[60] By 1970, economist Juanita Kreps, later commerce secretary under Jimmy Carter, testified that productivity and computerization should in a few years allow Americans to retire by age thirty-eight.[61]

Galbraith became the voice for 1950s liberal consensus politics, and helped end liberal suspicion of concentrated financial power. In 1952, he simply sliced the great fights of Wilson, and Brandeis, and Patman, and Pecora, and all the other antimonopolists right out of the history books. Instead, he mocked Brandeis's "somewhat tenuous belief in a 'money trust,'" and praised corporate monopolies. "There must be some element of monopoly in an industry," he wrote, "if it is to be progressive."[62]

Galbraith's progressive politics, including his lifelong alliance with big business, were forged in the 1930s, magnified during World War II, and solidified by the Red Scare. Galbraith, as ambitious as he was talented, understood that the Red Scare was not merely a threat to free expression, but to his own career. He understood the vitriol of right-wing conservatives earlier than most, tangling with Congress in the 1930s and 1940s.

Before the war, Galbraith, by training an agricultural economist, worked in the Agriculture Department, and saw liberal allies purged by southern conservatives over an attempt to distribute farm supports to black sharecroppers.[63] Galbraith later went to Harvard, and then traveled to England to learn from John Maynard Keynes. At Harvard, he became a believer in corporate planning, working with Henry Dennison, a liberal businessman who would be involved in the business-planning group the Committee for Economic Development, as well as the Twentieth Century Fund.

His first significant position was to run one of the key planning institutions during the war, the Office of Price Administration (OPA), under famous New Deal liberal Leon Henderson. This was a high-profile and important role for which Galbraith became famous. "From the spring of 1941, I controlled all prices in the United States," he said. "You could lower a price without my permission, but you couldn't raise a price without my permission or that of my staff."[64]

Galbraith's job was to fight inflation, a difficult task in a war-time economy straining to produce consumer and military goods at maximum volume. The OPA under Galbraith put in place a structure for restraining price increases of farm products and canned foods, but one that was especially confusing to farmers and small stores.

This experience reinforced his belief in command-and-control statism and the virtues of concentration. It was far easier to work with chain stores such as A&P to fix prices. Galbraith wanted to standardize product quality and fix prices, instead of allowing independent brands and pricing. This put him in direct conflict with thousands of independent retailers and manufacturers who sought to make and sell what they wanted. He came to believe America's economic system was composed of big, powerful, and efficient corporate enterprises willing to work with government, and smaller reactionary ones run by men who had decided to, as he put it, "self-exploit."[65] And since Galbraith had organized wartime price controls, he felt confident that a top-down, centrally planned system delivered a progressive social order.

While he was at OPA, conservatives in Congress began attacking the entire OPA as having "Communistic" leanings, singling out Galbraith for special scorn (an irony, as the U.S. was then allied with the Soviet Union). Much of the problem stemmed from industry carping by the smaller businessmen who bucked Galbraith's diktats. The head of the National Retail Dry Goods Association accused Galbraith, somewhat accurately, of trying to "change the business structure of the nation under the guise of war necessity."[66] And their criticisms were not without foundation. Their fear that the OPA was discriminating in favor of big chain stores was rooted in hard experience. In World War I, war mobilization had been used to enlarge the power of monopolies, because it was simply easier for a government board to deal with a smaller number of larger players. Patman himself, who headed a special committee on small business and otherwise supported the OPA, caught on fast, expressing frustration that OPA was favoring a "relatively few larger distributors to the detriment of the rank and file of retailers and wholesalers."[67]

But it wasn't only small retailers who targeted Galbraith. His imperious manner incurred the wrath of everyone from pig farmers to large food processors.[68] When Henderson was forced out of the OPA, it was only a matter of time for Galbraith. He resigned. Patman, who actively supported price controls and the administration, and who would later count Galbraith among his favorite economists, commented, "It certainly won't hurt OPA to have [Galbraith] resign. There is a general feeling that he has been OPA's fly in the ointment and I am sure his action will be constructive rather than damaging."[69] Galbraith's resignation brought him fame as a liberal martyr.

Galbraith is rightfully viewed as a hero, in many respects. After the war he found himself as a fact-finder in a dispute within the military, over whether the large strategic bombing campaigns by the British and American air forces in Germany had succeeded. He found, through captured documents and interviews with Nazi officials, that they had not. German war-making production had increased throughout the war; Galbraith estimated that only 5 percent of the damage inflicted had been done by the U.S. Army Air Force.[70] Because of these experiences, Galbraith had the confidence to stand up against nascent Cold War militarism, and later became an early opponent of the war in Vietnam, which endeared him to the emerging New Left.

To avoid a repeat of his experience being fired from the OPA, Galbraith insulated himself, at least partially, in networks of fellow elites, including Berle's. For several years, he had a key role as an organizer of the progressive big business alliance. Galbraith worked for Republican media magnate Henry Luce at the business publication *Fortune,* where he convinced business leaders to accept a business–friendly form of Keynesian economics.

Galbraith also, to help protect his own career and those of key allies from McCarthyite attacks, helped form Americans for Democratic Action, Berle's anticommunist group full of ex–New Dealers, union leaders, and many allies from the OPA, drawing in the progressive anticommunist left. In 1952, he followed the path of many of the egghead liberals, from general apathy and disdain toward the uneducated Truman, to campaign advisor for Adlai Stevenson. In 1953, he was hired along with Hofstadter by the Twentieth Century Fund to study monopoly in the American economy. He would eventually join the think tank's board.[71]

Returning to Harvard from *Fortune,* Galbraith ran into more difficulties with the McCarthyism of the business world. Business leaders on the board of the Harvard Corporation opposed his bid for tenure.

They pointed to his Keynesian outlook and the bombing survey as evidence of radicalism. Finally, in the name of academic freedom, the conservative president of Harvard, James Conant, threatened to resign if Galbraith wasn't appointed. His appointment went through.[72]

Galbraith benefited from the new direction of economics. The newly professionalizing field of economists stopped writing for a mass audience. Galbraith seized the opportunity to write for the public. While economists increasingly hid their political ideas inside of formulas under the pretense that they were physicists and thus doing science impenetrable to the layman, Galbraith wrote best-sellers in plain English with clear and playfully sardonic passages about power.

Galbraith's first best-seller, published in 1952, was called *American Capitalism*. It became a big hit, ultimately selling 400,000 copies. His next book, 1955's *The Great Crash 1929,* doubled that number. Just three years after that, *The Affluent Society* sold over a million copies.

Galbraith's fame and pugnacity buttressed his liberal bona fides. What Galbraith said, mattered. In the 1950s, he testified before the Senate on a run-up in the stock market, warning of another possible crash. As he spoke, the market lost the then-substantial sum of $7 billion of value. *The New York Times* put him on the front page the next day, and some readers associated Galbraith with the drop itself.[73]

A conservative Republican Indiana senator named Homer Capehart took advantage of this event to resurrect the charge that Galbraith was a communist because of some remarks Galbraith had once given at Notre Dame. J. Edgar Hoover called for the FBI's file on Galbraith, but found that there was nothing suspicious. "Investigation favorable except conceited, egotistical and snobbish," came the report.[74]

Galbraith, unlike most liberals who were afraid of attacks from the right, responded with verve and flair. Instead of cowering, he mocked Capehart, noting that he had delivered the speech in Indiana, and that Capehart's accusation was impugning Catholics of his own state. The senator retreated. Nevertheless, the high-profile conflicts, over OPA, his liberal corporatist economic outlook, the bombing survey, and his Harvard tenure, hardened in Galbraith a disdain not only for Cold War militarism, but for small businessmen.

Galbraith's corporatist outlook began to endear him to big business executives. In 1954, he had a series of private correspondences with an executive at the former Mellon-aligned company Bethlehem Steel on merger policy. Bethlehem Steel had tried to buy Youngstown Steel, a transaction the government successfully challenged in its first use of the new Celler-Kefauver law against anticompetitive mergers. Galbraith told Bethlehem Steel executives that they had been too soft in fighting the government. They should have claimed that the merger would have given the company sufficient size to challenge the largest steel producer, U.S. Steel. "The end product of an argument fully developed along these lines would have been extremely serious for the Government," he wrote, foreshadowing arguments later made in the 1980s by the Ronald Reagan administration.[75]

Despite left-wing leanings, Galbraith downplayed the idea of class conflict, or even conflict within the political economy in general. As he put it in a paid speech to a group of bankers in 1958, trying to assess blame for monetary problems "is futile and more than a trifle childish."[76]

By the 1960s, Galbraith was, as Princeton historian Sean Wilentz put it years later, "the most renowned and, arguably, most influential liberal economist in the United States during the decades after the Second World War."[77] He advised JFK in office, and then was appointed by JFK to serve—briefly—as ambassador to India. He became—compared to any other economist of his time—ludicrously famous, a television talk show star and a *New York Times* contributor, a "skier, wit, and bon vivant."[78] Businessmen at the heights of power, at companies like IBM and DuPont, sought his autograph and paid him lavishly to speak at company events, even as he served as an inspiration for the economic theories of the radical New Left.[79]

Almost every college student from the 1950s to the 1970s read him. There was even a brief public flurry of excitement over a possible Galbraith presidential campaign in 1968. In 1974, Galbraith was put on a list of "Too much of a good thing department" by trend journalists, along with Levi's, Coca-Cola, Johnny Cash, Szechuan cooking, and the Mafia.[80]

But what Galbraith was really known for was his ability to frame political ideas, to create language itself. In 1952, with his best-seller

*American Capitalism,* Galbraith replaced the Jeffersonian tradition of using antimonopoly law and policy to decentralize commercial and political institutions with a concept on the virtues of bigness that he called "countervailing power."

He defined countervailing power as the process by which concentrated private economic power would naturally and organically generate a counterbalancing force. A steel company might grow very large, but this wouldn't matter. Eventually, its employees would unionize, balancing out the power of the company with the power of a union. A big maker of cereal might be able to set prices because of its size and power. Soon, however, it would find that a large chain store had emerged to bargain those prices back down.

Dismissing long decades of political struggle by workers and anti-monopolists, Galbraith posited that countervailing power was an inevitable and automatic process that happened concurrently with industrial concentration. "The long trend toward concentration of industrial enterprise in the hands of a relatively few firms," he wrote, "has brought into existence not only strong sellers," but strong buyers.[81]

Part of the germination of countervailing power came from Galbraith's disdain for the fight against A&P. The power of large cereal makers to control prices led to the creation of large chain stores, which then could bargain with cereal makers for better prices, on behalf of the consumer. Echoing A&P's own PR campaign at the height of the FTC's antitrust case, Galbraith mocked the government for charging the company with the "crime" of "too vigorous bargaining . . . on the consumer's behalf." The case against the company was a "serious embarrassment to friends of the antitrust laws. No explanation, however elaborate, could quite conceal the fact that the effect of antitrust enforcement, in this case, was to the disadvantage of the public."[82]

Galbraith extended this theme across the entire economy. Countervailing power left no room for agency, but was a story of inevitability. Big buyers generated strong sellers, and big business created big labor as a balance. This process was automatic, and "as a common rule, we can rely on countervailing power to appear as a curb on economic power."

Bigness was modern and progressive, with smart new technology.

Smallness was dingy and reactionary. As Galbraith put it, the giant corporation was not an independent merchant writ large, but a new type of institution that could wield increasingly complex capital-intensive technology. A&P was not a corner grocer, but something newer, bigger, a friend of the consumer, a scourge of powerful food suppliers like canning companies.[83]

Galbraith would assert the virtues of bigness his whole life. "Half a century ago," he argued in 1938, "the ambitious workman might reasonably hope to be able in time to set up in business for himself, but today even the white collar man has little prospect of ever becoming an independent enterprise."[84] He continued this argument into *American Capitalism* and then *The Affluent Society* in the late 1950s.

The American reality of 1958, with strong unions, a strong and democratic government, and industrial corporations run by patriotic, even somewhat selfless men, was natural, right, and a permanent state of things. At least in terms of productivity, it was according to Galbraith an unchanging utopian end state.

In the 1960s, the idea of affluence began to dominate American politics. "No other economic text found such immediate response," wrote Peter Drucker about *The Affluent Society*, which encouraged more and more government spending.[85] Massive expenditures during the Lyndon Johnson administration to both fight overseas in Vietnam and address poverty at home was a function of affluence. The War on Poverty was a program rooted in Galbraithian views, in some sense a direct outgrowth of his 1958 book.

And even as politicians took up his ideas, Galbraith's own analysis became ever more deterministic in nature, with ever less room for the politicians. By 1967, Galbraith was openly disdaining the idea that democratic deliberation had anything to do with commerce. "It is part of the vanity of modern man that he can decide the character of his economic system." Technology and organization meant that "much of what happens is inevitable and the same . . . on all societies."[86] The Cold War was foolish, as the Soviet Union's large bureaucracy and the modern Western corporation were increasingly similar.

Man's "area of decision is, in fact, exceedingly small."[87]

## THE TRIUMPH OF THE EGGHEADS

Hofstadter and Galbraith together created a new language and new frame of analysis designed to eliminate the antimonopoly tradition in American politics. A new villain, the grubby racist small businessman, had replaced the money trust. The antimonopolists, far from noble, were just motivated by status anxiety. Countervailing power, operating automatically, addressed any ills from concentrated corporations, which brought modernity, wealth, and technological progress. The real political questions for liberals centered on how to promote art and beauty, end racial bigotry, stop environmental pollution, and promote peace. Corporate power nowhere on the list.

This death blow came together in a 1964 essay by Hofstadter, or what one scholar called "an obituary" for antimonopolism, titled "What Happened to the Antitrust Movement? Notes on the Evolution of an American Creed."[88]

With consensus history, Hofstadter had taken a bastardized clinical frame to airbrush the ideological importance of mass movements out of American history. He diagnosed groups as disparate as abolitionists, nativists, Greenbackers and populists, the popular left-wing press during World War I, white supremacists, and black Muslims as essentially suffering from mental disorders.[89] And in an era increasingly characterized by the politics of affluence, Hofstadter and his ilk framed those with ideological goals outside that of consensus historians as mentally ill cranks.

"What Happened to the Antitrust Movement?" was the intellectual culmination of the progressive big business alliances formed in the late 1930s, and would come to shape the attitude of two generations of American legal scholars. Antitrust, he wrote, "is one of the faded passions of American reforms." The essay then set out to explain why this was so, and why it was a sign of progress. Hofstadter first mocked the liberal historians who, in a "kind of mythological history" were "entirely misleading" about the history of corporate concentration. The attempt to constrain bigness, far from important, was laughable. Antitrust "as an ideology and a movement of reform, always contrasted so sharply with its actual achievements in controlling business that it tempted our powers of satire."

The essay was riddled with contradictions. Roosevelt's anti-monopoly message in 1938, and Thurman Arnold were to be ridiculed, Hofstadter wrote, their actions born of "desperation" and "regarded as substantial failures." And yet, Hofstadter continued, without missing a beat, "managers of the large corporations do their business with one eye constantly cast over their shoulders at the Antitrust Division." Nothing was mentioned about the antifascist arguments of Roosevelt, let alone Patman's notions of how A&P represented fascism in the American retail realm. The essay mentioned fascism only once, ascribing the fascist movement to small independent retailers seeking fair trade laws to compete with chain stores.

A key animus behind antitrust, Hofstadter argued, was not the desire to protect democracy, or promote a more open and innovative economy. It was, he wrote, the traditional Anglo-Saxon belief that competition formed "character," a view due to the "Protestant background of our economic thinking." In the late nineteenth century, it was steel and oil barons who venerated Herbert Spencer, the infamous preacher of the "Social Darwinism" interpretation of competition, in which the rich win out because they are smarter and stronger. Yet now Hofstadter linked the antimonopolists to this model of thinking. Hofstadter, in short, entirely flipped the arc of American history. Populist farmers seeking to regulate railroads were the ancestors of the proto-fascist McCarthy-era right-wing cranks. The monopolists were now the protectors of democracy.

Hofstadter then told Americans why they should venerate big business. His main argument was simple—that all the material progress of the last seventy-five years was the result of bigness and top-down control. "The steepest rise in mass standards of living has occurred during the period in which the economy has been dominated by the big corporation," he argued. "Whatever else may be said against bigness, the conception of monopolistic industry as a kind of gigantic, swelling leech on the body of an increasingly deprived and impoverished society has largely disappeared."

Big business, in popular surveys, was now a good employer, it kept prices down, and it had little influence on government.[90] Like Galbraith, Hofstadter made his arguments without bothering to acknowledge a single one of the myriad legal changes over the previous forty years to how corporations were governed, both externally and internally. Instead, borrowing from Galbraith's concept of countervailing power, he argued that big government and big labor had simply offset the sway of big business, automatically.

As Bull Moose progressives had done, Hofstadter strove to focus his liberal audience on "large corporations, with their programs of research," with being "technologically progressive." Small business, by contrast, in seeking fair trade laws or ending abusive practices through the Robinson-Patman Act to block the power of chain stores, were just attempting to protect old and obsolete methods and means.

Hofstadter also restructured what politics meant, removing corporate power as a central public concern and emphasizing "other issues"—like "foreign policy, urban development, civil rights, education"—as core social challenges. The moral danger to America, he said, came not from big business but from a callous lack of a social safety net. He blamed the failure to "render certain humane, healing, humanly productive and restorative social services" on, what else? "The ethos of competition." Galbraith had named the politics of affluence, Hofstadter provided its historical narrative.

Perhaps most important for the emerging politics of antimonopoly, Hofstadter borrowed liberally from a new and emerging school of corporatists on the right, approvingly citing the work of economists from the University of Chicago, G. Warren Nutter and George J. Stigler, who had expressed skepticism on the importance of monopoly power. And he heartily embraced a future darling of neoliberals, the Austrian economist Joseph Schumpeter, who in 1942 published one of the greatest paeans to big business in his book *Capitalism, Socialism and Democracy*. Wrote Hofstadter, "that gale of creative destruction about which Joseph Schumpeter wrote so eloquently, when he described the progressive character of capitalist technology, has driven both the liberal and the conservative ideologies before it."

Since the turn of the century, New Nationalists had sought to build an alliance between monopolists and big government in favor of a politics of command and control, where political arguments would be solely about distribution and consumerism. But they had never been able to fully win the hearts of liberals, because the Brandeis-influenced populists who believed in democracy and industrial liberty had stood in the way.

Men trained in Brandeis's thinking still ran policy in government agencies, the courts, and law schools, and would remain in control for the next generation. In no small part, this was driven by the older generation's still-potent fear of domestic fascism. As late as 1961, Kennedy's Antitrust head reminded the public that the "cartels of Western Europe led directly to the corporate fascist states of Mussolini and Hitler, that represented extremes in concentration of power."[91] Populists with long memories remained in powerful positions in Congress.

But now, a new language existed to shape liberalism. Whether through Hofstadter's consensus history or Galbraith's resurrection of Bull Moose–style technocratic governance, politics was no longer an avenue for structuring society but rather more a means of ratifying what technologically driven organizations already saw as an optimal governing arrangement.

From the 1880s until the 1930s, the "trust problem" was an obsession among economists, lawyers, and historians. Most believed, whatever the cause of concentration, in the "prevailing view that large size carried with it market power and potential for abuse." Under the influence of Galbraith and Hofstadter, that flood of work stopped. As one scholar noted in the 1980s, the postwar years saw "only a handful of pieces" emerge from the Ivory Tower, and most of those "mark a noticeable shift away from the problem that most agitated earlier scholars: monopoly power."[92]

The politics of affluence and consensus history deeply shaped many of the key postwar social movements that touched on political economy, such as consumer rights and environmentalism. They also, over the course of the next generation, entirely changed how liberals viewed the world, and themselves within it.

Liberals lost touch with the politics of commerce. They believed Hofstadter's arguments that America was free from ideological conflict over political economy, and Galbraith's arguments that the great questions over production and Wall Street had been solved.

In the 1970s, when the great postwar economy began to sputter, when banks broke free from their New Deal constraints, when the railroads collapsed, and credit and speculation spun out of control, they had no framework to understand, or even to see, the monopolists and financiers who were slowly reemerging and taking control of the big banks and giant corporations they so deeply trusted. Consensus history and affluence would leave American liberals confused, cynical, and helpless. Liberals, and even business leaders, would turn to the only people who had been thinking about the morality of corporate power and the politics of production. They turned to the men who would resurrect Mellonism.

But that would be in a few years. America in the postwar era was rich. Unfortunately, it was increasingly also blind.

## CHAPTER NINE

# THE FREE MARKET STUDY PROJECT

"I am not as discouraged as people think I should be. I think our general attitude should be that of the Bolsheviks after 1905."

**—Robert Bork, after Barry Goldwater's loss in the 1964 presidential election[1]**

■ ■ ■ ■ ■ ■ ■ ■ ■ ■ ■ ■ ■ ■

The counterrevolution was quiet at first. In 1946, a group of men came together to form the Free Market Study, centered at the University of Chicago. They did not agree on what was needed, or the path forward. Four in particular would come to lead the project. These four did not agree on the role of the state, or the problem of monopoly and corporate power. But all believed the world was heading toward leftist totalitarianism.[2]

The man who pulled the project together was an Austrian economist, Friedrich Hayek. He was visiting Chicago to build a global network of thinkers. In the 1930s, the University of Chicago was one of the few places where conservative intellectuals could feel a bit less isolated. Economists Frank Knight, Jacob Viner, and Henry Simons were a small group of economists in the U.S. academy who rejected the New Deal, and still believed in governing according to classical nineteenth-century liberal principles. The university was an institutionally flexible place, where people at the law school and the economics department collaborated.

Simons and some of his colleagues watched in fear of the New Deal, as unions grew, government ballooned, and leftists imposed authoritarian wartime price controls and regulations. But this older generation of conservatives, while opposed to central planning, had an egalitarian streak, opposing private monopolies as fiercely as labor unions. Simons was no fan of the New Deal, but neither did he appreciate Herbert Hoover's governance.

When Hayek visited this conservative intellectual community, it was the left that was ascendant. In 1944, Wright Patman might have faced a rabid right wing, and the Republicans might take back Congress in 1946, but workers nearly took control of General Motors, and virtually shut down the steel industry. There were strikes, bad ones, among electrical, packing house, and telegraph workers.[3] It was the greatest wave of labor unrest in U.S. history.

Leftism was also ascendant globally. England elected a left-wing Labour government, which socialized swaths of industry. In Europe, the winter of 1947 induced famine, coal shortages, and impassable roads, along with threats of communism.[4] Conservatives in England were petrified; the Anglo-American tradition of protecting property rights was in jeopardy.[5]

Hayek had expected this chaos. During World War II, Hayek had written a book, *The Road to Serfdom,* in which he had diagnosed the cause of mass social dysfunction as too much central direction of economic activity, or collectivism, which inherently led to totalitarianism. He traced this back to nineteenth-century intellectual debates; bad ideas, he believed, were at the core of the autocracies of the twentieth century.

The totalitarianism Hayek feared had most afflicted the Soviet Union and Nazi Germany, but it was also apparent among the left-wing Keynesian planners of the liberal democracies. Victory over the Nazis was only a first step, he believed. Now came the harder part, uprooting the central planning impulse in the democracies as well. Hayek wanted a thorough study of political economy to find out where power in the economy lay, and this was his goal with the Free Market Study, which could best be situated at Chicago.

Hayek's struggle was global. In 1947, he invited conservatives from Sweden, Germany, France, and all over Europe to meet American conservative intellectuals in the town of Mont Pèlerin, Switzerland.[6] These were largely isolated men, surrounded by leftism. So meeting together created an instant bond, in the knowledge that each member was not alone.[7]

The international group called itself the Mont Pelerin Society, and began meeting every year. The Mont Pelerin Society, and the Free Market Study, were part of the same movement to restore nineteenth-century liberalism, which came to be known as "neoliberalism."[8] But it was not born in plutocracy; the German variant of this line of thinking, known as ordoliberalism and inspired by Simons, came from men like Hayek who were dissidents against Nazi ideology, who saw in an aggressive decentralization of both state and monopoly power a means of protecting themselves against the return of fascism.[9]

By 1946, Hayek had become largely irrelevant in the economics world, having lost influence to Keynesians.[10] Keynes was no socialist (and even praised *The Road to Serfdom*), but Keynes had died, and now the central-plan-oriented John Kenneth Galbraith was emerging as one of the more widely published famous economic thinkers.

Hayek's specialty was the then-obscure field of the economics of information. His insight was on the purpose of pricing. A market-based price system carried information from large numbers of buyers and sellers to one another. No central planning agency, or private monopoly, Hayek realized, could replicate such coordination, because no one had all of the information contained in the heads of millions of free-acting agents. Thus did Hayek link individual freedom, free will, and economic coordination through markets.

In *The Road to Serfdom,* Hayek moved away from economics and toward philosophy, arguing, like Brandeis, that human beings were imperfect, that too much power in too few hands—either by the state or by monopoly—would lead to autocracy. His vision likely drew upon Brandeis, as Brandeis's views circulated in a key French salon attended by Hayek in the 1930s.[11] *The Road to Serfdom* opened with a quote from Franklin Delano Roosevelt's 1938 speech against monopolies.

Though mainstream economists didn't care about Hayek's views, he and Simons began collaborating on the possibility of putting together the Free Market Study. Both men were fiercely anticorporate, seeing private corporate power as an equally dangerous form of central planning as state socialism. Simons favored strict, almost puritanical restrictions on banking, and even nationalizing the train system and utilities.

But Hayek and Simons would not shape the ultimate path of the project. Two other men would do that. In 1945, Hayek toured the United States to promote *The Road to Serfdom*. Right-wing American businessmen loved the Austrian, who seemed to rail against the New Deal. In Detroit, Hayek met the key moneyman behind what would become the Free Market Study, the Missouri businessman and Baptist Harold Luhnow, who ran a foundation called the Volker Fund.

Luhnow had inherited large sums from his wealthy progressive uncle in Kansas City, and had become something of a megalomaniac. He used his money to organize a fighting force against communism, liberalism, corruption, Keynesian economics, and godlessness.

In the 1930s, while facing the local Kansas City political machine, Luhnow had become a fierce anti-leftist, falling in with a network of anti–New Deal business groups focused on "good government" technocracy. From the 1940s to the 1960s, the Volker Fund spent about a million dollars a year supporting right-wing books, speaking tours, and causes, of both libertarians and the nascent religious right.[12]

Over the course of several decades, Luhnow morphed into a strange figure. He eventually began telling subordinates he had "unique but unspecified spiritual power" to secretly influence world leaders.[13] He helped finance the Red Scare in the 1950s, sponsoring William F. Buckley's attacks on Keynesian economics—or the use of government deficits to manage economic downturns as illustrative of a socialistic threat in America.

In 1945, when Luhnow saw Hayek speak against central planning, he grew enthralled by the Austrian. He decided he wanted an American version of *The Road to Serfdom,* dumbed down and simplified. Hayek convinced Luhnow to fund the Free Market Study as a substitute. To run it, Hayek and Simons recruited a third economist, Aaron Director, who had been one of Simons's disciples. Luhnow agreed to fund Director's salary as a professor for five years, an unusual arrangement at the University of Chicago.

Director would be the last piece of the puzzle, the key to making the Free Market Study work. Director is an obscure figure who wrote little and left little of a written record. But he, through his students and converts, would play the key role in rebuilding Mellonism.

Director was a Russian-born Jew who immigrated to the United

States in 1913 as a boy, settling in Portland, Oregon. He did well in school, but Portland in his youth was a deeply reactionary, xenophobic, and racist town, one of the more important centers of the KKK and anticommunist post–World War I hysteria. Growing up Jewish and an immigrant in an atmosphere of enforced conformity was not easy; Director encountered anti-Semitic slurs and was kept out of social circles due to racial exclusion and overly zealous patriotism.

In 1921, Director attended Yale, where, again resentful of the wealthy Anglo-Saxon exclusionary culture, he came under the influence of Thorstein Veblen and H. L. Mencken. Both Veblen and Mencken were radical and elitist; Mencken did not believe humanity had the free will and intelligence to make democracy work. Director came to see the world this way as well; in a satirical newspaper he anonymously published at Yale called *The Saturday Evening Pest,* he and his friends used mockery and elitism, writing "the definition of the United States shall eternally be H. L. Mencken surrounded by 112,000,000 morons" and calling for "an aristocracy of the mentally alert and curious" to lead the way forward.[14]

Director joined the socialist-leaning IWW union in the Pacific Northwest, and continued developing his sense of self as an elite and heroic educator. In 1927, he married these instincts to conservative politics, heading to the economics department at the University of Chicago, finding a political home on the right for his radical ambitions. In many ways, Director's path mirrored that of the historian Richard Hofstadter, with Hofstadter becoming a corporatist on the left, and Director becoming one on the right.[15]

Director deeply respected Hayek and Simons. With their support, and Luhnow's money, Director would turn Chicago into a center of political power.

At first, the Free Market Study, Director, Simons, and Hayek were unified around the older conservative antimonopoly tradition of classical liberalism.[16] But in 1946, Simons committed suicide. This did not destroy the project, and probably spurred it along; Luhnow's close advisors had been skeptical of Simons's antimonopoly streak, and Director, though a conservative antimonopolist, was far more ideologically malleable.

In 1950, Luhnow threatened to "eject Director from his leadership role in the Free Market Study" because Director still retained tenets of Simons's philosophy.[17] Director eventually jettisoned Simons's anti-monopoly views, and in 1953, Luhnow funded a new study, called the Antitrust Project, to restructure the antitrust laws. It was in this period, in the late 1940s to the early 1950s, that Director broke from a classic conservative ethos, fusing conservative rhetoric with the radical elitism of Veblen and Mencken. The Chicago School transformed into a vehicle to rebuild Mellonism and corporate power.

Director soon began making the argument that private monopolies could only emerge and exert power due to government action. Private corporate monopolies would, for Director, cease being a problem. Director's organizing strategy was a two-step process. First, he would relentlessly recruit both scholars and willing funders of them. Second, he would have these scholars use the same Mencken-like frame as Director had at *The Saturday Evening Pest* at Yale, mocking key targets as ignorant elitists. As one Chicago Schooler put it, the strategy was "to ridicule the Supreme Court's treatment of antitrust as well as of other forms of government interference with the market."[18]

The money and the marketing worked. Director began gaining converts. Two initial recruits were part of the older Chicago conservative tradition. Milton Friedman and George Stigler had been part of the anti–New Deal school of conservative antimonopolists at the University of Chicago in the 1930s. In 1946, Friedman and Stigler made their first foray into aggressive public-policy advocacy on the Volker payroll, in a pamphlet blaming rent control for the immediate postwar housing shortage. Still, Friedman and Stigler, as classical liberals, were antimonopolists, as nearly all were in those days. Stigler even testified before Emanuel Celler's antimonopoly subcommittee on the need to break up the steel industry.

Director easily pulled them into the neoliberal orbit. Friedman was a brilliant marketer and statistician; like Director, Friedman was Jewish (and Director's brother-in-law); his career had been held back due to anti-Semitism. In the early 1950s, Director persuaded Friedman of the irrelevance of private monopoly power, and Friedman began seeing in the nascent neoliberal framework an opportunity for self-promotion.

In the late 1950s, Director convinced Stigler. From then on, Aaron Director would serve as ideological enforcer for the Chicago School, Milton Friedman would be the key rhetorician of this new philosophy, and George Stigler the economic visionary.[19]

Director had a remarkable ability to inspire and convert thinkers into conservative preachers of neoliberal doctrine. "A lot of us who took the antitrust course or the economics course underwent what can only be called a religious conversion," said one convert, Robert Bork, of Director's converts. "It changed our view of the entire world."[20] Bork had been a Pittsburgh socialist. After studying with Director, he turned into a conservative. He specialized in antitrust law, becoming the most important antitrust lawyer of the postwar era. Joked a Nobel Prize–winning economist heavily involved in the project named Ronald Coase, "I regarded my role as that of Saint Paul to Aaron Director's Christ. He got the doctrine going, and what I had to do was bring it to the gentiles."[21]

The Free Market Study was exciting, tantalizing, and a challenge to stultifying liberal orthodoxy. At first it was housed in the Chess Room of the Quadrangle Club, a historic faculty room with thick leather chairs at the University of Chicago. In a few years, it would spread to the main floor of the law school, with excited young scholars stuffed together in cubicles, talking, arguing, shouting, "stirring" over a lot of "coffee and some beer," both damaging and repairing egos.[22]

A sense of victimization, infused from the beginning, unified the members of the project. They saw themselves as radicals up against an all-powerful establishment of liberals. "The phrase Chicago Economics was often uttered with the same contempt that commonly characterized unsavory ethnic and religious epithets," wrote Chicago Schooler Henry Manne.[23]

This aggrieved posture served to make their ideas sound tantalizing and risky in later decades, even after they had conquered the world. It was, rhetorically, identical to Galbraith's use of the term "conventional wisdom" to distance himself from responsibility, even as he was at the center of power. This resentful anti-establishment pose would always color the movement these men built, later syncing well with the politicians who grew up in the anti-establishment culture of the 1960s.

Luhnow's money was enormously well spent; the Volker Fund would finance five different Nobel Prize winners in economics. Director's students were also impressive, and not just Bork. Henry Manne would reorganize how politicians understood Wall Street's relationship with the corporation, Ward Bowman would undermine the idea of corporate concentration as a political problem, and John McGee would reorganize American pricing law.

Still, as exciting as the project might be in 1946, returning to a pre–New Deal world seemed impossible. To reconstruct the system over which Andrew Mellon reigned required an architecture with three components.

The first component was the ability to rule an entire market through a specific corporate monopoly, or shared control of a market through a small set of corporations (which was known as an oligopoly rather than a monopoly). Each monopolistic company would be a mini-government, governing the prices, quality, labor, and supply chain of an industrial product or service, such as aluminum, oil, steel, ships, and magnesium. But during the New Deal, robust antitrust enforcement kept concentration and monopolization at bay.

Each company had in turn been controlled by one of a small number of oligarchs or banks, such as the House of Morgan, DuPont, Rockefeller, or Mellon himself. This was done through the second component, the connective power that turned each monopoly into a networked whole, with mechanisms to discipline wayward corporate structures. This was Wall Street, with tools such as holding companies, interlocking directorates, stock watering, debt issuance, and various forms of financial instruments. Wall Street, however, was deeply constrained by financial rules.

The third piece was the rhetorical machinery, a set of intellectual concepts and political institutions that would protect financial empires from democratic influence. Money would be necessary, money to develop and sell this ideology, not only to fund new academic departments, but to buy politicians and lawyers, to influence voters and newspapers, to set up institutions to persuade judges and professors. Even more critical was rhetoric to explain the world in ways that would organize citizens to seek not freedom from capital, but freedom for capital. But this was difficult to imagine, as New Dealers seemed to rule the centers of cultural capital, the newspapers and academic institutions.

It was their task to imagine it nonetheless. They saw themselves as up against the world, and they were going to conquer it. The Free Market Study, and then the Antitrust Project, would serve as the intellectual testing ground for the set of ideas that would eventually burst out of the academy and generate a political and financial revolution. "The Antitrust Project," said Yale Law professor George Priest, "was, perhaps, the most successful research program in the history of legal scholarship."[24]

## UNDER SIEGE BY LIBERALS

And yet, the counterrevolutionaries found their struggle against leftism agonizingly slow.

No one upset Chicago Schoolers like the luminous and hated John Kenneth Galbraith, who continued to become more famous and important. Galbraith's Keynesian planners had been effortlessly defeating Chicago conservatives for years. During the war, George Stigler encountered Galbraith at the Office of Price Administration, surrounded by his New Deal leftist allies. Stigler called Galbraith a "fox in the henhouse," and retreated to academia to get away from the man.[25]

In 1953, Galbraith promoted his notion of countervailing power, the quasi-Marxist notion that bigness in one area of the economy automatically generated bigness in other areas to tame it. He refused to work within the methodological constraints of economics and popularized the concept through his best-selling work *American Capitalism*. At the American Economic Association conference, they debated; Stigler was one of five different economists who sought to "clobber" Galbraith. He failed. As one economist observed, "it soon became hard to find a business or sociological piece of writing that did not make use of Galbraith's idea."[26]

The Chicago School lived in Galbraith's shadow. In the 1950s, Republicans, despite defeating Democrat Adlai Stevenson, expressed concern that their "egghead" intellectuals were not as luminous as those of the Democrats, like Galbraith. In 1958, Galbraith's *The Affluent Society,* which preached central planning and public spending to promote art and education, was a best-seller. It was immediately embedded into the intellectual fabric of young intellectuals within both parties. George Stigler expressed despair, exclaiming it was "shocking that more Americans have read 'The Affluent Society' than 'The Wealth of Nations.'"[27] Galbraith responded, "Professor Stigler's sorrow may be not that so many read Galbraith and so few read Smith but that hardly anyone reads Stigler at all." It was a brutal, and brutally effective, putdown.[28]

It was no better for Director's younger students. After his time at Chicago, Bork had trouble getting a job. "We consider your qualifications to be of the highest and placed you in the top echelon of the men we have interviewed," wrote the personnel committee of the prestigious law firm Covington & Burling.[29] But they hired someone else.

Eventually Bork caught on at another law firm, Kirkland & Ellis, where he worked for seven years. But it was not a fun experience. Practicing corporate law brought him, as he later put it in advising a young lawyer, "thoughts of despair and the rope."[30] Bork tried to get a teaching job, but, as he wrote in 1961, the job market was "frustrating."[31] Bork was rejected by Northwestern law school the next year, with a somewhat insulting note that they had hired "a young man who has only been out of Law School two or three years."[32] Bork was reduced to writing the "monopoly" entry for the *Encyclopaedia Britannica.*[33]

But it wasn't just the legal academic establishment, and Galbraith, that stood athwart the plans and careers of the Chicago Schoolers. The New Deal had been accepted, internalized everywhere. In 1954, the Republican president, Dwight Eisenhower, consigned to irrelevance those few "Texas oil millionaires" and the "occasional politician or business man" who wanted to eliminate the New Deal era of reforms. "Their number is negligible and they are stupid," he said.[34]

Chicago Schoolers sought to do what they could do within the constraints of economics, which was to build their own forums for publication away from the cloistered liberal establishment. In 1958, Director started *The Journal of Law and Economics,* with money from the Volker Fund, and then the Eli Lilly fortune.[35]

The liberal establishment, and the business world, paid little heed.

Chicago Schoolers held to their immediate postwar paranoia, believing that the New Deal regulatory and antitrust apparatus was leading the West to a left-wing totalitarianism. But leaders, even those whom Chicago Schoolers thought should know better, barely noticed. "Even the business community," wrote Bork and Bowman, "appears to understand neither the nature nor the immediacy of the threat."[36] Big businessmen saw Chicago scholars as a bit like a crazy old relative, to be cared for and shown respect, but only in private.[37]

The Committee for Economic Development, the dominant business trade association of the 1950s, came out with a report, "Soviet Progress Versus American Enterprise," in 1958 predicting that the USSR would overtake America. "When I really feel gloomy, I think that five years from now they will be obviously superior to us in every area," said the author of the study, Professor Jerome Wiesner.

This was the age of Sputnik, when the Soviets sent a satellite into space first, with the Red Army menacing Western Europe, and with John F. Kennedy about to mock Nixon over a presumed "missile gap" that played on fears of American inferiority. "When I am optimistic, I feel it will take ten," concluded Wiesner.[38]

Director answered the charge. In the second issue of the journal, Warren Nutter, a Director student, questioned this commonly held view that the Soviet Union system was superior. It didn't matter. A decade later, though the Soviet Union had not overtaken the United States, *Newsweek* listed which books were being read by famous businessmen. The list included not only Keynes, but Karl Marx's *Capital*.[39] Arjay Miller, the president of the Ford Motor Company, encouraged his colleagues to read Keynes's *General Theory of Employment, Interest, and Money*.

And it would get worse, or at least seem worse. Democratic president Lyndon Johnson, he of the "Great Society" welfare state, would not be succeeded by the liberal Hubert Humphrey, but by the conservative foe of the eastern establishment, Richard Nixon. Nixon installed a corporate lawyer named Richard McLaren to run the Antitrust Division, and McLaren, continuing with the Eisenhower model, wielded antitrust authority aggressively and assertively. Then Nixon imposed price controls on virtually every good, service, and wage in the economy, earning the grudging admiration of none other than the devil himself: John Kenneth Galbraith.

Nixon, though conservative, would not deviate from the New Deal status quo on political economy. "We're all Keynesians now," he said. The New Deal consensus was part of how business leaders organized their politics. The main lobbyist for Sears Roebuck, John Wheeler, pursued "corporate statesmanship," seeking to strengthen his company's political posture by supporting consumer protection legislation. The Republican majority whip, Senator Ted Stevens, attacked Nixon's FTC for being weak, saying he hoped enforcers would get more aggressive, and that "some of these big business people will complain to us you are going too far."[40]

But even as Chicago School scholars expressed common frustration and revulsion at the world around them, as they discussed their common crusade, they were succeeding, burrowing into the consciousness of the American business world and important young leaders. And as lonely as they felt, they knew of the progress they were making.

By the early 1960s, this nascent conservative movement would finally have the basic ideas in place to overturn much of the New Deal. By the 1970s, they would have the institutions to promote those ideas.

## THE MAKING OF THE NEW MELLONISM

The Chicago School oriented themselves around two different stylistic choices. The first was to use the language of Jeffersonian democracy, framed around attacks on monopolies and the promotion of individual liberty. They appropriated this language through Hayek.[41] In the 1950s, this rhetoric was willingly ceded by younger members of the Democratic establishment, as Galbraith-dominated liberal intellectuals increasingly began orienting around command-and-control elitism and disdain for commerce.

What Director constructed was a highly sophisticated rhetorical movement. Like Hofstadter, Director realized the key to subverting populism was to alter language itself. Actual competition might be, as

Director student McGee put it, "a false God," but co-opting the rhetoric of liberty was essential in persuading Americans who had been
raised on populist suspicion of centralized power.[42]

Hayek, as had Jefferson and Brandeis, saw potential danger among
all concentrations of power, from unions to corporations to government agencies. Director used Hayek's language, but removed corporate
power from the list of potential threats to liberty. To someone unaware
of the meaning behind the rhetoric, this new Director-altered language made it sound like Chicago Schoolers opposed monopolies and
collusive arrangements, and that it fit squarely within a conservative
tradition. But Director was creating an elaborate rhetorical trap. Monopolies and collusive arrangements had been understood as emerging
from the corporate sphere. Chicago Schoolers, led by Director, used
monopolies to refer to things like public schools and labor unions.
Director was, as Hofstadter had on the left, making corporate monopolists the protectors of liberty.

As important as the Jeffersonian political rhetoric was, the Chicago
School also relied on the apolitical language of science. George Stigler,
Ronald Coase, and Robert Bork saw enormous rhetorical power in
the scientific aesthetic and would use language oriented almost entirely around technocratic economics. They named their school of
thought the law and economics movement.

The history of the movement would be told and constantly retold
as one where Director and associated scholars had penetrating scientific insights, insights rejected by the dirty and unscientifically minded
world. As George Priest, another Chicago Schooler, argued, Director
was uninterested in changing the law; in fact he was no more interested in the law than "in, say, molecular biology." Court opinions provided nothing but data to disinterested scientists; "the law served the
Project as a subject of ridicule," but nothing more.[43] "I use the word
'science' deliberately," wrote Bork, in one of his many lambastings of
prosecutors and courts.[44]

The idea of a scientific consensus was a key rhetorical weapon, used
to exclude those who disagreed with the underlying political assumptions. The problem was, to make this argument, Chicago Schoolers had

to pretend that economic analysis was new, so they could claim they had discovered it. But it wasn't new.

Antimonopolists were also deeply interested in economics and science, from Louis Brandeis's emphasis on empiricism to commonly accepted theories by scholars like Joe Bain that showed a link between concentration in an industry and high profits.[45] Wright Patman had helped write the initial legislation creating the National Science Foundation.[46] But Brandeis and Patman understood that political economy was about power structures. While Brandeis believed in science, he did not believe in overly applying technocratic tools to political decisions. Corporations and markets were engineered, and they could be structured to promote a free and self-governing people capable of making intelligent decisions about politics. But they could also become mechanisms of oppression. The forum for such discussions was that of law and politics, where human beings could use their liberties and free will to come together and make such decisions.

The law and economics movement of the Chicago School was metaphysical, designed to replace law with science in the form of economics, with measurements of efficiency. Director had a deterministic view of human nature, ironically like Galbraith's, in which free will was superseded by the scientific unspooling of market developments; he imparted this vision to the Chicago School.

Director's group finessed the earlier embrace of empiricism by populists. They argued that, yes, there may have been some economics prior to the appearance of the Chicago School. But such work was either methodologically suspect, or incomplete. "Prior to the late 1950s, the science of economics was not adequate to the task of forming a comprehensive new interdisciplinary field with law," wrote Henry Manne. "There were few important works of 'applied economics' largely because many of the tools needed to do convincing analysis had not yet been invented."[47]

The advance of Chicago School policies would be couched in scientific terms, as economic expertise, as incorporating science and fancy terms such as "price theory" into legal rhetoric. This replacement of the democratic structuring of power by pseudoscience was evident from the beginning. In the first issue of *The Journal of Law and Economics,* one author proved logically that democratic systems shouldn't address private monopolies while another author proved there was a method to determine the scientifically correct size of a firm.[48]

This seeming embrace of science, and the discarding of those disagreed to the dustbin of the superstitious and emotional (or "populistic" as Bork once put it), was a means of winning arguments. Bork later said the use of a key one of these pseudoscientific tools—price theory—was "a powerful form of rhetoric."[49]

With this new science, the Enlightenment tradition was wiped out in bold strokes. George Stigler discussed Adam Smith's theories, and James Madison's ideas, and then concluded that only since 1958, coincidentally the year of his arrival at the University of Chicago, "has a general theory of the behavior of governments begun to appear. Three scholars, Anthony Downs, James Buchanan, and Gordon Tullock, began the task of constructing such a theory."[50]

The Chicago School was a reconstruction of the thinking of the nineteenth century, when opposition to concentrations of capital seemed as foolish as opposing the creation of clouds or the flowing of rivers.

Director had an unerring sense of how to use this scientific rhetoric, and ridicule, to persuade elite liberals, and undermine a forceful application of public power to private monopolies. Warren Nutter, for instance, was a student of Director, and his doctoral dissertation, *The Extent of Enterprise Monopoly in the United States, 1899–1939,* argued that monopoly power had not increased during that period, eroding concern over the problem of concentration.[51] Hofstadter approvingly cited Nutter in his pivotal 1964 essay, "What Happened to the Antitrust Movement?"

Director had his student John McGee rewrite the history of America's greatest monopolist, John D. Rockefeller of Standard Oil. McGee would purportedly prove that Standard Oil, contrary to nearly all scholarship and common understanding, had not engaged in predatory behavior. McGee claimed he looked at the trial record, and found no evidence of predatory pricing, or cutting prices in certain markets to drive rivals out of business. Later scholars examined McGee's claim, and found it false.[52] But liberals, and then courts, and then the Supreme Court, accepted McGee's narrative, and overturned key precedents on monopoly rules around predatory pricing.

Yet another seminal work, this one by Harold Demsetz, proved that corporate concentration didn't matter. Large firms were more profitable than small ones not because they had market power, as anti-monopolists assumed, but because their size was evidence of superior efficiency and good management.[53] Once again, this conclusion was highly disputed, but it helped lead to a wholesale change in perception and practice of antitrust.

Behind the rhetoric of science was an attack on democracy. Considerations of equity, democracy, and social stability became, as Bork put it, "vague, squishy, and dangerous," a "reckless and primitive egalitarianism."[54] In 1947, at Mont Pèlerin, James Buchanan, founder of public choice theory and one of the Chicago School's later Nobel Prize winners, referred to the need to ensure that wealthier citizens must not be forced to shoulder a disproportionate tax burden. Freedom, particularly economic, required "the removal of certain decisions from majority-vote determination."[55] He and Gordon Tullock later used a scientific veneer in *The Calculus of Consent* to argue a one-person, one-vote system was inefficient.[56]

Voting no longer represented part of the process of self-government—it became a chance for voters to maximize their welfare by bargaining with public officials to effect wealth transfers using politics rather than free markets. And those public officials, be they elected leaders, antitrust enforcers, regulators, or anyone else, had little interest in leadership, but were reflecting the will of the bargaining coalitions who had brought them to office and could enhance their power.

Director and his colleagues had a fundamentally nihilistic view of human nature, and introduced into political economics a language flowing from this conception. All humans sought to maximize their individual well-being. Legal systems should be modeled not on squishy notions such as justice, fairness, equity, or social stability, but on scientific measurements of individual welfare. In this brutal framework, those who succeeded were simply the most talented (a foreshadowing of the later fetishizing of meritocracy). Perhaps this reality might be sad, perhaps it might be unfair, but it was truth, and thus, scientific.

The key policy choices of the Chicago School flowed from this view of humans as inherently selfish and atomistic. In the 1960s, George Stigler began developing a new theory of why most public regulations to constrain corporate power were problematic, and in 1971 he popularized it with the notion of "regulatory capture." The meaning of regulatory capture was the phenomenon of public officials attempting to operate in the public interest by writing rules, but instead serving to enhance the power and wealth of the industry they were hired to regulate. What good was regulation at all, since regulators were just as self-interested as anyone else and would inevitably take bribes or do the bidding of the powerful. Similarly, rent controls protected low-income tenants from landlords. In the Chicago School's capable hands, this became "rent seeking," a selfish way for politicians to maximize their own power to gain votes from special interests, aka poor people. Rent seeking and regulatory capture were ways of denigrating the ability of democratic states to protect citizens.

Sometimes, old language, such as "free trade," would be redefined to airbrush out concentrations of power that were inconvenient to acknowledge, such as the need for national security and sovereignty. Neither could be measured by Chicago School economists, so they were defined out of existence in Milton Friedman's new version of free trade. Cordell Hull's carefully crafted trading regime, which sought to preserve low tariffs, restrict cartels, and prevent sovereign powers from seizing American industrial might through predatory pricing tactics, was tossed. The Chicago School version of free trade would be a new global utopian world, without concern for private monopoly power or national sovereignty.

Director assembled an entirely new discourse for politics. He understood that business leaders, though sympathetic to their social vision, were in an intellectual trap, caught in the powerful vise of liberal rhetoric. He knew that for business leaders, social respectability came with liberal sensibilities, requiring them to make comments about social responsibility, statesmanship, respect for democracy, and unions. So the Chicago School had to allow business leaders to have both social respectability and reassert their right to rule. Achieving their social vision would require reorienting language itself.

The key figure to break down the liberal legal establishment's adherence to the religion of antitrust was Bork, one of Director's first converts. In time there would be tens of thousands more, including some of the country's most important liberals, and eventually the entire Supreme Court.[57]

But Bork would be the tip of the spear.

## BORK AND GOLDWATER

In the 1950s, Robert Bork seemed destined for a frustrating if well-paid life as a corporate lawyer. But in 1962, he caught a lucky break, and was hired to be a law professor at the perceived liberal bastion of Yale. A fellow conservative from the University of Chicago, Ward Bowman, hired at Yale because the economics department had thought Bowman an antimonopolist, managed to get Bork onto the faculty.[58]

The hiring of Bork at Yale was a big deal for the Chicago network, and Bork would serve as a key piece in Director's empire building. Immediately, Bork plunged into controversy, and over the next four years turned himself and the Chicago School first from fringe academics to the respectable opposition, and then, the government in waiting. It was one of the most successful persuasion jobs in American history, a triumph of sheer rhetoric and persistence.

Bork used his brilliance, charm, and politeness to cultivate three important constituencies. The first was the corporate legal fraternity, with whom he had close ties from his seven-year run at Kirkland & Ellis. His academic work, with his platform at the liberal Yale Law School, buttressed his background and professional relationships. In 1963, he gave a speech to the New York City Bar attacking criminal sentences for price-fixing, just a few years after GE and Westinghouse executives had gone to jail for colluding on prices of electrical equipment. Bork, rather than bow to the liberal orthodoxy against antitrust violations, pronounced these sentences "unjust and an emotional overreaction."[59] This kind of attack was helpful to the corporate world, since it would remove the threat that the

Department of Justice had to force settlements upon clients with the fear of jail time.

For his performance, Bork received accolades from the corporate legal establishment. The legendary Howard Ellis of his former firm showered him with praise. "Thank you so much for your paper defending the 'Malefactors of Great Wealth,'" Ellis wrote.[60] Corporate titan Taggart Whipple at Davis Polk, who had represented Standard Oil of New Jersey before the Truman Committee during World War II (as well as arguing against Thurgood Marshall in *Brown v. Board of Education*), expressed his appreciation for noting the absurdity of government action.[61]

Bork's relationships with the corporate legal world were essential. He kept his former firm in the loop with his work, both promoting the interests of their clients through his academic work and pulling in favors from them at the same time. He then asked his former firm to help him join the influential American Bar Association Antitrust Section. This self-appointed ABA Antitrust Section was a key forum for inserting ideas into the antitrust establishment. Kirkland's Hammond Chaffetz was the chair of the section, and offered Bork entrée to this citadel of liberal power. Federal Trade Commission chairman Paul Rand Dixon and Department of Justice Antitrust chief Lee Loevinger were members of the section.[62] Bork would begin building relationships within the institutions.

Aside from the legal fraternity, Bork wooed corporate leaders themselves. He would often ask corporate counsels for their legal briefs, as a way of both studying the arguments he could then popularize and establishing relationships. He did this with Procter & Gamble on its merger with Clorox, and with Reynolds Metals.[63] Eventually, he would work with Alcoa, to attempt to discredit the decision in 1945 calling the company a monopoly and therefore guilty of Sherman Act violations.[64]

In late 1963, Bork and Bowman authored an article for *Fortune*. The article appeared at the right cultural moment. With "The Crisis in Antitrust," Bork and Bowman created a rhetorical structure that Bork would use for the rest of his life, the notion of a contradiction in the antitrust laws.

Antitrust was incoherent, they argued. The law sought to promote competition. Yet, it also sought to protect small businesses, thus preventing competition for those small enterprises against larger and more efficient rivals. Antitrust law was also subversive, gnawing away at the foundations of America. It reinforced "populistic" and "anti-free market strains in American thought," and had large, dangerous, and hidden costs.[65]

After decades of uniform pro-antitrust sentiment, such a clear articulation of potential problems in the law had a ready audience. Nineteen sixty-three was a key period for the Chicago School; the year before, Milton Friedman published his series of lectures that had been financed by the Volker Fund, under the title *Capitalism and Freedom,* which would eventually become a best-seller.

"The Crisis in Antitrust" was a big hit. "It is one of the best antitrust articles I have ever read," wrote one corporate lawyer. "You have launched a frontal assault on the fallacious 'new economics' which the 'pseudo liberals' have been using as a vehicle for their anti-competitive doctrines. . . . The asinine doctrines that are being spawned by the F.T.C. in Robinson-Patman cases in the name of 'free competition' need to be blasted to hell."[66]

The power of the argument extended Bork's influence beyond the legal fraternity. Think tanks and schools of management asked for reprints.[67] The New York City Bar invited Bork to discuss the question, "Is Antitrust Anti-competitive? A Hard Look at the Philosophy and Propriety of our Federal Antitrust Laws." Congressman Emanuel Celler attacked him on the House floor.[68] A seminar at the University of Rochester for executives offered Bork a lucrative speaking opportunity on mergers.[69] And he was asked to help direct money from the General Electric Foundation to fellow academics.[70] Businessmen were beginning to get interested.

The third constituency group was what put Bork into the political world, his cultivation of southern elites and the presidential campaign of Republican Barry Goldwater. And this came not through any arguments about antitrust, but one about the relationship between property and race. In August of 1963, Bork published a piece in *The New*

*Republic* titled "Civil Rights—A Challenge." In this article, he made the case against Title II of the Civil Rights Act, the public accommodations part of the bill, which prohibited racial discrimination in privately owned hotels and restaurants.

This part of the bill was, he argued, "legislation by which the morals of the majority are self-righteously imposed upon a minority." This attack on property rights, he argued, is "likely to be subversive of free institutions." Bork used the scientific style that he had adopted to sell Mellonism. Proponents of the bill, however well-meaning, were not considering the "cost in freedom that must be paid for such legislation." The Civil Rights Act would force businessmen to "deal with and serve persons with whom they do not wish to associate."[71] And that, Bork felt, was wrong.

Though Bork saw a "justifiable abhorrence of racial discrimination" as the motivation behind advocates for the law, his argument appealed to segregationists in the South. Bork argued that owning a public-facing business meant that the owner had no obligations to the public, and could discriminate at will. In 1963, in America, this argument was an endorsement of Jim Crow and a terror-filled South. But by putting the argument in the scientifically sounding welfare utilitarian framework of the Chicago School, Bork evaded having to address the fear and humiliation of what it was like to be black in America without using overtly racist rhetoric.

Nevertheless, Bork in this article aimed at nothing less than using his deep knowledge of antimonopoly law to deprive the civil rights movement of a powerful tool, the ability to use the law to block economic discrimination. This tradition of nondiscrimination by race or economic power suffused the civil rights movement and the New Deal. It was known as "common carriage," from when carriages and public accommodations facilities like inns were required to serve all comers. This was an Anglo-American tradition that stretched back hundreds of years.

When New Dealers passed the Civil Aeronautics Act of 1938 to regulate the nascent airline industry, the laws prohibited racial segregation on airplanes.[72] In 1960, Thurgood Marshall litigated a case seeking the desegregation of a restaurant in a bus terminal, successfully arguing that such a restaurant was part of the interstate bus system, and thus, a common carrier subject to nondiscrimination principles. Martin Luther King drew direct analogies from the Sherman Act when desegregating lunch counters.[73] In opposing the Civil Rights Act, Bork was standing all at once against the New Deal, the movement for racial equality, and the long tradition of common carriage law.

The backlash to this article was, at first, brutal, and marked the only time early in his career that Bork found himself the target of liberal outrage. It was a mark of Hofstadter's profound influence over liberals that when Bork put forth no less ideologically aggressive pronouncements about the need to unleash corporate power, it seemed like a conservative but polite technical disagreement. But Bork's attacks on the Civil Rights Act brought him into an explicit alliance with unapologetic racists, and put him at odds with liberals during the focal point of public debate over what justice meant in 1963. The controversy embarrassed Bork, with some of the most pointed reactions coming from Bork's own world of the legal fraternity.

One note from a New York lawyer summed up the feeling from the liberal legal world, noting that Bork overlooked a "recent costly experience the world had to undergo with people who built a plan of world conquest around a theory of a master race and policies of racial discrimination." The "vile poison" of "racial discrimination" should not be "spewed forth with impunity under the mantle of freedom."[74]

Bork was upset, and felt he might have made a political misstep. "I badly need some readers who might agree with me," he wrote to Howard Krane, a friend at Kirkland & Ellis. "Your own silence leads me to believe that either you haven't read it, you don't agree with it, or you don't like—and in any of those contingencies, to hell with you."[75] But singed as he might feel, Bork's article gave him credibility with another important opponent of the Civil Rights Act: Barry Goldwater, the Republican nominee for president.

Goldwater was the political analog to the Chicago School intellectuals. His was a radical takeover of the Republican Party, the rejection of milquetoast compromise, and the bold assertion of a different vision, a rejection of the philosophy peddled by every major president since FDR. Eisenhower had been a Republican New Dealer, but

Goldwater brought a different value system to the American public, the first time that laissez-faire Mellon-style arguments had been presented to the public since 1932. Goldwater asserted vehemently that he favored freedom and liberty, and used a hard-core anticommunist and anti-collectivist set of arguments.

Milton Friedman became an aggressive promoter of Goldwater, and saw the candidate as representing the first triumph of a new conservative ideological movement, with organizers such as Clifton White attempting to wrest power within the party from the moderate Republicans that had put Eisenhower in office.[76] This shift was not only ideological but also geographic; Goldwater was from Arizona, the Southwest, whereas Republicans such as Mellon, Morgan, and Rockefeller had often come from the Midwest or Northeast. The South and West had been industrializing rapidly because of New Deal policies, bringing in a new generation of white-collar managers to the region. The Sunbelt, not the Industrial Belt, was becoming the base of the GOP and modern conservatism.

Even if the Goldwater campaign failed to line up public support from big business, a quieter, more radical part of the business world was paying close attention to the new language Goldwater was using, and the policies he was promoting. This effort was organized by a policy entrepreneur named William Baroody, at an institution called the American Enterprise Institute (AEI). Founded in 1938 by businessmen to oppose the New Deal, in the early 1960s, AEI was one of the few right-wing think tanks in Washington, D.C. AEI received funds from Allen-Bradley, Ford, General Motors, General Electric, Socony Mobil, U.S. Steel, Procter & Gamble, Armstrong Cork, Youngstown Sheet & Tube, and from the Eli Lilly fortune.[77] But it was not influential, considered on the fringe of policymaking.

Within the Goldwater campaign, Baroody ran policy, and brought in the Chicago network. Milton Friedman and Yale Brozen joined, and Warren Nutter even became the campaign's director of issue analysis.[78] Baroody brought in Bork specifically to work against the Civil Rights Act. Bork dove right in, writing a seventy-five-page legal analysis of the Civil Rights Act to back up the arguments against the law by another Goldwater lawyer, William Rehnquist.[79]

Goldwater was so reviled by the legal establishment that at first, Bork denied publicly being an advisor.[80] But Goldwater relied on Bork's analysis for his opposition to the Civil Rights Act, and gave Bork influence on policy and the candidate's speeches.[81] Bork had sought to enter Republican politics for years, but he was looking for the right conservative candidate. Eventually he realized Goldwater was his man.[82]

Despite initial embarrassment, Bork organized for Goldwater, coming up with lists of potential academics who might sign on as advisors. This list included most of the Chicago School network, as well as a Harvard law school faculty member named Phillip Areeda, who would become critical to the project a decade later.[83]

Goldwater lost the election, badly. But Goldwater's defeat validated the Chicago network, including Bork. As one South Carolina banker put it, "For us to have a Goldwater man at Yale is indeed encouraging."[84]

Goldwater wrote Bork after the campaign, saying, "I assure you that a hard-rock core of twenty-seven million people in this country will be looked at and respected by the opposition and we've at least made a start."[85] Twenty-seven million people was not enough to win a presidential election, but it was a huge audience. Bork understood how important he had become, and how the Chicago School ideology had advanced, telling a law firm friend, "I am not as discouraged as people think I should be. I think our general attitude should be that of the Bolsheviks after 1905."[86]

These three constituency groups—the corporate legal fraternity, business elites, and the new conservative grassroots—provided critical institutional power for the projection of this renewed style of Mellonism. Bork and the Chicago School network were becoming the credible opposition, the ones to stand outside the affluent society and question its workings. In 1964, George Stigler became the president of the American Economic Association. Milton Friedman asked Bork to speak to the AEA the next year, even though Bork was not an economist.[87] Three years later, the president of the AEA was Milton Friedman.

Big business finally came calling, through the nascent network of conservative business-funded think tanks being set up to reorient politics and through traditional business forums. In 1964, toward the end of the Goldwater campaign, AEI asked Bork to join as an antitrust policy advisor to help guide the think tank on where policy research might be useful.[88] Within a month, Bork was receiving funding from AEI to rewrite the history of antitrust. He chose to do a historical study, in theory to determine what Congress meant when it passed various antitrust statutes, starting with the Sherman Act in 1890. The correct rational way to do antitrust, he said, would "grow naturally out of this study."[89]

Over the course of the next year, AEI kept offering Bork money, as much as he needed to finish the study. The result was the germ of the book that, beginning a decade later, would entirely change how Washington elites understood—and enforced—America's antimonopoly laws. In the study, Bork contended, supposedly from a close reading of the legislative history, that just about everyone who had ever looked at the antitrust laws before him had misunderstood them. The "intent of Congress underlying the Sherman Act has been misrepresented by some authors," Bork argued, "and all authors seem to have missed the full implications of what was said in the debates leading up to the act."[90]

Bork argued that when Congress first passed the law in 1890, its sole intent was to promote what he now called "consumer welfare," which he defined as meaning solely efficient production.[91] Congress intended the Sherman Act, Bork went on, not as a means of protecting democracy, or markets, or the rights of citizens to produce and exchange free from interference by a monopolist. The only thing antitrust was meant to do was get consumers more stuff.

Bork's study of the legislative intent of the antitrust laws was, like John McGee's revisionist view of Standard Oil, a fiction. But in October 1966, the Chicago *Law and Economics Journal* published Bork's argument.

Bork's argument began to pay off almost immediately. On March 14 of that year he was invited to respond to Donald Turner, the Antitrust chief at the Department of Justice, in front of the National Industrial Conference Board, to discuss "Antitrust Issues in Today's Economy" at the Waldorf-Astoria in New York. In attendance were the most powerful executives in American business, including executives from U.S. Steel, Bechtel, B. F. Goodrich, Kimberly-Clark, Standard Oil of New Jersey, GM, and General Electric.[92] Bork's conservative ideas had not won, but this gathering was not the fringe. His views were now mainstream, heard in the Waldorf-Astoria by the most powerful businessmen in the land and debated by the nation's top antitrust cop. And his friendly relationship with Turner would soon ripen.

Bork assailed the recent Supreme Court's decisions in support of strong antitrust enforcement. "The court has come very close in its actions," he said, "if not in its words to the position that anything is illegal if the Government says it is."[93] A little less than three weeks later, the government argued a famous case against a grocery store merger, known as *Von's Grocery*. The Supreme Court ruled once again for the government, but a justice, Potter Stewart, wrote a dissent, saying "The sole consistency that I can find is that, in litigation under §7, the Government always wins."[94]

And the Court listened, with Justice Harlan citing Bork in the case requiring Procter & Gamble to divest itself of Clorox.[95] Bork and the Chicago Schoolers were on their way to capturing the heart of the corporate world and the legal establishment.

Corporate leaders began to warm to the new ideas. Alcoa VP and general counsel William Unverzagt pronounced himself "in substantial agreement with you in your philosophy of antitrust and thus am quite anxious to be of assistance to you." Unverzagt noted that he was in "a select circle of people who have read the entire trial record in the Roosevelt Administration's antitrust case against Alcoa," as Unverzagt had been a young lawyer indexing the transcript during the trial.[96] Bork wasn't just rethinking antitrust; he was double-checking it with Mellon lawyers.

That year, General Electric executives became much more serious about working with the Chicago School, inviting Bork to a corporate meeting to help "academicians . . . get a little better understanding of the operating procedures and problems of one large diversified firm as an aid in developing research problems."

GE gave Bork and Bowman a grant with specific instructions on research topics. When Bork pushed back on the explicitness of the instructions, a GE representative noted that the money was of course to "underwrite any phase" of their "research efforts as you deem best." This was important to GE. "Our top executives," said GE consultant

Donald Watson, "are very much interested in promoting research into this particular area." The financing of Bork was the beginning of a broader campaign by corporate America to grow the law and economics movement. Union Carbide, Chase Manhattan, ITT, GM, U.S. Steel, and Pfizer soon showed interest in the burgeoning movement.[97] So did top media executives in the business press; Louis Banks, the managing editor of *Fortune,* worked with Bork to promote his ideas, financing and cheering on Bork's articles and discussing "our continuing campaign to get people thinking afresh on antitrust policy."[98]

This corporate funding and business support paid off. The law and economics program at Chicago created a Government-Business Relations program, financed by the General Electric Foundation. By 1975, the dean of the law school, Norval Morris, was offering lavish praise to GE for its funding, noting that the school's law and economics program had both "great scholarly strength and substantial impact in practice."[99] This funding allowed Chicago scholars to continue to take down and ridicule opponents. One of these Chicago scholars, the Director-influenced John Peterman, attacked a key Supreme Court decision on corporate concentration. Peterman wrote a 1975 paper titled "The Brown Shoe Case" to continue the crusade.[100]

The Chicago School was ascendant, and in antitrust, Bork, though he was at Yale, was the legal star. The Department of Justice Antitrust Division began asking for his articles, and in 1966 the liberal senator Philip Hart requested his help on the intersection between antitrust and foreign trade. Bork and Donald Turner became closer. Turner asked for his recommendation on personnel appointments, and in return offered help to Bork.[101] Philip Elman, an elitist Federal Trade commissioner who would later leak damaging information about the FTC to Ralph Nader, began a friendly correspondence with Bork. Elman found Bork students "a lively, critical bunch. More power to you!"[102]

Bork's students were also beginning to spread out, continuing his crusade on their own. His students, in the private bar and in regulatory agencies, carried on his mission, as he had carried Aaron Director's. By the late 1960s, Bork detected that the ideological mettle of the antitrust bar was "weakening."[103]

## THE CAPTURE OF THE LIBERALS

The Chicago network saw as key foes John Kenneth Galbraith and the planner left. But what Galbraith had done to liberalism actually helped pave the way for the acceptance of this radical conservative movement. Galbraith and Chicago School thinkers loathed each other, but their philosophies synced well. Behind Galbraith's frame of affluence was an elitism he drew from Thorstein Veblen, and that same elitism from the same source animated Director's project.

This broad philosophical alignment reflected a shared approval of concentration of capital and the deployment of that capital by a technical elite. Stigler and Demsetz argued that economies of scale were understated in the economic literature. Galbraith agreed, noting "that there must be some element of monopoly in an industry if it is to be progressive."[104] They disagreed vehemently on who should be in control of American political economy, but, quietly, agreed that control should be in the hands of the few.

They also had a similar view of the history of capitalism. George Stigler called it "churlish" to argue that J. P. Morgan's $62 million fee for the creation of U.S. Steel was excessive.[105] Galbraith found such sums tacky and did a TV special insulting the boorish manners of the robber barons, but by and large agreed that fears of an earlier money trust were overblown."[106]

Galbraith also shared the Chicago School's appreciation for the power and usefulness of creating an entirely new system of language, if one's goal was to steer people's attention away from great concentrations of private corporate power. The following sentence could have been written by any author at the Chicago School: "It is part of the vanity of modern man that he can decide the character of his economic system."[107] But it was written by Galbraith. Both the corporatists on the right, and the corporatists on the left, believed that history, in some sense, unspooled according to knowable scientific rules. Chicago Schoolers hated Galbraith, but he had kicked open the door through which they would enter.

In the late 1960s, Bork began the process of working on the person who would become his most important convert: Donald Turner, the liberal economist and lawyer in charge of Johnson's Antitrust Division. Turner was the most influential lawyer in the liberal firmament, a key carrier of the argument that the market power of big companies was dangerous. He had argued since the 1950s that, effectively, corporate size should be restricted, and America's corporate apparatus was too concentrated. Policymakers, he argued, should pursue a radical plan of decentralization. Should he change his mind, much of the liberal legal establishment would follow.

As it proved, Turner was an easy mark. Although charming, Turner was also complacent, intellectually arrogant and indecisive, interested more in efficiency than questions of political power. Turner did not necessarily believe the antitrust laws were the way to decentralize corporate America, even if he thought that would be good policy. Turner was both an economist and a lawyer, and thus became the first economist to ever have significant policymaking power at the Department of Justice. He was thus easily seduced by the premise of science as law. He was also good friends and a collaborator with Harvard professor Phillip Areeda, who had been a conservative Republican on Bork's list of potential Goldwater supporters in 1964.

Staff attorneys in the division disliked their new boss. Turner had imposed a bureaucracy of young and bright lawyers to review all subpoenas and briefs under the guise of "rationalizing antitrust." Line attorneys came to detest Turner's technocrats, who they called, variously, "the Gold Coast," the "Harvard-Stanford axis," and "a tribe of pencil-pushers." Turner would shelve cases without telling the staff attorney, and settle cases with defense attorneys, in private, without the trial attorney for the case present. And he was a procrastinator, brilliantly examining all sides of an issue without making a decision. Attorney General Ramsey Clark, Turner's boss, summed up his tenure with the line, "I would not select a professor to run the Antitrust Division."[108]

Turner was quite comfortable with corporate power, and rumors were that LBJ had appointed him to the DOJ as a favor to corporate America.[109] His behavior didn't dissuade critics. Even as he ran the Antitrust Division, Turner was accepting favors from large corporations. In 1966, just after dropping an antitrust suit against big brewer

Anheuser-Busch, Turner took a trip to St. Louis to see the baseball All-Star game, flying on the Anheuser-Busch private plane.

When an Eisenhower official, FCC chair John Doerfer, was a guest on the Storer yacht while tasked with regulating the Storer broadcasting empire, Eisenhower demanded his resignation.[110] LBJ didn't like Turner, referring to him dismissively as a "Harvard professor," an ineffective and dishonest egghead. But he wouldn't fire him.[111] Turner's former law partner, Lloyd Cutler, represented General Motors, the largest company in the world, and would drop by the DOJ to argue that Turner should drop the antitrust case against the company for monopolizing the locomotive market.[112] Turner was going easy on GM, refusing to act on a draft complaint at the Department of Justice to break up the company. The wreckage of the company's anticompetitive behavior would only become clear after Turner had left office, with the bankruptcy in the 1970s of railroads GM had injured.[113]

In 1966, Turner came under rhetorical assault from one of the most powerful and well-connected muckrakers in D.C., Drew Pearson. Pearson was an antimonopolist, and thought that Turner was far too comfortable with corporate power.[114] Pearson reported a scandal surrounding Turner. A former law partner of Turner hired conservative economist and Bork writing partner Ward Bowman to write a secret memo meant to influence Turner on General Motors.[115] Pearson also accused Turner of "sitting on" a case involving the control over the biggest liquid petroleum pipeline in the world, running from Texas to New Jersey and jointly owned by the largest oil companies in the country.[116]

Pearson lambasted Turner for letting it be known that "he will bring no more criminal prosecutions and that he will let business plead nolo contendere (no contest) if it is caught redhanded." This was, as Pearson noted, "exactly what business has been asking Santa Claus for but never really expected to get."[117] The antitrust division, Pearson said, was becoming the "deadest division in Justice."[118]

Almost simultaneously Turner found himself attacked, mocked even, from the corporatist left, most damagingly by Galbraith, who pronounced the antitrust laws a charade and a joke. In 1967, Galbraith came out with *The New Industrial State,* a book considered so important the Senate held a debate between Turner and Galbraith over the merit of the antitrust laws.

In the hearing, Galbraith made fun of Turner, noting that if he were serious about addressing concentration, he would break up the biggest companies in the country, like IBM and General Motors.[119] It was a rhetorical masterstroke worthy of Milton Friedman and Robert Bork. Thurman Arnold, the great trustbuster and one of Turner's key influences, tried to buck up Turner's spirit by mocking Galbraith, saying, "he apparently thinks he has a set of abstract documents which is going to cure everything. It just shows that no economist should be permitted to practice unless he has a law degree."[120]

Attacked by populist muckraker Pearson for being passive, mocked by the corporate left-winger Galbraith for being aggressive, Turner didn't know what to do.[121] *The Wall Street Journal* soon called the lack of antitrust urgency an "antitrust slowdown," and Congressional critics attacked Turner.[122] The *Journal* revealed that there was a suit to break up General Motors sitting fallow at the Justice Department, one that would have undone some of the three hundred acquisitions by GM going back to the turn of the century.[123] Turner had the department "scrambling" to issue a statement. "The matter is indeed sitting in the Antitrust Division because of some very difficult issues," he said.[124] Turner never filed the suit.

Turner responded by retreating into technocratic solutions. In 1968, he wrote formal merger guidelines to give instructions to industry, angering the populist trustbusting staff in the division.[125] Enforcers saw these guidelines as a retreat from recent Supreme Court decisions that had created precedent for much stricter merger prohibitions.

He turned to friends in the academy for support, such as law professor Alexander Bickel, who authored a piece in *The New Republic* defending Turner and arguing his critics didn't understand that the law didn't assert that "big is bad."[126] Bork also penned supporting letters to Turner, who appreciated it while under political attack.[127] By the end of the Johnson administration, Turner was saying that Bork, aside from being "one of the five or six leading figures in the field of antitrust law and antitrust policy" was a "personal friend." He talked with him on various issues, and "valued these discussions very highly."[128]

Despite the progress Chicago Schoolers were making, and Turner's frustrations, the New Deal consensus was still solid, and Bork, though respected, was still a dissenting voice. In the final year of the Johnson administration, LBJ advisors considered a broad restructuring of industry, in the form of a task force that the Johnson administration put together to deal with corporate concentration. This task force was led by Chicago Law School dean Phil Neal, and its conclusion became known as the Neal Report. The report recommended a law called the Concentrated Industries Act to address the problem of big business, interlocking directorates, and the rising conglomerate movement. Robert Bork was a member of the task force, as well as the only dissenter. The Johnson administration shelved the report, perhaps until his second term, which would never come. Still, spurred by Attorney General Ramsey Clark, on the last business day of the Johnson administration (and after Turner had left his position), the Department of Justice filed a major antitrust suit against one of the most powerful companies in the world, IBM.

His time in the LBJ administration would be the high point of Turner's belief in economic structuralism. Later that year, Thurman Arnold, the trustbuster and mentor to so many liberals, including Turner, died, leaving a void in the liberal trustbusting pantheon.

Soon after Nixon took office, he appointed a rejoinder to the Neal Commission, this one led by George Stigler. Stigler attacked the idea of doing anything on conglomerate mergers. The Stigler report, like the Neal Report, came to nothing. But Nixon did appoint four Supreme Court justices who joined Potter Stewart to create a Bork-friendly majority on the court. In 1975, Gerald Ford appointed John Paul Stevens to the court. Stevens had co-taught a course with Aaron Director in what Stevens called the most important intellectual experience of his life.[129] In the mid-1970s, the high court began striking down precedents that had made it easy to block mergers.

Under Nixon, Bork, who once had been told he would never get a job at the Department of Justice, became solicitor general, one of the most important legal positions in the government.[130] But by this point, Bork had done most of the key intellectual work on antitrust economics. In the mid-1970s, he captured his prize when, under the "chastening" influence of the Chicago School's Donald Turner, he reversed himself on the problem of concentration, having become "significantly more skeptical about the benefits of aggressive judicial intervention."[131]

Turner and Areeda were then hired by IBM and set to work.[132] They wrote a key academic journal article encouraging courts to loosen rules against the use of below-cost pricing designed to drive competitors out of business, a traditionally illegal practice known as "predatory pricing." According to a colleague of Turner's, the two men wrote the paper to make it impossible for courts to ever rule against an incident of predatory pricing.[133] This change in court interpretation aided their client IBM, which had been found guilty of engaging in predatory pricing in a parallel private suit that mirrored the government's case. Influencing the IBM case was, as a colleague put it, "almost certainly" their intent.[134]

In their paper on predatory pricing, Turner and Areeda cited McGee's earlier work on Standard Oil, published in 1958, in the first edition of the University of Chicago's *Journal of Law and Economics*. Aaron Director had trained Robert Bork, who seduced Donald Turner. Director trained Ward Bowman, the lobbyist-economist for GM. And Director trained McGee, who wrote the initial attack on predatory pricing in 1958. Now, all these pieces came together; Aaron Director had won.

Then in 1978, Turner and Areeda published what became the most cited set of books on antitrust of all time, *Antitrust Law: An Analysis of Antitrust Principles and Their Application,* more often known as the Areeda-Turner Treatise.[135] Since Turner was an LBJ Democrat, no one understood the books to be in any way linked to Robert Bork's work, or the Chicago School project more widely.

But Aaron Director couldn't have planned it any better. The Chicago School counterrevolution was ready to regear American society. All it would take would be a crisis to open the door.

## CHAPTER TEN

# THE REBIRTH OF WALL STREET

"Last year the level of merger activity reached an all-time high, even surpassing the previous peak of 1929. Most of the acquisitions have been of the conglomerate variety."
—**Senator Philip Hart**[1]

■ ■ ■ ■ ■ ■ ■ ■ ■ ■ ■ ■ ■

In 1946, as scholars at the University of Chicago began restructuring the intellectual edifice of Mellonism, a young twenty-six-year-old veteran named Walter Wriston set out with equally assertive ambitions. While not immediately clear where to direct his boldness, Wriston eventually took upon himself the task of rebuilding the power of Wall Street. He did this from the sleepy remnant of the bank that from the days of J. P. Morgan until those of Mellon had dominated Wall Street, but had been disgraced during the Pecora hearings. When Wriston started his work, the bank's name was National City. Its nickname then—which harkens back to its original name at its 1812 founding—is now its official name, Citibank.[2]

Rebuilding the power of Wall Street was not Wriston's original plan. He didn't even really want to be a banker. Like millions of World War II veterans, he was just looking for something interesting to do. "I came in looking for a job so I could eat," he recalled later, noting how he pledged to leave after a year if the work was as boring as he feared it would be. Lean, tall, and nervously energetic, Wriston entered a staid, boring institution that did what it did because that's how it had always been done.

And banking did not seem to be a place to do interesting things. When Wriston arrived, Citibank was still recovering from the embarrassment of Charles Mitchell and the Pecora hearings, twelve years before. The bank hadn't hired for nearly twenty years, since the great crash.[3] Most older employees were lifers, deeply cautious, or newly arrived veterans like Wriston.

The glamorous roles at the bank were essentially selling banking services to the big companies. This kind of job wasn't for Wriston. Wriston was sharp-elbowed and argumentative, not considered "pretty enough" to cater to the corporate men in charge of the large deposits Citibank eagerly sought.[4] He spent his first few years as a bank branch inspector, in the guts of the bank, doing audits of branches and learning about loans that had gone sour.

He got his first big taste of risk-taking around 1950, when he was moved out of the bank's backwater operations area and eventually assigned the account of an aggressive and wild Greek businessman, Aristotle Onassis. Onassis saw the postwar boom in shipping, and was buying every tanker he could find to handle the burgeoning oil trade, profiting enormously from the demand.

The only limit on Onassis's business expansion was financing. The cautious bankers with whom he worked would only lend to him based on the value of the ship he sought to buy, severely restricting how quickly he could grow. In Wriston, Onassis finally had a banker as aggressive as he was a businessman.

Wriston and Onassis worked not only to borrow money for Onassis's fleet, but to generate a new model of financing for the postwar era. Instead of lending against the replacement value of a ship, Wriston would lend against the cash flow value of what that ship could earn by being leased out to oil companies. Wriston had come up with a way to make lending seem less risky, and Onassis was able to buy more and larger ships by borrowing more money.

The new lending model was a subtle but transformative shift in the politics of banking and business, from caretaking to profit maximizing. Lending against the replacement value meant that businesses would focus on making sure that they took care of their property, and on the quality of their ships and factories. Lending against cash flow, however, meant that businesses would focus on maximizing cash-generating activities, like tax avoidance. A ship was not valuable because it was well-maintained, but because it could quickly generate more cash.

What's more, Onassis built ships offshore for half the price of American ships, and would domicile them in tax havens like Liberia and Panama. "You wouldn't have to be a brilliant person to make money in a business where you never paid taxes," said one lawyer who worked with Wriston.[5] By using this new model of financing, Wriston and Onassis helped undermine the American-flag tanker fleet.

Eventually, Wriston's model of lending would be used in everything from Boeing airplanes, supertankers and shipping, petroleum industry assets, and eventually Manhattan skyscrapers.[6] Wriston's new financing model could push businesses to make bolder decisions that often did pay off, but it also began the process of focusing business leaders on short-term horizons.

In his dealings with Onassis, Wriston began revealing an aggression absent from the banking business since the crash. Wriston, despite telling others that he went to work in the bank so he could eat, had grown up in a powerful, ambitious family. He was an old-line aristocrat whose father had deep links to the State Department. Both he and his father bemoaned Franklin Delano Roosevelt's interventionist New Deal. Wriston would carry this loathing of centralized government power throughout his life. Onassis offered him a million dollars a year; Wriston turned him down, preferring to gain power within Citibank. He was not just after money, but power.

In 1953, Citibank shifted its internal structure to focus on specific industry sectors. As the bank was the leading financier for transportation, "anything that flew, floated, or rolled" anywhere in the country and often overseas would now be financed by a small group of men, including Wriston.[7]

One of the companies Wriston handled was United Parcel Service. In 1953, UPS sought to resume its air service, seeking financing from Citibank. But the loan to UPS was simply too big for the bank to take on itself. So Citibank organized a syndicate of banks, each of whom would lend part of the money. This was, again, a subtle shift in the politics of banking, because interstate banking restrictions—implemented to block the reemergence of J. P. Morgan–like power—had largely kept lending restrained within geographic markets. With the UPS loan, Citibank loosened interstate banking restrictions, ever so slightly.[8]

In 1955, Wriston completed one of the most important merger deals of the decade, a complex $42 million takeover of a big shipping line, the Waterman Steamship Corporation, by an aggressive trucking magnate named Malcolm McLean. The stock market was so sleepy and companies were so cautious that Waterman had more cash on hand than the entire value of its stock. National City lent McLean the entire purchase price of Waterman, meaning McLean had to put almost no money of his own down to gain control of the corporation.[9]

Upon its acquisition, Waterman paid out a special $25 million dividend, covering much of the loan with the margin of safety the conservative company had stashed away. McLean was an innovative manager, and later introduced important innovations in shipping containers, but the Waterman deal was the beginnings of the reconversion of the corporation, from a legal institution chartered to build a product or run a service for profit, to a financial asset meant solely to generate cash for its investors. McClean had bought a corporation by borrowing against that corporation's own assets.

In 1959, Wriston became head of the bank's international division, where he gained an understanding of what an unregulated banking order could look like. He oversaw branches in countries that didn't have strict banking rules and where Citibank could even underwrite securities. He also oversaw the trading of foreign currencies, the return of a bank to speculative endeavors.

In Europe, something new and interesting was going on. Europeans were lending and borrowing from one another, but in dollars, and with American banking regulators absent. This credit market soon acquired a name: the Eurodollar market. By 1959, Europeans began lending these "euro-dollars" back to American companies, once again outside the regulated banking system. "American corporations that are long on prospects but short of cash," wrote Albert Kraus, a *New York Times* reporter, "are turning increasingly to foreign sources of funds to augment bank credit hard to find in the United States."[10] This new foreign market of dollar-based banking would contribute to something that would come to be known as "deregulation."

Banking was still sleepy, but Wriston was noticing, and increasingly forcing, interesting changes, becoming more influential within Citibank as he did so. An aggressive young man in his position was placed well to take advantage of a new political context. In the early 1950s, there were signs of a loosening New Deal regime. The Fed had been subservient to Roosevelt and then Truman, setting interest rates at what the president chose. The central bank was responsive to elected officials. But in 1951, after a baroque series of political conflicts, the Federal Reserve broke from President Truman's control, with its board making decisions without taking orders from the White House. Senator Joseph O'Mahoney and Wright Patman opposed this change, but did not have the ability to reverse it.[11]

President Eisenhower, though no extreme conservative, was friendlier to bankers than Truman. By 1956, he was asserting it would be inappropriate for a president to publicy criticize Federal Reserve policies, arguing the Fed should not be "responsible to the political head of the state." A more conservative regime, in which private bankers had more influence, would run the Fed.[12] Eisenhower was not Herbert Hoover, and most of the Glass–Steagall regime remained, but it was a small and significant return of power to financiers.[13]

Eisenhower also thought bankers, and not the government, should set interest rates.[14] Bankers tend to like higher interest rates because the interest rate is the price of money, which is what they sell.[15] Higher interest rates mean higher profits for bankers. Patman, by contrast, thought high interest rates were immoral. Since everything required money to be built, increasing the cost of money increases costs of borrowing to businesses, municipalities, utilities like water, gas, telephone, and electricity, as well as government borrowing. Taxpayers, businesses, and citizens get hurt, to the benefit of bankers.[16]

It wasn't just Patman who sought low interest rates. Low rates had been a goal of Democratic Party policy since the 1800s. At one point, Truman attacked the Fed for increasing the cost of money, saying in an era of communist fears that higher rates "is exactly what Mr. Stalin wants."[17]

To fight higher rates, Patman organized within Democrats in the House. In 1955, he attempted to create a new money trust probe similar to that done in the House with the aid of Brandeis and Wilson. Patman's goal was to restructure the banking system and lower interest rates for borrowers. Eisenhower opposed Patman's resolution, and the House voted against him 214-178, with a coalition of Republicans and southern Democrats defeating the probe.

Rates headed higher, and in the fall of 1956, Congressmen were "flooded with protests from state and local governments" who could no longer afford to finance the building of schools, roads, hospitals and other facilities, as well as farmers, small businessmen, and home builders, all of whom were angry with the administration's "tight-money policies." Patman reintroduced his resolution in early 1957. Eisenhower cut off Patman with an announcement in the State of the Union for his own money probe, run by his more bank-friendly allies, like corporate liberals at the Committee for Economic Development. "We're in awful shape when we put our financial studies in the hands of Patman," Eisenhower privately told aides. "Makes me shudder."

Patman, backed even by powerful allies like House Speaker Sam Rayburn, once again lost the vote, but created constant pressure on policymakers for lower rates. "The administration worked harder to defeat the Patman resolution," said Rayburn deputy and Democratic whip Carl Albert, "than any other legislation proposed during this session of Congress—it feared a Congressional probe into its manipulations of interest rates and government borrowings." Patman never stopped his crusade against high interest rates, creating a steering committee of fellow Congressmen to oppose increases in interest rates by the Federal Reserve, clashing not just with Eisenhower, but with his successors LBJ and Nixon in the process.[18] Drew Pearson wrote that "Patman . . . is as homey as an old shoe," but with high interest rates, "he becomes passionate and indignant." Pearson sympathized with Patman's view that "high rates were threatening the American economy, preventing home building, indirectly causing racial unrest in Cleveland, Detroit, and Watts because of poor housing."[19]

More political cracks appeared. Set free from their wartime constraints, and then from the constraints imposed by White House control over the Fed, bankers tried to seize more power. In the 1950s, several banks attempted to escape from restrictions on where they could gather deposits by creating bank holding companies. This legal structure allowed a bank to form a parent company, and that parent company would purchase a series of banks, or even nonbank businesses. For years, antimonopolists and the Fed had recommended this loophole be closed. These "multi-bank holding companies" could expand outside a bank's home area to get deposits, and even buy nonbanking companies.[20]

In 1956, Congress responded by passing the Bank Holding Company Act, a bill to, as one lawyer put it, close the "key routes to a national banking empire."[21] This bill strengthened the prohibition against banks engaging directly in nonbanking businesses. It also restricted interstate banking by bank holding companies. Memories of fascism colored the debate. Patman ally Sam Rayburn gave a speech to independent bankers in which he walked them through the logic that financial concentration led to industrial concentration which led to fascism. "Policies and important credit decisions are made hundreds or thousands of miles from many of the branches," he said. "This inevitably tends toward concentration in all lines, cartels, the stifling of new enterprises, and stagnation. When forced to choose between such monopoly and some ism, countries invariably have chosen the ism."[22]

In 1957, a powerful Democratic senator on the banking committee named Willis Robertson proposed a 250-plus-page banking reform bill that he told colleagues was a set of technical fixes. The bill was not just a set of modest technical shifts, but would have revamped the banking system, eliminating usury laws and virtually immunizing banks from antitrust scrutiny. It sailed through the Senate, but Patman bogged down the bill in the House Banking Committee. He told Rayburn, an ally in the low interest rate caucus, that it was not just a technical bill, but "a big bankers bill that will destroy the Democratic Party." The bill died.[23]

Politically, the 1950s were a stalemate, with bankers attempting to regain their political power, and New Dealers holding the line. The American economy was doing well. Credit was expanding. The Fed began looking the other way when banks would break rules, so it was a good moment for an aggressive younger banker like Wriston to learn his trade.

## CREATING THE SHADOW BANKING SYSTEM

In 1961, the forty-three-year-old John F. Kennedy, a new youthful symbol of American power, became president. Kennedy had with him a set of liberal technocratic economic advisors. These men believed they knew just which knobs in government—taxes, spending, interest rates—to twist to make sure the economy hummed along and everyone had a job. These men airbrushed power out of their analysis; their highly mathematized models of the economy even excluded banks.[24]

Kennedy's advisors thought class conflict and robber barons were history. One popular idea at the time was called "convergence theory," by economist Simon Kuznets. This theory rested on the assumption that economic equality just happened naturally as the economy produced more. It was a technocratic theory to match John Kenneth Galbraith's arguments about affluence.

This generation of economist aimed to depoliticize banking, which is how Wriston wanted it. Six months after Kennedy's inauguration, Wriston took another step up, becoming an executive vice president of the bank, and in the line of succession for the leadership. Wriston was a conservative, but he liked John F. Kennedy, and thought his freshness was "a pick-me-up for the country."[25] Kennedy pledged to get the country moving again. In his own way, Wriston wanted to get banking moving again. Wriston also liked one of Kennedy's key banking regulators, James Saxon at the Office of the Comptroller of the Currency (OCC), an obscure but powerful regulatory agency with a mandate over national banks. Saxon saw Citibank as his client, and he fought as hard as Wriston to strip New Deal rules constraining the banking sector.

Just weeks after Kennedy's inauguration, Wriston announced what looked to most outsiders as a small, technical product for corporate treasurers. It was called the negotiable certificate of deposit, or the CD. Though seemingly abstruse, the CD, as the OCC put it years later, "revolutionized the world of finance," providing a way for banks to get deposits that had heretofore been restricted from them.[26]

The CD solved an existential dilemma for Citibank. By the late 1950s, the bank was shrinking, shackled by regulation, unable to get enough deposits to conduct its banking business. It had lost tremendous market share in finance to other institutions. Between 1945 and 1960, the assets of life insurance companies tripled, savings and loan banks increased by nine times, and pension funds went up fifteen-fold. Commercial banks, in contrast, increased by just 60 percent. Even worse, a major source of their deposits was evaporating. Big corporations had, until the late 1950s, kept pools of cash on deposit with New York banks such as Citibank and Chase. But as interest rates increased, corporate treasurers began to engage in "cash management," finding alternatives to keeping deposits on hand.[27] The Marshall Plan, and expanding European markets, created demand for banking services to facilitate trade. But without deposits, New York banks couldn't service the demand. "Money center" banks, as they were known, were in danger of becoming irrelevant.

The key problem for Citibank was Regulation Q. This rule made big banks like Citibank just like every other bank, able to gather deposits from its own local area. It could not access all the cash being earned by a vibrant middle class. Citibank simply wasn't allowed to pay for deposits, so people and corporations put their cash in local banks, or alternatives such as Treasury bills. "We looked at the data," Wriston said, "and it turned out that demand deposits in New York City had not grown for ten years. You didn't have to be a rocket scientist to know we were going to go out of business."[28] Citibank was not in danger of going out of business, but it was in danger of becoming far less important, a regulatory design choice made because New Dealers wanted it that way.

At first, New York money center banks tried to grow their deposit base through mergers. In early 1955, one of the largest and most storied banks in American history, the Bank of Manhattan Company, merged with Chase Bank to form the second-largest bank in the country (the largest being Citibank). In an oddly structured merger, Chase ended up surrendering its bank charter and operating under the 1799 Manhattan bank charter secured by Aaron Burr to challenge Alexander Hamilton's banking monopoly.

Aggressive consumer-focused banks, stuffed with deposits from an increasingly wealthy middle class, were now merging with staid big-business-oriented ones to solve the deposit shortage. Chemical Bank and Trust absorbed the Corn Exchange Bank Trust Company, while Manufacturer's Trust acquired the Brooklyn Trust Company. New York City banks began lobbying to loosen state rules against expanding outside of the five boroughs, hoping to capture fat consumer deposits in the growing suburbs.[29]

Wriston's National City followed the Chase Manhattan purchase with a merger of its own, with First National.[30] But this marriage wouldn't be nearly enough. Limiting deposit growth to what New Yorkers decided to hold in their bank accounts couldn't hope to fulfill a global bank's ambitions.[31]

In 1961, Wriston and a former Federal Reserve official turned Citibank executive named John Exter found a solution. They noticed that European banks were issuing bondlike instruments known as certificates of deposit. These CDs paid an interest rate. Wriston and Exter realized that, if structured correctly, a CD could basically act like a high-interest deposit account, and help Citibank blow through Regulation Q. Citibank could begin attracting deposits from big corporations again (and eventually it would offer CDs to middle-class individuals).

The key was to make the CD act like a deposit account. The CD had to become "negotiable," meaning sellable in a secondary market, just like Treasury bills that were bought and sold every day. In front of the scenes, the depositor would put money into a Citibank CD, which seemed like a savings account. Behind the scenes, Citibank was actually trading on behalf of the depositor. To deposit money, a corporation could go to Citibank or a secondary market and buy a Citibank CD; to withdraw it, they could sell their CD to someone else who wanted it.[32] A negotiable CD would then function like a deposit yielding a higher rate of interest.

But there was a catch. To buy and sell CDs, there had to be a financial market for CDs. And there wasn't one. And there was no one interested in taking the risk to create such a market. In every financial market with lots of buyers and sellers, someone always has to stand in the middle, to make sure the trading is orderly, to set rules, and to make sure buyers and sellers follow them. This was often done by independent trading firms. These firms were a bit like a financial warehouse, temporarily holding bonds that someone might want to buy or taking in bonds that someone wants to sell, managing financial inventory.

Citibank couldn't create a market for CDs itself, because that was against laws set up by New Dealers that blocked commercial banks from trading. And no one would create a market in CDs without an incentive to do so. After all, to create a market, you have to have access to money. You have to be able to buy the inventory in the first place, and you have to be able to buy and sell financial instruments all the time. It can also be a risky business; if the market drops, you can be left holding an inventory of financial instruments that are worth less than you paid.

Wriston and Exter asked Herbert Repp, the chairman of Discount Corporation, one of the most important Treasury bill dealers in the country, to create a market for CDs. Repp agreed, under one condition. He wanted a $10 million loan, which was both a violation of Citibank's policy of not lending to unsecured brokers and a violation of conflict of interest provisions in New Deal regulations.[33] Wriston said yes anyway.

This transaction was a way to avoid New Deal laws and rules designed to stop hot money from corrupting the banking system. But in the new and more permissive environment, the Fed, while not pleased, condoned it. The Fed was concerned about money center banks losing deposits. Salomon Brothers and First Boston Corporation then announced they would also make a market in CDs. Wriston bet that by the time the Fed decided to act, the CD would be too important for the Fed to kill it off.[34]

"The new instrument," according to *Fortune,* "took the banking community by storm." Cash flooded into the big banks, with $5.8 billion of CDs outstanding by the end of 1962, $18 billion by August 1966, and $90 billion by 1974.[35] There was now no limit on what money center banks could lend, because they were no longer tethered to a local deposit base. *Barron's* observed that "these certificates gained such widespread acceptance that their rates became the money market's most keenly watched indicator, more so even than the traditional bellwether, Treasury bill yields."[36] As they had been able to in the 1920s, banks could now buy money anywhere in the world.

The CD was considered a tremendous financial innovation, but it was really just a clever way of getting around New Deal constraints.

More such "innovations" occurred later in the decade. But all of these were variants of the negotiable CD, a way of creating a redeemable deposit-like instrument that was not regulated, as regulators looked the other way.

Large banks could now buy deposits again, and take much bigger risks.[37] "The tremendous inflow of money into commercial banks was a form of energy," said a banking consultant. Banks began "breaking or bending" traditional barriers, entering high-margin businesses such as credit cards, leasing, and mortgage services.[38] As banks gained power, the ability for public controls over finance, and the plain people to access money, began to decline.

Citibank transformed from a regional bank dependent on regional and corporate relationships to one that exported money globally. Attempts to restrict lending by raising interest rates, or changing reserve requirements, no longer worked on the banks. If there was loan demand, the big banks could now find a way to meet it.[39]

The CD opened the spigots for the Kennedy boom, spurring a stock market frenzy. It allowed the big banks to speculate again, offering them the ability to get around the strict regulated banking system, and build up a new unregulated parallel banking system just for the powerful. As Wriston, enabled by timid regulators, gradually broke the highly compartmentalized financial order of the New Deal, a new system began springing up, a parallel banking world, side by side with the old regulated one. Like two people fighting over control of the steering wheel of a car, private financiers in their largely unregulated money markets began grappling for power with public regulators. The result was an increasingly unstable financial system.

In 1967, Wriston became the president of Citibank, one of the most influential men in American business. As he grew more powerful, Wriston grew more aggressive about fighting government regulation. "There was something emotional about his drive," said Albert Wojnilower, one of the few Wall Street economists who saw the dangers in what Citibank was doing. "I felt Wriston wanted simply to dismantle the financial system as we knew it."[40]

Under his leadership, Citibank officials would constantly try to think of creative ways to get around regulations. At one point, Wriston mused on whether Citibank could *buy* a foreign country and write its own rules in its own domicile.[41] This idea was ridiculous, because Citibank depended on the American government, through the Federal Reserve and the Federal Deposit Insurance Corporation, for its very ability to exist. Still, such musings spoke to the lengths to which Wriston wanted to go. Wriston would encourage a sense of lawlessness among his subordinates, telling them, "Clerks follow the rules. You guys are hired to break the rules."[42]

By the 1970s, Wriston would eventually become friends with Milton Friedman, and draw inspiration from the network of Chicago scholars.[43] Wriston became the key organizer of finance, law, and industry of his time, much in the vein of J. P. Morgan or Andrew Mellon, only without the massive personal financial holdings. Wriston was, as another bank chairman put it years later, "the acknowledged leader of our generation of bankers."[44] Unlike his predecessors, Wriston was no cultural conservative; he fought to bring women, Jews, and Catholics into Citibank, saying talent has "no passport, gender, color, or anything else."[45]

By the time Wriston became head of Citibank, bank credit was expanding much faster than the economy. The long boom of the 1960s was fueled by the funds being pumped into the banking system.[46] In 1961, commercial banks had started offering CDs only in large denominations of over $100,000; by the mid-1960s, they were offering CDs in $1,000 lots that ordinary people could afford.

But just as money center banks had been losing funds in the 1950s to other institutions, now they began to take funds that had been going to finance housing, small business lending, and government spending for the war in Vietnam. A host of factors—including an economic boom and spending on the war—were already straining demand for the nation's savings. But this early deregulation allowed and even forced banks to compete for this limited pool, pushing up interest rates much further and faster. The Kennedy business expansion fed on itself, as high interest rates caused companies to borrow and spend before interest rates went even higher. A class speculative boom developed, with private financiers increasingly dominating the economic boom.

Commercial banks were taking more deposits that had been going to savings and loan associations, and mortgage lending from S&Ls was dropping. S&Ls made long-term mortgage loans, and their portfolios turned over slowly. They could not compete in a high-interest world with sudden changes in rates. A housing shortage was developing. The compartments that had kept specialized credit institutions separate by making sure they had separate pools of deposits and different lending markets broke down. In May of 1966, Wright Patman attempted to pass a law banning the negotiable certificate of deposit.

The S&Ls and small bankers both worried as their financing fuel dried up. The head of the American Bankers Association warned that "unrealistic generous rates paid on CDs threaten to siphon funds out of smaller banks, and therefore, disrupt the flow of credit in many of the communities of the country."[47] Norman Strunk of the United States Savings and Loan League warned of another 1929-type situation, with a battle over hot money among banks.[48]

Regulators realized the massive growth in hot money had become a threat to the economy and the banking system.[49] As one Federal Reserve official noted, hot money from CDs was the "most vulnerable" type of bank funding because corporations and holders of CDs were likely to respond quickly to small changes in interest rates.

CDs were technically regulated under Regulation Q. The Federal Reserve, however, began to worry that if it tried to stop banks from offering these high-interest deposits, it would cause a sort of bank run in this parallel financial system. Depositors in CDs would flee the banks and banks would stop lending, causing a credit crunch. As Wriston had foreseen, by the time the Fed tried to step in, the CD had become so entrenched in the gears of the credit system that regulating it might cause significant damage.

Every time the interest rate of CDs came close to the limit set by Regulation Q, the Federal Reserve would avoid a conflict with money center banks by raising the rate ceiling. The standoff grew more intense.[50] The Fed was supposed to be in control of the financial system. In the 1950s, bankers would recoil in terror at an arched eyebrow from a Federal Reserve official. By the 1960s, the Fed was increasingly being held hostage.

The situation came to a head in 1966, when Patman's fears over high interest rates and dwindling central bank power were realized. In the first eight months of the year, both business and government borrowed heavily. Corporations raised $13 billion from selling securities, an increase of 25 percent from the previous year. They also borrowed from banks to prepay taxes, which the government required to finance the Vietnam War. In August, usually a light month, the government, corporations, and states and cities borrowed an especially large amount. Interest rates jumped.

The interest rate hit the rate ceiling of Regulation Q. This time the Fed decided it would not allow banks to continue to raise deposit rates in CD accounts. This caused a bank run in the new parallel banking system. Corporations withdrew their CD deposits from banks, so banks had to curtail their lending. Lending to all but the most secure customers stopped. Bank CEOs began to beg corporate customers not to let their certificates of deposit run off.

The credit crunch in the financial system moved quickly into the real economy. People looking to borrow money for a home, even with good credit, couldn't find it. Cities had a harder time borrowing money, as interest costs increased and bankers unloaded their holdings of municipal bonds. Business lending collapsed. Regulators and members of Congress panicked. Representative Thomas Rees of Los Angeles sought to crack down on CDs; "over-investment in CDs," he said, meant that "new mortgage money is very hard to find."[51] Responding to Americans' fears over drying-up credit, Lyndon Johnson appeared on television and said, "I pledge to the American people that I will do everything in the President's power to lower interest rates and to ease money in this country."[52] The banking system had come to depend on the hot money Wriston had unleashed.

Finally, the Fed acted. On September 1, 1966, its twelve branches sent identical "fist-in-glove" letters inviting banks to the discount window where they could borrow from the government. The panic subsided. Still, business investment collapsed, dropping at an annual rate of 26 percent in the fourth quarter of 1966 and the second quarter of 1967.[53] It didn't look like a recession, because increased spending on the war in Vietnam picked up the slack. But Americans were experiencing a confusing economic period, with high inflation and interest rates, layoffs, credit crunches, and a recession in some parts of the economy, but a boom in the military sector.[54]

The old boom-and-bust cycle of the robber barons had returned, but with a twist. During boom times, the private financiers would steer money into speculation and away from public priorities such as housing. But when the bust came, private bankers would turn the wheel over to public officials. Instead of nineteenth-century bank failures, because of the regulated banking sector, there would now be twentieth-century bank bailouts.

A few months after the Fed acted, as California continued to suffer from the overhang of a mortgage crisis, conservative Republican Ronald Reagan crushed Pat Brown in the state's gubernatorial race.[55] Democrats all over the country were routed. The election was, in part, a "backlash" election against the Great Society and the civil rights movement. But progressive Republicans won as well. Edward Brooke, the first African American in the Senate since Reconstruction, took the Senate seat in Massachusetts as a Republican. Political economy as much as race was on the ballot, which is why Democrats lost to both right-wing and progressive Republicans.

Soon the economy veered into a new boom. And for the first time since the 1920s, the stock market played a central role.

## THE GO-GO YEARS OF THE STOCK MARKET

In the 1920s, the New York Stock Exchange was in many senses a private club, aristocratic, based on insider ties. J. P. Morgan's preferred list showed that profits came to those who were well-connected. Disgraced during the 1930s, the New York Stock Exchange managed to return to cultural relevance because it was democratized by the New Dealers.

The Securities and Exchange Commission, created in 1934, enforced rules ensuring that all investors, from the smallest to the biggest, had equal access to information about the companies they were investing in. There were a host of new rules, like margin requirements, making it harder to borrow for speculative purposes. The Investment Company Act of 1940 regulated investment trusts, which were pools of money managed by professionals, to prevent the looting of the small investor.

As banks returned to vigor in the placid 1950s economy, so did the stock market. Stocks had done well in the 1950s, but most Americans ignored the opportunity. This reticence was both a cultural hangover from the depression, and because it was logistically hard to put money into stocks.

By 1958, there were tremors of a new model of financial entrepreneurship. A debonair, Chinese-born, twenty-nine-year-old named Gerald Tsai Jr. started the Fidelity Capital Fund, which was a product known as a mutual fund, a mass market means to invest in stocks similar to the pools of the 1920s. Mutual funds had existed for decades, but since the crash had been mostly unimportant. The Investment Company Act barred the pyramiding of investment pools that had allowed financiers to use a small bit of capital to wield large sums of investment money. In 1940, there was roughly $450 million in mutual funds, a paltry sum. The gradually increasing market and increasing ease of investment drew notice. By the end of the 1950s, Americans held $13 billion in mutual funds.

Within a month of Kennedy's inauguration, the stock market was on fire. It had increased by 15 percent from its October lows. The "Kennedy boom" continued. By mid-April, a week after the Bay of Pigs, it was up 25 percent.[56] For much of the rest of the decade, with expanding bank credit and higher spending on the Vietnam War, the stock market exploded. And there were now mass market means to participate and send some of that rich American savings into stocks. The amount of money in such funds doubled from 1963 to 1968.[57]

Fidelity began a marketing campaign to make investing sexy, as John Raskob had done in 1929. Tsai was a reporter's dream, wearing "elegant French cuffs," posing for photographs for reporters, and manicuring his hands while pandering to the orientalist instincts of reporters who described him as "inscrutable." "Gerald Tsai Jr.," wrote *Newsweek*, "radiates total cool."[58] And Tsai's celebrity status rose because his gunslinging style generated much larger returns than even the buoyant market would normally generate. In 1962, Tsai's fund gained 68 percent in just three months, and in 1965 it jumped 50 percent. This was not investing as prudent conservative bankers saw it; it was gambling. But in a bull market, Tsai looked less like a lucky opportunist, and more like an investment genius.

The gunslinger model of mutual fund performance investing began changing the American relationship with money. Savings and investing started becoming personal finance. Instead of holding stocks for decades, mutual funds would seek performance, selling stocks and bonds as necessary to do so. In 1966, Tsai set out on his own. He sought $25 million. Excited investors clamored to get in, and he raised ten times as much. It was a democratic form of fund; eventually he attracted over 200,000 shareholders. Tsai was the first celebrity fund manager, riding the wave of speculation induced by exploding bank credit.[59]

The rise of mutual funds was not the only institutional shift. Specialized brokerage services, like trading in large blocks of shares, popped up. And banks took advantage of the rising stock market of the 1950s and then 1960s to build out their own trust departments, which managed the portfolios in trust for wealth investors. In 1967, bank trust departments owned at least 5 percent of hundreds of the biggest industrial corporations. Bank trust departments were held in check, at least somewhat, by studies done by congressional committees controlled by Wright Patman.[60]

Much of this was fueled by the bank credit Wriston had unleashed. The credit crunch of 1966, which could have cratered the economy and the stock market, instead proved only a momentary pause. Government spending and Federal Reserve support of the banking system meant that panic didn't turn to caution. Not long after the crunch, both bankers and speculators once again began gambling.

Toward the end of the decade, the roaring market got a name. It was called the "Go-Go" stock market, named perhaps after a lively and free form of dancing, often in cabarets or clubs.[61]

In many respects, the 1960s stock market boom was different than that of the 1920s, or previous financial periods of euphoria. It was more democratic. More people took part. But it also marked the beginning of a new degree of concentration of power and control. The rise of mutual funds and bank trust departments enabled a small number of people to control billions of dollars of financial instruments. By the late 1960s, a serious merger industry had developed as a result of the growth of mutual funds and bank trust departments, or what one business professor at the time called a "concentration of financial securities among relatively few people." These institutional developments made it possible for, he said, "a small group of men working together to readily amass the huge amounts of money and establish the new issuances of securities" necessary to take over corporations.[62]

Once again a financier could, over a lunch with the right men in New York, locate most of the shares needed to buy a company. And that's what started happening.

## THE CONGLOMERATE CRAZE AND
## THE RECONSTRUCTION OF THE MONEY TRUST

In the second weekend of February 1969, New York City hotel bars were full of bored bankers. The brutal Sunday blizzard across the Northeast—fifteen inches of snow in the city alone—had closed the airports, clogged the roads, and delayed commuter rails.[63] Hundreds of bankers from all over the country, in town for the annual American Bankers Association trust conference, were trapped. There was nothing to do but talk, and the only subject anyone wanted to talk about was the hostile takeover attempt of Chemical Bank by a conglomerate raider, Saul Steinberg.

The takeover attempt was not normal. Ridiculous, perhaps. Frightening, maybe. Unusual, certainly. The third great merger wave in twentieth-century America had been going on since 1965, with 4,400 corporations disappearing in 1968 alone.[64] But a takeover such as this one? First there was the corporate raider himself, Saul Steinberg. He was twenty-nine and Jewish. Commercial banking just didn't have very many Jews, especially at the top levels.[65] While there were some Jews in investment banks, it was unthinkable for a man like Steinberg to buy such a revered commercial institution.

Steinberg's company, Leasco, was just eight years old, and had been tiny until the year before. Steinberg buying Chemical would be a minnow swallowing a whale. And Steinberg wasn't just trying to buy any old bank. He was going after an icon of America, Chemical Bank New York Trust Company. On this Sunday in early February of 1969, when bankers were chattering with snowdrifts outside in the New York City streets, Chemical held $9 billion in assets, and was the sixth-largest commercial bank in the country. Chemical had been a leader in American banking since before the Civil War. It was one of the largest single capital pools in the nation.

The directors included a DuPont, the chairman of AT&T, the president of IBM, the finance chair of U.S. Steel, and the former president of the New York Stock Exchange.[66] The chairman of the bank was William Renchard, a handsome sixty-one-year-old Princeton graduate from Trenton with iron-gray hair. Renchard had middle-class roots, but he had climbed up the social respectability ladder to the top. He had spent nearly his whole life at Chemical, since the depression, even.

Steinberg, ironically, was also in New York for a corporate event, but he wasn't a banker, so he wasn't invited to any of their parties. He was from Brooklyn, the son of a maker of rubber products. The takeover attempt seemed absurd.

Steinberg's business, started in 1961, was computer leasing, which meant he bought expensive computers and then rented them out. It wasn't much of a business, being what one economist called "an accounting gimmick." But in a sense, that was the point. Steinberg used accounting assumptions to make his company look like a highly profitable and fast-growing "tech" company. In 1965, Leasco raised $750,000 by going public, and by the late 1960s Steinberg's company was a hot stock traded on the New York Stock Exchange. Steinberg might not have had much of a business. But investors thought he did.

Steinberg began to use his stock to buy companies with real assets. He hired a management consultant and tasked him with finding companies to take over. Gerald Tsai would gamble in stocks. Steinberg began to gamble with entire companies. Steinberg would no longer just buy computers and use them as financial vehicles; he would now do so for entire corporations. In doing so, he was riding the hot new "conglomerate" trend of the decade, a repurposed pre–New Deal financial strategy.

In the 1920s, shaky "financial pyramids," known as investment trusts or holding companies, and built with little cash and huge amounts of borrowed money, took advantage of the investing public's desire to be a part of the bull market. These rickety structures accelerated the swings of the stock market, both driving the euphoria of 1928 and 1929 and the collapse from 1929 to 1933.

In the 1960s, men like Steinberg re-created this investment trust model, similarly built on borrowed money. But he and his ilk called them conglomerates. The conglomerate craze would be a sustained financier-led attack on the New Deal.[67]

Conglomerates weren't exactly new. These corporate structures had been around since the early days of the modern industrial era. A conglomerate is simply a holding company or corporation that operates in multiple different industries, usually owning individual divisions that could stand apart as separate businesses on their own. Early conglomerates were initially focused on a suite of related activities, like GE and electrical systems in the 1900s or branded food conglomerates of the 1920s.

But in the early 1960s a new type of conglomerate emerged, although this time these corporations were shaped by strict antitrust laws. In this instance, cash-rich corporations like RCA and LTV invested in entirely unrelated lines of business—Hertz or Wilson Sporting Goods, say—the argument being that an excellent executive team could manage any line of business well. One of the highest-flying conglomerates at the time, LTV, bought business lines in missiles, electronics, electrical cable, sporting goods, meat and food processing, and pharmaceuticals. As long as the stock market went up, this arrangement looked great.

At the center of this trend were the large banks. Chase Manhattan used its newfound power to organize its own pet conglomerates. Gulf and Western was one. Chase gave the fast-growing conglomerate an unsecured loan of $84 million to buy New Jersey Zinc. In return, Gulf and Western pressed all its subsidiaries to do business with Chase, and shared information about upcoming takeovers with the bank (which could use that information in its trust department). Chase was using its financial power to run swaths of businesses, through its business alliance with Gulf and Western.[68]

Power, as one analyst put it, was shifting "from the managers to the financial interests." Wall Street loved the new firms, though as one banker noted, whether one conglomerate "for example, can really run the best meatpacking business and the best steel business remains to be seen."[69] In reality, conglomerates were financial vehicles taking advantage of lax accounting and tax rules in a rising stock market.

These conglomerates were shaped by strict antitrust laws. There were strict restrictions on market shares in any one market, and strict limits on acquiring suppliers or customers in the same industrial supply chain. So one response by financiers was to buy totally unrelated lines of business so as to avoid scrutiny by antitrust agencies. The main point of the mergers was not to monopolize, but to create deal flow and profits for bankers, and to justify higher salaries and bonuses for executives, who now in theory had bigger portfolios of responsibilities.

By the late 1960s Steinberg was riding this new wave of conglomeration. As long as the stock market went up, this looked great. "No creation of the U.S. economy reflects the vigor, imagination, and sheer brass of the 1960s more than the conglomerate corporations," blared *Business Week*. "Wheeling and dealing with panache and merging with seeming haste all over the lot, they have shattered the cautious business clichés that have prevailed since the Depression. In so doing, they have mushroomed suddenly into some of the nation's largest industrial empires."[70] The actual business model underlying these business arrangements was the same as that of John Raskob or any other speculator. They were borrowing money to buy assets when the stock market was going up. Conglomerates were just doing it with entire companies. Sometimes conglomerates would, rather than borrow money, issue strange combinations of debt and stock, nicknamed "corporate underwear," "funny money," "Chinese money," and use it to buy real businesses. As *Business Week* put it, "They have a remarkable facility for creating profits seemingly out of thin air."

The conglomerate accounting illusion and a booming stock market were Steinberg's tools. He would use Leasco's high-flying stock, or its borrowing capacity, to buy actual assets earning income, and then use that income to justify his company's stock price. The business press and policymakers noted this chicanery, but it went unnoticed elsewhere. The month Lyndon Johnson decided not to run for reelection over the tumult over the Vietnam War, Steinberg's Leasco began a takeover attempt of the $350 million giant Reliance Insurance Company, which was a conservatively managed fire-and-casualty insurance company that had too much capital on hand to back its policies.[71]

For the country, the spring of 1968 was traumatic; the country mourned the assassinations of Martin Luther King and Robert Kennedy. But Steinberg was busy buying Reliance stock. By August, he had won the company, and Steinberg was worth $50 million at age twenty-nine. Steinberg bought a twenty-nine-room South Shore estate on Long Island, with two saunas, Picassos and Kandinskys, and a tennis court, and bragged about it constantly. Steinberg was the leading edge of a new post-depression generation on Wall Street, one that didn't know not to show open greed.

In the process, he inspired a generation of other young men. Steinberg had used his overvalued stock to buy real assets, and he became the conglomerate king. Leasco became one of the best-performing stocks through 1968, jumping in value fifty-four times in five years. If Steinberg could do it, so could almost anyone.

The conglomerate wave was the training ground for an entire generation who would build a new Wall Street. A young Arthur Levitt, who became SEC chair under Bill Clinton, and a young Sandy Weill, who finally broke down Glass-Steagall in 1999 as the CEO of Citigroup, both helped spur this movement along. Their small brokerage authored a key report encouraging conglomerate takeovers of insurance companies to grab a steady stream of cash for investing purposes. In 1967, their report landed on Steinberg's desk. (In this period, another young investor named Warren Buffett used a small holding company called Berkshire Hathaway to purchase an insurance company, with which he would seed an empire with investment capital.)

For the first time since the 1920s, a merger industry was developing, with large firms beginning to hire staff concerned with acquisitions. The stock market was changing, with institutional brokerages developing the ability to buy and sell large blocks of shares to accommodate large institutional investors and the new merger business. Management consultants, lawyers, and accountants began learning how to offer technical advice on mergers and acquisitions, and even to promote them. A magazine titled *Mergers & Acquisitions* launched.[72]

The takeover of Reliance wasn't enough for Steinberg. He wanted more, and set his sights on Chemical Bank. Reliance was part of Chemical's insurance portfolio, and they held a good chunk of the bank's stock; in November of 1968, while the nation fixated on the dramatic presidential contest among Richard Nixon, Hubert Humphrey, and segregationist George Wallace, Reliance began buying more.[73] In early 1969, bank chairman William Renchard got word the takeover attempt was on.

At the Plaza in snowy February, Chemical was hosting its reception for bankers at the ABA conference. Mostly they thought Steinberg was ridiculous. "Don't joke," Renchard warned them. "If this is successful, the next target may be you." The high-flying upstart conglomerate Resorts International had just considered buying venerable American corporation Pan Am. Goodrich Tire and Rubber was a potential target for Northwest Industries. Takeover targets weren't just mom-and-pop operations; this new breed of moneymen was targeting American royalty.

Renchard had his own weapons, and he wasn't about to let a man like Steinberg run such an illustrious board, or command the power of a money center bank. On February 5, Renchard struck. Mysteriously, from February 6 to February 28, 1969, Leasco's stock fell from $140 to $99. Large round blocks of stock were sold virtually every day, sold by operators of the newest and hottest mutual funds.[74] No one could prove it (though Wright Patman asked), but it looked like a classic "bear raid," or the now-illegal manipulation of a stock common on Wall Street from the 1860s to 1920s.[75]

Soon, Steinberg began feeling pressure not just from his falling stock price but from his creditors. Donald Graham, the chairman of Continental Illinois Bank and Trust and the lead bank on Leasco's $131.5 million revolving credit line, told him on February 7, 1969, that an acquisition of Chemical Bank would be bad for banking.[76] First Boston, Kuhn Loeb, and Hornblower & Weeks began organizing

Chemical stockholders and proxy firms to get pledges to vote against any merger, Selvage and Lee was to conduct public relations, and Joe Flom of Skadden, Arps was preparing Chemical's legal defense.[77] New York governor Nelson Rockefeller, brother of Chase Manhattan's David Rockefeller, swung into action, as did the Nixon administration and the Senate Banking Committee chairman.

Chemical lobbied for anti-takeover legislation to be introduced in both New York state and in the United States Congress.[78] Nixon's Department of Justice sent Leasco a letter asking for information on the merger and whether it violated the Clayton Act. All the while, Leasco's stock was dropping. Steinberg received angry calls from bankers and businessmen, attacking him for considering buying Chemical. "I always knew there was an Establishment," he said. "I just used to think I was part of it."

When Steinberg traveled to Washington to talk to Federal Reserve officials and Banking Committee senators about his proposed takeover, he realized he was done. He found unanimous opposition. Steinberg recalled one conversation in which Senator John Sparkman, chair of the Banking Committee, told him, "A couple of weeks ago I had a fellow in here complaining that somebody moved in and took over his bank and then fired him. Now, we can't have things like that." He then called to his secretary, "Where's that bill the lawyer for Chemical Bank sent in? I want to show it to Mr. Steinberg."[79] The next day, Steinberg met with Chemical's management team, including Renchard, and said he was no longer interested in buying the bank.

Steinberg lost. But the amount of firepower it took to defeat this nobody Steinberg—the Federal Reserve, the Senate, the Nixon administration, the governor of New York, the assembled aristocracy of banking and their archrivals the Wall Street investment banks—was shocking. And Steinberg still might have won had he persevered.

The possibility that Steinberg's attempt could have succeeded was a lesson to the men who had beaten back the merger. Soon, banks themselves sought to turn into conglomerates, led, as always, by Wriston.

But in this swinging decade, with the centralization of power in the hands of the new money lords, there would be a wrinkle. His name was Congressman Wright Patman.

## CHAPTER ELEVEN

# WRISTON VERSUS PATMAN

"Patman must have been frightened by a banker while a fetus."

**—An anonymous
enemy of Wright Patman**[1]

■ ■ ■ ■ ■ ■ ■ ■ ■ ■ ■ ■ ■

I n 1963, Wright Patman achieved a lifelong goal, ascending to the chairmanship of the House Committee on Banking and Currency. Patman took over from a mild Kentucky Democrat, Brent Spence, who for years had kept Patman from wielding significant power over banking legislation. Power in Congress flows largely to the majority party, which operationalizes that power by choosing the chairman of each legislative committee. Beyond simple party affiliation and majority status, chairmanships had usually been determined by seniority, or length of service on that committee. Spence had entered Congress after Patman, but Patman's high-profile fights with Mellon and his refusal to knuckle under to FDR and drop the Bonus Bill made him enemies, and those enemies kept him off the Banking Committee until 1938. Patman would sometimes ask Spence how he was feeling and Spence would respond, "Wright, you have an undue interest in the state of my health."[2] Patman's populist posture kept him from leading the committee he had dreamed of running for twenty years.

When Patman took the chairman's gavel, he knew what he wanted to do. Like Brandeis, Patman believed that the power of bankers was based on the public's perception of banking as complex and mysterious. He intended to break this power by teaching the public how banks actually operated. By this point, Patman had grown heavy around the waist. His hair had thinned. He had the same gentle air, and the same sturdy yet polite ways of exhibiting his dislike of Wall Street. His endlessly loyal staff of banking radicals was used to being worked to the ground by Patman, who got to work by 6 a.m. And he still had that secret weapon that few in Congress or in business could tolerate: Patman was not afraid to lose.

The Patman Banking Committee produced reports explaining the workings of financiers who had grown less powerful if not less greedy than during Andrew Mellon's time. He hired a staff of experts, investigators, and economists to churn out reports. There was Paul Nelson, the staff director and a PhD in economics from Columbia; Jake Lewis, a tall, lanky writer who knew the corridors of Washington; Benet Gellman, a former White House staffer and an expert in banking laws; Jane D'Arista, the first female researcher and economist hired by the committee; and Curtis Prins, a hard-nosed, foul-mouthed investigator who would travel around the country sniffing out financial scams.

Before Patman took over, the committee was largely passive, reacting to demands by industry and the Federal Reserve. Patman revamped the committee, using his staff to seize the legislative initiative from the bank lobby and the executive branch bureaucracy. He produced original research and reports, some of which turned out to be foundational in terms of the understanding of the banking industry in the era. Under the previous chairman, the committee spent just $200,000 per year.[3] Within a few years, it was spending $1.695 million. Patman's staff published over thirty independent research reports on Federal Reserve policy, federal financial policy, and banking. In his first year, the committee published reports on the scope of bank holding company ownership, the extent of chain banking, commercial bank reporting practices to stockholders, and bank regulations. He was, as even his opponents admitted, "a remarkable teacher."[4]

The expertise of Patman's committee frustrated the banking lobby. In 1964, Patman issued a primer on money, and distributed 200,000 copies of his speech, "The ABCs of Money," many to schoolteachers. The American Bankers Association responded with its own pamphlet, handing it out to its eighteen thousand banker members.[5] Patman also went into the guts of academia, seeking to understand and examine how money and banking were being taught in universities by doing Congressional studies of textbooks.[6]

As chair, Patman didn't hesitate to make enemies. He investigated bank control over the stock market through their trust departments, and called for a "full-scale, top-to-bottom, A-to-Z investigation of the entire banking lobby."[7] He angered colleagues by attacking corruption in Congress, which was rampant. As Drew Pearson reported, freshmen members were "approached within hours of their arrival in Washington and offered quick and immediate loan service," with banks telling members, "Just write a check, we will honor it." Committee members were offered bank stock for free and given directorships on local bank boards. Representative Henry Gonzalez, an ally of Patman, told a journalist what it was like to become a member of the committee. Upon joining, a local San Antonio banker praised his business acumen, and said, "we would like you to be chairman of the board" of a new bank.[8]

Despite his official control over the flow of legislation, Patman's power over the committee was always tenuous. During Patman's tenure as chair, the committee usually had many more Democrats than Republicans. For instance, in the 92nd Congress, there were thirty-seven members of the committee, roughly fifteen Republicans and twenty-two Democrats. But many of the Democrats were people whom the staff called "Ivy League liberals," ranking well on civil liberties and on scorecards for groups such as the Americans for Democratic Action, but voting in committee to further the interests of commercial banks.

Thomas "Lud" Ashley, an Ohio Democrat who later became a bank lobbyist, was the prototypical example. "These guys come to Congress in their thirties as promising attorneys and businessmen with high ideals and great enthusiasm," said one observer. "But after six or seven years they find themselves approaching middle age with decent incomes but no real security, while their former law partners back home are secure and prosperous."[9] Patman's archenemy Congressman Wilbur Mills filled committee slots for all committees, and stacked the Banking Committee with members who would vote against Patman. Patman had to outwit or outlast his opponents.[10]

Patman play-acted the fuzzy-headed simpleton. But his willingness to draw out hearings and use complex legislative tactics to foil bank-friendly legislation was highly effective and enraged his opponents. The general press ignored banking, and the financial press scorned Patman. But he took advantage of the fact that fear of concentrated banking power and the new developments in the financial space was widespread, especially among the old guard.

By the late 1960s, few liberal intellectuals were paying attention to finance and the conglomerate trend, but Patman and older political leaders like Emanuel Celler—who held hearings on Steinberg and Chemical Bank—kept up the pressure. So did the new Nixon administration, with Attorney General John Mitchell and his assistant attorney general for antitrust, Richard McLaren, expressing "deep concern over the current merger movement." Mitchell went so far as to tell the Georgia Bar Association in 1969 that the "future vitality of our free economy may be in danger."[11] There were ten separate investigations into the conglomerate trend.[12] Nixon feared conglomerates could allow bankers to breach the traditional line between commerce and finance.

## ROUND ONE: THE BANK MERGER FIGHT

In the early 1960s, Patman intuitively understood that something was wrong with the financial system. Wall Street was beginning to recentralize as bankers quietly weakened New Deal–era controls. When he became chair, he started to hit back by attempting to address a simple problem: too many bank mergers.

The bank merger problem had been long-lasting, and reflected a split over merger authority between bank regulators and the Department of Justice Antitrust Division. Kennedy's chief bank regulator at the Office of the Comptroller of the Currency, James Saxon, was a strong proponent of bank mergers. From 1960 to 1966, bank regulators approved 1,001 out of 1,035 merger requests, rejecting only 34, despite the Department of Justice finding antitrust problems in over half of the proposed mergers.[13]

Finally, in 1961, the DOJ had had enough. In *United States v. Philadelphia National Bank,* the DOJ sought to block a bank merger, interfering in what bank regulators thought was their area. The DOJ declared a host of mergers, including several concentrated banking powers in major cities, illegal. The antitrust division even sought to undo an already completed large 1961 merger between Manufacturers Trust and Central Hanover.[14]

The bank lobby immediately acted and Patman called them out. "When [the DOJ] stepped on the toes of the nation's fourth largest bank," said Patman, "the roar from Wall Street was heard in every Congressional district."[15] The Senate Banking Committee chairman introduced a bill to remove bank mergers from the antitrust laws, and to legalize these six mergers retroactively. The American Bankers Association and twenty-nine state bank associations supported it. The bill went through the Senate with just a few senators, including William Proxmire, Philip Hart, and Robert F. Kennedy, trying to retain antitrust agency jurisdiction over the banks.[16] It looked like a smooth passage, an uncontroversial reversion to bank regulator control of the banking system.

That is, until Patman spoke. "If you exempt banks from anti-trust," he said, "you might as well also shoot the policeman on the corner." The bill had to go through his committee, so at first, he refused to hold hearings.[17] Then his committee members demanded he act, so he spent more than a month, stretching through August and September of 1965, doing so. He brought in Robert Kennedy and independent businessmen and bankers to testify against the bill, eliciting a wide range of opinion for a bill that had until this time been without opposition.[18]

The banking industry was split on the merger trend. Smaller bankers were unhappy with the concentration of power. The Independent Bankers Association expressed "great alarm." Patman himself genially used apocalyptic rhetoric. "My great fear," he said, "is that for the control of such vast power for the benefit of our competitive, free enterprise economy, democratic government may prove inadequate, with the result that it will be superseded by a collectivist form of government, Socialist or Fascist in character."[19] The hearings led to the revelation that a special antitrust subcommittee of the American Bar Association had been pressured by bank law firms to water down a report on bank mergers.

The bank lobby acted through Thomas "Lud" Ashley. Ashley introduced legislation to strip merger authority over banks from the Department of Justice.

Over the course of several months, Patman used his chairman's prerogative to delay action, facing off with an increasingly bitter Ashley. "The banks have spent more money on these bills than any other banking legislation in the history of Congress," noted Patman.[20] It got so heated and ugly that in October 1965, Ashley convened a rump session of the committee with the lights off in the Banking Committee room while Patman was at the hospital attending to his wife. This act was an unprecedented breach of congressional procedure and decorum, all to retroactively legalize the $5.6 billion merger between Manufacturers Trust Company and the Central Hanover Bank.

But a committee staffer walked in during the meeting and alerted a Patman ally, who stopped the proceedings. Ashley's arrangement of a rump session of the committee left Capitol Hill watchers agog. Nothing like it had ever been seen in Congress. Patman denounced the illegal session, but financial writers, as usual, mocked Patman, writing it up as a "pint-sized melodrama." The furor and the controversy caused the fight to drag on for months, until the Johnson administration brokered a compromise.

Bankers thought they had gotten the better of Patman. But Patman had outsmarted the bank lobby by outworking them. With a twinkle in his eye, Patman told a colleague, "It's true the bankers control a majority of the committee members, but I still control the staff. And my staff has included some language in the merger bill that will give the bankers fits. But they will not figure that out until after the bill is being enforced."[21]

And it was true. The Supreme Court found that, under the just-passed law, the Bank Merger Act of 1966, bank mergers still remained under the jurisdiction of the Department of Justice. Bankers thought that the bill would restrict bank merger challenges, but because of Patman's language, it had the opposite effect.[22]

But the bank merger fight proved to be merely a warm-up for the fight over Walter Wriston's plan to have Citibank turn into a conglomerate, and do away with Glass-Steagall once and for all.

## ROUND TWO: THE ONE-BANK HOLDING COMPANY FIGHT

In the late 1960s, bankers, jealous of Saul Steinberg and other high-fliers, sought to create conglomerates, so their corporations could enter any industry they chose. And they had discovered a loophole in the law to make this wish come true. While the Bank Holding Company Act of 1956 placed restrictions on any holding company that owned multiple banks, it allowed a holding company to own a *single* bank. In theory, this meant banks could create a holding company parent, and then that parent could buy insurance companies, travel agencies, computer companies, and so forth.

This loophole was known, but it was theoretical because no large bank dared to use it. The month before protesters and police clashed at the Chicago Democratic National Convention in 1968, Walter Wriston's Citibank announced it would become a bank holding company. By December, over fifty banks followed. "Commercial banks," wrote *Business-Week,* "looked strangely exciting this week as they began to try out the role of the freewheeling conglomerate."[23] Chemical Bank, which would shortly rally its fellow banks to fight off becoming part of Saul Steinberg's conglomerate, now formed its own holding company, Chemical New York Corporation.

A bank could now, through its holding company, own any business it chose, and use its control over credit to give that business a competitive advantage. The new bank strategy struck at the heart of Glass-Steagall, as well as the even longer-standing separation of banking and commerce. An anonymous banker made this clear in *The New York Times,* writing "We're spending our time worrying about the problems of the 1930s. This is wrong. Times have changed."[24]

Wriston's move sparked the second war between Patman and the big money center banks. Senator William Proxmire, the Federal Reserve, and the Nixon Treasury and Justice Departments were all heavily involved, building on suspicion of conglomerates that had emerged throughout the decade.

Emanuel Celler's Antitrust Subcommittee wrote a staff report on corporate power, showing how often board members of giant banks sat on boards of giant industrial corporations.[25] Willard Mueller, a former Patman staffer turned head economist at the FTC, developed new antitrust theories to address financial concentration in unrelated markets. Nixon Treasury Secretary David M. Kennedy said that unless the line between banking and commerce was strictly enforced, America would be "dominated by some fifty to seventy-five huge centers of economic and financial power, each of which would consist of a corporate conglomerate controlling a large bank . . . controlling a large nonfinancial conglomerate."[26]

The general counsel of the FTC, who had been the head of the Antitrust and Cartels Division in postwar Japan when Americans restructured the Japanese economy, warned that conglomerate mergers were creating something similar to the situation in prewar Japan, with informal coalitions of corporations known as *zaibatsu*, centered around a large bank but encompassing every other part of the economy.[27]

But the stampede toward the single-bank holding company structure generated special concern in Washington. This time it wasn't just banks attempting to get bigger by merging with other banks. Nixon's assistant attorney general for antitrust, Richard McLaren, observed that the nation's largest banks had formed one-bank holding companies. Their goal was to become "unregulated, financial, commercial, industrial power centers." Not only did it pose "serious antitrust questions," but it was against the "traditional American policy of keeping banking separate from other business activities."[28]

On January 20, 1969, the day Nixon was inaugurated as president, Citibank sought to obliterate Glass-Steagall with a bid through its holding company for the large insurance company Chubb Corporation. Wriston sought to combine Citibank's power over lending and borrowing with the large portfolio controlled by Chubb's property and casualty insurance. It was the classic empire-building move, based on the use of other people's money to build the empire.[29]

Patman proposed blocking single-bank holding companies from owning nonbank businesses. As usual, he held long and extensive hearings.[30] At first, most large banks refused to send anyone to testify, hoping the furor would go away and funny moneyman Patman wouldn't be able to generate sufficient power to force a law. But they were wrong.[31] They did face opposition. Patman used his hearings, which took place over seventeen days and produced 1,600 pages of testimony, to organize the opposition to the large bankers. Data processing executives, travel agents, courier services, insurance companies, and even smaller banks testified to support Patman's approach, and that of his Senate ally William Proxmire.[32]

Milton Shapp, a Pennsylvania entrepreneur running for governor, told members of the Banking Committee about pressure put on him by banks to buy alternative services when he needed financing. An Indianapolis travel agent, Othmar Grueninger, talked about how bank-owned travel agencies were driving independent agencies out of business because of their unparalleled access to data about who traveled and who was creditworthy. "Any time I deposited checks from my customers," he said, "I was providing the banks with the names of my best clients."[33]

There were even splits within the banking lobby. The American Bankers Association had members who supported strict regulation of bank holding companies, and large banks that did not. In 1968, the large banks broke from the ABA and formed an association named the Association of Corporate Owners of One Bank. This association would be their vehicle to fight, both within the ABA and Congress.[34] They also went on a public relations campaign to leak stories favorable to the banks and to attack Patman. George Moore, the chair of Citibank, lobbied *The New York Times, The Wall Street Journal,* and *The Washington Post,* while asking not to be identified, but was revealed by *American Banker* magazine.[35]

The large bankers worked through their usual allies on the committee, the Republican minority, and a rump faction of Democrats. On June 24, chairman Patman convened the House Banking Committee to begin marking up a bill.

Republican congressman William Stanton obediently worked with Patman's Democratic opponents on a bill incorporating all of the demands of the American Bankers Association, the large banks, and the conglomerates. The top Republican on the committee, William Widnall, used an unusual parliamentary trick to cut short debate. He put forward Stanton's bill as a "second substitute" for Patman's legislation, which would mean that no more votes could be taken on any part of the legislation. The committee had to vote to replace the entire bill with the bank-friendly Stanton version, before the committee could even debate any particular section. On June 26, the committee backed the Stanton banker bill 20–15. Executives at the ABA, based in New York City, and bank lobbyists all over D.C., celebrated this humiliation of Patman.[36]

The Stanton bill passed to the floor of the House to be scheduled for floor debate, which most assumed wouldn't matter. Months passed. And then, there was a stunning reversal. First, Patman passed to Drew Pearson's successor, Jack Anderson, the story of the sordid nature of the Stanton bill. Then, lobbyists for insurance and travel agencies, data processors, and industry groups mobilized. Insurance agents, afraid of being undercut if big banks were able to enter their business, were so effective and aggressive that Stanton himself said he had received more telegrams on the legislation than on anything else he had ever worked on.

Patman's staff worked with friendly Republicans, handing them key amendments for which they could take credit. On the floor of the House, Patman and his staff put back everything from his original bill.[37] By the time the rout finished, only three lines remained of the Stanton legislation that passed out of the committee. This reversal stunned the bank lobbyists, who were not paying attention. The American Bankers Association didn't learn what happened until the next day. The banks faced a humiliation far greater than what Patman had suffered in his committee.[38]

Bankers turned to the Senate, and their ally Alabama's John Sparkman.[39] But before the Senate could act, the conglomerate boom came to a sharp end. The stock market crashed, with conglomerates such as LTV and Leasco down 80 to 90 percent. Over a hundred Wall Street brokerage firms were revealed to be insolvent. A massive train system, Penn Central, that had been turned into a conglomerate, went bankrupt. In the midst of this gathering storm, on July 7, 1970, the Senate Banking Committee took up its version of Patman's bank holding company legislation.[40]

The bank lobbyists and the lobbyists for conglomerates went to work on much more favorable terrain. Senator Sparkman had the legislation written in private.[41] Sparkman was a sophisticate, a somewhat paternalistic man who sought more money for housing for the middle class, but also, as an analyst put it, a man with "an irrepressible faith in the essential goodness of the man of means."[42] And a committee full of similarly inclined men joined him. Stalwart liberals such as Ed Muskie, Ernest "Fritz" Hollings, and Walter Mondale, in this age of affluence, were consumer rights advocates, but mostly inattentive to issues of corporate and banking power.

The markup of the bill in committee was done in "executive session." This meant essentially that the votes were secret and the members could have their positions kept from the public.[43] This approach—highly common in that era—granted enormous power to the chair of the committee, who could then cut deals and present a finished product to the entire House or Senate. Mini-fiefdoms in Congress were common.[44]

These fiefdoms didn't always benefit powerful interests, but they could. In this case, they did. The legislative print introduced by Sparkman was favorable to the banks and conglomerates. It allowed for grandfathering in of existing privileges, weakened the Fed's authority to regulate, and let banks continue to buy into any industry they wished. The Senate committee markup culminated in the passage of what became known as the Green Stamp Amendment, so named because it was done at the behest of a conglomerate known for offering customers reward cards in the form of green stamps. It was also known as the "conglomerate exemption" amendment.

Senator William Proxmire, one of the few opponents of the bank lobby, said he had "never witnessed a more intensive lobbying campaign on behalf of a special interest amendment." Lobbyists "for the conglomerate amendment," he said, "were practically falling over one another in an effort to get it into the bill."[45] The amendment would have exempted 900 of the existing 1,116 bank holding companies from any additional rules. In committee, the amendment was adopted. Nearly all bank holding companies were exempted from any restrictions.[46]

On the floor of the Senate, the coalition assembled by Patman attempted the same trick they had accomplished in the House, under the leadership of Proxmire. But Proxmire proved to be less adept at legislative maneuvering than Patman. Proxmire attempted to strip out the worst part of the bill, the Green Stamp Amendment. In committee, bank advocates outnumbered him, but on the floor, where the full Senate voted, he had the votes.

Sparkman and conservative Wallace Bennett from Utah, however, outfoxed Proxmire. They persuaded Senate leaders to schedule the vote for a time when twenty-nine senators were absent.[47] Then, at the last minute, three populist midwestern senators who had pledged to vote against the conglomerate exemption amendment, including George McGovern, provided the margin for the 37–34 vote in favor of the bankers. The reason, it turns out, was that the National Farmers Union, a powerful liberal farm group, had made some bad pension investments and gotten into debt with a Denver bank, which was then acquired by a conglomerate in 1968. The bank then collected its favor from the NFU; the NFU asked the three liberal senators to change their votes.[48]

The Senate thus produced a bill supported by much of the banking and conglomerate lobby, one opposed by Patman, the Nixon administration, and the business coalition worried about unfair competition from banks and conglomerates. Nonetheless, it passed the Senate by a vote of 77–1, with only Proxmire registering disapproval.[49] The final legislative package would come down to a meeting between the House and the Senate, where Patman and Sparkman would face off to iron out the differences between the final legislation in the House and the Senate. Seven House members and four senators would be in the conference. The ABA mobilized, with a special Action Letter sent out; dozens of local bankers were dispatched to talk to conference committee members, in person if possible, on the phone if not.[50]

Patman and his staff were again relentless. Patman's staff, led by Benet Gellman, negotiated with Sparkman's staff lead, Hugh Smith. Patman's staff volunteered to write the agenda, to which Smith acceded. So the debate was structured by Patman; members of Congress and senators on the committee were presented with tradeoffs that framed exemptions as dangerous and embarrassing loopholes.[51]

Then, the Patman forces attacked the Green Stamp Amendment. The Senate had attached to their bill a noncontroversial provision to coin 150 million commemorative Eisenhower dollars with 40 percent silver content. A major contractor for the silver jacketing material for the coins was a company owned by a contributor to New Jersey senator Harrison Williams, a sponsor of the Green Stamp Amendment. Patman staffers informed the contractor that the commemorative coin provision would be stripped if the Green Stamp Amendment stayed in the bill. On the first day of the conference, Williams pulled his support for the amendment, and it was dropped. It was an ugly deal to get rid of a dangerous banking amendment, in return for a few million in profit to the backer of a senator.[52]

The negotiations were, according to *American Banker* magazine, among "the most contentious ever held on banking legislation." Bennett at one point berated Patman for making the "same old speech" against bankers, and accused Patman of planting hostile stories about him in the press (which his staffers were likely doing, with Patman's tacit approval). As Patman tried to respond, Bennett angrily told Patman to shut up. It wasn't supposed to be this hard to pass a bill supported by the banking lobby. All during the negotiations, more than a dozen lobbyists waited, in what seemed like a vigil, in the hall outside the conference room. They were depending on the Senate conferees to save their conglomerates.[53]

Banks continued their part of the fight by doing more favors for congressmen. In 1969, when the prime rate was 8.5 percent (meaning most borrowers paid much more than that), one Washington, D.C., bank was lending money to over a hundred congressmen at a little over 6 percent. Banks tried to donate hundreds of thousands of dollars just before the election through their political action committee, BANK-PAC, which backfired in what one member called a "combination of arrogance and stupidity" that was "straight out of the days of the robber barons."[54] Citibank, whose head lobbyist, John Yingling, was considered the most effective in Washington, was more suave. He worked *The New York Times* for favorable coverage.[55] Even the Nixon Antitrust Division got involved—on Patman's side this time—with the head of policy planning for the Department of Justice attacking the "special interest" Green Stamp conglomerate exemption amendment.[56]

Ultimately, Patman's side offered what seemed to be a concession to end the conference committee. The original Patman bill had listed lines of business that banks could not enter; Patman dropped this in committee, and instead delegated the authority to regulate bank holding companies to the Federal Reserve.[57] It seemed like a reasonable compromise to the bankers, as the Fed was already their regulator. But once again, Patman proved victorious. The Fed kicked eighty-nine conglomerates out of the banking business in the next two years. The rush of banks into the one-bank holding company structure had been "sidetracked."[58]

Patman felt satisfied with the basic aims of the legislation. His counsel, Benet Gellman, was ebullient. "We accomplished almost everything," he gloated. "We got the one-bank holding companies covered, which was the main thing." Walter Wriston had sought to use the one-bank holding company as a way around regulatory constraints and let Citi do things like get into mutual funds and to buy Chubb Insurance, but the Fed wouldn't allow either. The Fed also blocked entrance by one-bank holding companies into other key parts of the insurance business, land development, and management consulting. Gellman crowed, "There were no major exceptions, either, in the final bill, and everybody who formed a holding company after June 30, 1968, had to divest and the Federal Reserve began its case by case review after the bill was passed."[59]

The Bank Holding Company Act Amendments of 1970 was one of the most important antimonopoly laws of the twentieth century, stopping the banking industry and conglomerates from breaking down the traditional barrier between commerce and banking. Just before the law passed, four of the largest New York City banks were negotiating to buy major insurance companies through holding companies.[60] The bill stopped these mergers. It would not be until 1998, when libertarian Federal Reserve chairman Alan Greenspan would use the power granted by the compromise between Patman and Sparkman not to keep finance segmented, but to let a giant insurance and brokerage company, Travelers Group, merge with Citibank.

While a massive legislative achievement for Patman, the bill didn't carry the public force that the banking reforms had in the 1930s. Walter Wriston was no Charles Mitchell, the disgraced head of National City whose frauds were still being discovered tucked away in foreign branches of the bank as late as the 1960s.[61] Wriston didn't appear as a robber baron, but a cosmopolitan executive who believed in racial tolerance, liked rock 'n' roll, and wanted to be a responsible business leader in a technologically advanced society. Citibank, as he told governors and local politicians, didn't pollute, and it went without mention that the bank didn't send soldiers to Vietnam.[62] So while Wriston lost this battle, unlike Mitchell, he didn't lose his public reputation and influence. He could return to the political arena to once again fight to loosen rules on bankers.

And so Patman didn't get popular credit for constraining banking power, because there was not a broad sense that this power was necessary to constrain. And it would not be the only work that would go unacknowledged. During this same period, Patman forced through a piece of legislation called the Bank Secrecy Act, a core law to block money laundering and the evasion of tax and margin requirements.[63] He slipped the Fair Credit Reporting Act, a bill to regulate credit reporting, into a conference committee because his own committee wouldn't pass it. He took on Wilbur Mills, the most powerful member of the House, who ran the secretive Ways and Means Committee on taxation, blocking the standard unanimous passage of a special tax loophole for an individual company.[64]

But fear of robber barons or monopolists was not meaningful to a younger generation. In 1972, New York congressman and antimonopolist Emanuel Celler, who had been in the House for forty-nine years, was defeated in a Democratic primary by a young attorney named Elizabeth Holtzman, who ran against him as a feminist based on Celler's opposition to the Equal Rights Amendment. It would prove a harbinger.

Financial power was beginning to slam into the real economy. In 1970, it would soon ruin the railroad system, turning much of America's transportation infrastructure in the Northeast into one of the biggest corporate frauds of the century. Penn Central would set up the debates of the 1970s about an increasingly crisis-prone and destructive economic order. Patman would play his role, and would have one more victory. But the financiers were gaining power, and there were no political or intellectual reinforcements behind him.

## CHAPTER TWELVE

# PENN CENTRAL

"Rumor has it that a red carpet was chosen for the House
Banking Committee's hearing chamber to hide the blood
spilled during chairman Wright Patman's frequent jousts
with the nation's money lords."

—**Lester Salamon**, *The Money Committees*[1]

■ ■ ■ ■ ■ ■ ■ ■ ■ ■ ■ ■ ■

On June 20, 1970, Paul Volcker, a tall man with a low voice,
headed to Capitol Hill on a mission. It was a Saturday, and
he was going to an office where people worked on week-
ends, that of Banking Committee chairman Wright Patman. Volcker,
an undersecretary of the treasury for Nixon, wasn't there to talk about
the heated debate over bank holding companies. He was overseeing
a $200 million emergency loan to the nation's biggest transportation
network and seventh-largest company, the Penn Central railroad.

Penn Central was one of the oldest and grandest companies in
America, with roots going back to the 1840s. Banks considered it an
honor to lend to the company. Nevertheless, five Penn Central executives were on their way to the same office for the same reason. The
Penn Central executives were gathering to beg for their company's life.
Volcker, and the Penn Central executives, knew Patman was unlikely
to approve a transfer of government money. But they had nowhere else
to turn.[2] If Penn Central went down, the whole banking system, and a
number of weak large corporations, might go down as well.

The collapse had taken years, decades even. First, the economy
had changed; trains now competed with trucks and airplanes, in addition to the fact that industry—as well as the need to ship industrial goods—had moved away from the Northeast. Second, regulators

hadn't kept pace, forcing railroad companies to run empty passenger trains on certain routes when commuters were taking cars. Third, union contracts often forced the railroads to pay workers who didn't work.[3] Most importantly, railroad managers themselves began stripping their companies of value, trading stocks on inside information, rewarding themselves with lavish pay, and engaging in empire building through unworkable mergers. Finally, the CEO of Penn Central tried to turn the train company into a conglomerate, to gamble his way out of insolvency. The Penn Central collapse involved deception by accountants, lies to regulators, customers, and passengers, and the sell-off and demolition of one of the most beautiful train stations in the world, all to keep the fraud going for as long as possible. And Wall Street had been knee-deep every step of the way. Walter Wriston at National City was Penn Central's banker.

The corporation had fouled up its giant train system by engaging in a classic railroad robber baron technique: paying dividends instead of maintaining the track and rolling stock. Its executives had also rediscovered old ways to ruin a balance sheet. Penn Central had borrowed at high interest rates to buy land, buildings, pipelines, and even that long-time signal of American financial greed and idiocy, Florida real estate. Everything the corporation owned was mortgaged, and no one would lend Penn Central another dime. Now, bleeding cash, the company went begging for a bailout from the government. But the last-ditch strategy had a flaw, one common in the banking world of the 1960s and 1970s. Penn Central and its bankers had to go through Patman.

This moment revealed what Patman had feared, that the New Deal was rotting away under the influence of big business, big bankers, and high interest rates. For years, Walter Wriston had been working to let loose the demons of unregulated finance. These demons were now free. They could be ignored as long as the problem was an esoteric one of interest rates and amendments on bank holding companies, as long as a stock market boom enthralled the bankers to sustain ever-expanding credit. But unregulated finance had now smashed into something real, America's train system, and broke it. In this moment, Patman had a choice. He could assent to a bailout of a mismanaged train system and its bankers. Or he could say no, and risk a financial crash.

## A DYING RAILROAD BUSINESS

The Penn Central problem was more than an inconvenience, considering its importance in the American transportation system. Every weekday the company transported 300,000 rail passengers on 1,280 trains, comprising 65 percent of rail passengers living east of the Mississippi and 35 percent of all rail travelers nationwide. Commuters in New York City made 175,000 trips a day, 15,000 in Boston, and 13,675 daily between New York City and Washington, D.C. It had 20,570 miles of track through sixteen states and two provinces in Canada. Without the company, the northeastern United States "would be paralyzed."[4] And this traffic did not include its freight business, which carried the coal and steel that made up the industrial sinews of the region.

In terms of its place in the financial and business structure of the nation, Penn Central was perhaps more important. It was the largest real estate company in the country. It had 100,000 creditors, 118,000 stockholders, and had paid a dividend for over one hundred years. It employed 95,453 people belonging to twenty-three different unions, with an aggregate annual payroll of more than a billion dollars. As a financial holding company, it owned pipelines, trucks, barges, water companies, coal mines, factories, hotels, amusement parks (Six Flags Over Texas and Six Flags Over Georgia), part of the New York Rangers and the New York Knicks, real estate in Florida, the eighth-largest crude oil producer in the nation, and California warehouses. In New York City, the company held land on top of which sat Grand Central Terminal, the Pan Am Building, the Yale Club, the Union Carbide Building, the Chemical Bank New York Trust Building, Pennsylvania Station, the Graybar Building, the Vanderbilt Building, the Vanderbilt Concourse Building, the Bankers Trust Building, and buildings on Lexington Avenue, Madison Avenue, and Park Avenue.[5]

For years, Americans had noticed that something was wrong with the trains. In New York City, the trains were always late. Or hot. Or cold. "Filthy" was a common complaint from commuters. "Absolutely disgusting."[6] One day in 1969, thousands of commuters in New York had to find alternative routes home at the height of rush hour because all electrical train service had been canceled. Police had to quell a near riot. Prosperous commuters picketed the company when it sought to raise fares. One advertising executive said that he was picketing because "the running time of the trains has not changed since 1899" and he was tired of being late. "I have an 1899 schedule to prove it."[7]

Passengers blamed executives who—even while speculating in roller coasters—had not spent enough to maintain its equipment, or buy new equipment, for decades. Management, in turn, blamed regulators for keeping fares too low, subsidizing competitors in the trucking industry, and preventing them from dropping unprofitable routes. At one point, an irate neighbor called the chairman of the railroad, Stuart Saunders, about the local passenger service, which was late yet again. Saunders responded by offering to give away the company's passenger service commuter rail, as it was a massively unprofitable cash drain.[8]

To be sure, the railroad business was not an easy one. The Interstate Commerce Commission (ICC) favored shippers in its rate making. World War II was a briefly and incredibly profitable moment for the rail system, because war production pushed shipping to its maximum. But the heavy wartime demand also exhausted much of the equipment, and the executives were loath to pay for maintenance and upkeep in the less profitable years after the war.

Railroads lost market shares in freight to trucking, and passenger revenue between 1951 and 1957 among Northeast railroads tumbled.[9] Textile mills moved to the South, as did newer industrial plants, hurting demand for Penn Central's freight services, which were centered in the Northeast and Midwest.[10] Yet the ICC, pressured by Congress, forced railroads to maintain service to all parts of the country, and regulated the companies in much the same way they did in the 1920s, when they enjoyed quasi-monopolies over transportation. By the early 1960s the government had begun to guarantee loans to much of the industry.[11]

All of this was true enough, but not the whole story. The executives at Penn Central had contempt for their own business. Despite living close to a commuter stop, the corporation's CEO refused to ride the train to work, instead taking a limousine. His central ambition, he said one night, was to put passenger and freight revenue into real estate investments "instead of putting it in the fucking railroad."[12] The men who ran the Pennsylvania Railroad lived in the same neighborhoods, attended church together, and had gone to the same colleges. The man who served as president of Penn Central in the 1960s got his career break when he was noticed by senior management for his prowess on the company baseball team.[13]

When these clubby executives complained about regulators bleeding the corporation of cash, it didn't square with the perks they awarded themselves, like the costly, temperature-controlled palatial private train car used by the president of Penn Central, Alfred Perlman.[14] It didn't square with a continually increasing dividend, which impressed fellow Philadelphia society members who were holders of the stock. And it didn't square with obvious bad management, such as managers regularly losing track of boxcars and equipment. In late 1968, for instance, Penn Central lost one hundred cars in a coal train for ten days outside of Syracuse because of misplaced paperwork.[15] In another instance, hundreds of boxcars were stolen from Penn Central, repainted, and then rented back to the corporation.[16]

Even those who did focus on the railroad business remained stuck in the nineteenth-century military culture.[17] Much of the newer business, like shipping merchandise, food, appliances, and textiles, tended to go with trucking, while railroad men concentrated on what they knew, which was shipping coal and steel.

The sheer arrogance of Penn Central's executives—indeed, their almost barbarian disregard for their corporation's role in society—all but forced the public to reject the corporation's claims. Saunders enraged New Yorkers when he tore down the grand landmark of that city, the "Greco-Roman temple to railroading," Pennsylvania Station, to sell development rights for an ugly, boxy set of office buildings and the Madison Square Garden sports arena. Passengers, rather than striding from their trains into the iron-and-glass arches of a cathedral of transportation, scuttled out into an overcrowded rat warren.[18]

All of these failures carried a larger symbolic meaning. Americans loved their railroads, the blue-coated man in brass buttons shouting "All ah-board," names of famous routes like the Manhattan Limited from New York to Chicago, the Wabash Cannon Ball in the Midwest, and the Super Chief out to California. The sight of the black, powerful locomotives chugging through a curve was enough to make a man weep.[19] And yet, in 1970, when Paul Volcker paid his visit to Wright Patman, the system had been stripped to the point of collapse.

## FROM A RAILROAD TO A CONGLOMERATE

Penn Central was created out of two railroads in the Northeast, the Pennsylvania and the New York Central. These two companies first started discussing a potential merger in 1957. In 1962, the two announced the deal, the largest railroad merger in American history up to that time, and one that would allow the two companies to close down duplicate facilities and consolidate traffic.[20] It seemed like a good idea at the time, but in retrospect it was more like two drunks trying to stay standing up by leaning on each other.

At first, the railroad men, and the public, believed that the merger would be a great success. And for a while it looked like it was. By 1968, the stocks of the railroads had quadrupled.[21]

But problems cropped up. The rationale for the merger was to shutter facilities and services no longer needed. But Saunders was a glad-hander, not a railroad operations person, and the company was riven by factional disputes at the top. Saunders and the entire management team, not paying attention to the railroad itself, mishandled the merger process. The federal regulator, the Interstate Commerce Commission, held 128 days of public sessions in 18 cities, with 461 witnesses, 290 prepared statements, and 347 exhibits, filling 40,000 pages. The entire merger process took eleven years.[22]

Every state and many cities had jurisdiction over its area of the merger, so each could extract concessions. New Jersey, for example, agreed to support the merger if the railroad promised not to cut service, even though cutting service was the point of the merger.[23] Railway unions threatened a "catastrophic" strike unless they got a written guarantee their jobs would be preserved. All seventeen unions got job security, for life. To get the merger approved, Saunders even agreed to hire back one thousand employees who handled mail, though the Postal Service had moved its mail contracts to planes and trucks.

By the time the deal went through, the ICC had actually forced the new Penn Central to buy more than it originally intended, as they required the corporation to take over the money-losing New Haven Railroad for $140 million.[24] Saunders should have said no, and so should have the company's bankers. But he had made promises to Wall Street.

The Penn Central would become arguably one of the most poorly run private train systems in the industrialized world. "It was just a goddamned operating mess," said one veteran of the industry. As a yardmaster at Selkirk put it: "They'd get a car for Harrisburg, which wasn't on the old Central, and they'd say, 'Where the hell is Harrisburg? I know where Pittsburgh is. Shit! I'll send it to Pittsburgh.'" Complaints of dirty restrooms and unheated coaches shot up, and trains were constantly late. It was also the most expensive, spending 66 cents of every dollar on labor costs, compared to 58 cents by its railroad competitors.[25]

By the late 1960s, it became clear that the merger would not deliver on its operational promises. Inflation and high interest rates were beginning to rattle the economy. Patman believed high interest rates wrecked industry, and they were tearing through the railroad. By the end of the decade, the corporation was losing roughly half a million dollars a day.[26]

The flip side of this newfangled financial environment was that the CEO and CFO of the corporation had far more freedom to focus on financial manipulations, and on nonrailroad lines of business. One result was that executives from the Pennsylvania refused to put money into operations or maintenance, seeing any cash going into actual railroading as a diversion from potential profit. A second result was the plan to turn the Penn Central into a conglomerate. The banks gushed over this strategy. In the era of a euphoria induced by the stock boom, investors saw more danger in being left out of the loan syndication than in underwriting risk.

David Bevan, the CFO, organized this conglomerate effort, which in total used $144 million to buy nonrailroad businesses. Penn Central used borrowed money to buy real estate investment businesses such as Great Southwest Corporation, Arvida Corporation, and Macco Corporation, and pipeline business Buckeye Pipeline. Interest on this money cost a total of $51 million.[27] The company launched, through a holding company, an airline named Executive Jet (with George Wallace's vice presidential candidate, Curtis LeMay, on the board), losing $21 million and incurring the second-largest Civil Aeronautics Board fine in history for attempting to start an airline illegally.[28]

All the borrowing led to corruption at an almost comically petty scale. Bevan organized a group of Penn Central executives and their friends who would pool their money into a mutual fund, named PenPhil, and engage in insider trading. Chemical Bank lent PenPhil $1.8 million on preferential terms, because of Bevan's ability to move Penn Central business into any bank he chose. The fund would then buy stocks just before Penn Central did, leading to guaranteed returns. PenPhil bought stock in Tropical Gas, Kaneb Pipeline, National Homes Corporation, and the Arvida-held Boca Raton Hotel and Club.

To get the money to organize all of this, Bevan took advantage of the new financial world Wriston had created. Penn Central borrowed in the newest and most exotic financial markets, the "commercial paper" market and the "Eurodollar market," which only existed because of the more permissive environment Patman had been battling. When the old regulated sources of funds were tapped out, Bevan pushed the limits of the new system. Penn Central was the first large-scale example of "financialization," or the turning of a company from a producer of goods or services into one that viewed all its activities through the lens of Wall Street.[29]

At first, this maneuvering seemed to work. The merger and conglomerate strategies looked profitable, because of Bevan's imaginative accounting schemes. Bevan masked losses on the railroad with non-railroad income. He engaged in tricks like buying up older bonds of Penn Central selling at a discount because they offered low interest rates. He then recorded a profit for the difference between the cost of each bond and the higher face value of the older but equally costly obligation. "His imaginative accounting," said an official, "is adding millions of dollars annually to our reported income." The corporation's accountant, Peat Warwick, blessed these fraudulent schemes because it was being paid off with consulting contracts, and Penn Central failed to disclose problems in its investor reports. In 1968, the railroad was secretly losing $400,000 a day.[30]

As the conglomerate craze cratered, so did Penn Central. By the end, Bevan and Saunders were borrowing against any fixed asset owned by the railroad. And they knew this was illegal. Bevan convinced the board to buy liability insurance to protect high-ranking executives and directors in the event they were personally sued. Until 1968, Pennsylvania corporations were prohibited from paying the full premium on officers' liability insurance, but a Penn Central lawyer successfully lobbied the state legislature to change the law.[31]

In 1968, Penn Central was still an investment darling. But the political context was shifting. In 1969, Saul Steinberg lost not only Chemical Bank but also what he called his "$24 million mistake," an ill-fated bid for British publishing giant Pergamon Press.[32] The conglomerate game was up. Leasco stock hit $7 that summer, down from $57. James Ling had resigned from the once mighty LTV, the merger-mad pace-setter of conglomerates of the 1960s. Most conglomerates, high-fliers who had terrified and titillated corporate America with an acquisition streak unparalleled since the 1920s, were down 80–90 percent. By 1969, Bevan was selling his stock in the railroad, as were fifteen other executives.

By May of 1969, Penn Central was paying $260,000 a day in interest payments. By November, the corporation confirmed it would miss its dividend, which had not happened since 1848. An act of God pushed the railroad over. The winter of 1969–1970 was the worst in decades. Freight didn't move for days, causing the railroad to burn through cash. Penn Central was desperate. On the last day of 1969, Bevan borrowed $59 million of Swiss francs through a subsidiary established in Curaçao.[33]

The end came in the spring of 1970, when a bond issue by Penn Central failed to sell. Up until the middle of March, Bevan had been able to distract bankers by hiding debt offerings in the complexity of Penn Central's corporate structure, using accounting tricks to show better financial results when there was a dangerous cash bleed. Finally, a senior attorney for Penn Central's prestigious law firm, Sullivan & Cromwell, balked, and wouldn't approve the bond offering.

There was a run on the corporation's commercial paper, and vendors were no longer accepting its checks. Panic selling of the stock ensued, with the powerful Standard & Poor's ratings agency that analyzed corporate securities on behalf of investors downgrading the bonds of the railroads. Bank trust departments, presumably with access to advanced knowledge of the railroad's deteriorating condition, sold stock ahead of the panic. Goldman Sachs, one of the key investment banks for Penn Central, liquidated its position in commercial paper. Penn Central's loss for the year would be a staggering $431 million.

Every piece of property, every real estate parcel it owned—and it owned a lot—was mortgaged. The commercial paper market had dried up. In May, Saunders approached David Kennedy, Nixon's treasury secretary and the former head of Penn Central creditor Continental Illinois Bank, and asked for emergency assistance. Kennedy and Nixon's transportation secretary, John Volpe, began putting together rescue plans.[34]

At this point, the bankers stepped in. Walter Wriston called Volpe, and together they had Bevan and Saunders fired. Paul Gorman, a former high-level AT&T executive, was tapped to head the corporation. Multiple board members resigned, citing conflicts of interest in either the railroad's shipping business or borrowing habits. Directors, regulators, and the public were all about to find out the extent of the fraud. No banker in his right mind would lend the company another nickel. The only thing standing between bankruptcy, and potentially catastrophic consequences for U.S. financial markets, was the prospect of a government bailout.

## THE BAILOUT FIASCO

The railroad was in trouble, but it still had immense political resources. Penn Central's power extended into the Nixon White House. Eisenhower budget director and later Nixon campaign finance chief and commerce secretary Maurice Stans owned $570,000 of stock in a company controlled by Penn Central, and Nixon's closest friend at his old law firm was on retainer to the company. When the Department of Transportation needed to deal with the details of the Penn Central's business, it found it nearly impossible to find lawyers and accountants who did not have relationships with the company. It was "like a gigantic octopus, its tentacles reaching into hundreds of board rooms, affecting universities, touching virtually every major bank in the nation, influencing government."[35] The railroad had relationships with Attorney General John Mitchell and Treasury Secretary David Kennedy. The company nearly, but not entirely, controlled the Pennsylvania congressional delegation.

And increasingly, policymakers within Congress and the executive branch agreed that as unseemly as it might look, a bailout was the only choice for this vital piece of the nation's transportation and financial infrastructure. Penn Central was too big to fail. To speed the process, the Nixon administration tried to act without Congress, expecting to get retroactive permission from the legislative body. Volpe sought to persuade the deputy secretary of defense, David Packard, to use a law Patman had worked on decades before, the Defense Production Act, to guarantee a consortium of bank loans to the railroad.[36] Under this law, the Pentagon could guarantee loans to any operation necessary for national defense.

The Vietnam War was on, and a forty-six-year-old assistant attorney general of the Office of Legal Counsel, William Rehnquist, offered a legal interpretation stretching the law to cover a Penn Central bailout.[37] This interpretation of the law angered southern legislators, who supported Nixon on funding the unpopular Vietnam War, and did not want that money to go to eastern bankers.[38]

Patman, who was among the southern legislators who voted to fund the war, began asking questions, and administration officials got nervous. No one wanted to take responsibility for going around Congress. Nixon's attorney general, John Mitchell, had worked with the railroad as a private lawyer, so he recused himself. Packard had the Navy, musing on granting the money to the railroad, ask the Federal Reserve about the likelihood of being repaid. Fed examiners initially said they expected no problems, since the eminently respectable Citibank was the railroad's lead creditor. But after the examiners peered at

Penn Central's books, the Fed told the Navy that Citibank had no idea what it was doing.[39]

The decision about whether to use the law in this controversial manner was elevated to the president. Nixon, however, was distracted, having just ordered an invasion of Cambodia, which he considered an exemplary American armed forces operation, unrivaled since Mac-Arthur's amphibious landing at Inchon in Korea decades before. He was angry the stock market wasn't responding by going up.[40] Nixon wouldn't authorize a bailout without Congressional approval, and that meant getting approval from Patman.

Penn Central was led by very powerful, well-connected men. But their political allies, their close friends, in the bright harsh glare of the public spotlight, wouldn't help. So Penn Central executives had no choice but to deal with Wright Patman, whose position on the Banking Committee meant he had jurisdiction over the problem that Saturday in June, when Paul Volcker was heading to Congress.

Gorman wore a lovely suit, as did the other board members. Volcker, their contact within the administration, showed up in what he happened to be wearing that Saturday morning: dirty gardening clothes. Chairman Patman looked like an owl, with his cherubic face, glasses, and cheerfully polite disdain for the men who had come to beg.

The problem, as all knew, was deadly serious. Penn Central was vital to the nation's financial and commercial arteries, and the company simply had no cash and no hope of getting any more cash unless the government stepped in. The assembled political leaders had known for some time that the previous team of executives had looted the corporation. But until this moment, none knew how badly.

They also did not know what it would mean for other companies that relied on commercial paper if Penn Central defaulted. The corporation's bankruptcy could set off a chain reaction of other bankruptcies as frightened banks pulled credit lines, and as corporations that had been lending to each other through an unregulated $40 billion commercial paper market froze up. This was the curse of hot money, promulgated since the early 1960s and Citibank's invention of the CD (and then Eurodollar deposits, and commercial paper). Corporations exposed in this way included Pan Am, Chrysler, and large numbers of rickety Wall Street brokerage firms—and who knows how many banks? A severe credit crunch could be the result, worse than the one in 1966, perhaps another 1929.[41]

Patman and his staff of young liberals had been tangling with the WASP business elite for nearly a decade, but this time was different. While 1966, with the drying up of lending to homeowners and cities, was worrisome, it was not terrifying. But this was. New Deal regulations were supposed to prevent such possible meltdowns. Financiers weren't supposed to be able to mismanage and loot corporations to such an outrageous extent, let alone endanger the entire economy. But the banking system had somehow started to morph back into its old, dangerous form. Conglomerates, mutual funds, computerization— the financiers had broken out of their box. The old regulations hadn't disappeared; most Americans and businesses existed within a heavily regulated banking system, but a new unregulated system, in parallel, was growing up, and it was now a threat not just to America's railroad system, but to the nation as a whole.

Patman didn't panic. Just two years earlier, Patman's staff had investigated interlocking directors among major corporations and banks. The railroad, or at least its predecessor, loomed in this study. Patman found that the Pennsylvania Railroad had seventeen interlocking directorships with major banking institutions.[42] In April of 1970, a new review of the situation showed fourteen such relationships involving eleven board members with twelve commercial banks. Seventeen of the largest stockholders were commercial banks, "through their trust departments for the benefit of others."[43] "The operations of the Penn-Central conglomerate and the heavy involvement of the banking community," Patman argued, "is strikingly similar to the tragic holding company scandals of the 1930s."[44]

By now Patman had been in office for forty years, and he well remembered Andrew Mellon's chicanery. In his first campaign for Congress in 1928, Patman had run "against monopolies, trusts, branch banking and excessive and discriminatory freight rates," and opposed the "money barons of the East."[45] The Penn Central was an example of the white-shoe money lords he hated, so prestigious that banks considered it an honor to lend their railroad money. The corporation even had a Mellon on its board, Richard King Mellon. Patman was not about to change now. Railroads were, in his view, as incompetent in 1970 as they had been in Brandeis's day.

Patman met with the executive leadership of the railroad for an hour and forty-five minutes. Gorman was not a railroad man by background and was still finding out the extent of the corporation's financial problems. He was frustrated, but he just couldn't get Patman to agree to the bailout. Volker tried to lobby Patman, to no avail. "Paul," he said, "you are wasting your time. It ain't gonna happen."[46] The answer was no. As Patman explained later, his reasoning for rejecting help was simple. "Why not small business, why not housing?" he asked. "Why pick out a big, rich corporation and help it with taxpayer's money?" There was no good answer.[47]

Gorman, and the rest of the Penn Central executives, were angry. They had expected to get their way. Gorman was so coddled he wasn't even carrying money. He had to borrow change from a Patman staffer to call the headquarters in Philadelphia to let them know they had been turned down.[48] The Penn Central would not get its bailout. The next day, on June 21, 1970, the Penn Central released an anodyne press release, saying the company would be filing for bankruptcy under Section 77 of the U.S. Bankruptcy Code. It was front-page news, with railroad officials later blaming high interest rates and the recession. The corporation asked 94,000 workers to stay on the job, and pledged to continue passenger service as the court began its restructuring.

The crisis didn't end but immediately shifted from the railroad to its creditor banks, as well as corporations that were in similar dire circumstances after having used the same exotic borrowing techniques as Penn Central. All of these institutions were now in trouble. The corporation's bankruptcy filing caused its over 100,000 creditors, including every major Wall Street bank, to lunge for safety in the commercial paper market, the first economy-wide liquidity crisis since 1933. Even the banks, because of the bank holding company loophole Patman was trying to block, financed themselves with commercial paper.[49]

Banks and big corporations weren't insolvent, but they had been relying on an unregulated financial system, and there was now panic, similar to the bank runs of the 1930s, only this time the run was on exotically named instruments such as commercial paper. Arthur Burns, the head of the Federal Reserve, acted, as he had in 1966. The Fed let it be known to all banks that it would not look askance should any bank need to borrow from the Fed to replace any borrowing needs from large companies that had been filled by commercial paper. The Fed kept its discount window open over the following weekend, and in doing so, prevented a credit crunch. There was a pullback in lending, but there was no domino effect, and no depression.

Bankers and business executives were furious with Patman. Didn't he realize how close he had pushed corporate America into insolvency? But those who Patman called the "plain people," the large undefined mass of citizens who rode the trains, supported him. Piles of correspondence lauded Patman for standing up to greedy bankers and railroad executives who ran "filthy" trains that were constantly late.

"I could have kissed you" ... "Imagine a struggling railroad that owns billions in real estate" ... "Keep pounding on this great conspiracy of money lenders" ... "The Penn-Central affair stinks to the high heavens. All the administration wants to do is bail out the bank" ... "Thank God for Congress!" The letters came from scholars and businesspeople, retirees and workers, Democrats and Republicans, even small bankers. The vice president of the National Federation of Independent Business congratulated Patman, saying, "You have never been more important to the future."[50]

Some complained about their retirement savings being savaged by greedy executives. Others groused that they couldn't get loans, while big corporations could. Workers for Penn Central wrote in supportively, noting mismanagement of the corporation. Some stated, in letters written to Patman in all caps, that foreign conspirators were ripping off America. All were horrified at the greed, the bad leadership, and the corrupt nexus between Wall Street and politics. And all were grateful to Patman.

Liberal intellectuals such as Hofstadter and Galbraith had argued that people no longer cared about monopolies, or the "so-called money trust." But they were wrong. Americans from across the spectrum did care. Anger at Wall Street, while submerged in the cultural debates of the 1960s, had not gone away. It was always there, bubbling.

## CHAPTER THIRTEEN

# THE COLLAPSE OF THE NEW DEAL CONSENSUS

"A lot of thinkers in the ivy-covered towers led the growing consumer advocates down the primrose path of specious thought."

—**Congressman J. J. Pickle, 1975**[1]

■ ■ ■ ■ ■ ■ ■ ■ ■ ■ ■ ■ ■

The failure of the Penn Central surprised people who shouldn't have been surprised, like officials from the railroad's regulator, the Interstate Commerce Commission. The credibility of the ICC was shattered. It had overseen the catastrophic merger and the disastrous conglomerate strategy. It had not recognized the danger of new financial instruments, and had not stopped Penn Central from lying to investors. The ICC had even helped the corporation evade scrutiny from other government regulators.[2] "The record of the ICC," said one congressional report, "is a shocking chronicle of bureaucratic disregard for the protection of the public."[3]

But Congress blamed high-level bankers and corporate officers as much as, if not more, than the ICC. "Powerful people in the Administration and in the business and banking community . . . are hurt," said Patman staffer Jake Lewis. "What we have now is a rare emergency situation which has all kinds of possible ramifications—both good and bad."[4] Patman's Banking Committee investigators conducted wide-ranging interviews and combed the corporate archives of the railroad and its banks. Toward the end of 1970, Patman began rolling out reports.

Some were simply embarrassing, like the exposé of insider trading by the PenPhil club and a blow-by-blow of the Executive Jet subsidiary (including nude photographs of stewardesses, free airline trips for a buxom blonde known as "Miss Hurst Golden Shifter" for her appearances at auto shows, and a Miami employee of the airline who procured attractive young women to accompany executives on trips to Europe and then tried to blackmail corporate leaders). Others revealed more systemic problems in corporate America, showcasing the failure of the conglomerate strategy, and insider trading among banks that had been lending to Penn Central while trading its stock.[5]

Aside from Patman's Banking Committee, the Securities Exchange Commission and an additional Congressional oversight committee run by West Virginia congressman Harley O. Staggers also conducted investigations, as did the new bankruptcy trustees of the Penn Central. Reporters and academics wrote books, including *The Wreck of the Penn Central, No Way to Run a Railroad,* and *The Fallen Colossus.*

And the episode crystallized a feeling that had existed since the mid-1960s that something was wrong with the American economy. Reliable industrial systems themselves were breaking down. In 1965, New York's Con Edison electric utility experienced a grueling twelve-hour blackout, snarling subways and commuter trains, diverting planes and panicking citizens. Executives at General Motors spent their time fighting laws mandating seat belts and antipollution measures, even as they lost market shares to Toyota and Mercedes, vehicles made by former enemies Japan and Germany.

The economy was out of kilter in other ways. Real wages for manufacturing workers started falling in the mid-1960s, as did labor productivity.[6] Bank of America mailed millions of unsolicited credit cards across America, part of a dizzying array of new and confusing financial choices in what would eventually be called "personal finance." Imports flooded in from Western Europe, Japan, and Taiwan, as America ran its first postwar trade deficit in 1971. In 1968, third-party presidential candidate George Wallace ran on a segregationist platform. But his angry bromides against bankers resonated not just in the South, but also, in a replay of the 1920s spread of the KKK, in the North as well, with workers facing stagnating wages, import competition, and layoffs.

The stock market had its own crisis in 1970 as the conglomerate stocks cratered. The brokers who had conducted much of the trading activity turned out to be insolvent, and required bailouts of their own. In that ill-tempered spring, the New York Stock Exchange chair Bernard Lasker met with Nixon about the financial chaos, letting him know the country was "five minutes till midnight of another 1929." In the 1960s, the mutual fund boom had spread stock ownership. By the time of the crash in 1970, thirty million households unhappily held stock. Before he met with Nixon, Lasker visited the vice president, whose secretary pleaded with him to restore the value of her fund.[7]

The economy recovered quickly after the Penn Central collapse. But something subtle had changed. The Federal Reserve had allowed bankers to recentralize credit risk, remaking corporate America and creating dangerous fragility in finance. And then when this newly fragile system nearly collapsed in 1966 and again in 1970, the Fed bailed out the credit instruments it had allowed to become systemically important. Any unregulated instrument or bank, if it became critical enough, was now effectively guaranteed.

One consequence of this shift in behavior by the Fed was a change in the politics of who could access money, and how they could access it. There was now one financial system for normal people, which was heavily regulated in the lending and borrowing one could undertake. There was another for big banks and corporations, who could operate in an unregulated land of exotic financial instruments, all backed by the Fed in the event of a crash.

Another consequence was a change in the boom-and-bust cycle. Recessions in the 1970s would be accompanied with something no one had ever experienced in a downturn: inflation. The Fed was now simply too afraid to cut off borrowing channels in a crisis in the unregulated system, so it would bail out bankers after each crunch. Bankers became much less cautious and much more willing to lend money, even when times were bad. In addition, the government ran large budget deficits in every recession, which immediately countered the fall in private spending. The combination of government spending and the willingness of private bankers to lend money to big businesses even in downturns flooded the economy with money, leading to accelerating bouts of inflation.[8]

In 1973, as part of the Yom Kippur War against Israel, Arab

countries banded together to embargo oil against Israel's Western allies, and eventually simply raised the cost of petroleum. Oil quadrupled in price, generating inflation and moving $60 billion of surplus dollars mostly from oil-importing countries to those in the Middle East.[9] Middle Eastern leaders then reinvested much of this money into the now-unregulated financial system, making it even easier for big corporations and banks to borrow for speculative purposes.[10]

This new speculation, beginning shortly after the Fed contained the Penn Central fall-out and supercharged by petrodollars, ended just as Penn Central had. With a crash. In 1973, one of the largest developers of apartments in the country, the Kassuba Corporation, failed, as did a series of new institutions designed to get around banking regulations, such as real estate investment trusts. From 1972 to 1974, the stock market lost nearly half its value. The failure of the nation's twentieth-largest bank, Franklin National, in 1974 nearly caused a crisis in the banking system. Franklin National had borrowed enormous amounts in the unregulated Eurodollar markets and lost money on speculation and fraud. When the bank's problems went public, there was a run similar to that on Penn Central.[11]

The Penn Central collapse had been merely a prelude to the psychological shock Americans now experienced. Cheap gas and an endless real estate boom were hallmarks of the thirty years of postwar American dominance and prosperity; both ended in 1973–1974. There were shortages of gasoline, electricity, and even onions, and rumors of insufficient stockpiles of everything from mustard to vegetable oil to cat food. In November of 1973, *The Tonight Show* host Johnny Carson made a joke about a toilet paper shortage, prompting a run on toilet paper as Americans rushed to buy every roll they could find.[12]

With the crash of Franklin National, the Fed stepped in once again, to make sure anyone who lent to Franklin National was fine. "The entire financial world," Arthur Burns, the chairman of the Federal Reserve Board, said after the bailout, "can breathe more easily, not only in this country but abroad."[13] The Fed was beginning to stand behind anyone whose losses were so big they could crater the system. Or as first put in a 1975 hearing on bank reform by Ralph Nader, "Too Big to Fail."[14]

For much of 1974 and 1975, Penn Central–like failures seemed almost commonplace.[15] Electric utility Consolidated Edison had to sell assets to New York state to stay solvent, and iconic airline Pan Am struggled to service its debts.[16] In 1975, New York City itself, the icon of American capitalism, went through a financial crisis in the high-interest-rate environment, and nearly went bankrupt (prompting the famous *Daily News* headline—"Ford to City: Drop Dead"—after Ford rejected a federal bailout for the city). Like Penn Central, the problem was both secular—economic activity had moved out of the city—and financial—interest rates were too high. The city placed its budget under the control of an independent board run by bankers to cut social spending and labor costs, and, at the behest of among others Ford's chief of staff Dick Cheney, begin charging tuition at the city university system that had been tuition-free since 1847.

The Penn Central crisis, as two journalists put it at the time, reached "far beyond railroads, challenging deep-rooted and basic assumptions of American corporate life." It caused "the nation and its business and political leaders to take a fresh look" at "the condition of American capitalism."[17] As Americans struggled in the 1970s to find answers to destructive new financial trends, a debate erupted about how to address the collapse of New Deal financial and industrial arrangements.

Part of this debate involved resurrecting old ideas. There was, for instance, a mini-boomlet on behalf of Teddy Roosevelt Bull Moose–style planning, beginning in the late 1960s and cresting into the next decade. In an article in *New York* magazine titled "Richard Nixon and the Great Socialist Revival," John Kenneth Galbraith archly lauded Nixon for socializing Penn Central with a proposed bailout, and praised similar bailouts of Lockheed and the New York Stock Exchange. These were the precursors, he argued, of a large-scale nationalization of industry, a planned economy to take the place of a competitive one.[18] Galbraith had broached the notion in his 1967 book *The New Industrial State*.[19] He dubbed his solution a "New Socialism," unveiled in his 1973 best-seller, *Economics and the Public Purpose*.

The president seemed to go in all directions at once. At times, he could be like a New Dealer. In the fall of 1972, Nixon approved moving forward on LBJ's antitrust suit against IBM, asserting that he should get "credit for attacking business." Nixon also sought to protect local retailers by defending pricing laws. "This is an old-fashioned attitude," he told his antitrust chief, "but I would rather deal with an entrepreneur than a pipsqueak manager of a big store." Nixon could also be downright populist, reflecting less his own early career as a lawyer on Wall Street and more his father's failure as an impoverished farmer and then grocer. "Supermarkets may sell Wheaties at a cent less, but I just don't think we want a nation of supermarkets." And of the conglomerates and Wall Street, he told Richard McLaren that policy concentrating economic power reflected "the selfish interests of the top people."[20]

Sometimes, however, Nixon went along with the nascent Chicago School. In 1971, a commission he appointed recommended deregulation of the entire banking system (opposed, of course, by Patman). He also appointed George Stigler to run a commission on antitrust laws, which Stigler promptly used to attack the administration's own assertive use of antimonopoly rules against conglomerate mergers.[21]

The president could even be a planner. Nixon had as a young attorney during the war been one of many seeking to control prices at the Office of Price Administration, under Galbraith. As interest rates continued to increase along with inflation, Nixon announced a plan to resurrect the OPA. With the unveiling of the "New Economic Policy" in August of 1971, Nixon assembled a board to oversee all wages and prices in the country, calling for intrusive price controls. Even Galbraith applauded. "I am sensitive about giving Mr. Nixon credit for anything," he said. But "we should be grateful" to Nixon for good policy.[22]

Nixon's price controls did temporarily control inflation, and as the economy recovered he was reelected in a landslide. But when Nixon lifted price controls, inflation shot back up. In truth, Nixon had no clear philosophy, or interest, in economic policy, and neither did key administration political leaders such as Henry Kissinger, who believed thinking about production beneath him. The debate over Penn Central and the increasingly obvious crisis of capitalism would have to be led by others. How this debate ended would mark a forking of the path for the American, and global, political economy. "The questions raised," Patman said, "are extremely serious not only for the current Penn-Central case, but for the entire U.S. economy."[23]

There would be three groups in the debate. Populists like Patman and allies like Michigan senator Philip Hart would propose one path, to decentralize American political economy once again. Chicago School intellectuals, meanwhile, would argue for a world without public constraints on private capital. But now a third group would participate in these debates, the consumer rights movement, influenced by Galbraith and elite postwar liberals, and organized by Galbraith's friend Ralph Nader.[24]

## THE POPULIST PATH

Populist political leaders, as they had during the 1930s in the last great era of ideological ferment, attacked bigness. "Under the umbrella of the economic talk, all we are trying to figure out is why our economy is in—and this is a harsh word—such a mess." So said trustbusting senator Philip Hart, in 1973, to open his hearings on the Industrial Reorganization Act.[25] Hart argued, in his bill, that bigness "contributed to unemployment, inflation, inefficiency, the under utilization of economic capacity and the decline of exports."[26] It made monetary and fiscal policy unworkable and forced the government to exert direct control over major sections of the economy.

Big business should be smaller. Hart and his allies looked beyond Nixon, tracing the increasing chaos and instability to the big corporation. "The economic strength of these large corporations, both foreign and American, is immense," said Hart's colleague, Senator Abraham Ribicoff of Connecticut. "They control huge financial resources and shift capital, technology, and management skills across borders, sometimes contrary to the interest of the nations in which they operate."[27]

Hart's answer was simple. His bill, the Industrial Reorganization Act, aimed to implement the Neal Commission's recommendations of breaking up most large corporations in the U.S. legislation to "responsibly restructure industry," Hart wrote in the bill's preamble, which was necessary not only to preserve a market economy but "a democratic society." Hart's bill was seen as anything but radical. It was based on the work of mainstream antitrust economists, and was supported even by the conservative chairman of the Federal Reserve, Arthur Burns.

The first witness was a former Patman staffer, Willard Mueller, who had been the head economist at the FTC for much of the 1960s. "America," he said, "is at one of those unique turning points in history when, by action or inaction, we must decide which road we shall travel to achieve our national objective." The Industrial Reorganization Act was the right road, he said.

Hart held six days of hearings. And as part of these hearings, his staff investigated large institutions, like IBM and AT&T. Hart saw the suit against IBM as analogous to that against Standard Oil or Alcoa, with the computer giant—as Rockefeller's giant had in 1911—monopolizing the most technologically advanced and important piece of American industry. And AT&T was the definition of a big and slothful monopoly.

Hart, heading back and forth between votes on the Senate floor, argued with witnesses, debated big ideas, and held forth on the large problems bedeviling the collapsing New Deal framework. The next year, the Department of Justice filed suit to break up the telephone giant, using some of the material Hart's staff gathered during the hearing. With continual congressional pressure, the Antitrust Division would wage war with IBM and AT&T for the rest of the decade.

Hart was savvy, but also old. "All of us remember the action after World War II in disposing of aluminum plants to Kaiser and Reynolds, RFC loans, and guaranteed government purchases for a limited period of time," he said, as witnesses nodded their heads. But there was an increasingly evident age gap. Hart remembered the fights, but younger liberals did not. The fight against Alcoa in the 1930s and 1940s, with the titanic clashes of the Mellon system in the shadow of the Nazis, seemed ever less relevant in the days of Cold War rivalry with the Soviet Union and cheap Japanese imports.[28]

As Hart sought to rescue the industrial system, Patman worked to plug the gaps in the law that financiers had been exploiting to build their conglomerates. His staff produced a report both to address the banking debates of the 1960s and rebut Nixon's emerging attempt to loosen financial rules. The increasingly lax regulatory framework and concentrated financial apparatus was undermining a stable economy. As Patman's report noted, it caused "frequent, almost predictably periodic inflationary booms and recessions that have beset the Nation's economy," damaging "both the financial institutions themselves and the people who depend on them."

Patman aimed to restore the regulated banking system, and public controls over the allocation of credit. He sought to break off bank trust departments from banks; reform the Fed and make the central bank an arm of the Treasury Department, as it had effectively been under Eccles; eliminate conflicts of interest through interlocking directors; change how foundations, bank holding companies, and pension funds operated; and guarantee that states, cities, and people trying to buy homes could borrow money.[29]

Hart's Industrial Reorganization Act and Patman's reform ideas to restructure the financial system were a path to reduce the new 1960s-style concentrations of economic power. But while in 1933, Pecora and Roosevelt had helped solidify an intellectual consensus in favor of restricting financial and corporate power, there were no such leaders to help out in 1973. "We will find a series of witnesses with Ph.D.'s in economics," said Hart, "disagreeing among themselves." But their ideas would be shelved; Hart's bill would never get a vote.

## THE PATH OF BIG BUSINESS

Hart's hearing was also a moment when the ascending Chicago School and the old New Deal antimonopolists met. By 1973, the Chicago School had made enormous progress in wooing the corporate world. These scholars had been attempting to persuade big business leaders for over a decade that they should reject their accommodations to New Deal regulations and labor unions, or they would face oblivion. Penn Central and Nixon's price controls showed oblivion wasn't far away.

In 1972, John Harper, the CEO of Alcoa, Henry Ford II of Ford, and Fred Borch of General Electric combined three older corporate networking groups into a trade association called the Business Roundtable. The Business Roundtable was an organization not of corporate lobbyists, but corporate CEOs themselves, reflecting a new dedication to politics by corporate leaders. It drew from the most powerful men in business, like Reginald Jones of General Electric, Thomas Murphy of General Motors, Walter Wriston of Citibank, and Irving Shapiro of DuPont.[30]

As DuPont's Shapiro put it, politics had become increasingly intrusive into business, so he would respond by taking business into politics. The big business lobby radicalized and professionalized across the board, turning from primrose New Deal corporate "statesmanship" to aggressive advocacy. After the embarrassing loss over bank holding companies, the American Bankers Association moved its headquarters from New York to Washington.[31] Lewis Powell, later a Nixon Supreme Court pick, authored a memo for the U.S. Chamber of Commerce, now known as the "Powell Memo," making the explicit case for big business to seize the organs of cultural and legal power through aggressive public advocacy, litigation in the courts, and a campaign to reorient the ideology of academic institutions.

This organizing happened just as the Chicago School was making inroads among business leaders. In 1962, George Stigler first made his arguments that banking, trucking, railroads, electric utilities, and airlines should no longer be subjected to public regulations. This seemed a bit like madness when he first proposed it; companies had structured their business models around such rules. But after Penn Central's collapse, Nixon's brief experiment with price controls in 1972, and the first hints of "stagflation," the prospect of less regulation became much more widely attractive.

So did the fight against antitrust, a moderate level of which had been accepted by the business community. One of the key strategic priorities of the Business Roundtable was to stop the de-concentration initiative that came from the Neal Report. The Roundtable fought against the Federal Trade Commission's collection of detailed statistics on the revenues of the 250 largest companies in the country. A Chicago School–trained FTC chairman named James Miller killed it in the 1980s.[32]

The rapidly organizing big business community mobilized against Hart's bill. The U.S. Chamber of Commerce, the traditional lobbying group for large businesses, had its chief economist, Carl H. Madden, testify against the de-concentration initiative. Chicago School scholars were the front line in the assault. In his testimony, Madden cited Robert Bork, Yale Brozen, and George Stigler. Harold Demsetz, having written a paper justifying the virtues of big business in 1973, testified against the bill directly, as did Henry Manne. The populist Mueller scoffed at them, arguing anyone who had any sense and studied the matter saw the obvious link between size and market power.[33]

The next year, in 1974, Exxon, IBM, Mobil Oil, and Xerox, each of which was targeted by an FTC or DOJ suit, cemented an alliance with Chicago scholars. These corporations sponsored a Columbia Law School convening known as the Airlie House conference on industrial organization, on the grounds of an old plantation in the Virginia countryside.[34]

At Airlie House, Chicago School scholars and antimonopolist economists held a series of debates. John McGee, who in a 1958 paper had "proved" Standard Oil was not predatory, attacked the Bureau of Economics director, F. M. Scherer, on the question of the minimum efficient size of firms. Yale Brozen, who had "proved" concentrated industries didn't show high profit rates, went at H. Michael Mann, an ex–Bureau of Economics director, on barriers to entry. Harold Demsetz went at the correlation of high profits and concentration, "proving" that large firms had higher profits because of efficiency, not market power.[35] The debates were published in a book, *Industrial Concentration: The New Learning*.[36]

The Chicago Schoolers didn't win the substantive argument against antimonopolist economists. Despite the language of science, little of what the Chicago School economists put forward was ever rooted in empirical proof. But they gained a marketing coup in the use of the term "The New Learning," which persuaded much of the political world that there was no longer a consensus, or need, for strong antitrust enforcement.

## THE NEW POLITICS AND THE NADER ATTACK ON THE FTC

The final group in the debate was the leaders of a rising generation of baby boomers influenced by the countercultural form of politics, young, numerous, self-righteous, dubbed "The New Left." Much of the political energy in the 1960s was oriented around race relations, environmentalism, and the war in Vietnam, often organized on the college campuses the leaders of this generation attended. "We are people of this generation," wrote Tom Hayden in what became a famous manifesto, the Port Huron Statement, "bred in at least modest comfort, housed now in universities, looking uncomfortably to the world we inherit."[37] These were the children of affluence.

In the 1960s, it was hard to go into a college dormitory at the time without seeing a copy of a Galbraith book. Many young leaders were inspired by John F. Kennedy's message of government service as an honorable calling. Many of these college graduates revered the seeming brilliance of the liberal intelligentsia, attracted to egghead technocracy.

The war in Vietnam shaped the children of affluence in two ways. It disillusioned them toward the leaders who had inherited the political economy legacy of the New Deal, like LBJ. It was hard to imagine labor unions, liberal political leaders, and Democratic Party machine hacks as illustrative of some grand experiment in industrial liberty, when they were part of the political coalition behind sending them to fight an immoral war in Vietnam. They saw socialists like Galbraith, who was a critic of the war, as far more in tune with their generational needs. Second, it created solidarity among the affluent and split them from the working class. Higher education was their province, and attending college or graduate school, until 1971, exempted one from military service. White-collar youth opposed the war while young, working-class people fought it.

In the presidential election of 1968, the Democratic Party's nominating contest served as the forum for a great debate on the future of the country. Robert Kennedy attempted to win the primary with a "black-blue" coalition, of poor blacks and working-class whites. Kennedy had been one of the few senators opposing bank deregulation when Patman was fighting his lonely battles. Kennedy's approach was to unite the old New Deal policies of protecting independent farmers, retailers, and workers with newer political goals of promoting equal social rights for African Americans and opposing the war in Vietnam.

But he was murdered by an assassin in California. Democrats nominated LBJ's vice president, and Vietnam War supporter, Hubert Humphrey. Like Kennedy, Humphrey embraced the New Deal philosophy; indeed Humphrey was a legendary liberal populist and antimonopolist who had ushered in the era of civil rights for the Democrats in 1948. The war in Vietnam weakened Humphrey, and George Wallace's racist third-party candidacy cost Humphrey the election by attracting angry white workers nationwide.

After Nixon won, Democrats put together the Commission on Party Structure and Delegate Selection, also known as the McGovern-Fraser Commission, which sought to heal the party's wounds. An influential Democratic strategist, Fred Dutton, took control of the process. Dutton, who had managed Robert Kennedy's campaign, blamed unions and white working-class voters for the party's problems. In the commission, Dutton actually sought to eject the white working class from the Democratic Party, which in true Galbraithian form he saw as "a major redoubt of traditional Americanism and of the anti-negro, anti-youth vote." The workers, he argued, were now "the principal group arrayed against the forces of change."[38] So he designed a party process that would reduce the power of organized labor in picking the Democratic nominee.

Dutton was the perfect specimen of the emerging corporate liberal. He had helped conceive of Earth Day when working for John F. Kennedy, but would later become an oil lobbyist. In his view, the future would be a Democratic coalition of African Americans, feminists, and affluent college-educated whites, many of whom would work for giant, technologically sophisticated, progressive corporations. Dutton's strategy was a break from the basic class-conscious Democratic coalition of independent farmers, shopkeepers, and unionized workers that Franklin Delano Roosevelt had structured in the 1930s. For Dutton, this new Democratic Party coalition, born in affluence, had moved beyond material needs. The "balance of political power," he argued, had shifted "from the economic to the psychological to a certain extent—from the stomach and pocketbook to the psyche, and perhaps sooner or later even to the soul." To Dutton, the small businessman and blue-collar worker represented the past.[39]

In 1972, George McGovern won the Democratic nomination through the process that Dutton designed, with the coalition Dutton envisioned. It was an utter disaster for Democrats. McGovern, detached from the working class, was simply not very interested in economic questions, seeking to run on the moral question of the war in Vietnam. Nixon had partially defused the political potency of the war in Vietnam by pulling out some troops. On the economic side, Nixon imposed price controls to hold back inflation. Americans trusted Nixon to do a better job on the economy, and voted for Nixon overwhelmingly.[40] Nevertheless the 1972 presidential contest, as well as campus politics and the antiwar, civil rights, and environmental movements, were the training grounds for a host of New Left politicians.

As the ideological debate kicked off by the Penn Central collapse occurred within the corporate and financial sector, for young people it was increasingly the Vietnam War that shaped what it meant to be a liberal or a conservative. To the extent that corporate power mattered, it was through the consumer rights movement, led by Nader.

Nader was one of the great heroes to emerge from the 1960s, operating in some ways as Brandeis had, as a crusading public interest lawyer. In 1964, Nader had launched the consumer movement by revealing malfeasance in corporate America with his book on General Motors, *Unsafe at Any Speed*. His book, and GM's clumsy attempt to blackmail him, began turning the social energy of the decade to consumer rights. "Suddenly, if you were having difficulties in the marketplace," said one consumer rights leader, "and by no means just with automobiles, you were no longer just a schlemiel who couldn't make it in the world—you suddenly were in the best company of all—your two hundred million fellow Americans who were all now willing to admit that they were in the same boat. It was that perception, articulated and presented to us first by Nader, that made possible the massive bursting forth of energy that became the consumer movement of the 1970s."[41]

Car companies did not care if their customers died in accidents. Soda makers refused to put warning labels on bottles that would explode at random. A common story was that a maker of infant cribs, who, upon being told by the Department of Health, Education, and Welfare that his cribs were strangling babies, replied, "So what?" Hundreds of thousands were drawn to the notion that businessmen were hostile to consumers, charging higher prices for substandard products. Activist groups mushroomed, and in just a few years, consumer rights departments popped up in states and counties all over the country.[42]

Advocacy for consumer rights was not new, having existed at the turn of the twentieth century and been encoded in such bills as the Pure Food and Drug Act of 1906. Consumer advocates sought to protect shoppers from poor-quality products. Some, however, had much more profound aims, seeing consumer consciousness as a mechanism to reorient American political philosophy toward socialism. Fifty years before Nader, social planners Walter Lippmann, Herbert Croly, and Walter Weyl sought to create a form of consumer-dominated politics in service of Teddy Roosevelt's Bull Moose pro-monopoly movement. This vision stripped the citizen of any role in the production process and situated the citizen as simply a consumer of goods and services. Consumerism left behind important institutions—like Consumers Union—to protect the American shopper from price gouging and unsafe products, but American political philosophy remained oriented around the role of the citizen as a producer.

The aims of Nader's new movement, like those of Lippmann and Croly, were broader than price and safety. Consumer rights were a function of the politics of affluence. Organizers sought products that were made to be ecologically sound, coming as many of them had from environment groups, like Friends of the Earth, the League of Conservation Voters, and Zero Population Growth. And they were utopianists. When asked by an AT&T official about its end goal, one veteran of the movement replied, "What I see is that one day instead of the United Auto Workers sitting across the table from the auto makers every few years to negotiate a new contract, there will be three people at the table. The one who will speak first will be the representative of the national organization of consumers, and he will say something like this: 'The democratically selected representatives of the American car-buying public have met in their annual conference, and they have agreed on behalf of their constituents that the people of America are willing in this next year to pay seventy-five dollars more per car. Now you gentlemen may decide among yourselves how you wish to divide that up.'"[43]

The leader of this movement, throughout the 1960s and 1970s, was Nader. Nader was in many ways a populist, expressing skepticism toward big business, big government, and big labor. He would quote Brandeis on a generalized fear of bigness. Nader was close with Brandeis disciple Patman, working with Patman to oppose bailouts and supporting and advocating for the breakup of large firms such as General Motors.[44] But unlike Brandeis, who had represented small firms and had experience in business, Nader's career was not rooted in promoting fair commerce and protecting the citizen producer. Brandeis believed citizens needed control of production and commerce, so they could have the autonomy necessary to be citizens and protect their communities. Nader did not particularly care who had control of commerce as long as the consumer was protected.[45] "People first had to get it that corporations were rapacious and government corrupt," he said in 1975. The goal was to "replace corporations, break them up," so they could be "owned by workers or better yet consumers." In truth, Nader had not thought carefully about who would control commerce.[46]

Nader came to disdain rules that would enable small businesses to engage in fair trade, such as the Robinson-Patman Act or anti-chain-store pricing rules. Like the New Left, he seemed to oppose politics itself as dirty. Only a cadre of public interest lawyers, he believed, could look out for the interest of consumers in the face of a rapacious and corrupt governing and business elite. Nader's strategy was to take leverage of the liberal judiciary created by the New Dealers to bring business to heel.

This new form of politics, idealistic and ignorant, slammed into the antimonopoly policy world in 1968. That year, Nader had seven student volunteers, dubbed by the press "Nader's Raiders," do a four-month investigation of the Federal Trade Commission and produce a report. Commissioner Philip Elman, who was a friend of Bork and an opponent of the Robinson-Patman law, offered help. He set up the Nader researchers in a room in his office at the FTC, and "just gave them all the dirt I had."[47]

For years, powerful corporate lawyers had attacked the Federal Trade Commission, reserving special venom for the Robinson-Patman

Act, which the commission enforced. What opponents of Robinson-Patman missed was the delicate institutional balance the law provided. Because of the law, the FTC had strong grassroots political support from thousands of small businesses who knew they were protected from chain stores by the commission. The chairman of the Small Business Committee, a Tennessee congressman named Joe Evins, who held the purse strings for the commission, made sure that the agency was funded if it enforced the act.[48] "I think it compares favorably with the Magna Carta or the Sherman Act," FTC chairman Paul Rand Dixon, a populist southerner, said of Robinson-Patman.[49]

But Nader missed the political balance provided by small business, influenced as he was by Galbraithian liberals and the anti-institutional and elitist biases of the 1960s counterculture New Politics. The report framed the FTC as incompetent and a fount of illegal political fundraising.[50] His investigators portrayed Dixon as a purely political operative, biased against Ivy League graduates and in favor of the southern populist "ruling clique" of the commission.[51]

The new consumer rights movement simply didn't see value in the FTC's role in organizing fair trade by and for independent small businesses, which the report called derisively "the 'noble savages' of the business community."[52] While it was "true that historically the Act has given the FTC a recognized constituency, the small businessman," the report argued, "this in itself has misdirected the Commission away from the man who is to benefit most from competition and a free enterprise system—the consumer."[53] Fair trade laws were, according to Nader ally Michael Pertschuk, a "disreputable remnant of recession-inspired price fixing."[54] Or as the key author of the report put it, "The maximization of consumer welfare was our talisman."[55]

Shortly after the Nader report on the FTC, the powerful American Bar Association leveraged Nader's work, and set up an independent commission to restructure the FTC.[56] In the 1960s, the FTC had helped win a series of important merger cases that made it hard for big companies to buy competitors. It had also prosecuted the Robinson-Patman Act on behalf of small businesses. The ABA and the Nader report created the opportunity for Nixon officials to usher in a period of "dramatic organizational change" at the FTC. Elite-trained lawyers and economists became much more important, small-town concerns less so.[57] In 1963, the FTC issued 215 complaints and 252 orders on Robinson-Patman violations; by 1972, the number of complaints dropped to one and the number of orders to four.[58] As one Texas congressman put it, "The unknowing, unwitting coalescing of big business and consumer advocates resulted in the silent repeal of Robinson-Patman."[59]

To Nader, and increasingly younger political leaders alienated from the political economy of the New Deal over the Vietnam War, protecting citizen sovereignty in the form of local retailers seemed like protecting special interests at the expense of consumers. This priority came to be reflected in more than just the consumer rights area. The Chicago School began to influence the intellectual organs of the New Left. The hot new magazine for the younger liberal policy elite of the 1970s was *Washington Monthly,* founded by Charlie Peters, a Roosevelt admirer who sought to renew and restore liberalism. *Washington Monthly* would be, as it advertised, "the liberal magazine that questions liberal orthodoxy." But this questioning often meant, in reality, repealing the New Deal. One ad for the *Monthly* bragged, "Our case against social security was made two years before *Harper's*."[60]

*Washington Monthly* asserted, as Nader had, that government bureaucracy was overwhelmingly smug. So too were unions. Teachers in white-collar unions were resisting accountability for performance, corporate managers were overpaid, American companies were less competitive internationally, and Democrats were afraid of risk and obsessed with status. Washington was broken. "Yesterday, Penn Central. Today, Pan Am. Tomorrow? The American system is in trouble and we all know it," Peters wrote. He wanted, in some undefined manner, to tear it down. The ship was sinking and it was time to try "crazy, impossible" ideas.[61]

Hart- and Patman-style populists focused foremost on political economic structures; they saw corporate power, Wall Street, and financial corruption as foundational problems leading to not only inflation and high interest rates but an antidemocratic concentration of power. The newer generation diagnosed the crisis as generational, cultural, a lack of youthful vigor within American institutions. Taylor Branch, in *Washington Monthly,* wrote in 1970 an article titled "We're All Working for the Penn Central" on how dispiriting it was to work not at a giant railroad conglomerate but in a government bureaucracy.

The upstarts viewed Penn Central as a symbol of a generalized stagnation, a moral curse, rather than a practical problem that could be addressed by reducing the size of business and constraining concentrations of power. "We've grown fat and sloppy," Peters argued. "General Motors and the Post Office each have over 700,000 employees. One turns out lemons. The other loses packages. . . . The old organizations—public or private—simply aren't doing the job." In the 1970s, his writers were trying to find something new, something different, something interesting to address the congealed and increasingly ossified society. But oriented by the politics of affluence rather than the memory of Mellon, they ignored antimonopolist elders and did not fully understand the danger of concentrated financial power.

Gradually an antigovernment and anti-union trend emerged within the liberal intelligentsia. Milton Friedman authored his attack on Roosevelt's Social Security program in *Washington Monthly,* as the liberal magazine became a regular host to Chicago School–influenced economists. Galbraith, in his 1973 book, *Economics and the Public Purpose,* accepted Stigler's contention of "regulatory capture." Corporate managers, he argued, though sometimes authoritarian, were also increasingly and naturally progressive, and far more competent than the regulators who had allowed the Penn Central collapse.[62]

Chicago School arguments took off not just among the Business Roundtable, but within the consumer rights world, which saw rules like Regulation Q, fair trade rules, and restrictions on airline behavior as "cartel regulations."[63] "Throughout the land," Nader said, "people are repulsed by arrogant and unresponsive bureaucracies serving no useful public purpose, and they are looking at this Congress to get on with the national house cleaning job that is needed."[64]

The Chicago School law and economics movement also penetrated liberal thinking through Democratic technocrats in academia, like the deregulation-promoting liberal Alfred Kahn, who flourished in an era where political economy was being depoliticized. Kahn taught legions of young liberal lawyers, and influenced thousands more with his classic 1970 textbook *The Economics of Regulation.*[65] The Penn Central collapse had seemed to crush the legitimacy of regulators. Rather than stand up for the smart use of state power to regulate the behavior and size of private enterprise, the left-leaning Galbraith helped the Chicago School deliver a death blow to Brandeis's ideal of regulated competition.

Brandeis had put together a theory whereby American politics attacked bigness in industry and protected citizens by preserving fair markets. Only by preserving fairness in commerce, he believed, could democracy survive. This idea had lasted, in its twentieth-century form, from the election of 1912 into the 1970s. But Galbraith and Robert Bork had prepared tools to tear it apart. And Nader was the unwitting mass marketer who was teaching a young generation to join them.

## CHAPTER FOURTEEN

# WATERGATE BABIES

"In general the liberal democratic position is to harmonize the interests of large corporations and big government, to tinker and 'improve' what they perceive to be a basically sound machine. Essentially their argument is for a gradual, continued concentration of industry and government. From this ideological viewpoint a person such as Patman, whether in fact old or ineffectual, seems an absurd anomaly, to be swept aside in the year of the 'revolution.'"

—**Alexander Cockburn and James Ridgeway,** *The Village Voice,* **1975**[1]

∎ ∎ ∎ ∎ ∎ ∎ ∎ ∎ ∎ ∎ ∎ ∎ ∎

I n January 1975, a seventy-eight-year-old Pennsylvania congressman from Philadelphia named William A. Barrett was working in the chamber of the U.S. House of Representatives. Barrett was busy, and had to get some documents back to his desk. He flagged down one of the hundreds of roving young pages in Congress, and handed him some documents. "Here," he said, barely looking up from his work. "Take these papers to my office."[2]

"Go fuck yourself!" replied the young man. "Take them yourself!"

Barrett had just met Thomas J. Downey of Long Island, the youngest member of the new class of congressmen elected in the wake of the Watergate scandal. The youth movement of the 1960s had slammed into Washington, D.C.

Nicknamed the Watergate Babies, the newly elected officials were young, idealistic, fierce, and aggressive, disgusted by Nixon and the Vietnam War. But they weren't just in the capital to attack Nixon, or his successor, Gerald Ford. They were here to end business as usual. They were going after the whole establishment, Democrats and all. Downey's colleague George Miller, a twenty-nine-year-old new member from California, later recalled the anger of the young members. They had, he said, "a million grievances."[3]

This class of Democrats was not like those who had arrived in 1932, 1934, 1936, 1958, or 1964. "We were the children of Vietnam, not World War II," explained Timothy E. Wirth, an incoming member from Colorado.[4] The new members understood modern messaging technologies; McGovern had built a massive direct mail list, and as Wirth put it, "We were products of television, not of print." Mainly from upper-middle-class suburbs and often Republican-leaning districts, they had learned their politics on college campuses, angry about government overreach and spying, veterans of the bitter battles of the 1968 and 1972 primaries. "We were young. We looked weird," said a new member named Toby Moffett, just thirty years of age and a community activist in Connecticut. "I can't even believe we got elected!"

They flooded into the House, the Senate, governor's mansions, and state legislatures. The raw numbers of pickups understated the change to the Democratic Party. Due to retirements, there were seventy-five new Democrats in Congress, many young, eager, and disdainful of the party hierarchy. More than 40 percent of the entire Democratic Caucus had served for less than four years.[5] There would be another large class of Democrats in 1976. This surge was a launching pad for a political generation: a twenty-eight-year-old law professor and *Washington Monthly* reader named Bill Clinton had nearly pulled off what had been imagined as an impossible upset for a congressional seat in Arkansas.

It was a process-driven class that believed in Nader's form of anti-politics. Many opposed party labels. New Hampshire freshman Norman D'Amours never once asked Georgia governor Jimmy Carter, when Carter was stumping for him, to mention the Democratic Party.[6] Bob Edgar was a thirty-one-year-old Methodist minister who began his campaign by going to the phone book to look up "Democratic" to find the local party headquarters.[7] "Virginal assholes" was what one old strategist called the wave of young Democrats.[8]

The new Democrats entered a fractured Democratic Party and

swung the balance of power to the liberals. Until 1974, the liberal faction in the House had been held down not by the Republican opposition but by their own party. For decades, it had been committee chairmen, largely from the conservative South, who controlled the House, from the flow of legislation, to budgets, parking spots, floor debates, even committee seating. "The winds of change have arrived in the House of Representatives," said California congressman Phillip Burton. New York congresswoman Bella Abzug, an antiwar feminist and one of the first members of Congress to call for Nixon's impeachment, rejoiced at the arrival of the newcomers, exclaiming, "The reinforcements have arrived." There were so many Democrats that it was inconceivable to imagine the Republicans as a serious problem. Nixon was gone, Ford was weak. The problem was now the old guard inside the Democratic Party.

Wright Patman was also excited. These were the Watergate Babies, the men and women that his campaign against the Nixon White House had helped elect. When no one in the party would dare stick their neck out about Watergate, before Nixon's reelection in 1972, Patman had used his Banking Committee staff to investigate the break-in. He had wound up on Nixon's enemies list in the process. The Speaker of the House, Carl Albert, thought Patman's investigation had started the president's downward spiral, forcing Nixon to live, as Albert put it, "in constant torture" from the moment the committee began looking into the matter.[9]

Patman, as usual, had faced opposition from not only Republicans but Democrats on his own committee. On a critical vote on October 3, 1972, Patman had tried to get subpoena power to compel the Nixon administration to turn over documents and produce witnesses to answer questions posed by his investigators. But he lost the vote; the GOP stayed unified, while six Democrats on his own committee voted to turn Patman down.[10]

Having lost the ability to investigate, Patman turned his files over to Senator Sam Ervin, who later broke open the scandal. Patman's investigation, while unsuccessful in the short term, framed all subsequent investigations of Watergate, and the president's later downfall. Patman had been proven right, and President Nixon had fallen. But there were signals that Patman wasn't picking up about his own waning influence. The new energetic liberals were not taking direction from Patman.

The Democratic newcomers were angry. It was a moment for ideological realignment, not just because of Nixon's corruption but the high interest rates and the recession, the conglomerate mania turned to dust, the collapse of Penn Central and the bailouts. It was time for a new class of Democrats to fix the world. Patman had worked with some of the youngsters, like Bill and Hillary Clinton, two organizers in Texas for George McGovern in 1972. "It isn't just the Democrats that will be elected, but the kind of Democrats," Wright Patman said. "They'll come in here mad as biting sows."[11]

Patman was right about one thing. The new Democrats were mad.

## THE "RED GUARD OF THE REVOLUTION"

The week of the 1974 midterm elections, the great villain himself, Richard Nixon, lay in a hospital in critical condition, mute, with pneumonia-related complications after emergency surgery to treat a blood clot. Nixon was perhaps in better shape than his party. After the elections, just 18 percent of voters identified themselves with the GOP, and two thirds of voters, when asked to think of something positive about the party, couldn't name anything.[12] The Capitol Hill Club, the informal social club of congressional Republicans, was under threat of foreclosure, and prominent Republicans at a group called the Committee on Conservative Alternatives began researching the requirements to set up a third party.[13]

Yet the elections did not suggest a rousing endorsement of the Democrats. While just 15 percent of voters thought that Republicans would do a better job addressing corruption, and 35 percent believed Democrats would do so, 43 percent of voters believed neither party would.[14] Turnout was the lowest it had been in three decades.[15]

Nixon's resignation in August of 1974, and his later pardon, colored the election, but these events happened in the midst of financial turmoil, just as a mild recession was turning into a severe downturn. The oil embargo contributed to a rise in food prices of 2.3 percent in October 1974 alone, a shockingly high increase for a recessionary environment.[16] On Election Day, 80 percent of voters cited the economy or inflation as the main issue.[17]

Americans did not have faith in their political leaders, or the ability for the election to lead to change. "Why should I go down to the polling place and help them weave a rope for my own noose?" asked one California voter.[18] Americans were pessimistic on the economy, that great postwar engine of wealth, around which both parties had framed their political concept of affluence. "I don't think these people in Washington get it," said one Detroit housewife. "We can see that inflation is serious, because we have to make hard decisions in our daily household budgets."[19]

There weren't obvious answers, at least not among the politicians who had grown up on Hofstadter's consensus history. "I don't really know what to do about inflation, and [my opponent] doesn't either," an unnamed candidate in the Midwest said the month before the election. "So we both haul out our clichés and hope we'll get the best of it." It was all process talk, "personal integrity," no program.[20] But the lure of the politics of affluence was strong. The week of the election, Oregon Republican senator Mark Hatfield proposed that wealthy nations eat less, and send the surplus to poor nations.[21]

The week after the midterm election, bad economic news showered the nation. Industrial output continued its decline; and the Ford administration finally acknowledged a recession was on.[22] Inflation was running at over 10 percent a year, but not because the economy was overheating. There was a recession, with record unemployment, paired with the price hikes. The price of sugar jumped, and auto sales were worse than expected. New York state was running out of money, and borrowing costs for New York City were spiking.[23] Economic growth shrank sharply in the first quarter of 1975, and unemployment would hit nearly 9 percent by May.

In the face of this moral, economic, and political meltdown, neither party had a clear leader or clear philosophy. "No one can effectively lead or even work in the Republican Party today, because no one can possibly say what it stands for," said *National Review* publisher William Rusher.[24] In March, at a Republican leadership conference,

President Gerald Ford and California governor Ronald Reagan debated the future of the Republicans, without a clear resolution.[25]

The Democrats seemed a bit better. They knew what they were not. "Much of what the government has tried to do over the past 15 years has failed," said Michael Dukakis, the new Massachusetts governor. "We're not a bunch of little Hubert Humphreys," quipped Gary Hart, a newly elected senator who had run the presidential campaign of George McGovern in 1972. At a Democratic issues conference in 1975, keynote speaker Alvin Toffler, author of the best-seller *Future Shock,* told attendees to "throw out all the old New Deal claptrap." Some called the new House members the "Red Guard of the Revolution," seeking to tear down the old.

But while these new members were liberal and antiwar, few had been schooled in political economics and none remembered the depression. "The kinds of things that would motivate, say, [House Speaker] Tip O'Neill were not part of our experience." said Paul Tsongas, elected that year in Massachusetts even as he irritated the local party apparatus.[26] "The populism of the 1930s doesn't really apply to the 1970s," said Pete Stark, elected in 1972. Stark had gained acclaim by putting a neon peace sign atop the skyscraper that housed his bank.[27] The influence of the consumer rights movement was significant; Toby Moffett had been a Nader's Raider, running a consumer and environmental advocacy group in Connecticut before his election.[28]

Yet the new members were, as one advocate put it, "scared shitless about the economy in their district."[29] Despite Democrats holding an overwhelming majority in the new House of Representatives, there was no stated approach to the problems of corruption and economic stagnation. "I'm not entirely sure what my political philosophy is," said new Michigan congressman James Blanchard.[30] These new Democrats had no answers, no vision of political economy. They just knew that the economy was doing badly, and they were frightened.

A new generation was entering politics, one that had, since the 1950s, been taught an entirely different story about the nature of political economy, and America, than had the generations before. Gone was the conflict between Jefferson and Hamilton over monopoly and banking, gone was the class conflict and the robber barons, gone even was Brandeis, replaced by vapid discussions about the power of television and the microchip. "We were products of computer politics, not courthouse politics," said Wirth years later.[31] Gary Hart, the star of the class of 1974, dismissed those who "clung to the Roosevelt model long after it had ceased to relate to reality."[32]

Hubert Humphrey reflected on this McGovern generation without the optimism of Patman. "If you were old," he said, "you had to be gotten rid of. If you were new and different, that was good. If you had done something, if you had experience, you were unacceptable."[33]

The eighty-year-old leader of the AFL-CIO, George Meany, was deeply embittered by the massive Democratic wave. He snapped at a reporter, "Who said I was optimistic? Do I look optimistic? I'm disillusioned."[34]

## ORGANIZING A REVOLUTION

A few days after the election, months before the new members of Congress would be sworn in, two young members of Congress began setting the stage for a revolution. Wirth and New York's Edward W. Pattison headed to Washington, D.C., sharing the anger of the voters and determined to do something even before they were sworn in as congressmen. Their agenda was, in essence, to matter.

It was a cold day when they arrived. Wirth and Pattison went to see the Speaker of the House, Oklahoma Democrat Carl Albert. Albert was weak, seeking to please all sides of his fractious party. Wirth remembers, in that first meeting, Albert rocking back and forth in a comically huge chair, the Speaker's feet not quite hitting the ground. As the chair moved back and forth, the Speaker's pant leg would pull up, showing a great expanse of white long underwear. Back and forth. After the fights over Nixon, the assassinations of Bobby Kennedy and Martin Luther King, the McGovern defeat, the riots, the chaos, to talk to this old man in charge of the Democrats was, Wirth later said, "surreal."

Albert sent them to see an assistant who seemed to Wirth to be nice but stuck in the nineteenth century. This divide wouldn't do, the rift between new members in touch with an alienated America and the old guard. Wirth, Pattison, and a third member, Gladys Spellman, set up an office for the class of 1974 as an organizing base. "Out of nowhere, we just did it," said Wirth.[35]

Wirth, Patterson, and Spellman had help and mentorship from members with experience, including Congressman Richard Ottinger, an anti-Patman member of the Banking Committee. And it was here where it became clear that what Wirth and his allies really opposed was not Patman's age, but Patman's populism. Ottinger had worked with Thomas "Lud" Ashley in 1965 to pass the bill legalizing the Manufacturers Trust Company merger in the dark with Patman at the hospital. And now Ottinger was mentoring the Watergate Babies, and helping them define their political strategy.[36] Wirth, Pattison, and Spellman organized a number of speakers, most notably David Broder, the relentlessly centrist Pulitzer Prize–winning columnist for *The Washington Post* who was the "single most powerful and respected political journalist in Washington."[37]

Broder spent many of his columns lamenting the intellectual vacuousness of both parties and encouraging Democrats to reorient their views on political economy. To a proposal for a new New Deal, he jeered, "If there are many Americans in this jaded age who can believe in the New-New Deal, then, logically, the Tooth Fairy is a cinch to be elected President."[38] He held up an anti–New Deal Democratic advisor, Ted Van Dyk, and urged Democrats to expend "political energy as great as that which went into the creation of the New Deal-Fair Deal-New Frontier-Great Society" to slash government radically.[39]

The first target of the Watergate Babies was the way that committee chairmen were chosen. While congressional process was not a big issue in the 1974 campaign and seemed tangential to core policy questions, thinking about congressional process was a natural fit for incoming politicians who had run without much of a program. The year before, in *Economics and the Public Purpose,* Galbraith had called for an end to the seniority system. His suggestions included open votes, the establishment of a budget committee to do planning, and doing away with the seniority system that allowed committee leaders to exclude "younger men" from power who were more in touch with public views on how to distribute resources.[40] Broder and Galbraith both pushed a kind of politics opposed to class conflict and focused on process questions, which synced well with the new class. At a postelection dinner, five new Democratic members were "drooling all over" John Gardner, the chairman of the process reform group Common Cause.[41]

The older liberal members who tutored the newcomers also emphasized the importance of congressional process reforms. Watergate Babies weren't a majority, but they entered as a large bargaining bloc into a split Democratic Party. Liberals from the North, the Midwest, and the West had been organized since the late 1950s into a faction called the Democratic Study Group. The DSG had cemented around a commitment to liberalism and racial equality, but had mushroomed into a full shadow party, with vote-counting operations, legislative analysis, and political campaign advice. DSG members picked fights within the Democratic Party, defeating conservatives who had been using complex procedural techniques to bottle up civil rights legislation.[42]

The DSG had a number of leaders, with a key force being San Francisco representative Phil Burton. Since the 1950s, the goal of the DSG had been to overthrow the seniority system and allow for a stronger Congress to rein in both segregation and the Cold War. Burton had used complex parliamentary tactics to have a full House vote in 1973, ending war funding for Vietnam.[43] The first day the new Congress was in session, Burton achieved a long-term goal, terminating the House Un-American Activities Committee.

In December, Burton was elected—with the votes of nearly every freshman—to be the chair of the entire Democratic Caucus.[44] At the first caucus meeting, this group joined together to demonstrate their power by firing the official doorkeeper of the House of Representatives, William "Fishbait" Miller, an incompetent crony of a Mississippi Dixiecrat, who was paid a lavish salary of $40,000 a year, and who controlled 340 patronage positions. The intraparty war was on.[45]

The liberals were on the march, aided by circumstance as much as anything. One of the key figures holding the seniority system together had been the most powerful chairman, Wilbur "Mr. Tax" Mills of the Ways and Means Committee. Ways and Means not only handled all tax legislation, and health care programs such as Medicare, but it also allocated committee assignments. Few dared challenge Mills on anything. But Mills had a serious problem: he was an alcoholic, and his addiction was out of control.

Just before the election, in October, Mills was caught drunk driving in D.C. In the car with him was Fanne Foxe, a dancer nicknamed the "Argentine Firecracker," who jumped into the Tidal Basin to try to escape the police.[46] Despite widespread reporting of the incident, Arkansas voters reelected Mills. Foxe used the publicity to attract attention for a strip show in Boston. Political reporters showed up. To their shock, Mills jumped onstage to join the show. He held a press conference, seemingly drunk, from her dressing room.[47] Mills was stripped of his power, the Ways and Means Committee enlarged to dilute the influence of the existing membership, and then Mills resigned from Congress in December and joined Alcoholics Anonymous. The threat of retaliation from Mills was gone.

Committee chairs would now be decided by a vote of every Democrat in the House, instead of just picking the most senior member of the committee. The Watergate Babies took advantage. They invited every sitting committee chair to answer questions from the new members. Ostensibly, every chairman was elected by their colleagues, but it was a pro forma process. "If you were senior enough," Wirth said, "you got elected, and that was it." The Watergate Babies changed this system. "Why don't we question these guys, and see what they're like, and see if we ought to vote for them or not?" Wirth asked. The Watergate Babies class sent out invitations to sitting chairman to come and talk to the group; the chairmen refused. Wirth said the group responded by saying, "Well that's fine, we'll vote against every one of you."[48]

## THE KILLING OF WRIGHT PATMAN

In January 1975, the new Democratic Caucus met to make decisions about getting rid of committee chairs. The old bulls began cutting deals, offering favors to new members to win their votes. Wayne Hays of Ohio, nicknamed the "meanest man in Congress," was the chairman of the Administration Committee. Hays kept a mistress on staff for $14,000 a year, and allowed members to take cash from their office supply budget so he could retain his power. *The New York Times* called him "a disgrace to Ohio, the Democratic Party, and the House of Representatives."[49] Members of the class of 1974 pledged to vote against Hays, but he was one of the most powerful members of the House, because his committee dispensed critical favors to members, like the location of their parking space. Hays launched a lobbying campaign, offering perks and a pay hike for members of Congress. He kept his chairmanship.[50]

Two reactionary members lost their positions. Armed Services chairman Edward Hebert attacked the freshmen as "boys and girls," and refused to allow amendments against the war in Vietnam to come up for a vote. A vote of 152–133 turned him out. The conservative Agriculture chairman, W. R. Poage, who voted against the Democratic Party more than he voted with it, went down by 144–141.

The fight over Patman, however, was different. The attack on Patman didn't come from the freshmen or the DSG, but from the leadership and from the liberal establishment. Patman had used his control over staff to investigate concentrated financial power. This attack on finance angered many fellow Democratic members who were often given honoraria—speaking fees and cash payments—by local banks, or were added to their lavishly compensated boards of directors. These long fights had left scars, and pro-bank liberals took advantage of the naïveté of the freshmen.

One of the demands from the freshmen was to open up committees to sunlight. Pro-bank liberal Democrats on the Banking Committee told the Watergate Babies that Patman ran the committee autocratically.[51] Yet in 1966, it had been the pro-bank liberals on Patman's committee who had attempted to scuttle a subpoena into large banking institutions. After noticing newsmen in the committee room, Ashley sought a secret vote to withdraw the subpoena. "I don't know of any rule requiring a closed session," replied Patman. "The public has a right to know what we do here. I want the press to attend."[52] Embarrassed, opponents of the subpoena withdrew their request.

For years, pro-bank liberals had cooperated with southern reactionary Democrats and Republicans to try to gut Patman's authority, stripping him of subpoena power and attempting to fire his staff.[53]

Patman and his staffers fought back, with publicity. Patman ally Drew Pearson exposed liberals on the Banking Committee, especially Ashley.

Ashley, Pearson wrote, was a "man about town," along with his "pals" at the American Bankers Association. He had become "the darling of the big bankers," so bent on getting Patman that he had been able to get "all 14 Republican committee members in his pocket," as well as several Democrats, to block Patman from controlling the organization of his own committee.

Then, Pearson plunged in the knife, and twisted. He wrote that after Ashley arrived in Washington, "one of the first things he did was to throw out his wife, who was put in the position of telephoning the Congressman's friends to ask for help."[54] Ashley blamed Patman for the embarrassing column. It wasn't just Ashley and Ottinger; Patman regularly lost votes within the committee, as he had over bank holding company fights in 1970, and over the Watergate subpoena in 1972.

The constant battles with bankers, and with his own party members, had cost Patman support among Democratic leaders. When populist and Patman ally Sam Rayburn was Speaker, this didn't matter. But now it did. Patman assumed his long record as a populist Democrat who fought Nixon and the big bankers would be more than enough to win support among the new members. It did the opposite.

When Patman's enemies on the committee saw the opportunity presented by the Watergate Baby incoming class, they mobilized. They told the youngsters that Patman wasn't up to the job, and pointed to the bank holding company bill, and how Patman had written much of the legislation on the floor instead of through his committee. Rather than this episode being illustrative of the corruption of House Banking Committee Democrats and the power of the bank lobby, it was framed to the newcomers as Patman being unable to control his committee.

Few of the Watergate Babies knew anything about banking, or corporate concentration, and fewer of them cared. Economic concentration questions were not important; what mattered was Vietnam, government bureaucracy, the seniority system, and civil liberties. And to the extent members of the new class thought about political economy, they were likely to have been deeply influenced by Galbraith.

"[Patman's] economic ideas were not in pace with modern concepts," said Pete Stark. Just hearing from older members that Patman was old and out of touch was enough. Older pro-bank liberals were also showering attention on the incoming members. "We didn't know a lot about what was going on," said one member of the new class. "We were well-manipulated by the older guys."[55]

This anti-Patman sentiment was buttressed by Common Cause and Americans for Democratic Action (the group Berle and Galbraith had helped form). Common Cause had supplied a report on transgressions by committee chairs, with their main targets southern conservatives who abused their committee positions for personal gain or opposed core Democratic goals civil rights legislation. But one was Wright Patman, who was placed on the list because of rumors from liberal members on the committee that he was out of touch and violating committee rules. "He's a pathetic old man," said one lobbyist for Americans for Democratic Action.[56]

Every committee chair had to be renominated by the Democratic Steering and Policy Committee, and then put to the full Democratic Caucus for a vote. Nearly every committee chair was renominated by Steering and Policy, which was heavily influenced by the Speaker, Carl Albert, not the new members. But Patman was turned out by a vote of 11–13.

When the full caucus convened, Patman tried to get his chairmanship back. But Ottinger, Reuss, Common Cause, and Ashley had already made the case among the young Watergate Baby class that Patman was a bad chairman. No one seemed to be able to explain exactly why he couldn't or shouldn't continue leading the committee. "You can't have an 81-year-old chairman," said one young member. "He was an old, old gentleman," said Joan Claybrook of the consumer watchdog group Public Citizen. "Not senile, but not in command. He had done his thing. He had had his day."[57]

Moffett warmly praised the old man to reporters, but when pressed, admitted he organized against him. Ed Koch, a member of the Banking Committee who would become the mayor of New York City, said "philosophically I agree with Patman, but I voted against him because he was a bad chairman. I am philosophically opposed to Wayne Hays, but I voted for him because he was a good chairman." Another anonymous member said, "Patman couldn't sell pussy on a troop train."[58]

The young freshmen "revolutionaries" seemed to want to get rid of Patman, but without articulating why. Spellman, a newcomer from Maryland, said that "it broke my heart to vote against Mr. Patman," though in fact she had lobbied against him. "He was my father's hero. But our decision was based not on heart but on logic. Mr. Patman is 81 and that's a time when minds begin to wander." When asked about Patman's long-standing fights against the concentration of power in big corporations and banks, she said, "To be real honest, I don't know. I haven't had a chance to study that."[59]

Barbara Jordan, the renowned representative from Texas, and the first black woman from the South to serve in Congress, spoke eloquently in Patman's defense.[60] One of the few populist Watergate Babies, California's Henry Waxman broke with his class and supported Patman. "I was taken aback that so many liberal friends were against him," he later commented.[61] Missouri congresswoman Leonor Sullivan said Patman was "the most liberal chairman in this House, most courageous in public interest." One member compared him to King Lear, and Texas congressman Jim Wright talked about Patman bravely opposing the Ku Klux Klan in Texas in the 1920s. But even though Patman had been the first Democrat to investigate Watergate, his colleagues crushed him 152–117, a far worse showing than any of the other deposed chairmen.

Ralph Nader was irate. "The bank lobbies would take anyone as long as it isn't Patman," he said, noting that liberals had turned against a "bastion of progressivism and courage that is Wright Patman." Congressman Charlie Wilson, a fellow Texan, commented, "the irony is that the most liberal Democratic Caucus in history has done something that will cause great celebration in the First National Bank in Dallas."[62]

Killing Patman was one of the few actions for which the Watergate Babies received praise. Broder, in a widely circulated column titled "The Good News of a Troubled Capital," called the moves of the new caucus to fire veteran leaders "an act of extraordinary political and legislative responsibility. . . . A liberal like Wright Patman was not spared just because most in the caucus share his distaste for high interest rates.

The vagaries of his leadership had become an embarrassment to his party—and his railing against the banks could not save him."[63] Broder did not mention that he had spoken with the Watergate Babies to help organize their thinking at their first meeting.

Patman's goal had been to become chairman of the Banking Committee, to fight the bankers. He'd done that, and for decades he'd held the New Deal financial system together with savvy political maneuvering and vigor. But in 1975, with the help of dozens of fresh "reformer" members of Congress, the bankers got him. The genial and weak Henry Reuss, who had liberal sympathies and an air of academic detachment (as well as stock in a Buffalo bank called Niagara Shares), took over the committee. A week later, the bank-friendly members of the committee completed their takeover, and ousted Leonor Sullivan—a Missouri populist, the only woman on the Banking Committee, and the author of the Fair Credit Reporting Act, from her position as the subcommittee chair. "A revolution has occurred," noted *The Washington Post.*[64]

And a revolution had occurred. The Watergate Babies were angry. Patman had been right about that. But they were angry at people like him. Patman's removal from his committee chairmanship was devastating. He lost the institutional power and voice he had worked so hard to achieve. A year later, he was planning to retire from Congress when, on February of 1976, he was taken to Bethesda Naval Medical Center, ill with influenza. The flu turned into streptococcal pneumonia. Diabetic and eighty-two years of age, he died on March 7.

A United States Air Force transport plane flew Patman's body to Texarkana from Bethesda. Local papers covered every aspect of the funeral, including the batch of carnations sent by President Gerald Ford. A thousand people attended the funeral, with over five hundred more outside. One witness noted that "as the funeral procession made its way from the church to the cemetery," constituents who had elected and reelected him twenty-four times stood "reverently, some with their hands over their hearts in tribute to their departed friend and Member of Congress."[65]

Jim Wright, who was to become Speaker of the House, gave a commemoration that even Republicans praised. Patman "early in life began a lifelong love affair with the plain and simple, unpretentious average men and women of this land who sensed with some unerring instinct that here was a man whom they could trust." Indeed, when the plane touched down bearing Patman's body, his close friends insisted the hearse tour the African American section of town. Patman would have wanted to stop one last time at the Quonset hut "where he had always gone for beer and catfish on trips home and, more important, so that he could pay his respects to all of his constituents. The gesture was returned in kind: the streets were lined several deep."[66]

Jake Lewis, his close aide, later commented on Patman's sense of optimism that "the last breath he drew out at Bethesda he must have been thinking, what will I do tomorrow." And Leonor Sullivan, one of his closest allies in Congress, eulogized him by noting that "the American people—small business, the wage earner, the average-income family, the veteran, the poor, and the unprivileged—were the beneficiaries of his prodigious efforts. And so, I might add, were all businessmen who sincerely believe in competitive enterprise."[67]

But while the memory of Patman would endure, his policies would not. "The whole financial structure should be made more competitive and less segmented," said the new chairman, Henry Reuss, as he laid out the new committee agenda, with a nod to the fashionable new trend toward deregulation. He did want to direct the Fed to move more lending to "socially desirable" purposes like housing, rather than corporate takeovers and speculation.[68] But his attempt to do so was smashed thoroughly by the banking lobby, and unlike Patman, Reuss gave up.

In February 1978, Reuss did something Patman would never have done. He declared a truce. In a speech to the American Bankers Association, Reuss told the three hundred assembled members, "As bankers and Congressmen, let's forget our differences and concentrate on our opportunities." Reuss followed up his speech with a private session in March with bank executives at the posh International Club in D.C. "Reuss just got tired of fighting the lobby, which was getting him nowhere, and decided to be a statesman," said an observer.[69]

## CHAPTER FIFTEEN

# THE LIBERAL CRACK-UP

"I suggest that a philosopher of many years ago pointed out this phenomenon, and said that there is something about the intellectual mind that induces it to focus on the obscure at the expense of the obvious. And this is why I am glad that no one has ever accused me of being intellectual."

**—Thomas Rothwell,
small business lobbyist, 1975**[1]

■ ■ ■ ■ ■ ■ ■ ■ ■ ■ ■ ■ ■

Within a few months of the 1974 election, the Watergate Babies, along with the older liberals who had mentored them, had removed Patman and reorganized Congress. Now it was time to restructure the rules for who could do business in America.

In late March of 1975, during the beginning months of the new Congress, a successful businessman sat before the House Judiciary Subcommittee on Monopolies, chaired by liberal New Jersey powerhouse Peter Rodino, who had presided over Nixon's impeachment. This businessman's name was Curtis Bruner, and his company, Classic Chemicals, produced Classic Car Wax, a high-quality, well-known product sold all over the country. Bruner was there to tell Congress not to repeal the fair trade law (called Millard–Tydings) that allowed makers of branded products and independent retailers to block unfair practices by chain stores.

Bruner told the assembled congressmen how he built his business. In 1965, when Bruner began trying to sell his high-quality car wax, most of the large chains wouldn't even talk to him, preferring to sell cheap wax in a market dominated by DuPont and three other giants. Smaller retailers wouldn't stock it either, because they feared being undercut by discounters. Then Bruner discovered fair trade contracts.

When he began promising small stores that his high-quality car wax would be sold at the same price in small stores and discount stores, small stores stocked the item and told customers about it. Bruner's product became popular, and discount stores began stocking it. Bruner could now break into what had been a monopolistic market in car wax, by competing on quality, not just price. It was the same basic story that retailers and producers of branded goods had been telling for a hundred years, the same story that motivated Brandeis to call predatory discounting "the competition that kills."

Bruner was telling the members of Congress that the laws against predatory pricing were working. Discount chains, supermarkets, and large department stores existed side by side with independently owned retailers with good service and local roots. But if the fair trade laws disappeared, he said, the country would be "dominated by big businesses." He was not asking for protection from big business. He was telling Congress how he would react if forced to compete in a country dominated by big businesses. "I intend to be one of them," he said.[2]

Bruner was joined in his critique by small business lobbyist Edward Wimmer, a former Patman ally, who added his own warning in a letter to the committee. "Lenin," Wimmer argued, "said that small business was the only real obstacle in the path of Communism in the U.S. and that it would be removed."[3]

Most of the new members barely noticed the warnings. The men testifying were old, the laws were old, and it was out with the old. They would soon pass the Consumer Goods Pricing Act of 1975, which invalidated state-level fair trade laws.

The movement to repeal the laws had started before the new Congress convened. In 1974, prepping for the incoming class of Watergate Babies, the legislative director of the Consumer Federation of America said repeal of the fair trade laws is "one of the things we will work hardest on." Public Citizen, a new consumer rights group started in 1971 by Ralph Nader, announced a "great deal of interest" in the law's repeal. In November, a Senate staffer told the press that one of the first items on the agenda was hearings on repealing the fair trade laws.[4]

Republicans joined these consumer groups. Ford's Council on Wage and Price Stability, established to fight inflation, had years earlier recommended their repeal as part of the broad attack on price hikes.[5] Ford's attorney general said that repealing those laws could "make a swift and meaningful impact on our inflationary problems." Meanwhile, major business groups were silent, with the U.S. Chamber of Commerce and the National Retail Merchants Association taking no position either way.[6] Druggists, marketers, independent retailers, and newspapers protested the potential repeal bitterly; even Robert Bork argued in favor of the right of companies to set their own prices. But as one liberal congressman put it, laws protecting small stores from unfair trade practices are bad because they simply don't "help the consumer."[7]

And when the new Congress convened, so did the movement toward repealing these laws. "This simple repealing legislation may be the most effective single action the Congress can take to combat inflation in certain areas of the economy," announced Rodino.[8] Liberals Ted Kennedy and George McGovern joined in. Only the hoary old Hubert Humphrey, who had been a local pharmacist before entering politics, supported fair trade.[9]

Fear of chain stores had become a quaint, nostalgic, black-and-white picture of the Great Depression, as relevant as soup lines. Senator Edward Brooke, a liberal Republican from Massachusetts, sponsored the fair trade repeal law in the Senate.

On the surface, the repeal of fair trade laws was driven by a fear of inflation. By the end of 1974, prices were increasing at roughly 12 percent a year. This was due to a series of disruptions, from spending on the war in Vietnam to an increasingly unregulated credit boom, culminating in an oil embargo and a spike in prices for fuel. But nothing happens overnight in politics. Inflation fell throughout 1975, collapsing to 6 percent by the beginning of 1976.[10] The overthrow of fair trade, which had been won with so much struggle fifty years earlier, was the culmination of a consistent push by Wall Street and the left to remove the citizen from having control over production. Courts had already been striking down fair trade laws for decades (with Congress responding immediately to restore them); in the 1970s, the number of Robinson–Patman cases brought by the FTC declined rapidly.[11]

In many respects, the entire edifice of twentieth-century antimonopolism stood on the foundation of fair trade and other laws designed to keep the capitalist—and the trading companies they controlled—from interfering in the process of pricing a good. Brandeis had warned in 1913 of the shortsightedness of consumerism. "Far-seeing organized capital secures," he wrote, "the cooperation of the short-sighted unorganized consumer to his own undoing. Thoughtless or weak, he yields to the temptation of trifling immediate gain; and selling his birthright for a mess of pottage, becomes himself an instrument of monopoly."[12]

Similarly the command-and-control left had understood almost as long the ways in which pricing—and the concept of the consumer—allowed for consolidation of power. Walter Lippmann, struggling with his own lack of faith in democratic self-government, argued that America's best hope lay in the ability of big corporations to devise "administrative methods by which the great resources of the country can be operated on some thought-out plan."[13]

Big business representatives had been attacking fair trade laws and the Robinson–Patman Act since the laws were passed.

The laws aimed at two different price harms. The first was predation, where a corporation like Standard Oil or A&P could use discounting to drive competitors out of business. The second was price discrimination, where a railroad or corporation could charge different prices to favor bigger companies that did their bidding. Both predation and price discrimination helped companies with access to capital, which meant that these tactics placed control over commerce in the hands of the money trust of Wall Street. The antimonopoly laws were designed to block both harms, and thus, restrict Wall Street.

But predatory practices and price discrimination can lower prices for consumers, at least on a temporary basis. Naive new consumer rights groups and political leaders, in thrall to command-and-control philosophies of political economy, were easily persuaded by the legal establishment that fair trade laws were simply protectionist rackets designed to help special interests.[14] The new liberals eagerly took apart the system of laws designed to protect the little guy. "These are the people that wouldn't think of committing discrimination in a sociological context and that would horrify them," said a small business advocate, "but in an economic context, it becomes the thing to do."[15]

Though most members didn't know it, the Democratic Congress of 1975 had just taken the single biggest step toward the destruction of the independent business enterprise—and the small producer and small retailer—in the history of America. With the passage of the Consumer Goods Pricing Act, the nation's small retailers could no longer protect themselves against well-capitalized chain stores, and producers no longer had the ability to control what middlemen did with their products.

## WALMART POLITICS

The congressional attack on fair trade opened up opportunity for a new retail emperor, a man living in Bentonville, Arkansas, on the western edge of the Ozarks mountain range. The Ozarks were a poor area, splitting Arkansas, Oklahoma, Missouri, and Kansas. These states, plus Mississippi, Louisiana, Tennessee, and Texas, would become the base of what the man called his company—Walmart. Sam Walton was an eager and aggressive retailer who had been evading fair trade laws since the 1950s. Like Andrew Mellon, Walton was a ruthless competitor. As a child, he had traveled throughout Missouri with his father, a debt collector foreclosing on defaulting farmers during the Great Depression.[16] It trained him for a life of hard work and brutal competition.

In the 1950s, when Walton began learning how to retail, many poor farmers were leaving the land for jobs in the new poultry farms, clothing factories, or resorts that brought Chicago retirees south. People in the region needed to stretch every penny, a perfect launching pad for Walton's discounting empire.[17] It is where the kind of folks Patman called the "plain people" lived; the Robinson of Robinson-Patman had been an Arkansas senator. There were also thousands of independent stores in the South protected by the fair trade and Robinson-Patman laws, many of them just shacks near dirt roads. Here Walton sought his fortune. In 1962, the same year K-Mart and Target launched, he opened his first real Walmart discount store in Rogers, Arkansas. The irony was Walton could pay a small amount of money for a lease on a store and succeed because of the system that populists put in place to protect independent shopkeepers.

Walton had an innovative strategy, a flair for theatrics, and a willingness to work harder than anyone else in the business. His weapon was price, a belief that selling the goods that people need a little bit cheaper would draw crowds of eager shoppers. Walton was willing to buy directly from manufacturers and get around middlemen, and had an obsessive zeal for controlling costs.[18] It was a great business because Walton enforced a ruthless efficiency in his stores, but Walmart was a moderate-sized regional retailer with no buying power across the economy at large. The Consumer Goods Pricing Act of 1975 set the corporation free.

In 1976, Walmart sent a thank-you note, of a sort, to consumers. In advertisements blaring "Spring fabric prices to suit your budget," the chain noted, in small type, that "the repeal of fair trade laws nationally made it possible for Walmart to discount all patterns."[19]

This legal shift reshaped American commerce; over the next thirty years, it allowed capitalists to use chains to kill small retailers focused on service. It concentrated power in the hands of much larger discounters, and ultimately manufacturers who could match scale with the new goliaths. From 1970 to 1979, Walmart went from $44 million in annual sales to $1.2 billion. By 1985, Sam Walton, now a billionaire, was the richest man in America.[20] By 1993, Walmart achieved an average of over $1 billion in sales every week.[21]

But in 1975 in Congress, few thought much about the likely consequences of taking apart America's fair trade laws. The new members were from the suburbs in the Northeast, not the Ozarks; they looked down on southerners and people in rural areas. And the rights of producers, of small business or small banks or credit unions, did not matter next to the need to hold down prices for the consumer.

The Senate did not bother to find small business groups to testify, though "a couple submitted statements expressing fear that there would be vicious price-cutting without fair trade."[22] The hearings were so sloppy that data about aspirin was used in the Senate hearing, despite aspirin not even being a fair trade product.[23]

This philosophical shift to consumer consciousness was across the board, not just on fair trade laws in retail. The consumer movement sought to get rid of rules restricting banks and those restricting chain stores. As one Consumers Union representative told the Senate Banking Committee, "In many ways, Regulation Q ceilings, like fair trade laws, are anti-competitive, anti-consumer vestiges of the Depression and have long outlived any usefulness they may once have had."[24] The consumer movement dismissed both the New Deal achievement of constraining Wall Street, and the populist achievement of restraining mass-buying monopolies. Citibank and Walmart seemed to offer better deals to consumers, and that was more important to these advocates than restraining corporate power.

With the loss of Patman, there were few Democrats left who were able to understand the nature of the political power of the retailer and trading company. White southern retailers and pharmacists had been independent of concentrated power since the 1930s. To them, the New Deal meant fair trade laws that protected their livelihood from the chain store "menace." White independent merchants often supported the Democratic Party even when disagreeing on racial segregation, unions, or other policies. Black merchants and independent farmers were protected in part by these laws. As a political by-product, many ended up serving as a class who had the money, experience, property, and ambition to support civil rights activists in innumerable practical ways.[25]

Ultimately, the embrace by the Democrats of discounting—for the sake of the "consumer"—helped to remake the political structure of both parties. As this civic leadership class that had been buttressed by fair trade and similar laws fell apart, so did the Democratic organizing base in the South. Walmart spread, first in the rural South, and then into the Midwest, the Rocky Mountains, and Rust Belt cities, paralleling the Republican conquest of the same territory.[26] The Republicans became rooted in a far more right-wing base in the South, and the Democrats began moving away from their long support for the small businessperson and small farmer.

The 94th Congress did deliver one final populist piece of legislation, passing the Hart-Scott-Rodino Antitrust Improvements Act, a long-sought reform to require companies to notify the government

upon seeking a merger.[27] This was part of new, more assertive antimonopoly rhetoric, but this rhetoric was increasingly focused on keeping
consumer prices low. Watergate Babies thought the antimonopolist
posture was to help discount chain stores subvert local businesses. They
viewed Americans as consumers, not citizens.

## THE LAST HURRAH FOR ANTITRUST

On January 17, 1969, the last business day of Lyndon Johnson's administration, Attorney General Ramsey Clark charged IBM with
monopolization of the general-purpose digital computer market.[28]

The DOJ complaint was, as one lawyer put it to Congress, "equal
in significance to the Standard Oil case of 1911."[29] Standard Oil was
the high-tech story of the 1880s, IBM the high-tech leader of the
1960s. The company had 74 percent of the market for general-purpose
digital computers, selling $2.3 billion in 1967. Its closest competitor
had 5 percent, or $156 million.[30]

In the late 1960s, IBM was one of the most powerful companies
on the planet, commandeering the market for computation, the very
brain of corporate America and the military. It terrified competitors
with its tactics. IBM offered its products in a bundle, with software,
hardware, and services at one price, to prevent other companies from
being able to compete in any part of the industry. IBM would also
slash prices below cost anywhere there might be competition, and
often preannounced products, later known as "vaporware," simply to
scare customers away from buying untested computing products from
rivals. It dominated computing, printing, memory, peripherals, and
software, keeping its suppliers on a tight leash.

Unbeknownst to any of the participants, the creation of the personal computer in the 1970s would open up the digital age to hundreds
of millions of people, putting computers in reach of every business in
the West, and eventually much of the world. But this might never have
come to pass had the PC industry been monopolized by IBM using its
traditional tactics. PCs might have been locked down and under the
control of IBM, forever.

The case against IBM was one of the most important in world

history. Practically just the bringing of the suit resulted in a huge win for humankind, which was the decision to open up personal computing, the final chapter in the running from the 1930s to the 1970s to ensure that the fruits of science and engineering would flow to the public instead of monopolists.

On the one hand, policymakers liberated this new technology from the grasp of a would-be monopolist, and made sure it was accessible to humankind. On the other, ironically, the law and economics movement on both sides of the aisle used the case to bludgeon and destroy the rationale for similar future liberating activities. These thinkers had matured, and by the end of the case, they had largely destroyed antimonopoly philosophy as it had been understood in America since the founding of the nation.

Since the 1930s, IBM had been under constant antitrust scrutiny, first for its monopolization of the punch card market. The government had taken a sticks-and-carrots approach to structure the technology industry. In 1952, the government launched a suit against IBM for monopolizing punch card technology, but also pushed the corporation, as well as its competitors, into the digital computer market with defense contracts. By the 1960s, IBM had acquired monopoly power in digital computing. It used a strategy of bundling software with expensive hardware, as well as a range of pricing games, to prevent competitors from emerging or gaining a foothold in the fast-growing computer business.

The government claimed IBM shut out rivals by offering one price for an entire computer system, including software, processing units, as well as memory and printing. This bundling allowed the company to use market power in one area of computing to retain share in all of them. The company also undercut potential competition through predatory pricing, lowering products to near cost or potentially below cost to drive out rivals (strategies reprised decades later by Microsoft).[31] There were a host of private suits from IBM rivals, like Telex and the Control Data Corporation.

At first the suit went reasonably well. Early on, the government was working with the Control Data Corporation (CDC), which had a private suit against IBM that mirrored the government's.[32] In June, IBM unbundled its hardware and software, changing its pricing formula so that customers could purchase the products separately. Unbundling these two products was a "major restructuring" of the computer market, and led to the creation of an independent software industry.[33] In 1973, in a private antitrust suit with Telex, federal judge Sherman Christensen found IBM guilty and ordered the company to pay $352.5 million in damages.[34] IBM even began musing on which parts it could sever as part of a potential breakup.[35]

But the case eventually set the stage for a change in the philosophy of antitrust practitioners. Thurman Arnold died the year of the IBM complaint, ending the influence of the key New Deal–era official. IBM penetrated the Democratic legal establishment immediately, hiring Johnson's attorney general Nicholas Katzenbach as a vice president, as well as bringing former LBJ antitrust chief Donald Turner and his academic partner Phillip Areeda onto their legal team.

The company then hit at a vulnerability within the antitrust laws, which was the difficulty and length in administering a complex case of business law. IBM hired a phalanx of attorneys and economists to undermine, delay, and embarrass the Department of Justice. IBM subverted the cooperation between the government and private litigants by paying off CDC, including a payment of $15 million just for attorney's fees, which was larger than the annual budget of the Antitrust Division. As part of the settlement, IBM was apparently permitted to destroy the computer index of 27 million documents gathered by CDC so the government couldn't use it.[36] It sought complex mini–trials over matters such as market definition; it took a little over five years before both sides had even completed their depositions, meaning interviews with witnesses. IBM also took aim at one of the judges in the trial, claiming he was hostile to the company. Six years after the original 1969 filing, the case went to court. The government's side took 473 days in court, 52 witnesses, more than 3,200 exhibits, and 72,000 pages of transcripts. It went through four lead counsels. The case became a full-employment act for antitrust lawyers and economists, with one economist buying himself a boat and naming it "Section Two," after the section of the Sherman Act which enabled the suit.[37]

With a ferocious pushback against the Department of Justice, IBM sought to reorient the ideological foundations of antitrust law itself.

This included financing of Chicago School–influenced conferences and scholars. After the trial its economic experts came out with a book, *Folded, Spindled, and Mutilated: Economic Analysis and U.S. v. IBM,* with recommendations on elevating the importance of economists in antitrust cases so that the precedent of the 1945 Alcoa decision against the aluminum company's monopoly would have less influence on the courts. But even before the suit ended, IBM reoriented the ability of private litigants to win cases. The company's hiring of Areeda and Turner proved effective. They wrote a key paper in 1975 on the use of predatory pricing, which cited the *IBM v. Telex* case. Then the Telex decision against IBM was reversed on appeal. As antitrust scholar William Kovacic noted in 2014, "IBM's well-funded litigation (not a timid, indifferent operation) by 1978 had crushed various private plaintiffs."[38]

By 1980, the IBM suit seemed to have been going on endlessly. The liberal Katzenbach was telling Democrats, like Peter Rodino, how out-of-control young lawyers at Justice unfairly hectored a giant of American commerce. IBM argued the computer industry was changing so quickly, with mainframes giving way to minicomputers to personal computers, that it wasn't even clear what the DOJ wanted.[39] IBM's arguments about the government resonated in the increasingly antigovernment 1970s. Citibank's Walter Wriston said, "The government is suing to dismember IBM. The question is, what is the public good of knocking IBM off? The ultimate conclusion to all this nonsense is that people cry, 'Let's break up the Yankees—because they are so successful.'"[40]

Decades later, the importance of the IBM suit to the development of the American economy would become clear. In 2001, one of the most important business historians of the twentieth century, Alfred Chandler, would note that this suit led to IBM's decision to unbundle its software, and that decision "became and remained central to the evolution of the computer industry worldwide."[41] The suit, as Ed Black of the Computer and Communications Industry Association put it in 1997, also "signaled to both venture capitalists and key, talented individuals that they could, in fact, start new firms and not be stifled by Big Blue."[42]

Like GM and U.S. Steel, both hulking giants perceived as

management marvels until nimble foreign and smaller competitors undermined them, IBM would have been better off had it been broken up. In the 1980s, the firm's scientists won two more Nobel Prizes, but its large bloated bureaucracy did not adjust to changes in the market. It was late entering minicomputers, personal computers, engineering workstations, and laptops, because the company's executives were focused on protecting its high-margin mainframe business.

The successes of the suit did not register among the new economists and antitrust lawyers trained in the Chicago School framework. They could no longer tell the difference between healthy markets and big companies, and chalked up the competition in the technology industry to nature, rather than antitrust policy. A mythos emerged around Silicon Valley, that a set of institutions built on democratic protection of the engineer and scientist from the monopolist was instead born from antigovernment garage tinkerers.

Bork used the length of the IBM case to undermine antitrust enforcement by dubbing the case the equivalent of the Vietnam War for the Antitrust Division. It was not an accurate framing, but it stuck. The Carter administration would hand over the flagging case to an unenthusiastic Reagan Justice Department.

## THE CHICAGO SCHOOL TAKEOVER

In the middle of the 1970s, Democrats held almost two thirds of Congress. The Republican Party was in disgrace. But the Chicago School could do no wrong. Milton Friedman won the Nobel Prize for economics in 1976, setting the stage for multiple Mont Pelerin members to win it over the next few decades. Even though Republicans were losing elections, conservative ideas—or rather, radical libertarian ideology—were ascendant.

The 1970s were a time of intellectual and ideological ferment around political economy, unrivaled since the 1930s. Galbraith was calling for outright socialism. He was joined by a significant number of liberal economists who did not know what to do now that Kennedy-era "New Economics" had failed.[43] Young liberals saw antitrust and regulatory policy, and antimonopolism more broadly, as

irrelevant, in the face of environmentalism, civil rights, antiwar organizing, and consumerism. This attitude left most areas of business law
wide open to Chicago School arguments.

Behind the glitter of Nobel Prizes awarded to Chicago School adherents was a sophisticated, well-funded political organizing campaign.
There was the New Learning, when big business and the new scholars
had allied to dismiss the Brandeis-style antimonopolists. There was the
movement for "deregulation," supported not just by Stigler but by the
Nader consumer movement. The concept of "deregulation" was naturally incoherent—there is no such thing as a market without regulation;
the question had always been whether public institutions or financiers
organize market rules. But like most Chicago School concepts, "deregulation" was a rhetorical strategy designed to undermine traditional
American political philosophy. And underneath all of it was hard-core
institution building, through the capture of and control over the curric-
ula of law schools and the creation of groups like the Federalist Society,
founded in 1982, to reach into the long-cloistered judiciary, and edu-
cate thousands of state and federal judges in the new thinking.

The campaign to capture the universities and the judiciary was
being run largely by director-disciple Henry Manne. In the early 1970s,
Manne had created an "Economics Summer Camp" to teach economics to law professors. A dozen companies concerned about antitrust
funded the "camp," and the professors, from top law schools such as
Harvard, Yale, and Duke, were paid, as Manne proudly explained, the
"then princely sum of $1,000, plus all expenses and some very fancy
meals." Liberal law professors found themselves, almost unwittingly,
imparting the new learning to their students. Manne saw this educational process as "wholesaling" law and economics to professors, who
would then "retail" it to students.[44]

In 1976, Manne extended his "summer camp" to judges, setting
up the Economics Institute for Federal Judges. Over the next fifteen
years, over 40 percent of sitting federal judges eventually took Manne's
classes and learned how to use "economics" to help guide their judicial decision making, to substitute "science" for law.[45] Manne invited lecturers Milton Friedman, whose Nobel Prize made him seem
an apolitical scientist. The new law and economics rhetoric helped

conservative judges more persuasively make their arguments; at one dinner event, a judge pounded his fist on the table and said, "What I want to know is why in hell hasn't anyone told me about this before now." But more importantly, it helped—especially in tandem with the teachings of Galbraith and Nader—to rearrange how many liberal judges saw the law. As one judge from the Southern District of New York told Manne, "Henry and I don't see eye to eye on a number of policy issues, but he has made me understand for the first time that everything I want has its cost."[46]

The Chicago School continued to make progress among elite legal scholars as well. After the New Learning conference in 1974, the consensus shifted rapidly. Donald Turner moved away from his earlier suspicions of concentrated corporate power. By 1977, Stanford Law professor William Baxter expressed regret for signing onto the Neal Report. "It seems particularly appropriate that I recant," he said. "The state of economic art has changed." By 1978, Chicago School professor turned judge Richard Posner claimed, accurately, that antitrust policy had come to a basic agreement that one would find in a "totally non-ideological field."[47]

The Chicago Schoolers made especially swift progress within the Republican Party. Under Nixon and Ford, mainstream Republican politicians and enforcers were still largely attached to the Brandeisian antimonopoly status quo. Then in 1978, the Republicans experienced their own Watergate Baby year, with a slug of new young eager baby boomers, radicalized in the 1960s as children of affluence, entering politics. This cohort came in under the moniker the New Right, mimicking the label of the New Left. Walking around a key Republican conference, the Tidewater Conference in April of 1978, young Republicans were carrying around a new and important book, Robert Bork's magnum opus, *The Antitrust Paradox.*

*The Antitrust Paradox* was an elaboration of Bork's earlier arguments in "The Crisis in Antitrust." New Right politicians saw Bork's crusade to shrink the antitrust laws and to subvert antimonopolism as part of their cultural crusade to attack liberalism, and to save America from godless crypto-communism.

Bork brought an apocalyptic tone to his work. Militant leftists, he argued, entrenched by the Supreme Court, had blocked private initiative and freedom, stopping large businesses from being able to grow, making corporate mergers "practically impossible," and harassing business as a matter of routine. Antitrust enforcement, he claimed the Supreme Court believed, "is in the good old American tradition of the sheriff of a frontier town." The sheriff did not try to find out who had done wrong, he simply "walked the main street and every so often pistol-whipped a few people."[48]

Antitrust, Bork preached, was symptomatic of an out-of-control culture of nihilism, a militant "sub-category of ideology," and "one of the most elaborate deployments of governmental force" in American life. It was wrecking the American economy and American society, encouraging "trends dangerous to our form of government and society."

Bork's arguments were not unusual, for he had been making them for decades. But it was unusual that the voices in opposition, though there were some, didn't resonate anymore. Originally, Bork had meant the book to come out in 1970.[49] But he had put it aside so he could work as the solicitor general in the Nixon administration. By 1978, the book was a bit dated. The courts, spurred by Manne's seminars, new Nixon judges, and the Chicago influence, had changed. With Patman and Arnold dead, Areeda and Turner had already led the liberal antitrust establishment to accept a modified form of Bork's theories. Areeda and Turner's broad and influential treatise on antitrust law, written when they were both at Harvard and first published in 1978, incorporated Bork's pro-concentration framework. Widely used across the profession, the Areeda-Turner treatise allowed courts and Democrats to accept a lighter version of the Chicago School. This milder but essentially similar model of thinking became known as the Harvard School of antitrust.

The corporatists on the right and the left, from the consumer rights movement to Robert Bork to John Kenneth Galbraith, stood ready to finally demolish the antimonopoly tradition in American life. Monopoly power existed, they argued, because it was efficient. This argument wasn't a political statement, it wasn't liberal or conservative, or Republican or Democrat—it had become accepted "science." Chicago School law and economics was now internalized by all, with some minor variants. All they needed now was a friendly administration to help introduce the new way of thinking. Over the course of four years, they got two.

## THE CARTER CATASTROPHE

From 1974 onward, despite Democratic Party victories, the reaction against the New Deal and antimonopolism gained traction. Shorn of a small business constituency, the Democrats began to drift.

A new type of thinking focused on efficiency, consumerism, and technocracy was taking hold. Congress created a budget and planning office, the Congressional Budget Office, in 1974 to constrain its own ability to wield taxing and spending power, and placed Alice Rivlin, a corporate technocrat, in charge of it.[50] Conservative ideas were on the ascent. In 1975, Congress created the Earned Income Tax Credit, a refundable tax credit to subsidize the wages of the poor, which was a welfare-style program conceived by conservative economist Milton Friedman.

In the late 1970s, Congress was deluged with crises. New York City went bust. To deal with the Penn Central mess, Congress passed a bill to nationalize passenger rail traffic through Amtrak and some freight traffic through Conrail, while "deregulating" much of the rest of the railroad industry. Policymakers were desperately attempting to hold down inflation and address the industrial and financial crises that had been shocking the American economy since 1970. In a handwritten note on his announcement on the Consumer Goods Pricing Act, President Ford wrote in the margin, "In particular, I hope the Congress will support my program of regulatory reform in such important areas as air transportation, trucking, and financial institutions."[51] Congress would, and so would Jimmy Carter, who radically expanded upon Ford's ambitions.

Conservative politics were also on the ascent. In November of 1975, the House passed for the third time a bill to create a new federal consumer agency. In 1971 and 1974, the bill went through with a better than two-to-one margin. In 1975, with a much larger Democratic Caucus, it passed only by 208–199. The bill lost eighty Democratic votes, many from liberal northerners. "There has grown up, especially in the last six months, a strong anti-government, anti-bureaucracy, anti–new agency phenomenon in this country," said the sponsor of the bill, Representative Ben Rosenthal.[52]

In 1976, the Democrats nominated Jimmy Carter for the presidency. When he ran for office, he echoed the consumer populism of the left, promising to "take my cues for regulatory appointments" from Nader. He and Nader were so close during the campaign that Nader stayed over at Carter's house, and then played the umpire at a softball game between Carter's campaign staff and the press corps.[53] At a rally put together by Nader, Carter said that "consumers will now have a voice in the Oval Office."[54] Carter made good on his promise. A host of Nader allies went into the administration. Michael Pertschuck became chairman of the FTC.

The new kind of politics that Carter and Nader brought in devastated the institutional power of the enforcers. In the 1960s and early 1970s, the FTC's management cultivated a broad constituency among small businesses who had begun to feel the competitive squeeze from national chains, mass merchandisers, and other capital-intensive large businesses.

In 1983, Donald Randall, an antitrust lawyer who worked for Senator Phil Hart as a general counsel in his monopoly subcommittee, explained what happened next. Ralph Nader, Randall said, attacked these FTC actions as "trivial," leading a groundswell in academia and among consumer movement groups against the commission. In 1977, the Carter FTC began broad industrywide rules focused on the consumer, abandoning its grassroots constituency of small businesses. At the same time as the Carter FTC weakened its own support base, it took on the most powerful interests in the country with rules on cereal, funerals, used cars, toothpaste, cigarettes, debt collection, children's toys, and children's advertising. This change "opened a hornet's nest of opposition," Randall said, but there was no counterbalancing support except a "weak, poorly financed and disorganized consumer movement."[55]

The consumer rights movement wiped out the small business grassroots constituency that had protected the FTC. When big business went on the attack, there was no one to defend antimonopoly tradition. Carter's consumer thrust failed. And the consumer rights movement, which never really had a committed grassroots base, found no sustainable institutional way to keep going. When asked why the consumer rights movement fell apart, Ralph Nader simply noted, "Our theory was wrong."[56]

More broadly, Carter, like the Watergate Babies and the liberal establishment, had no answer to the rolling series of financial crises and oil shocks of the decade. These two problems—inflation and oil prices—were conjoined. Inflation had been raging since the late 1960s, but under Carter, it got much worse. In 1979, America suffered a major geopolitical defeat, as revolutionaries in Iran overthrew the American-backed leader of the country and drove up oil prices once again. Americans watched their influence ebb throughout the 1970s, with the oil shock of 1973, the fall of Saigon in 1975, the Cuban intervention in Angola in 1975, the Nicaraguan revolution by the Sandinistas, and the Soviet invasion of Afghanistan in 1979. The Iranian revolution led to long lines at the gas pump, touching Americans more directly.

Nothing Carter did seemed to work. In 1977, Democrats reduced unemployment, but couldn't address worsening productivity and a flood of foreign imports.[57] Long-sought Democratic policy goals, like full employment, urban renewal, national health insurance, a national consumer agency—all had to wait. In 1979, the intellectual emptiness of the Democrats was underscored when Chrysler required a $1.5 billion loan guarantee from the government.

In response, Jimmy Carter oversaw a large capital gains tax cut in 1978, followed by "deregulation" of the banking, telecommunications, railroad, trucking, and airline industries, and a strong dose of fiscal austerity. Carter was using conservative ideas to govern. Nixon treasury secretary William Simon had inspired this large tax cut for financial capital with a theory known as "capital shortage," in which he argued that financiers were simply afraid to invest in new businesses because of high tax rates and overregulation. This worsened inflation.

Carter also nominated Paul Volcker to run the Federal Reserve. Volcker was an inflation hawk who Carter advisor Stuart Eizenstat said was perceived of as a conservative and "the candidate of Wall Street." (Volcker would later, for instance, keep in his pocket a list of recent union contracts, so he could show politicians who asked why he had to continue to cause unemployment with higher interest rates.[58]) Volcker believed that the prosperity of the 1950s and 1960s was a "game of mirrors" and that "the standard of living of the average American must decline."[59] Volcker fought inflation by using interest rates to bring the economy to a screeching halt, with Carter supporting the campaign even though it would end up helping cost him the reelection.

Carter pursued a host of policies Ronald Reagan would later build on. The Paperwork Reduction Act of 1980 and the Regulatory Flexibility Act made public rules harder to write and enforce. The Bankruptcy Act of 1978 made it easier for financiers to recover new financial instruments (derivatives) in bankruptcy proceedings than they could normal loans, pushing even more lending and borrowing outside of regulated channels. The Staggers Act destroyed a suite of rules around railroads. The Airline Deregulation Act dismantled the structure that Harry Truman had helped craft in 1938 to protect small- and medium-sized towns from predatory financiers manipulating airline routes. The Motor Carrier Act of 1980 eliminated the power of the Teamsters union, and turned the job of trucking from a middle-class profession into what one academic called "Sweatshops on Wheels."[60]

In 1980, two Texas billionaires, Nelson and Herbert Hunt, tried to corner the silver market, backed by yet another oil power—Arab oil barons. They did so much damage to the commodities markets that Volcker as head of the Federal Reserve had to supervise yet another financial bailout. The Hunt brothers' bailout ratified a radical shift in power. As economist Albert Wojnilower explained in 1980, "It is now everywhere taken for granted that no monetary authority will allow any key financial actor to fail. In 1980 the markets paid virtually no attention to the silver (Hunt brothers), First Pennsylvania, and Chrysler debacles, each of which would have had traumatic consequences not many years before."[61]

Carter collapsed politically; Ted Kennedy ran a primary against a sitting leader of his own party, a rare event. By the end of the administration, Carter had abandoned his promises to help the consumer. He was listening to financially oriented Democratic advisors Charles Schultze and Hamilton Jordan, who were promising bankers that

Carter was better for banks than his primary challenger, Ted Kennedy. Carter, they said, would balance the budget, and while he would not grant them another tax cut now, perhaps one could be negotiated in the future.[62]

But Kennedy, even though challenging Carter, was as enthralled by the Chicago School thinking as Carter. Carter officials, Nader, Kennedy, and a Kennedy aide named Stephen Breyer teamed up to "deregulate" the airlines, gutting routes to small cities and beginning an era of regional inequality. Kennedy would then push the Motor Carrier Act to get rid of rules for trucking, which Carter signed. While full of intra-party recriminations, the 1980 primary had little actual ideological disagreement.[63] A Carter aide summarized the Carter strategy toward Kennedy as "Fuck the Fat, Rich Kid." A Kennedy aide responded with "Fuck the Cracker."[64]

Nor was there really that much difference between Carter and Ronald Reagan, who beat Carter in one of the worst landslides in the history of American presidential politics. One of Ronald Reagan's first acts after taking the presidency in 1981 was to fire America's air traffic controllers after they went on strike. Today this action is widely seen as illustrating the radical nature of the change from Democratic Carter to the Republican Regan. Yet in fact, before leaving office, Carter had already agreed to the same plan if the strike took place on his watch.[65]

Even before the "Reagan revolution" of 1980, the political culture of the Democrats had already shifted, radically, away from explicit governing through making public rules, taxing and spending, and shaping markets through competition policy. Instead, Carter had opened the door to a new vision, where private concentrations of power would govern. His advisors, like domestic policy chief Stuart Eizenstat, were puzzled how his "populist consumerism" didn't catch on.[66] Instead, Carter was perceived as weak, rudderless, unwilling to govern.

This was part of a broader, partywide phenomenon. As *The Washington Post* reported in 1978, "This overwhelmingly Democratic Congress chose to raise Social Security taxes while cutting the tax on capital gains. It rejected virtually every proposal put forward by organized labor; on many issues, it gave ground to business. It gave the oil companies a natural gas price deregulation bill they had sought unsuccessfully for 25 years. It willingly voted for large increases in defense spending but shied away from expensive domestic initiatives and concentrated on cutting the federal budget deficit."[67]

A new school of technocratic liberals had emerged, led by anti-labor technocrats like economist Alice Rivlin, Charlie Schultze, Lester Thurow, and Alfred Kahn. Kahn, for instance, was Jimmy Carter's anti-inflation czar, a household name, hilarious, charming, and deeply antagonistic toward labor unions. "I'd love to see the Teamsters to be worse off," he once said. "I'd love the automobile workers to be worse off."[68] Kahn, a self-described liberal Democrat influenced in his early work by Joseph Schumpeter and Thorstein Veblen, was most known for being disdainful of regulations. In his academic work in the early 1970s, he adopted much of the Chicago School framework on efficiency, describing regulations as "typically...a decision to restrict competition."[69]

Another scholar, Lester Thurow, was one of the new generation, a link between the Chicago School and younger Democrats (who would eventually call themselves neoliberals). In an influential 1980 book titled *The Zero-Sum Society,* Thurow argued government and business activities were simply zero-sum contests over resources and incomes. The title of the book was a nod to Galbraith's *The Affluent Society.* Like Galbraith, Thurow came out against the antitrust laws, asserting the laws had failed, imposing costs that "far exceed any benefits." He adopted, in part, Milton Friedman's preferred substitute strategy, which was to erode public trade rules and encourage unfettered imports. Foreign imports of steel and autos, went his logic, had produced far more competition than antitrust. "In markets where international trade exists or could exist," Thurow argued, "national antitrust laws no longer make sense."[70] Thurow was reframing the arguments of Chicago Schoolers for a Democratic audience.

By 1978, a leading intellectual light in the Democratic Party—Stephen Breyer—was questioning the most high-profile success of the consumer rights movement, the mandate for seat belts.[71] Donald Turner had made Breyer's career in 1965 by bringing him into the Antitrust Division as part of his "brain trust."[72] By 1980, Breyer was a key advisor to Ted Kennedy, and had worked with Kahn and Nader to get rid of public rules on airlines. Breyer advised Kennedy to make "deregulation" a key theme in his primary challenge to Carter.[73]

Democrats were concluding that their role as a party was not to govern the political economy. They could fight with the GOP over how to redistribute the fruits of what a concentrated corporate sector could produce, but it was morally wrong to go against economic "science" and to meddle with how complex systems functioned.

In 1980, Lloyd Bentsen, a Texas Democrat, came out with a report from the Joint Economic Committee (JEC) called "Plugging in the Supply Side," introducing the world to "supply side economics." Bentsen made sure that all Republicans and Democrats on the committee endorsed the report. It was a unanimous and bipartisan conclusion from the JEC, which Wright Patman had helped create to let Congress think about broad problems. The report endorsed the idea of a "regulatory budget" to reduce public demands over the corporate sector, changes in the tax code to promote investment, and moving power away from public institutions and toward private ones. It was an ideological document, yet one upon which everyone, by the end of the decade, agreed.

Everyone, that is, but the people. Americans didn't like the new ideas, at least not when proposed by a Democrat. With farmers, workers, bankers, business leaders, and liberals upset in 1980, Carter's reelection attempt collapsed. It would fall to a new president, Ronald Reagan, to implement these ideas, now with only minor resistance from the opposition.

Looking back from the perspective of 1993, Bork acknowledged the magnitude of the ideological victory that he and his allies won during these years. In a new introduction for a revised edition of *The Antitrust Paradox,* called "The Passing of the Crisis," Bork wrote that "what has happened to antitrust amounts to a revolution in a major American policy."[74] And so it had. It wasn't that Republicans gained political power, and implemented Bork's philosophy, though that happened. It was that Bork convinced not just the right wing but the left that antitrust, and more broadly democracy, as practiced in the middle of the twentieth century was not only inefficient, but countered the dictates of natural economic systems and science itself.

The final proof of victory had come only a few years earlier, after President Reagan had nominated Bork for the Supreme Court. In 1972, Donald Turner had told the Senate he was not a "fan" of Bork's antitrust work. In 1987, he said he found himself "more and more impressed with the insight in many of [Bork's] antitrust writings."[75] And he concluded by endorsing Bork's nomination to the court.

The intellectual and political debate was over.

# THE REAGAN REVOLUTION

"It's been a hard day all around. First, my wife's pet kanga-
roo has to go and get poisoned, and then somebody stole
my midget butler's stepladder."

**—Unnamed Texas oil man, 1957[1]**

"Antitrust seldom resembles art, but Bill Baxter's 1982
Merger Guidelines were every bit as significant in the
field of antitrust as the recording of *Giant Steps* was in the
field of modern jazz."

**—Charles James, Assistant Attorney General,
Antitrust Division[2]**

■ ■ ■ ■ ■ ■ ■ ■ ■ ■ ■ ■ ■

O n Election Day in 1980, Americans rejected Jimmy Carter.
The story of the election was the economy. Few alive, except the old-timers, had seen anything like it. Unemployment jumped to levels not seen since the Great Depression. Housing
starts collapsed, factories closed across the country, and yet, inflation
wouldn't go down.

Real personal income fell in 1980. Nationally, as one senator noted,
personal income fell in 1980 by 2.6 percent, more in some areas than
others. In Arkansas, the hit was nearly 5 percent.[3] Voters didn't know
if Reagan had the right answers, but they knew that Carter had the
wrong ones. Reagan took forty-four states and stunned the Democrats, who could not have imagined such a rebuke.

At the post-inaugural balls, Nancy Reagan wore a one-shouldered
sheath gown of lace over silk satin designed by James Galanos, who
said he wanted to make her look "elegant in keeping with the new

formality."[4] Fashion reporters awaited Nancy Reagan's stated plans to redecorate the White House. A veritable "air force" of corporate jets, some four hundred in total, carried partyers to "lavish white-tie inaugural celebrations."[5] Mellonism was back.

Ronald Reagan attacked the New Deal coalition with a relish far beyond what Carter had ever dared. The political economy framework for Reagan was derisively known as "trickle-down" economics, which meant that if the government ensured wealth and power flowed upward, the people at the bottom might eventually benefit. Reagan cut taxes on the wealthy and on corporations, and slashed government spending on the poor. He embraced antiabortion activists, and began the rollback of civil liberties protection by staffing the Department of Justice with men who opposed civil rights laws.[6]

He also attacked a deeply weakened union movement. Early in his term, when twelve thousand federal air traffic controllers went on strike to demand a pay raise and safer working conditions, Reagan did not negotiate. He simply fired them, had their union decertified, and hired replacement workers. Over 125,000 people applied for these jobs, as unions were no longer able to dissuade people from becoming "scab" replacements.[7] Reagan's harsh anti-union stance was a signal to the private sector; Phelps Dodge and International Paper imitated Reagan by replacing strikers rather than negotiating.[8] When Reagan took office, roughly a quarter of American workers were in a union; by the end of the decade it had fallen to 16 percent.

And when Reagan didn't attack the New Deal coalition, he insulted it, saying on PBS in 1982 that the Roosevelt administration had been full of fascists and communists.[9] But this was just the visible part of what his administration would do. Reagan would usher in an assault on just about every part of the New Deal regulatory apparatus, a rollback of the political economy protections against concentrated capital that had existed in one form or another since the rise of the giant corporation.

By this time, the intellectual debate over how to structure power in the political economy had been won by Reagan's allies. In March of 1981, the original Chicago School gang, Aaron Director, Ronald Coase, Milton Friedman, Robert Bork, Richard Posner, and Harold Demsetz among others, got together to look back and honor the work they had accomplished over thirty years. As the convener of the event put it, "the basic views of the world of a Coase, a Director, or a Friedman never really changed. The world changed, and for some reason we do not understand, became receptive."[10]

Perhaps it was more direct. University of Chicago professor Melvin Reder explained the success of the Chicago School differently. Their "policy position was too attractive ideologically, and too successful as propaganda, for hesitant conservatives to refuse support. . . . In 'support' I include grants for research, conferences, and so forth. But also, and more important, I include access to conservative politicians and business leaders, and to the media."[11] It was certainly a lucrative path to follow; Phillip Areeda, part of the Democratic-leaning Harvard School of antitrust, in 1995 endowed his own department at Harvard Law School with a $5 million donation, the second-largest gift the school had ever received. This came from legal advising and consulting in a life the Harvard Law professor described as dedicated almost entirely to "teaching and writing."[12]

In an era of affluence, under the sway of Galbraith, liberals stopped caring or talking about corporate concentration, leaving critiques of questions of monopoly to the Chicago School and their new "science." So in the 1970s, when chaos reigned, only these self-proclaimed "scientists" seemed to have any answers. The field of political economy was theirs. "Indeed," said George Stigler, whose Nobel Prize in 1982 would be celebrated at the White House, "it can be said that they conquered the field; by 1980 there remained scarcely a trace of the" old antimonopoly framework in the economic literature.[13]

Beyond the literature, the new institutions the Chicago Schoolers had forged were training judges and churning out law students. Business allies, such as Walter Wriston of Citibank, had become key advisors to the new president. The dominance of the business class, which the Chicago Schoolers had cultivated since the 1950s, was overwhelming. "The broad issues on which business tends to have a significant impact are no longer issues," said Wall Street economist Alan Greenspan. "Government regulations, wage and price controls, and business tax policy—all that is behind us."[14]

A new generation of business leaders, inspired, oddly, by the counterculture of the 1960s and 1970s, comfortable with politics and overturning the established order, was coming to power. The hippies of the 1960s became yuppies in the 1980s. Michael Milken, who would become the most important financier since J. P. Morgan, challenged his radical activist classmates in 1970, writing, "Unlike other crusaders from Berkeley, I have chosen Wall Street as my battleground for improving society."[15]

The triumph of the Chicago Schoolers wasn't just a matter of Reagan's election, but the collapse of all coherent intellectual opposition. Leading Democratic thinkers sounded exactly like leading Republican thinkers. Stigler had high praise not only for economists James Miller, who would chair the Federal Trade Commission, and George Shultz, who would lead the Department of State, both under Reagan, but also for economists Darius Gaskins and Alfred Kahn, who had, respectively, chaired the Interstate Commerce Commission and run the Civil Aeronautics Board, both under Carter.[16] Harvard School antitrust scholar Stephen Breyer, appointed an appeals judge by Carter (and eventually landing on the Supreme Court in the 1990s), had cited Stigler, as well as key "public choice" theorists promoting deregulation—James Buchanan and Gordon Tullock—in his textbook on regulation.[17]

One of the first targets of the Reaganites were restrictions on the banking industry. The administration attacked the problem of regulation from two directions. It both allowed banks to do more and allowed nonbank institutions to enter traditional banking businesses. In 1982, Reagan allowed banks to essentially pay whatever they wanted on deposits, and stripped away the rules restricting savings and loan banks to their core business of helping Americans finance homes.[18] At a Federal Home Loan Bank, an ex-banker turned regulator immediately allowed savings and loans to offer an adjustable rate mortgage. And quietly, at the Office of the Comptroller of the Currency, the government began allowing banks to speculate in financial derivatives and commodities.[19]

Financial institutions could now gamble, move into unrelated lines of business, and get much bigger. Where Carter sought to shift the rules somewhat to solve technocratic dilemmas, Reagan pushed much harder to openly aid plutocrats. His administration drew back dramatically on white-collar enforcement and banking regulation. American Express bought Shearson Loeb Rhoades, a brokerage firm. Sears, the giant retailer, bought brokerage Dean Witter, organizing its business strategy to become a financial supermarket, offering credit cards, deposit-like instruments known as money market funds, and insurance, along with a retail catalogue.

Citibank made much of its profits in the decade not from traditional banking services, but from the credit card. Bankruptcies roughly doubled in ten years, after the Supreme Court effectively eliminated state usury caps in 1978, and neither Carter nor Reagan responded.[20] Charge and credit card dollar transactions went from $155 billion in 1982 to $400 billion in 1990. Average outstanding consumer credit jumped from $7,660 to $10,880 in the decade, growing at an annual rate of 6 percent. Credit card debt grew even faster, at 21 percent a year, from $580 in 1982 to $2,430 in 1990 per household.[21]

Democrats in Congress had also largely embraced the new ways. In July of 1981, the Senate Banking Committee worked together to remove a limit on interest rates that had been in the Arkansas Constitution since 1874, a limit placed there to block financial power in the state. John Tower, the first Republican senator from Texas since Reconstruction, speaking to Arkansas Democrat Dale Bumpers, took the occasion to invoke the ghost of Wright Patman, for comic effect. "I think we probably both remember a late colleague of ours," he said. "Patman, who of course thought bankers were the incarnation of the devil." The hearing room erupted in laughter.[22]

Years before, letting banks charge usurious high interest rates might have been controversial. By 1981, letting them do so wasn't just correct, but according to Stigler, it was done for the benefit of poor people who needed to borrow.[23] There was resistance. "We don't have much to brag about here except our interest rates and University of Arkansas football," said Bill Becker of the AFL-CIO in Arkansas. "The bankers and the retailers are too greedy, they want too damned much."[24] But Tower, Bumpers, and Bill Clinton (who as a young law professor had done legal work to help monopolize the credit card industry), embraced deregulation.[25]

Democrats and Republicans at all levels were now both focused on freeing financial capital from the New Deal's carefully forged chains. Citibank had been grappling with New York state lawmakers to lift that state's usury cap for years, but the state wouldn't budge. Finally the bank moved its credit card operation to South Dakota, and New York politicians took notice. As New York assemblyman Denny Farrell put it, "suddenly I became in favor of deregulation. I got into the flow."[26]

Reagan solidified the power of concentrated financial capital, effectively guaranteeing the balance sheet of large banks that lent too much money to third-world nations when oil prices were high. The expression "Too Big to Fail" would be popularized in 1984, just a few years later, named for an institution that could borrow for free while failing. For everyone else there would be credit cards. The ability to borrow, for a reasonable price, would be based on your proximity to wealth and power, rather than on the rule of law.

## THE MERGER BOOM

In early February of 1981, Reagan picked his antitrust chief. He chose William Baxter, whom journalist Steve Coll described as "a severe-looking man in his early fifties, with coal-black slicked-down hair, cold, dark eyes, sunken cheeks, and a sallow complexion."[27] Baxter was ideological, strident, unquestionably bright, and cold. Though not trained in economics, he would often refer to himself as an economist. His coldness extended to his personal life. Baxter lived with a Stanford statistician, and when asked why he did not marry her, replied that to do so would raise his tax bill.

Baxter's arrival signified the reconstitution of monopoly power in America. Over a series of congressional hearings in 1981 and 1982, Baxter explained that he would be restructuring antitrust and merger law to prioritize economic efficiency, and no longer enforce the law consistent with congressional purpose of restraining corporate size and power. Neither courts nor Congress deterred Baxter. He called Supreme Court decisions "rubbish" and "wacko," and circulated a memo in the department calling one such precedent "idiocy."[28] The Supreme Court might assert that certain forms of price-fixing were illegal, but Baxter didn't care and said he wouldn't enforce the law regardless.[29] And he simply would not enforce laws he didn't like, such as Robinson-Patman, which he called an attempt "to put lead weights in the saddle bags of the fastest riders."

Democratic senator Howard Metzenbaum and Republican senator Arlen Specter both objected to what they saw as a subversion of law through executive fiat. But they didn't have the votes to stop Baxter's revolution. Law and economics scholar Richard Posner noted that Baxter's tenure was, along with the firing of the air traffic controllers, one of the "defining moments of the Reagan administration."[30]

Under Baxter, the division dramatically slowed its activity. Baxter ordered the dismissal of a suit against Mack Trucks, which had been accused of price-fixing. He cleared the acquisition of two brickmakers. He dropped a suit against Jack Welch's General Electric. In its opening months, the Nixon administration's antitrust enforcers had gone after ITT, U.S. Steel, and the Crocker National Bank, filing fourteen major cases. In a similar period, Carter's team had launched twenty-four cases, including one against Schlitz Beer. By contrast, the Reagan administration filed just four, and all were minor complaints against highway contractors.[31] Over the course of the decade, the administration cut the division's staff by nearly half.[32]

Baxter had not originally supported Bork's crusade. In 1968, Baxter had signed on to an Attorney General antitrust study that called for a massive restructuring of corporate America, to de-concentrate American business. But like Donald Turner and Phillip Areeda, Baxter had gone in the other direction since, a convert of the New Learning. Baxter was more an intellectual than a litigator, and attorneys practicing under him referred to him as a "space cadet" for his academic veneer. When yet another story of an off-the-wall suggestion for a trial would circulate in the department, an antitrust litigator would cup his mouth and say, "Earth to Baxter. Earth to Baxter. Come in." But he was not hired to litigate, or to run the Justice Department's Antitrust Division, the crown jewel in America's elaborate system of competition enforcement. He was hired to restructure it.[33]

Baxter made two significant changes to the division. First, he elevated the role of economists. Like Bork, Baxter held that economics was a science and that the law should conform to that science, regardless of what the political intent of lawmakers was. Once confirmed, Baxter elevated the head economist to a full deputy assistant attorney general, on par with the enforcement and litigation chief. Economists reviewed every outstanding case under the new lens, and the DOJ dropped many of them. Attorneys took to calling the economists "case killers." He also did what Henry Manne had done for law professors and judges, by organizing economics courses for staff attorneys.[34] As one of Baxter's students said, "No lawyer worth his salt would consider going to an important meeting at the division without at least one economist in tow."[35]

His second key innovation was a shift in the merger guidelines. Baxter's new 1982 guidelines were, as a Department of Justice official put it twenty years later, a "revolutionary leap." These guidelines made it much harder to challenge mergers. The 1968 guidelines had been simple and based on market shares. The Baxter guidelines "integrated the new economic learning" by introducing the need for complex economic analysis of costs and benefits of any particular potential mergers and/or market structure.[36] This change generated minor opposition. "John D. Rockefeller would have liked a trust-buster like Baxter," wrote *The Economist,* meaning it as a compliment.[37] Baxter's changes to the division would last, supported as they were by erstwhile liberals such as Don Turner. "I'd say his rhetoric may be a little more conservative, but the law may have been drifting that way anyway," Turner told the press.[38]

One of the most important signals to corporate America of a new era of monopolization occurred on January 8, 1982, when Baxter dropped the thirteen-year suit against the monster of technology, IBM. The dropping of the IBM suit catalyzed an attitude on Wall Street. "Bigness apparently wasn't going to be a problem in the new era of unbridled capitalism," wrote *Wall Street Journal* reporter James Stewart. "Suddenly, economies of scale could be realized in already oligopolistic industries such as oil, where mergers wouldn't even have been considered in the Carter years."[39]

The practical result of this signaling was a merger boom to concentrate power within industries. Baxter himself couldn't encourage mergers fast enough. He rejected corporate concentration as a factor in merger analysis, despite congressional fears of concentrated power when crafting the antitrust law.[40] Merger activity, he said, "is a very, very important feature of our capital markets by which assets are continuously moved into the hands of those managers who employ them most efficiently and interfering in a general way with that process would, in my judgment, be an error of substantial magnitude."[41]

Baxter told a House subcommittee that the merger of financial services giants American Express and Shearson Loeb Rhoades was likely not a violation of the antitrust laws; and neither was the possible merger of Prudential and Bache Group.[42] The Department of Justice went out of its way to assert it was creating "a more favorable atmosphere for mergers."[43]

Baxter supercharged a merger trend already under way. Stock prices had been low in the 1970s, and inflation high. This dynamic made it easier to buy a corporation, especially one with assets like the rights to oil or factories, than to build assets and attempt to secure scarce industrial materials and labor. As one Wall Street analyst noted, "It has been widely recognized that the price of a target is likely to go up in an inflationary environment. It may be cheaper to buy now and pay back creditors with deflated dollars."[44] High oil prices also meant Chase and Citibank were flush with money deposited by oil-rich Arab countries, and this money could be profitably loaned out for mergers.

There were significant policy changes at work as well, changes that often reinforced one another. Four new conservative Supreme Court Justices appointed by Nixon made mergers a bit easier with a series of court decisions starting in 1974.[45] In 1982 the Supreme Court in *Edgar v. MITE Corp.* got rid of most state-level antitakeover statutes. Carter and Reagan deregulation in trucking, oil, airlines, trains, telecommunications, and banking opened up opportunities for mergers. And financial deregulation allowed savings and loans, formerly confined to simple home mortgages, to invest in mergers by buying "junk bonds."

The merger wave of the 1980s was distinct in two ways. In the 1960s conglomerate mania avoided antitrust law by buying businesses unrelated to their core industry. Conglomerates acquired subsidiaries because they could take advantage of lax accounting rules to make their earnings look better than they were. In the 1980s, corporations took advantage of the erosion of merger law by buying their competitors and concentrating industries. Also, a growing number of acquisitions were "hostile," meaning the existing management and board did not want to sell the company's independence.

From 1929 to 1974, a big respected company doing a hostile deal was, as merger specialist Martin Lipton said, "like spitting on the floor. It just wasn't done."[46] This began to change in the late 1960s, most famously with Saul Steinberg's aborted takeover of Chemical Bank. But Steinberg never had top-tier advisors, bankers, or lawyers, and he failed. In 1974, hostile takeovers became normalized. International Nickel, with the help of blue-chip investment bank Morgan Stanley, made a hostile offer for battery maker ESB Inc. When Morgan Stanley signaled to corporate America that it would take part in hostile takeovers, it meant that making an offer that upset other executives would not make one a Saul Steinberg–type. One could still be invited to the club.

Reagan's election sent another signal to corporate America and Wall Street. As Baxter put together the Reagan Antitrust Division, raiders attempted three of the largest hostile takeovers in history, launching a merger wave similar to that of the 1890s. In 1981, Standard Oil of Ohio bought Kennecott Copper for $1.77 billion, while Standard Oil of California bought Amax Inc. DuPont bought Conoco for $7.5 billion. This was followed by U.S. Steel, which was tired of running a steel company, purchasing Marathon Oil for $6.3 billion. Cities Services Company sold out to Occidental for $4 billion.

The new rule in corporate America was not to build products or services—it was to buy or be bought. An entire industry of takeover specialists, including arbitrageurs who could manipulate stock prices, emerged to restructure corporate America. And this trend began affecting every facet of American culture. Hospitals began a furious merger wave, and costs in the American health care began exploding.[47]

Business goliaths restructured in the 1980s to take advantage of this new merger wave. The leader was a young and aggressive new CEO at one of the oldest and biggest conglomerates in America, General Electric, the corporation that had financed much of Bork's research.

Jack Welch was trained as an engineer, and had made it to the top at GE by selling a new type of plastic. Walter Wriston was on the board of GE, and had helped Welch become CEO.[48] Welch made his mark as CEO not by engineering products, but by financial engineering. Welch understood earlier than almost any other business leader what the new pro-merger legal environment meant, and announced at his first meeting with security analysts in 1981 that under his leadership, GE's strategy would be to stop competing in markets where the company wasn't number one or two.[49] In any business in which GE wasn't or couldn't become the market leader, he would either have the manager find a way to get to number one, sell the division, or shut it down.

Within four years, Welch shut down a dozen of the company's 217 factories, and cut 18 percent of total employment at the company. As Wriston said, Welch wasn't "waiting around until the changes are too late and too little."[50] Welch sold all mass market manufacturing lines, except big appliances and light bulbs. GE ditched its consumer electronics business. Under Welch, the company began a policy of firing 10 percent of its employees every year, as well as spending billions of dollars to buy back stock.[51] In the press, Welch became known as "Neutron Jack," with his strategy of mass layoffs reminding reporters of the neutron bomb, which was reputed to kill people while leaving buildings intact. Journalists sometimes called him "Trader Jack" for his strategy of buying and selling companies, treating GE less as an industrial giant and more as a portfolio of financial assets. In six years, he bought and sold nearly six hundred business and product lines.[52] But he also, as author Barry Lynn noted, set the pattern for mergers and acquisitions in old-line industrial America.

In 1985, at the height of fears about the Japanese "invasion" of corporate America, Welch took over television maker RCA, assuring Congress he would combine GE and RCA to compete more effectively with Japanese television manufacturers. Instead, Welch traded the entire GE-RCA TV division to France's Thomson Electronics in return for Thomson's medical device business. He kept NBC, which was not subject to international competition. As Lynn put it, "in two strokes, Welch remade multiple world-spanning industries. The rationale behind his moves was simple: concentrate power, avoid direct competition with firms backed by mercantilist states (as Japan's electronics companies were), and focus on industrial activities that could be protected through interaction with regulators (Thomson's medical device business) or the Pentagon (RCA's defense business, which Welch kept)."[53]

Welch also began to outsource much of GE's work to other companies, often those abroad with lower labor and environmental costs. "If I had my way, I'd put every GE plant on a barge," he famously said. Eventually, GE would do even better. By the 2000s, the company founded by Thomas Edison didn't even manufacture light bulbs, sourcing them from Chinese contractors and branding them as GE products.[54]

Other leading companies, such as General Motors, followed Welch's path. In the mid-1980s, GM bought both Electronic Data Systems and Hughes Aircraft, attempting to diversify away from the auto industry in which it was up against foreign competitors backed by governments into regulated industries with government contracts. What it couldn't do by diversifying it did by offshoring, moving production to low-wage areas like northern Mexico starting in the early 1980s.[55] The steel industry did the same thing. U.S. Steel bought not only Marathon Oil for $6.3 billion but paid $3.6 billion for Texas Gas and Oil; National Steel bought United Financial Corporation of California, and another steel company, Armco, went into insurance. Meanwhile, in 1986, the Reagan administration's Commerce Department invited 38,000 American companies to a trade fair in Acapulco, encouraging them to explore moving factories to Mexico.[56] American business was getting bigger, hollower, and more concentrated. Corporations were consolidating power over individual markets. This was not just true in the industrial sector. It happened, as it had in the 1920s, through the chain store.

## CRAZY EDDIE AND THE SHOPPING MALL

In the 1970s, New Yorkers became familiar with advertisements by "Crazy Eddie," an excitable fast-talking electronics salesman who ran late-night television commercials for his discount chain with the tagline "Crazy Eddie's Prices are Insaane!!!!!!!!!!!" And his prices were astonishingly low. They were also a violation of the law.

Around 1970, Eddie Antar started discounting electronics, gleefully ignoring the fair trade prices set by manufacturers. When manufacturers refused to sell him inventory, he would go to gray-market suppliers, find surplus from other businesses, or portray used or defective products as new. His outrageous ads were entirely focused on low consumer prices. Fair trade wasn't the only place where he found the rules an inconvenience. He paid his employees off the books, lied to the government to avoid paying sales taxes, and hassled shoppers. His stores, violating not-often-enforced Blue Laws, were open on Sunday, as well as Christmas, New Year's, and Thanksgiving, a rarity for major chains.

Crazy Eddie had found a business model incompatible with fair trade laws. When these laws changed in 1975, and when the government stopped enforcing the Robinson–Patman laws against price discrimination, Crazy Eddie capitalized and opened up more stores.[57] Crazy Eddie's tagline about insane prices was onto something. With its large volume of purchases, the chain was able to use its buying power to demand volume discounts from suppliers, as well as crush independent retail store competitors.

More policy levers tilted the world toward Crazy Eddie. The Federal Reserve's high interest rate policies strengthened the dollar, allowing for an even greater flood of cheap imports of electronics and adding leverage to the new chains like Crazy Eddie. By 1987, the chain was in four states and had $353 million in revenue. Crazy Eddie's run ended abruptly, not due to retail improprieties, but because of tax cheating and securities fraud. But in the new environment, much of the business model was sound. With its emphasis on low prices instead of quality products and service, Crazy Eddie created a template for who would have power in American retail in the 1980s. It would not be the maker of things, or the community store. It would be the middleman.[58]

Crazy Eddie was in the Northeast, but elsewhere the same trends were obvious, if less tacky and crooked. In much of America, the 1980s was synonymous with the platform of this low-priced consumer paradise: the shopping mall. First built in the 1950s, the indoor shopping mall was a platform for commerce, a replacement for downtown shopping areas. In the 1970s, merchants began taking credit cards for payment en masse, which made it easy to shop anywhere. In 1975, there were 16,400 shopping centers that accounted for a third of all retail. By 1987, there were 30,000 malls, which took over half of all spending, 8 percent of the labor force, and 13 percent of all national output of goods and services.

*Consumer Reports* called these malls the "air-conditioned, sanitized, standardized . . . new Main Streets of America." In 1986, "along with power mowers, 'the pill,' antibiotics, smoke detectors, transistors, and personal computers, the shopping mall was selected as one of the top 50 wonders that has revolutionized the lives of consumers."[59]

The stores that succeeded were chains that, like Crazy Eddie's, based their business on volume, scale, and price. The Gap, Benetton, Ann Taylor, Banana Republic, and The Limited grew in the legal environment that allowed bullying of suppliers and encouraged offshoring of the apparel industry. By 1985, The Limited was the top seller of women's clothing and accessories in the world. In 1986, the company was producing 200 million items of clothing, which amounted to three pieces for every single woman between the ages of fifteen and fifty-five in America. The founder of the chain described his strategy as choosing clothes to sell based on what "we could copy and sell the hell out of," and creating private label brands manufactured in Asia. [60] The Limited did its own merger binge, buying Victoria's Secret, Abercrombie & Fitch, Henri Bendel, and Lane Bryant.[61]

And then there were the "big box" stores: Kmart, Toys "R" Us, Target, and of course Walmart, as well as warehouse discounters such as Costco, Sam's Club, and BJ's Wholesale Club. These stores were bigger, had fewer clerks to help customers, and offered even lower prices.

Fair trade laws had allowed makers and manufacturers to set their retail prices. This meant that independent retailers competed on service, since they couldn't really discount. Customers paid the same price for the item no matter where they went, so retailers had an incentive to invest in skilled salespeople who could offer advice on which items to buy and how to service those items. In the 1970s, liberals got rid of these fair trade laws. And when manufacturers could no longer set prices, customer service disappeared. Customers could now get free advice from a smaller store, and then do the buying at the big ones who sold cheap.

One irony was that Baxter supported fair trade laws, while liberals fought against them on behalf of chain stores. At the behest of large discounters like Kmart, Democrats and Republicans in Congress put pressure on the Reagan Department of Justice and the FTC to prosecute those who used fair trade practices.[62] The 1980s was thus a strange brew, with Chicago School advocates encouraging corporate consolidation in a merger boom, and consumer-rights-influenced liberals encouraging consolidation through chain stores.

Wall Street began attacking department stores, a process heralded by a merger battle between Federated Department Stores and Campeau Corporation (owner of Allied Stores), which ended up saddling formerly well-run companies with unpayable amounts of debt. The battle ended by putting Bloomingdale's, Jordan Marsh, Burdines, and an entire series of smaller department stores into one giant debt-laden empire, which soon went bankrupt. And in this new discount world, what replaced customer service? Branding.

The independent retailers that Patman and the Democratic Party had fought so hard to protect began to vanish en masse. In 1972, shortly after Crazy Eddie opened its doors, there were a little over 1.9 million retail establishments. Ten years later, that number had fallen by about a quarter, and didn't recover. And the sales volume per store skyrocketed.

In the 1980s, the shopping experience changed, as did the experience of producing something for sale. Manufacturers had to sell through a smaller number of chain stores. Those stores had limited personnel to help customers choose among various items, so making something now also meant having a large advertising operation to do the work that retail clerks used to do. And chain stores could now bully manufacturers, legally, and exploit the strong dollar induced by Reagan and Volcker policies to threaten even the largest ones with the flood of cheap foreign goods.[63] It became much harder to be an independent retailer or manufacturer. Congress in 1975 ended the American system of commerce, put in place between 1914 and 1937, that was designed to modernize the ability to make, shop, and sell while retaining the traditional political independence of the shopkeeper or merchant.[64] In the 1980s, Wall Street merger specialists pillaged the existing temples of commerce, the grand department stores, while newly empowered chain store proprietors devastated the local store and small manufacturer.

## HIGH-TECH MONOPOLIES

Baxter did digress, in one important exception, from the Chicago School. He inherited an antitrust suit from the Carter administration against the largest company in the world: American Telephone and Telegraph. And in contravention to what most of the other officials in the Reagan administration wanted, he refused to drop it. Instead, to the surprise of nearly everyone involved, he pledged to litigate the case "to the eyeballs."

The case against AT&T had started partly as a result of the Neal Commission, the LBJ-convened commission of antitrust economists that recommended large-scale de-concentration of the economy. In 1973, Senator Phil Hart introduced the Industrial Reorganization Act to break up all large American corporations. Hart, who saw himself as an heir to trustbusting Senator John Sherman, was persuaded to include AT&T's monopoly in his hearings over the legislation. His committee staff passed files about AT&T to the Department of Justice Antitrust Division.[65] For seven and a half years, the battle over AT&T's power raged in the courts, in Congress, and at the FCC. The Carter administration's FCC chairman, Charles Ferris, began chipping away at the 1956 decree, the conclusion to an earlier antitrust case and one that confined the company to the telecommunications field and prohibited it from entering the computer business. In 1979, Ferris allowed AT&T to offer data and information services through subsidiaries.[66]

For Baxter, the case to break up AT&T had strong economic and conservative underpinnings. The company had in effect four businesses: a series of regulated local telephone monopolies, a long-distance telephone network, a telecommunications equipment arm called Western Electric, and a research division known as Bell Labs. Prior to the 1960s, the company's monopoly seemed to make sense; it was technologically impossible or at least impractical to create a parallel telecom network.

But technology had eroded the importance of a single integrated system for telecommunications, and thus the need for the existing regulatory and monopoly model. AT&T's competitor MCI used microwave technology to compete in long distance. It was a billion-dollar company. Japanese competitors in the equipment business were going after AT&T's Western Electric telecom manufacturing subsidiary.

What earlier policymakers had seen as a necessary telephone and telecom monopoly, Baxter saw as an entrenched incumbent using regulations to protect its high margins. Baxter believed AT&T was using the revenue from the regulated local telephone networks to subsidize its other businesses. Baxter also felt that A&T's current structure protected IBM as well, since AT&T was restricted from challenging IBM in the computer business by the 1956 consent decree.[67] At the time, IBM was a giant, and Baxter believed that only another giant trusted by corporate America, such as AT&T, could compete with the computer behemoth.

By breaking up AT&T, Baxter would end the anticompetitive cross-subsidies and create a new competitor to IBM in one stroke. While not normally a proponent of assertive antitrust action, Baxter felt that, as one antitrust lawyer in the division put it, the AT&T case was "the one good thing the Antitrust division had done in the last thirty years."[68] In 1981, AT&T essentially lost the case, and AT&T's leadership accepted that the old monopoly telephone system was over.[69] It settled with the government. The company agreed to split off its regulated local subsidiaries into seven "Baby Bell" local service companies, each of which would be regulated as a local monopoly. In this one case, a case opposed by nearly all adherents of the Chicago School at the time, Baxter represented a throwback to the trustbusting legacy of New Dealers.

The consequences of the breakup were complex, and staggering. The most obvious and immediate impact was the end of cross-subsidization in the telephone business, and a hit to the pocketbooks of most Americans. Local phone rates increased by 35 percent, while the cost of long-distance phone service fell.

Another more important consequence was the burst of competition and innovation in the communications and technology industries.

Sprint and MCI grew into major long-distance competitors, and eventually a whole wireless cell phone industry and internet service providers like America Online and CompuServe emerged. There were fears AT&T would cut its research and development if it lost its natural monopoly; the opposite occurred, as the company feared competitive pressure.[70] It also deployed technology, like fiber-optic networks, much faster. Prior to the breakup, AT&T bought telecommunications equipment largely from its own subsidiary, Western Electric. But the Baby Bells created in the breakup were now willing to buy telecom equipment from anyone who could make it. Now, others could compete to get a share of the communications technology industry, and did. The corporation eventually broke itself up even further, spinning off Western Electric and Bell Labs into separate corporations.

It is difficult to imagine that AT&T, had it remained a monopoly, would have allowed the remarkable shifts in telecommunications over the following decades, including cell phones, pagers, voicemail, and the commercial internet. The information revolution had been bottlenecked by AT&T; Baxter broke the bottleneck and unleashed the rest of the electronic century.

An equally significant consequence of the end of the suit was, paradoxically, the clear signal to business leaders in these new areas that their goal should be the acquisition of monopoly power. The same day Baxter announced the AT&T settlement, he also announced the dropping of the IBM suit, and conceded he was dramatically relaxing antitrust enforcement. AT&T would be broken up because it had been subject to public utility rules, but IBM would be left alone to act as it wanted, since it had not been subject to such regulatory scrutiny.

The Reagan Department of Justice, by ending its pursuit of monopolization after the AT&T case, set the trajectory of the ongoing information revolution toward monopoly. New computing companies focused, as GE had, on acquiring strategically pivotal positions in the burgeoning electronics field. The burst of innovation and competition released after the breakup was temporary, a free-for-all to see who would become the new monopolists.

Finally, the AT&T breakup had another ironic effect. It added to the merger wave, as the Baby Bells began reconsolidating. The original long-distance business was eventually swallowed by Southwestern Bell, which renamed itself AT&T.

## LOCKING IN THE REAGAN REVOLUTION

Ronald Reagan oversaw a revolution in political economy, implementing in the 1980s what Aaron Director had conceived in the 1950s. Reagan locked in his policies by stacking the courts with conservative Chicago School–oriented judges who believed in the New Learning and had deep disdain for populism. Reagan put four judges on the Supreme Court, including Bork ally Antonin Scalia. Perhaps as importantly, he seeded the lower courts with law and economics adherents like Douglas Ginsburg, Frank Easterbrook, and Richard Posner.

In the late 1960s, Aaron Director's strategy of mocking the Supreme Court and liberal judges for not understanding economics began to work, as law and economics scholarship began appearing in judicial dissents. The next decade, Nixon, Ford, and Carter judicial appointments accepted the arguments of Chicago School advocates on mergers and antitrust. By the 1980s, Chicago School advocates could watch the merger wave unfold with the satisfaction that some unelected judge couldn't block it by substituting his or her preference for economic science.

Within a year of his inauguration, Reagan put Bork on the highly influential Court of Appeals for the D.C. Circuit. Bork, along with a new generation of law and economics thinkers put on the courts as judges, would structure antitrust doctrine directly. Aaron Director's disciples were now in control of the law.

## CHAPTER SEVENTEEN

# THE MORGANS, THE MELLONS, AND THE MILKENS

"The fetters which bind the people are forged from the people's own gold."

—**Louis Brandeis**[1]

■ ■ ■ ■ ■ ■ ■ ■ ■ ■ ■ ■ ■

It was 1986, and one of the most popular television shows was *Dallas,* about the oil tycoon J. R. Ewing and that most Texan of dreams, to get rich through scheming. At a Beverly Hills conference for Wall Street financiers, the actor Larry Hagman, who played J. R., riffed on a popular commercial for the American Express credit card, speaking instead of his "Drexel Express titanium card," named after the most powerful investment bank of those days, Drexel Burnham Lambert. The card, he said, "has a ten-billion-dollar line of credit ... don't go hunting without it." The men in the audience admired J. R.'s daring, wealth, scheming, and most of all, perhaps, his use of borrowed money to ruthlessly capture or crush rival corporations.

This was anything but Wright Patman's Texas, which traced back to the late nineteenth century and the Farmers' Alliance demands for low interest rates and fair markets. J. R.'s Texas culture was formed in the 1940s, with billionaire financiers in short sleeves play-acting cowboy on Wall Street, as captured in books with titles such as *The Lusty Texans of Dallas, Houston: Land of the Big Rich,* and *The Super-Americans.* By the 1980s, it was no longer just Texas oil fraud, but Texas land fraud and Texas savings and loan fraud that minted the new millionaires.

After the Iranian revolution in 1979, the skyrocketing of the prices of oil resulted in one of the largest transfers of wealth in history, from oil consumers in the West to oil producers. No one but Arabs, Venezuelans, and Texans seemed to be doing well. The stock market was catatonic, inflation and interest rates catastrophic. In such an environment, the Federal Reserve couldn't even really print money without stoking more inflation. But the Texans and the Saudis could always pump more oil.

The new culture of greed in the oil patch reverberated across America, and around the world. The 1980 episode of *Dallas* "Who shot J. R.?" was the second-highest-rated prime time show in American history. The mother of the Queen of England begged Larry Hagman to tell her who did it. He refused. Hagman later claimed that the show, broadcast in communist Romania, helped bring down the country's dictator by illustrating to the forlorn people the luxuries available in the West.

Hagman was a special guest at the 1986 party of the biggest names on Wall Street, nicknamed the "Predators' Ball." More formally, it was called the "Drexel High-Yield Bond Department Annual Conference," high-yield debt being the preferred name for junk bonds. *Dallas* and J. R. were a perfect bridge between the oil-shock-driven 1970s and the "Greed is good" Wall Street–oriented decade of the 1980s.

The gathered wealth represented, according to one participant, three times the GNP of the U.S.[2] So powerful was this combination of financial firepower and lax merger rules that the Predators' Ball—held annually and increasing in prestige until the end of the decade—became a forum for thousands of the most important people in finance, as well as those trying to peek into this world of luxury. Attendees included oil magnate and corporate raider T. Boone Pickens, media barons Rupert Murdoch, Barry Diller, and Ted Turner, cell phone pioneer Craig McCaw, financial kingpin Ronald Perelman, revolutionary corporate raiders Carl Icahn and Henry Kravis, Las Vegas casino magnate Steve Wynn, and countless CEOs, celebrities, and politicians, as well as striking workers to picket them.[3]

By 1986, the conference had become an orgy of fame, money, sex, arbitrage, politics, and mergers. Frank Sinatra once made an appearance for a cool $150,000 fee. Diana Ross sang, changing outfits twice during her routine.[4] Country music star Dolly Parton performed. A Madonna look-alike danced and lip-synced to her famous song

"Material Girl," changing the lyrics to "I'm a double-B girl living in a material world," in a nod to both bra sizes and junk bond ratings.[5]

On the second night, the VIPs of the event, some hundred of the "real players"—people with large amounts of money, access to money, or deal lawyers—attended a private party and dinner. Arbitrageur Martin Weinstein made a wry comment, noting that a corporate raider named Irwin Jacobs "had been in deep conversation for hours with one of these women at the far end of the room." Weinstein said, "Tell Irwin he doesn't have to work so hard. She's already paid for."[6]

Such was life among financial raiders, schemers, looters, and fraudsters of the 1980s who were not content with yachts and private jets, but sought entire corporations to fit into burgeoning industrial empires. The investment bank Drexel Burnham Lambert was the center of the swirling greed, the industry leader and near monopolist of the corporate restructuring of the 1980s. And Drexel was run in all but name by the most influential banker on Wall Street since Andrew Mellon: Michael Milken. The J. R. Ewing sketch was Milken's doing. It was symbolism, and potent, at that.

Milken represented the return of the final component of Mellonism, the unbridled power of the financier to shape the real economy to serve his own ends. Milken used the corporation and the bank as a means of moving investors' capital—other people's money—into his own pocket. Unlike Saul Steinberg in the 1960s, Milken was free from restrictions on financial capital, and free from antitrust rules or banking regulations. He could use borrowed money or trading instruments however he saw fit.

Milken got his start in 1969, entering a second-tier Wall Street firm as a trader in bonds of high-risk companies. Because the bonds Milken traded were risky, they paid a high interest rate. Often these were companies known as "fallen angels" that had been considered good credit risks, like Penn Central, but had defaulted. There was no public listing for these bonds, which Wall Street soon dubbed "junk bonds." In the 1970s, most of the midlevel investment banks that raised money for these kinds of firms disappeared, leaving a funding gap for smaller and younger companies.[7]

Smaller and medium-sized companies presented a special challenge for financial markets. For one, they didn't have enough of a reputation or track record that investors could rely on. These kinds of companies typically borrowed money via direct lending through banks. A banker could monitor a company directly, unlike atomized investors who held small bits of these corporations' paper. But as banking declined in importance versus the increasingly unregulated financial system, so did the financing channels for newer and riskier ventures.

In another era, Milken would have become a modestly successful specialist in a backwater area of Wall Street, or perhaps a small-scale white-collar crook. But Milken would take advantage of, and pushed, the newly lax legal context for finance. There was another risk in lending to unknown, lesser known, or weaker companies without adequate supervision. This kind of lending could be easily corrupted. Two economists, George Akerlof and Paul Romer, observed the danger. As they put it in 1993, a "limited liability corporation could borrow money, pay it into the private account of the owners, and then default on its debt."[8] This danger was especially acute when the person in charge of lending the money was in on the scam. He or she could get money from investors, "lend" it to unknown companies, and then transfer the money to his or her own pocket by taking a cut. New Deal financial reforms were designed to block just such behavior, which had been done by the financiers of the 1920s.

Michael Milken became the architect of a complex and corrupt financial system based on engaging in this kind of looting. It started relatively small. He would entice investors into buying junk bonds of unknown companies that yielded high interest, and then take large fees from the deal flow. Milken had to ensure that these bonds paid out their interest, or at the very least, that investors who held these bonds could sell them in a market. Otherwise, investors would stop buying junk.

Milken somehow made this work by standing in between the junk bond buyer and the company issuing the debt. If you bought Drexel junk, Milken would always be willing to buy back your bonds, no matter how the underlying corporation that issued the bonds did. Somehow, even if the bond was outlandishly risky or close to worthless, Milken could always find a willing buyer, or take you out of it himself. Bond buying is a form of lending, and, normally, bond buyers care about whether the borrower will pay them back. But Milken stood in the middle between a lender and a borrower, and would ensure bond buyers were paid back regardless of how the borrower did. He could do this because he was stashing losses within captive pools of capital he controlled, like mutual funds, insurance companies, thrifts, and pension funds, aka other people's money.[9]

But who were these buyers willing to buy worthless junk bonds? Milken realized he needed to find men who controlled pools of other people's money and who were willing to hide losses for him. He found them among the dregs of Wall Street, the scam artists who lived in the gray areas of the financial world. These men wanted access to junk bond financing, so they had an incentive to help Milken create what looked like a vibrant market and draw real investors in. One such Milken vessel was Saul Steinberg, who still owned Reliance Insurance, a giant pool of other people's money. There were others—Carl Lindner, Meshulam Riklis, Victor Posner—who owned insurance companies and banks whose deposits and premiums they could use to buy junk bonds.

Milken also took advantage of a laxer environment to build pools of capital he would control. For instance, he helped build up an early junk bond mutual fund, First Investors Fund for Income (FIFI), and cultivated a relationship with the fund manager, David Solomon. After Milken got involved, "almost overnight, Solomon was transformed into a seeming portfolio wizard," wrote investigative reporter Connie Bruck. In those first few years, "Drexel employees claimed it was Milken who pulled Solomon's strings." In 1975–1976, FIFI was the most successful bond fund in America, with Solomon and Drexel doing a road show to sell investors on the fund. A few years later, FIFI had so much money from investors that Solomon "could not afford to be choosey" and had to buy "the diciest bonds" Milken had to offer, the "junkiest of the junk." In the 1980s, with billions of investors' money, Milken was using FIFI and other captive funds to buy junk bonds Drexel issued. While the First Investors Fund offered seemingly miraculous returns at first, it eventually collapsed, with ordinary investors losing hundreds of millions of dollars, some their life savings.[10]

The junk bond looked like an active market, with lots of buyers and sellers. But as Akerlof and Romer put it, "The junk bond market of the 1980s was not a thick, anonymous auction market characterized by full revelation of information. To a very great extent, the market owed its existence to a single individual, Michael Milken, who acted, literally, as the auctioneer."[11]

Milken spun a theory that he was so good with numbers, such a hard worker, and had discovered that investors undervalued junk bonds due to an irrational preference for quality bonds. This bias seemed to explain the exceptional performance of junk bonds, and how Milken could also seem to find a buyer if a seller wanted out.[12] For roughly fifteen years, from 1974 to 1989, Milken got bigger and stronger, and he became a money machine, the junk bond king.

Other investment banks couldn't figure out how he did what he did. Eventually, they simply started to emulate his aggressive tactics, putting up their own capital to get into junk bonds. But they couldn't compete, as Akerlof and Romer pointed out, because the market was rigged. Junk bond buyers were confident when they bought Milken's bonds that they would be paid back. A host of side payments to those running the institutions hiding the losses kept the network functional. Milken's network—including Milken's top salesman in Beverly Hills and two Milken-involved thrifts—even quietly purchased an interest in a bond rating company, Duff & Phelps, which then proceeded to rate the bonds of those thrifts favorably (both thrifts eventually collapsed).

Others who tried to compete with Milken by selling junk bonds didn't have places to stash losses, and were just trying to match lenders and borrowers. If there were defaults, junk bond buyers lost money. So junk bond buyers bought from Milken, who came to control the entire market.[13]

In 1983, Drexel, which had been a second-tier investment bank, issued $4.69 billion of junk offerings, three times what it had done the year before, including a billion dollars for a young telecommunications upstart named MCI and $400 million for MGM/UA Entertainment Company, entities that could not otherwise access capital markets effectively at the scale they sought. By 1987, the junk bond market had grown from $7 billion in the mid-1970s to $125 billion.[14]

Looser financial regulation greatly helped Milken, as did lax enforcement of laws that remained on the books. But two changes helped truly super-size Milken's scheme. The first was the transformation through financial deregulation of the savings and loan industry into giant pools of unregulated government-backed money.

These S&Ls were designed to finance the American home, and Patman had sought to carefully fence them off so they could continue to do so in perpetuity. But they were set loose by a series of laws, including one signed by Carter in 1980 and one signed by Reagan in 1982. S&Ls could now pay depositors any interest rate, and more importantly, they could enter any line of business they wanted, from commercial real estate to junk bonds. And the U.S. taxpayer backed all of it, through deposit insurance.

Across the country, real estate developers took control of S&Ls and began looting them by having the banks make loans to insiders. As they had with Penn Central, accountants looked the other way while the new S&L bosses lied about their balance sheets, and the great law firms, from New York to Chicago to Texas, bullied regulators and threatened suits against them. "For half a million dollars you could buy any legal opinion you wanted from any law firm in New York," an anonymous lawyer turned banker said in the 1980s.[15] Their clients could pay anything for the legal and accounting help, because "deposit insurance gave them the key to the U.S. Treasury."[16]

Top politicians on both sides of the aisle, from Republican John McCain to House Democratic leader and former Patman ally Jim Wright, took money from the S&Ls and in turn helped bully regulators. As Banking Committee chair, Patman had fought to preserve the financial channel for homes, and to investigate fraud where he found it. Just six years later, in 1982, Banking Committee chief Fernand St. Germain wrote the bill deregulating Savings and Loans while allegedly being supplied with prostitutes from S&L lobbyists. A few years later, newspapers exposed him as using his power as committee chair to become a millionaire. The scandal caused his popularity to plummet. He fought back, with help from the now-big-business-funded party establishment. His allies ran antiwar ads, accusing his opponent of seeking to bog down the U.S. in Nicaragua, which would become "Another Vietnam."

Consumer groups meanwhile ignored St. Germain's corruption because St. Germain criticized bankers for charging high interest rates on credit cards, and offered "trivial but crowd-pleasing bills to regulate unpopular commercial practices." Congress Watch, a Nader-backed group, said that questions of his personal finances "were unlikely to interfere with his banking work." Another Nader spin-off, the Public Interest Research Group, practically apologized for noting St. Germain took financial industry money, writing "not everyone who receives a large amount of PAC contributions will be anticonsumer," and applauding his willingness to put a particular consumer issue "high on the agenda." St. Germain buried his opponent, surfing to reelection on a flood of business donations, many from large financial institutions.[17]

A *New York Times* op-ed satire explained the problem with the 1982 Garn–St. Germain Depository Institutions Act: "We all know now why the old Prudential National Trust company changed its name to Crazy Louie Bank N.A. because by now everybody's heard the commercials: 'Shop the banks! Shop the savings banks! Shop the money market funds! Then take your money to Crazy Louie's. He'll beat them all! Crazy Louie's Maniacal Money Account will *always* pay the highest interest rates in town! And that interest is *guaranteed,* because Crazy Louie is a member of the FDIC, an agency of the Federal Government, which insures your deposits—not only the principal, but the interest, too.'"[18]

S&L fraud remade the American landscape, funding white elephant shopping centers and luxury hotels built mainly to be looted. The total cost ran into the hundreds of billions of dollars. For Milken, S&Ls were a perfect place to stash losses. When necessary, he could put toxic junk bonds in Columbia Savings and Loan of Beverly Hills, CenTrust Federal Savings of Miami, Executive Life Insurance Company, or any of the more than fifty financial institutions that eventually went bankrupt under the weight of tens of billions of defaulted Drexel bonds.[19] As writer Benjamin Stein told Congress, "Thanks largely to well-meant but extremely unfortunate legal changes at the beginning of the 1980s, the federal government basically repealed Glass-Steagall if an investment bank just called its commercial banking captive a 'savings and loan.'"[20]

Milken now had a virtually unlimited pool of money under his command. He had over a hundred billion dollars in direct financing through junk bonds. More importantly, corporate America and investors believed he could at any point raise as much as needed for any purpose, vastly increasing his power.[21] He turned toward the opportunities presented by the relaxation of both anti-merger law and rules surrounding stock market trading. Starting in 1983, Milken staked aggressive corporate raiders and arbitrageurs who would launch raids on companies backed by Drexel junk bonds.[22] In 1985, a Drexel banker told the hundreds of assembled financiers that the bank had figured out how to easily "finance the unfriendly takeover," which earned the conference's "Predators' Ball" nickname.[23] These bankers looked to Morgan and Mellon as inspiration. A guiding theme of Drexel's corporate finance department was to find and stake, as one banker put it, the "robber barons of the future."[24]

These new raiders looked for a specific type of company. They wanted to buy corporations that generated cash, had little debt, and owned assets. Conservatively managed companies with an engineer–CEO at the helm and that focused on producing industrial goods, such as National Can, were perfect. Then, Milken would find a stalking horse, usually a short, ambitious man who needed to conquer the world. He would either go to his network of junk buyers and raise hundreds of millions of dollars, or write what was called a "highly confident letter" saying that he could do so. The raider would take the money and buy a large slug of shares. Sometimes the company would pay the raider to go away, sometimes the raider would lose to another bidder, and sometimes the raider would win the prize.

If the raider lost, he would still make money by having his shares bought out at higher prices. Carl Icahn earned hundreds of millions this way. If the raider won the company, he would then saddle it with the debt he had incurred. It worked like buying a home with a mortgage. Essentially he would buy the company by borrowing against the company's own assets. This was a massive leveraging operation, buying corporations with other people's money. But unlike most attempts to buy stock with borrowed money, there were no margin requirements.

Once the acquisition was complete, the company would pay out large salaries, fees, and service the extremely high-cost junk bonds.

Sometimes the companies would go bankrupt and disappear, sometimes the debt would be restructured. It didn't matter. The deals benefited insiders, who were simply shifting corporate assets to themselves. Fees to the dealmakers, including investment advisors, bankers, underwriters, specialized fund managers participating in the buyouts, and lawyers, came to roughly 6 percent of the purchase price of a firm.[25]

All of Wall Street changed to accommodate this new and highly profitable activity. Investment bankers and lawyers pioneered a range of tactics to fight against or enact hostile takeovers, colorfully known as "greenmail," "the PacMan strategy," "shark repellents," "the poison pill," "the golden parachute," and so forth. But all of these were essentially ways of loading corporate America with debt, or looting the companies outright. Investment bankers were now in the business of selling deals for the fees.

Corporate CEOs, most of whom were initially resistant to the takeover wave, were bribed into submission. In 1977, banker Martin Siegel, who eventually landed at Drexel and, along with Milken, would be criminally convicted, invented the golden parachute. The golden parachute was, as journalist James Stewart put it, "essentially a lucrative employment contract for top corporate officers, [and] provided exorbitant severance payments for the officers in the event of a takeover. Supposedly, the contracts were intended to deter hostile takeovers by making them more expensive. In practice, they tended to make the officers very rich."[26]

As important as the fees was the information Milken acquired about which companies were being sold before raiders bid up the price of bonds or stock. This information, as well as deal structures Drexel controlled, gave Milken both money and power. He set up partnership structures outside Drexel, with names like Otter Creek, and allowed favored colleagues and family members to put money into them. These partnerships were then, as sociologist Mary Zey wrote, "used for the purpose of skimming warrants and equities in several of the Drexel underwritings," such as that of Beatrice Foods.[27] Congressman John

Dingell found Drexel had twenty to thirty such partnerships allowing employees to profit on the side from deals in which they were involved; Otter Creek held a balance of $145 million, and one account bought and sold a billion dollars of stocks and bonds in a single year.[28]

According to writer Benjamin Stein, SEC staff attorney John Hewitt was collecting a "mountain of research" about Drexel showing "stupendous price fixing and bond-price rigging" by Milken. There was, he wrote, "clear-cut—or at least impressive—evidence that a Milken partnership, Otter Creek, was trading illegally on inside information."[29] Yet the Reagan Securities and Exchange Commission and Department of Justice had pulled back on enforcement of laws against white-collar crime. While Drexel paid high salaries, it was impossible not to notice the lucrative profits of a Milken partnership. Milken combined allies from inside Drexel and throughout Wall Street into these partnerships, making this entire apparatus dependent on him personally. These partnerships were akin to the House of Morgan's preferred list, a way to funnel payments by helping favored individuals get guaranteed returns on stock investments. Milken now had yet another lever to control captive pools of capital, whether those were S&Ls, mutual funds, insurance companies, or corporate pensions. He simply showered the men who controlled these pots of other people's money with an unending stream of favors.

Well-placed speculators could participate in the merger frenzy whether they were involved in the deal or not. Through arbitrage departments, investment bankers could bet on whether a deal would close, and with insider trading tips, these bets would often pay off. Much of Wall Street got involved, directly or indirectly, with Milken's network. Robert Rubin, who later became the treasury secretary under Bill Clinton, climbed the ladder at Goldman Sachs as an arbitrageur. His protégé, Robert Freeman, accused of being part of the Milken-influenced network of traders, eventually pleaded guilty to insider trading.[30]

To those around him, it seemed as if Milken had figured out how to grow money on trees, and hand it to his favored clients. In the 1980s, junk bonds became the mechanism for reorganizing corporate America, and brought a new generation of leaders into the forefront of American finance and business with a different philosophy about power. "In a few short years," wrote pro-Milken journalist Edward Jay Epstein, he "had reshaped the financial world in a way that no one else had done since J. P. Morgan in the nineteenth century."[31]

The Predators' Ball conferences were a celebration of debauchery, money, and power, but they became more than that. They became a celebration of financial capitalism, and an explicit nod to the original robber baron spirit that had created corporate America in the 1880s and 1890s. And they illustrated the increasing political power of this new raider class on Wall Street, not just over their traditional Republican allies, but among the new class of Democrats.

Attendees also included Tim Wirth of Colorado, Bill Bradley of New Jersey, and Alan Cranston of California. Howard Metzenbaum of Ohio, a staunch antimonopolist, went. Ted Kennedy of Massachusetts attended, to "listen and learn." The mayor of Los Angeles, Tom Bradley, the only African American mayor of the city, gave a speech and introduced Michael Milken as "that man of genius, that man of courage, that man of vision, that man of conviction."[32] These were the young rock stars of the party, the future leaders of America.

The corruption of these politicians was gradual. At first, politicians watched the takeover wave with alarm. Members of Congress introduced over thirty anti-takeover bills.[33] The Reagan administration was strongly supportive of the raiders, but Congress wasn't. Wirth, who chaired an important subcommittee, expressed concern that "shareholders, companies, employees, and entire communities have been harmed in these battles for corporate control." His key staffer, David Aylward, sought a strong probe and helped organize high-profile hearings. "We really don't know where this money is coming from, and whether it could be better used for something else in the long term," he told the press.

Drexel had a lavish political operation. After the hearings, Aylward took a lobbying job working for the Alliance for Capital Access, a trade association of junk bond users. He offered paid speeches to senators and House members, testified before committees, and spread money around. He had become a Milken lobbyist. The congressional push to restrict the use of junk bonds in takeovers ended.[34] In 1986, Paul Volcker attempted to impose restrictions on the use of junk bonds. The Reagan administration and Congress pressured him to back down.[35]

Milken rewarded congressmen directly. As the *Los Angeles Times* reported, "Two members of Congress, Reps. Stephen L. Neal (D-N.C.) and Carlos J. Moorhead (R-Glendale), were paid $2,000 each in honorariums in 1986 to stroll through the command center of Drexel's junk bond operation in Beverly Hills and chat with employees." Neal later spoke on the floor of the House "against provisions in an omnibus spending bill that were designed to discourage the use of junk bonds in financing corporate takeovers."[36]

Milken's money—and takeover fever—spread far and wide within the Democratic Party.[37] For instance, in 1990, Carter-era trade representative and former Democratic national chair Robert Strauss received $8 million representing both sides in the acquisition of MCA by Matsushita Electric.[38] Strauss's law firm, Akin, Gump, Strauss, Hauer & Field, had earlier earned $431,058 in 1986 lobbying for Drexel.[39]

The political machinery of the 1980s Democratic Party was financed in part with Milken money; Drexel executives on the West Coast were responsible for raising between $35,000 and $50,000 apiece for California fundraising events for Tony Coelho, the congressman in charge of making sure that House Democrats kept their majority through the Democratic Congressional Campaign Committee. When Milken had to plead the Fifth Amendment in a committee hearing in Congress so as not to incriminate himself, Coelho remained loyal. At a Drexel conference just a few weeks before Milken testified, Coelho gave a speech in Los Angeles, saying, "I am here tonight to show my respect and deep admiration for Michael Milken, my very good friend. . . . He is constantly thinking about what can be done to make this a better world." Coelho got $2,000 for the speech. In 1989, Coelho resigned due to questions about his personal finances. A $100,000 junk bond underwritten by Drexel somehow wound up in his possession, with the bond bought with money borrowed from Columbia Savings and Loan, a thrift run by Milken's protégé Thomas Spiegel. After Coelho's resignation from Congress, he went to work on Wall Street for a million dollars a year.

"I'm determined to be as successful here as I was in the political world," he said.[40]

Meanwhile, arbitrage merger specialist Robert Rubin was everywhere in Democratic politics. He became a close advisor to Democratic presidential hopefuls Walter Mondale and Michael Dukakis and went on to New York governor Mario Cuomo's competitiveness commission.[41]

As Milken became more powerful, he became a philosopher-king of the decade. He mimicked the weird political language developed of the era, talking about job formation, education, and "human capital."

Milken also benefited from Milton Friedman's success in the 1970s at insisting that the main goal of business leadership should be the well-being of the shareholder. Michael Jensen, a conservative Harvard Business School professor, was a prime conduit and refiner of this thinking, and now argued the takeover wave was essential for attacking entrenched corporate management and restructuring corporations to make them more responsive to shareholders.

Jensen's theory was that corporate managers had an incentive to run the company inefficiently because shareholders were dispersed and powerless. Jensen saw companies with lots of cash, factories, research departments, and/or unionized workforces as poorly managed. The New Deal–era corporation was, in his view, run by undisciplined non-financially-oriented leaders. One solution was the leveraged buyout firm, a pool of capital run by a financier who could buy these fat and happy companies. A financier would load up these companies with debt and pay out cash dividends, thus, in Jensen's theory, disciplining corporate management. In reality the leveraged buyout firm was just a mechanism for financiers to loot corporations and strip them of their assets, but Jensen provided a fig leaf useful in the press and on Capitol Hill.

The 1985 Predators' Ball led to a flurry of dealmaking. Just weeks after the conference, Milken-backed raiders launched takeover bids of Unocal, National Can, Crown Zellerbach, and Northwest Industries.[42] The deals got so big that, by the end of the decade, investment bank KKR's takeover of RJR Nabisco with Drexel debt went for $25 billion, an amount so large that "the electronic transfer of funds necessary to complete the deal exceeded the physical capacity of the Federal

Reserve wire transfer."[43] One young Drexel banker half-joked about going after the titans of corporate America, saying "maybe we'll take a run at IBM."[44]

American corporate strategists began to worry about the effects of financiers pillaging corporations. "The hostile tender offer," said management consulting legend Peter Drucker, "has become a dominant force—many would say the dominant force—in the behavior and actions of American management, and almost certainly a major factor in the erosion of American technological leadership.[45]

Even corporations that didn't get taken over restructured to load themselves up with debt. Between 1984 and 1985, 398 of the 950 largest companies in North America restructured, only 52 in response to actual takeover bids. The rest were self-initiated. In 1984, the amount of equity, or the part of the ownership structure that wasn't debt, shrank by $85 billion. The level of debt in corporate America increased from 73 percent to 81.4 percent just between 1983 and 1984.[46]

To give a sense of what this did to the American corporation, consider the Goodyear Tire and Rubber Company. In 1986, a British raider named James Goldsmith attacked the company, claiming that management had taken their focus off the tire business. Goldsmith admitted he knew nothing about the tire business, but he did smell cash flow. What was going on was that Goodyear had put too much capital into its tire business, accounting for 25 percent of the research and development of the entire industry. Goodyear was the industry leader, and aimed to stay that way by making ever safer, longer-lasting tires.[47]

But Goodyear management's very success made the corporation a target for the raiders, as the one-two combination of low debt and high levels of investment was perfect for looting. The company defended itself. As the head of business planning put it to Congress in the face of Goldsmith's claims, "I do not believe that our 120,000 employees, tens of thousands of dealers and suppliers, and hundreds of thousands in communities who depend on Goodyear expected anything less than the defense we mounted. We all felt shocked and somewhat helpless in the face of one man backed by billions of dollars raised essentially by pledging our own assets."

Goodyear defended itself, aggressively, using a "shareholder rights plan." They sold their energy and aerospace divisions, borrowed money, and bought back their own stock. The shares more than doubled. But in the process, the company took its debt up from 33 percent in 1986 to 80 percent of the total value of the company. Goodyear cut research, capital investment, advertising, training, closed three plants, and reduced employment by 4,300 workers. It had been a well-managed company. There were plant expansions in Alabama in 1976, Tennessee in 1981, and North Carolina in 1982. In 1977, they built a $260 million plant in Oklahoma, and a $250 million plant in Texas to take on Korean competition. But, for three years after the raid, the company announced it would undertake no new investment to "focus on debt repayment."

"Did we create wealth?" a Goodyear executive wondered later about these years. "I think not. In the long run, I think we destroyed wealth."[48]

The junk bond market, and the savings and loan banks, did ultimately collapse. The looting was profound. One analyst noted that nearly all savings and loan banks that were major buyers in the junk bond market collapsed. According to Benjamin Stein, Drexel issued around $220 billion in debt, with a loss to investors and taxpayers of between $40 billion and $100 billion.[49] Milken went to jail for insider trading, partly due to his domination of the junk bond market and his unwillingness to share spoils with the rest of Wall Street as much as his own crooked ways. But by the end of the 1980s, Wall Street had permanently changed corporate America. A new type of business model existed. The leveraged buyout industry, stung with bad publicity, rebranded as "private equity." While some PE firms made productive investments, they were largely pools of floating capital that sought to use the corporation for the purpose of the financier.[50]

Strategically, the only businesses that were sustainable in the new legal environment were those that could withstand the pressures of financial raiders. Large-scale monopolistic corporations such as General Electric and Walmart could use the new tools to their advantage. So could high-tech concerns such as Microsoft that had taken advantage of the technology revolution to acquire choke holds over new vital arteries of commerce. Private equity firms and financial intermediaries who could use the new capital market structure to their advantage increasingly controlled American business.

In previous eras in American history, the wreckage caused by such widespread looting would have led to substantial legal reforms. And there were some. But the key innovation, that the corporate structure exists as a mechanism for the extraction of cash for insiders from either the company itself or from a market that company monopolized, was here to stay.

## CHAPTER EIGHTEEN

# TECH GOLIATHS AND TOO BIG TO FAIL

"A partnership with Microsoft is like a Nazi non-aggression pact. It just means you're next."

—**Anonymous partner of Bill Gates**[1]

■ ■ ■ ■ ■ ■ ■ ■ ■ ■ ■ ■ ■

In 1985, the Dow Jones average jumped 27.66 percent. Making money in stocks, as a journalist put it, "was easy." With lower interest rates, low inflation, and "takeover fever," investors could throw a dart at a list of stocks and profit.[2] The next year was also very good. The average gain of a Big Board stock in 1986 was 14 percent, with equity market indexes closing at a record high.[3]

For the top performers, the amounts of money involved were staggering. In 1987, Michael Milken awarded himself $550 million in compensation. In New York City, spending by bankers—a million dollars for curtains for a Fifth Avenue apartment, a thousand dollars for a vase of precious roses for a party—was obscene. A major financier announced in the Hamptons one night that "if you have less than seven hundred fifty million, you have no hedge against inflation." In Paris, a jeweler "dazzled his society guests when topless models displayed the merchandise between courses." In west Los Angeles, the average price of a house in Bel Air rose to $4.6 million. There was so much money it was nicknamed "green smog."[4]

Ambitious men now wanted to change the world through finance. Bruce Wasserstein had been a Nader's Raider and had helped write the original FTC study in 1969. He now worked at First Boston as one of the most successful mergers and acquisitions bankers of the 1980s. Michael Lewis wrote his best-seller *Liar's Poker* as a warning of what unfettered greed in finance meant, but instead of learning the lesson, students deluged him with letters asking if he "had any other secrets to share about Wall Street." To them, the book was a "how-to manual."[5]

Finance was the center, but its power reached outward everywhere. The stock market was minting millionaires in a collection of formerly sleepy towns in California. Sunnyvale, Mountain View, Los Altos, Cupertino, Santa Clara, and San Jose in the 1960s had been covered with "apricot, cherry and plum orchards," and young people there often took summer jobs at local canneries.[6] Immediately after Reagan's election, in December of 1980, Apple Computer went public, instantly creating three hundred millionaires, and raising more money in the stock market than any company since Ford Motor had in its initial public offering of shares in 1956. A young Steve Jobs was instantly worth $217 million.[7]

In upper midwestern farming country, up in the Corn Belt and High Plains, the power of finance had very different impacts. The winter of 1985 had been bitter and harsh, with farmers often encountering days with a windchill factor of 50 degrees below. Worse than the weather was the dreaded monthly payment to the bank. The mid-1970s had been good, with high commodities prices and a land boom, so farmers borrowed money to buy land, planted as much as they could, and watched the cash roll in. But farm debts had more than doubled, and as interest rates increased, the problems began to build up fast in the late 1970s.[8]

Like the old populists of the 1890s, farmers in the late 1970s began getting together, and talking about the cost of equipment and how much of their crop revenue was going to the processors. A wave of farm strikes began, with signs known as "John Deere Letters." "Crime Doesn't Pay . . . Neither Does Farming." Farmers wanted supply management, which would guarantee them payments based on the cost of production, and which for much of the twentieth century had been the policy of the U.S. government. In February 1979, thousands drove to Washington in a "tractorcade," parking their tractors on and tying up the National Mall. President Carter then made things much worse by imposing an embargo on grain shipments to the Soviet Union, in response to the Soviet invasion of Afghanistan. Many farmers responded by ditching the Democratic Party in 1980 and voting for Reagan, hoping for something, anything, to get better. That was a mistake.

Reagan paid the farmers back by breaking the back of farm country. In the early 1980s, wheat production boomed, but prices for wheat collapsed. At the same time, interest rates went even higher. Higher costs and less revenue meant many farmers couldn't pay their mortgage. Rural high schools closed, churches lost membership, as families and young people left the farms. The news constantly covered sad stories about the end of the family farm. There were still faint memories of the Great Depression, with old-time farmers talking about "the thirties," when the cattle starved and corn wasn't worth selling, the price was so low. In Worthington, Minnesota, 250 farmers gathered to "hear an activist tell them that they 'have no moral obligation to repay an unjust debt' and that they would be right to use a gun to defend their farms from foreclosure."

The Reagan administration responded by cutting payments to farmers. But who could you shoot? A young Farmers Home Administration supervisor from New York relocated to Union County, South Dakota, a county named for the cause of the Civil War. The government had moved him around the state in the hope that he would get tough with local farmers behind on their mortgages. His wife had been fired from two separate jobs, and his daughter wrote poems expressing sadness she had to keep leaving new friends behind. He caused a stir when he killed his wife, daughter, and dog, and then went to the office to shoot himself. "The job has got pressure on my mind, pain on my left side," he wrote in his suicide note.[9] The news media focused on the plight of the farmers. The government sent in officials to make it worse.

The family farmer had lots of people who said they were friends at election time—even the glamorous music industry put on a giant "Farm Aid" concert in 1985 to raise money for bankrupt growers. But there was no Wright Patman in the Democratic Party anymore. On the contrary, "new" Democrats like Dale Bumpers and Bill Clinton of Arkansas worked to rid their state of the usury caps meant to protect the "plain people" from the banker and financier.[10] And the main contender for the Democratic nomination in 1988, the handsome Gary

Hart, with his flowing—and carefully blow-dried—chestnut brown hair, spoke a lot about "sunrise" industries like semiconductors and high-tech, but had little in his vision incorporating the family farm.[11]

It wasn't just the family farmer who suffered. On the South Side of Chicago, U.S. Steel, having started mass layoffs in 1979, continued into the next decade, laying off more than 6,000 workers in that community alone. Youngstown, Johnson, Gary—all the old industrial cities were going, in the words of the writer Studs Terkel, from "Steel Town" to "Ghost Town." And the headlines kept on coming. John Deere idled 1,500 workers, GE's turbine division cut 1,500 jobs, AT&T laid off 2,900 in its Shreveport plant, Eastern Air Lines fired 1,010 flight attendants, and docked pay by 20 percent. "You keep saying it can't get worse, but it does," said a United Autoworker member.[12]

And all the time, whether in farm country or steel country, the closed independent shop and the collapsed bank were as much monuments to the new political order as the sprouting number of Walmarts and the blizzard of junk-mail-holding credit cards from Citibank. As Terkel put it, "In the thirties, an Administration recognized a need and lent a hand. Today, an Administration recognizes an image and lends a smile."[13]

Americans were experiencing, once again, what it felt like under Mellonism. Regional inequality widened, as airlines cut routes to rural, small, and even medium-sized cities. So did income inequality, the emptying farm towns, the hollowing of manufacturing as executives began searching for any way to be in any business but one that made things in America. It wasn't just the smog and the poverty, the consumerism, the debt and the shop-till-you-drop ethos. It was the profound hopelessness.

Within academic and political institutions, Americans were taught to believe their longing for freedom was immoral. Power was recentralizing on Wall Street, in corporate monopolies, in shopping malls, in the way they paid for the new consumer goods made abroad, in where they worked and shopped. Yet policymakers, reading from the scripts prepared by Chicago School "experts," spoke of these changes as natural, "scientific," a result of consumer preferences, not the concentration of power.

And the law and economics world celebrated. In 1988, Reagan accepted an award from the American Enterprise Institute, the think tank that had financed Bork's legislative history, built by the man who would elevate the Chicago School's intellectuals during the Goldwater campaign. "We have come a long way together," the president said. "From the intellectual wilderness of the 1960s, through the heated intellectual battles of the 1970s, to the intellectual fruition of the 1980s. The American Enterprise Institute stands at the center of a revolution in ideas of which I, too, have been a part."[14]

## THE CORRUPTION OF THE DEMOCRATS

And what of the party of the people, the Democrats? The scandals of the 1980s should have enabled the party to hit back against Reagan and the GOP. Throughout American history, the triumph of plutocrats in a decade provoked a backlash, and the opposing party would win a series of elections and reorient political economy. But the Chicago School had dismantled this political fail-safe. By the 1980s, the Democrats as a party had lost the ability even to think about the problem of concentrated economic power, so they did not understand what was happening, hence could not oppose the process even if they wanted to.

The psychological shock of Reagan's victory in 1980 had caused a soul-searching among party leaders, the defeat much worse than McGovern's landslide loss to Nixon. Democrats in the 1970s had largely abandoned their New Deal alliances of small businesses, family farmers, and unionized workers, and had lost the ideological core of the party. Now they had to build something new.

Into this vacuum stepped a new generation of leaders. In 1982, Randall Rothenberg wrote an *Esquire* cover story titled "The Neoliberal Club: Bleeding Hearts Need Not Apply." This article featured, accurately, the young major new leaders for the party: Paul Tsongas, Bill Bradley, Gary Hart, and Tim Wirth. Rothenberg's follow-up writing, which included a book titled *The Neoliberals*, discussed the politicians Bill Clinton, Bruce Babbitt, Al Gore, and Dick Gephardt, and the writers and intellectuals Charlie Peters, Robert Reich, Lester Thurow, and James Fallows. It was these leaders who would dominate the next thirty years of Democratic politics. These were the men successfully grooming themselves for the post-Reagan presidency, and they began calling themselves "New Democrats." The common denominator of the group was that they were "pragmatic," which meant they believed in the "end of the New Deal."[15]

Paired with these political leaders were economists like Alice Rivlin, as well as consumer-oriented advocates like Ira Magaziner, who styled themselves as technocrats able to float above dirty old politics. These operators adhered to the Boston Consulting Group's framework that older industries such as steel and automobiles were low-value "sunset" industries, and that it was smart to allow Wall Street to milk these older industries for cash to be invested in "sunrise" industries such as computer chips and video games.[16]

As Rothenberg noted, neoliberal thinking, though sounding fresh, was not actually new. It was what Teddy Roosevelt argued in 1912 when he ran as a Bull Moose progressive and sought to abolish antitrust laws and organize business and government into a cooperative whole under the slogan "concentration, cooperation, and control." New Democrats saw cooperation between business and government as a compelling alternative to Reaganism, and as a means of addressing international financial problems. Thurow had drawn from Galbraith, who in turn had drawn directly from such Bull Moose thinkers as Walter Lippmann.

Like Teddy Roosevelt and Galbraith, Thurow preached the abolition of the antitrust laws. All used the same excuse for doing so. "In markets where international trade exists or could exist, national antitrust laws no longer make sense," wrote Thurow. This was a direct echo of TR's statement, in accepting the Bull Moose nomination in 1912, that if we "do not allow cooperation, we shall be defeated in the world's markets."[17] As Rothenberg pointed out, Bill Bradley, Gary Hart, and Paul Tsongas made the same argument, all proposing to relax antitrust and banking laws.[18]

There was one big difference, however. Whereas Teddy Roosevelt believed big government should rule concentrated capital, in the era of Reagan, New Democrats preached the idea that government should serve concentrated business institutions, under the guise that the job of political leaders was to cooperate with big business and forge consensus. New Democrats thought of the government's assertion of public power against big business as illegitimate, as picking "winners" and "losers," as unfair and unproductive redistributionism, and as a problem of "entrenched bureaucracies and narrow interests in Washington." They used concepts, many from the Chicago School and repackaged by Thurow, to shield corporate executives, bankers, and financiers from democratic oversight.[19] As shopping malls and mergers spread, these New Democrats found it repugnant to consider bringing back the New Deal model of attacking corporate concentrations of power.

A young operative named Al From organized the political operation of the New Democrats. From had worked in the Carter White House. After the Carter debacle, an old Louisiana politician, Gillis Long, recruited From to run the House Democratic Caucus, and they put together something called the "Committee on Party Effectiveness" to bring fresh ideas into the party. This forum included many of the key future leaders of the Democratic Party: Tim Wirth, Dick Gephardt, Al Gore, Geraldine Ferraro, Martin Frost, Les Aspin, Tony Coelho, Barney Frank, and many others. Advised by Thurow, Rivlin, and Charles Schultze, the group produced reports designed to infuse the Democratic Party with this new vision of political economy.[20]

The Committee on Party Effectiveness adopted new language for the party, a language of flabby, difficult-to-follow technobabble. Smart leaders of tomorrow should speak of "infrastructure," and "human capital," and "public-private partnerships," and "high-technology entrepreneurship." The concepts of "competition" and "the market" were reconceived to mean financial speculation and the free flow of capital, not social structures designed to support the independence and well-being of ordinary Americans. And big business was now "good." As Thurow put it, "'Small is beautiful' sounds beautiful, but it does not exist because it does not jibe with human nature. Man is an acquisitive animal whose wants cannot be satisfied."[21]

The language of the New Democrats was like Jell-O, impossible to nail down, vague, though always opposed to anything that sounded like populism or New Dealism. But the intent to insiders was clear. "Make no mistake about it," wrote From in a memo about his strategy, "what we hope to accomplish . . . is a bloodless revolution in our party. It is not unlike what the conservatives accomplished in the Republican Party during the 1960s and 1970s."[22]

In 1984, Walter Mondale, the vice president under Jimmy Carter, ran a campaign incorporating some of these new themes. Mondale, like the neoliberals, argued strongly for reducing the budget deficit. He also focused on cooperation between industry and government, proposing a technocratic sounding "Economic Cooperation Council." The new council would of course not be "picking winners and losers," but would among other things help, as the 1984 Democratic platform put it bloodlessly in the midst of ugly layoffs, "smooth the transition of workers and firms to new opportunities." Voters didn't like the new technobabble and gave Reagan forty-nine states instead of forty-four as they had in 1980.[23]

In the wake of this loss, financiers like Michael Steinhardt and Robert Rubin recruited From to take his organizing work outside Congress and establish the Democratic Leadership Council (DLC), an independent group designed to put neoliberal philosophy at the core of Democratic policymaking. The DLC now became the center of anti-populist political thinking for rising Democratic stars, the technobabble wielded to compete with Republicans for finance-friendly yuppies. As DLC's chairman, Virginia politician Chuck Robb, said in 1986, "the New Deal consensus which dominated American politics for 50 years has run its course."[24]

The DLC was an elite-driven organization, without a grassroots core. Populist senator Howard Metzenbaum opposed the DLC, and high-profile activist Jesse Jackson derided the DLC as the "Democrats for the Leisure Class." But the Democratic betrayal of farmers, small business, and labor meant there was no longer institutional working-class support for the Democratic Party, except a fast-shrinking core group in labor. The result was that the DLC proved to be spectacularly successful. Groups of DLC politicians dubbed "the cavalry" traveled around the country to talk to reporters, activists, and operatives with a message of "change and hope." Babbitt explained it by saying, "We're revolutionaries. We believe the Democratic Party in the last several decades has been complacent. . . . We're out to refresh, revitalize, regenerate, carry on the revolutionary tradition." Media elites loved it; the *Washington Post*'s David Broder headlined his column: "A Welcome Attack of Sanity Has Hit Washington."[25]

Along with From came a new architecture for political campaigns, the systemization of legal business donations to Democrats through the political action committee, or PAC. Democratic congressman Tony Coehlo had begun coordinating business PACs in 1981, directing them to Democratic candidates who fit the New Democrat mold. A close ally of Michael Milken, Coehlo was transactional, creating a patronage machine. With large annual donations to the "Speaker's Club," donors could become "trusted, informal advisors" to top Democrats, and though he never said it explicitly, able to influence policy. Coelho trained future Virginia governor Terry McAuliffe (who was the finance director of the DCCC in the mid-1980s) and a host of young operatives in what increasingly was viewed as a pay-to-play system.[26] For the next generation, the Democratic Party's main strategy was to attempt to outbid the equally craven Republican Party for the smiles—and money—of the new plutocrats.

When the junk bond market crashed at the end of the 1980s, the Democrats could have turned the collapse of this economy-wide Ponzi scheme into a political cudgel to use against Republicans. But they not only had no ideological framework to do so, many top Democrats were now implicated. Shortly before Coehlo's own resignation in the face of investigations into financial improprieties, his close ally, Speaker of the House Jim Wright, also resigned in a cloud of scandal, having taken gifts from corrupt savings and loan bankers and then bullying regulators on their behalf (in one instance accusing a regulator of being part of a corrupt "ring of homosexual lawyers in Texas").[27] Thomas "Lud" Ashley, the old nemesis of Patman, was by this time a bank lobbyist, and he worked to protect one of George H. W. Bush's sons, Neil Bush, from fraud charges for his involvement in Silverado Banking, Savings and Loan Association. Wirth, as well as Senators Bob Graham of Florida and John Kerry of Massachussetts, were caught having flown on the corporate jet of Miami's CenTrust bank, which stood at the center of a multibillion-dollar savings and loan disaster.[28]

In 1988, Democratic presidential nominee Michael Dukakis was advised by Rubin, and few others had any interest in talking about the corruption. Jesse Jackson, the only thorn in the side of the DLC, did not organize his campaign around opposition to corporate power; his son took a summer internship with Drexel in 1989. "Scarcely a word about the smoldering S&L issue [was] said by either candidate during the 1988 election campaign," according to *The Washington Post*. Even in the recession of the early 1990s, with a very slow recovery because of the overhang of junk debt and the S&L failures, Democrats had little to say.

It took a Republican, Representative Jim Leach of Iowa, to point out what the Democrats had missed. "The irony is that the biggest domestic public policy mistake of the century was effectively a non-issue in the 1988 election and appears likely to be a non-issue in the '92 election."[29]

## THE REVOLUTION OF 1992

As the new decade began, Reagan's successor, George H. W. Bush, presided over what seemed to be a remarkable series of foreign policy successes. The Berlin Wall fell in 1989, and communism collapsed across Eastern Europe. By 1991, the Soviet Union transformed into the independent state of Russia; the Cold War was over. At the same time, Bush exorcized the ghosts of Vietnam. During the First Gulf War, America put over half a million troops in the Middle East and pushed the Iraqis out of Kuwait using technological wonders like smart bombs and Patriot missiles. America lost fewer than 250 troops. Americans were euphoric, able to use military might at will, and no longer needing to worry about the great communist opponent sowing chaos in the rest of the world. By March of 1991, Bush had an approval rating of 89 percent, the highest ever measured by Gallup.

But the euphoria was short-lived. The end of the junk-bond-fueled real estate boom of the 1980s brought forth a new kind of recession. After the economy started growing again, jobs didn't come back in what became known as a "jobless recovery." America had military might, but its economic power seemed to be ebbing. Bush was a figure of potency on the world stage in 1991. A week into the new year and just before the New Hampshire primary, Bush collapsed at a state dinner in Japan, vomiting into the lap of the Japanese prime minister. His approval rating by July of 1992 dropped to 29 percent, a fall of sixty points in a little over a year.[30]

By the time of the 1992 election, there was a sullen mood among the voters, similar to that of 1974. "People are outraged at what is going on in Washington. Part of it had to do with pay raises, part of it has to do with banks and S&Ls and other things that are affecting my life as a voter," said a pollster.[31] That year, billionaire businessman Ross Perot ran the strongest third-party challenge in American history, capitalizing on anger among white working-class voters, the Democrats who had switched over to Reagan in the 1980s. He did so by pledging straightforward protectionism for U.S. industry, attacking the proposed North American Free Trade Agreement (NAFTA) and political corruption. Despite a bizarre campaign in which he withdrew and then reentered the race, Perot did so well he shattered the Republican coalition, throwing the election to the Democrats. There would be one last opportunity for the Democrats to rebuild their New Deal coalition of working-class voters.[32]

The winner of the election, Bill Clinton, looked like he might do so. He had run a populist campaign using the slogan "Putting People First." He attacked the failed economic theory of Reagan, criticized tax cuts for the rich and factory closings, and pledged to protect Americans from foreign and domestic threats. "For too long, those who play by the rules and keep the faith have gotten the shaft," Clinton said. "And those who cut corners and cut deals have been rewarded." His campaign's internal slogan was "It's the economy, stupid," and the 1992 Democratic platform used the word "revolution" fourteen times.[33]

As a candidate, Clinton's Democratic platform called for a "Revolution of 1992," capturing the anger of the moment. But the platform was written by Al From, and for the first time since 1880 there was no mention of antitrust or corporate power, despite a decade with the worst financial manipulation America had seen since the 1920s. This revolution would be against government, in government, around government.

When Clinton took office, the Democrats finally had a majority in the House, a majority in the Senate, and the presidency. Clinton not only entrenched Reagan's antitrust principles into the DOJ by making them bipartisan, but expanded the Reagan revolution more broadly. With the end of the Cold War, Clinton took neoliberalism global. Through the North American Free Trade Agreement, the restructuring of relationships with China, and the creation of the World Trade Organization, the

Clinton administration sought to do its part in building a New Economy, a borderless world everywhere where capital would flow freely.

Bill Clinton's politics were those of Al Smith, not FDR. In New York state as governor, Roosevelt had fought with financial interests. In Arkansas, Clinton coddled them, solicited them, lavished them with attention. His wife, Hillary, was on the board of Walmart, and he had even appointed Sam Walton an honorary brigadier general in the Arkansas National Guard.[34] And now, as president, he led the Democrats in repudiating their traditional populist distrust of concentrated capital in politics. In 1993, a book came out on lobbying in Washington. Wayne Thevenot, a Clinton donor and a former campaign manager for Gillis Long, laid out the new theme of the modern Democratic Party: "I gave up the idea of changing the world. I set out to get rich."[35]

Like Reagan, Clinton went after restrictions on banking. Reagan sought to free restrictions on finance by allowing banks and nonbanks to enter new lines of business. Clinton continued this policy, but over the course of his eight years attacked restrictions on banks themselves. In 1994, the Clinton administration and a Democratic Congress passed the Riegle-Neal Interstate Banking and Branching Efficiency Act, which allowed banks to open up branches across state lines. Clinton appointed Robert Rubin as his treasury secretary, super-lawyer Eugene Ludwig to run the Office of the Comptroller of the Currency, and reappointed Alan Greenspan as the chairman of the Federal Reserve.

All three men worked hard through regulatory rulemaking to allow unfettered trading in derivatives, to break down the New Deal restrictions prohibiting commercial banks from entering the trading business, and to let banks take more risks with less of a cushion.[36] Citigroup, now led by Walter Wriston's successor, John Reed, finally got an insurance arm, merging with financial conglomerate Travelers Group, approved by Greenspan, who granted the authority for the acquisition under the Bank Holding Company Act.[37] In 1999, Clinton and a now-Republican Congress passed the Gramm-Leach-Bliley Act, which fully repealed the Glass-Steagall Act that had shattered the House of Morgan and the House of Mellon. The very last bill

Clinton signed was the Commodity Futures Modernization Act of 2000, which removed public rules limiting the use of exotic gambling instruments known as derivatives by now-enormous banks.

Clinton signed the Telecommunications Act of 1996, which he touted as "truly revolutionary legislation," and this began the process of reconsolidating the old AT&T as the Baby Bells merged. At the signing ceremony, actress Lily Tomlin reprised her role as a Ma Bell operator. Huge pieces of the AT&T network came back together, as Baby Bells merged from seven to three. Clear Channel grew from forty radio stations to 1,240. In 1996, the Communications Decency Act was signed, with Section 230 of the act protecting certain internet businesses from being liable for wrongdoing that occurred on their platform. While not well understood at the time, Section 230 was one policy lever that would enable a powerful set of internet monopolies to emerge in the next decade.

Clinton also sped up the corporate takeover of rural America by allowing a merger wave in farm country. Food companies had always had some power in America, but before the Reagan era, big agribusinesses were confined to one or two stages of the food system. In the 1990s, the agricultural sector consolidated under a small number of sprawling conglomerates that organized the entire supply chain. Cargill, an agricultural conglomerate that was the largest privately owned company in America, embarked on a series of mergers and joint ventures, buying the grain-trading operations of its rival, Continental Grain Inc., as well as Azko Salt, thus becoming one of the largest salt production and marketing operations in the world.

Monsanto consolidated the specialty chemicals and seed markets, buying up DeKalb Genetics and cotton-seed maker Delta & Pine Land. ConAgra, marketing itself as selling at every link of the supply chain from "farm gate to dinner plate," bought International Home Foods (the producer of Chef Boyardee pasta and Gulden's mustard), Knott's Berry Farm Foods, Gilroy Foods, Hester Industries, and Signature Foods. As William Heffernan, a rural sociologist at the University of Missouri, put it in 1999, a host of formal and informal alliances such as joint ventures, partnerships, contracts, agreements, and side agreements

ended up concentrating power even further into "clusters of firms."
He identified three such clusters—Cargill/Monsanto, ConAgra, and
Novartis/ADM—as controlling the global food supply.[38]

The increase in power of these trading corporations meant that
profit would increasingly flow to middlemen, not farmers themselves.
Montana senator Conrad Burns complained his state's farmers were
"getting less for our products on the farm now than we did during
the Great Depression." The Montana state legislature passed a resolution demanding vigorous antitrust investigations into the meatpacking,
grain-handling, and food retail industries, and the state farmer's union
asked for a special unit at the Department of Justice to review proposed
agricultural mergers. There was so little interest in the Clinton antitrust
division that when Burns held a Senate Commerce Committee hearing on concentration in the agricultural sector, the assistant attorney
general for antitrust, Joel Klein, didn't bother to show up. "Their failure to be here to explain their policies to rural America," said Burns,
"speaks volumes about what their real agenda is."[39]

In the Reagan era, Walmart had already become the most important chain store in America, surpassing the importance of A&P at the
height of its power. But it was during the Clinton administration that
the company became a trading giant. First, the corporation jumped in
size, replacing the auto giant GM as the top private employer in America, growing to 825,000 employees in 1998 while planting a store in
every state. The end of antitrust enforcement in the retail space meant
that Walmart could wield its buying power to restructure swaths of industries and companies, from pickle producers to Procter & Gamble.[40]
Clinton allowed Walmart to reorder world trade itself. Even in the mid-
1990s, only a small percentage of its products were made abroad. But the
passage of NAFTA—which eliminated tariffs on Mexican imports—as
well as Clinton's embrace of Chinese imports allowed Walmart to force
its suppliers to produce where labor and environmental costs were lowest. From 1992 to 2000, America's trade deficit with China jumped
from $18 billion to $84 billion, while it went from a small trade surplus
to a $25 billion trade deficit with Mexico. And Walmart led the way.
By 2003, consulting firm Retail Forward estimated more than half of
Walmart merchandise was made abroad.[41]

Clinton administration officials were proud of Walmart, and this new generation of American trading monopolies, dubbing them part of a wondrous "New Economy" underpinned by information technology. "And if you think about what this new economy means," said Clinton deputy treasury secretary Larry Summers in 1998 at a conference for investment bankers focusing on high-tech, "whether it is AIG in insurance, McDonald's in fast-food, Walmart in retailing, Microsoft in software, Harvard University in education, CNN in television news—the leading enterprises are American."[42]

The Clinton administration also went deep into the heart of the American military establishment, undoing the work of Clifford Durr, the New Dealer who had fought to decentralize corporate power in the defense industry in order to ramp up against the Nazi threat in the late 1930s. With the end of tensions with the communist regimes and the perceived ascendance of worldwide liberal democracy, the U.S. industrial base would have to undergo a radical shift. The direction of that shift would be left to the policy choices of the new administration. In 1993, Clinton's deputy secretary of defense, William Perry, gathered CEOs of top defense contractors and told them that they would have to merge into larger entities because of reduced Cold War spending. "Consolidate or evaporate," he said at what became known in military industrial lore as "The Last Supper." Former secretary of the navy John Lehman noted that "industry leaders took the warning to heart." Defense contractors hollowed out and concentrated. Along with cutting two million jobs, the number of U.S.-based prime contractors went from sixteen to six. These prime contractors then demanded that their subcontractors merge—subcontractor mergers quadrupled from 1990 to 1998.[43]

The defense industrial base turned from focusing on engineering wonders like cruise missiles and B-2 Stealth Bombers to balance sheet engineering. Private equity as a business model had been popularized by Milken. In 1993, this financial force moved into concentrating the defense industrial base. Lehman, for instance, presided over Reagan's massive defense buildup in the 1980s as secretary of the navy. In the 1990s, he ran a private equity firm that raised money from investors to rearrange the corporate assets of defense contractors.

It was also under Clinton that the last bastion of the New Deal coalition—a congressional majority held by the Democrats since the late 1940s—fell apart as the last few holdout southern Democrats were finally driven from office or switched to the Republican Party. And it was under Clinton that the language of politics shifted from that of equity, justice, and potholes to the finance-speak of redistribution, growth and investment, and infrastructure decay.

The Democratic Party embraced not just the tactics, but the ideology of the Chicago School. As one memo from Clinton's Council of Economic Advisors put it, "Large size is not the same as monopoly power. For example, an ice cream vendor at the beach on a hot day probably has more market power than many multibillion-dollar companies in competitive industries."[44]

During the twelve years of the Reagan and Bush administrations, there were 85,064 mergers valued at $3.5 trillion. Under just seven years of Clinton, there were 166,310 deals valued at $9.8 trillion.[45] This merger wave was larger than that of the Reagan era, and larger even than any since the turn of the twentieth century when the original trusts were created.[46] Hotels, hospitals, banks, investment banks, defense contractors, technology, oil, everything was merging.

The Clinton administration organized this new concentrated American economy through regulatory appointments and through nonenforcement of antitrust laws. Sometimes it even seemed they had put antitrust enforcement itself up for sale. In 1996, Thomson Corporation bought West Publishing, creating a monopoly in digital access to court opinions and legal publishing; the owner of West had given a half a million dollars to the Democratic Party and personally lobbied Clinton to allow the deal.[47] The DOJ even approved the $81 billion Exxon and Mobil merger, restoring a chunk of the Rockefeller empire.

Clinton also appointed pro-monopoly judges. When Clinton appointed Supreme Court justices, he picked Stephen Breyer and Ruth Bader Ginsburg. Both sailed through the Senate, not because of a tradition of bipartisanship, but because neither worried powerful business interests. Both were adherents of the same basic monopoly-friendly philosophy promoted by the Chicago School. And once on the bench, in 2004, both signed one of the most pro-monopoly opinions in the

history of the court, one authored by Antonin Scalia. "The mere possession of monopoly power, and the concomitant charging of monopoly prices, is not only not unlawful," said the court, "it is an important
element of the free-market system. The opportunity to charge monopoly prices—at least for a short period—is what attracts 'business
acumen' in the first place; it induces risk taking that produces innovation and economic growth."[48]

Clinton advisor James Carville very early on in Clinton's first term
noted what was happening. "I used to think if there was reincarnation,
I wanted to come back as the president or the pope or a .400 baseball
hitter," he said. "But now I want to come back as the bond market. You
can intimidate everybody." Toward the end of Clinton's second term,
with a transcendent stock market, bars in the United States began
switching their television sets from sports scores to CNBC, to watch
the trading in real time. In the 1990s, it wouldn't be Herbert Hoover
overseeing a bubble, it would be a Democrat.

## THE RISE OF THE TECH GIANTS

Like the rest of the Clinton administration, the DOJ Antitrust Division in the 1990s talked populist, but governed with a deference
to monopoly. Clinton's first appointment to run the division was a
Washington lawyer named Anne Bingaman. Antitrust was not particularly important to the administration, and it seemed to some that
Bingaman got the job as a political favor to her husband, New Mexico senator Jeff Bingaman. "Hmph," Attorney General Janet Reno
said to *The Wall Street Journal,* "there's the White House trying to
push a Senator's wife on me."[49]

Nevertheless, when she took office, Bingaman was ready to entirely
remake the dormant division. She "fired up" the staff, and opened up
new investigations. "Anne Bingaman has a blunt message for corporate
America: The antitrust cops are back on the beat," said the *Journal.*[50]
One of Bingaman's first goals was to open up the most important
new area of the economy, the one where Reagan had allowed nascent robber barons to not only seize power over industry but over the
future of technology. She would take on the big bad monopolist of

the computer industry, Microsoft, which was frightening Silicon Valley, and increasingly, much of corporate America.

In the 1960s, Silicon Valley was a middle-class area populated by farmers and engineers. Up until the early 1980s, the personal computing industry was largely a world of hobbyists, composed of tinkerers who played with what most businessmen thought were toys. Hobbyist culture was pervasive and utopianist, a combination of both the San Francisco counterculture scene and the Cold War–era New Deal high-tech can-do spirit. One of the early forums for the personal computer, for instance, the Homebrew Computer Club, inspired the design of the Apple I. Tinkerers passed around software to each other for free, updating and improving it collectively.

New Deal enforcers had enabled this freewheeling culture. AT&T and IBM were both under constant threat by antitrust authorities, with IBM sued on the last business day of the Lyndon Johnson administration, and both companies being sued throughout the 1970s. Both developed software standards and languages, like COBOL and UNIX, widely available at little or no cost.[51] Xerox, like AT&T and IBM, had been the target of aggressive antitrust actions. The corporation, through its Xerox PARC lab, developed core aspects of personal computing like the mouse and the graphical user interface, and allowed its technologies to be commercialized by others (including some of its employees who left to start their own companies). In the early 1980s, IBM, meanwhile, stepped gingerly into personal computing, afraid of new antitrust actions. The company worked to transfer enormous programming, manufacturing, and technical skills to the nascent personal computer supply chain of independent companies, without its usual vicious disciplinary tactics. It even indirectly financed the production of PC "clones," competitors to its own PCs.

Information technology, like the railroad, the telephone, or the telegraph, is based on networks. Operating systems, software, memory chips, disk drives, videotapes—these are not just products but systems organized around common standards. The value of a piece of software is not just what you can do with the software, but whether it is compatible with other software and with various hardware platforms. When the market for personal computers exploded in the 1980s, it opened the way for a host of new software and hardware products, everything from memory to microchips to spreadsheets and word processing. The technical dynamics were similar to the digital computer market of the 1950s and 1960s, but with a much bigger market and more possibilities for entrepreneurs.

The key political economy question was whether industry standard setting would be public and open, or proprietary and monopolistic. This was not a new problem; there was a reason John D. Rockefeller named his company Standard Oil. New Dealers had forced standards to be relatively open. The fax standard, for instance, and that of TV broadcasting, were not proprietary.

The legal context of the Reagan era, however, returned business to Rockefeller's era. In 1980, Congress passed a law applying copyright restrictions to software, and in 1982, Reagan dropped the IBM antitrust suit that had pressured the company to retain its open architecture model for computing. It also broke up AT&T, creating a burst of competition in communications, but for the purpose of "deregulating" the telecommunications field.

The rest of the industry took notice. As with Rockefeller leveraging the network of railroads to monopolize the oil industry, entrepreneurs used the exploding personal computer market to seize monopoly power around key bottlenecks. Spreadsheets, word processors, and operating systems became costly software monopolies. There were rivals in these markets—Lotus 123 and Boland in spreadsheets, for instance—but competition took place through lawsuits as they battled over who would control standards, not over whose product was better.[52]

These nascent monopolies were lucrative and did extremely well under the finance-friendly Reagan political economy. Software and computer companies sold shares on the frothy stock market; by the mid-1980s there were so many millionaires in Silicon Valley that there were shortages of high-end housing.[53]

The industry consolidated quickly. The key alliance dominating the technology industry, like that between the Pennsylvania Railroad and John D. Rockefeller in the 1880s, was that of Bill Gates's Microsoft software producer and Intel microchip company. In 1980, IBM, wary of being accused of controlling the personal computer business, signed a deal with Microsoft to produce an operating system—known as DOS—for its personal computer, and standardized its PC chips on Intel. IBM then transferred enormous programming and technical know-how to both companies, and even protected Intel throughout the 1980s from Japanese competition.[54] Gates was the more powerful of the two. He had gotten his start commercializing software in the late 1970s, fighting against the sharing culture of the early personal computer hobbyists.

The operating system (OS) is the basic controlling software for a computer, setting the specifications by which other software operate. IBM allowed Gates to sell his OS to other producers of personal computers. By 1983, Microsoft controlled the industry standard on-ramp to the personal computer. Gates soon realized how powerful this intermediary position was, and he moved quickly to entrench his monopoly power by forcing computer makers to take a "per processor" license fee. Under this arrangement, computer makers paid Microsoft for every computer shipped, regardless of whether it had a Microsoft operating system. The per processor contract excluded competitors from the operating system market.

By 1987, Gates, not IBM, controlled what customers sought in a personal computer, which was not the computer itself or the IBM brand or even the operating system, but the ability to do different things with their machine, like write documents using a word processor or play games with video game software.[55] All software producers would essentially have to write software applications for Microsoft's DOS operating system.

Gates then began to leverage his monopoly position. Over the course of the 1980s, Microsoft launched software applications that competed with the most popular business applications, like Lotus 123 spreadsheets, or WordPerfect word processing. It gave its own internal teams secret information about upcoming changes to its operating system product, Windows, leveraging its monopoly in operating systems into another monopoly for business software. Programmers at Microsoft used to say, "DOS ain't done till Lotus don't run."[56] Gates was aiming for two key monopolies—operating systems and business applications—in the most important and fastest-growing product market in history, the personal computer.

In 1991, spurred by Microsoft's rivals in Silicon Valley, the Federal Trade Commission started investigating the corporation's practices. Gates was openly contemptuous of the FTC, reportedly calling one commissioner a "Communist" and telling *Business Week,* "The worst that could come of this is that I could fall down on the steps of the FTC, hit my head, and kill myself."[57] The commission could not reach an agreement about whether to move forward with a case. In 1993, with support from Republican and Democratic senators, Bingaman took over the case from the FTC.

This was the moment when the Clinton administration could have turned back the Reagan-era monopolization free-for-all. Bingaman could have sent a powerful signal to corporate America. Despite her pledge to stiffen the division's work on antitrust, there were signs that Bingaman, like Clinton, was no populist. For one thing, she studied antitrust under William Baxter. More than his student, she was also his admirer, praising his brilliance and his "monumental" legacy. She did not veer from Baxter's merger guidelines, which had helped unleash the merger boom, asserting they "appeared economically sound." Her only area of disagreement was that Reagan-era antitrust was insufficiently supportive of chain stores and consumerism. She pledged to prosecute fair trade agreements where merchants maintained a minimum price for their products.[58]

Bingaman also had little intellectual support for taking on the largest and most powerful company in the personal computing industry. While many of Microsoft's Silicon Valley competitors backed the suit, intellectuals and commentators did not. Frank Fisher, an important economist at MIT, argued that "you don't want to confuse Microsoft's success with monopoly." Rob Shapiro, an operative who worked in Al From's orbit at a New Democrat think tank, warned DOJ that it would damage America's software industry with an ill-advised suit, noting that Microsoft's high market share in operating systems was a sign not of dysfunction, but that the "market is working well." And liberal legend Alfred Kahn said the costs of inaction were worth it. Should Microsoft turn slothful, he said, "We'll just have to deal with the problem if and when it comes."[59]

In July of 1994, the DOJ settled with the company, allowing

Microsoft to retain its market position in operating systems and its ability to leverage that into new application markets. Bingaman earned a modest concession, where Microsoft stopped its per processor licensing fee structure. But by 1994, this contractual arrangement was irrelevant; Microsoft's operating system had become the industry standard. Bingaman claimed victory and lawyers at DOJ cracked open champagne to celebrate, but it was a hollow and embarrassing announcement, undercut a few days later when Bill Gates mocked her. No one will change anything they are doing at Microsoft, he said, though he would have one official deign to read the agreement. Microsoft soon dominated the market for key business tools, including databases, presentation software, and word processing, with massive monopoly profits to match. Its stock jumped from $48 to $62 in the four months after the settlement.[60]

In the months to come, Bingaman would reveal herself as an ardent Chicago School adherent, seeing little wrong with Microsoft's increasing market power. In 1995, Microsoft tried to buy Intuit, the leading personal finance software maker. The goal was to dominate the then-nascent internet. The company, as one executive said in 1997, was trying to get a "vig," a mobster's term for a share, of every transaction made on the internet. Bingaman reached a deal with Microsoft to allow the transaction to go through, but when she went before a court to have the settlement approved, she ran into Judge Stanley Sporkin, a former SEC enforcer and adamant opponent of white-collar misdeeds. Sporkin delayed the deal, and even allowed corporate opponents of the deal, led by lawyer Gary Reback, to argue against the merger in his court. Bingaman angrily demanded the judge allow Microsoft to leverage its monopoly power into control of the internet, but he would not. She soon left the DOJ, and a new chief, Joel Klein, filed suit to block the acquisition. Gates abandoned the merger attempt.

But Microsoft wasn't chastened. Gates had decided that his company would dominate the internet. A small start-up called Netscape had created something called a browser, a piece of software letting a user look at websites easily. This would be the on-ramp to the internet, much as the operating system was the on-ramp to the personal computer. Gates decided to create a competitive product, Internet Explorer, and leverage his power to destroy Netscape. The company updated its operating system, Windows 95, bundling its browser and seeking to, as one rival executive testified he heard from a Microsoft executive, "cut off Netscape's air supply." It used the same exclusionary tactics as it had to defeat other creators of applications, bullying a host of PC makers and internet service providers. Netscape soon hired Reback to see what he could do to get enforcers to pursue a case against Microsoft.

Microsoft then began its next strategic move to leverage its monopoly power, this time into swaths of the nondigital economy. Gates understood that Americans would one day do their shopping, banking, news consumption, and social interactions online, and he wanted to rule it all. Microsoft launched a travel company called Expedia, and began investing in media, including a company called Sidewalk, which was intended to dominate the lucrative classified advertising market. It brought together over a hundred venture capitalists and implied strongly they should refrain from investing in areas Microsoft intended to dominate.[61] The extent of Gates's ambition and power finally scared old-line corporate America as well as state-level officials.

In 1998, the Texas attorney general became interested in Microsoft's monopolization of the browser market; some key PC makers were located in his state. More state attorneys general followed his lead. In 1998, the Department of Justice, spurred by Reback, gathering interest from state attorneys general and angry venture capitalists, launched an antitrust suit against the company. Klein presided over the largest trial since that against AT&T. In 2000, the court ruled for the government, and put forward a plan to split up Microsoft into two companies, one that held the operating systems and the other that controlled the Microsoft software businesses that ran on top of the operating system, similar to how Congress had split railroads from other businesses. It was a cautious decision; Microsoft would still retain its monopolies, even if they were now in separate companies. But Gates appealed the decision anyway, and the most conservative circuit court in America overturned the breakup order. In 2001, the George W. Bush administration essentially dropped the remainder of the case.

The Microsoft suit had two critical impacts on the development of the American political economy. Microsoft never dominated the internet the way it had the personal computer, because it was never able to leverage its hold over the browser market to control how users interacted with third-party websites. Like IBM, which under fear of antitrust had allowed an open computer industry, Microsoft allowed an open internet. It did not block a new company dedicated to selling books called Amazon and a new company with an innovative search engine called Google from accessing customers through Internet Explorer.

But the suit also signaled an end to antimonopoly prosecutions. The Clinton administration clearly had little interest in prosecuting monopoly, and had to be embarrassed and cajoled into doing something about an obvious monopoly in a key sector of the economy. The Bush administration was even less inclined to do anything about monopoly power. While Microsoft's internal culture was reoriented away from predatory action, after this case the Department of Justice would cease bringing forward monopolization cases entirely.

In 2003, Larry Ellison, the CEO of large software maker Oracle, said he had no choice but to copy Microsoft's tactics. "We have to roll up our industry," he said. Like every industry, the business software market was going to have just one key company. "We will be that dominant player."[62]

## THE ROARING 2000S

To most Democrats, and the majority of Americans, Bill Clinton's years in power seemed to have been the most successful for any president since the 1960s. During the eight years that Clinton was president, the country grew twenty-three million jobs in the longest economic expansion in American history. Unemployment fell to a thirty-year low, with unemployment for blacks and Hispanics at the lowest point measured up until that point. There was the largest expansion of college opportunity since the GI Bill, and crime rates dropped to a twenty-six-year low. Industrial productivity jumped.

The median family income rose by $6,338 over eight years, adjusted for inflation. All income brackets had double-digit growth. The poverty rate fell to its lowest in twenty years. The budget went into surplus, and the number of families owning stock jumped by 40 per-cent.[63] Goldman Sachs called this the "best economy ever," and *Business Week* lauded a "New Age economy of technological innovation and rising productivity." When George W. Bush came into office after Clinton, the satirical website *The Onion*'s headline read, "Bush: 'Our Long National Nightmare of Peace and Prosperity Is Over.'"[64]

During his second term, Clinton took his "third way" politics global, and leaders all over the world copied his model of success. A popular television show, *The West Wing*, written with heavy influence from Clinton insiders, inspired a younger generation to embrace the ideals of the Watergate Baby generation, the closeness to business, the lack of willingness to assert public power. In the show, corporate lawyers and lobbyists were cool, heroic, sexy.

But below the surface, something was off. Toward the end of the Clinton administration, a Harvard Law professor named Elizabeth Warren, specializing in bankruptcy law, noticed something odd about this new wonderful 1990s economy. She was conducting the first mass-scale research project asking the question, Why are Americans going bankrupt? In the midst of plenty she saw that many Americans were still falling behind. It turns out that Americans, with a record high stock market and a record low unemployment rate, weren't doing well. The "trick and traps" of Wall Street were preying on their finances.

Meanwhile, in 1999, consumer groups began hearing complaints of predatory lending, specifically on mortgages, and particularly in a new segment called subprime lending. Protesters and dissidents were still on the margins, as they had been in the late 1920s. But other signs suggested that there was an awakening. Protesters shut down a World Trade Organization meeting in Seattle. These hints, however, did not add to much but a quiet dissent to the prevailing order. Even the shock of Bush winning the election in 2000, in the midst of an economy of plenty, did not disturb the prevailing neoliberal ideology of the Democrats.

By the time the George W. Bush administration took power in 2001, little remained of populism, or even memories of populism. Lawyers occasionally looked back at New Deal policies, baffled by how strange they seemed. Democrat Willard Tom called an FTC case against Xerox forcing the company to divest its patent portfolio like finding a "previously undiscovered ancient culture." It was unsettling, he argued, because apparently the FTC's remedy "seems to have done a world of good."[65]

The roll-up of power in the political economy accelerated with more high-level tax cuts, deregulation by Bush, and monopolization. In 2005, the Bush administration finally repealed the New Deal–era Public Utility Holding Company Act, clearing the way for the rise of massive new multistate electricity corporations with ever more ability to resist local regulators. The Bush White House also passed bankruptcy legislation that made it easier for banks to use derivatives but harder for normal people to get out of credit card debt. Financiers and regulators thoroughly corrupted the mortgage industry, inflating a bubble that masked underlying deterioration of American industry.

And digital technology, once channeled into the public domain by the government, was now layered on top of the Reagan revolution of political economy that Clinton had completed. New giants, as powerful, or perhaps even more powerful than those originally built by John D. Rockefeller, J. P. Morgan, and Andrew Mellon, emerged in the post-Microsoft era. Though Gates didn't get a "vig" on every piece of commerce online, the successor monopolies to Microsoft did. Amazon, Google, and Facebook followed the business model of Microsoft, leveraging their essential platforms to take power throughout swaths of the economy.

All of this seemed to represent a tremendous success, the equivalent of the endless prosperity of the Roaring Twenties. In 2004, Ben Bernanke, the conservative economist who in 2006 would be named chair of the Federal Reserve, announced that American policymakers had conquered the business cycle, and, it seemed, the world. Humans in 2004 were living in the "Great Moderation."

On April 5, 2006, Barack Obama—then a young senator hoping to be president—gave a speech at the Brookings Institution's new wing, the Hamilton Project. The Hamilton Project was financed and organized by Clinton's economic policy team, with Robert Rubin as the key leader. Obama's ideological framework was straight out of the 1970s, using rhetoric from Reich, Thurow, and From.

"The forces of globalization have changed the rules of the game," said Obama, including "how we compete with the rest of the world." The national competitiveness frame was in there, as was the globalization as inevitable framework. "For those on the left," he continued, "and I include myself in that category, too many of us have been interested in defending programs the way they were written in 1938." He called for straightforward Mellon-style policies—eliminating the budget deficit and keeping public debt low. He did not mention monopoly. The thoughtful bankers and policymakers in the audience were, he said, a "breath of fresh air."[66] It was those same people who, in the 1990s, "[took] on entrenched interests" and ushered in the prosperity of that decade. Hopefully, in two years, they could reenter the White House under a Democratic administration and do it again.

Then, in 2007, the loosening of financial rules and the merger of financial power induced a global financial crisis, centered in some of the world's most powerful financial institutions. Concentration of power in the private sector, it turned out, had its downside.

## TOO BIG TO FAIL

In retrospect, the fissures in the system had been obvious for years. Financial crises had been getting worse, from Mexico to East Asia, as "hot money" flowed across borders. The stock bubble collapsed almost as soon as Clinton turned over the White House to Bush. Starting with the recession in 2001 and continuing through the recovery, the total share of income in the entire economy going to workers—a measure that had been stable for fifty years—began declining.[67] Part of the problem was that economists had lost the ability to measure economic activity accurately. A significant amount of the "computer-driven" productivity increases measured in the American economy during the 1990s came from just one corporation: Walmart. The store's influence, as one journalist put it, had "reached levels not seen by a single company since the 19th-century."[68]

Then the real crack-up happened. On September 15, 2008, the old-line investment bank Lehman Brothers declared bankruptcy. Lehman's fall was the largest collapse in American corporate and banking history, a super-sized Penn Central, setting off a bank run that threatened every single commercial institution in the world. The art of modern politics had become so disconnected from any understanding of commerce that the president, George W. Bush, simply didn't understand what was happening. Speaking at the UN less than a week later, he downplayed financial turmoil as irrelevant.

Foreign leaders weren't fooled. Gloria Macapagal Arroyo, the president of the Philippines, discussed the terrifying global implications of the crisis. She was followed by the head of Argentina, and the president of France, both of whom pointed the finger at the intellectual consensus of unregulated financial capitalism then dominant in America (though also, as European leaders were loath to admit, dominant in Europe as well).[69]

Wall Street was too panicked to notice foreign disapproval. American International Group (AIG), the largest insurance company in the world, hovered on the brink of collapse, and if AIG fell, then so would every major bank. The unregulated markets where corporations borrowed froze up. Activity in the nonfinancial "real" economy—factories, shipping yards, housing—took a sickening slide, as millions of Americans began liquidating their savings in an unsuccessful battle to ward off foreclosures. Under pleading from Bush, Congress passed a $700 billion bailout for the treasury secretary to do with largely as he pleased.

A little less than two months after Lehman collapsed, Barack Obama won the presidency. With the firepower of the bailout, and the hope of the world, he had remarkable latitude to restructure the global political economy. The parallels with the Hoover-to-FDR handover of power were eerie. The shadow banking system, first unleashed in the early 1960s, had frozen up, similar to how the banks had collapsed in the early 1930s. George W. Bush was asking for cooperation from Obama, just as Hoover had of Roosevelt.

What path would the new president choose? For there were multiple possibilities. This crisis was centered in the most basic institution FDR had saved, the American home. Promoting homeownership had been a bedrock policy framework since at least the 1930s, a key link in the social contract between Americans and their political and financial elites, but also a mechanism to ensure social stability. Policymakers were now caught in a bind. There was now roughly $5–7 trillion of mortgages Americans could not repay, and if these mortgages were not repaid, large banks would become insolvent.[70]

In 2008, political leaders discussed a new Reconstruction Finance Corporation, mortgage write-downs. Meanwhile, academics, policy-makers, and business leaders were open to a new intellectual framework. Richard Posner, the inheritor of Robert Bork's mantle as the main organizer of the law and economics movement, published *A Failure of Capitalism,* in which he asserted that capitalism was not a self-correcting system. Alan Greenspan told a congressional oversight committee that he was in a "state of shocked disbelief" that the "self-interest of lending institutions" had not protected the integrity of finance.[71] Former General Electric CEO Jack Welch told the *Financial Times* that the shareholder value movement was the "dumbest idea in the world."[72]

But by the time Barack Obama took the oath of office, the ideas that took hold in the 1970s had been political orthodoxy for two generations. Obama had started his career in the early 1980s as a community organizer in Chicago, trying to work with poor families being ruined by the Reagan-era corporate looting and deindustrialization. Obama had been unable to do much to ameliorate the suffering, and turned to law. By the time he ran for Senate he had discovered the New Democratic movement. In his book *The Audacity of Hope,* he praised Bill Clinton's third-way framework as "pragmatic" and "non-ideological." Obama mimicked the arguments of the Democratic Leadership Council, attacking Democrats as bereft of ideas, ridiculing defenders of the New Deal and Great Society—a group that had become all but extinct—as adherents of a hokey "old-time religion."[73]

When Obama took office, most of his advisors barely knew an earlier economic tradition had existed, and those who did—like Rubin—had built their careers rejecting it. His advisors, and Democrats writ large, accepted the solidity and importance of large corporations and banks; the idea of using public power to structure markets was not only off the table, it was outrageous. He would work with a Democratic Congress led by Watergate Babies. Both his major financial reform bill and his major push for health care went through committees chaired by members of the class of 1974 (Chris Dodd, Henry Waxman,

Max Baucus, and George Miller). Barney Frank, elected a few years after the Watergate Baby class, had sat on the Committee on Party Effectiveness in the 1980s, and chaired the Financial Services Committee in the House during the crisis.

Not surprisingly, Obama's policy choices ended up pushing wealth and power upward. Under Obama's leadership, the Democratic Party continued Bush's bank bailout, but without a populist restructuring of the monetary, debt, or industrial systems that had led to the crisis. In 2008, to secure the votes Bush needed for his bailout, Obama asked congressional allies to support the $700 billion Troubled Asset Relief Program. One newly elected member, Donna Edwards, demanded that he also attach to the bailout protections for homeowners by allowing people to write off their mortgage debt in bankruptcy, which they could not now do. This would give borrowers negotiating leverage with the banks in restructuring their mortgage to something they could pay. Obama demurred but promised her that he would get it done later. She voted for the bailout. Unbeknownst to her, Obama's transition team, those who had been in the audience two years earlier, had already ruled out such changes to bankruptcy laws. The result was upward of nine million foreclosures. America's middle class lost between $5 and $7 trillion in wealth.[74]

The lack of a populist wing in the Democratic Party meant that Obama received little criticism over these choices. But when asked why he didn't address the foreclosure crisis, it became clear that Obama had chosen a remarkable ideological path for any Democratic president. He drew a comparison between his own immediate task and that of the last president to take office during a financial crash. Rather than come up with some sophisticated excuse for not following FDR's model, Obama instead embraced long-disproven Republican libels of the New Deal, and criticized FDR for not working with Herbert Hoover and causing a banking crisis. We "didn't do what Franklin Delano Roosevelt did, which was basically wait for six months until the thing had gotten so bad that it became an easier sell politically."[75]

Obama's treasury secretary, Tim Geithner, joined the attack on FDR, whom he charged with refusing to "lift a finger to help the outgoing administration relieve the suffering of the Depression."[76] Instead, he lauded the architect of concentrated financial power in America, Alexander Hamilton, calling him the "original Mr. Bailout." Bill Clinton, who mentored many of the figures in the Obama administration, got together with Geithner and mocked the "bloodlust" of Americans who wanted justice for top-tiered bankers. [77]

Like Bill Clinton, Obama ended up prioritizing the stability of a concentrated financial system over risking an attempt to end the foreclosure wave threatening the American housing market, or engaging in white-collar criminal prosecution, antitrust enforcement, or any sort of crackdown on concentrated financial power. The Democratic Party had become the party of Hamilton and Mellon. [78] To the extent there was a reformist element in the Obama administration, it was limited to creation of a new Consumer Financial Protection Bureau, which was oriented around the consumerist framework that the Watergate Babies understood.

At the height of the Great Recession, Obama's antitrust officials, who had drawn from their experience in the Clinton era and their training under the influence of Chicago and Harvard schools of law and economics, helped to engineer another merger boom, in telecoms, pharmaceuticals, airlines, event ticketing, media, and technology. Big Tech did especially well. During Obama's years in office, Google, Facebook, and Amazon acquired hundreds of companies, growing to dominance over advertising markets, retail, and information technology, and in the process pushing forward another round of defensive consolidation in the rest of corporate America.

Notionally "progressive" corporations like Google became key pillars of a cosmopolitan liberal culture. This was the world of the Watergate Babies and the corporatist thinkers who shaped their intellectual understanding of it. Toward the end of the administration, Obama even helped a popular artist, Lin-Manuel Miranda, popularize a smash-hit theater production about Alexander Hamilton, portraying the founding monopolist—and onetime slave owner—as a sexy and daring warrior for racial justice. [79]

Unchecked, the great private monopolies made the social dysfunction of the Reagan era even worse. Americans became more obese, pumped full of sugary industrially processed foods by a small number of corporate giants. Independent black businesses collapsed; black-owned banks were a tenth as likely to get bailout money as other banks. A gruesome heroin epidemic spread in rural areas, spurred by hopelessness and corruption among pharmaceutical monopolies. Toward the end of Obama's second term, the life span of white men and women without a college education began dropping as suicide, alcoholism, and drug addiction caused a die-off, what policymakers began calling "deaths of despair." This epidemic approached, and then exceeded, the height of the death toll of the AIDS crisis.[80]

Meanwhile, the gilded elites who controlled the Democratic Party mused about theories projecting the natural inevitable unspooling of history, like the idea that "superstar cities" just innately attracted talented engineers, versus rural backwaters that would naturally lose out due to ignorant bigotry. The administration and bipartisan leaders in Congress continued to support the by-now-old framework, including working on behalf of corporatist trade deals and progressive tech monopolists.

In an era in which the Democratic Party was perhaps the strongest support pillar for the new Mellonism, the American people had nowhere to turn but the street. Republicans were the first to rebel, as self-described Tea Partiers—backed by billionaires—attacked the Bush-Obama bailout of the banks. Then came social movements on the left—Occupy Wall Street in 2011, and Black Lives Matter in 2013. At the ballot box, Americans voted for change in 2006, 2008, 2010, 2014, and 2016, veering from party to party in a desperate search for someone to address their fears and anxieties. This rebellion of protest and at the ballot box was inchoate, and did not point the finger at the real ideological culprit, which was the hold monopolies had over American business, politics, culture, even the family.

When Donald Trump ran for office, his platform of "America First" and his slogan, "Make America Great Again," with its undertones of soft authoritarianism, seemed at first a joke to the gilded elites. But the Democratic Party had been gradually weakened during the Obama administration, with more than a thousand elected officials at every level but that of the presidency falling to conservative Republicans. Then in June 2016, Great Britain voted to leave the great postwar project of the European Union, revealing deep populist anger at the status quo worldwide. And in January 2017, it was Trump who took the oath of office over the heavily favored Hillary Clinton.

The Democratic Party, and American democracy, would have to be built anew.

# CONCLUSION

"A nation's greatness can be measured by the happiness and prosperity of the people who produce the nation's wealth."

**—Wright Patman**[1]

■ ■ ■ ■ ■ ■ ■ ■ ■ ■ ■ ■ ■

Wright Patman was an optimist, but the rise of soft authoritarianism globally would not have surprised him. Dictatorship in politics is consistent with how the commercial sphere has developed since the 1970s. Americans are at the mercy of distant forces, our livelihoods dependent on the arbitrary whims of power. Patman once attacked chain stores as un-American, saying, "We, the American people, want no part of monopolistic dictatorship in . . . American business."[2] Having yielded to monopolies in business, we must now face the threat to democracy Patman warned they would sow.

The plutocratic winds blowing across the global landscape were formed from Michael Milken–staked takeover barons and their descendants, as well as Sam Walton's Walmart, a deregulated transportation and telecommunications world, and an endless merger wave. We have concentrated markets in everything from airlines to coffins to candy to hospitals.[3]

But we also face a challenge even more significant than the consequences of a four-decade-long Reagan revolution, because layered on top of the political revolution wrought by the Chicago law and economics school and their left-wing allies is a technological revolution that has enabled a far more dangerous concentration of power. While Bill Gates never got his "vig" over every commercial transaction, the next generation of monopolists is closer than ever to doing so. The pace-setting political institutions in our culture are tech platforms, in particular Amazon, Google, and Facebook. These companies are information monopolies, manipulating the free flow of information, and our ability as citizens to think and come together to do politics.

Tech platforms are rewiring our culture. As Senator Richard Burr lectured tech executives in 2018, "The information your platforms disseminate changes minds, hardens opinions, helps people make sense of the world." Or, as a reporter tweeted, "My friend's toddler babbled 'don't forget to subscribe' as he was put to bed. The kid watches so much YouTube he thought it means 'good bye.'"[4] This is not just a domestic problem; earlier in 2018 Sri Lanka banned Facebook because the company was unable to prevent the use of its platform to foment ethnic hate crimes.[5] Journalism and politics are centralizing all over the world, on top of centralized intermediaries of our information, commerce, and advertising revenue.

Google and Facebook, in 2018, took roughly 60 percent of all online ad revenue in America, and online ad revenue is the largest and fastest-growing source of advertising money. Google has about 90 percent of the search ad market, can track users across 80 percent of websites, and its ad subsidiary AdMob has 83 percent of the market for Android apps and 78 percent of iOS apps. Facebook has 77 percent of mobile social networking trafficking, and roughly two thirds of Americans get news on social media.[6]

As *Wired* magazine editors Nick Thompson and Fred Vogelstein put it, "Every publisher knows that, at best, they are sharecroppers on Facebook's massive industrial farm. . . . And journalists know that the man who owns the farm has the leverage. If Facebook wanted to, it could quietly turn any number of dials that would harm a publisher— by manipulating its traffic, its ad network, or its readers."[7]

Roughly 1,800 local newspapers in America have disappeared since 2004, and over 2,000 of the 3,143 counties in America now have no daily newspaper.[8] Pittsburgh has become the first midsized regional city without a daily newspaper. Specialty newspapers are dying as well; from 1999 to 2009 the number of black newspapers was cut in half.[9] From 2005 to 2015, roughly 26 percent of newspaper journalists— including digital outlets—were laid off. There have also been massive

declines in the workforce of related industries, like radio, book publishing, magazines, and music.

In other words, America is increasingly a news desert. This may
not be obvious from the surfeit of seeming outlets for information, the
endless number of websites, cable channels, and the stream of information coming from social media. But the reality is the increasing number of seeming options for information masks a smaller and smaller
amount of original reported news. As journalist and media researcher
Tom Rosenstiel put it in 2009, "A good deal of what is carried on
radio, television, cable, wire services begins in newspaper newsrooms."
Today, most of what we read on Twitter or Facebook originates there
as well.

Meanwhile Amazon captures nearly one of every two dollars
Americans spend online, and it is the leading seller of books, toys,
apparel, and consumer electronics in the nation. Its cloud computing subsidiary has over one million enterprise customers, it is a major
movie producer and defense contractor, and it has 100 million U.S.
customers that are members of its Prime bundling service. It is the
number one threat to independent retailers.[10]

Book publishing and distribution, media financed by advertising,
and social media are how we communicate ideas with one another,
and all three channels for information are increasingly in the hands of
a monopolist.

## THE RISE OF AMAZON

Amazon, like Google and Facebook, exists because of the legal shift
enabling and promoting bigness in structure and monopoly in business
strategy. But while new, these companies are, like the railroads or Standard Oil, network industries very much like their antecedents.

In 1994, Jeff Bezos, working at a hedge fund, conceived of the
idea of building an "Everything Store" that would serve as the monopoly intermediary for commerce. He started by selling books, but
his plan was to expand into every possible item. As Bezos's hedge fund
boss, who helped conceptualize the notion, put it in 1999, "The idea
was always that someone would be allowed to make a profit as an

intermediary. The key question is: Who will get to be that middle-man?"[11] Amazon was born to be a monopolist. Bezos, like John D. Rockefeller, sought every competitive advantage. He noticed a 1992 Supreme Court decision allowing mail order companies to avoid sales tax, and used it to create a pricing advantage against his competitors.[12]

Bezos drew inspiration from Sam Walton, hiring hordes of Walmart executives to build out his retailing and logistics infrastructure. Venture capitalists also pushed Bezos toward monopoly. After the first major investment by Kleiner Perkins, an important investment firm, the company's internal slogan became "Get Big Fast." The end of Robinson-Patman enforcement meant Amazon could use bulk discounts to monopolize product markets. Bezos also used predatory pricing either to drive his competitors out of business or acquire them, in one case on track to losing $100 million in three months selling diapers below cost to force a company called Diapers.com to sell to him, in an acquisition approved by the toothless Federal Trade Commission.

In the late 1990s, Bezos began repurposing his logistics capacity to sell DVDs, music, and toys, and opened its storefront to third-party merchants, turning the retail business into a "platform" where multiple buyers and sellers come together to interact. Amazon also competes on this platform, so the corporation has unparalleled surveillance into its competitors' business. Railroads in 1908 had been prohibited from this kind of vertical integration; so had A&P in 1949. But Amazon exploded in a legal environment crafted by Bork, where vertical integration was a signal not of monopolization but efficiency.

Today, Amazon is an infrastructure and data conglomerate that is well on its way to becoming the intermediary for all commerce. It is a gatekeeper to online buying, with roughly half of all online retail coming through Amazon. This means that Amazon can impose conditions on any merchant that seeks to sell online, and it does so with abandon. To sell in a prominent place on the site known as the "Buy Box," merchants and manufacturers are encouraged to use Amazon's fulfillment and logistics services and its advertising services. Amazon also creates private-label versions of the hot-selling products on its platform, using its surveillance monopoly power.[13]

The corporation sells hundreds of millions of products, both directly and by managing its "marketplace." It owns a delivery and logistics network to serve its own retailing operation and those of its third-party merchants, including a growing shipping fleet. It has retail stores and owns the Whole Foods supermarket chain, and is the largest book retailer in the world and one of the largest publishers in America.[14]

The corporation's business strategy is to emulate its takeover of the online retail business, where it first established a powerful market position using aggressive pricing strategies and then vertically integrated into new business lines by opening up its system to third-party merchants. Bezos has built or bought a series of similar platforms that Amazon both controls and on which Amazon competes.

Amazon manufactures Kindle e-readers, Fire tablets, and controls the Alexa voice-assistant platform. It runs the dominant cloud computing business, which hosts the websites and services of millions of businesses (as well as the CIA and much of the U.S. government), a sort of operating system for the web. It is also one of the largest producers of television and film, electronics, fashion, and advertising services, as well as a credit lender to small businesses. Its advertising business and cloud computing businesses are by themselves separately worth hundreds of billions of dollars apiece.[15]

There is no perfect analogy to Amazon, but it is a mixture of Standard Oil, the A&P chain store, the Microsoft software monopoly, and the Mellon system of interlinked businesses. Bezos came from the hedge fund world, learned from Walmart and Microsoft, and took advantage of the legal framework structured by Director, Bork, and the law and economics movement.

## A GOD'S-EYE VIEW: THE RISE OF GOOGLE AND FACEBOOK

Bezos was also one of the original investors in the dominant information intermediary formed in 1998, Google. As Google cofounder Larry Page put it, "Jeff was very helpful in some of those early meetings."[16]

The company originated as a computer science project by Page and his academic partner, Sergey Brin, to map the internet more effectively than had been done until that point. Brin and Page realized that existing search engines were riven by a structural conflict of interest, because they were advertising-supported. They would thus manipulate their search results in service to their advertising business. They decided to start a company using their academic research.

Google was, like the "Everything Store," monopolistic from inception, with a goal of "organizing the world's information." Its business model emerged as a result of this libertarian legal environment, fused with progressive cultural tolerance and a key antitrust suit. While the corporation was started by two computer scientists, Larry Page and Sergey Brin, it was Eric Schmidt, an executive at Microsoft-opponent Novell, who built the monopolistic business model. He recruited to Google Sheryl Sandberg, a Clinton Treasury official who would later help organize Facebook. Schmidt, Page, and Brin soon turned Google toward an advertising-supported model, despite earlier misgivings about the basic conflict of interest such a model would inherently incur.

The regulatory framework for what would become Google's business, online advertising, emerged in the mid-1990s, after the Bork revolution was complete. In the 1990s, the FTC explored how to update its mission in the context of the rise of the internet. The Federal Trade Commission's 1996 report on consumer protection policy in the "new, high-tech global marketplace" framed the job of the commission as fostering self-regulation of industry. While the FTC staff report noted the possibility of "online entry barriers through search engines designed to push competitors out of the way," it also quoted an expert hailing interactive media as "the first intelligent media on the consumer side."[17] The recommendations largely confined the FTC to encouraging self-regulation and policing consumer fraud.

At the same time, the antitrust suit against Microsoft by the state attorneys general and the Department of Justice set the stage for the innovative environment in which the search giant would emerge. After the suit, Microsoft executives began sharing software plans proactively with competitors, and decided against an early plan to use its control over the now-dominant Internet Explorer browser to crush new entrants to the internet economy, including Google.[18] In the late

1990s, entrepreneurs rushed into the online advertising and internet space, propelled by the internet boom and no longer afraid of being squashed by Microsoft.

Over the course of the 2000s, Google grew into a significant advertising-fueled search engine, and eventually a data conglomerate. It bought companies to build out its advertising business in 2002–2003, software companies that would become Google Maps in 2004 and internet video monopoly portal YouTube in 2006. Google had the ability to advertise effectively because it knew what its users were thinking. As users did searches, Google accumulated a vast store of knowledge about the thoughts and questions of hundreds of millions of people. It became, as influential writer John Battelle put it, a "database of intentions." In 2007, encouraged by industry lobby groups, the FTC offered principles for self-regulation in the behavioral advertising market, largely oriented around the industry regulating itself voluntarily.[19]

The legal environment was favorable to monopoly and did not have significant public rules structuring advertising markets, which meant that there was a scramble for dominance. What followed was, similar to the creation of U.S. Steel in 1901 from the thousands of independent iron and steel companies, a merger wave. AOL, Yahoo!, Microsoft, Verizon, WPP, and Oracle all became major buyers of behavioral targeting analytics companies, ad exchanges, publishers, and ad networks. But Google led the pack. From 2004 to 2014, Google spent at least $23 billion buying 145 companies.[20]

The most important acquisition was when, in 2007, the FTC permitted Google to purchase its rival in the online advertising space, DoubleClick.[21] DoubleClick was becoming a key railroad-like marketplace for internet advertising, a facilitator for newspapers and publishers to sell their advertising online and for ad buyers to buy advertising online. Google, in buying DoubleClick, combined its "database of intentions" with a vast trove of knowledge on how advertising campaigns and user behavior worked across third-party websites. The merger allowed Google to leverage its dominance in search advertising to third-party display advertising in which DoubleClick specialized.

It was a controversial decision. As FTC Commissioner Pamela

Jones Harbour wrote, "I dissent because I make alternate predictions about where this market is heading, and the transformative role the combined Google/DoubleClick will play if the proposed acquisition is consummated."[22]

While multiple players were vying for online advertising supremacy, it was largely Google, and Facebook, that won. In 2004, Facebook emerged as a nascent competitor to Google in a new set of online markets: social media, or the sharing of social information. Facebook piggybacked on this libertarian legal framework and purchased over seventy companies to attain monopoly power over social media advertising. Its key acquisitions were Instagram in 2012 and WhatsApp in 2014. While each company has its own complex dynamics, Facebook and Google are both essential infrastructures for the digital economy, with little public accountability.

Today, Google has eight products with more than a billion users apiece.[23] It knows what you think through its much larger "database of intentions." It knows where you go in the physical world through its two billion constantly roaming Android phones and its mobile ad app and Google Maps subsidiaries. It knows where you go online through its tracking businesses, and it has information about business ad campaigns through its advertising technology subsidiaries. This provides Google with a God's-eye view of behavior. Married to this surveillance power is the ability to organize the distribution of information through YouTube, Google Maps, Google search, email, and its own popular browser. As Schmidt put it, "We know where you are. We know where you've been. We can more or less know what you're thinking about."

Google, Amazon, and Facebook are conglomerates who monopolize ad markets, and have done so through a range of tactics and mergers that were until very recently illegal. And in doing so, they have become governing powers. Mark Zuckerberg, the CEO of Facebook, put it this way. "In a lot of ways," he said, "Facebook is more like a government than a traditional company. We have this large community of people, and more than other technology companies we're really setting policies."[24]

While there are analogies, this concentration of power over the sinews of information is new. In 1831, Alexis de Tocqueville visited America and was astonished at the number and diversity of newspapers, later writing, "There is scarcely a hamlet which has not its own newspaper." He contrasted that to the centralized newspaper systems in Europe, which were designed to insulate kings from public criticism. In America, there were so many newspapers that wealthy and famous people could not use the power of dominating information channels to, as he put it, "excite the passions of the multitude to their own advantage."[25] Americans rebelled against the British, in part, because of taxes the British levied on newsprint, which was the mechanism for organizing speech.

Today, with Google, Amazon, Facebook, we find ourselves in America, and globally, with perhaps the most radical centralization of the power of global communications that has ever existed in history. One company controls roughly 90 percent of what we search for. And they also know what we think, because we tell them, through our searches. Another company controls our book market, and a third controls how we interact with our social worlds. Meanwhile, the free press is dying.

## TOWARD A NEW DEMOCRACY

In 1912, Americans understood that they were in the midst of a crisis, similar to those they had faced prior to the Civil War and during the revolutionary era. Theirs was a crisis of concentration of power, and they faced the decision of moving toward autocracy or democracy, a free society or a slave society. Today we face a similar moment of reckoning. There are different technical, social, and physical characteristics, but we can recapture the ability that our forebears had to demand democracy in the political and the commercial sectors.

The Watergate Babies rejected the lessons of Patman's generation for many reasons, conflating economic populism with an antiquated vision of the economy. But there was wisdom in Patman's lessons. In the 1930s, he said that restricting chain stores would prevent "Hitler's methods of government and business in Europe" from coming to the United States. For decades after World War II, preventing economic concentration was understood as a bulwark against tyranny. From the 1970s until the financial crisis, this rhetoric seemed ridiculous. No longer. Financial crises occur regularly now, and prices for essential goods and services reflect monopoly power rather than free citizens buying and selling to each other. People worldwide, sullen and un-moored from community structures, are turning to rage, apathy, pro-test, and angry tribalism.

The reason for this dissatisfaction, the anxiety, is clear. The institu-tions that touch our lives are unreachable. We organize our social net-works through Facebook, our information through Google, our health care from complex bureaucracies, our seeds and chemicals through seed monopolists. We sell our grain through Cargill and watch movies, buy groceries, books, and clothing through Amazon. Open markets are gone, replaced by a handful of corporate giants. We are increasingly addicted to opioids, sugary processed foods, and alcohol. We have no faith in what was once the most democratically responsive part of gov-ernment, Congress. We cannot begin to address perhaps the most im-portant existential challenge humanity has ever faced, climate change. Steeped in centralized power and mistrust, people all over the world face demagogues selling blame and hatred.

But even more profound than the anxiety is the confusion. Our policymakers, until recently, saw giants like Google, Amazon, and Goldman Sachs as exemplars of the American spirit, instead of the dangerous re-creation of trading corporations seeking to control and enslave us—like the East India Company—against which we rebelled. They confused charity for justice, meekly asking our munificent plu-tocrats to raise our wages or donate their ill-gotten gains to charitable foundations plastered with their names. We have asked for new laws to offer welfare to the poor, instead of seeing poverty itself as a lack of freedom, as a denial of the basic rights of citizenship. This is not democracy. This is servitude.

And yet, paired with this profound discouragement and confusion is a moment of tremendous opportunity. While today our monop-olists use our scientific genius to encourage us to click on ads, the technology of our age is unimaginably powerful. Each of us carries a supercomputer disguised as a phone in our pocket, connected through satellites and wireless towers to the most extensive information network in human history. This grid can become a tool of liberation, or it can become the most sophisticated set of leashes ever invented. Across our commerce, our industries can be remade, and remade in remarkably innovative ways, if we would but move aside the entrenched status quo of monopolists and unleash the talents and genius of a free people upon them.

For forty-seven years in Congress, Patman got up early every morning to make sure that the "plain people," as he put it, could live a secure middle-class life, not just in material comforts, but as an independent self-governing people. He drew upon a founding tradition, which was that the basis of a democratic social order was not just the right to vote, but the wide dispersal of private property among citizens.

Under this Enlightenment idea, property did not just mean the ability to dominate or use a parcel of land or a piece of capital, but also the responsibility to take care of it. The ability to use property and one's labor to produce wealth created political independence. A citizen who could grow food and make money with a farm or store was not dependent on any social better or aristocrat for her livelihood. Carefully and publicly regulated markets that protected the rights of buyers and sellers were the forums by which citizens formed communities, freely trading goods, services, crops, information, their own labor, and ideas. Citizens as individuals had the ability to say no, and because they had that power, they had the ability to come together as a society.

The coming together to protect our property and liberty—from monopolists, financiers, or foreign powers—by a government we controlled was the American experiment. This Enlightenment ideal has been continually updated to take advantage of modern technology and new political and social contexts. After World War II, we exported this model globally, so that it became the basis for seventy-five years of prosperity and peace in Europe, and so that we would not have another world war. The American experiment, born in the Enlightenment, was, and is still, based on a radical philosophy of self-government. It is still who we are. We are coded for peaceful rebellion. We are born to fight against power. As a people, we expect our government to uphold justice. And we are angry, and sullen, when it does not.

We have challenges Patman did not face. There was no worldwide threat of climate change. And Patman did not have to face a society so alienated from itself as we are today. It was not outlandish in the 1930s to imagine restructuring corporate America, as corporate America was relatively new. Family farms existed, and corporations, while enormous, had not stretched across the globe in dangerous fragile webs of production, as they have today.

Still, we have one remarkable cultural advantage. Patman grew up in an era when citizenship meant being a straight white male. Being gay, or black, or female, or falling in love with someone from another race, or refusing to conform to any number of social norms, meant being excluded from social rights and becoming a political target. Patman was not a racist. He faced down the Ku Klux Klan in the 1920s, he ensured broad economic rights regardless of race, and he helped put the first black man on the Federal Reserve board in the 1960s. But he did not make racial equality a core mission of his life, and he voted for segregation in the 1950s and 1960s because he would have lost his seat in Congress had he not, even as he faced candidates claiming he was insufficiently committed to white supremacy.[26]

Patman had to make a cynical, ugly choice because most white Americans of his era would not tolerate racial or gender equality. Today, because of sacrifices going back generations, this is a choice we no longer have to make. We can form a multiracial democracy based on equality. We have not done so, but it is within our ability.

There are other reasons for hope today. The financial crisis induced new ways of thinking. In 2008, Elizabeth Warren was appointed by Senate majority leader Harry Reid for a job chairing an oversight board on the bank bailouts. She was from Oklahoma, one of the key centers of populism, and she grew up on the teetering edge of the middle class. In 2009, as chair of the Congressional Oversight Panel, she helped organize the first broad attack on financial power in decades, exposing bad behavior of banks and systemic criminal practices during the foreclosure crisis. Vermont senator Bernie Sanders then ran a campaign in 2016 based on opposition to Too Big to Fail banks, a phrase that came to culturally resonate and in doing so channeled popular American frustration with corporate gigantism. The antimonopoly movement is rising everywhere. The Democratic Party platform had an antimonopoly plank in 2016 for the first time since 1988, and most major Democratic Party figures are expressing concern over the power large technology companies have. So are important Republicans, such as Senator Josh Hawley of Missouri and Congressman Doug Collins of Georgia. The Department of Justice and the Federal Trade Commission are arising from their decades-long slumber, and Representative Emanuel Celler's old stomping grounds, the Judiciary Committee, announced an investigation of big tech in June of 2019. In Europe, Australia, Japan, Israel, and India, antitrust enforcers are bringing suits and investigations. All of this is being spurred by a rising popular frustration with corporate concentration. The people are waking up.

The vision put forward by Warren and Sanders of a financial system under control by democratic institutions is fundamentally organized by the New Deal framework and its populist legacy. Even Donald Trump is a throwback, looking like a faint echo of the Mussolini that New Dealers feared. The rise of corporatism, and the backlash, has sparked a search for ideas and a new generation of leaders. In the 2018 midterm elections, a wave of young post-financial-crisis politicians took office. They may not know exactly what they want, but they are eager to find a new tradition, and merge what made sense about the Watergate Baby frame with a new populist understanding of power.

There is also now a new intellectual community. In the latter part of the Clinton administration, a business journalist named Barry Lynn began studying the problem of monopolization in the supply chains that moved goods from East Asia to the United States. In 2010, Lynn published *Cornered,* a book that inspired a new antimonopoly movement that draws its inspiration from what has come before.

Since then, a group of antimonopoly historians, economists, law professors, business leaders, politicians, policymakers, and writers has emerged, rediscovering our traditions and updating them for the age in which we live today. The book you are reading is a product of that community. It is intended both as a history but also as an invitation to join us.

In 2017 at, ironically, the Stigler Center at the University of

Chicago, the first meeting of the intellectual core of this movement came together to examine the question, "Is there a concentration problem in America?" This new group of antimonopolists debated, for three days, with the Watergate Baby generation experts, who by now had become the old guard. And for the first time, the technocratic children of Bork, Areeda, and Turner had to debate the wisdom of Brandeis.

Join us. Make this your tradition, wherever you live and whatever you do. Because it is your tradition, it is your birthright, as an American, or just as someone who believes that free individuals can come together and govern themselves. If you are dissatisfied, if you seek a better world, you are not alone.

I'm not going to lie. We are in a bad spot. It isn't just that we have to contend with plutocrats. It's that we have divorced property ownership from caretaking itself. Our industrial supply chains are fragile, concentrated and full of dangerous and hidden risks. The Chinese Communist Party, with its highly sophisticated and vast industrial power, has integrated surveillance into a nascent totalitarian model, with not only concentration camps full of ethnic minorities but immense leverage over Western corporations. Democracies are falling globally, in part because people understand that the formal mechanisms of voting do not matter when decisions about political economy are reserved to a coddled elite. But we can fight back.

What that means is not just protest, or elections. It means learning. Whoever you are, whatever interest you have, you have the ability to do that. There are tens of thousands of markets, local, national, international, and a democracy requires people to think and learn about the policies underpinning each one of them.

Use your identity. Every subgroup—whether white, black, gay, straight, immigrant, male, female, genderqueer—interacts with market structures that can discriminate, integrate, liberate, or not. If you are experienced in an area, you see with experienced eyes, and can guide policymakers into building a more just way to do commerce. If you are building a business, think about the right way to do commerce, and make that your politics. If you are young, take your interest, whatever it is—law, politics, sports, history, business, engineering, farming, art—and learn not just about the technical specifics of the field, but about the moral choices you can make in that field. If you want to enter politics, think about the glorious life you could have if you emulate Patman, a man who loved his constituents, and fought for the plain people and against monopolists, or any of the staffers, regulators, business leaders, or lawyers who were his allies. Our monopoly problem is a massive one, but it can be solved by breaking it down into person-sized chunks.

Fighting back also means not falling into the trap of elitism. The weakness of the technocrat is "imposter syndrome," a feeling that he or she doesn't belong in a position of power, that his or her expertise is a pretense. This insecurity is what Aaron Director identified as his key to power. "Beautiful smugness" is how John Kenneth Galbraith and Richard Hofstadter persuaded a generation to give up their liberties. These men, Director in particular, understood that powerful liberal lawyers, well-respected and arrogant, were susceptible to mockery by their colleagues. Director made fun of lawyers who subscribed to common sense, creating a social context where an embrace of complex-seeming models by credentialed experts who were working for oligarchs overrode respect for justice, democracy, or basic human decency. In doing this, Director reoriented the elitist liberal brain, rewiring it for plutocracy without liberals even knowing.

The only immunization against this is a democratic form of populism. I do not mean the toxic fake version of populism, demagogues and frauds blaming ethnic groups. I mean old-school populism, the belief that citizens, educated and responsible, know what is best for themselves. And united they come together in a system of democracy and use the law to protect and develop themselves.

This populism does not disdain expertise, but embraces it. But expertise must serve the people; it must not be oriented to confuse them, to erect a new aristocracy. And that means you must never be afraid to say "I don't know," and you must do your best to remember that men in suits with impressive credentials can and often do lie, cheat, and steal. It's true that humanity has a remarkable amount of accumulated knowledge, but as individuals, we're all making it up as we go along.

To do the work of being a citizen, each of us has to work hard, learn, build up a working body of knowledge.

We have created and re-created our republic many times in our history. We did it in 1776 when we declared independence, not just from a king but from the idea of aristocracy itself. We did it in freeing ourselves from the Slave Power, and again in 1912 and during the New Deal and World War II, when we liberated ourselves from industrial barons and fascists. Today, we must choose whether we have the courage, wisdom, and discipline to govern ourselves, both as individuals, as communities, and as a nation. That is our choice, as a people.

Nothing about monopolization is inevitable. Our increasingly dystopian and corrupt corporate apparatus was brought to us by people selling a fantasy of inevitability. Some of them sold us a right-wing fantasy of corporate monopolies and bigness as a sign of progress. Some of them sold us a left-wing fantasy of corporate monopolies as an unstoppable feature of capitalism. But these fantasies are, in the end, the same. They both are designed to sell you on the idea that you have no power, that you are nothing but a consumer.

And that is not true. It has never been true. America has always been a nation of tradespeople. We embed social justice in our banks, our corporations, our markets, in how we exchange goods, services, crops, ideas, and labor with one another. Each of us is a worker, a businessperson, a consumer, and a citizen. The real question is not whether commerce is good or bad. It is how we are to do commerce, to serve concentrated power or to free ourselves from concentrated power.

This is the choice that has always confronted the American people, liberty for all or a small aristocracy governing our commerce and ourselves. To choose wisely, we must unlearn much of the history we have been taught. Many of us learned a version of our history as one of inevitable progress, goodness, and triumph. Many of us learned the inverted version, that our history is one of inevitable sin, racism, conquest, greed. Neither of these is true, because both versions airbrush out our own free will. The truth is, America is a battle, a struggle for justice. And we choose, every generation, who wins.

# ACKNOWLEDGMENTS

I really enjoyed writing this book, though it's easy to say that now, since it's done. There are a lot of people to thank, but I'll first explain where this book really came from.

My parents used to drag me to art and history museums when I was young, telling me that one day I'd appreciate it. I never liked most of the museums with classical art, but eventually I got interested in the ones that had to do with history. My mom would tell me that learning a piece of history is like getting a piece of a puzzle or a quilt, the more you learn the more you'll start to see bigger patterns. She inspired me with a deep love of the past, and a sense of wonder at always discovering more. In those same museums, meanwhile, my dad made jokes about toilet paper. My dad showed me . . . history can be fun? Whatever.

Starting in 2002, I accidentally got into politics as a profession. I was at an accounting software company, and I got to arguing with people on internet message boards about the war in Iraq. Eventually I realized that what I was doing was a form of online political organizing, and online political organizing was more interesting to me than accounting (though don't sleep on accounting; it is actually fascinating, I just didn't know it at the time). In 2003, I left my job and bounced around political campaigns, congressional offices, media outlets, and think tanks, learning from the people around me about why the world is structured as it is. I got into housing policy and banking, and then monopoly power. I picked up different pieces of what looked to me like a puzzle, and I started to see larger patterns, exactly like my mother told me I would.

This book is my attempt to pay back those who taught me what I know. Now, all the things authors say about the process of writing a book are true. It's painful, draining, and confidence-sapping. It's also . . . joyful to work out thoughts and research in a coherent way. And it's impossible to do it without a community around you, because a book is inherently part of a larger conversation with others. This section of the book is all about thanking some of the people who helped.

My wife, Sophia Lin, did two equally important things. First, she helped make this book understandable. Sophia is brilliant, but more important, she's *organized*. In the spring of 2018, faced with a mess of pages with a lot of scribbles about monopoly power in the twentieth century, she was willing to use her vacation and spare time to help me turn them into something that was coherent. I am in awe of her ability to tease out the compelling argument from words put in semi-random order. Sophia also helped support me emotionally as I went through the painful process of wrestling to get the stuff in my head onto paper. I often wondered whether I could ever finish, had various crises of confidence, did large amounts of whining, and had many dinner table conversations about random parts of history to which Sophia patiently, or in some cases not so patiently, listened.

There are a bunch of other people who played critical roles in this project. Two stand out in terms of helping me shape the ideas in this book. Jane D'Arista taught me how to think about banking during the financial crisis. In doing so, and in our many conversations, she helped me understand the legacy of Wright Patman and a whole other tradition of politics. Barry Lynn taught me about monopoly power, political economy, and political philosophy, and helped rearrange my mind. Before Barry got ahold of me, I never understood why ideas mattered, and didn't grasp the details of power. Barry helped me conceptualize some of the key aspects of the book, and spent copious amounts of time on the manuscript, making the arguments and stories cleaner and more interesting. Barry supported me, encouraged me, and changed the way I see the world. Jane and Barry are both writers, and I encourage you to read their work.

I wrote this book while a fellow at a think tank called the Open Markets Institute. Think tanks are places where people studying policy can talk to one another and learn, and from that intellectual community can come ideas about how to restructure the levers of power for a more just world. That's the theory of think tanks, anyway. In the middle of the writing of this book, OMI split off from a larger think tank in a somewhat high-profile scandal involving the use of corporate money to censor views critical of powerful interests. This split was an experience that reinforced what I was learning in the archives about power. In the split, and in guiding Open Markets, a few people played key roles. Sarah Miller had a keen sense of strategy and focus, and along with Barry, made my work possible. Thanks also to Eddie Vale, Kat Dill, Kevin Carty, Leah Douglass, Brian Feldman, Matt Buck, Stella Roque, and Jess Wertheim. OMI researcher Claire Kelloway helped me understand the politics of agriculture and the Homestead Act, and OMI legal director Sandeep Vaheesan helped me better understand the history of the courts and antitrust law. And Phil Longman taught me about trains, health care, and the 1980s, read chapters, and gave me feedback throughout. Phil is the best editor I have ever worked with.

My first agent, Will Lippincott, gave me the confidence to try and write this book. My current agent, Farley Chase, helped me through the process to complete it in every way he could. My editor, Ben Loehnen, took a manuscript that was a somewhat coherent set of stories and made sure it made sense to people that don't spend all their time thinking about monopoly power. All three were consummate professionals and deeply supportive, which gave me the confidence to be bold. Jonathan Karp, Caitlyn Reuss, and the whole Simon & Schuster team were wonderful partners, and the production department was patient and careful. And to Farah Amjad and Lauren Gurley, I am immensely grateful for your detailed fact-checking work. Any errors in this book are of course all mine.

Scholars Richard John, Gerald Berk, Adam Tooze, William Hogeland, and Eric Rauschway read chapters and helped me understand the broader historical and economic trends involved in these debates, in the process sharing their breathtaking knowledge and expertise. Tooze invited me to a wonderful seminar at Columbia University where I was able to discuss some of the early chapters with a variety of scholars. Lina Khan, Rohit Chopra, Andy Green, Guy Rolnick, and Teddy Downey read parts of the manuscript and gave me essential feedback. Lina, you give me hope. Rohit and Andy, you inspire me that governing is possible. And Teddy, I've never met anyone who hates corruption and is as relentlessly optimistic about life.

Paul Glastris helped me with access to the *Washington Monthly* archives and gave me useful historical perspective on the role of the magazine. Jamie Galbraith, Michael Lind, Bob Borosage, Luigi Zingales, Lori Wallach, Beth Baltzan, Alan Riley, Richard Parker and Dean Baker were generous with their time and insights on questions of political economy. I relied on the fine work of David Dayen, Zach Carter, and Ryan Grim, and also benefited from many conversations in which they helped me refine my ideas and thinking about politics. Jen Howard taught me the power of the press, and Zephyr Teachout taught me to understand that we have wrestled with corruption in sophisticated ways for hundreds of years. Many people did essential work critical to this project, whether they know it or not. I want to single out Chris Leonard, Laura Philip Sawyer, Jonathan Tepper, Tim Wu, Bert Foer, Frank Foer, Susan Webber, Joe Nocera, Jesse Eisinger, Sven Beckert, Saule Omarova, Greta Krippner, Robert Van Horn, Neil Barofsky, Ira Katznelson, and Elizabeth Warren.

Thomas Frank, Glenn Greenwald, and Chris Lehmann encouraged me in this project. Chris edited my piece *The Hamilton Hustle* which helped me get key thoughts together about how we as liberals understand history. Rebecca Rosen, Sacha Zimmerman, and Yoni Applebaum helping me publish *How the Democrats Killed Their Populist Soul* in *The Atlantic* in 2016, which was the article on which this book is based. Peggy Noonan was immensely encouraging, going out of her way to help someone out of her political and social orbit for no reason other than she believed the work mattered.

This book emerged from my experienced working in politics and media over fifteen years. I learned enormous amounts from friends and colleagues in that time. For teaching me about politics, political economy, technology, law or journalism, thank you to Hal Singer, Slade Bond, Rafi Martina, Jason Kint, Stacy Mitchell, Chris Arnade, Lucas Kunce, Pierre Sprey, Zach Freed, David Segal, Jeff

Hauser, Daniel Schulman, Alex Lawson, John Wonderlich, Tom Perriello, Tim Wu, Umberto Gambini, Christian D'Cunha, Luther Lowe, Lillian Salerno, Asher Schechter, Johnny Ryan, Frank Pasquale, Frank Pasquale, Siva Vaidhyanathan, Megan Gray, Fiona Scott Morton, J.D. Scholten, Dina Srinivasan, Tommaso Valletti, Cristina Caffarra, Daniel Crane, Steve Teles, Jonathan Kanter, Michael Kades, Sally Hubbard, Sanjukta Paul, Jen Harris, Trisan Harris, Roger McNamee, Andrew Kentz, Nathan Rickard, Marshall Steinbaum, Amanda Fischer, Ro Khanna, Alan Grayson, Bernie Sanders, Keith Ellison, Syd Terry, Lauren Doney, Julie Tagen, Aysha Moshi, David Bagby, David Sirota, Mike Darner, Graham Steele, Lindsay Owens, Roger Alford, Vittorio Cottafavi, James Gee, Justin Slaughter, Adrienne Christian, Corey Frayer, Rebecca Kelly-Slaughter, Ganesh Sitaraman, Allen Grunes, Jonathan Martin, David Leonhardt, Mike Isaacs, Nick Confessore, Rana Foroohar, Matthew Klein, Chris Hayes, Lydia Polgreen, Dave Weigel, Noah Kulwin, Dylan Ratigan, Brad Miller, Francine McKenna, Gretchen Morgenson, Nicholas Shaxson, William Greider, Steve Hilton, Nick Hanauer, Ben Smith, Ryan Cooper, Noah Smith, Farhad Manjoo, Nancy Scola, Matt Taylor, Ken Vogel, Nitasha Tiku, Sascha Meinrath, Marvin Ammori, Craig Aaron, Harold Feld, Tim Karr, Helen Brunner, Nancy Bagley, Sheila Bair, Mark Steckel, Damon Silvers, Barry Ritholtz, Lisa Epstein, Mike Konczal, Joshua Rosner, Ty Gellasch, Dan Geldon, Pete Conti-Brown, Adam Levitin, Nova Daly, Jacob Reses, Daniel Kishi, Scott Cleland, Mike Jones, Steve Wamhoff, Stephanie Kelton, Elizabeth and Matt Bruenig, Karen Kornbluh, Marty Kaplan, Mark Egerman, Robert Reich, Zaid Jilani, Rob Johnson, Thomas Ferguson, Judd Legum, Duncan Black, Ben Rahn, Mark Schmitt, Ryan Morgan, Faiz Shakir, Ari Rabin-Haft, Rick Perlstein, Lee Fang, Jon Walker, Brad Johnson, Murshed Zaheed, Mike Elk, Micah Sifry, Stirling Newberry, Andrew Rasiej, Tim Tagaris, Marc Laitin, Kevin Murphy, Ben and Beth Wikler, Lorelei Kelly, Howie Klein, Ellen Miller, Steve Clemons, Simon Rosenberg, Chris Bowers, Dave Meyer, Jane Hamsher, Christopher Lydon, Mike Lux, Debra Cooper, Jessamyn Conrad, Shamus Khan, Simon DeDeo, Katrina Baker, Casey Seltzer, Megan Downey, James Adomian, and Judith Freeman.

And thank you to my brother, Nick, and sister-in-law, Francesca, as well as Penny, Freddie, and Lydia.

And now some advice. What's it like to write a book? Well, it is far more fun to have written a book than to actually be writing it. Still, if you have an idea you need to get out into the world, do it.

# BIBLIOGRAPHY

## BOOKS

Abels, Jules. *In the Time of Silent Cal.* New York: Putnam, 1969.

Adams, Stephen B. *Mr. Kaiser Goes to Washington: The Rise of a Government Entrepreneur.* Chapel Hill: University of North Carolina Press, 1997.

Adams, Walter, and James W. Brock. *The Bigness Complex: Industry, Labor, and Government in the American Economy,* 2nd edition. Stanford: Stanford University Press, 2004.

Allen, Frederick Lewis. *Only Yesterday: An Informal History of the 1920s.* New York: Harper & Row, 1931.

Applebaum, Eileen. *Private Equity at Work: When Wall Street Manages Main Street.* New York: Russell Sage Foundation, 2014.

Barlett, Donald, and James Steele. *America: What Went Wrong?* Kansas City: Andrews McMeel, 1992.

Batchelor, Bob, and Scott Stoddart. *The 1980s.* Westport, CT: Greenwood Press, 2007.

Beckert, Sven. *Empire of Cotton: A Global History.* New York: Alfred A. Knopf, 2014.

Belzer, Michael. *Sweatshops on Wheels Winners and Losers in Trucking Deregulation.* New York: Oxford University Press, 2000.

Berk, Gerald. *Louis D. Brandeis and the Making of Regulated Competition, 1900–1932.* Cambridge: Cambridge University Press, 2009.

Bernstein, Irving. *The Lean Years: A History of the American Worker, 1920–1933.* New York: Da Capo, 1960.

Birnbaum, Jeffrey. *The Lobbyists: How Influence Peddlers Get Their Way in Washington.* New York: Random House, 1993.

Black, Edwin. *IBM and the Holocaust.* New York: Crown, 2001.

Bork, Robert. *The Antitrust Paradox: A Policy At War with Itself, with a New Introduction and Conclusion.* New York: Free Press, 1993.

Brandeis, Louis. *Other People's Money—and How the Bankers Use It.* New York: Frederick A. Stokes, 1914.

Breyer, Stephen. *Regulation and Its Reform*. Cambridge: Harvard University Press, 1982.

Brinkley, Alan. *The End of Reform: New Deal Liberalism in Recession and War*. New York: Vintage, 1996.

Brooks, John. *The Go-Go Years: The Drama and Crashing Finale of Wall Street's Bullish 60s*. New York: Open Road Media, 2014; originally published, 1973, by Weybright and Talley.

Brown, David S. *Richard Hofstadter: An Intellectual Biography*. Chicago: University of Chicago Press, 2006.

Bruck, Connie. *The Predators' Ball: The Inside Story of Drexel Burnham and the Rise of the Junk Bond Raiders*. New York: Penguin, 1989.

Buchanan, James, and Gordon Tullock. *The Calculus of Consent: Logical Foundations of Constitutional Democracy*. Ann Arbor: University of Michigan Press, 1962.

Burgin, Angus. *The Great Persuasion: Reinventing Free Markets Since the Depression*. Cambridge: Harvard University Press, 2015.

Butler, Smedley. *War Is a Racket*. New York: Round Table Press, 1935.

Burrough, Bryan. *The Big Rich: The Rise and Fall of the Greatest Texas Oil Fortunes*. New York: Penguin, 2009.

Califano, Joseph. *Governing America: An Insider's Report from the White House and the Cabinet*. New York: Simon & Schuster, 1981.

Cannadine, David. *Mellon: An American Life*. New York: Alfred A. Knopf, 2006.

Celler, Emanuel. *You Never Leave Brooklyn: The Autiobiography of Emanuel Celler*. New York: John Day, 1953.

Chandler, Alfred. *Inventing the Electronic Century: The Epic Story of the Consumer Electronics and Computer Industries, with a new Preface*. Cambridge: Harvard University Press, 2009.

———. *The Visible Hand: The Managerial Revolution in American Business*. Cambridge: Belknap Press of Harvard University Press, 1977.

Chernow, Ron *The House of Morgan: An American Banking Dynasty and the Rise of Modern Finance*. New York: Simon & Schuster, 1990.

Clark, John. *Social Control of Business*. New York: McGraw-Hill, 1939.

Coll, Steve. *The Deal of the Century: The Breakup of AT&T*. New York: Simon & Schuster, 1988.

Constantine, Lloyd. *Priceless: The Case That Brought Down the Visa/MasterCard Bank Cartel*. New York: Skyhorse, 2012.

Conti-Brown, Peter. *The Power and Independence of the Federal Reserve*. Princeton: Princeton University Press, 2016.

Cooper, John Milton, Jr. *Pivotal Decades: The United States, 1900–1920*. New York: W. W. Norton, 1990.

———. *Woodrow Wilson: A Biography*. New York: Alfred A. Knopf, 2009.

Costigliola, Frank. *Awkward Dominion: American Political, Economic, and Cultural Relations with Europe, 1919–1933*. Ithaca: Cornell University Press, 1988.

Crane, Daniel A., ed. *The Making of Competition Policy: Legal and Economic Sources.* New York: Oxford University Press.

Croly, Herbert. *The Promise of American Life.* New York: MacMillan Company, 1909.

D'Arista, Jane W. *Federal Reserve Structure and the Development of Monetary Policy: 1915–1935.* Originally published 1971; reprinted as *The Evolution of U.S. Finance, Volume 1.* Armonk, NY: M. E. Sharpe, 1994.

Daughen, Joseph R., and Peter Binzen. *The Wreck of the Penn Central.* Boston: Little, Brown, 1971.

Davidson, Kenneth. *Megamergers: Corporate America's Billion-Dollar Takeovers.* Cambridge, MA: Ballinger, 1985.

Dickson, Paul, and Thomas Allen. *The Bonus Army: An American Epic.* New York: Walker, 2004.

Diggins, John P. *Mussolini and Fascism: The View from America.* Princeton: Princeton University Press, 1972.

DiNunzio, Mario, ed. *Woodrow Wilson: Essential Writings and Speeches of the Scholar-President.* New York: New York University Press, 2006.

Doherty, Brian. *Radicals for Capitalism: A Freewheeling History of the Modern American Libertarian Movement.* New York: PublicAffairs, 2007.

Dong, Tian-jia. *Understanding Power Through Watergate: The Washington Collective Power Dynamics.* Lanham, MD: University Press of America, 2005. Drucker, Peter. *The Concept of the Corporation.* New York: John Day, 1946.

———. *The Unseen Revolution: How Pension Fund Socialism Came to America.* New York: Harper & Row, 1976.

DuBois, W.E.B. *Black Reconstruction in America: An Essay Toward a History of the Part Which Black Folk Played in the Attempt to Reconstruct Democracy in America, 1860–1880.* New York: Russel & Russel, 1935.

Durr, Clifford. *The Early History of the Defense Plant Corporation.* Washington, DC: Committee on Public Administration Cases, 1950.

Dutton, Frederick. *Changing Sources of Power: American Politics in the 1970s.* New York: McGraw-Hill, 1971.

Eccles, Marriner. *Beckoning Frontiers: Public and Personal Recollections.* New York: Alfred A. Knopf, 1951.

Edwards, Lee. *Goldwater: The Man Who Made a Revolution.* Washington, D.C.: Regnery, 1995.

Eisner, Marc Allen. *Antitrust and the Triumph of Economics: Institutions, Expertise, and Policy Change.* Chapel Hill: University of North Carolina Press, 1991.

Eizenstat, Stuart. *President Carter: The White House Years.* New York: Thomas Dunne Books/St. Martin's Press, 2018.

Elias, Christopher. *The Dollar Barons.* New York: Macmillan, 1973.

Ellis, Charles D. *The Partnership: The Making of Goldman Sachs.* New York: Penguin Press, 2008.

Evans, David S. and Richard Schmalensee. *Paying with Plastic: The Digital Revolution in Buying and Borrowing*. Cambridge, Mass.: MIT Press, 1999.

Ferberg, Mark Franklin. "The Democratic Study Group: A Study of Intra-Party Organization in the House of Representatives." PhD thesis, University of California, 1964.

Ferguson, Charles, and Charles Morris. *Computer Wars: How the West Can Win in a Post-IBM World*. New York: Times Books, 1993.

Finan, Christopher. *Alfred E. Smith: The Happy Warrior*. New York: Hill and Wang, 2002.

Fisher, Franklin M., McGowan, John J., and Greenwood, Joen E., *Folded, Spindled, and Mutilated: Economic Analysis and U.S. vs IBM*. MIT Press, Cambridge, MA, 1983.

Fishman, Charles *The Wal-Mart Effect: How the World's Most Powerful Company Really Works—and How It's Transforming the American Economy*. New York: Penguin, 2006.

Foner, Eric, and John A. Garraty, eds. *The Reader's Companion to American History*. Boston: Houghton Mifflin, 1991.

Foroohar, Rana. *Makers and Takers: How Wall Street Destroyed Main Street*. New York: Crown Business, 2017.

Frank, Jerome. *Fate and Freedom: A Philosophy for Free Americans*. New York: Simon & Schuster, 1945.

Frank, Thomas. *Listen, Liberal: Or, What Ever Happened to the Party of the People?* New York: Metropolitan Books, 2016.

Freyer, Tony. *Antitrust and Global Capitalism, 1930–2004*. Cambridge: Cambridge University Press, 2006.

From, Al. *The New Democrats and the Return to Power*. New York: Palgrave Macmillan, 2013.

Galbraith, John Kenneth. *The Affluent Society*. Boston: Houghton Mifflin Harcourt, 1958.

————. *American Capitalism: The Concept of Countervailing Power*. Boston: Houghton Mifflin, 1952.

————. *The Great Crash 1929*. Boston: Houghton Mifflin, 1955.

————. *The New Industrial State*. Boston: Houghton Mifflin, 1967.

————. *Economics and the Public Purpose*. Boston: Houghton Mifflin, 1973.

————. *The Age of Uncertainty*. Boston: Houghton Mifflin, 1977.

Gaughan, Patrick A. *Mergers, Acquisitions, and Corporate Restructurings*. Hoboken, NJ: Wiley, 2018.

Geithner, Timothy. *Stress Test: Reflections on Financial Crises*. New York: Crown, 2014.

Gerhart, Eugene C. *Robert H. Jackson: Country Lawyer, Supreme Court Justice, America's Advocate*. Indianapolis: Bobbs-Merrill, 1958.

Giersch, Herbert, ed. *Merits and Limits of Markets*. Berlin: Publications of the Egon-Sohmen-Foundation 1998.

Green, Mark J., Beverly C. Moore, and Bruce Wasserstein. *The Closed Enterprise*

*System: Ralph Nader's Study Group Report on Antitrust Enforcement.* New York: Grossman, 1972.

Greider, William. *Come Home, America: The Rise and Fall (and Redeeming Promise) of Our Country.* New York: Rodale Books, 2009.

———. *Secrets of the Temple: How the Federal Reserve Runs the Country.* New York: Simon and Schuster, 1987.

Gross, James. *The Making of the National Labor Relations Board: A Study in Economics, Politics, and the Law, 1933–1937.* Albany: State University of New York Press, 1974.

Grubbs, Donald H. *Cry from the Cotton: The Southern Tenant Farmers' Union and the New Deal,* Chapel Hill: University of North Carolina Press, 1971.

Haeg, Larry. *Harriman vs. Hill: Wall Street's Great Railroad War.* Minneapolis: University of Minnesota Press, 2013.

Hart, Gary. *A New Democracy: A Democratic Vision for the 1980s and Beyond.* New York: William Morrow, 1983.

Hayward, Steven F. *The Age of Reagan: The Fall of the Old Liberal Order, 1964–1980.* New York: Prima Publishing, 2001.

Helferich, Gerard, *An Unlikely Trust: Theodore Roosevelt, J. P. Morgan, and the Improbable Partnership That Remade American Business.* Guilford, CT: Lyons Press, 2017.

Hofstadter, Richard. *The American Tradition and the Men Who Made It.* New York: Vintage, 1954.

———. *The Paranoid Style in American Politics.* New York: Alfred A. Knopf, 1965.

Horwitz, Robert Britt. *The Irony of Regulatory Reform: The Deregulation of American Telecommunications,* New York: Oxford University Press, 1989.

Hoyt, Edwin P. *That Wonderful A&P!* New York: Hawthorne Books, 1969.

Hull, Cordell. *The Memoirs of Cordell Hull.* New York: Macmillan, 1948.

Hyman, Sidney. *Marriner Eccles: Private Entrepreneur and Public Servant.* Stanford: Graduate School of Business, Stanford University, 1976.

Irons, Peter, *The New Deal Lawyers.* Princeton: Princeton University Press, 1982.

Jackson, Brooks. *Honest Graft: Big Money and the American Political Process.* New York: Alfred A. Knopf , 1988.

Jacobs, John. *A Rage for Justice: The Passion and Politics of Phillip Burton.* Berkeley: University of California Press, 1995.

Jackson, Robert. *That Man: An Insider's Portrait of Franklin D. Roosevelt.* New York: Oxford University Press, 2003.

John, Richard. *Network Nation: Inventing American Telecommunications.* Cambridge: Belknap Press of Harvard University Press, 2010.

Kahn, Alfred. *The Economics of Regulation: Principles and Institutions, Volume II: Institutional Issues.* New York: Wiley, 1970–71.

Katznelson, Ira. *Fear Itself: The New Deal and the Origins of Our Time.* New York: Liveright, 2013.

Kaufman, Burton Ira. *The Carter Years.* New York: Facts on File, 2006.

Kiechel, Walter. *Lords of Strategy: The Secret Intellectual History of the New Corporate World*. Boston: Harvard Business Press, 2010.

Kiesling, Roy A. *Report to Those Most Concerned: A Memoir of the U.S. Consumer Movement, 1970–1980*. Amazon Digital Services, 2012.

Kintner, Earl W. *Legislative History of the Federal Antitrust Laws and Related Statutes*. New York: Chelsea House Publishers, 1978.

Kitch, Edmund W. "The Fire of Truth: A Remembrance of Law and Economics at Chicago, 1932–1970." *Journal of Law and Economics* 26, no. 1 (1983).

Klein, Maury. *A Call to Arms: Mobilizing America for World War II*. New York: Bloomsbury, 2013.

Kornbluth, Jesse. *Highly Confident: The Crime and Punishment of Michael Milken*. New York: William Morrow, 1992.

Kotz, David. *Bank Control of Large Corporations in the United States*. Berkeley: University of California Press, 1978.

Krippner, Greta. *Capitalizing on Crisis: the Political Origins of the Rise of Finance*. Cambridge: Harvard University Press, 2011.

Krugman, Paul. *Peddling Prosperity Economic Sense and Nonsense in the Age of Diminished Expectations,* New York: W.W. Norton, 1994.

Lamoreaux, Naomi. *The Great Merger Movement in American Business, 1895–1904*. New York: Cambridge University Press, 1985.

Lawrence, John A. *The Class of '74: Congress After Watergate and the Roots of Partisanship*. Baltimore: Johns Hopkins University Press, 2018.

Levinson, Marc. *The Great A&P and the Struggle for Small Business in America*. New York: Hill & Wang, 2011.

——————. *The Box: How the Shipping Container Made the World Smaller and the World Economy Bigger*. Princeton: Princeton University Press, 2006.

Lewis, Michael. *The Big Short: Inside the Doomsday Machine*, New York: W.W. Norton, 2010.

Lichtenstein, Nelson. *The Retail Revolution: How Wal-Mart Created a Brave New World of Business*. New York: Metropolitan Books, 2009.

Lilienthal, David. *Big Business: A New Era*. New York: Harper, 1953.

Lippmann, Walter. *Drift and Mastery*. New York: M. Kennerley, 1914.

Lippmann, Walter and Rossiter, Clinton. *The Essential Lippmann: A Political Philosophy for Liberal Democracy.* New York City: Random House, 1963.

Lisio, Donald. *The President and Protest: Hoover, MacArthur, and the Bonus Riot*. New York: Fordham University Press, 1994.

Loving, Rush, Jr. *The Men Who Loved Trains: The Story of Men Who Battled Greed to Save an Ailing Industry*. Bloomington: Indiana University Press, 2006.

Lynn, Barry C. *Cornered: The New Monopoly Capitalism and the Economics of Destruction*. Hoboken, NJ: John Wiley & Sons, 2010.

MacDonald, Scott B., and Jane E. Hughes. *Separating Fools from Their Money: A History of American Financial Scandals*. New Brunswick, NJ: Transaction Publishers, 2007.

Madrick, Jeff. *Age of Greed: The Triumph of Finance and the Decline of America, 1970 to the Present.* New York: Alfred A. Knopf, 2011.

Markusen, Ann, Peter Hall, Scott Campbell, and Sabina Deitrick. *The Rise of the Gunbelt: The Military Remapping of Industrial America.* New York: Oxford University Press, 1991.

Mayer, Martin. *The Bankers.* New York: Weybright & Talley, 1974.

_____. *The Greatest-Ever Bank Robbery: The Collapse of the Savings and Loan Industry.* New York: Maxwell Macmillan International, 1990.

McClenahan, William M., Jr., and William H. Becker. *Eisenhower and the Cold War Economy.* Baltimore: Johns Hopkins University Press, 2011.

McDonough, Frank, ed. *The Origins of the Second World War: An International Perspective.* New York: Continuum International, 2011.

McGee, John. *In Defense of Industrial Concentration.* New York: Praeger, 1971.

McKenna, Christopher. *The World's Newest Profession: Management Consulting in the Twentieth Century.* New York: Cambridge University Press, 2006.

Mellon, Andrew W. *Taxation: The People's Business.* New York: Macmillan, 1924.

Merkley, Paul. *Reinhold Niebuhr: A Political Account.* Montreal: McGill-Queen's University Press, 1975.

Merritt, Keri Leigh. *Masterless Men: Poor Whites and Slavery in the Antebellum South.* New York: Cambridge University Press, 2017.

Migone, Gian Giacomo. *The United States and Fascist Italy: The Rise of American Finance in Europe.* New York: Cambridge University Press, 2015.

Mills, Charles Wright. *The New Men of Power: America's Labor Leaders.* New York, Harcourt, Brace, 1948.

_____. *The Power Elite.* New York: Oxford University Press, 1956.

_____. *White Collar: The American Middle Classes.* New York: Oxford University Press, 1951.

Minsky, Hyman. *Stabilizing an Unstable Economy.* New Haven: Yale University Press, 1986.

Mirowski, Philip, and Dieter Plehwe, eds. *The Road from Mont Pèlerin: The Making of the Neoliberal Thought Collective, With a New Preface.* Cambridge: Harvard University Press, 2015.

Mishel, Lawrence, Jared Bernstein, and Sylvia Allegretto. *The State of Working America, 2006–2007.* Ithaca: Cornell University Press, 2006.

Monsen, R. Joseph. *Modern American Capitalism: Ideologies and Issues.* Boston: Houghton Mifflin, 1963.

Moreton, Bethany. *To Serve God and Wal-Mart: The Making of Christian Free Enterprise.* Cambridge: Harvard University Press, 2009.

Mueller, Robert W. ed. *A & P: Past, Present and Future,* New York: Progressive Grocer Magazine, 1971.

Mueller, Willard. *Fighting for Antitrust Policy: The Crucial 1960s.* Bloomington, IN: Xlibris, 2009.

Murillo, Mario. *Colombia and the United States: War, Unrest and Destabilization.* New York: Seven Stories Press, 2004.

Neuse, Steven. *David E. Lilienthal: The Journey of an American Liberal.* Knoxville: University of Tennessee Press, 1996.

Noah, Timothy. *The Great Divergence: America's Growing Inequality Crisis and What We Can Do about It.* New York: Bloomsbury Press, 2013.

Nocera, Joseph. *A Piece of the Action: How the Middle Class Joined the Money Class.* New York: Simon & Schuster, 1994.

Nugent, Walter. *The Tolerant Populists: Kansas Populism and Nativism.* Chicago: University of Chicago Press, 1963.

Obama, Barack. *The Audacity of Hope: Thoughts on Reclaiming the American Dream.* New York: Crown, 2006.

O'Connor, Harvey. *Mellon's Millions: The Biography of a Fortune; the Life and Times of Andrew W. Mellon.* New York: John Day, 1933.

Ortiz, Stephen R. *Beyond the Bonus March and GI Bill: How Veteran Politics Shaped the New Deal Era.* New York: New York University Press, 2010.

Packard, Vance. *The Naked Society.* Brooklyn, NY: Ig Publishing, 2014.

Paper, Lewis. *Brandeis: An Intimate Biography of Supreme Court Justice Louis D. Brandeis.* Upper Saddle River, NJ: Prentice-Hall, 1983.

Parisi, Francesco, and Charles K. Rowley. *The Origins of Law and Economics: Essays by the Founding Fathers.* Northhampton, MA: Edward Elgar, 2005.

Parker, Richard. *John Kenneth Galbraith: His Life, His Politics, His Economics.* New York: Farrar, Straus & Giroux, 2005.

[Pearson, Drew, and Robert Allen]. *Washington Merry-Go-Round.* New York: Horace Liveright, 1931.

Pecora, Ferdinand. *Wall Street Under Oath: The Story of Our Modern Money Changers.* New York: Simon & Schuster, 1939.

Pederson, William D., ed. *A Companion to Franklin D. Roosevelt.* Malden, MA: Wiley-Blackwell, 2011.

Perlstein, Rick. *Before the Storm: Barry Goldwater and the Unmaking of the American Consensus.* New York: Hill & Wang, 2001.

———. *The Invisible Bridge: The Fall of Nixon and the Rise of Reagan.* New York: Simon & Schuster, 2014.

Pertschuk, Michael. *Revolt Against Regulation: The Rise and Pause of the Consumer Movement.* Berkeley: University of California Press, 1982.

Phillips-Fein, Kim. *Invisible Hands: The Businessmen's Crusade Against the New Deal.* New York: W. W. Norton, 2009.

———. *Fear City: New York's Fiscal Crisis and the Rise of Austerity Politics.* New York: Metropolitan Books, 2017.

Pitofsky, Robert, ed. *How the Chicago School Overshot the Mark: The Effect of Conservative Economic Analysis on U.S. Antitrust.* New York: Oxford University Press, 2008.

Prins, Nomi. *All the Presidents' Bankers: The Hidden Alliances That Drive American Power.* New York: Nation Books, 2014.

Purcell, Edward A., Jr. *The Crisis of Democratic Theory: Scientific Naturalism and the Problem of Value*. Lexington: University Press of Kentucky, 1973.

Raff, Daniel M. G., and Philip Scranton, eds. *The Emergence of Routines: Entrepreneurship, Organization, and Business History*. Oxford: Oxford University Press, 2017.

Ralph Nader Congress Project. *The Money Committees: A Study of the House Banking and Currency Committee and the Senate Banking, Housing and Urban Affairs Committee*. Directed by Lester M. Salamon. New York: Grossman, 1975.

Rauchway, Eric. *Winter War: Hoover, Roosevelt, and the First Clash over the New Deal*. New York: Basic Books, 2018.

Reback, Gary L. *Free the Market!: Why Only Government Can Keep the Marketplace Competitive*. New York: Portfolio, 2009.

Reeves, Richard. *President Nixon: Alone in the White House*. New York: Simon & Schuster, 2001.

Ritchie, Donald A. *Electing FDR: The New Deal Campaign of 1932*. Lawrence: University Press of Kansas, 2007.

Rohatyn, Felix G. *Dealings: A Political and Financial Life*. New York: Simon & Schuster, 2010.

Rosen, Jeffrey. *Louis D. Brandeis: American Prophet (Jewish Lives)*. New Haven: Yale University Press, 2016.

Rothenberg, Randall, *The Neoliberals: Creating the New American Politics*. New York: Simon & Schuster, 1984.

Ruddy, Daniel, ed. *Theodore Roosevelt's History of the United States: His Own Words, Selected and Arranged by Daniel Ruddy*. New York: HarperCollins, 2010.

Sadler, Spencer. *Pennsylvania's Coal and Iron Police*. Charleston, SC: Arcadia Publishing, 2009.

Samuelson, Paul. *Economics*. New York: McGraw-Hill, 1948.

Sawyer, Laura Phillips. *American Fair Trade: Proprietary Capitalism, Corporatism, and the 'New Competition,' 1890–1940*. Cambridge: Cambridge University Press, 2017.

Scharoun, Lisa. *America at the Mall: The Cultural Role of a Retail Utopia*. Jefferson, NC: McFarland, 2012.

Schlesinger, Arthur M., Jr. *The Crisis of the Old Order, 1919–1933: The Age of Roosevelt, Volume I*. New York: Houghton Mifflin Harcourt, 1957.

———. *The Coming of the New Deal, 1933–1935: The Age of Roosevelt, Volume II*. Boston: Houghton Mifflin, 1957.

Schwarz, Jordan. *Liberal: Adolf A. Berle and the Vision of an American Era*. New York: Free Press, 1987.

Shapiro, Irving. *America's Third Revolution: Public Interest and the Private Role*. New York: Harper & Row, 1984.

Shesol, Jeff. *Supreme Power: Franklin Roosevelt vs. the Supreme Court*. New York: W. W. Norton, 2010.

Silk, Leonard. *The Economists*. New York: Basic Books, 1976.

Skrabec, Quentin. *Aluminum in America: A History*. Jefferson, NC: McFarland, 2017.

Sloan, Allan. *Three Plus One Equals Billions: The Bendix–Martin Marietta War*. New York: Arbor House, 1983.

Smith, Adam. *Supermoney*. Hoboken, New Jersey: John Wiley, 2006 (originally published by Random House, 1972).

Smith, George David. *From Monopoly to Competition: The Transformations of Alcoa, 1888–1986*. New York: Cambridge University Press, 2003.

Smith, Yves. *ECONned: How Unenlightened Self Interest Undermined Democracy and Corrupted Capitalism*. New York: Palgrave Macmillan, 2011.

Sparrow, James, ed. *See Boundaries of the State in US History*, Chicago: University of Chicago Press, 2015.

Stein, Benjamin. *A License to Steal: The Untold Story of Michael Milken and the Conspiracy to Bilk the Nation*. New York: Simon & Schuster, 1992.

Stein, Judith. *Pivotal Decade: How the United States Traded Factories for Finance in the Seventies*. New Haven: Yale University Press, 2010.

———. *Running Steel, Running America: Race, Economic Policy, and the Decline of Liberalism*. Chapel Hill: University of North Carolina Press, 1998.

Stewart, James B. *Den of Thieves*. New York: Simon & Schuster, 1991.

Stigler, George. *Memoirs of an Unregulated Economist*. New York: Basic Books, 1988.

Stone, Brad. *The Everything Store*. New York: Back Bay Books/Little, Brown, 2014.

Stone, Isidor Feinstein (I.F.). *Business as Usual: The First Year of Defense*. New York: Modern Age Books, 1941.

Tarshis, Lorie. *The Elements of Economics*. Boston: Houghton Mifflin, 1947.

Teles, Steven. *The Rise of the Conservative Legal Movement: The Battle for Control of the Law*. Princeton: Princeton University Press, 2008.

Terkel, Studs. *Hard Times: An Oral History of the Great Depression*. New York: Pantheon, 1970.

Thurow, Lester C. *The Zero-Sum Society: Distribution and the Possibilities for Change*. New York: Basic Books, 1980.

Tooze, Adam. *Crashed: How a Decade of Financial Crises Changed the World*. New York: Viking, 2018.

———. *The Deluge: The Great War, America and the Remaking of the Global Order, 1916–1931*. New York: Penguin, 2014.

Traflet, Janice M. *A Nation of Small Shareholders: Marketing Wall Street after World War II*. Baltimore: Johns Hopkins University Press, 2013.

Tugwell, Rexford. *Democratic Roosevelt: A Biography of Franklin D. Roosevelt*. Garden City, NY: Doubleday, 1957.

Van Hise, Charles. *Concentration and Control: A Solution of the Trust Problem in the United States*. New York: Macmillan, 1914.

Van Horn, Robert, Philip Mirowski, and Thomas A. Stapleford, eds. *Building Chicago Economics: New Perspectives on the History of America's Most Powerful Economics Program*. Cambridge: Cambridge University Press, 2011.

Varian, Hal. *Information Rules: A Strategic Guide to the Network Economy*. Boston: Harvard Business School Press, 1999.

Wartzman, Rick. *The End of Loyalty: The Rise and Fall of Good Jobs in America*. New York: PublicAffairs, 2017.

Wells, Wyatt. *Antitrust and the Formation of the Postwar World*. New York: Columbia University Press, 2002.

White, Gerald. *Billions for Defense: Government Financing by the Defense Plant Corporation During World War II*. Tuscaloosa: University of Alabama Press, 1980.

White, Richard. *Railroaded: The Transcontinentals and the Making of Modern America*. New York: W. W. Norton, 2011.

Whitham, Charlie. *Post-War Business Planners in the United States, 1939–48: The Rise of the Corporate Moderates*. London: Bloomsbury Academic, 2016.

Wilson, Mark R. *Destructive Creation: American Business and the Winning of World War II*. Philadelphia: University of Pennsylvania Press, 2016.

Wilson, Woodrow. *The New Freedom: A Call for the Emancipation of the Generous Energies of a People*. New York and Garden City: Doubleday, 1913.

Winerman, Marc. *The Origins of the FTC: Concentration, Cooperation, Control, and Competition*. Washington, DC: Federal Trade Commission, 2003.

Winslow, John F. *Conglomerates Unlimited: The Failure of Regulation*. Bloomington: Indiana University Press, 1973.

Wolf, Thomas P., William D. Pederson, and Byron W. Daynes. *Franklin D. Roosevelt and Congress: The New Deal and Its Aftermath*. Armonk, NY: M. E. Sharpe, 2001.

Wolfson, Martin H. *Financial Crises: Understanding the Postwar U.S. Experience*. Armonk, NY: M. E. Sharpe, 1986.

Wood, Gordon S. *The Radicalism of the American Revolution*. New York: Vintage, 1991.

Wright, Jim. *Balance of Power: Presidents and Congress from the Era of McCarthy to the Age of Gingrich*. Atlanta: Turner Publishing, 1996.

Yergin, Daniel. *The Prize: The Epic Quest for Oil, Money & Power*. New York: Simon & Schuster, 1992.

Young, Nancy Beck. *Wright Patman: Populism, Liberalism, & the American Dream*. Dallas: Southern Methodist University Press, 2000.

Zey, Mary. *Banking on Fraud: Drexel, Junk Bonds, and Buyouts*. New York: Aldine de Gruyter, 1993.

Zweig, Phillip. *Wriston: Walter Wriston, Citibank, and the Rise and Fall of American Financial Supremacy*. New York: Crown, 1995.

## DIGITAL ARCHIVES

American Presidency Project, University of California, Santa Barbara.

Clinton Presidential Library Online.

Eisenhower Presidential Library Digital Collections.

Gerald Ford Presidential Library and Museum Digital Collections.
Harry Truman Library Digital Collections.
Henry Morgenthau Diaries, FDR Library Online.
Jack Rabin Collection on Alabama Civil Rights and Southern Activists.
Joseph C. O'Mahoney Papers, American Heritage Center at the University of Wyoming.
LBJ Library Oral Histories, LBJ Presidential Library.
Oklahoma Historical Society.
The King Center.
Theodore Roosevelt Digital Library. Dickinson State University.
Walmart Digital Museum.

## ARCHIVES

Aaron Director Papers, University of Chicago.
Century Foundation Archives, New York Public Library Manuscripts and Archives.
Cordell Hull Papers, Library of Congress.
David Finley Papers, Library of Congress.
Don Turner Papers, LBJ Presidential Library.
Emanuel Celler Papers, Library of Congress.
Franklin D. Roosevelt Presidential Library & Museum.
Homer Cummings Papers, University of Virginia Library.
James Landis Papers, Library of Congress.
John Kenneth Galbraith Papers, John F. Kennedy Presidential Library and Museum.
Leon H. Keyserling Papers, Harry S. Truman Library and Museum.
*Mellon tax trial transcript, A. W. Mellon v. Commissioner of Internal Revenue,* National Archives (RG200 Gift of Judge Bolon B. Turner).
Ramsey Clark Papers, LBJ Presidential Library.
Ray Stannard Baker Papers, Library of Congress.
Richard Hofstadter Papers, Columbia University Archives.
Robert Bork Papers, Library of Congress.
Robert Jackson Papers, Library of Congress.
Ronald H. Coase Papers, University of Chicago.
Sam Rayburn Papers, Briscoe Center for American History.
Theodore Schultz Papers, University of Chicago.
William Edgar Borah Papers, Library of Congress.
Wright Patman Papers, LBJ Presidential Library.

## GOVERNMENT DOCUMENTS

Regulation of Stock Ownership in Railroads, Part 2, 71st Congress, 3rd Session, February 20, 1931, Committee on Interstate and Foreign Commerce.
Bowers, Douglas E., Rasmussen, Wayne D., and Baker, Gladys L. *History of Agricultural*

*Price-Support and Adjustment Programs, 1933-84,* Economic Research Service, U.S. Department of Agriculture. Agriculture Information Bulletin No. 485, Washington, D.C. December 1984.

Committee on the Judiciary, *Eligibility of Hon. Andrew Mellon.* United States Senate: U.S. Government Printing Office, May 7, 1929.

*Congressional Record.*

"Dwight D. Eisenhower: 1956 : containing the public messages, speeches, and statements of the president, January 1 to December 31, 1956. Eisenhower, Dwight D. (Dwight David), 1890-1969., United States. President (1953-1961 : Eisenhower) United States, Office of the Federal Register." Washington: Office of the Federal Register, National Archives and Records Service, General Services Administration.

Federal Reserve Annual Report, 1921.

Federal Reserve Annual Report, 1946.

Federal Trade Commission, *Final Report on Chain Store Investigation,* S. Doc. No 4-74. Washington, DC: U.S. Government Printing Office, 1934.

Federal Trade Commission, *Report of the Federal Trade Commission on the Merger Movement.* Washington, DC: U.S. Government Printing Office, 1948.

Field hearing before the Committee on Commerce, Science, and Transportation, United States Senate, 106th Congress, 1st Session, How Mergers in the Nation's Agricultural Industry Impact Consumers, July 24, 1999.

Final Report on the Reconstruction Finance Corporation. Washington, DC: U.S. Government Printing Office, 1959.

Hearings before the Ad Hoc Subcommittee on Antitrust, the Robinson-Patman Act, and Related Matters, House Committee on Small Business, Recent Efforts to Amend or Repeal the Robinson-Patman Act—Part 1, November 5, 6, 11, 12, 19, 1975, p. 25.

Hearings before the Antitrust Subcommittee of the Committee on the Judiciary, "Investigation of Conglomerate Corporations" House hearings, October 15, 16, 22, 23, 1969, Serial No. 23, Part 2.

Hearings before the Senate Banking and Currency Committee, 89th Congress, 1st Session, on S. 1698 (1965).

Hearings before the Committee on Banking and Currency, House of Representatives, Eighty-Ninth Congress, Second Session, on H.R. 14026, "To Eliminate Unsound Competition for Savings and Time Deposits" May 9, 10, 11, 12, 19, 24, 25, 31; June 1, 2, 7, 8, 9, 16, and 23, 1966.

Hearing before the Committee on the District of Columbia and Its Subcommittee on the Judiciary House of Representatives, 71st Congress, "Real Estate, Mortgage Foreclosure, and Blue Sky Legislation," February 24, 25, 26, 27, March 3, 7, 10, 12, 19, 1931.

Hearings before the Committee of Interstate Commerce, United States Senate, "Conditions in the Coal Fields of Ohio, West Virginia, and Pennsylvania," 1928.

Hearings before the Committee on the Judiciary, "Charges of Hon. Wright Patman Against the Secretary of the Treasury," January 13, 14, 15, 18, 19, 1932.

Hearings before the Committee on the Judiciary, United States Senate, 100th Congress, 1st Session, Nomination of Robert H. Bork to Be Associate Justice of the Supreme Court of the United States, September 15, 16, 17, 18, 19, 21, 22, 23, 25, 28, 29, 30, 1987.

Hearing before the Joint Commission of Agricultural Inquiry. Washington, DC: U.S. Government Printing Office, August 2, 3, 4, 5, 8, 9, 11 1921.

Hearing before the Joint Economic Committee of the Congress of the United States, "The Future of Newspapers: The Impact on the Economy and Democracy," September 24, 2009.

Hearing before the Committee on Rules, Investigation of Activities of Those Engaged in Purchasing Cottonseed Oil, etc., February 10, 1930.

Hearing before the Committee on the Judiciary, The Conglomerate Merger Problem, Part Eight. U.S. Senate, Government Printing Office, 1970.

Hearing before the House Committee on Small Business, Impact of Federal Antitrust Enforcement Policies on Small Business, September 9, 1982.

Hearing before the Select Committee on Small Business, U.S. Senate, A Seminar Discussion of the Question: "Are Planning and Regulation Replacing Competition in the New Industrial State," June 29, 1967, and "The Question: Are Planning and Regulation Replacing Competition in the American Economy? (The Automobile as a Case Study)," July 10, 23, 1968.

Hearing before the Senate Judiciary Committee, Competition, Innovation, and Public Policy in the Digital Age: Examining the Impact of High-Growth Technology and the Internet on Antitrust, Intellectual Property, Competition Policy, and Enforcement, November 4, 1997; March 3, July 23, 1998.

Hearing before the Subcommittee of the Select Committee on Small Business, A Seminar Discussion of the Question: "Are Planning and Regulation Replacing Competition in the New Industrial State?," June 29, 1967.

Hearing before the Subcommittee on Commerce and Finance, House Interstate and Foreign Commerce Committee, 91st Session, "Mutual Fund Amendments Part One," November 12, 13, 14, 17, 18, 19, 20, 21, December 8, 9, 10, 11, 1969.

Hearings before the Subcommittee on Antitrust and Monopoly, Senate Judiciary Committee, March 27, 28, 29, 30, May 7, 8, 1973.

Hearing before the Subcommittee on Commerce, Consumer, and Monetary Affairs of the Committee on Government Operations, "Oversight of Federal Trade Commission Law Enforcement: Fiscal Years 1982 and 1983," November 9, 1983.

Hearing before the Subcommittee on Economic Stabilization of the Committee on Banking, Finance, and Urban Affairs, "Oversight Hearing on Mergers and Acquisitions," May 12, 1987.

Hearings before the Subcommittee on Financial Institutions of the Committee on

Banking, Housing, and Urban Affairs, Credit Deregulation and Availability Act of 1981 in U.S. Senate, July 9, 15, 21.

Hearings before the Subcommittee on Financial Institutions of the Senate Committee on Banking, Housing, and Urban Affairs, July 24, 25, 1974.

Hearings before the Committee on Finance, United States Senate, "Investigation of Economic Problems," February 13, 28, 1933.

Hearing before the Subcommittee on Monopolies and Commercial Law, Committee on the Judiciary, 94th Congress, 1st Session, on H.R. 2384, Fair Trade Repeal, March 25, 1975.

Hearing before the House Banking Subcommittee on Financial Institutions, Supervision, Regulation, and Insurance, Financial Institutions and the Nation's Economy: "Discussion Principles," Part 2, December 11, 12, 16, 17, 1975.

Hearings before the Subcommittee and Antitrust and Monopoly, Senate Judiciary Committee, March 27, 28, 29, 30, May 7, 8, 1973, p. 1.

Hearings before the Subcommittee on International Trade of the Senate Finance Committee, Multinational Corporations, February 26, 27, 28, March 1, 6, 1973, p. 1.

Hearing in the House Banking Committee, "Eliminate Unsound Competition for Savings and Time Deposits," 89th Congress, 2nd Session, May 9, 10, 11, 12, 19, 24, 25, June 1, 2, 7, 8, 9, 16, 23, 1966.

Hearings before the Subcommittee on Surface Transportation of the Committee on Interstate and Foreign Commerce, U.S. Senate, Jan 13, 14, 15, 16, 17, 1958.

Investigation of the Lobbying Activities of the American Retail Federation, Hearings before the Special Committee To Investigate the American Retail Federation, House of Representatives, June 5, 6, 25, 27, July 9, 10 1935.

"Industrial Relations: Final Report and Testimony Submitted to Congress by the Commission on Industrial Relations" Volume VIII, Senate, 64th Congress, 1st Session, Document No. 415, U.S. Government Printing Office, 1916.

Interstate Commerce Commission: *No. 6569 Report of Investigation of the Financial Transactions of the New York, New Haven & Hartford Railroad Company.* Washington, DC: U.S. Government Printing Office, 1914.

Joint Economic Committee, The Federal Reserve: A Study Prepared for the Use of the Joint Economic Committee, January 3, 1977. Washington, DC: U.S. Government Printing Office, 1976.

Lebergott, Stanley. *Annual Estimates of Unemployment in the United States, 1900–1954.* Washington, DC: Bureau of the Budget, 1957.

Money Trust Investigation: *Investigation of Financial and Monetary Conditions in the United States Under House Resolutions Nos. 429 and 504 before a Subcommittee of the Committee on Banking and Currency,* House of Representatives, 1912–1913.

National Emergency Council, *Report on Economic Conditions of the South.* Washington, DC: U.S. Government Printing Office, 1938.

Oversight Hearing before the Subcommittee on Monopolies and Commercial Law of the Committee on the Judiciary, House of Representatives, 97th Congress, 2nd Session, on Corporate Takeovers, June 10, 1982.

Oversight Hearing on Mergers and Acquisitions House Banking Committee, Subcommittee on Economic Stabilization, May 12, 1987.

"Report of the Special Outside Counsel in the Matter of Speaker James C. Wright, Jr." Committee on Standards of Official Conduct, U.S. House of Representatives, February 21, 1989.

Senate Committee Report No. 94-466, 94th Congress, 1st Session.

Senate Subcommittee of the Committee on Manufactures, June 20, 1932, "Federal Emergency Measures to Relieve Unemployment."

Staff Report of Antitrust Subcommittee No. 5, House Committee on the Judiciary, 89th Congress, 1st Session, Interlocks in Corporate Management, March 12, 1965.

Staff Report of the SEC to the Special Subcommittee on Investigations, The Financial Collapse of the Penn Central Company, August 1972.

Staff Report of the Committee on Banking and Currency, House of Representatives, The Penn Central Failure, Parts 1–5, 1970.

Staff Report of the Subcommittee on Domestic Finance, Committee on Banking and Currency, August, Financial Institutions: Reform and the Public Interest, 1973.

Staff Study for the Special Subcommittee on Investigations of the Committee on Interstate and Foreign Commerce, U.S. House of Representatives, Inadequacies of Protections for Investors in Penn Central and Other ICC-Regulated Companies, July 27, 1971, pp. iv, 36.

Subcommittee on Monopolies and Commercial Law, Committee on the Judiciary, 94th Congress, 1st Session, on H.R. 2384, Fair Trade Repeal, March 25, 1975.

Temporary National Economic Committee, Final Report and Recommendations of the Temporary National Economic Committee, 77th Congress, 1st Session, 1941.

U.S. Senate, Select Committee on Investigation of the Bureau of Internal Revenue, Part One. Washington, DC: U.S. Government Printing Office, 1924.

# NOTES

## ABBREVIATIONS USED IN THE NOTES

RBP    Robert Bork Papers, Library of Congress
RJP    Robert Jackson Papers, Library of Congress
WPP   Wright Patman Papers, LBJ Presidential Library

## PREFACE

1   John Adams to Thomas Jefferson, with Postscript by Abigail Adams, February 2, 1816, https://founders.archives.gov/documents/Jefferson/03-09-02-0285.

2   Mary Russell, "Freshman-Led Drama Yet to Play Out," *Washington Post,* 1/19/1975.

3   Barbara Sinclair, "Majority Party Leadership Strategies for Coping with the New U. S. House," *Legislative Studies Quarterly,* vol. 6, no. 3, 1981, pp. 391–414. JSTOR, www.jstor.org/stable/439482, p. 392.

4   Norm Brewer, "Class of '74 Under Attack," Gannett News Service, printed in *San Bernardino County Sun,* June 14, 1992, p. A9; John Lawrence, "How the 'Watergate Babies' Broke American Politics," *Politico Magazine,* May 26, 2018, https://www.politico.com/magazine/story/2018/05/26/congress-broke-american-politics-218544.

5   Jim Wright, *Balance of Power: Presidents and Congress from the Era of McCarthy to the Age of Gingrich,* p. 239. The "greatest political speech" line comes from author interview with Tom Downey.

6   Mark Stanley, "The Death of Wright Patman: Mourning the End of an Era," *East Texas Historical Journal* 42, no. 1 (March 2004).

7   Benjamin Lady, "A Tale of Two Recoveries: Wealth Inequality After the Great Recession," The Century Foundation, August 28, 2013, https://tcf.org/content/commentary/a-tale-of-two-recoveries-wealth-inequality-after-the-great-recession/?agreed=1.

8   Kenneth Jackson, *Crabgrass Frontier: The Suburbanization of the United States* (New York: Oxford University Press, 1985), p. 231.

9   Phil Longman, "Time to Fight Health-Care Monopolization," *Democracy Journal* 42 (Fall 2016), https://democracyjournal.org/magazine/42/time-to-fight-health-care-monopolization/.

10  "The Third-Leading Cause of Death in US Most Doctors Don't Want You to Know About," CNBC, February 22, 2018, https://www.cnbc.com/2018/02/22/medical-errors-third-leading-cause-of-death-in-america.html.

11  Phil Longman, "How Big Medicine Can Ruin Medicare for All," *Washington Monthly,* November 2017, https://washingtonmonthly.com/magazine/novemberdecember-2017/how-big-medicine-can-ruin-medicare-for-all/.

12  See Centers for Disease Control database, CDC WONDER, for 2017 numbers, https://www.drugabuse.gov/related-topics/trends-statistics/overdose-death-rates; "CNN Exclusive: The More Opioids Doctors Prescribe, the More Money They Make," March 12, 2018, https://www.cnn.com/2018/03/11/health/prescription-opioid-payments-eprise/index.html.

13  Brittany Shoot, "OxyContin Billionaire Granted Patent for Opioid Addiction Treatment," *Fortune,* September 7, 2018, http://fortune.com/2018/09/07/oxycontin-opioid-addiction-treatment-patent-richard-sackler-purdue-pharma/.

14  Sam Collins, "Pharmaceutical Company with Monopoly on Lifesaving Treatment Jacks Up Prices," *Think Progress,* March 3, 2015, https://thinkprogress.org/pharmaceutical-company-with-monopoly-on-lifesaving-treatment-jacks-up-prices-3883e95f88c7/; "Profiteering from the Opioid Crisis," *USA Today,* May 16, 2018, https://www.usatoday.com/story/opinion/2018/05/16/opioid-crisis-drug-makers-jack-up-naloxone-prices-putting-beyond-reach-those-trying-rescue-overdose/611871002/.

15  "The Business of Voting," Penn Wharton Public Policy Initiative, https://trustthevote.org/wp-content/uploads/2017/03/2017-whartonoset_industryreport.pdf.

16  Siddhartha Mahanta, "New York's Looming Food Disaster," *Citylab,* October 21, 2013, https://www.citylab.com/equity/2013/10/new-yorks-looming-food-disaster/7294/.

# CHAPTER ONE
## 1912

1   Woodrow Wilson, *The New Freedom: A Call for the Emancipation of the Generous Energies of a People.*

2   Schlesinger described Teddy Roosevelt's "squeaky voice, his gleaming teeth, his overpowering grin, and his incurable delight in self-dramatization." Arthur

M. Schlesinger Jr., *The Crisis of the Old Order, 1919–1933, The Age of Roosevelt, Volume I.*

3    "Roosevelt Out with Platform: Declares for More Drastic Control of Corporations, in Speech at Osawatomie," *New York Times,* 9/1/1910, pp. 1, 2.

4    Gerard Helferich, *An Unlikely Trust: Theodore Roosevelt, J. P. Morgan, and the Improbable Partnership That Remade American Business.*

5    Larry Haeg, *Harriman vs. Hill: Wall Street's Great Railroad War.*

6    See Teddy Roosevelt essay, "The Most Brilliant American Statesman Who Ever Lived," Daniel Ruddy, ed., *Theodore Roosevelt's History of the United States: His Own Words, Selected and Arranged by Daniel Ruddy,* p. 47.

7    Ibid., p. 78.

8    Andrew Glass, "Alice Roosevelt is married in the White House, Feb. 17, 1905," *Politico,* 2/17/2019, https://www.politico.com/story/2019/02/17/this-day-in-politics-february-17-1170475.

9    One reporter called Mussolini a "Latin Teddy Roosevelt." "Calls Mussolini Latin Roosevelt; Isaac F. Marcosson Says Fascist Chief and Kemal Pasha Are Both Autocrats. Declares League Doomed. Italian Occupation of Corfu Its Death Blow, Says American Magazine Writer," *New York Times,* 10/7/1923, p. 10; Tim Wu, *The Curse of Bigness: Antitrust in the New Gilded Age,* (New York: Columbia Global Reports, 2018), p. 76.

10    "Roosevelt Out with Platform: Declares for More Drastic Control of Corporations, in Speech at Osawatomie."

11    Lewis L. Gould, "1912 Republican Convention: Return of the Rough Rider," *Smithsonian,* August 2008.

12    Cordell Hull, *Memoirs of Cordell Hull, Volume One,* p. 46.

13    "West Virginia's Monongah Mine Disaster Was Nation's Worst But Also Prompted Change," *WeHeartWV,* December 6, 2017, http://weheartwv.com/2017/12/06/west-virginias-monongah-mine-disaster-was-nations-worst-but-also-prompted-change/; Adriana Colindres, "A Century Later: The Cherry Coal Mine Disaster," *Journal Star,* 11/1/2009; Carolina Miranda, "The 1910 bombing of the Los Angeles Times has been the subject of books and film. Now it's a bus tour," *Los Angeles Times,* 11/22/2017; "The Triangle Shirtwaist Factory Fire," U.S. Labor Department, March 23, 2012, https://www.osha.gov/oas/trianglefactoryfire-account.html.

14    "Our Modern Railroads as Juggernauts," *New York Times,* 1/16/1910, p. 2, magazine section.

15    "Gaynor Shot – X-Ray Shows Bullet Split – His Condition Good – Assailant Shows No Regret," *New York Times,* 08/10/1910, p. 1.

16    John Milton Cooper, *Pivotal Decades: The United States, 1900–1920,* p. 146.

17    "Woodrow Wilson, Presidential Possibility," *Munsey's Magazine* 46, no. 1 (1911): p. 4.

18    "Barnes Attacks Roosevelt Openly," *New York Times,* 9/3/1910, p. 1.

19  Ruddy, *Theodore Roosevelt's History of the United States,* p. 299.

20  "From the Archives: President Teddy Roosevelt's New Nationalism Speech of August 31, 1910," White House Archives, republished on December 6, 2011, https://obamawhitehouse.archives.gov/blog/2011/12/06/archives-president-teddy-roosevelts-new-nationalism-speech.

21  Ibid.

22  W. E. B. DuBois, *Black Reconstruction,* p. 26.

23  Sven Beckert, *Empire of Cotton: A Global History,* p. 104. "Natchez: In 1850 Half of the Millionaires in the US Lived Here," *Christian Science Monitor,* 3/22/1983.

24  "From the Archives: President Teddy Roosevelt's New Nationalism Speech."

25  Mayer, *The Bankers* pp. 27–28; "Morrill Act," Primary Documents in American History, Library of Congress online, https://www.loc.gov/rr/program/bib/ourdocs/morrill.html; "Homestead Act," Primary Documents in American History, Library of Congress online, https://www.loc.gov/rr/program/bib/ourdocs/homestead.html.

26  "From the Archives: President Teddy Roosevelt's New Nationalism Speech."

27  See Alfred Chandler, *The Visible Hand: The Managerial Revolution in American Business.*

28  Richard White, *Railroaded: The Transcontinentals and the Making of Modern America,* p. 24.

29  The scandal implicated Speaker James G. Blaine, Vice President Schuyler Colfax, and future President James Garfield. White, *Railroaded,* p. 64.

30  Bruce Bartlett, "Money And Politics," *Forbes,* June 12, 2009, https://www.forbes.com/2009/06/11/terry-mcauliffe-virginia-primaries-opinions-columnists-fundraising.html#627ed8242b77.

31  Spencer J. Sadler, *Pennsylvania's Coal and Iron Police,* p. 46.

32  Marc Winerman, *The Origins of the FTC: Concentration, Cooperation, Control, and Competition,* p. 6.

33  Quoted in Laura Phillips Sawyer, *American Fair Trade: Proprietary Capitalism, Corporatism, and the "New Competition," 1890–1940,* p. 23.

34  Ibid., pp. 2–3, 66.

35  William L. Letwin, "Congress and the Sherman Antitrust Law: 1887-1890," *The University of Chicago Law Review,* vol. 23, no. 2, 1956, pp. 221–58, JSTOR, www.jstor.org/stable/1598473; William Kolasky, "Senator John Sherman and the Origin of Antitrust," *Antitrust,* vol. 24, Fall 2009, p. 87.

36  See Winerman, *The Origins of the FTC,* p. 8.

37  Eric Foner and John A. Garraty, eds., *The Reader's Companion to American History.*

38  Ron Chernow, *The House of Morgan: An American Banking Dynasty and the Rise of Modern Finance,* p. 55.

39  Ibid., pp. 66–67.

40  Ibid., p. 54.

41 William Jennings Bryan, "Democratic National Convention Address: 'A Cross of Gold,'" July 8, 1896, American Rhetoric Online Speech Bank, https://www.americanrhetoric.com/speeches/williamjenningsbryan1896dnc.htm.

42 "1900 Democratic Party Platform," American Presidency Project, https://www.presidency.ucsb.edu/documents/1900-democratic-party-platform.

43 Naomi Lamoreaux, *The Great Merger Wave in American Business, 1895–1904*, pp. 2–3.

44 See Chapter 10 of Brandeis's *Other People's Money*.

45 Ruddy, *Theodore Roosevelt's History of the United States*, p. 217.

46 "Mr. Roosevelt Is Now President," *New York Times*, 9/15/1901, p. 1.

47 Larry Haeg, *Harriman vs. Hill*, chapters 1, 12.

48 "$150,000 Given by Morgan to Elect Colonel," *New York Times*, 10/4/1912, p. 1.

49 Winerman, *The Origins of the FTC*, pp. 13, 15.

50 Jerome Frank, *Fate and Freedom: A Philosophy for Free Americans*, p. 62.

51 Charles Van Hise, *Concentration and Control: A Solution of the Trust Problem in the United States*.

52 "From Alexander Hamilton to Theodore Sedgwick, 10 July 1804," Founders Online, National Archives, accessed April 11, 2019, https://founders.archives.gov/documents/Hamilton/01-26-02-0001-0264.

53 Gordon Wood, *The Radicalism of the American Revolution*, p. 30.

54 See Roosevelt essay, "The Most Brilliant American Statesman Who Ever Lived": "I have not much sympathy with Hamilton's distrust of democracy."

55 Barry C. Lynn, *Cornered: The New Monopoly Capitalism and the Economics of Destruction*, p. 102.

56 "First Inaugural Address" in *The Papers of Thomas Jefferson, Volume 33: February to April 1801*, Barbara B. Oberg, ed., (Princeton University Press, 2006), pp. 148–52.

57 Herbert Croly, *The Promise of American Life*, chapter 12.

58 "Address by Theodore Roosevelt Before the Convention of the National Progressive Party in Chicago, August, 1912."

59 Helferich, *An Unlikely Trust*, p. 174.

60 See Eugene Debs, "The Social Democracy" republished in the *Fort Wayne Evening Sentinel*, March 8, 1900, p. 4; "The Workers and the Trusts," *Jamestown* [ND] *Weekly Alert* 23, no. 6 (Aug. 31, 1899): "Labor (and I am talking about intelligent labor) will take no hand in 'smashing the trusts.' Labor's voice will not be heard in the political pickpockets' clamor to 'down the trusts.' They have sense enough to know that they might as well attempt to force the waters of the Mississippi back into the millions of tributaries when they come."

61 John Milton Cooper Jr., *Woodrow Wilson*, pp. 98, 134, 142–43. While W. E. B. DuBois endorsed Wilson for president in 1912, he quickly came to regret that decision.

62 "Woodrow Wilson, Presidential Possibility," *Munsey's Magazine,* p. 12.

63 "Governor Wilson Agrees with Mr. Brandeis: Lunch at Sea Girt Together and Discuss Means of 'Accomplishing Industrial Freedom,'" *New York Times,* 8/29/1912, p. 3. For the origin of his nickname, Brandeis himself used the term "the People's Lawyer" to contrast it to the corporation lawyer, and it stuck. Footnote 3, John Braeman, "'The People's Lawyer' Revisited: Louis D. Brandeis Versus the United Shoe Machinery Company," *The American Journal of Legal History* 50, no. 3 (2008): pp. 284–304, www.jstor.org/stable/25734127.

64 Interstate Commerce Commission: No. 6569, "Report of Investigation of the Financial Transactions of the New York, New Haven & Hartford Railroad Company," 1914, p. 4.

65 Helferich, *An Unlikely Trust,* p. 151.

66 "The People Versus the Railroads," *Hearst's Magazine* 24 (July 1913–December 1913); "21 Killed in Bar Harbor Express, 50 Hurt, As White Mountain Flier Cleaves Pullmans on the New Haven," *New York Times,* 9/3/1913, p. 1.

67 Interstate Commerce Commission: No. 6569, "Report of Investigation of the Financial Transactions of the New York, New Haven & Hartford Railroad Company," 1914.

68 Gerald Berk, *Louis D. Brandeis and the Making of Regulated Competition, 1900–1932,* pp. 41–43.

69 Interview with Brandeis, Ray Stannard Baker Papers, Box 101.

70 "Industrial Relations: Final Report and Testimony Submitted to Congress by the Commission on Industrial Relations," vol. 8, Senate, 64th Congress, 1st Session, Document No. 415, 1916, Government Printing Office, p. 7659.

71 For a good discussion of Brandeis's philosophy, see Berk, *Louis D. Brandeis and the Making of Regulated Competition;* "Governor Wilson Agrees with Mr. Brandeis," *New York Times.*

72 Cooper, *Woodrow Wilson,* p. 163.

73 Mario DiNunzio, ed., *Woodrow Wilson: Essential Writings and Speeches of the Scholar-President,* pp. 347–50.

74 Cooper, *Woodrow Wilson,* p. 163.

75 Money Trust Investigation: *Investigation of Financial and Monetary Conditions in the United States Under House Resolutions Nos. 429 and 504 Before a Subcommittee of the Committee on Banking and Currency,* House of Representatives 1912–1913, p. 4.

76 Lewis Paper, *Brandeis: An Intimate Biography of Supreme Court Justice Louis D. Brandeis.*

77 Richard John, *Network Nation: Inventing American Telecommunications,* p. 359.

78 Cooper, *Woodrow Wilson,* p. 8.

79 Paul Abrahams, "Brandeis and Lamont on Finance Capitalism," *The Business History Review* 47, no. 1 (Spring 1973): 94. Still, they retained "one directorship on each of the corporations with which it had been affiliated."

80  Quote from Washington observer at the time Gus Karger in Cooper, *Woodrow Wilson*, p. 329.

81  "Wilson Message Excites Criticism from Republicans," *New York Times*, May 21, 1919, p. 1.

## CHAPTER TWO
### Mellonism

1   G. K. Chesterton, *The Man Who Was Thursday: A Nightmare* (London: J. W. Arrowsmith, 1908), p. 53.

2   Willis Fletcher Johnson, *The Life of Warren G. Harding: From the Simple Life of the Farm to the Glamor and Power of the White House* (Wilmore, 1923), p. 206.

3   John Milton Cooper Jr., *Woodrow Wilson*, p. 574.

4   "Wilson's Exist Is Tragic," *New York Times*, 3/5/1921, p. 1.

5   Interview with Brandeis, Ray Stannard Baker Papers, Box 101.

6   Ibid.

7   Cooper, *Woodrow Wilson*, p. 375.

8   John Kenneth Galbraith, *The Age of Uncertainty*, p. 133.

9   Edward A. Purcell Jr., *The Crisis of Democratic Theory: Scientific Naturalism and the Problem of Value*. See chapter 7.

10  Ibid.

11  See for instance H. L. Mencken, *Notes on Democracy*: "Democracy is a pathetic belief in the collective wisdom of individual ignorance."

12  Purcell, *The Crisis of Democratic Theory*. See chapter 7.

13  See Chapter 1, "Shadows of the Great War," on the extensive regulatory state imposed on businesses during World War I, in Mark R. Wilson, *Destructive Creation: American Business and the Winning of World War II*.

14  Ibid., pp. 18–19.

15  Interview with Brandeis, Ray Stannard Baker Papers, Box 101. It would not be until 1920 that the first commercial radio station would launch.

16  Matt Phillips, "The Long Story of U.S. Debt, From 1790 to 2011, in 1 Little Chart," *Atlantic*, November 13, 2012.

17  Federal Reserve Annual Report, 1921, pp. 1, 101.

18  Adam Tooze, *The Deluge: The Great War, America and the Remaking of the Global Order, 1916–1931*.

19  Ibid., chapter 18.

20  Frederick Lewis Allen, *Only Yesterday: An Informal History of the 1920s*, p. 42.

21  Michael Bordo and Andrew Filardo, "Deflation in a Historical Perspective," Bank for International Settlements Working Papers, No. 186, November 18, 2005.

22  Tooze, *The Deluge*. See chapter 18.

23  "The Federal Reserve: A Study Prepared for the Use of the Joint Economic

Committee," January 3, 1977 (Washington, D.C.: U.S. Government Printing Office, 1976), p. 41.

24  Jane D'Arista, *The Evolution of U.S. Finance,* p. 39; 1921 Report of the Federal Reserve Board, p. 104.

25  Tooze, *The Great Deluge,* see chapter 18.

26  Emanuel Celler, *You Never Leave Brooklyn: The Autobiography of Emanuel Celler,* p. 80.

27  Allen, *Only Yesterday,* p. 40.

28  Arthur M. Schlesinger Jr., *The Crisis of the Old Order, 1919–1933,* p. 45.

29  "Harding for World Court," *New York Times,* 3/5/1921, pp. 1, 2.

30  "The Case of Andrew Mellon," *New Republic,* January 20, 1926, http://www.newrepublic.com/article/politics/93808/the-case-andrew-mellon.

31  Harvey O'Connor, *Mellon's Millions: The Biography of a Fortune; the Life and Times of Andrew W. Mellon,* pp. 117, 177.

32  "Eligibility of Hon. Andrew Mellon, Report on the Committee on the Judiciary, May 7, 1929, United States Senate," (Washington, D.C.: U.S. Government Printing Office), p. 29. Mellon was able to address objections upon his appointment by divesting himself of his board positions and selling much of his stock. He thus claimed that he was not conducting business and had no control of any corporations. This was not true.

33  O'Connor, *Mellon's Millions,* p. 123.

34  Jules Abels, *In the Time of Silent Cal,* p. 215.

35  O'Connor, *Mellon's Millions,* p. 213.

36  David Cannadine, *Mellon: An American Life,* p. 40.

37  Ibid., p. 143.

38  Ibid., p. 232.

39  Ibid.

40  George David Smith, *From Monopoly to Competition: The Transformations of Alcoa, 1888–1986,* p. 42.

41  Ibid. Also see O'Connor, *Mellon's Millions,* pp. xi–xv.

42  "Report on Economic Conditions of the South by National Emergency Council (U.S.)," 1938, p. 54.

43  W. E. B. DuBois and Martha Gruening, "Massacre at East St. Louis," *The Crisis* 14 (September 1917), pp. 219–38. The Central Trades and Labor Union protested the influx of "undesirable negroes . . . used to the detriment of our white citizens by some of the capitalists and a few of the real estate owners."

44  Drew Pearson and Robert Allen, *Washington Merry-Go-Round,* pp. 163–83. This references the book, not the syndicated column of the same name.

45  Select Committee on Investigation of the Bureau of Internal Revenue, U.S. Senate, Part One, 1924 (Washington, D.C.: U.S. Government Printing Office), pp. 5–8. The court was called the Board of Tax Appeals.

46  For Mellon's personal rebate, see Pearson and Allen, *Washington Merry-Go-Round,* pp. 163–83. This references the book, not the syndicated column of the

same name. For Gulf oil amount, see "Select Committee on Investigation of the Bureau of Internal Revenue," p. 93.

47   *Nation* 122, No. 3167, March 17, 1926, p. 281.

48   Mario A. Murillo, *Colombia and the United States: War, Unrest and Destabilization,* p. 139; Daniel Yergin, *The Prize: The Epic Quest for Oil, Money & Power.*

49   O'Connor, *Mellon's Millions,* p. 184.

50   Andrew W. Mellon, *Taxation: The People's Business,* p. 79.

51   Ibid., pp. 71–72.

52   Calvin Coolidge, Address to the American Society of Newspaper Editors, Washington, D.C., January 17, 1925, http://www.presidency.ucsb.edu/ws/?pid=24180.

53   "The Case of Andrew Mellon," *New Republic,* January 20, 1926.

54   "Annual Estimates of Unemployment in the United States, 1900–1954," Bureau of the Budget; Stanley Lebergott, National Bureau of Economic Research, 1957.

55   Schlesinger, *The Crisis of the Old Order, 1919–1933,* p. 67.

56   "The Soaring Twenties," *Forbes,* July 29, 2009.

57   Hearing before the Joint Commission of Agricultural Inquiry, August 2, 3, 4, 5, 8, 9, 11, 1921, pp. 12–14; quote by Comptroller of the Currency John Skelton Williams.

58   Pearson and Allen, *Washington Merry-Go-Round,* p. 164. This references the book, not the syndicated column of the same name.

59   Eric Foner, "Bush emulates the worst on track to bottom rung," *Times Tribune,* 12/24/2006, D4.

60   "Report of the Federal Trade Commission on the Merger Movement," 1948.

61   Clark, *Social Control of Business,* p. 6.

62   Keyserling to Truman, undated memo, "Proposed Message by the President on Anti-Monopoly Policy," Leon H. Keyserling Papers, Box 9, p. 30.

63   "Report of the Federal Trade Commission on the Merger Movement," 1948.

64   *Dr. Miles Medical Co. v. John D. Park & Sons Co.,* 220 U.S. 373 (1911).

65   Paul B. Ellickson, *The Evolution of the Supermarket Industry from A&P to Wal-Mart,* in *Handbook on the Economics of Retail and Distribution* (Cheltenham: Edward Elgar Publishing, 2016), pp. 101–4.

66   Federal Trade Commission, *Final Report of Chain Store Investigation,* 1934.

67   Arthur J. Keeffe and Mary S. Head, "What Is Wrong with the American Banking System and What to Do About It," 36 *Maryland Law Review* 788 (1977), http://digitalcommons.law.umaryland.edu/mlr/vol36/iss4/5, p. 801.

68   Irving Bernstein, *The Lean Years: A History of the American Worker, 1920–1933.*

69   Final Report and Recommendations of the Temporary National Economic Committee, 77th Congress, 1st Session, 1941, p. 27.

70   Winthrop Lane, *Civil War in West Virginia* (New York: B. W. Huebsch, 1921), p. 15.

71   Ibid., p. 8.

72   "Conditions in the Coal Fields of Ohio, West Virginia, and Pennsylvania,"

1928, Hearings Before the Committee of Interstate Commerce, United States Senate.

73 O'Connor, *Mellon's Millions*, p. 208.

74 "Conditions in the Coal Fields of Ohio, West Virginia, and Pennsylvania," 1928.

75 Schlesinger, *The Crisis of the Old Order, 1919–1933*, p. 67.

76 Kim Phillips-Fein, *Invisible Hands: The Businessmen's Crusade Against the New Deal*.

77 "Report on the Economic Conditions of the South," p. 23. This report was written in the 1930s, but there's no reason to assume the conditions were substantially different ten years before.

78 Ibid., p. 24.

79 Ibid., p. 30.

80 Frank Costigliola, *Awkward Dominion: American Political, Economic, and Cultural Relations with Europe, 1919–1933*, p. 134.

81 Jon Patrick Diggins, *Mussolini and Fascism: The View from America*.

82 Ibid., p. 206.

83 "An Apology for Fascism," *New Republic,* January 12, 1927, pp. 207–8.

84 Gian Giacomo Migone, *The United States and Fascist Italy: The Rise of American Finance in Europe*, p. 59.

85 "Secretary Mellon Admires the Boss of Sunny Italy," *Brooklyn Daily Eagle,* June 28, 1925.

86 Frank Costigliola, *Awkward Dominion: American Political, Economic, and Cultural Relations with Europe, 1919–1933*, p. 134.

87 "Mussolini Most Remarkable Says Secretary Mellon," *St. Petersburg Times,* August 12, 1926.

88 David Finley Papers, Box 68; *New York Times*, March 12, 1926; "Mussolini Most Remarkable Says Secretary Mellon," *St. Petersburg Times.*

89 David Finley Papers, Box 71; "Republican Policies," speech of A. W. Mellon, from station WRC, October 29, 1928.

90 David Finley Papers, Box 73; interview with John Sinclair of the North American Newspaper alliance, November 8, 1928.

## CHAPTER THREE
### The Impeachment of the Old Order

1 Brandeis dissent in *New State Ice Co. v. Liebmann*, 285 U.S. 262 (1932), U.S. Supreme Court, decided March 21, 1932.

2 Statement of Wright Patman, "Mellonism," upon Mellon's resignation from the Treasury and appointment as ambassador to England, WPP, Box 1511C.

3 "Asks Mellon's Impeachment on 1789 Law," Associated Press, reprinted in *New York Daily News,* January 7, 1932, p. 2.

4   Nancy Beck Young, *Wright Patman: Populism, Liberalism & the American Dream,* p. 23.

5   "Demands That House Impeach Mellon," *New York Times,* January 7, 1932, p. 9.

6   Janet Schmetzer, "Wright Patman and the Impeachment of Andrew Mellon," *East Texas Historical Journal* 23, no. 1 (1985); Young, *Wright Patman,* p. 43; Paul Dickson and Thomas Allen, *The Bonus Army: An American Epic,* p. 50.

7   Eligibility of Hon. Andrew W. Mellon Secretary of the Treasury, Report of the Committee on the Judiciary, May 7, 1929 (Minority report was Norris, Caraway, Walsh, Blaine), p. 17.

8   Dickson and Allen, *The Bonus Army,* p. 49.

9   Emmanuel Saez, "Striking it Richer: The Evolution of Top Incomes in the United States (Updated with 2014 preliminary estimates)," Technical Notes 201506, *World Inequality Lab,* 2015.

10  See Jane D'Arista, *The Evolution of U.S. Finance,* vol. 1. In 1920, the Fed was dominated by what became known as the "real bills" doctrine, meaning that the Fed, rather than pulling the country out of recession when times were bad or cooling off a boom when times were good, did the opposite. Several branches of the Fed did not even realize they were conducting monetary policy, and just sought to make money to fund their operations while helping their local member banks.

11  Frederick Lewis Allen, *Only Yesterday: An Informal History of the 1920s,* p. 237.

12  Ibid., p. 239.

13  Cordell Hull Papers, reel 3, letter from Judge George Anderson, November 20, 1925, response November 23, 1925. Hull called it a "Mark Hanna period of psychology."

14  Nomi Prins, *All the Presidents' Bankers: The Hidden Alliances That Drive American Power,* p. 94.

15  John Kenneth Galbraith, *The Great Crash 1929,* p. 37

16  Prins, *All the Presidents' Bankers,* p. 95.

17  David Cannadine, *Mellon: An American Life,* p. 390–91.

18  Studs Terkel, *Hard Times: An Oral History of the Great Depression,* p. 20; Cannadine, *Mellon,* p. 305.

19  See the chapters "The Big Bull Market" and "Crash!" in Allen, *Only Yesterday.*

20  Terkel, *Hard Times,* p. 6.

21  See, for instance, "William Guggenheim Says to Stop 'Soaking the Rich,' Only Big Business Can Pull the Country Out of Depression," *New York Times,* January 13, 1933.

22  Senate Subcommittee of the Committee on Manufactures, "Federal Emergency Measures to Relieve Unemployment" hearing, statements of Dr. Edward Israel, Chairman of the Committee on Social Justice of the Central Conference of American Rabbis; Dr. James Myers of New York, for the Federal Council of Churches in Christ; Dr. R. A. MacGowan of Washington, D.C., of

the National Catholic Welfare Conference; and Dr. Sidney Goldstein of New York, Chairman of the Joint Committee on Unemployment, June 20, 1932.

23  Ibid., p. 21.

24  *Garment Worker: Official Organ of the United Garment Workers of America,* vol. 31, 1931, p. 18.

25  Senate Subcommittee of the Committee on Manufactures, "Federal Emergency Measures to Relieve Unemployment," hearing. The numbers on the unemployed come from the statement of Edward McGrady of the Federation of Labor, June 20, 1932.

26  "After the Dearborn Massacre," *New Republic,* March 30, 1932.

27  Senate Subcommittee of the Committee on Manufactures, "Federal Emergency Measures to Relieve Unemployment," hearing, statement of John Edelman, starting on p. 20.

28  William Manchester, "Rock Bottom in America," *New York,* 8/5/1974, pp. 24–32, 41–46.

29  Schlesinger, *The Crisis of the Old Order, 1919–1933,* p. 205.

30  Dickson and Allen, *The Bonus Army,* p. 160.

31  Schlesinger, *The Crisis of the Old Order, 1919–1933,* p. 256.

32  Dickson and Allen, *The Bonus Army,* p. 52; Lisio, *The President and Protest.*

33  "Federal Emergency Measures to Relieve Unemployment," Senate Subcommittee of the Committee on Manufactures, June 20, 1932.

34  Young, *Wright Patman,* p. 12.

35  Arnold B. Sawisklak, "Patman Pulls No Punches In Fight for 'Little Man,'" *Daily News-Journal,* August 29, 1967.

36  Young, *Wright Patman,* p. 7.

37  Letter to voters from Patman in campaign to retain District Attorney seat, undated, WPP, Box 77.

38  Campaign materials, "Wright Patman Opens Campaign for Congress" WPP, Box 77.

39  Oral history transcript, Wright Patman, interview 1 (I), August 11, 1972, by Joe B. Frantz; oral history transcript, Wright Patman, interview 2 (II), February 4, 1976, by Michael L. Gillette, LBJ Library Oral Histories.

40  Oklahoma Historical Society, August 29, 2014, https://web.archive.org /web/20140829191410/ and http://digital.library.okstate.edu/encyclopedia /entries/S/SO001.html.

41  Young, *Wright Patman,* p. 5.

42  Oral history transcript, Wright Patman, interview 1 (I), August 11, 1972, by Joe B. Frantz, LBJ Library Oral Histories, accessed January 12, 2019, https:// www.discoverlbj.org/item/oh-patmanw-19720811-1-74-97, p. 5.

43  Oral history transcript, Wright Patman, interview 1 (I), August 11, 1972, by Joe B. Frantz, LBJ Library Oral Histories, accessed June 4, 2019, https://www .discoverlbj.org/item/oh-patmanw-19720811-1-74-97.

44    See Young's analysis of the census, *Wright Patman,* p. 23, note 33.

45    "Mr. Patman of Texas," *The Calhoun County News,* 1/29/1932, WPP, Box 1511C.

46    "Real Estate, Mortgage Foreclosure, and Blue Sky Legislation," Committee on the District of Columbia and Its Subcommittee on the Judiciary House of Representatives 71st Congress, 2nd and 3rd Sessions, on H.R. 4950, H.R. 10476, S. 3490, S. 3489, S. 3491, March 3, 7, 10, 12, 19, 1930, February 24, 25, 26, and 27, 1931.

47    Investigation of Activities of Those Engaged in Purchasing Cottonseed Oil, Etc., Hearing Before the Rules Committee, February 10, 1930.

48    "Attacks Probe of Power Trust," *The Pittsburgh Press,* October 6, 1930, p. 11.

49    Ibid., p. 2.

50    "Memorial Services Held in the House of Representatives and Senate of the United States, Together with Tributes Presented in Eulogy of Wright Patman, Late a Representative from Texas," (Washington, D.C: United States Government Printing Office, 1976).

51    "Charges of Hon. Wright Patman Against the Secretary of the Treasury," Hearings before the Committee on the Judiciary, January 13, 14, 15, 18, 19, 1932, p. 24.

52    *Congressional Record,* February 29, 1932, p. 4968.

53    Ibid., January 11, 1933, p. 1585.

54    This is according to Secretary of War Newton Baker. Mitchell Yockelson, "Military Service in the United States Army During World War I, 1917–1919" Genealogy Notes, *Prologue Magazine* 30, no. 3 (Fall 1998), https://www.archives .gov/publications/prologue/1998/fall/military-service-in-world-war-one .html.

55    Dickson and Allen, *Bonus Army,* p. 4.

56    I. J. Grompine and J. Donald Edwards, "Terminations After World War I," http://scholarship.law.duke.edu/cgi/viewcontent.cgi?article=2204&context =lcp.

57    Stephen R. Ortiz, *Beyond the Bonus March and GI Bill: How Veteran Politics Shaped the New Deal Era,* p. 17.

58    Mellon's views were similar to those of Democrats, as he wrote in his book on economics: *Taxation: The People's Business.* "My own recommendations on this subject were in line with similar ones made by Secretaries Houston and Glass, both of whom served under a Democratic president."

59    John W. Dean, "President Vetoes Bonus Bill Benefitting Soldiers," *The History Reader,* April 29, 2011, http://www.thehistoryreader.com/modern-history /president-vetos-bonus-bill-benefiting-soldiers/.

60    Dickson and Allen, *The Bonus Army,* p. 26.

61    Smedley Butler, *War Is a Racket* (1935).

62    Full speech reprinted in *New Outlook,* July 21, 1922.

63    John W. Dean, "President Vetoes Bonus Bill Benefitting Soldiers," *Historical*

*Reader,* April 29, 2011, http://www.thehistoryreader.com/modern-history/president-vetos-bonus-bill-benefiting-soldiers/.

64 Donald J. Lisio, "A Blunder Becomes Catastrophe: Hoover, the Legion, and the Bonus Army," *Wisconsin Magazine of History* 51, no. 1 (1967): 37–50, www.jstor.org/stable/4634286.

65 Dickson and Allen, *The Bonus Army,* p. 23.

66 Ibid. It was nicknamed the Tombstone Bonus because a veteran could get the money early and leave it to his next of kin should he die before 1945. Patman discussed this in his 1934 pamphlet "Patman's Appeal to Veterans."

67 Lisio, *The President and Protest,* p. 28

68 Patman would give these kinds of speeches routinely over several years. For specific quotes cited here, see *Congressional Record,* December 30, 1932, p. 1135. On January 17, 1933, he said, "Every community will get a share. It will go to every class, race, and creed; every occupation, avocation, and trade will be benefited; it will be deposited in the banks, which will increase the reserves of the banks, make the depositors' money safer and credit easier to obtain."

69 See Ortiz, *Beyond the Bonus March and GI Bill,* as well as Young, *Wright Patman*; Lisio, *The President and Protest,* p. 32.

70 Ortiz, *Beyond the Bonus March and GI Bill,* p. 39.

71 Letter to Lon Boynton in Paris, Texas, WPP, Box 1115C.

72 Letter to Joint Committee on Revenue Taxation, October 7, 1931, WPP, Box 1511A (Gulf, Koppers, Standard Steel Car, Mellon National Bank, Bethlehem Steel).

73 Letter to Patman from I. Jalonick, Republic Insurance Company, September 29, 1931, WPP, Box 1511A.

74 Letter from Douglas Van Horne to Wright Patman, January 19, 1932, WPP, Box 1511C; letter from J. Rossman, undated, WPP, Box 1511A.

75 Undated statement from J. A. Truesdell, WPP, Box 1511C. The company was Pacific Oil Company, which went out of business after Comptroller Daniel Crissinger ordered banks not to accept its stock or bonds as collateral.

76 Letter to Patman from Evan Humphreys, January 15, 1931, WPP, Box 1511C.

77 Letter from Carlos Melguizo, December 29, 1931, WPP, Box 1511B; letter to Henry Stimson from Wright Patman, October 7, 1931, WPP, Box 1511A.

78 Telegram from Clarence Cannon to Wright Patman, September 9, 1931, WPP, Box 1511A.

79 Letter from Ben Miller to Wright Patman, July 14, 1931, WPP, Box 1511A.

80 Letter from Wright Patman to Hon. Jus. Allred, Attorney General of Texas, February 6, 1933, WPP, Box 1511C.

81 Ortiz, *Beyond the Bonus March and GI Bill,* pp. 42–44.

82 Schmetzer, "Wright Patman and the Impeachment of Andrew Mellon," p. 37.

83 Dickson and Allen, *The Bonus Army,* p. 45.

84   Ibid., p. 49.

85   Young, *Wright Patman,* p. 43.

86   Schmetzer, "Wright Patman and the Impeachment of Andrew Mellon."

87   Terkel, *Hard Times,* p. 271; Schmetzer, "Wright Patman and the Impeachment of Andrew Mellon," p. 39.

88   "Charges of Hon. Wright Patman Against the Secretary of the Treasury," Hearings before the Committee on the Judiciary, January 13, 14, 15, 18, 19, 1932.

89   Letter from Patman to I. Jalonick, October 3, 1931, WPP, Box 1511A.

90   Cannadine, *Mellon,* p. 451.

91   Ibid., p. 297.

92   George David Smith, *From Monopoly to Competition: The Transformations of Alcoa, 1888–1986,* p. 143.

93   Schmetzer, "Wright Patman and the Impeachment of Andrew Mellon," p. 41.

94   Drew Pearson, "Mellon Oil Concession Figured in Colombian Credit, Witness Says," *Baltimore Sun,* January 13, 1932, p. 1.

95   "Olaya's Oil Version Disputed by Mellon," *New York Times,* January 16, 1932; "Special Cable to the New York Times," *New York Times,* January 16, 1932.

96   Dickson and Allen, *The Bonus Army,* p. 52

97   Statement of Wright Patman Regarding Appointment of Andrew W. Mellon As Ambassador to Great Britain, WPP, Box 1511C.

98   *The Saco News* (Saco, Maine), WPP, Box 1511C.

99   Telegram from The American Legion, Luckette Cochrane Post, February 4, 1932, WPP, Box 1511C.

100  Hoover press conference, April 15, 1932: "Another one of the contributions to the setback in confidence has been the agitation of the bonus."

101  Dickson and Allen, *The Bonus Army,* p. 1.

102  Terkel, *Hard Times,* p. 2.

103  Senate Subcommittee of the Committee on Manufactures, June 20, 1932, "Federal Emergency Measures to Relieve Unemployment," statement of Roy Wilkins, assistant secretary, NAACP, p. 21; Dickson and Allen, *The Bonus Army,* p. 118.

104  Cody Carlson, "This week in history: President Hoover orders the Bonus Army dispersed," *Deseret News,* July 31, 2013.

105  William Manchester, "Rock Bottom in America," *New York,* August 5, 1974, p. 28.

106  Dickson and Allen, *The Bonus Army,* p. 187.

107  Ibid., p. 175; Manchester, "Rock Bottom in America," pp. 23–42, 41–46.

108  Manchester, "Rock Bottom in America," p. 31.

109  "Coming Civil Rights March in Capital," *CQ Almanac,* http://library.cqpress.com/cqalmanac/document.php?id=cqal68-1282236; William Manchester, "Rock Bottom in America," *New York,* August 5, 1974, p. 24.

110   Statement of Wright Patman (issued after the clash with the Bonus army), WPP, Box 1511A.

111   Letter from Patman to American Veterans Association National Commander Charles Kinsolving, August 15, 1934, WPP, Box 1511A.

112   Thomas Phillip Wolf, William D. Pederson, and Byron W. Daynes, *Franklin D. Roosevelt and Congress: The New Deal and Its Aftermath*, p. 86.

113   Joshua K. Hausman, "Fiscal Policy and Economic Recovery: The Case of the 1936 Veterans' Bonus," June 17, 2013.

114   Martin Luther King Jr., "The Crisis in America's Cities: An Analysis of Social Disorder and a Plan of Action Against Poverty, Discrimination, and Racism in Urban America," Atlanta, Southern Christian Leadership Conference, August 15, 1967: "If they are developed as weekly events at the same time that mass sit-ins are developed inside and at the gates of factories for jobs, and if simultaneously thousands of unemployed youth camp in Washington, as the Bonus Marchers did in the thirties, with these and other practices, without burning a match or firing a gun, the impact of the movement will have earthquake proportions. (In the Bonus Marches, it was the government that burned down the marchers' shelters when it became confounded by peaceful civil disobedience.)"

## CHAPTER FOUR
### Populists Take Power

1    Eugene C. Gerhart, *Robert H. Jackson: Country Lawyer, Supreme Court Justice, America's Advocate*, p. 474.

2    Democratic State Convention Keynote, File #251, September 27, 1926, Franklin D. Roosevelt Presidential Library & Museum.

3    "Roosevelt Orders Merger Inquiry," *New York Times*, June 30, 1929, p. 20; "Roosevelt's Radio Address on Power," *New York Times*. 4/8/1931; "State Inquiry Urged Into Utility Board," *New York Times*. 1/28/1929.

4    "Morgan Buys Power Chain Fought by Smith in 1926, Now Controls Vital Sites," *New York Times*, 9/14/1929.

5    "Franklin Roosevelt on Public Utilities: Democratic Governor of New York Plans to Make This Question, Instead of Prohibition, His Chief Issue in Campaign for Reelection," *Hartford Courant*, 5/25/1930.

6    "The Governor States the Power Issue," *New York Times*, 1/12/1930.

7    "Highlights of Governor Roosevelt's Message, Dealing with State and National Affairs," *New York Times*, 1/7/1932, p. 1.

8    "Issue to Be Forced," *Cincinnati Enquirer*, 3/6/1931.

9    "Washington Notes," *New Republic*, 4/1/1931.

10   "Howard Urges Favorite Sons Give Roosevelt Right of Way," *New York Times*, 1/5/1932, p. 1.

11    Letter to the Editor, *Hartford Courant,* 5/17/1932, p. 12.

12    "Monopoly and the Public Welfare," Address by Hon. C. N. Haskell, Oklahoma City, March 11, 1931, WPP, 1511B.

13    Hull, *The Memoirs of Cordell Hull,* Chapter 11, "Steering the Party Towards Roosevelt."

14    "Governor Ritchie's Jackson Day Dinner Speech," *New York Times,* 1/8/1932, p. 16; Arthur M. Schlesinger Jr., *The Coming of the New Deal, 1933–1935,* p. 284.

15    "Governor Ritchie's Jackson Day Dinner Speech"; "Ritchie Comes Out for the Presidency, Hailed at Big Rally: Attacking 'Over-regulation,' He Urges a 'Return' to First Democratic Principles," *New York Times,* 1/8/1932, p. 1.

16    Donald A. Ritchie, *Electing FDR: The New Deal Campaign of 1932,* p. 60.

17    Christopher Finan, *Alfred E. Smith: The Happy Warrior,* 2002, p. 235. Raskob opened a special investment account for Smith. The winnings went to Smith, the losses were absorbed by Raskob. Just one transfer to Smith, presumably one of many, was $118,000.

18    Columbus, Ohio, Campaign Speech (speech file 490), August 20, 1932, FDR Presidential Library.

19    Hull, *The Memoirs of Cordell Hull,* p. 141.

20    "Raskob Proposal for State Liquor Rule Starts a Storm in National Committee; Robinson Attacks, Smith Defends Him," *New York Times,* 3/6/1931.

21    Hull, *The Memoirs of Cordell Hull,* p. 143.

22    Ibid., p. 144.

23    "Raskob Is Repudiated," *Cincinnati Enquirer,* 3/6/1931, p. 1.

24    "National Breakdown Seen by La Follette At Progressive Meet," AP, as printed in the *Wausau Daily Record-Herald,* 3/12/1931, pp. 1, 8.

25    Schlesinger, *The Crisis of the Old Order, 1919–1933,* chapter, "Decision in Chicago"; Ritchie, *Electing FDR,* Chapter 2.

27    Ritchie, *Electing FDR,* p. 105.

28    Ritchie, *Electing FDR,* Chapter 3.

29    "Acceptance Speech for Presidential Nomination" (speech file 483A), Chicago, Illinois, July 2, 1932, FDR Presidential Library, http://www.fdrlibrary .marist.edu/_resources/images/msf/msf00494.

30    Schlesinger, *The Crisis of the Old Order,* p. 416.

31    Ritchie, *Electing FDR,* p. 120; Allen and Dicksen, *Bonus Army,* p. 193.

32    "Columbus, Ohio—Campaign Speech" (speech file 490), August 20, 1932, Franklin D. Roosevelt Presidential Library & Museum.

33    Salt Lake City, Speech at Mormon Temple (speech file 508), September 17, 1932, FDR Presidential Library.

34    "London Police Repel Raid by Jobless on Parliament in Three Hours of Rioting," *New York Times,* 11/2/1932, p. 1; "Insull Is Arrested; To Go to Hospital," *New York Times,* 11/5/1932; "Johnson Denounces Hoover's Audacity," *New York*

*Times,* 11/5/1932; Stern's on 42nd Street was holding a "landslide" sale on furniture and coats, ad, *New York Times,*11/6/1932, p. 10; "Cox Sees Faith Lost in Government," *New York Times,* 11/3/1932, p. 8; "Crowd Faces Storm to Cheer Roosevelt," *New York Times,* 11/2/1932, p. 1.

35  Eric Rauchway, *Winter War: Hoover, Roosevelt, and the First Clash over the New Deal,* p. 199; Studs Terkel, *Hard Times: An Oral History of the Great Depression),* p. 57.

36  Federal Deposit Insurance Corporation, *Managing the Crisis: The FDIC and RTC Experience—Chronological Overview,* https://www.fdic.gov/bank/histori cal/managing/chronological/pre-fdic.html.

37  "Los Angeles Stores Guarded," *New York Times,* 3/3/1933.

38  "Iowa Governor Asks Halt on Foreclosures," *New York Times,* 1/20/1933.

39  Schlesinger, *The Crisis of the Old Order,* p. 460.

40  "Railroads Demand 10 Percent Pay Cut Stand; Hint Move for 20%," *New York Times,* 12/13/1932, p. 1; "Tammany Yields to Bankers' Demands; Drastic Pay Cuts, Abolition of 3 Boards Among Reforms Up for Adoption Today," *New York Times,* 12/5/1932; "Aldermen Vote Pay Cuts; $20,000,000 More Planned; Banks Still Cool on Loans," *New York Times,* 12/6/1932. "Anti-Saloon League Hard Up; Hit by Bank Crash, Asks Help," *New York Times,* 1/6/1932.

41  Clarence Streit, "8 Killed, 45 Injured In Battle In Geneva," *New York Times,* 11/10/1932.

42  "Hitler Gets Chance to Form a Cabinet but Rejects Terms," *New York Times,* 11/22/1932, p. 1.

43  "Aldrich Hits at Private Bankers In Sweeping Plan for Reforms, *New York Times,* 3/9/1933.

44  Col. Edward M. House, "Does America Need a Dictator?," *Liberty* 10 (January 7, 1933).

45  "Long Range Social Plan for Nation Urged by Hoover Board to Stabilize Economic System and Curb Unrest," *New York Times,* 1/2/1933.

46  Rex Tugwell, *Democratic Roosevelt: A Biography of Franklin D. Roosevelt,* pp. 349–50.

47  Ibid.

48  Eric Rauchway, *Winter War: Hoover, Roosevelt and the First Clash over the New Deal,* p. 216.

49  For a good discussion of the bitter relationship between Hoover and FDR during the lame duck period, see Eric Rauchway, *Winter War.*

50  Schlesinger *The Crisis of the Old Order, 1919–1933,* p. 467.

51  76 *Congressional Record,* 3110, 1933, floor speech, February 1, 1933.

52  76 *Congressional Record,* 2538, 1933, floor debate, January 25, 1933. One of the key borrowers from the RFC was Charles Dawes, a former vice president and the winner of the Nobel Peace Prize in the 1920s. Hoover fought a losing battle to keep records of its lending secret.

53  "City Bank Officer Bares Ramsey Loan," *New York Times,* 3/2/1933, p. 8.

54 Ferdinand Pecora, *Wall Street Under Oath: The Story of Our Modern Money Changers*.

55 "Man Who Trapped Kreuger Describes Deals to Senators," *New York Times*, 1/12/1933, p. 1.

56 "Insull Is Arrested; To Go to Hospital," *New York Times*.

57 Pecora, *Wall Street Under Oath,* chapter, "Superbank"; *New York Times*, 2/22/1933, p. 1.

58 "Senator Wheeler Assails Mitchell," *New York Times, 2/22/1933*.

59 "Federal Inquiry on National City and Insull Starts," *New York Times*, 2/25/1933; Pecora, *Wall Street Under Oath*; "National City Lent $2.4M to Save Stock of Officers," 2/23/1933.

60 Pecora, *Wall Street Under Oath*.

61 "Morgan Foreign Financing Detailed, Fees Disclosed; Coolidge on One Stock List," *New York Times*, 5/26/1933.

62 "Glass and Pecora Battle as to Goal of Morgan Inquiry," *New York Times*, 5/27/1933.

63 "You and the House of Morgan," *Pittsburgh Press*, June 2, 1933, p. 2.

64 "'Sympathy' Voted to Morgan by the West Virginia House," *New York Times*, 5/24/1933.

65 Pecora, *Wall Street Under Oath*; "British Creditors Offered," *New York Times*, 5/26/1933, p. 1.

66 "Morgan Foreign Financing Detailed, Fees Disclosed; Coolidge on One Stock List," *New York Times*, 5/26/1933.

67 "20 Companies Lent 20 Billions in 1929 in Call Loan Boom," *New York Times*, 2/24/1934, p. 1.

68 Pecora, *Wall Street Under Oath*.

69 "Inaugural Address," March 4, 1933, speech file 610, FDR Presidential Library, http://www.fdrlibrary.marist.edu/_resources/images/msf/msf00628.

70 "Fireside Chat on Banking March 12, 1933," speech file 616a, FDR Presidential Library; "Emergency Banking Act of 1933" by the Federal Reserve Bank of Richmond, 2013, https://www.federalreservehistory.org/essays/emergency _banking_act_of_1933.

71 "Chicago Teachers Lay Siege to Banks," Associated Press, *Baltimore Sun*, April 25, 1933, p. 5.

72 Emanuel Celler, *You Never Leave Brooklyn: The Autobiography of Emanuel Celler*, p. 11–12.

73 "So They Say," *The Bakersfield Californian*, June 16, 1933, p. 18.

74 "Cummings Surveys Mitchell Evidence," *New York Times*, 3/18/1933.

75 Thoams F. Huertas and Joan L. Silverman, "Charles E. Mitchell: Scapegoat of the Crash?," *The Business History Review* 60, no. 1 (1986): 81–103, www.jstor .org/stable/3115924.

76 "New York Banker Loses Court Fight," *Cumberland Evening Times*, 8/8/1935.

77  "Harriman Stabs Himself as He Is Found in Roslyn; His Wounds Not Serious," *New York Times*, 5/21/1933, p. 1.

78  History of the Mellon Tax Case, memo, RJP (Robert Jackson Papers), Box 67.

79  Ibid.

80  Drew Pearson and Bob Allen, *Washington Merry-Go-Round* (syndicated column of Drew Pearson), June 5, 1933.

81  "Mellon, Walker, T. S. Lamont Face Actions on Taxes," *New York Times*, 3/11/1934, p. 1.

82  "Andrew Mellon Indictment Fails," *Indianapolis News*, 5/8/1934, p. 2.

83  Cannadine, *Mellon*, p. 512–13.

84  Ibid.

85  Ibid., p. 523.

86  Ibid.

87  "Senators Bitterly Debate Gold Cases," *New York Times*, 2/21/1935, pp. 1, 2

88  Cannadine, *Mellon*, p. 525.

89  September 6,1934, letter to Morgenthau, RJP, Box 67.

90  Eugene C. Gerhart, *Robert H. Jackson: Country Lawyer, Supreme Court Justice, America's Advocate*, p. 74.

91  *Pittsburgh Press*, 2/20/1935, p. 2.

92  Opening statement of Jackson, RJP, Box 68.

93  February 22, 1935, letter to Oliphant from Jackson, RJP, Box 67.

94  August 20, 1934, letter to Jackson from the head of the Appeals Division, RJP, Box 67.

95  *Muncie Evening Press*, 2/7/1935, p. 9.

96  Cannadine, *Mellon*, p. 534.

97  "Bars Bank Records in Mellon Tax Suits," *New York Times*, 2/20/1935, pp. 1, 7.

98  "Whip-Lash Tongues, Rapier-Like Minds of Hogan and Jackson Liven Mellon Fight," *Pittsburgh Press*, 2/20/1935, p. 2.

99  David Finley Papers, Box 65.

100 April 11, 1935, letter to Oliphant, RJP, Box 12: "The death of Mr. Ochs was felt by us owing to the attitude he had taken in the Mellon case. . . . We were confidentially informed that A. W. Mellon himself had written a bitter letter complaining of the publicity being given by the *New York Times*, and asking that Daniel be withdrawn. We were also advised from the same confidential source that Mr. Ochs had sent a man to Pittsburgh who could neither be intimidated nor bought, and that he would not suppress the stories or change the reporter. Unfortunately for Jackson, Ochs died in the middle of the trial, and Daniell was reassigned to Arkansas to investigate tenant farming. Jackson noted that he then had to rely "on Associated Press reports which we have good reason to believe are censored or at least are carefully written to suit the other people."

101 See for instance January 11, 1935, letter from *Washington Post* publisher Eugene

Meyer to David Finley asking for Mellon to have a Mellon company, the Pittsburgh Plate Glass Co., advertise in his newspaper, and May 29, 1934, letter from Finley to Mellon on a request by Meyer for Mellon to talk to Heinz about advertising. David Finley Papers, Box 17.

102 "Eugene Grace Called in Mellon's Hearing," Associated Press, 4/18/1935; Fred Perkins, "Steel to Rise to New Highs, Schwab Says," *Pittsburgh Press*, 5/20/1935; Fred Perkins, "British Expert on Art Works Helps Mellon," *Pittsburgh Press*, 5/10/1935.

103 February 22, 1935, letter to Oliphant from Jackson, RJP, Box 67.

104 *Pittsburgh Press,* 2/20/1935, p. 2.

105 *Green Bay Press-Gazette,* 2/18/1935, p. 9; opening statement of Frank Hogan, trial transcript, p. 12.

106 Opening Statement by Frank Hogan, trial transcript, pp. 90–92.

107 Letter to Oliphant from Jackson, February 22, 1935, RJP, Box 67; and in addition an interview with Carrin Patman. For an alternative perspective, see Cannadine, *Mellon.*

108 "$19M Art Gift Planned by Mellon," *New York Times,* 2/19/1935, pp. 1, 23.

109 Opening statement, RJP, Box 67.

110 "Charges Mellon Aided Own Banks While Secretary," *New York Times,* 2/27/35.

111 "Mellon Accused of Selling Short," *New York Times,* 2/21/1935, p. 1. Mellon's witness denied Mellon was betting against the market, but Jackson's cross-examination was devastating. "Wasn't it entered on the broker's account as a short position?" he asked. "Yes," said Mr. Johnson. Before Jackson could get more details, Van Fossan, the board head, excused the witness.

112 "Twelve Ways to Dodge the Income Tax," *New Republic,* May 29, 1935, pp. 74–75.

113 "Mellon Millions Given to Children, but He Got Income," *New York Times,* 2/26/1935.

114 February 25, 1935, letter, RJP, Box 67.

115 February 22, 1935, letter to Herman Oliphant, RJP, Box 67.

116 "Mellon's Hearing to Be Shifted Here," *New York Times,* 3/22/1935, p. 8.

117 Gerhart, *America's Advocate*, pp. 76–78.

118 Letter from Jackson to Oliphant, April 11, 1935, RJP, Box 67.

119 See front page of *Pittsburgh Press* on 5/1/1935: "Big Business Rips New Deal," "13,000 Are Idle in Auto Dispute," "Police on Guard In Milk Strike," "Morgenthau Stand on Tax Hit by Mellon." See also telegram from Morgenthau to Jackson, 4/30/1935, RJP, Box 67; letters from Jackson to Oliphant, 5/29/1935, RJP, Box 67.

120 "Morgenthau Stand on Tax Hit by Mellon," *Pittsburgh Press*, 5/1/1935.

121 "Mellon Assailed on 'Panic' Defense," *New York Times,* 5/3/1935, p. 42.

122 "Many Tax Cases Hinge on Mellon's," *New York Times,* 3/18/1935.

123 "Du Pont Tax Sale to Raskob Scored," *New York Times,* 4/4/1937, p. 3.

124 Letter from Jackson to Morganthau, RJP, Box 67; and in addition an interview with Carrin Patman.

125 Conversation between Treasury Secretary Henry Morgenthau and Senator James Couzens, 48 A-B 3/7/1935, Henry Morgenthau diary, Volume 4, March 1–April 22, 1935, Part One, where Couzens asks for a transcript of the trial and says it will be "very helpful" for the Senate's legislative program.

126 "Mellon Tax Fight Renewed in Briefs," *New York Times*, 5/2/1936, p. 2.

127 Gerhart, *America's Advocate*, p. 80–82.

128 "Du Ponts $144,430 Tops Landon Gifts," *New York Times*, 12/2/1936, p. 10. For discussion of new appointees, see "History of the Mellon Tax Case," p. 3, RJP, Box 67; and letters to Jackson from Ottamar Hamele, Head, Appeals Division, 8/20/1934 and 8/16/1934, RJP, Box 67.

129 "Landon Is Assailed by Six Governors in Party Broadside," *New York Times*, 7/26/1936, pp. 1, 8.

130 Madison Square Garden Address (2 parts), speech file 1007A and 1007B, FDR Presidential Library, October 31, 1936

131 "Industry Gives Up Fight on New Deal," *New York Times*, 12/10/1936, pp. 1, 36.

132 "Mellon Gives Art to U.S.; $27,000,000, With Gallery—President 'happy at Project'," *New York Times*, 1/3/1937.

133 Memo for the Attorney General, "Matter of Offer of A.W.M,.," 1/4/1937, RPJ, Box 67.

134 February 11, 1937, letter from La Guardia to Patman, WPP, Box 1511A.

135 History of the Mellon Tax Case, memo, RJP, Box 67. The seven dissenters said the board "undertook to prejudge evidence" that would have sustained the government's contentions.

136 Memo to the Secretary of the Treasury, June 6, 1938, Henry Morgenthau Diaries, FDR Presidential Library, http://www.fdrlibrary.marist.edu/_resources/images/morg/md0173.pdf; Morgenthau Papers, Box 406, Grossman memo summarizing Morgenthau's view that the tax trial forced Mellon to create the National Gallery, November 18, 1946.

137 Message to Congress on Tax Evasion Prevention, June 1, 1937; Roy G. and Gladys C. Blakey, "The Revenue Act of 1937," *American Economic Review* 27, no. 4 (1937): 698–704, www.jstor.org/stable/1801981.

138 "I.C.C. Investigates Mellon Railroads," *New York Times*, 5/19/1936, p. 33.

139 "'Oil Trust' Trial Opens Tomorrow," *New York Times*, 10/3/1937, Business Section, p. 1; Cannadine, *Mellon*, pp. 571–72; Smith, *From Monopoly to Competition*, pp.188–89.

140 "Strike Threatens Rolling Rock Hunt," *New York Times*, 4/11/1937, p. 74; "Rolling Rock Farms to Be Given Up—Sit-Down Closes Steel Man's Potato Cellar," *New York Times*, 4/2/1937, p. 15; "R. K. Mellon, Sportsman Nephew, Seen as Head of Family Finances Instead of Scholar Son," *New York Times*, 8/29/1937, p. 4.

141 Lecture of John Q. Barrett on Robert H. Jackson Prosecuting Andrew W. Mellon, Youtube.com, 2001 (minute 3:30), https://www.youtube.com/watch ?v=EsduLzolIAU).

142 Author interview with Jane D'Arista.


## CHAPTER 5
### Trustbusters Against Hitler

1 "Fireside Chat #12—New Spending Program" (2 parts), speech file 1129A and 1129B, April 14, 1948, FDR Presidential Library.

2 William Edgar Borah Papers, Box 801.

3 Maury Klein, *A Call to Arms: Mobilizing America for World War II,* p. 161.

4 February 28, 1935, memo to Morgenthau, RJP, Box 67.

5 "121-Year-Old Bank Closes in Pittsburgh," *New York Times,* 9/21/1931.

6 "Pittsburgh Doors Closed to Conserve Funds," *Pittsburgh Press,* 9/21/1931.

7 "Stock Exchange Forbids Short Selling After England Suspends Gold Standard; Prices Rally Sharply After Early Drop," *Ithaca Journal,* 9/21/1931.

8 Cannadine, *Mellon,* p. 441.

9 February 28, 1935, memo to Morgenthau, RJP, Box 67.

10 Ibid.

11 Gerhart, *Robert H. Jackson,* pp. 80–81.

12 See undated memo, "Monopoly versus Democracy," Homer Cummings Papers, Box 222.

13 "The Menace to Free Enterprise," Robert Jackson before the American Political Science Association, December 29, 1937, p. 6, RJP, Box 79.

14 Robert Jackson, *That Man: An Insider's Portrait of Franklin D. Roosevelt,* p. 122.

15 Laura Phillips Sawyer, *American Fair Trade: Proprietary Capitalism, Corporatism, and the "New Competition," 1890–1940,* p. 252.

16 Ibid., pp. 279, 289.

17 Arthur M. Schlesinger Jr., *The Coming of the New Deal, 1933–1935,* p. 280.

18 Sidney Hyman, *Marriner Eccles: Private Entrepreneur and Public Servant,* p. 240.

19 See Alan Brinkley, *The End of Reform: New Deal Liberalism in Recession and War,* pp. 89–91.

20 75 *Congressional Record* 747, 1931, December 18, 1931.

21 Henry Wolfe, "Hitler Looks Eastward," *The Atlantic,* February 1937.

22 "'No Hope' in Europe, Baruch Reports," *New York Times,* 9/7/1937, p. 14.

23 Confidential memorandum for the secretary of the treasury, September 12, 1938, Morgenthau Diaries, http://www.fdrlibrary.marist.edu/_resources/images/morg/md0184.pdf.

24 Memorandum of a Fishing Trip with President Roosevelt Leaving Washington, D.C., on Saturday November 27, 1937, and Returning on Monday, December 6, 1937, RJP, Box 189.

25 December 31, 1937, letter to Thurman Arnold from Robert Jackson, RJP, Box 77.

26 "Ickes Lashes Out At Big Business," Associated Press, as printed in the *Boston Globe*, 12/31/1937,

27 "Robert H. Jackson at the Antitrust Division," *Albany Law Review*, June 27, 2005, p. 795.

28 Fireside chat, April 14, 1938.

29 April 29, 1938, Message to Congress on Curbing Monopolies.

30 Speech by Joseph O'Mahoney, July 11, 1938, Joseph C. O'Mahoney Papers, University of Wyoming, American Heritage Center, Accession Number 00275, Box 22, Folder 17, pp. 4–5.

31 William Pederson, ed., *A Companion to Franklin D. Roosevelt*; Frank McDonough, ed., *The Origins of the Second World War: An International Perspective*, p. 483.

32 Norman Littell, "The German Invasion of American Business," January 25, 1941, Temporary National Economic Committee final report, p. 182.

33 An Address by Francis Biddle, Attorney General of the United States, to Be Given at the Annual Dinner of the Harvard Law School Alumni Association, Harvard Club, New York, New York, February 23, 1944, Emanuel Celler Papers, Box 53.

34 Clifford Durr, *The Early History of the Defense Plant Corporation*, p. 7.

35 Maury Klein, *A Call to Arms: Mobilizing America for World War II*, p. 65.

36 This includes John Maynard Keynes, who wrote *The Economic Consequences of the Peace*, a bestseller, in 1919, and Woodrow Wilson, who predicted another war if the Treaty of Versailles failed. Keynes reiterated his fear in 1933, when an open letter to Roosevelt he wrote was published in the *New York Times*, warning that if FDR failed, rational discourse would disappear, and the forces of revolution and orthodoxy would fight it out.

37 April 12, 1935, letter to Bruce Bliven, RJP, Box 67.

38 "Campaign Address at Columbus, Ohio, August 20, 1932. Columbus, Ohio—Campaign Speech" (speech file 490), FDR Presidential Library.

39 John Maynard Keynes, "Letter of February 1 to Franklin Delano Roosevelt," in *Collected Works XXI: Activities 1931–1939* (London: Macmillan, 1982).

40 Report of the Assistant Attorney General Robert H. Jackson in charge of the Antitrust Division, Homer Cummings Papers, Box 222, p. 13.

41 Diary 66, April 23–30, 1937, p. 64, Henry Morgenthau Diaries, FDR Library Online, http://www.fdrlibrary.marist.edu/_resources/images/morg/md0090 .pdf.

42 "Just How Mr. Mellon Controls the Aluminum of All the World," *Milwaukee Journal*, 5/9/1937.

43 Klein, *A Call to Arms*, p. 160.

44 *Early History of the Defense Plant Corporation*, Committee on Public Administration Cases, 1950, p. 21; Klein, *A Call to Arms*, p. 63.

45 Final Report on the Reconstruction Finance Corporation, p. 126.

46 See, for instance, Robert Nathan's comments on planning for key raw materials, which were steel, aluminum, and copper. Oral History Interview with Robert R. Nathan, Chairman, Planning Commission War Production Board, 1942–1943, Deputy Director, Office of War Mobilization and Reconversion, 1945, UN Korean Reconstruction Agency, 1952–1953, Harry Truman Library, https://www.trumanlibrary.org/oralhist/nathanrr.htm.

47 George David Smith, *From Monopoly to Competition: The Transformation of Alcoa, 1888–1986*, p. 3.

48 Harvey O'Connor, *Mellon's Millions: The Biography of a Fortune; the Life and Times of Andrew W. Mellon*, p. 80.

49 George David Smith, *From Monopoly to Competition*, p. 10.

50 O'Connor, *Mellon's Millions*, p. 84.

51 Ibid., pp. 90–92.

52 Ibid.

53 George David Smith, *From Monopoly to Competition*, p. 131.

54 Quentin Skrabec, *Aluminum in America: A History*, p. 178.

55 George David Smith, *From Monopoly to Competition*, p. 138–40.

56 O'Connor, *Mellon's Millions*, p. 78.

57 Ibid., p. 80; "Just How Mr. Mellon Controls the Aluminum of All the World," *Milwaukee Journal*, 5/9/1937.

58 "Flock of Vice-Presidents Support Aluminum Chief," *Pittsburgh Press*, 10/3/1933, p. 16.

59 "Just How Mr. Mellon Controls the Aluminum of All the World," *Milwaukee Journal*, 5/9/1937; for the price change, see complaint *United States of America v Aluminum Company of America*, Homer Cummings, Box 71, for the "aluminum standard" joke, see O'Connor, *Mellon's Millions*, p. xiv.

60 "Roosevelt's Radio Address on Power," *New York Times*, 4/8/1931.

61 Memo to Mr. Stevens from Homer Cummings, July 8, 1933, and letter to George Haskell from Homer Cummings, February 7, 1934, Homer Cummings Papers, Box 71.

62 George David Smith, *From Monopoly to Competition*, p. 192.

63 Letter to the President from Homer Cummings about a legal proceeding in the case, June 1, 1937, RJP, Box 77.

64 *United States v. Aluminum Company of America, et al.,* petition.

65 See Romeneike Press Clipping Bureau cartoon in Homer Cummings, Box 71.

66 Uncompleted Jackson autobiography, RJP, Box 189, p. 94; "Mellon Company Is Sued as Aluminum Monopoly; Its Dissolution Is Sought," *New York Times*, 4/24/1937, p. 1; Eugene C. Gerhart, *Robert H. Jackson: Country Lawyer, Supreme Court Justice, America's Advocate.*

67 Mark R. Wilson, *Destructive Creation: American Business and the Winning of World War I*, p. 43.

68 See memos by Walter Rice to Robert Jackson, correspondence between the

attorney general and the secretary of war, FBI file on an investigation of Donald Davenport at Harvard Business School, letter from HWT Eglin, Colonel, to Alcoa—in Homer Cummings Papers, Box 71.

69  Peter Irons, *The New Deal Lawyers*, pp. 3, 13.

70  Jeff Shesol, *Supreme Power: Franklin Roosevelt vs. The Supreme Court.*

71  July 15, 1922, letter from the attorney general to the president, RJP, Box 77: "Mr. Gibson is endorsed by both the Pennsylvania Senators and by Mr. Mellon, Secretary of the Treasury."

72  June 1, 1937, letter to the president from Homer Cummings, and December 9, 1937, memo for the attorney general, RJP, Box 77.

73  August 10, 1937, memo for Mr. Jackson, RJP, Box 77.

74  See correspondence with Patman in RJP, Box 77.

75  June 1, 1937, letter to the president from Homer Cummings, RJP, Box 77.

76  December 9, 1937, memo for the attorney general, and December 8, 1937, Confidential Memo for Assistant Attorney General Jackson from Walter Rice, RJP, Box 77.

77  August 10, 1937, memo for Mr. Jackson, RJP, Box 77.

78  See H.R. 2271, introduced January 8, 1937, and memo by Walter Rice Re: Judge Gibson, August 10, 1937, RJP, 77.

79  December 17, 1937, Memorandum for Mr. Jackson from Walter Rice, RJP, Box 77.

80  Tony Freyer, *Antitrust and Global Capitalism, 1930–2004,* p. 16.

81  Daniel M. G. Raff and Philip Scranton, eds., *The Emergence of Routines: Entrepreneurship, Organization, and Business History,* p. 75.

82  Klein, *A Call to Arms,* p. 161.

83  June 20, 1939, memo for Mr. Arnold by Robert Jackson RJP, Box 77; Raff and Scranton, eds., *The Emergence of Routines,* p. 75. For more on Caffey, see Elihu Lauterpacht, International Law Reports, pp. 175–77; and "Many Alien Enemies Now Liable to Arrest," *New York Times,* 2/17/1918, p. 3.

84  George David Smith, *From Monopoly to Competition,* p. 205.

85  "Arnold Assailed by Alcoa Counsel," *New York Times,* 1/14/1942, p. 28.

86  As quoted in Ellis Hawley, *The New Deal and the Problem of Monopoly* (Princeton: Princeton University Press, 1966), pp. 156–57.

87  "Bankers Elevate Critic of New Deal," *New York Times,* 11/15/1935, pp. 1, 36. See also Marriner Eccles's autobiography, *Beckoning Frontiers: Public and Personal Recollections.*

88  Eccles, *Beckoning Frontiers,* p. 252.

89  Ibid., p. 92.

90  Hearings before the Committee on Finance, United States Senate, "Investigation of Economic Problems," February 13–28, 1933, p. 730; "Urges Slump Cure by Gold Embargo," *New York Times,* 2/25/1933.

91  Hyman, *Marriner Eccles,* p. 105.

92  Eccles, *Beckoning Frontiers,* p. 298; Stephen B. Adams, *Mr. Kaiser Goes to Washington: The Rise of a Government Entrepreneur.*

93  Hyman, *Marriner Eccles,* p. 245.

94  Klein, *A Call to Arms,* pp. 243–44.

95  I. F. Stone, *Business as Usual: The First Year of Defense,* pp. 49–52; Smith, *From Monopoly to Competition,* p. 192.

96  Klein, *A Call to Arms,* p. 60.

97  I. F. Stone, *Business as Usual,* p. 65.

98  Kenneth M. Keisel, *Wright Field,* p. 89.

99  Stone, *Business as Usual,* pp. 49–52; Smith, *From Monopoly to Competition,* p. 192.

100  I. F. Stone, *Business as Usual,* pp. 52–54.

101  "O'Mahoney Links Aluminum, Air Lag," *New York Times,* 1/13/1941, p. 7.

102  Gerald White, *Billions for Defense,* p. 42; Ann Markusen, Peter Hall, Scott Campbell, and Sabina Deitrick, *The Rise of the Gunbelt: The Military Remapping of Industrial America.* p. 29; Durr, *Early History of the Defense Plant Corporation,* p. 6; Smith, *From Monopoly to Competition,* pp. 216–17.

103  *Congressional Record,* May 16, 1941, p. 4161; *Congressional Record,* May 28, 1941, p. 4510; Gerald T. White, "Financing Industrial Expansion for War: The Origin of the Defense Plant Corporation Leases," *The Journal of Economic History,* vol. 9, no. 2, 1949, pp. 156–83, JSTOR, www.jstor.org/stable/2113638.

104  Gerald White, *Billions for Defense: Government Financing by the Defense Plant Corporation During World War II,* pp. 26, 35.

105  Ibid., p. 80.

106  Stone, *Business as Usual,* pp. 49–52; Smith, *From Monopoly to Competition,* p. 192.

107  "Nazi Influence in U.S. Industry Nearly Wiped Out," *St. Louis Dispatch,* 1/9/1942.

108  "Arnold Asks Legislative to Ban Cartels," Associated Press, 3/28/1942.

109  Virginia Paisley, "Truman Hurls Treason Charge at Standard Oil," *New York Daily News,* 3/28/1942.

110  "La Follette Urges Aluminum Authority to Aid Plane Output," Associated Press, June 15, 1942.

111  Internal meeting minutes of the Subcommittee on Monopoly, August 9, 1951, Emanuel Celler Papers, Box 52.

112  "Meet Thurman Arnold, Trust-Buster Extraordinaire," by Drew Pearson and Robert Allen, "The Merry-Go-Round," syndicated column of Drew Pearson, April 18, 1942; See discussion of the 'goon squad' by Robert Nathan, "Oral History Interview with Robert R. Nathan Chairman, Planning Commission War Production Board, 1942–1943," Deputy Director, Office of War Mobilization and Reconversion, 1945, UN Korean Reconstruction Agency, 1952–1953, https://www.trumanlibrary.org/oralhist/nathanrr.htm.

113  Address Business Confidence and Government Policy, for Broadcast over Mutual Broadcasting System, December 26, 1937, Homer Cummings Papers, Box 75.

114  Oral History Interview with H. Graham Morison, August 4, 1972, Harry Truman Presidential Library and Museum.

115  Guy Rolnick, "Antitrust, Growth and Inequality," interview with Harvard Law School professor Einer Elhauge on the ProMarket blog, July 1, 2016, https://promarket.org/horizontal-shareholding-antitrust-growth/.

116  "Harriman Good Peacemaker," by Drew Pearson, "Washington Merry-Go-Round," syndicated column of Drew Pearson, May 12, 1968.

117  Hand did not absolve Alcoa of anticompetitive conduct, he merely said that was not the issue at hand.

118  Gerald White, *Billions for Defense,* pp. 76, 106–07; see letter from FDR to the secretary of commerce, March 23, 1942, Presidential's Official Files (OF) 1050, FDR Presidential Library.

119  Marquis Childs, "Skillful Intervention Shown in Aluminum Case," *Pittsburgh Post-Gazette,* 1/18/1946, p. 8.

120  Gerald White, *Billions for Defense,* p. 42.

121  See Mark Wilson, *Destructive Creation,* p. 88: "Far from being monopolized by the largest corporations, the business of war was distributed broadly and deeply."

122  Durr, *Early History of the Defense Plant Corporation,* pp. 28–29.

123  Cannadine, *Mellon,* p. 571.

124  James Gross, *The Making of the National Labor Relations Board: A Study in Economics, Politics, and the Law, 1933–1937,* p. 16.

125  Markusen et al., *The Rise of the Gunbelt,* p. 33.

126  Report of the Committee Appointed to Review the Decartelization Program in Germany, a committee partially staffed by FTC officials appointed by the Army, James Landis Papers, Box 45.

127  Documents from James Landis Papers, Box 45.

128  "Smash I. G. Farben Empire, Eisenhower Advises Allies," *New York Times,* 10/21/1945, p. 1.

129  See Wyatt Wells, *Antitrust and the Formation of the Postwar World.*

130  "La Follette Says Cartels Are Far from Removed: Senator Warns That Pattern of Postwar Trade Must Be Set," *Green Bay Press-Gazette,* p. 1.

131  "An Address by Francis Biddle, Attorney General of the United States, to Be Given at the Annual Dinner of the Harvard Law School Alumni Association, Harvard Club, New York, New York," February 23, 1944, Emanuel Celler Papers, Box 53.

132  Testimony of W. G. Brown, Director, Office of International Trade Policy, State Department, 1950, Emanuel Celler Papers, Box 53.

133  Clifford Durr discusses the Defense Plant Corporation with John Imhoff, Part 1, Jack Rabin Collection on Alabama Civil Rights and Southern Activists,

1941–2004; "Principles to Guide Selection of Sites for Defense Industries," August 3, 1940, John Kenneth Galbraith Papers, Box 1.

134    "Principles to Guide Selection of Sites for Defense Industries," August 3, 1940, John Kenneth Galbraith Papers, Box 1.

135    Smith, *From Monopoly to Competition,* chapter 6; "Will the Old South Live on in New?," *News Leader,* 3/31/1955.

136    C. P. Trussell, "Jackson Subpoenaed as Congress Probes War Plant Blacklist Threat," *Baltimore Sun,* 10/8/1940; Charles Ellis, "Knox and Patterson Deny Violators of Labor Act Will Be Blacklisted," *Philadelphia Inquirer,* 10/9/1940.

137    Klein, *A Call to Arms,* pp. 2, 4, 141; Margo, Robert A. "Explaining Black-White Wage Convergence, 1940-1950." *Industrial and Labor Relations Review,* vol. 48, no. 3, 1995, pp. 470–81, JSTOR, www.jstor.org/stable/2524775.

## CHAPTER SIX
### A Democracy of Small Businesses

1    Richard Oulahan, "Bowers in Democratic Keynote Scores Corruption; Smith Certain on First Ballot as Convention Opens, Picks Robinson as Running Mate, Dictates Platform," *New York Times,* 6/27/1928.

2    Ibid.

3    Keri Leigh Merritt, *Masterless Men: Poor Whites and Slavery in the Antebellum South,* p. 329.

4    "Land Tenure History," Indian Land Tenure Foundation, https://iltf.org/land -issues/history/, accessed 6/9/2019.

5    Merritt, *Masterless Men,* p. 362.

6    Brandeis dissent in *Liggett* (1933).

7    Douglas E. Bowers, Wayne D. Rasmussen, and Gladys L. Baker, *History of Agricultural Price-Support and Adjustment Programs, 1933–84,* Economic Research Service, U.S. Department of Agriculture, Agriculture Information Bulletin No. 485, Washington, D.C., December 1984; "Historical Statistics of the United States, 1789–1945 - Census Bureau," p. 31, https://www2.census.gov/library /publications/1949/compendia/hist_stats_1789-1945/hist_stats_1789-1945 -chL.pdf. Farm products had by far the largest decline in price.

8    See speech by Patman, January 13, 1933, 76 *Congressional Record* 1584, p. 193; Rauchway, *Winter War,* p. 236.

9    https://www.brookings.edu/articles/black-progress-how-far-weve-come -and-how-far-we-have-to-go/.

10    Donald H. Grubbs, *Cry from the Cotton: The Southern Tenant Farmers' Union and the New Deal,* p. 25.

11    Rauchway, *Winter War,* p. 108.

12    For a good narrative of structural racism within the New Deal, see Ira Katznelson, *Fear Itself: The New Deal and the Origins of Our Time.*

13    See for example *Corsicana Semi-Weekly Light,* 11/10/1949, p. 19; and *Daily Times* (Davenport, Iowa), 1/1949, p. 29.

14    Dave Kansas, "A&P Heading to the Checkout Counter?," *Wall Street Journal,* 12/10/2010, https://blogs.wsj.com/marketbeat/2010/12/10/ap-heading-to -the-checkout-counter/. For the lyrics to the song, see Edwin P. Hoyt, *That Wonderful A&P!,* p. 103; "Red Circle & Gold Leaf," *Time,* November 13, 1950.

15    Hoyt, *That Wonderful A&P!,* pp. 123, 136, 150; Kansas, "A&P Heading to the Checkout Counter?"

16    Hoyt, *That Wonderful A&P!,* p. 139.

17    Marc Levinson, *The Great A&P and the Struggle for Small Business in America.*

18    Hoyt, *That Wonderful A&P!,* p. 92.

19    Ibid., p. 96.

20    See 1909 speech before the American Hardware Manufacturers Association at Atlantic City by R. E. Shanahan of the Bissell Carpet Sweeper Co., "A Policy Beneficent in Results and Worthy the Support of All Manufacturers, Jobbers, and Retailers," in which he describes how his company has pursued price maintenance for thirty-three years, since 1876. Speech reprinted in Subcommittee on Monopolies and Commercial Law, Committee on the Judiciary, 94th Congress, 1st Session, on H.R. 2384 Fair Trade Repeal, March 25, 1975.

21    Hoyt, *That Wonderful A&P!,* p. 129.

22    *Dr. Miles Medical Co. v. John D. Park & Sons Co.,* 220 U.S. 373 (1911).

23    Paul B. Ellickson, *The Evolution of the Supermarket Industry: From A&P to Wal-Mart* in *Handbook on the Economics of Retail and Distribution,* Chapter 15, Edward Elgar Publishing, Cheltenham, pp. 368–91, https://ssrn.com/abstract=1814166 or http://dx.doi.org/10.2139/ssrn.1814166; Hoyt, *That Wonderful A&P!,* p. 102.

24    Levinson, *The Great A&P and the Struggle for Small Business in America,* p. 288.

25    "Psychological Warfare: A&P Brand," *New Republic,* November 14, 1949.

26    Barry Lynn, "The Case for Breaking Up Walmart," *Harper's,* 2006; Edward Krugman, "Soap, Cream of Wheat and Bakeries: The Intellectual Origins of the Colgate Doctrine," *St. John's Law Review*: Vol. 65: No. 3, Article 10, https:// scholarship.law.stjohns.edu/lawreview/vol65/iss3/10; Hoyt, *That Wonderful A&P!.*

27    Hoyt, *That Wonderful A&P!,* p. 114.

28    Robert W. Mueller, ed., *A & P: Past, Present and Future,* p. 19.

29    Hoyt, *That Wonderful A&P!,* pp. 119–21.

30    Walter Lippmann, *Drift and Mastery,* p. 74.

31    "The Week," *New Republic,* February 17, 1926, p. 341.

32    Hoyt, *That Wonderful A&P!,* p. 134.

33    "Chain Stores: Final Report on the Chain-Store Investigation," Federal Trade Commission, December 14, 1934, p. 25.

34  Investigation of the Lobbying Activities of the American Retail Federation, Hearings before the Special Committee on Investigation American Retail Federal, House of Representatives, June 5, 6, 25, 27, July 9, 10, 1935, p. 505.

35  Levinson, *The Great A&P and the Struggle for Small Business in America*, p. 164.

36  Barry Lynn, "The Case for Breaking Up Wal-Mart," *Harper's*, July 24, 2006.

37  Thomas W. Ross, "Winners and Losers Under the Robinson-Patman Act," *Journal of Law and Economics* 27, no. 2 (1984), Article 2, p. 257.

38  Levinson, *The Great A&P and the Struggle for Small Business in America*, p. 159; Ross, "Winners and Losers Under the Robinson-Patman Act."

39  Levinson, *The Great A&P and the Struggle for Small Business in America*, p. 165.

40  Ross, "Winners and Losers Under the Robinson-Patman Act," p. 258.

41  1939 Retail Census, Volume 1, Part 1, 57, "Changes in Wholesaling," quoted in Levinson, *The Great A&P and the Struggle for Small Business in America*.

42  "Fair Trade Laws," address by James Mead, Chairman of the Federal Trade Commission, before the New York State Pharmaceutical Association, June 11, 1951, https://www.ftc.gov/system/files/documents/public_statements/684181/19510611_mead_the_fair_trade_laws.pdf .

43  Lina M. Khan, "Amazon's Antitrust Paradox," *Yale Law Journal* 126 (2016), http://digitalcommons.law.yale.edu/ylj/vol126/iss3/3; "Testimony of Thomas Rothwell, Executive Director of the Counsel of the Marketing Policy Institute," p. 24; Subcommittee on Monopolies and Commercial Law, Committee on the Judiciary, 94th Congress, 1st Session, on H.R. 2384, Fair Trade Repeal, March 25, 1975.

44  "A&P Opens Fight on Chain Tax Bill," *New York Times*, 9/15/1938.

45  Levinson, *The Great A&P and the Struggle for Small Business in America*.

46  Ross, "Winners and Losers Under the Robinson-Patman Act," p. 249.

47  Ronn Torossian, "Hitler's Nazi Germany Used an American PR Agency," *New York Observer*, 12/22/2014.

48  Hoyt, *That Wonderful A&P!*, p. 196; Levinson, *The Great A&P and the Struggle for Small Business in America*, pp. 192–97.

49  Levinson, *The Great A&P and the Struggle for Small Business in America*, p. 180.

50  Ibid.

51  Hoyt, *That Wonderful A&P!*, p. 152.

52  Levinson, *The Great A&P and the Struggle for Small Business in America*. p. 187–89.

53  "Red Circle & Gold Leaf," *Time*, November 13, 1950.

54  Levinson, *The Great A&P and the Struggle for Small Business in America*.

55  "Psychological Warfare: A&P Brand," *New Republic*, p. 12.

56  Marc Levinson, *The Great A&P and the Struggle for Small Business in America*.

57  "Red Circle & Gold Leaf," *Time*, November 13, 1950.

58  Hoyt, *That Wonderful A&P!*, p. 202.

59  "Labor Leaders Oppose A&P Anti-Trust Suit," *Meyersdale Republican,* October 13, 1949, p. 4.

60  Levinson, *The Great A&P and the Struggle for Small Business in America,* p. 245.

61  Edwin P. Hoyt, *That Wonderful A&P!,* p. 203.

## CHAPTER SEVEN
### The New Deal Constitution

1  Keyserling to Truman, undated memo, "Proposed Message by the President on anti-monopoly policy," Leon H. Keyserling Papers, Box 9, p. 6.

2  "The Women Ask the President," originating at Broadcast House, CBS, October 24, 1956, Eisenhower Presidential Library Digital Collections, https://www.eisenhower.archives.gov/research/online_documents/women_in_the_1950s/1956_10_24.pdf.

3  Ibid.

4  American National Election Studies Guide to Public Opinion and Electoral Behavior." All statistics are for the population in 1958, except for the question on whether the government is rigged. When that question was first asked in 1964, 64 percent thought government was run for the benefit of all, while 29 percent thought it was run for a few big interests. See also "Pew Research Center: Beyond Distrust: How Americans View Their Government, 1. Trust in government, 1958–2015," 11/23/2015, https://www.people-press.org/2015/11/23/1-trust-in-government-1958-2015/.

5  Leah Platt Boustan, "Competition in the Promised Land: Black Migration and Racial Wage Convergence in the North, 1940–1970," *The Journal of Economic History* 69, no. 3 (2009): 755–782, www.jstor.org/stable/40263942.

6  See chapter "The Great Compression" in Judith Stein, *Pivotal Decade: How the United States Traded Factories for Finance in the Seventies;* Jackson, *Crabgrass Frontier,* p. 7; "Current Population Reports: Consumer Income," *Bureau of the Census* no. 77, May 7, 1971, p. 60, https://www2.census.gov/library/publications/1971/demographics/p60-77.pdf.

7  "'Tough' Aide Named U.S. Antitrust Chief," *New York Times,* 5/10/1960, p. 28.

8  Columbus, Ohio, Campaign Speech (speech file 490), FDR Presidential Library, August 20, 1932, p. 7.

9  Walter Lippmann and Clinton Rossiter, *The Essential Lippmann: A Political Philosophy for Liberal Democracy,* p. 436.

10  Tim Canova, "The Federal Reserve We Need," *American Prospect,* October 7, 2010.

11  Hyman Minsky, *Stabilizing an Unstable Economy,* p. 84.

12  Annual Report of the Board of Governors of the Federal Reserve System, 1946, pp. 95–98.

13  Jeff Madrick, *Age of Greed: The Triumph of Finance and the Decline of America, 1970 to the Present.*

14  Martin Mayer, *The Bankers*, p. 13.

15  Phillip Zweig, *Wriston: Walter Wriston, Citibank, and the Rise and Fall of American Financial Supremacy*, p. 50.

16  Ibid., p. 46. For the quote on air-conditioning, see Mayer, *The Bankers*.

17  Zweig, *Wriston*, p. 57.

18  Ibid., pp. 125–26; Brooks, *The Go-go Years*, p. 113.

19  Carl Kaysen, "Big Business and the Liberals, Then and Now," *New Republic*, November 22, 1954, pp. 118–20. For a good overview of the Committee for Economic Development, see Rick Wartzman, *The End of Loyalty: The Rise and Fall of Good Jobs in America*.

20  Mary Zey, *Banking on Fraud: Drexel, Junk Bonds, and Buyouts*, p. 47.

21  John F. Winslow, *Conglomerates Unlimited: The Failure of Regulation*, p. 4.

22  The percent of equities owned increased from 1.4 percent in 1945 to 5.7 percent in 1965, which was part of the broader increase in institutional investment. See "The Mutual Fund Industry 60 Years Later: For Better or Worse?," remarks by John C. Bogle, founder and former chairman, The Vanguard Group, from the January/February 2005 issue of the *Financial Analysts Journal*. Small shareholders were buy-and-hold investors: see p. 153 of Janice M. Traflet, *A Nation of Small Shareholders: Marketing Wall Street after World War II*. For a quick understanding of the change in managerial behavior, see Robert H. Hayes and William J. Abernathy, "Managing Our Way to Economic Decline," *Harvard Business Review*, July 1980; John Winslow, *Conglomerates Unlimited: The Failure of Regulation*, pp. xvii–xviii.

23  Walter Bagehot, *Lombard Street: A Description of the Money Market* (London: Henry S. King, 1873), p. 20.

24  Madrick, *Age of Greed*, p. 23.

25  Greta Krippner, *Capitalizing on Crisis: The Political Origins of the Rise of Finance*; R. Alton Gilbert, "Requiem for Regulation Q: What It Did and Why It Passed Away," *Federal Reserve Bank of St. Louis Review*, February 1986, pp. 22–37, https://doi.org/10.20955/r.68.22-37.zge.

26  Mayer, *The Bankers*, pp. 189–91.

27  Krippner, *Capitalizing on Crisis*.

28  Keyserling to Truman, undated memo, "Proposed Message by the President on anti-monopoly policy," Leon H. Keyserling Papers, Box 9, Truman Library, pp. 7–10, 26–30; March 13, 1952, Message to the Convention of the National Rural Electric Cooperative Association on Federal Power Policy, Harry S. Truman Papers, 1945–1953, https://www.trumanlibrary.org/publicpapers/index.php?pid=944&st=&st1=; Barry Lynn, "Antitrust: A Missing Key to Prosperity, Opportunity, and Democracy," *Demos*, pp. 7–10; Martin Watzinger, Thomas Fackler, Markus Nagler, Monika Schnitzer, "How antitrust enforcement can spur innovation: Bell Labs and the 1956 Consent Decree," February 2017, https://economics.yale.edu/sites/default/files/how_antitrust_enforcement.pdf.

29 White, *Billions for Defense*, pp. 106-7.

30 For a good overview of this arrangement, see Laura Phillips Sawyer, *American Fair Trade: Proprietary Capitalism, Corporatism, and the "New Competition," 1890–1940*.

31 For a full description of how this system worked, see Barry Lynn, "Antitrust: A Missing Key to Prosperity, Opportunity, and Democracy," paper for Demos, p. 7, http://www.demos.org/sites/default/files/publications/Lynn.pdf .

32 Kimberly Weisel, "Half of World War II's Veterans Started Businesses. Less Than 5 Percent of Today's Veterans Do," *Slate,* October 16, 2016, http://www.slate.com/blogs/moneybox/2016/10/10/fewer_veterans_are_becoming_entrepreneurs_a_lot_fewer.html.

33 Matt Stoller, "The Housing Crash and the End of American Citizenship," *Fordham Urban Law Journal* 1183 (2012), vol. 39, no. 4, available at: https://ir.lawnet.fordham.edu/ulj/vol39/iss4/8; Frank S. Levy and Peter Temin, "Inequality and Institutions in 20th Century America," June 27, 2007, MIT Department of Economics Working Paper No. 07-17, https://ssrn.com/abstract=984330 or http://dx.doi.org/10.2139/ssrn.984330.

34 "Special Message to the Congress: The President's Economic Report," January 7, 1949, *Public Papers of Harry S. Truman 1945–1953*, Harry S. Truman Presidential Library and Museum, https://www.trumanlibrary.org/publicpapers/index.php?pid=1016&st=&st1=.

35 Ibid., p. 3.

36 Smith, *From Monopoly to Competition*, p. 253; Richard Cooperman, "Why We Lack Aluminum," *New Republic*, October 8, 1951, p. 14.

37 "Address by Honorable Harry S. Truman of Missouri, Before Joint Session of Missouri Legislature, 3/22/1939," inserted into the 84 Cong. Rec. (Bound)—Appendix—Congressional Record (Bound Edition), Volume 84 (1939), p. 1105.

38 August 30, 1941, letter from Harry S. Truman to Bess W. Truman, Harry S. Truman Papers, Family, Business, and Personal Affairs, https://www.trumanlibrary.org/whistlestop/study_collections/trumanpapers/fbpa/index.php?documentVersion=both&documentid=HST-FBP_12-45_01.

39 Address at the Jefferson-Jackson Day Dinner, March 29, 1952, Harry S. Truman Papers, 1945–1953, https://www.trumanlibrary.org/publicpapers/index.php?pid=951.

40 Letter to the Chairman of the House Judiciary Committee on the Problem of Concentration of Economic Power, July 8, 1949, Harry S. Truman Papers, https://www.trumanlibrary.org/publicpapers/index.php?pid=1166.

41 See list of attendees, "Minutes of Meeting of Subcommittee on Study of Monopoly Power," August 9, 1950 and June 27, 1949 Emanuel Celler Papers, Box 52.

42 House Banking Committee, Subcommittee on Economic Stabilization, Oversight Hearing on Mergers and Acquisitions, May 12, 1987, p. 121. Bethlehem constructed a "completely new, modern facility at Burns, Harbor, Indiana," which was "the only integrated green-field blast furnace-oxygen converter rolling mill built during the 1960s and 1970s to provide a U.S. counterpart to the modern steel-making capacity growing by leaps and bounds abroad." See debate, "Big Business is Dangerous" by Emanuel Celler, p. 125, and "Big Business Is Essential," by Crawford H. Greenewalt, *Reader's Digest,* June 1950, p. 127, archived in Emanuel Celler Papers, Box 54.

43 "In Fight for 'Little Man,'" *The Times-News,* 8/29/1967.

44 The Defense Department argued that one of the company's industrial subsidiaries was managing the nation's atomic arsenal, and it was dangerous to be suing that same company for monopolization at the same time.

45 Drew Pearson, 1/25/1955 as well as 6/19/1952, "Washington Merry-Go-Round," syndicated column of Drew Pearson; Oral History Interview with H. Graham Morison, August 10, 1972, Harry S. Truman Presidential Library and Museum.

46 Anthony Leviero, "Smash I.G. Farben Empire, Eisenhower Advises Allies," *New York Times,* 10/21/1945.

47 Drew Pearson, "Eastland Blocked Confirmation of Justice Department Official," 8/27/1960, "Washington Merry-Go-Round," syndicated column of Drew Pearson. At the same time as he was holding up Bicks, Eastland was happy to let Harold Tyler, a civil rights advocate, run the Department of Justice Civil Rights Division at a time when the assault on segregation in the South was picking up steam.

48 Telephone conversation #11385, sound recording, LBJ and Ramsey Clark, January 20, 1967, 7:00 p.m., LBJ Presidential library. https://www.discoverlbj .org/item/tel-11385.

49 William M. McClenahan Jr. and William H. Becker, *Eisenhower and the Cold War Economy,* p. 175.

50 Hearings before the Subcommittee and Antitrust and Monopoly, Senate Judiciary Committee, March 27, 28, 29, 30, May 7, 8, 1973, p. 439, "Statement of Dr. Carl H. Madden in Behalf of U.S. Chamber of Commerce of the United States of America, Chamber of Commerce of the United States of America, Background Study on S. 1167, Industrial Reorganization Act."

51 Timothy Noah, *The Great Divergence: America's Growing Inequality Crisis and What We Can Do about It,* p. 129.

52 See Steven Neuse, *David E. Lilienthal: The Journey of an American Liberal,* p. 121.

53 Studs Terkel, *Hard Times: An Oral History of the Great Depression;* David Lilienthal, *Big Business: A New Era,* p. 17.

54 Ibid.

55　Franklin D. Roosevelt, Inaugural Address, January 20, 1937, in "The Great Communicator: The Master Speech Files, 1898, 1910–1945," File No. 1030, FDR Library.

56　Historical Census of Housing Tables, Sewage Disposal, U.S. Census Bureau, Housing and Household Economic Statistics Division, https://www.census .gov/hhes/www/housing/census/historic/sewage.html; Rick Wartzman, *The End of Loyalty*, p. 101.

57　Alan Derickson, *Health Security for All: Dreams of Universal Health Care in America* (Baltimore: Johns Hopkins University Press, 2005), p. 129.

58　Stephen R., Ortiz, *Beyond the Bonus March and GI Bill: How Veteran Politics Shaped the New Deal Era*; Kimberly Weisul, "Where Are All the Missing Veteran-Owned Businesses?," *Inc.*, October 2016.

59　"Roosevelt's First Year: 12 Epochal Months," *New York Times*, 3/4/1934, pp. 144, 150; Eric Rauchway, *Winter War: Hoover, Roosevelt, and the First Clash over the New Deal*, p. 108.

60　C. Vann Woodward, *The Strange Career of Jim Crow, Commemorative Edition* (New York: Oxford University Press, 2002), p. 8.

61　Brian Feldman, "The Decline of Black Business," *Washington Monthly*, March/April/May 2017.

62　"The Impact of the FCC's Chain Broadcasting Rules," *Yale Law Journal* (1951), https://digitalcommons.law.yale.edu/ylj/vol60/iss1/4.

63　"Oral History Interview with H. Graham Morison," August 10, 1972, Harry S. Truman Presidential Library and Museum.

64　Ibid.

65　Keyserling to Truman, undated memo, "Proposed Message by the President on anti-monopoly policy," Leon H. Keyserling Papers, Box 9, p. 6.

66　"Oral History Interview with H. Graham Morison," August 10, 1972, Harry S. Truman Presidential Library and Museum.

67　"Brownell Terms 1955 the 'Antitrust Year,'" *New York Times*, 1/3/1956.

68　"I.B.M. Trust Suit Ended by Decree," *New York Times*, 1/26/1956, pp. 1, 18; Alfred Chandler, *Inventing the Electronic Century: The Epic Story of the Consumer Electronics and Computer Industries*, Chapter 4; Oral History Interview with H. Graham Morison, August 10, 1972, Harry S. Truman Presidential Library and Museum; Edwin Black, *IBM and the Holocaust*.

## CHAPTER EIGHT
### Corporatists Strike Back

1　John Kenneth Galbraith, *The Affluent Society*.

2　"'Interests' Draw Stevenson's Fire," *New York Times*, 12/2/1956, p. 16.

3　"Congressional Race Hottest in Country," *Marshall News Messenger*, 7/16/1944.

4   "Abe Mays Warns That Bureaucrats Are Moving in on United States Fast," *The Paris News*, 7/14/1944, p. 1. Also see ad for Harold Beck opposing Patman, *Marshall News Messenger*, p. 5: "[Beck] will violently oppose the forces seeking to destroy States Rights."

5   The four men were Hugh Roy Cullen, Clint Murchison, Sid Richardson, and H. L. Hunt.

6   Bryan Burrough, *The Big Rich: The Rise and Fall of the Greatest Texas Oil Fortunes*, pp. 135–40; Nancy Beck Young, *Wright Patman: Populism, Liberalism, & the American Dream*, pp. 135–37; Lowell Mellett, "Reactionary Forces Fail to Get Public Okeh on Important Issues," *Tampa Bay Times*, 6/28/1945.

7   Office of the Chief of Military History, *American Military History*, chapter 24, "Peace Becomes Cold War, 1945–1950," United States Army, https://history .army.mil/books/AMH/AMH-24.htm.

8   Richard Parker, *John Kenneth Galbraith: His Life, His Politics, His Economics*, p. 261.

9   Vance Packard, *The Naked Society*, pp. 5, 14; Burrough, *The Big Rich*, pp. 227–28.

10  Ibid.

11  Radio transcript of Ed Hart and Wright Patman, October 6, 1946, WPP, Box 52B.

12  See letter of March 19, 1947, from Joe Rigdom of the International Union of Operating Engineers, WPP, Box 52B, and James Marlow, "Fascism in Action," *Salisbury Times*, 7/14/1947.

13  See a list of printings of *Communism in Action*, "Communism in Action," House Doc. No. 754-79/2," WPP, Box 52B.

14  Lorie Tarshis, *The Elements of Economics*. See in particular chapter 4, "Government and the Economy."

15  Yves Smith, *ECONned: How Unenlightened Self Interest Undermined Democracy and Corrupted Capitalism* (New York: Palgrave Macmillan, 2010).

16  Paul Samuelson, *Economics: The Original 1948 Edition*, (New York: McGraw-Hill, 1948) p. 132; Tarshis, *Elements of Economics*, chapter 45.

17  Catherine Lawson, "The 'Textbook Controversy': Lessons for Contemporary Economics," *Journal of Academic Freedom* 6 (2015); Yves Smith, *ECONned*; Richard Parker, *John Kenneth Galbraith: His Life, His Politics, His Economics*, p. 223.

18  Emanuel Celler, *You Never Leave Brooklyn*, pp. 153–54.

19  Paul Merkley, *Reinhold Niebuhr: A Political Account*, p. 154.

20  Mark R. Wilson, *Destructive Creation: American Business and the Winning of World War II*, p. 92.

21  Jordan Schwarz, *Liberal: Adolf A. Berle and the Vision of an American Era*, p. 14.

22  "Morgan and Co. Plus CIO," *Milwaukee Journal*, 1/19/1938, p. 8.

23  George Packer, "The New Liberalism," *New Yorker*, November 17, 2008, https://www.newyorker.com/magazine/2008/11/17/the-new-liberalism.

24    In 1939, for instance, it promoted chain stores in a study; A&P bought 500,000 copies to give to customers at the height of the fight over chain store taxes. Century Foundation archives, Box 26, Minutes of the Meeting of the Dissemination Committee, January 16, 1940. "In addition, the A&P Co. bought 500,000 copies of the bulletin on Chain Store Taxes for distribution to its customers." For an example of the publicity it generated, see for instance "Cost of Distribution" in the *New York Times,* 6/18/1939, p. 66, or "Chain Store Found to Excel in Wages," *New York Times,* 7/9/1939, p. 47. On the Century Foundation's planning legacy, see letters from Edward Filene and internal correspondence with Hoover Commerce Department, Century Foundation Archives, Box 110. For a broader discussion of corporate planners, see Charlie Whitham, *Post-War Business Planners in the United States, 1939–48: The Rise of the Corporate Moderates.*

25    See chapter 1 of Judith Stein, *Pivotal Decade: How the United States Traded Factories for Finance in the Seventies;* and Lawrence Mishel, Jared Bernstein, and Sylvia Allegretto, *The State of Working America, 2006–2007,* p. 55.

26    "U.S. May Reopen Anti-Trust Drive," *New York Times,* 6/10/1945, p. 75.

27    Helen Fuller, "Truman Makes Monopoly a 1948 Issue," *New Republic,* September 8, 1947, pp. 8–10; "200 Monopolies Menacing U.S. Free Enterprise, Truman Charges," *St. Louis Post-Dispatch,* 10/1/1948; "GOP Legislators Supply Long Rope," *Tennessean,* 7/2/1948. See Annual Message to the Congress on the State of the Union, January 7, 1948.

28    Marc Levinson, *The Great A&P and the Struggle for Small Business in America,* p. 245.

29    Crawford Greenewalt, "Big Business Is Essential to Our Economy," *Reader's Digest,* June 1950.

30    Reinhard Bendix, "The Public's Image of Big Business," *Nation,* December 15, 1951.

31    David Lilienthal, *Big Business: A New Era,* p. 99–101

32    James T. Sparrow, ed., *See Boundaries of the State in US History;* Richard R. John, *From Political Economy to Civil Society: Arthur W. Page, Corporate Philanthropy, and the Reframing of the Past in Post-New Deal America.*

33    Whitham, *Post-War Business Planners in the United States, 1939–48; Twentieth Century Fund: 75th Anniversary Celebration,* p. 51, https://tcf.org/assets/downloads/tcf-twentieth_century_fund.pdf.

34    Thomas Carskadon, "The Job Ahead in Dissemination: A Confidential Office Memorandum," June 1953, p. 17, Century Foundation, Box 26.

35    Twentieth Century Fund Newsletter, No. 33, Fall 1958, Century Foundation, Box 432. The report was favorable to monopoly power, saying that the hope of winning monopoly profits drove economic activity. This implied that blocking the formation of monopolies would have negative consequences. Specifically the report said that monopolies may "possess grave defects," but "the *hope* of

winning profits which certain kinds of monopolistic position provides is a driver force for both business firms and individuals without which our economy might well stagnate." The report concluded, "not competition alone, but the combined force supplied by competition and by ambitions of a noncompetitive nature, will make a progressive economy."

36   Peter Drucker's *The Concept of the Corporation* (1946); Richard Hofstadter's *The American Tradition and the Men Who Made It* (1948); sociologist C.Wright Mills's *The New Men of Power: America's Labor Leaders* (1948), *White Collar: The American Middle Classes* (1951), and *The Power Elite* (1956); David Lilienthal's *Big Business: A New Era* (1953); and John Kenneth Galbraith's *American Capitalism: The Concept of Countervailing Power* (1952).

37   Lilienthal, *Big Business,* pp. 113–14.

38   Mills, *White Collar,* p. 28; for information on the background of A.C. Hoffman, see "Monopoly, Unemployment, and the Welfare Burden: The Deindustrialization of America," 17 *Antitrust L. & Econ.* Rev. 95 (1985).

39   Mills, *White Collar,* p. xix.

40   See letter from 20th Century Fund director Evans Clark to Galbraith, January 23, 1953, Galbraith papers, Box 63.

41   "Anti-Intellectualism in American Life," pp. 3–4, draft in Richard Hofstadter Papers, Box 33.

42   Hofstadter, Richard, *The Paranoid Style in American Politics,* p. 43.

43   Drew Pearson, "U.S. Destroyer Strafed," 1/25/1955. Syndicated column of Drew Pearson, Washington Merry-Go-Round.

44   Parker, *John Kenneth Galbraith,* p. 256.

45   University Seminar on the State, Eleventh Meeting, 1953–1954 Series, March 24, 1954, Richard Hofstadter Papers, Box 24.

46   Brown, *Richard Hofstadter,* xx.

47   David S. Brown, *Richard Hofstadter: An Intellectual Biography,* p.40.

48   Ibid., p. 39.

49   Ibid., pp. 52–54.

50   As his biographer put it, Hofstadter "thought the 'heartland' a source of political reaction and organized his emotional and intellectual sympathies around a polyglot East." In one of his books, Hofstadter "used or invented more than a dozen categories to denounce the tactics favored by the Wasp hierarchy to solidify its superior position. They include: 'Anglo-Saxon mystique,' 'Anglo-Saxon clique,' 'Anglo-Saxon Saxon school,' 'Anglo-Saxon thesis,' 'Anglo-Saxon liberties,' 'Anglo-Saxon Saxon movement,' 'Anglo-Saxon lineage,' 'Anglo-Saxon power,' 'Anglo-Saxon heights,' 'Anglo-Saxon superiority,' 'Anglo-Saxon cult,' and the 'Anglo-Saxon myth.'" Brown, *Richard Hofstadter.*

51   Hofstadter, *The American Political Tradition,* p. xxvii.

52   Norman Pollack, "Hofstadter on Populism: A Critique of 'The Age of Reform,'" *The Journal of Southern History* 26, no. 4 (1960): 478–500, www.jstor

.org/stable/2204624. Pollack criticized Hofstadter for assuming that "material and ideological differences are non-existent in American society," and that "consensus upon capitalist values characterizes the basic pattern of American development."

53    Richard Hofstadter, *The Age of Reform: From Bryan to F.D.R.*, p. 82.

54    Hofstadter, *The American Political Tradition*, p. 412.

55    Norman Pollack, "Hofstadter on Populism: A Critique of 'The Age of Reform,'" Pollack, for instance, noted that "systematic treatment of Populist economic grievances would provide a necessary correction to this bias, but this is accorded a negligible role in Hofstadter's analysis." C. Vann Woodward commented that Hofstadter neglected to note virulent anti-Semitism among the elite so as to emphasize the bigotry of the populists. See also Walter Nugent, *The Tolerant Populists: Kansas Populism and Nativism,* in 1963, which showed that populists in Kansas were, at least for the nineteenth century, antiracist reformers.

56    Letter to Hofstadter from the Fund for the Republic, December 9, 1957, Richard Hofstadter Papers, Box 24.

57    Hofstadter, *The American Political Tradition*.

58    John Kenneth Galbraith, *The Affluent Society*, p. 65

59    Address by President John F. Kennedy, Yale University Commencement, June 11, 1962.

60    First Inaugural Address of Richard Milhous Nixon, January 20, 1969.

61    "Leisure Looms Large as Society Theme," *Tampa Times*, 2/9/1970.

62    Galbraith, *American Capitalism*, p. 88.

63    Parker, *John Kenneth Galbraith*, p. 67.

64    John Kenneth Galbraith Interview, *The Progressive*, April 13, 2000, http://www.progressive.org/mag_amitpalgalbraith. As a young economist, he had over fifteen thousand people working for him, overseeing the entire pricing structure of the economy (including a young lawyer named Richard Nixon).

65    John Kenneth Galbraith, *The New Industrial State*, Introduction to the Fourth Edition, p. xxxvii; Leonard Silk, *The Economists*, p. 101; John Kenneth Galbraith, *Economics and the Public Purpose*, p. 70.

66    Quoted in Silk, *The Economists*, p. 101.

67    "Small Merchants Suffer Under OPA Rules—Patman," *Minneapolis Star*, 5/18/1943, p. 23.

68    "Price Control Not 'Tough Enough,' OPA Deputy Tells the Retailers," *New York Times*, 1/14/1943.

69    "Critics Hail Galbraith's Resignation," United Press, *News-Journal* (Mansfield, Ohio), 6/1/1943, p. 7. Patman at this point was largely concerned with the effect of price controls and war procurement on small business, so it is likely that he was frustrated with the OPA's regulations in how they were undermining smaller retailers, food processors, and farmers.

70   Parker, *John Kenneth Galbraith*, p. 180.

71   See John Kenneth Galbraith Papers, Box 63; and Century Foundation Papers, Boxes 34 and 26; see letter from 20th Century Fund director Evans Clark to Galbraith, January 23, 1953, Galbraith Papers, Box 63.

72   Parker, *John Kenneth Galbraith*, p. 231.

73   Ibid., p. 270.

74   Ibid.

75   Correspondence with John C. Long, manager of publications of Bethlehem Steel, October 18, 1954, John Kenneth Galbraith Papers, Box 15. This is similar to the inclusion of what was called an "efficiencies" defense, which the Reagan administration incorporated into its merger guidelines in 1984. See "The Merger Guidelines and the Integration of Efficiencies into Antitrust Review of Horizontal Mergers," Department of Justice Antitrust Division, https://www.justice.gov/archives/atr/merger-guidelines-and-integration-efficiencies-antitrust-review-horizontal-mergers.

76   "Harvard Economist Declares Monetary Policy Fails Again" speech by John Kenneth Galbraith to Independent Bankers Association, *The Independent Banker,* April 1958, p. 31; A thank-you note for the honorarium is in Box 38 of the John Kenneth Galbraith Papers.

77   General Editors' Introduction to John Kenneth Galbraith, *The New Industrial State,* Introduction to the Fourth Edition.

78   Leonard Silk, *The Economists*, p. 89.

79   Letter from E. I. Du Pont De Nemours and Company Public Relations Director Glen Perry to Galbraith inviting him to give a speech, with a $2,500 honorarium, February 8, 1967, John Kenneth Galbraith Papers, Box 98; letter from A. J. Barr of IBM on March 7, 1969, offering an honorarium for his speech stressing the "growing importance of planning in our complex economy," John Kenneth Galbraith Papers, Box 120. See the June 12, 1969, letter from IBM product line planner J. F. McConnell. John Kenneth Galbraith Papers, Box 120.

80   Leonard Silk, *The Economists*, p. 89.

81   Galbraith, *American Capitalism,* p. 111.

82   Ibid., p. 143.

83   Ibid., p. 34.

84   "Statement of the Problem": 1938 course description by Galbraith when he was at Princeton, John Kenneth Galbraith Papers, Box 1.

85   Peter Drucker, *The Unseen Revolution: How Pension Fund Socialism Came to America,* p. 174. "By 1976, the only question was whether the official budget ceiling of $395 billion was too low, and whether any ceiling could be set and observed at all. States and cities have increased their expenditures perhaps even faster."

86   Galbraith, *The New Industrial State,* p. 483.

87   Ibid.

88    For the 'obituary' quote, see Daniel A. Crane, *The Making of Competition Policy: Legal and Economic Sources*, p. 500.

89    "With nothing productive to offer the nation, their opposition had to be destroyed, or at least delegitimized. Borrowing the language of the Frankfurt School—'clinical,' 'thematic apperception,' 'status,' 'possession,' 'identity,' 'projected,' 'complexes,' 'disorder,' and, of course, 'pseudo-conservative'—Hofstadter claimed that opponents of the liberal status quo suffered a kind of perversity resulting in 'a profound if largely unconscious hatred of society.'" Brown, *Richard Hofstadter*, p. 94. See also Richard Hofstadter, "The Paranoid Style in American Politics," *Harper's*, November 1964, p. 78.

90    "What Happened to the Antitrust Movement: Notes on the Evolution of an American Creed," in Crane, *The Making of Competition Policy*, p. 237.

91    "Antitrust and Economic Growth," address by Lee Loevinger at the Magazine Publishers Association, Greenbrier conference, May 9, 1961, pp. 4–5, Ramsey Clark Papers, Box 52.

92    Naomi Lamoreaux, *The Great Merger Wave in American Business, 1895–1904*, pp. 6–7. Also see Walter Adams, "Resale Price Maintenance: Fact and Fancy," *The Yale Law Journal* 64, no. 7 (June 1955): 969. From the late 1930s to the 1950s, it became "fashionable for such diverse groups as the Farm Bureau Federation, the National Grange, the CIO, the General Federation of Women's Clubs, the Consumers Union, the Antitrust Division, and the Federal Trade Commission" to attack the fair trade pricing laws, which had protected retailers and manufacturers against the A&P.

## CHAPTER NINE
### The Free Market Study Project

1    November 9, 1964, letter to James Beaver of Kirkland & Ellis, just after the Goldwater loss, RBP, Box i2.

2    See memos in Theodore Schultz Papers, Box 39. A typical announcement would be something like, "There will be a meeting of the Executive Committee of the Free Market Study on Monday, January 26th, in the Chess room of the Quadrangle Club." For a description of who really founded the school, see Robert Van Horne in chapters 4 and 6 of Philip Mirowski and Dieter Plehwe, eds., *The Road from Mont Pèlerin: The Making of the Neoliberal Thought Collective, With a New Preface* (Cambridge: Harvard University Press, 2015).

3    "CIO Unions of State Pledge Cash Aid in 5 Big Strikes," *New York Times*, 1/21/1946, p. 1.

4    Angus Burgin, *The Great Persuasion: Reinventing Free Markets Since the Depression*, pp. 102–3.

5    August 26, 1949, letter from John Jewkes to Aaron Director on Britain, Aaron Director Papers, Box 1. See also foreword to the 1956 American paperback

edition of Friedrich Hayek, *The Road to Serfdom: Text and Documents—The Definitive Edition: Text and Documents (The Collected Works of F.A. Hayek, Volume 2,)* original text 1944.

6   December 28, 1946, letter from Hayek to Director, Aaron Director Papers, Box 1.

7   John Davenport, "Reflections on Mont Pelerin," Mont Pelerin Society newsletter, July 1981, RBP, Box 438.

8   Quinn Slobodian, *Globalists: The End of Empire and the Birth of Neoliberalism* (Cambridge, Massachusetts: Harvard University Press, 2018).

9   "In fact, in the immediate postwar period, these two schools held relatively similar positions on these issues. One reason was their intellectual inspirations had a common ground: Henry Simons," in *The Road from Mont Pèlerin*, Philip Mirowski and Dieter Plehwe, eds., p. 209.

10   For a good account of Hayek's loss to Keynes, see Burgin, *The Great Persuasion*.

11   Jeffrey Rosen, *Louis D. Brandeis: American Prophet*, p. 195.

12   Brian Doherty, *Radicals for Capitalism: A Freewheeling History of the Modern American Libertarian Movement,* p. 183.

13   Michael J. McVicar, "Aggressive Philanthropy: Progressivism, Conservatism, and the William Volker Charities Fund," *Missouri Historical Review* 105 (2011).

14   Robert Van Horn, "Harry Aaron Director: The Coming of Age of a Reformer Skeptic (1914–24)," *History of Political Economy* 42, no. 4 (2010): pp. 601–30.

15   Ibid.

16   Edmund W. Kitch, "The Fire of Truth: A Remembrance of Law and Economics at Chicago, 1932-1970," *The Journal of Law and Economics* 26, no. 1 (Apr., 1983): pp. 163-234, 201.

17   Philip Mirowski and Dieter Plehwe, eds., *The Road from Mont Pèlerin: The Making of the Neoliberal Thought Collective, With a New Preface,* p. 208–9.

18   George Priest, "The Contributions of Robert Bork to Antitrust Economics," *The Journal of Law & Economics* 57, no. S3 (August 2014), S1–S17.

19   See profile of Friedman in Leonard Silk's *The Economists.*

20   Kitch, "The Fire of Truth," p. 183.

21   Ibid., p. 192.

22   Ibid., p. 202.

23   "Essays by the Founding Fathers: The Rise of Law and Economics," a memoir of the early years by George Priest in *The Origins of Law and Economics: Essays by the Founding Fathers,* edited by Francesco Parisi and Charles K. Rowley, p. 312.

24   Ibid., p. 353; Kitch, "The Fire of Truth," p. 201. Bork: "What I did with Aaron's group at Chicago in the law and economics project was an article on vertical integration. I cannot now recall exactly how that came about, although obviously the basic idea springs from the nonsense involved in the legal theory of the transfer for market power from one market to another—by foreclosure,

leveraging, tying, and so forth—all of the various mechanisms the law has imagined. It was that one year, 1953–1954, on the project, when we talked to Director one-on-one, that was the most stimulating experience, more so than the classes."

25  George Stigler, *Memoirs of an Unregulated Economist*, p. 60.

26  R. Joseph Monsen, *Modern American Capitalism: Ideologies and Issues*, pp. 29–30, as quoted in Richard Parker, *John Kenneth Galbraith: His Life, His Politics, His Economics*, p. 249.

27  George J. Stigler, "The Intellectual and the Marketplace," *Kansas Journal of Sociology*, vol. 1, no. 2, 1965, pp. 69–77, available at www.jstor.org/stable/23308504.

28  Floyd Norris, "An Economist Who Didn't Just Play by the Numbers," *New York Times*, 2/16/ 2005.

29  Letter to Bork from Ed Burling, January 7, 1954, RBP, Box i1.

30  Letter from Bork to Cynthia Jacob, August 23, 1967, RBP, Box i2.

31  Letter from Bork to Harlan, October 30, 1961, RBP, Box i1.

32  Letter from William Pedrick to Bork, January 23, 1962, RBP, Box i1.

33  Letter to Bork from John Dodge, May 9, 1955; letter from William Pedrick to Bork, January 23, 1962, RBP, Box i1.

34  Letter to Edgar Newton Eisenhower, November 8, 1954, *The Papers of Dwight David Eisenhower, Volume XV—The Presidency: The Middle Way, Part VI: Crises Abroad, Party Problems at Home; September 1954 to December 1954*, chapter 13, "A New Phase of Political Experience," (Baltimore: Johns Hopkins University Press, 2001).

35  Letter from Coase to Antony Sullivan of the Earhart Foundation, Ronald H. Coase Papers, February 8, 1977, Box 21.

36  Robert Bork and Ward Bowman, "The Crisis in Antitrust," *Columbia Law Review* 65, no. 3 (March 1965).

37  Even allies of these free marketers wouldn't lift a finger to help. Alan Greenspan, a business economist, could have been a key ally, since he was libertarian, an ideologue, a member of the National Association of Business Economists, and thus a link between the intellectual world of the Chicago School and the world of business leaders. But when asked, he refused to promote the journal to his fellow business economists. Conservatism was embarrassing. See correspondence between Greenspan and Coase, 1968, Ronald H. Coase Papers, Box 23.

38  "Onrushing Soviet Economy Threatens U.S. Existence," *Atlanta Constitution*, 5/17/1958, p. 4.

39  Richard Boeth, "What the Famous Read," *San Francisco Examiner*, 6/12/1968.

40  Michael Pertschuk, *Revolt Against Regulation: The Rise and Pause of the Consumer Movement*, p. 77.

41  In 1938, Hayek met Walter Lippmann to discuss Lippmann's book *The Good Society*. Lippmann by then had become an ardent Brandeisian antimonopolist.

Hayek called his later work a "trend of thought which may be said to have started twenty-two years ago when I read *The Good Society.*"

42  John McGee, *In Defense of Industrial Concentration,* p. 16.

43  *The Origins of Law and Economics: Essays by the Founding Fathers,* Francesco Parisi and Charles K. Rowley, eds., p. 354.

44  Robert Bork, "Antitrust in Dubious Battle," *Fortune,* September 1969.

45  Brown Shoe, Philadelphia National Bank, Consolidated Foods, Procter & Gamble all accepted this structuralist framework.

46  "The Science Mobilization Bill (H.R. 2100) – Its Salient Features" March 5, 1943, WPP, Box 52A.

47  "The Origins of Law and Economics," in Parisi and Rowley, eds., *Essays by the Founding Fathers,* 310.

48  Gary Becker, "Competition and Democracy," *Journal of Law and Economics* 1 (October 1958): 105.

49  Letter to Duncan Norton-Taylor of *Fortune,* June 15, 1963, RBP, Box i1; Robert Bork, *The Antitrust Paradox,* p. viii.

50  Stigler, *Memoirs of an Unregulated Economist,* p. 115.

51  Robert Van Horn, Philip Mirowski, and Thomas A. Stapleford, eds., *Building Chicago Economics,* p. 293.

52  James A. Dalton and Louis Esposito (2007), "Predatory Price Cutting and Standard Oil: A Re-examination of the Trial Record," in Richard O. Zerbe and John B. Kirkwood, eds., *Research in Law and Economics* 22, Emerald Group Publishing Limited, pp. 155–205.

53  For a roundup of views on this question, see "Department of Justice: Price-Concentration Studies: There You Go Again," https://www.justice.gov/atr/price-concentration-studies-there-you-go-again.

54  Robert Bork, *The Antitrust Paradox: A Policy at War with Itself,* pp. xiii, x.

55  Mont Pelerin Society records, as quoted by Burgin, *The Great Persuasion,* p. 118.

56  See James Buchanan and Gordon Tullock, *The Calculus of Consent: Logistical Foundations of Constitutional Democracy,* p. 95: "If individual intensities of preference are not equal over all voters, this unique feature of simple majority rule disappears. If minorities feel more strongly on particular issues than majorities, then any rule short of unanimity may lead to policies that will produce net 'harm,' even if the comparability of utilities among separate persons is still accepted as legitimate."

57  See *Verizon v. Trinko,* a unanimous decision authored by Antonin Scalia lauding the value of monopoly profits.

58  Kitch, "The Fire of Truth," p. 195.

59  Letter to Henry Reath, February 11, 1963, RBP, Box i1.

60  Letter from Howard Ellis to Robert Bork, March 4, 1963, RBP, Box i1.

61  Letter from Taggart Whipple, February 26, 1963, RBP, Box i1.

62    Letter to Frederick Rowe from Bork, March 6, 1963; and letter from Chaffetz to Bork where Chaffetz invites Bork to a section meeting, March 6, 1963, RBP, Box i1.

63    Letter to Richard Barrett on Procter & Gamble–Clorox merger with Reynolds metals, July 19,1963, RBP, Box i1.

64    See letters between Bork and Alcoa vice president and general counsel William Unverzagt, RBP, Box i2.

65    Letter to Duncan Norton-Taylor of *Fortune,* June 15,1963, RBP, Box i1.

66    Letter to Bork from Allan Trumbull, January 24, 1964, RBP, Box i1.

67    Letter to Bork from Priscilla Karb of the School of Industrial Management, February 7, 1964; letter to Bork from Sharon Washburn of the Brookings Institution, March 11, 1964, RBP, Box i1.

68    Letter from Joseph Taubman, editor of Antitrust Bulletin, May 12, 1964, RBP, Box i1.

69    Letter from William Meckling, July 8, 1965, RBP, Box i2.

70    Letter from Glen Weston to Bork, February 4, 1964, RBP, Box i1.

71    Robert Bork, "Civil Rights—A Challenge," *New Republic,* August 31, 1963.

72    Rebecca Maksel, "As Late as 1963, Some U.S. Airports Were Still Segregated," *Air and Space Magazine,* October 4, 2018.

73    Brian Feldman, "The Decline of Black Business," *Washington Monthly,* March/April/May 2017, https://washingtonmonthly.com/magazine/marchaprilmay -2017/the-decline-of-black-business/.

74    Letter from Bertil Westlin, August 27, 1963, RBP, Box i1.

75    Letter to Howard Krane from Bork, September 9,1963, RBP, Box i1.

76    For a good understanding of the importance of the Goldwater campaign, see Rick Perlstein, *Before the Storm: Barry Goldwater and the Unmaking of the American Consensus.*

77    Kim Phillips-Fein, *Invisible Hands: The Businessmen's Crusade Against the New Deal.*

78    See letter to Bork from Nutter, September 30, 1964, RBP, Box i2; "Scholars for Goldwater Include New Economists," *Simpson's Daily Leader Times,* 10/6/1964, p. 6; Rick Perlstein, *Before the Storm* pp. 417–18.

79    Lee Edwards, *Goldwater: The Man Who Made a Revolution,* p. 363.

80    Letter from Bork to the editor of *The National Observer,* July 6, 1964, RBP, Box i1.

81    See letter invitation to Bork from Edward McCabe of the Republican National Committee to discuss the "major issues of this campaign," August 12, 1964. RBP, Box i2.

82    Letter from Howard Krane to Bork, July 17, 1964, RBP, Box i1.

83    Letter from Bork to Glenn Campbell, August 21, 1964, RBP, Box i2.

84    Letter from Ernest Patton to Bork, July 9, 1964, RBP, Box i1.

85    Letter from Goldwater to Bork, November 20,1964, RBP, Box i2.

86 Letter to James Beaver of Kirkland & Ellis, November 9, 1964, just after the Goldwater loss, RBP, Box i2. Decades later, Bork said he got tenure at Yale because of the Goldwater campaign, analogizing his career to Mary McCarthy's *The Groves of Academe.* "When the fellow is about to be fired for incompetence, he suddenly announces he's been a Communist all those years, although he hadn't been. They couldn't fire him. In my case, I came out for Goldwater in 1964, which immunized me." Yale Law, apparently, was a lonely place for a free market man. But now one of the law professors there had tenure. See Kitch, "The Fire of Truth," p. 195.

87 Letter from Friedman to Bork, November 30, 1965, RBP, Box i2.

88 Letter to Bork from Thomas Johnson, October 5, 1964, RBP, Box i2. Bork received a $100 fee.

89 Letter to Thomas Johnson from Bork, November 4, 1964, RBP, Box i2.

90 Letter to Thomas Johnson from Bork, July 15, 1965, RBP, Box i2.

91 This required courts, he said, "to distinguish between agreements or activities that increase wealth through efficiency and those that decrease it through restriction of output." Robert H Bork, "Legislative Intent and the Policy of the Sherman Act," *The Journal of Law & Economics*, vol. 9, 1966, pp. 7–48, JSTOR, www.jstor.org/stable/724991.

92 Letter from Betty Bock, manager, Antitrust Department of the National Industrial Conference Board, July 22, 1965, RBP, Box i2.

93 "Market Power Is Merger Test," *Oil and Gas Journal*, March 14, 1966, pp. 65–66, RBP, Box i2.

94 United States Supreme Court, *United States v. Von's Grocery Co.* (1966), United States Supreme Court, No. 303, argued March 22, 1966; decided May 31, 1966.

95 Letter from Jim Gordon to Bork, May 5, 1967, RBP, Box i2. See Harlan's concurrence in *Federal Trade Commission, Petitioner v. The Procter & Gamble Company.*

96 See letters between Bork and Alcoa VP and General Counsel William Unverzagt, October 5 & 6, November 9, December 11, 1967, RBP, Box i2.

97 Letters between Donald Watson, Consultant Educational Relations, and Bork, February 8 and February 28, 1967, RBP, Box i2. The letter with the specific instructions is not in the Bork archives.

   In 1971, GE representatives, including Watson, sat down with Ron Coase, and the dean of the Chicago Law School, Phil Neal, sat with other corporate officers, including representatives from Union Carbide, Chase Manhattan, ITT, General Motors, U.S. Steel, and Pfizer. See note in the Ronald H. Coase Papers, Box 23, on a May 17, 1971, lunch.

98 Letter from Banks to Bork, July 13, 1967, RBP, Box i2.

99 Note from Norval Morris to Richard Kramer of the GE Foundation, October 23, 1975, Ronald H. Coase Papers, Box 23.

100 Peterman also did research showing that ownership restrictions in media markets were pointless. See note in the Ronald H. Coase Papers, Box 23

10/23/1975 note from Norval Morris to Richard Kramer of the GE Foundation, and note from John Peterman, Associate Professor, discussing his publication of his research in 1971. John L. Peterman, "The Brown Shoe Case," *The Journal of Law & Economics* 18, no. 1 (1975): pp. 81–146, available at www .jstor.org/stable/725247; John L. Peterman, "Concentration of Control and the Price of Television Time," *The American Economic Review* 61, no. 2 (1971), pp. 74–80, available at www.jstor.org/stable/1816978.

For an understanding of Director's strategy, see George Priest, "The Contributions of Robert Bork to Antitrust Economics," *The Journal of Law & Economics* 57, no. S3 (August 2014): S1–S17.

101 Letter from Turner to Bork, January 11, 1966, RBP, Box i2; and letter from Bork to Turner asking for Turner to recommend Bork for a Fulbright, June 9, 1967, which Turner filled out, Don Turner Papers, Box 2.

102 Letters from Elman to Bork, May 17, 1966, and July 1, 1966, RBP, Box i2. For a good profile of Elman's role in undermining the FTC, see Willard Mueller, *Fighting for Antitrust Policy: The Crucial 1960s*, pp. 80–81.

103 See letter from Frances Enseki, May 2, 1966, Bork papers i2, correspondence between Bork and Cynthia Jacob August 4, 1967, August 23, 1967, Bork papers i2.

104 John Kenneth Galbraith, *American Capitalism: The Concept of Countervailing Power,* p. 88.

105 George Stigler, "The Dominant Firm and the Inverted Umbrella," *The Journal of Law & Economics* 8 (October 1965), vol. VIII.

106 Galbraith, *American Capitalism,* p. 109; John Kenneth Galbraith, *The Age of Uncertainty,* "Episode 2: Manners and Morals of High Capitalism," British Broadcasting Corporation, 1977.

107 John Kenneth Galbraith, *The New Industrial State,* p. 483.

108 Mark J. Green, Beverley C. Moore Jr, and Bruce Wasserstein, *The Closed Enterprise System: Ralph Nader's Study Group Report on Antitrust Enforcement,* pp. 83–84, 88, 97.

109 Drew Pearson, "Rhodesian Issue Has U.S., Britain Jumping," 12/20/1965, "Washington Merry-Go-Round," syndicated column of Drew Pearson.

110 Drew Pearson, "General Motors Lawyer Wants Antitrust Case Dropped," 7/21/1966, "Washington Merry-Go-Round," syndicated column of Drew Pearson.

111 Telephone conversation # 8633, sound recording, LBJ and Nicholas Katzenbach, August 26, 1965, 1:20 p.m.: "This Harvard professor doesn't know what the hell to do about [rising prices]." LBJ waxed nostalgic for Thurman Arnold and his breaking of the Mellon aluminum monopoly. For LBJ complaining about Turner, see the following conversation: Telephone conversation #9039, sound recording, LBJ and Nicholas Katzenbach, October 22, 1965, 6:39 p.m., Recordings and Transcripts of Telephone Conversations and Meetings, LBJ

Presidential Library, accessed December 14, 2018, https://www.discoverlbj .org/item/tel-09039.

112  Drew Pearson, "Bobby Heads Kennedy Clan," 3/10/1967, "Washington Merry-Go-Round," syndicated column of Drew Pearson.

113  Louis Kohlmeier, "General Motors Next Target of Trustbusters?" *Wall Street Journal,* 11/1/1967. For a discussion of GM and trains, see upcoming chapter "Penn Central."

114  Drew Pearson, "Justice Department and Auto Exhaust," 5/27/1966, "Washington Merry-Go-Round," syndicated column of Drew Pearson.

115  Pearson, "Bobby Heads Kennedy Clan."

116  Drew Pearson Special, 5/31/1967, "Washington Merry-Go-Round," syndicated column of Drew Pearson.

117  Drew Pearson, "Rhodesian Issue Has U.S., Britain Jumping," 12/20/1965, "Washington Merry-Go-Round," syndicated column of Drew Pearson.

118  Drew Pearson, "Antitrust Fight a Dead Issue," 4/12/1966, "Washington Merry-Go-Round," syndicated column of Drew Pearson.

119  Hearing before the Subcommittee of the Select Committee on Small Business, A Seminar Discussion of the Question: "Are Planning and Regulation Replacing Competition in the New Industrial State?," June 29, 1967, p. 10..

120  Letter from Thurman Arnold to Turner, May 29, 1967, Don Turner Papers, Box 2.

121  Letter to Daniel Rezneck, January 7, 1966, Don Turner Papers, Box 1: "I suppose I should have said something about Drew Pearson, but what is there to say?" he wrote.

122  Louis M. Kohlmaier, "Antitrust Slowdown, Liberal Critics Score Trustbuster Turner for Inaction on Mergers," *Wall Street Journal,* February 10, 1967, and "Gentle Trustbuster," *Wall Street Journal,* March 7, 1967; Alexander Bickel, "Antitrust Slowdown?" *New Republic* vol. 156, issue 20, May 20, 1967, pp. 15–18.

123  Louis Kohlmeier, "General Motors Next Target of Trustbusters?" *Wall Street Journal,* November 1, 1967.

124  Letter to Harlan Blake from Don Turner, November 24, 1967, Don Turner Papers, Box 2.

125  Marc Allen Eisner, *Antitrust and the Triumph of Economics: Institutions, Expertise, and Policy Change,* chapter 5.

126  Bickel, "Antitrust Slowdown?," pp. 15–18.

127  Letter from Bork to Turner, June 9, 1967, and May 2, 1967, letter from Bickel to Turner with a draft of the *New Republic* piece saying, "I just went ahead and shamelessly plagiarized a lot of what you told me, without risking any embarrassing attributions." Don Turner Papers, Box 2.

128  See note in Don Turner Papers, Box 2.

129  George Priest, "The Contributions of Robert Bork to Antitrust Economics" *The Journal of Law & Economics* 57, no. S3 (August 2014): pp. S1–S17.

130 "Thank you so much for your paper defending the 'Malefactors of Great Wealth.' I have passed the paper on to our Antitrust men to read. I am sure they will agree with you but you will never be offered a job in the Department of Justice!'" Letter to Bork from Howard Ellis, 3/4/1963, RBP, Box i1.

131 Herbert J. Hovenkamp, "The Harvard and Chicago Schools and the Dominant Firm," Faculty Scholarship at Penn Law, 2007, https://scholarship.law.upenn.edu/faculty_scholarship/1771; Robert Pitofsky, ed., *How the Chicago School Overshot the Mark: The Effect of Conservative Economic Analysis on U.S. Antitrust* (New York: Oxford University Press, 2008), p. 107.

132 Giersch Herbert, ed. *Merits and Limits of Markets,* p. 218.

133 Kitch, "The Fire of Truth," p. 209.

134 Pitofsky, ed., *How the Chicago School Overshot the Mark*, p. 33.

135 Rebecca Haw Allensworth, "The Influence of the Areeda–Hovenkamp Treatise in the Lower Courts and What It Means for Institutional Reform in Antitrust," *Iowa Law Review* 1919 (2015), p. 100.

## CHAPTER TEN
### The Rebirth of Wall Street

1 "The Conglomerate Merger Problem, Part Eight," U.S. Senate Committee on the Judiciary (Washington, DC: U.S. Government Printing Office, 1970), p. 4532.

2 The original name for the bank was City Bank. In 1865, the company took a national charter and renamed itself National City Bank, though it was still nicknamed City Bank. In 1968, the bank itself went back to its original name, Citibank. Today, the consumer division is Citibank, within a conglomerate called Citigroup. Phillip Zweig, *Wriston: Walter Wriston, Citibank, and the Rise and Fall of American Financial Supremacy*, p. 31.

3 Martin Mayer, *The Bankers,* p. 192.

4 Zweig, *Wriston,* pp. 29, 49, 54, 67.

5 Ibid., p. 66; Rana Foroohar, *Makers and Takers: How Wall Street Destroyed Main Street,* p. 45.

6 Zweig, *Wriston,* p. 82.

7 Ibid., p. 71.

8 Ibid., pp. 77–82.

9 "Waterman Gets $42,000,000 Offer," *New York Times,* 4/2/1955, p. 35; Zweig, *Wriston,* pp. 71–73; Marc Levinson, *The Box: How the Shipping Container Made the World Smaller and the World Economy Bigger,* pp. 44–47; Patrick A Gaughan, *Mergers, Acquisitions, and Corporate Restructurings,* p. 349.

10 Albert Kraus, "U.S. Concerns Go Abroad for Funds; Traffic in 'Accommodation Dollars' Is Estimated at $100,000,000," *New York Times,* 11/8/1959.

11 Peter Conti-Brown, *The Power and Independence of the Federal Reserve,* p. 34. Also

see the Subcommittee on Domestic Finance's "A Primer on Money," August 4, 1964, p. 105.

12 "Dwight D. Eisenhower: 1956: containing the public messages, speeches, and statements of the president, January 1 to December 31, 1956. Eisenhower, Dwight D. (Dwight David), 1890-1969, United States. President (1953-1961: Eisenhower)," United States, Office of the Federal Register, (Washington: Office of the Federal Register, National Archives and Records Service, General Services Administration), p. 88.

13 Albert Wojnilower, "The Central Role of Credit Crunches in Recent Financial History," Brookings Institution, p. 282. Also see Mayer, *The Bankers,* and Hyman Minsky, *Stabilizing an Unstable Economy,* p. 84. On the lending side, loans became riskier. For instance, the typical car loan went from two to three years from 1954 to 1957. On the asset side, investments also became riskier. Government bonds fell from 57 percent of total financial assets in 1946 to 34.8 percent in 1955 to 19.8 percent in 1965.

In the 1950s, the Federal Reserve had a powerful set of levers over the banking system, based on large reserves held in depository institutions. In 1951, "when depository institutions held 65 percent of financial sector assets and liabilities, reserve balances accounted for 11.3 percent of bank deposits." See Jane D'Arista, "Setting an Agenda for Monetary Reform," p. 11.

14 "New U.S. Bond Seen of Major Import," *New York Times,* 4/12/1953, pp. 170, 179.

15 See, for instance, Paul Krugman, "Why Bankers Want Rate Hikes," *New York Times,* 10/2/2015, https://krugman.blogs.nytimes.com/2015/10/02/why -bankers-want-rate-hikes/.

16 *Congressional Record,* 90th Congress, p. 9235, August 23, 1967, LBJ White House Central Name File 75.

17 Conti-Brown, *The Power and Independence of the Federal Reserve,* p. 34.

18 See Thomas Stokes, "Fiscal Probe is Feared," *Coos Bay Times,* 3/9/1957; Barrow Lyons, "Patman's Fight for a New Banking Probe," *Gazette and Daily,* (York, PA) 6/13/1958; "A Showdown Is Coming in 'Tight Money' Probe," *Nashville Tennessean,* 3/7/1957. See also Memo to All House Democrats from Wright Patman, April 6, 1965, WPP, Box 622; Memo to All House Democrats from Wright Patman, July 17, 1969, WPP, Box 384A; Nancy Beck Young, *Patman,* pp. 174–80, 188. Truman and Patman corresponded on interest rates, with Truman angrily writing "The Secretary's of the Treasury of the present day have been trying to imitate Andrew Mellon by his actions. . . . And they have succeeded!"

19 Drew Pearson, "Grumbles About Packaging Bill," 9/6/1966, "Washington Merry-Go-Round," syndicated column of Drew Pearson.

20 Federal Reserve Annual Report, 1946.

21 Saule T. Omarova and Margaret E. Tahyar, "That Which We Call a Bank:

Revisiting the History of Bank Holding Company Regulations in the United States," *Cornell Law Faculty Publications* (2012): p. 1012, https://scholarship.law .cornell.edu/facpub/1012.

22   "Remarks of Speaker Sam Rayburn before the Convention of the Independent Bankers Association," Washington, D.C., March 26, 1955, Sam Rayburn Papers, Box 3U96.

23   Clarence Marshall, "Va. Senator Raps Attack on Bank Law," *Daily Press* (Newport News, Virginia), 7/24/1958; "Insiders' Made Millions On 'Leak' About Discount Rate Cut, Congressman Says," *Gazette and Daily* (York, Pennsylvania), 3/11/1958; Young, *Patman*, pp. 180–83.

24   Minsky, *Stabilizing an Unstable Economy*, p. 4; Judith Stein, *Running Steel, Running America: Race, Economic Policy, and the Decline of Liberalism*, p. 9.

25   Zweig, *Wriston*, p. 140.

26   Office of the Comptroller of the Currency website: "The Negotiable CD: National Bank Innovation in the 1960s," https://www.occ.treas.gov/about /what-we-do/history/150th-negotiable-cd-article.html.

27   Mayer, *The Bankers*, p. 190.

28   Madrick, *Age of Greed*, p. 17.

29   "Banks to Press Expansion Fight," *New York Times*, 11/13/1958.

30   Zweig, *Wriston*, p. 82; "Merger Confirms New Banking Era," *New York Times*, 1/16/1955, pp. 149, 152.

31   Jeff Madrick, *Age of Greed: The Triumph of Finance and the Decline of America, 1970 to the Present*, pp. 16–17.

32   Citigroup website, "Citi Turns 200: Negotiable Certificates of Deposit," https://blog.citigroup.com/citi-turns-200-negotiable-certificates-of-deposit. A time deposit or short-term bond, a CD would have a certain term, of say, twelve months. Corporate and foreign customers could buy a twelve-month $100,000 certificate of deposit at 4 percent, and after a year would get $104,000. So that same twelve-month $100,000 at 4 percent could be sold at any point, and so sold to a secondary buyer with a price incorporating the interest that had already accrued. Zweig, *Wriston*, pp. 141–44.

33   Madrick, *Age of Greed*, pp. 16–17.

34   Mayer, *The Bankers*, pp. 192, 195.

35   Ibid., p. 194; Citigroup website, "Citi Turns 200: Negotiable Certificates of Deposit"; Office of the Comptroller of the Currency website, "The Negotiable CD: National Bank Innovation in the 1960s."

36   "The Negotiable CD: National Bank Innovation in the 1960s, History: 150 Years of the OCC," website of the Office of the Comptroller of the Currency, https://www.occ.gov/about/what-we-do/history/150th-negotiable-cd .html.

37   Ralph Nader Congress Project, *The Money Committees: A Study of the House*

*Banking and Currency Committee and the Senate Banking, Housing and Urban Affairs Committees,* p. 112.

38  Ibid.

39  Zweig, *Wriston,* p. 143.

40  Madrick, *Age of Greed,* p. 14.

41  Zweig, *Wriston,* p. 693.

42  Ibid., p. 305.

43  Ibid., pp. 448–49.

44  "Walter B. Wriston, Banking Innovator as Chairman of Citicorp, Dies at 85," *New York Times,* 1/25/2005.

45  Zweig, *Wriston,* p. 124.

46  Minsky, *Stabilizing an Unstable Economy,* p. 85: "The growth of CDs in the early 1960s enabled bank credit to expand substantially faster than the reserve base."

47  Hearing in the House Banking Committee, "Eliminate Unsound Competition for Savings and Time Deposits," 89th Congress, 2nd Session, May 9, 10, 11, 12, 19, 24, 25, June 1, 2, 7, 8, 9, 16, 23, 1966.

48  Ibid. "The Federal Reserve has, in effect, lifted ceilings off of the savings market and opened the way for unrestrained competition in the savings market on the part of the commercial banks. The history is clear of what happened the last time we had competition of this type. The promotional-minded banks begin to pay unusually high rates and then in order to protect themselves, more conservative banks are forced to increase their rates to prevent their deposits from being siphoned away. Through this process, the price paid for savings money has skyrocketed even though the overall pool of savings may not have increased. Then to meet these higher costs, banks are forced to reach further and further for loans in order to secure the earnings and high interest rates to compensate for the higher deposit costs."

49  Ibid.

50  Wojnilower, "The Central Role of Credit Crunches in Recent Financial History."

51  Press release from the Office of Congressman Thomas Rees, "Legislation Regulating Bank Certificates of Deposit Introduced by Thomas Rees," May 19, 1966. To Eliminate Unsound Competition for Savings and Time Deposits: Hearings Before the Committee on Banking and Currency, House of Representatives, Eighty-Ninth Congress, Second Session, on H.R. 14026, May 9, 10, 11, 12, 19, 24, 25, 31, June 1, 2, 7, 8, 9, 16, and 23, 1966.

52  "Surge in Interest Rates Dramatizes Need for New Action by Washington," *New York Times,* 7/2/1967, pp. 63, 74.

53  Minsky, *Stabilizing an Unstable Economy,* p. 101; Wojnilower, "The Central Role of Credit Crunches in Recent Financial History."

54  Walter Rugaber, "G.M. To Cut Back Car Output 8.1% in Next Two Months,"

*New York Times,* 11/19/1966; H. J. Maidenberg, "New Layoffs Set In Auto Industry," *New York Times,* 2/18/1967; Martin Mayer, *The Bankers,* p. 197. Mayer asserted "the money crunch of fall 1966 did produce the mini-recession of early 1967 . . ."

55   See Mayer, *The Bankers,* p. 196–97 for the credit crunch effects on California home building.

56   John Brooks, *The Go-Go Years: The Drama and Crashing Finale of Wall Street's Bullish 60s,* p. 27.

57   See "Mutual Fund Amendments Part Two," Subcommittee on Commerce and Finance, House Interstate and Foreign Commerce Committee, 91st Session, November 12, 13, 14, 17, 18, 19, 20, 21, December 8, 9, 10, 11, 1969, p. 568.

58   Joe Nocera, *A Piece of the Action: How the Middle Class Joined the Money Class* (New York: Simon & Schuster, 1994), p. 47.

59   Ibid.

60   Bank trust departments owned at least 5 percent of the stock of 147 of the 500 largest manufacturing and mining companies. David Kotz, *Bank Control of Large Corporations in the United States,* p. 10.

61   Brooks, *The Go-Go Years,* p. 12.

62   John Winslow, *Conglomerates Unlimited: The Failure of Regulation,* p. xviii.

63   "15-Inch Snowfall Disrupts Travel," *New York Times,* 2/10/1969, p. 1.

64   Neil Jacoby, "The Conglomerate Corporation," *Center Magazine,* July 1969: "The third period of hyperactivity began about 1965. when the graph of annual mergers broke sharply upward from its long-term trend line."

65   "No Longer a WASP Preserve," *New York Times,* 6/29/1986.

66   Brooks, *The Go-Go Years,* p. 239.

67   Ibid., pp. 4, 356.

68   Winslow, *Conglomerates Unlimited,* Chapter 2, "Make Friends with a Bank."

69   "Conglomerates," *Business Week,* November 30, 1968. Article reprinted on p. 4963 of Hearings before the Antitrust Subcommittee, The Conglomerate Merger Problem, Nov 4, 5, 6, 1969, Jan 28, Feb 5, 18, 19, 1970; Winslow, *Conglomerates Unlimited,* p. xix.

70   Ibid.

71   "Investigation of Conglomerate Corporations," House Antitrust Subcommittee hearings, October 15, 16, 22, 23, 1969, Serial No. 23, Part 2, p. 31.

72   Ibid., p. xii.

73   Memo from John Leatham to Saul Steinberg, November 6, 1968, p. 320; "Investigation of Conglomerate Corporations," House Antitrust Subcommittee hearings, October 15, 16, 22, 23, 1969, Serial No. 23, Part 2; Brooks, *The Go-Go Years,* p. 240.

74   "Investigation of Conglomerate Corporations," House Antitrust Subcommittee hearings, October 15, 16, 22, 23, 1969, Serial No. 23, Part 2, pp. 537–40.

75   Brooks, *The Go-Go Years,* p. 242, Patman to Steinberg.

76　"Investigation of Conglomerate Corporations," House Antitrust Subcommittee hearings, October 15, 16, 22, 23, 1969, Serial No. 23, Part 2, pp. 105, 107.

77　Ibid., p. 516.

78　Ibid., p. 159.

79　Brooks, *The Go-Go Years,* p. 255. The basics of this dynamic are confirmed in Zweig, *Wriston,* p. 257. Bank lobbyist Charls Walker would later say of the defense of Chemical Bank, "we engineered it through Sparkman."

## CHAPTER ELEVEN
### Wriston Versus Patman

1　Ralph Nader Congress Project, *The Money Committees: A Study of the House Banking and Currency Committee and the Senate Banking, Housing and Urban Affairs Committees,* p. 28.

2　Young, *Wright Patman* p. 172.

3　Ralph Nader Congress Project, *The Money Committees,* pp. 34–39; Christopher Elias, *The Dollar Barons,* pp. 388–89; author interviews with former Patman staffers Jane D'Arista, Curtis Prins, and Peggie Lewis.

4　Ralph Nader Congress Project, *The Money Committees,* p. 36.

5　"Bankers Answer Patman Charges: Association Attacks Texas Representative's Comment on Interest Payments; Intense Battle Is Seen; Democrat Repeats His Belief That 'Money Powers Run the Federal Reserve,'" *New York Times,* 12/3/1964, p. 69.

6　See letter to Patman from Appleton-Century-Crofts referencing Patman's study of college textbooks on money and banking, June 23, 1960, WPP, Box 52A.

7　"Bank Lobby Investigation," *CQ Almanac,* 1969; "Patman Promises Full-Scale Probe of Banking Lobby," Associated Press, as published in the *San Antonio Express,* 8/1/1969.

8　Ibid.; Drew Pearson, "Filing Financial Returns" 5/26/1969, "Washington Merry-Go-Round," syndicated column of Drew Pearson; "Patman Promises Full-Scale Probe of Banking Lobby."

9　Ralph Nader Congress Project, *The Money Committees,* pp. 47–57.

10　Elias, *The Dollar Barons,* pp. 391–94.

11　John F. Winslow, *Conglomerates Unlimited: The Failure of Regulation,* pp. 18, 23.

12　Ibid., p. 7. The ten investigations of conglomerates came from the Senate Antitrust Subcommittee, the FTC, SEC, FCC, NYSE, House Ways and Means, DOJ, ICC, House Antitrust Subcommittee, and one within the White House.

13　Ralph Nader Congress Project, *The Money Committees,* p. 97.

14　Philip Marcus, "The Undermining of an Antitrust Bank Merger Policy," *Depaul Law Review* 16, no. 1 (Fall–Winter 1966). Note that DOJ brought the

*United States v. Philadelphia National Bank* in 1961; it was heard at the Supreme Court and won in 1963.

15   Ibid., p. 67.

16   Don Bonafede, "Banking Industry Dynamite," *Herald Tribune News Service*, as printed in the *Alexandria Daily Town Talk,* 7/12/1965.

17   From the *New York Herald Tribune,* May 19, 1965, p. 32, as reported in William T. Lifland, "The Supreme Court, Congress, and Bank Mergers," *Law and Contemporary Problems* 32 (Winter 1967), pp. 15–39.

18   See Hearings on S. 1698 before House Committee on Banking and Currency, 89th Congress, 1st Session, 2021 (1965).

19   Ibid.

20   Marcus, "The Undermining of an Antitrust Bank Merger Policy," p. 71.

21   Willard Mueller, *Fighting for Antitrust Policy: The Crucial 1960s,* p. 26; Willard Edwards, "Bank Merger Bill Passage Fantastic Job," *Chicago Tribune Press Service,* 2/13/1966; Rice Odell, "Dark Plots Emerge on Capitol Hill," *Washington Daily News,* 10/20/1965, 2/12/1966; Ralph Nader Congress Project, *The Money Committees,* p. 54; author interviews with former Patman staffers Peggie Lewis and Jane D'Arista.

22   Mueller, *Fighting for Antitrust Policy,* p. 167; Elias, *The Dollar Barons,* pp. 197–99.

23   Phillip Zweig *Wriston: Walter Wriston, Citibank, and the Rise and Fall of American Financial Supremacy,* p. 236.

24   Elias, *The Dollar Barons,* p. 148.

25   Staff of Antitrust Subcommittee No. 5, House Committee on the Judiciary, 89th Congress, 1st Session, Interlocks in Corporate Management (March 12, 1965).

26   *Fortune* magazine, in Zweig, *Wriston,* p. 256.

27   James Henderson and Willian Henderson, "Will a Zaibatzu Control Our Economy," *The Federal Bar Journal,* 1966, vol. 26.

28   Elias, *The Dollar Barons,* p. 147.

29   Zweig, *Wriston,* pp. 256–59, "Citibank to Acquire Chubb," *Dow Jones News Service,* 1/20/1969.

30   Ralph Nader Congress Project, *The Money Committees,* pp. 120–21.

31   Elias, *The Dollar Barons,* p. 146.

32   Ralph Nader Congress Project, *The Money Committees,* pp. 120–21.

33   Elias, *The Dollar Barons,* pp. 142–45.

34   Ralph Nader Congress Project, *The Money Committees,* pp. 122.

35   Elias, *The Dollar Barons,* pp. 148–49.

36   Ralph Nader Congress Project, *The Money Committees,* pp. 124–25.

37   Ibid., pp. 127–28.

38   Ibid., p. 129.

39   Ibid., p. 132

40   Ibid.

41   Elias, *The Dollar Barons*, p. 154; author interview with Peggy Lewis; Ralph Nader Congress Project, *The Money Committees*, p. 26–27.

42   Ralph Nader Congress Project, *The Money Committees*, p. 132.

43   Ibid., p. 26.

44   "Wilbur Mills, Long a Power in Congress, Is Dead at 82," *New York Times,* 5/3/1992, p. 53. Much legislation was written in executive session. Virtually all tax legislation, for instance, came from Ways and Means Committee chairman Wilbur Mills, who used executive session and his encyclopedic knowledge of the tax code, horse-trading, and autocratic management to run a "house within a House." ("I never vote against God, motherhood or Wilbur Mills," a House colleague once told a reporter.) Ralph Nader Congress Project, *The Money Committees*, pp. 134–36; Elias, *The Dollar Barons*, pp. 157–59.

45   Ralph Nader Congress Project, *The Money Committees*, p. 135.

46   Elias, *The Dollar Barons*, p. 159.

47   Ibid., p. 137.

48   "Senate OK's Bank-Holding Regulation," Associated Press, 9/17/1970.

49   Ralph Nader Congress Project, *The Money Committees*, p. 138.

50   Ibid., pp. 137–39.

51   Ibid., pp. 139–40.

52   Walter Shapiro, "The Profit Motive and the Public Interest: Wright Patman vs. the Bankers," *Ramparts,* May 1971 (located in the Patman Vertical File, Briscoe Center for American History).

53   Ibid., p. 18.

54   Ibid.

55   Elias, *The Dollar Barons*, p. 160.

56   See Elias, *The Dollar Barons,* pp. 159–62.

57   Ibid., p. 166.

58   Ibid., p. 163.

59   Shapiro, "The Profit Motive and the Public Interest."

60   Federal Reserve press release, 9/23/1998, https://www.federalreserve.gov/boarddocs/press/BHC/1998/19980923/19980923.pdf.

61   Zweig, *Wriston*, p. 126.

62   Shapiro, "The Profit Motive and the Public Interest: Wright Patman vs. the Bankers."

63   "After a Lapse, U.S. Begins Enforcement of Bank Secrecy Act, *New York Times,* 1/23/1978, p. 1. Liberals did not all support Patman on this; the ACLU opposed it on privacy grounds.

64   "'Mr. Tax' Faces Challenge to His Authority by Ralph Nader," *In the Public Interest,* April 19, 1972. See also Ralph Nader Congress Project, *The Money Committees,* p. 81.

## CHAPTER TWELVE
### Penn Central

1   Ralph Nader Congress Project, *The Money Committees: A Study of the House Banking and Currency Committee and the Senate Banking, Housing and Urban Affairs Committees,* 1975, p. 26.

2   The episode is described in Daughen and Binzen, *Wreck of the Penn Central,* pp. 273–74; Young, *Patman,* p. 256; author interview with former Patman staffer Pegg Lewis. The line about banks considering it an honor to do business with the company is on p. 180 of *Wreck of the Penn Central.* The size of the company is described in "The Penn Central Failure and the Role of Financial Institutions, Part V," 3/29/1971, p. iii.

3   Daughen and Binzen, *Wreck of the Penn Central,* pp. 187, 192–95, 297; Rush Loving Jr., *The Men Who Loved Trains: The Story of Men Who Battled Greed to Save an Ailing Industry,* pp. 45–46.

4   Daughen and Binzen, *The Wreck of the Penn Central,* pp. 6–7, 112, 113.

5   Ibid., pp. 7, 112, 194, 216.

6   Ibid., p. 2.

7   Ibid., p. 117.

8   See 1969 Penn Central Annual Report, p. 11: "Much of our commuter equipment is 50 to 60 years old and is simply wearing out"; Daughen and Binzen, *Wreck of the Penn Central* pp. 105–09, 111, 113, 118, 188–92, 283.

9   Rush Loving Jr., *The Men Who Loved Trains: The Story of Men Who Battled Greed to Save an Ailing Industry,* pp. 14–15.

10  Daughen and Binzen, *The Wreck of the Penn Central,* pp. 34–35.

11  Loving, *The Men Who Loved Trains,* p. 14, 120–23; "Problems of the Railroads," Hearings before the Subcommittee on Surface Transportation of the Committee on Interstate and Foreign Commerce, U.S. Senate, Jan 13, 14, 15, 16, 17, 1958, "Statement of Daniel P. Loomis, President Association of American Railroads," p. 26.

12  "A Tear for the Poor Railroad," *New Republic,* January 29, 1972, p. 25; Daughen and Binzen, *The Wreck of the Penn Central,* p. 115.

13  Loving, *The Men Who Loved Trains,* pp. 34, 57.

14  Daughen and Binzen, *The Wreck of the Penn Central,* p. 1.

15  Loving, *The Men Who Loved Trains,* p. 56.

16  "The Great Boxcar Mystery, Mixup, Theft, or Swindle," *Tampa Bay Times,* 4/16/1971, p. 14.

17  Loving, *The Men Who Loved Trains,* p. 21.

18  Ibid., p. 71.

19  Daughen and Binzen, *The Wreck of the Penn Central,* pp. 298, 318.

20  "The Financial Collapse of the Penn Central Company," Staff Report of the SEC to the Special Subcommittee on Investigations, August 1972, p. 15.

21  Daughen and Binzen, *The Wreck of the Penn Central,* pp. 1, 13–14.

22  "Penn Central's Hectic Courtship Lasted 11 Years," *Philadelphia Inquirer,* 1/16/1968, p. 4.

23  Daughen and Binzen, *The Wreck of the Penn Central,* pp. 50–51.

24  Loving, *The Men Who Loved Trains,* pp. 45–46.

25  Daughen and Binzen, *The Wreck of the Penn Central,* p. 95.

26  Ibid., pp. 95, 192, 203–05; Young, *Patman,* p. 256.

27  "The Penn Central Failure and the Role of Financial Institutions Part One," November 2, 1970, Staff Report of the Committee on Banking and Currency, House of Representatives, p. 28.

28  Penn Central itself was the best customer of Executive Jet, which was perhaps related to the airline company's employment of sex workers as stewardesses.

29  I'm using Greta Kippner's definition of financialization from "The Financialization of the American Economy," *Socio-Economic Review,* Volume 3, Issue 2 (2005): "I define financialization as a pattern of accumulation in which profits accrue primarily through financial channels rather than through trade and commodity production."

30  Daughen and Binzen, *The Wreck of the Penn Central,* p. 197; Loving, *The Men Who Loved Trains,* pp. 71, 86, 87.

31  Daughen and Binzen, *The Wreck of the Penn Central,* pp. 198–99.

32  Saul Steinberg, "My $24 Million Error," *Business Observer,* 11/22/1970.

33  Brooks, *The Go-Go Years,* 305; Daughen and Binzen, *The Wreck of the Penn Central,* pp. 205, 212, 225; Loving, *The Men Who Loved Trains,* 87.

34  Charles D. Ellis, *The Partnership: The Making of Goldman Sachs* (New York: Penguin Press, 2008), p. 102; Daughen and Binzen, *The Wreck of the Penn Central,* p. 202, 240–42; "The Penn Central Failure and the Role of Financial Institutions Part Five," 3/29/1971, Staff Report of the Committee on Banking and Currency, House of Representatives, pp. iii–v.

35  Ibid., pp. 7, 180, 216.

36  "Patman Bars Aid for Penn Central," *New York Times,* 6/21/1970.

37  Memo by William Rehnquist, June 4, 1970, "Authority of the Department of Defense to Guarantee Loans to Penn Central Company Under Defense Production Act of 1950," WPP, Box 634B.

38  Loving, *The Men Who Loved Trains,* p. 112.

39  Martin Mayer, *The Bankers,* p. 308.

40  John Brooks, *The Go-Go Years: The Drama and Crashing Finale of Wall Street's Bullish 60s,* p. 301.

41  Felix G. Rohatyn, *Dealings: A Political and Financial Life,* pp. 71–72; Adam Smith, *Supermoney,* p. 270.

42  "Commercial Banks and Their Trust Activities: Emerging Influence on the American Economy, Volume One," 7/8/1968, staff report for the Subcommittee on Domestic Finance Committee on Banking and Currency, House

of Representatives, 90th congress, 2d session, July 8, 1968., U.S. Government Printing Office, p. 379.

43 Memo to Members of the Banking and Currency Committee, June 26, 1970, WPP, Box 634B.

44 Ibid.

45 "Wright Patman Opens Campaign for Congress," campaign material, WPP, Box 70.

46 Young, *Patman*, p. 256.

47 Josh Guadiosi, "Cash Needed to Put Penn Central Back on Track" *UPI,* 7/12/1970.

48 Author interview with Peggy Lewis.

49 In 1971, a Fed survey of banks revealed that most banks had increased loan demand from corporate customers due to "uncertainties generated by the Penn Central crisis." Supplement: "Current Economic and Financial Conditions," April 20, 1971, FOMC material, p. A-3,https://www.federalreserve.gov/mon etarypolicy/files/fomc19710824gbsup19710820.pdf.

　　Almost immediately, the Penn Central liquidity guarantee became standard operating procedure at the Fed. In 1970–71, when Nixon took the U.S. out of the Bretton Woods post-war monetary system linking the dollar to gold at a fixed rate, economist Paul Samuelson argued, "The response of monetary authorities to the Administration's new economic plans should be analogous to what it was during the Penn Central crisis. Their role must be to assure everybody that there will be no credit, and no quality of credit, crisis." Current Economic Comment by District, Prepared for the Federal Open Market Committee by the Staff, August 18, 1971,https://www.federalreserve.gov /monetarypolicy/files/fomc19710824redbook19710818.pdf.

50 See letters, WPP, Box 508A and Box 508B.

## CHAPTER THIRTEEN
### The Collapse of the New Deal Consensus

1 "Recent Efforts to Amend or Repeal the Robinson-Patman Act—Part 1, Hearings before the Ad Hoc Subcommittee on Antitrust, the Robinson-Patman Act, and Related Matters," House Committee on Small Business, November 5, 6, 11, 12, 19, 1975, p. 25.

2 "The Financial Collapse of the Penn Central Company," Staff Report of the SEC, August 1972.

3 "Inadequacies of Protections for Investors in Penn Central and Other ICC-Regulated Companies," Staff Study for the Special Subcommittee on Investigations of the Committee on Interstate and Foreign Commerce, U.S. House of Representatives, July 27, 1971, pp. iv, 36.

4   Memo to Paul and Benet from Jake Lewis, June 24, 1970, WPP, Box 634B.

5   See Staff Reports of the Committee on Banking and Currency, "The Penn Central Failure and the Role of Financial Institutions," Parts 1–5, 1970–1971.

6   Judith Stein, *Pivotal Decade: How the United States Traded Factories for Finance in the Seventies*, chapter one.

7   John Brooks, *The Go-Go Years: The Drama and Crashing Finale of Wall Street's Bullish 60*, pp. 12, 298–99.

8   This is drawn from Hyman Minsky's observations in *Stabilizing an Unstable Economy*, pp. 15–17.

9   Phillip Zweig, *Wriston: Walter Wriston, Citibank, and the Rise and Fall of American Financial Supremacy*, p. 390.

10  Stein, *Pivotal Decade*; Zweig, *Wriston*, p. 441.

11  Andrew Malcolm, "The 'Shortage' of Bathroom Tissue: Classic Study in Rumor," *New York Times*, 2/3/1974, p. 29.

12  "Could a 40-Year-Old Bank Collapse Have Saved the U.S. Economy?," *Time*, October 8, 2014.

13  "Financial Institutions and the Nation's Economy: Discussion Principles," Part 2, p. 918, House Banking Subcommittee on Financial Institutions, Supervision, Regulation, and Insurance, December 11, 12, 16, 17, 1975.

14  Minsky, *Stabilizing an Unstable Economy*, p. 15.

15  M. H. Wolfson, *Financial Crises: Understanding the Postwar U.S. Experience*.

16  Kevin Baker, "The Near-Death of Grand Central Terminal," *Harper's* blog, June 19, 2014, https://harpers.org/blog/2014/06/the-near-death-of-grand -central-terminal/; Kim Phillips-Fein, *Fear City: New York's Fiscal Crisis and the Rise of Austerity Politics*, pp. 242–55.

17  Joseph R. Daughen and Peter Binzen, *The Wreck of the Penn Central*, p. 6.

18  "Richard Nixon and the Great Socialist Revival," *New York*, September 21, 1970, p. 24.

19  "A Seminar Discussion of the Question: Are Planning and Regulation Re-placing Competition in the New Industrial State," Select Committee on Small Business, U.S. Senate, June 29, 1967; "The Question: Are Planning and Regulation Replacing Competition in the American Economy? (The Automobile as a Case Study)," July 10, 23, 1968.

20  Richard Reeves, *President Nixon: Alone in the White House*, p. 79.

21  "Nixon Hangs Fire on Conglomerates," *Washington Post* service, reprinted in *Arizona Republic*, 6/16/1969.

22  "Galbraith Praises Nixon—Reluctantly," *Akron Beacon Journal*, 10/9/1971, p. 2.

23  Memo to committee, 6/26/1970, WPP, Box 634B.

24  Nader read Galbraith in school, and was deeply influenced. Nader was the sole witness at the 1968 Senate Small Business Committee hearing on Galbraithian planning in the auto industry. See Ralph Nader, "The Legacy of John Kenneth

Galbraith," *Counterpunch,* August 19, 2006; and "The Question: Are Planning and Regulation Replacing Competition in the American Economy? (The Automobile as a Case Study)."

25 Hearings before the Subcommittee and Antitrust and Monopoly, Senate Judiciary Committee, March 27, 28, 29, 30, May 7, 8, 1973, p. 1.

26 "S. 1167, The Industrial Reorganization Act," printed in Hearings before the Subcommittee and Antitrust and Monopoly, Senate Judiciary Committee, March 27, 28, 29, 30, May 7, 8, 1973, p. 4.

27 Multinational Corporations, Hearings before the Subcommittee on International Trade of the Senate Finance Committee, February 26, 27, 28, March 1, 6, 1973, p. 1.

28 Hearings before the Subcommittee and Antitrust and Monopoly, Senate Judiciary Committee, March 27, 28, 29, 30, May 7, 8, 1973, p. 4, 49, 58, 62, 127, 197.

29 "Financial Institutions: Reform and the Public Interest," Staff Report of the Subcommittee on Domestic Finance, Committee on Banking and Currency, August, 1973. Patman's report was written as a rebuttal to Nixon's own task force recommending restructuring the banking system, known as the Hunt Commission report.

30 See Irving Shapiro, *America's Third Revolution: Public Interest and the Private Role,* pp. 26–29. The Business Roundtable was a combination of three groups. The first was the Business Council, a meeting group that had existed since 1933. The second was the Construction Users Anti-Inflation Roundtable, which was composed of contractors and builders to crack down on unions to slow inflation. And the third was the March Group, an informal alliance of business leaders.

31 Elias, *The Robber Barons,* p. 154.

32 Mueller, *Fighting for Antitrust Policy,* p. 206.

33 Hearings before the Subcommittee and Antitrust and Monopoly, Senate Judiciary Committee, March 27, 28, 29, 30, May 7, 8, 1973, comments by Mueller, p. 46; "Statement of Dr. Carl H. Madden in Behalf of U.S. Chamber of Commerce of the United States of America," Chamber of Commerce of the United States of America, Background Study on S. 1167, Industrial Reorganization Act, pp. 396–452. See also Henry G. Manne and Geoffrey A. Manne, "Testimony on the Proposed Industrial Reorganization Act of 1973—What's Hip (in Antitrust) Today Should Stay Passé," *International Center for Law and Economics,* white paper 2018-2.

34 See footnote 90 in William Kovacic, "Out of Control? Robert Bork's Portrayal of the U.S. Antitrust System in the 1970s," *Antitrust Law Journal* 79 (2014): pp. 855–80.

35 Kenneth Davidson, *Megamergers: Corporate America's Billion-Dollar Takeovers,* pp. 121–24.

36     *ABA Journal,* September 1975, p. 1034.

37     Judith Stein, *Pivotal Decade.*

38     Fred Dutton, *Changing Sources of Power: American Politics in the 1970s,* p. 119. In the acknowledgments for the book, Dutton cites among others Galbraith, C. Wright Mills, and the National Planning Association.

39     Thomas Frank, *Listen, Liberal: Or, What Ever Happened to the Party of the People?,* p. 50.

40     Stein, *Pivotal Decade,* chapter two.

41     Roy A. Kiesling, *Report to Those Most Concerned: A Memoir of the U.S. Consumer Movement, 1970–1980.*

42     Ibid.

43     Ibid.

44     "Financial Institutions and the Nation's Economy: Discussion Principles," Part 2, House Banking Subcommittee on Financial Institutions, Supervision, Regulation, and Insurance December 11, 12, 16, 17, 1975, p. 918.

45     Haley Edwards, "The Corporate 'Free Speech' Racket, *Washington Monthly,* January 2014, https://washingtonmonthly.com/magazine/janfeb-2014/the-corporate-free-speech-racket/. The emerging consumer-oriented politics Nader championed had echoes in Walter Lippmann's writing in *Drift and Mastery* in 1914. A good example is how Nader helped create the idea of corporate free speech as a defense against public regulations.

46     Stein, *The Pivotal Decade,* chapter six.

47     Mueller, *Fighting for Antitrust Policy,* p. 80; Mark J. Green, Beverley C. Moore Jr., and Bruce Wasserstein, *The Closed Enterprise System: Ralph Nader's Study Group Report on Antitrust Enforcement,* p. 407.

48     Green et al, *The Closed Enterprise System,* p. 402.

49     Ibid., p. 407.

50     Mueller, *Fighting for Antitrust Policy* pp. 80–86; Green et al., *The Closed Enterprise System,* p. 330.

51     Edward F. Cox, Robert C. Fellmeth, John E. Schulz, *The Nader Report on the Federal Trade Commission* (New York: Grove Press, 1970), p. 151.

52     Ibid., p. 398.

53     Ibid., p. 409.

54     Michael Pertschuk, *Revolt Against Regulation: The Rise and Pause of the Consumer Movement,* p. 9. See also Green et al., *The Closed Enterprise System,* p. 409, where the authors misunderstand how predatory price cuts can undermine competition. The report criticizes the FTC by showing an incident where the Koppers Company "had a monopoly on resorcinol for 16 years, but only after a new competitor complained about being undercut did the Commission investigate Koppers, and then not for its monopoly prices but for its price cuts."

55     Green et al., *The Closed Enterprise System,* p. xviii.

56     Mueller, *Fighting for Antitrust Policy,* pp. 82–86.

57  Marc Allen Eisner, *Antitrust and the Triumph of Economics: Institutions, Expertise, and Policy Change.*

58  "Impact of Federal Antitrust Enforcement Policies on Small Business," September 9, 1982, House Committee on Small Business, pp. 16–18.

59  Recent Efforts to Amend or Repeal the Robinson-Patman Act—Part 1, Hearings before the Ad Hoc Subcommittee on Antitrust, the Robinson-Patman Act, and Related Matters, House Committee on Small Business, November 5, 6, 11, 12, 19, 1975, p. 25.

60  See advertisement for *The Washington Monthly* published in *Mother Jones* magazine, July 1976, p. 2.

61  Charlie Peters, "Putting Yourself on the Line," *Washington Monthly*, October, 1974, Charlie Peters, "A Neo-Liberal's Manifesto," *Washington Post*, September 5, 1982

62  For a discussion of regulatory capture, which Galbraith calls "bureaucratic symbiosis," see his *Economics and the Public Purpose*, pp. 138–39. For a discussion of how corporate management decision-making is "authoritarian . . . by sound instinct" and yet control in the hands of such management is a progressive change, see p. 81.

63  For example, see Naderite Mark Green on PBS in 1978, minute ten, https:// youtu.be/7Cnm_YWJiSQ?t=602.

64  Michael Arria, "The Surprising Collection of Politicos Who Brought Us Destructive Airline Deregulation," *Alternet*, July 3, 2016.

65  Robert H. Frank, "Alfred E. Kahn: Regulator and Language Maven." *Review of Industrial Organization*, vol. 42, no. 2, 2013, pp. 191–201, JSTOR, www.jstor .org/stable/41799508; Jonathan L. Rubin, "The Premature Post-Chicagoan: Alfred E. Kahn," American Bar Association, *Antitrust* 25, no. 3 (2011).

## CHAPTER FOURTEEN
### Watergate Babies

1  Alexander Cockburn and James Ridgeway, "Why They Sacked the Bane of the Banks," *Village Voice*, February 3, 1975.

2  John A. Lawrence, *The Class of '74: Congress After Watergate and the Roots of Partisanship*, p. 2.

3  Ibid., p. 70.

4  Ronald D. Elving, "Rebels of '94 and 'Watergate Babies' Similar in Class Size, Sense of Zeal," *CQ*, 1/24/1998, http://www.cnn.com/ALLPOLITICS /1998/01/26/cq/elving.html; John A. Lawrence, *The Class of '74: Congress After Watergate and the Roots of Partisanship*; "McGovern Campaign Marked Beginning Of Direct Mail," *All Things Considered*, 8/1/2012, https://www.npr .org/2012/08/01/157739995/mcgovern-campaign-marked-beginning -of-direct-mail.

5   "Albert Favors a Stronger Role for Newer House Members and the Dilution of Ways and Means Panel," *New York Times,* 11/22/1974, p. 17.

6   Joseph Califano, *Governing America: An Insider's Report from the White House and the Cabinet,* p. 15.

7   Ron Elving, "Congressman's Exit Closes Book on 'Watergate Babies,'" NPR, 1/31/2014, https://www.npr.org/sections/itsallpolitics/2014/01/30/269003155/congressmans-exit-closes-book-on-watergate-babies.

8   Richard Reeves, "Post-Watergate Morality: You Take the Low Road," *New York,* May 13, 1974, p. 80.

9   Tian-jia Dong, *Understanding Power Through Watergate: The Washington Collective Power Dynamics,* p. 28.

10   Ibid., p. 25.

11   Edmond LeBreton, "Patman Offers RX for Economic Ills," Associated Press, 7/21/1974.

12   Steven F. Hayward, *The Age of Reagan: The Fall of the Old Liberal Order, 1964–1980,* p. 448.

13   "GOP Seeks Path Out of Valley of Watergate," *New Castle News* (Pennsylvania), 3/20/1975; Rick Perlstein, *The Invisible Bridge,* p. 329.

14   NBC News Election Survey as quoted in Ron Docksai, "Third Party Urged for the Right," *Los Angeles Times,* 3/2/1975.

15   Lawrence, *The Class of '74 ,* p. 74.

16   "Food Paces 2.3 Percent Increase in Wholesale Price Index," *New York Times,* 11/15/1974.

17   Lawrence, *The Class of '74.*

18   Nicholas Von Hoffman, "Marshmallow Politics," *Springfield Leader and Press,* 10/17/1974.

19   "Mood of the Electorate: Anger Plus Frustration and Pessimism," *New York Times* 11/3/1974, p. 74.

20   Ibid.; Reeves, "Post-Watergate Morality: You Take the Low Road," p. 80. "The focus," said pollster Peter Hart, "has all been on personality and process, with nothing for program." Bloodless process. "Personal integrity" was the name of the game in 1974, wrote Richard Reeves. "That sounds nice—but try to prove you have it, or rather, try to disprove an accusation you don't. The best defense is to never have done anything except stay at home watching television."

21   "Reduced Diets in Affluent Lands Argued at Food Parley in Rome," *New York Times,* 11/7/1974, p. 1.

22   "Industrial Output Declines, Adding to Recession Data," *New York Times,* 11/16/1974, p. 1; "Recession Cited by White House for First Time," *New York Times,* 11/13/1974, p. 1.

23   Ronald Docksai, "3rd Party Urged for the Right," *Los Angeles Times,* 3/2/1975.

24   Phillips-Fein, *Fear City,* p. 152

25   "GOP Seeks Path Out of Valley of Watergate," *New Castle News,* 3/20/1975.

26   *Atlantic,* Vol. 263, 1989; Alan Ehrenhalt, "Last Hurrahs for the New Deal," *Washington Monthly,* January 1976.

27   Glenn Bunting, "Some Don't Buy Stark's Apology for Overdrafts: Congressional perks: The lawmaker, a banker and a multimillionaire, admitted to bouncing 17 checks over a year at the House's private bank," *Los Angeles Times,* 10/31/1991.

28   "Moffett's Political Mission Is Derailing Nader," *Hartford Courant,* 10/18/2004.

29   Alexander Cockburn and James Ridgeway, "Why They Sacked the Bane of the Banks," *Village Voice,* February 3, 1975, p. 20.

30   Rick Perlstein, *The Invisible Bridge: The Fall of Nixon and the Rise of Reagan,* p. 321.

31   Ronald D. Elving, "Rebels of '94 and 'Watergate Babies' Similar in Class Size, Sense of Zeal," *CQ,* 1/24/1998, http://www.cnn.com/ALLPOLITICS /1998/01/26/cq/elving.html.

32   Ibid., p. 317.

33   "Democrats Face Fight for Control," *New York Times,* 11/9/1972.

34   "Meany Says the Democrats Did Not Receive a Mandate," *New York Times,* 11/8/1974, p. 18; *Atlantic,* Vol. 263, 1989.

35   Author interview with Tim Wirth.

36   Alexander Cockburn and James Ridgeway, "Why They Sacked the Bane of the Banks," *Village Voice,* February 3, 1975; author interview with Tim Wirth. (Wirth said, "We scheduled a meeting of our class and we had David Broder come and speak and we had a couple of other people come and speak and then a lot of discussion about what it was that we ought to do as a group.)

37   Tim Crouse, "The Boys on the Bus," 10/12/1972, *Rolling Stone.*

38   David Broder, "Will Democrats Offer More Than a Bleak Alternative," 9/12/1975, syndicated column in the *Washington Post.*

39   David Broder, "Ted Van Dyke Could Be the Democratic Party's Mother Goose," 10/4/1975, syndicated column in the *Washington Post.*

40   John Kenneth Galbraith, *Economics and the Public Purpose,* pp. 288, 290.

41   Lawrence, *The Class of '74,* p. 87.

42   Mark Franklin Ferberg, "The Democratic Study Group: A Study of Intra-Party Organization in the House of Representatives," PhD thesis, University of California, 1964.

43   Perlstein, *The Invisible Bridge,* p. 327.

44   Ibid.

45   Ibid., p. 326.

46   Stephen Green and Margot Hornblower, "Mills Admits Being Present During Tidal Basin Scuffle," *Washington Post,* 10/11/1974.

47   Perlstein, *The Invisible Bridge,* p. 327; "Mills Derided in Congress Over Link to Stripper," *New York Times,* 12/3/1974.

48   Author interview with Tim Wirth.

49   "Half-Rebellion," *New York Times*, 1/19/1975; Edward D. Berkowitz, *Something Happened: A Political and Cultural Overview of the Seventies*, p. 102.

50   Author interview with Tim Wirth and author interview with Jane D'Arista; Perlstein, *The Invisible Bridge*, p. 328.

51   Alexander Cockburn and James Ridgeway, "Why They Sacked the Bane of the Banks," *Village Voice*, February 3, 1975; author interview with George Miller.

52   Drew Pearson, "Polls Reveal Viet Policy Losing Support," 6/18/1966, "Washington Merry-Go-Round," syndicated column of Drew Pearson.

53   Drew Pearson, "Sec. Udall Gets Soft on Oil," 2/27/1967, "Washington Merry-Go-Round," syndicated column of Drew Pearson; author interview with Curtis Prins.

54   Drew Pearson, "Hard-Working Legislator Is Penalized," 2/6/1967, "Washington Merry-Go-Round," syndicated column of Drew Pearson.

55   Lawrence, *The Class of '74*.

56   Cockburn and Ridgeway, "Why They Sacked the Bane of the Banks."

57   Ibid; Perlstein, *Invisible Bridge*, p. 328; author interview with George Miller.

58   Cockburn and Ridgeway, "Why They Sacked the Bane of the Banks."

59   Ibid., p. 20.

60   Bruce Freed, "House Democrats Not Easy for Party to Control," *Congressional Quarterly*, 2/7/1975.

61   Author interview with Henry Waxman.

62   Cockburn and Ridgeway, "Why They Sacked the Bane of the Banks."

63   David Broder, "The Good News of a Troubled Capital," 1/20/1975, syndicated columnist with the *Washington Post*.

64   Quoted by Julian Zelizer, "When Liberals Were Organized," *American Prospect*, January 22, 2015.

65   "Memorial Services Held in the House of Representatives and Senate: Of the United States, Together with Tributes Presented in Eulogy of Wright Patman, Late a Representative from Texas, United States," 94th Congress, 2d session, 1976, United States Congress, U.S. Government Printing Office, p. 19.

66   Mark Stanley, "The Death of Wright Patman: Mourning the End of an Era," *East Texas Historical Journal* 42, no. 1 (2004).

67   Young, *Wright Patman*, pp. 299–301; *Congressional Record*, March 22, 1976, pp. 7447–48; "Memorial Services Held in the House of Representatives and Senate: Of the United States, Together with Tributes Presented in Eulogy of Wright Patman, Late a Representative from Texas," p. 23.

68   "Size of Deficit Is Key: Reuss," *Milwaukee Journal*, 4/1/1975, p. 52.

69   "Banks Know How to Get Way on Capitol Hill," *Baltimore Sun*, 5/7/1978, p. 1.

## CHAPTER FIFTEEN
### The Liberal Crack-Up

1  "Recent Efforts to Amend or Repeal the Robinson-Patman Act—Part 1, Hearings before the Ad Hoc Subcommittee on Antitrust, the Robinson-Patman Act, and Related Matters," House Committee on Small Business, November 5, 6, 11, 12, 19, 1975, p. 215.

2  Subcommittee on Monopolies and Commercial Law, Committee on the Judiciary, 94th Congress, 1st Session, on H.R. 2384 Fair Trade Repeal, March 25, 1975, p. 73.

3  Ibid., p. 130.

4  David T. Cook, "Repeal of Fair-Trade Laws," *Christian Science Monitor,* 11/20/1974.

5  Congressional Research Service, Library of Congress, "The Council on Wage and Price Stability: A Background Analysis," 1975, p. 30.

6  Cook, "Repeal of Fair-Trade Laws."

7  "Recent Efforts to Amend or Repeal the Robinson-Patman Act—Part 1, Hearings before the Ad Hoc Subcommittee on Antitrust, the Robinson-Patman Act, and Related Matters," House Committee on Small Business, November 5, 6, 11, 12, 19, 1975, p. 212.

8  Ibid., p. 1.

9  "Bill to repeal fair trade finds it's fair sailing," *Newhouse News Service,* 3/27/1975.

10  U.S. Bureau of Labor Statistics, Consumer Price Index for All Urban Consumers: All Items, Federal Reserve Bank of St. Louis, https://fred.stlouisfed.org/series/CPIAUCNS, December 27, 2018.

11  For a good background on predatory pricing law, see Lina Khan, "Amazon's Antitrust Paradox."

12  Louis Brandeis, "Cutthroat Prices: The Competition that Kills," *Harper's Weekly,* November 15, 1913.

13  Walter Lippmann, *Drift and Mastery,* p. 141.

14  These groups were, as one expert put, exposed to only "one side of the story and seem astonished and incredulous when they learn that resale price maintenance and Fair Trade has a most distinguished ancestry" Subcommittee on Monopolies and Commercial Law, Committee on the Judiciary, 94th Congress, 1st Session, on H.R. 2384 Fair Trade Repeal, March 25, 1975, p. 29.

15  "Recent Efforts to Amend or Repeal the Robinson-Patman Act—Part 1, Hearings before the Ad Hoc Subcommittee on Antitrust, the Robinson-Patman Act, and Related Matters," House Committee on Small Business, November 5, 6, 11, 12, 19, 1975, p. 215.

16  Nelson Lichtenstein, *The Retail Revolution: How Wal-Mart Created a Brave New World of Business,* p. 24.

17  Ibid., p. 25.

18   For a good discussion of the "missionary zeal" Walton brought to the company and its larger strategy, see Charles Fishman, *The Wal-Mart Effect: How the World's Most Powerful Company Really Works—and How It's Transforming the American Economy,* p. 46.

19   Walmart ad in *The Mexico Ledger* (Mexico, Missouri), 3/22/1976, p. 6.

20   "Every Day Low Prices," Walmart Digital Museum, https://walmart museum.auth.cap-hosting.com/explore/#/timeline/artifact/55f18477 -7abf-46ff-ab41-d94f7cbd00af.

21   See Wal-Mart Annual Report, 1993.

22   Earl W. Kintner, *Legislative History of the Federal Antitrust Laws and Related Statutes,* p. 972.

23   Subcommittee on Monopolies and Commercial Law, Committee on the Judiciary, 94th Congress, 1st Session, on H.R. 2384 Fair Trade Repeal, March 25, 1975, pp. 30–31.

24   Consumers Union Statement by Peter Schuck, Hearings before the Subcommittee on Financial Institutions of the Senate Committee on Banking, Housing, and Urban Affairs, July 24, 25, 1974, p. 244.

25   Brian Feldman, "The Decline of Black Business," *Washington Monthly,* March/April/May 2017.

26   Nelson Lichtenstein, *The Retail Revolution: How Wal-Mart Created a Brave New World of Business* (New York: Metropolitan Books, 2009), p. 10: "Wal-Mart and the GOP worked symbiotically to roll back the wage standards and welfare systems established since the New Deal, while promoting a Protestant, evangelical sense of social morality, the deunionization of labor, and the global expansion not only of U.S. economic power of American cultural authority as well."

27   Pre-merger notification was a long-sought reform. See Mueller, *Fighting for Antitrust Policy* , pp. 133, 140–41.

28   "Justice Department Decides IBM Case 'Without Merit,'" *Computerworld,* January 18, 1982, p. 1.

29   Hearings before the Subcommittee and Antitrust and Monopoly, Senate Judiciary Committee, March 27, 28, 29, 30, May 7, 8, 1973, p. 127.

30   See DOJ complaint reprinted in, Franklin M. Fisher, John J. McGowan and Joen E. Greenwood, *Folded, Spindled, and Mutilated: Economic Analysis and U.S. vs IBM.* p. 356.

31   "IBM Named in Antitrust Suit," *Journal Herald,* 1/18/1969, p. 1.

32   Tim Wu, "Tech Dominance and the Policeman at the Elbow," February 26, 2019, Columbia Public Law Research Paper No. 14-623, https://ssrn.com /abstract=3342598 or http://dx.doi.org/10.2139/ssrn.3342598.

33   "IBM Readjusts Pricing Formula," *New York Times,* 6/24/1969, pp. 55, 58.

34   "I.B.M. Is Found Guilty in Antitrust Suit and Told to Pay Telex $352.5 Million," *New York Times,* 9/18/1973, p. 1.

35   Gary Anthes, "Rearview Mirror," *Computerworld,* 3/2/1998, p. 65.

36  Hearings before the Subcommittee and Antitrust and Monopoly, Senate Judiciary Committee, March 27, 28, 29, 30, May 7, 8, 1973, comments by Willard Mueller, p. 48.

37  Author conversation with Glenn Loury, an economist who worked on the case as a graduate student; "Milestones in the U.S. vs. IBM Case," *Computerworld*, January 28, 1982, p. 6.

38  William Kovacic, "Out of Control? Robert Bork's Portrayal of the U.S. Antitrust System in the 1970s," *Antitrust Law Journal* 79 (2014): pp. 855–80.

39  Hearing before the Committee on the Judiciary Subcommittee on Monopolies and Commercial Law, "Oversight on AT&T and IBM Settlements," February 4, 1982, pp. 8–9, 48 of "Joint Statement of Nicholas Katzenbach, Senior Vice President and General Counsel of IBM, and Thomas D. Barr, Cravath, Swaine & Moore," see comments on p. 25 of the hearing transcript.

40  Phillip Zweig, *Wriston: Walter Wriston, Citibank, and the Rise of American Financial Supremacy*, p. 649.

41  Alfred D. Chandler Jr., *Inventing the Electronic Century: The Epic Story of the Consumer Electronics and Computer Industries, With a New Preface*.

42  U.S. Senate Judiciary Committee Hearings, Competition, Innovation, and Public Policy in the Digital Age: Examining the Impact of High-Growth Technology and the Internet on Antitrust, Intellectual Property, Competition Policy, and Enforcement, March 3, 1997, November 4, 1997, July 23, 1998, p. 24.

43  See for instance "What's Left of the U.S. Left" *Vancouver Sun*, 10/28/1977; Kenneth Arrow's 1977 lecture "A Cautious Case for Socialism" reprinted in *Dissent*, https://www.dissentmagazine.org/wp-content/files_mf/1426269747ACau tiousCaseforSocialism.pdf.

44  *The Origins of Law and Economics: Essays by the Founding Fathers*, Francesco Parisi and Charles K. Rowley, eds., p. 312.

45  Henry N. Butler, *The Manne Programs in Economics for Federal Judges*, 50 Case W. Res. L. Rev. 351 (1999), https://scholarlycommons.law.case.edu/caselrev /vol50/iss2/19.

46  *The Origins of Law and Economics*, p. 320.

47  Davidson, *Megamergers*, p. 122.

48  Robert Bork, *The Antitrust Paradox: A Policy At War With Itself* (New York: Basic Books, 1978), pp. 4, 6.

49  William Kovacic, "Out of Control? Robert Bork's Portrayal of the U.S. Antitrust System in the 1970s," *Antitrust Law Journal* 79 (2014): p. 866 .

50  Rivlin would use CBO to oppose Jimmy Carter's plan to confront the oil crisis.

51  "Statement by the President," Box 33, folder "12/12/75 HR6971 Consumer Goods Pricing Act of 1975" of the White House Records Office: Legislation Case Files at the Gerald R. Ford Presidential Library https://www.fordlibrary museum.gov/library/document/0055/1669141.pdf.

52    Alan Ehrenhalt, "Last Hurrahs for the New Deal," *Washington Monthly,* January 1976, pp. 56–57.

53    Stuart Eizenstat, *President Carter: The White House Years,* p. 386.

54    Ibid.

55    Oversight of Federal Trade Commission Law Enforcement: Fiscal Years 1982 and 1983, November 9, 1983, p. 11; Richard Zoglin, "The Coming Battle Over TV Ads For Kids," *New York Times,* 1/1/1978.

56    Roy A. Kiesling, *Report to Those Most Concerned: A Memoir of the U.S. Consumer Movement, 1970–1980.*

57    Judith Stein, *Pivotal Decade: How the United States Traded Factories for Finance in the Seventies.*

58    William Greider, *Secrets of the Temple: How the Federal Reserve Runs the Country,* p. 47; William Greider, *Come Home, America: The Rise and Fall (and Redeeming Promise) of Our Country,* p. 49

59    R. Gregory Nokes, "Volcker Asserts Lower Standard of Living Only Answer to Runaway Inflation," Associated Press, published in the *Schenectady Gazette,* 10/16/1979; Paul A. Volcker, Chairman, Fed. Reserve Sys., Address at Kansas State University Alfred M. Landon Lecture Series on Public Issues: "Dealing with Inflation: Obstacles and Opportunities" (Apr. 15, 1981).

60    Michael Belzer, *Sweatshops on Wheels: Winners and Losers in Trucking Deregulation* (New York: Oxford University Press, 2000), preface and p. 29.

61    Wojnilower, "The Central Role of Credit Crunches in Recent Financial History."

62    Evans and Novak syndicated column in the *Chicago-Sun Times,* and syndicated nationally, September 23, 1979.

63    See Evans and Novak, "Kennedy Moving to the Center", column in the *Chicago Sun-Times,* syndicated nationally, September 25, 1979.

64    "Ted Kennedy's Final Round," *Rolling Stone,* July 24, 1980.

65    Ray Abernathy, "The PATCO Conspiracy Revisited: From Carter to Reagan . . . to Obama," *In These Times,* August 17, 2009, http://inthesetimes.com /working/entry/4764/the_patco_conspiracy_revisted_from_carter_to_ reagan . . . to_obama.

66    Robert Kaiser and Mary Russell, "Compromise Reached on Key Tax Cuts," *Washington Post,* 10/15/1978.

67    Eizenstat, *President Carter,* p. 357.

68    Burton Ira Kaufman, *The Carter Years,* p. 319.

69    Alfred Kahn, *The Economics of Regulation: Principles and Institutions, Volume II: Institutional Issues,* p. 1.

70    Lester C. Thurow, *The Zero-Sum Society: Distribution and the Possibilities for Change,* pp. 145–46.

71    Stephen Breyer, *Regulation and Its Reform,* 1982, p. 2.

72    Fred P. Graham, "2 Top Antitrust Lawyers Quit," *New York Times,* 12/9/1965.

73 Leonard Silk, "Economic Scene," *New York Times,*11/9/1979, p. 86.

74 Bork, *The Antitrust Paradox.*

75 Senate Judiciary Hearings, Nomination of Robert H. Bork to Be Associate Justice of the Supreme Court of the United States, Part III, p. 3313.

## CHAPTER SIXTEEN
### The Reagan Revolution

1 Bryan Burrough, *The Big Rich: The Rise and Fall of the Greatest Texas Oil Fortunes,* p. 250.

2 "Remarks of Charles A. James, Assistant Attorney General, Antitrust Division, U.S. Department of Justice, on the Occasion of the Twentieth Anniversary of the 1982 Merger Guidelines," June 10, 2002, https://www.justice.gov/archives/atr/giant-steps-remarks-charles-james-assistant-attorney-general-antitrust-division.

3 "Credit Deregulation and Availability Act of 1981," Hearings before the Subcommittee on Financial Institutions of the Committee on Banking, Housing, and Urban Affairs, U.S. Senate, July 9, 15, and 20, p. 30.

4 "Nancy Reagan: A Change of Style," The National Museum of American History, online exhibit of the First Ladies at the Smithsonian, http://americanhistory.si.edu/first-ladies/nancy-reagan.

5 Leslie Wayne, "The New Face of Business Leadership, *New York Times,* 5/22/1983, p. 172.

6 Justin Gomer and Christopher Petrella, "How the Reagan Administration Stoked Fears of Anti-White Racism," *Washington Post,* 10/10/2017, https://www.washingtonpost.com/news/made-by-history/wp/2017/10/10/how-the-reagan-administration-stoked-fears-of-anti-white-racism/?utm_term=.3ba5a49105c8.

7 "Reagan Stance on PATCO Causes Unions Anxiety," *New York Times,* 10/21/1981, p. 24.

8 Joseph McCartin, "The Strike That Busted Unions," *New York Times,* 8/2/2010.

9 "Reagan Says Many New Dealers Wanted Fascism," *New York Times,* 12/23/1981, p. 12.

10 Earl W. Kitch, "Fire of Truth," p. 231.

11 Mueller, *Fighting for Antitrust Policy* p. 209.

12 Andrew Wright, "Law Scholar Areeda, 'Antitrust Guru,' Dies," *Harvard Crimson,* January 5, 1996, https://www.thecrimson.com/article/1996/1/5/law-scholar-areeda-antitrust-guru-dies/.

13 George Stigler, *Memoirs of an Unregulated Economist,* p. 166.

14 Leslie Wayne, "The New Face of Business Leadership," *New York Times,* 5/22/1983, p. 172.

15 Kornbluth, *Highly Confident*, p. 42.

16 Stigler, *Memoirs of an Unregulated Economist*, p. 121.

17 Stephen Breyer, *Regulation and Its Reform*, pp. 382, 389, 394, 396, 431, 449, 459.

18 Paul S. Calem, "The New Bank Deposit Markets: Goodbye to Regulation Q," *Business Review*, Federal Reserve Bank of Philadelphia (November–December 1985): 19–29.

19 "Reagan Reversing Many U.S. Policies," *New York Times*, 7/3/1981, p. 8; Saule T. Omarova, "The Quiet Metamorphosis: How Derivatives Changed the 'Business of Banking,'" *University Miami Law Review*, 2009, p. 1058; UNC Legal Studies Research Paper No. 1491767, https://ssrn.com/abstract=1491767.

20 Diane Ellis, "The Effect of Consumer Interest Rate Deregulation on Credit Card Volumes, Charge-Offs, and the Personal Bankruptcy Rate (March 1998)," Federal Deposit Insurance Company, Bank Trends, No. 98-05, https://ssrn.com/abstract=92209 or http://dx.doi.org/10.2139/ssrn.92209.

21 David S. Evans and Richard Schmalensee, *Paying with Plastic: The Digital Revolution in Buying and Borrowing*, (Cambridge, Mass.: MIT Press, 1999).

22 Credit Deregulation and Availability Act of 1981, Hearings before the Subcommittee on Financial Institutions of the Committee on Banking, Housing, and Urban Affairs, U.S. Senate, July 9, pp. 15, 21.

23 Stigler, *Memoirs of an Unregulated Economist*, p. 192.

24 Robert Walters, "Arkansas Consumers Enjoy Low Interest Rates," Newspaper Enterprise Association, published in *Gadsen Times*, 12/5/1981.

25 Lloyd Constantine, *Priceless: The Case That Brought Down the Visa/MasterCard Bank Cartel*.

26 Phillip Zweig, *Wriston: Walter Wriston, Citibank, and the Rise of American Financial Supremacy*, p. 710.

27 Steve Coll, *The Deal of the Century: The Breakup of AT&T*, p. 136.

28 "Federal Antitrust Enforcement Policies and Small Business," Joint Hearing before the Committee on Small Business and the Subcommittee on State, Justice, Commerce, The Judiciary, and Related Agencies of the Committee on Appropriations, United States Senate, September 9, 1982. p. 13.

29 Ibid.

30 Richard A. Posner, "Introduction to Baxter Symposium," *Stanford Law Review* 51 (1999): p. 1007.

31 "U.S. Drops Trust Suits Against Mack, 2 Others," Associated Press, July 9, 1981; Gary L. Reback, *Free the Market!: Why Only Government Can Keep the Marketplace Competitive*, p. 45.

32 "Changes in Antitrust Enforcement Policies and Activities," United States General Accounting Office, October 1990.

33 Coll, *The Deal of the Century*, pp. 182–84.

34 Reback, *Free the Market!*, p. 35.

35    Ibid., p. 83.

36    Remarks of Charles A. James Assistant Attorney General, Antitrust Division, U.S. Department of Justice, on the Occasion of the Twentieth Anniversary of the 1982 Merger Guidelines, https://www.justice.gov/archives/atr/giant -steps-remarks-charles-james-assistant-attorney-general-antitrust-division.

37    Quoted in Reback, *Free the Market!*, p. 85.

38    Peter Grier, "Impact of AT&T, IBM Decisions," *Christian Science Monitor,* 1/11/1982, accessed May 12, 2018, https://www.csmonitor.com /1982/0111/011144.html.

39    James B. Stewart, *Den of Thieves*, p. 97.

40    William F. Baxter, "Responding to the Reaction: The Draftsman's View," *California Law Review* 71 (March 1983): p. 630.

41    Walter Adams and James W. Brock, *The Bigness Complex: Industry, Labor, and Government in the American Economy*, 2nd edition.

42    "Mergers and Acquisitions," Oversight Hearing before the Subcommittee on Monopolies and Commercial Law of the Commission on the Judiciary, House of Representatives, 7/8, 8/26, 9/23, 12/9, 1981 pp. 3–4.

43    "Do Oil and Chemistry Mix?," editorial, *New York Times,* 7/9/1981.

44    Corporate Takeovers: Oversight Hearing before the Subcommittee on Monopolies and Commercial Law of the Committee on the Judiciary, House of Representatives, 97th Congress, 2nd Session, June 10, 1982.

45    Debra Valentine, "The Evolution of U.S. Merger Law," Prepared Remarks before INDECOPI Conference, 8/13/1996.

46    Allan Sloan, *Three Plus One Equals Billions: The Bendix–Martin Marietta War,* p. 35.

47    Jonathan Baker, "The Antitrust Analysis of Hospital Mergers and the Transformation of the Hospital Industry," *Law and Contemporary Problems* (Spring 1988): 94; Alex Horenstein and Manuel Santos, "Understanding Growth Patterns in US Health Care Expenditures," Journal of the European Economic Association, Volume 17, Issue 1, February 2019.

48    Zweig, *Wriston*, p. 834.

49    Walter Kiechel, *Lords of Strategy: The Secret Intellectual History of the New Corporate World,* p. 72.

50    "Why Jack Welch Is Changing GE," *New York Times,* 5/5/1985, p. 190.

51    John Holusha, "Are We Eating Our Seed Corn?," *New York Times,* 5/3/1990, Section 3, p. 1.

52    Debra Whitefield, "GE's 'Trader Jack' Strikes Again with Move to Sell Electronics Unit," *Los Angeles Times,* 7/26/1987.

53    Barry C. Lynn, *Cornered: The New Monopoly Capitalism and the Economics of Destruction*, p. 67.

54    Peter Whoriskey, "Light bulb factory closes; end of era for U.S. means more jobs overseas," *Washington Post,* 9/8/2010.

55    Peter Applebome, "U.S. Goods Made in Mexico Raise Concern on Loss of

American Jobs," *New York Times,* 12/29/1986; Louis Uchitelle, "Mexico's Hope for Industrial Might," *New York Times,* 9/25/1990.

56  Applebome, "U.S. Goods Made in Mexico"; Daniel Cuff, "U.S. Steel to Acquire Texas Oil and Gas in $3.6 Billion Deal," *New York Times,* 10/31/1985; Agis Salpukas, "National Steel to Acquire United Financial Corp," *New York Times,* 3/7/1979.

57  See "Crazy Eddie Early Years," *White Collar Fraud,* blog, https://whitecollar fraud.com/crazy-eddie/crazy-eddie-early-years/.

58  For a discussion of the Crazy Eddie story, see Sam Antar, "The Crazy Eddie Fraud: Confessions of a White-Collar Criminal," Whitecollarfraud.com, 9/21/2014; Barry Meier, "Crazy Eddie's Insane Odyssey," *New York Times,* 7/19/1992; Wayne King, "Selling on Sunday Rising Despite Confusing Laws," *New York Times,* 5/22/1976. For a discussion of Crazy Eddie's exploitation of purchasing power, see SEC Amendment No. 1 to Form S-1, Crazy Eddie, Inc. filed on 3/13/1985 as published on Whitecollarfraud.com, https://white collarfraud.com/wp-content/uploads/2016/10/1985-03-13-Crazy-Eddie -Amendment-to-Form-S-1-Registration-Statement.pdf: "The Company believes that its purchasing power enables it to offer such merchandise at prices generally below those offered by such other stores. All products sold in Crazy Eddie stores carry a 30-day price guaranty pursuant to which the store will refund the difference between its sale price and any lower price for the same product that is demonstrated by a customer to be available at any other store."

59  See Richard Feinberg and Jennifer Meoli, "A Brief History of the Mall," *Advances in Consumer Research* 18 (1991): 426–27.

60  "The Limited's Wexner Sets No Limits on Success," *Des Moines Register,* 5/22/1985, p. 4x.

61  Bob Batchelor and Scott Stoddart, *The 1980s,* p. 75.

62  See testimony by Kmart CEO in "Oversight of Federal Trade Commission Law Enforcement: Fiscal Years 1982 and 1983," Subcommittee on Commerce, Consumer, and Monetary Affairs of the Committee on Government Operations, November 9, 1983.

63  Lisa Scharoun, *America at the Mall: The Cultural Role of a Retail Utopia,* p. 116; David W. Boyd, "From 'Mom and Pop' to Wal-Mart: The Impact of the Consumer Goods Pricing Act of 1975 on the Retail Sector in the United States," *Journal of Economic Issues* 31, no. 1 (1997): 223–32, www.jstor.org/stable /4227158.

64  In 1914, Congress enacted the Federal Trade Commission Act and the Clayton Antitrust Act, which included prohibitions against discriminatory pricing. There were state-level fair trade laws put in place over the next two decades, culminating in the Robinson-Patman Act in 1936 and the Miller-Tydings Act in 1937.

65 Steve Coll, *The Deal of the Century,* pp. 29–35, 60. The Neal Commission helped influence the Hart bill in 1973, and Hart's hearings then created pressure on the DOJ to go up against AT&T. Hart's staff also gave evidence to the DOJ, "typed transcripts of interviews with AT&T competitors who said they were afraid to testify in public before the antitrust subcommittee."

66 Eizenstat, *President Carter,* p. 383.

67 Steve Coll, *Deal of the Century,* pp. 182–83; Robert Britt Horwitz, *The Irony of Regulatory Reform: The Deregulation of American Telecommunications.* p. 242.

68 Coll, *Deal of the Century,* p. 182.

69 Ibid., p. 265; Ernest Holsendolph, "Judge Lets AT&T Case Go On; Sees Signs of Antitrust Violations," *New York Times,* 9/12/1981.

70 Ken Labich, "Was Breaking Up At&T a Good Idea?," *Fortune,* January 2, 1989, http://archive.fortune.com/magazines/fortune/fortune_archive/1989/01/02 /71446/index.htm.

## CHAPTER SEVENTEEN
### The Morgans, the Mellons, and the Milkens

1 Louis Brandeis, *Other People's Money,* Chapter One

2 Connie Bruck, *The Predators' Ball: The Inside Story of Drexel Burnham and the Rise of the Junk Bond Raiders.* p. 258.

3 Ibid., p. 183.

4 Scott B. MacDonald, *Separating Fools from Their Money: A History of American Financial Scandals.*

5 Mary Zey, *Banking on Fraud: Drexel, Junk Bonds, and Buyouts,* p. 5.

6 Connie Bruck, *The Predator's Ball,* p. 15.

7 Ibid., for a description of the opacity of the market, see p. 32, for a description of the decimation of small investment banks, see p. 43.

8 George A. Akerlof and Paul M. Romer, "Looting: The Economic Underworld of Bankruptcy for Profit," NBER Working Paper No. R1869, p. 5.

9 Bruck, *Predator's Ball* pp. 286–87, Zey, *Banking on Fraud,* pp. 158–59.

10 Bruck, *The Predator's Ball,* pp. 33, 46–47, 56–57; Stein, *License to Steal,* p. 70; Anthony Carideo, "First Investors is under fire," *Star Tribune,* 2/3/1991.

11 George A. Akerlof and Paul M. Romer, "Looting: The Economic Underworld of Bankruptcy for Profit," NBER Working Paper No. R1869, p. 5.

12 Ibid., p. 47; Stein, *License to Steal* pp. 31–35; Zey, *Banking on Fraud,* p. 158–59.

13 George A. Akerlof and Paul M. Romer, "Looting: The Economic Underworld of Bankruptcy for Profit," NBER Working Paper No. R1869; Stein, *License to Steal,* pp. 143–51; Richard Stevenson, "California Saving Unit Is Seized," *New York Times,* 2/24/1990; Michael Lev, "U.S. Seizes Columbia Savings," *New York Times,* 1/26/1991.

14    Bruck, *Predator's Ball,* p. 78, Altman, Edward I. "Revisiting the High-Yield Bond Market." *Financial Management,* vol. 21, no. 2, 1992, pp. 78–92, *JSTOR,* www.jstor.org/stable/3665667.

15    Martin Mayer, *The Greatest-Ever Bank Robbery: The Collapse of the Savings and Loan Industry,* p. 20.

16    Ibid., p. 19.

17    Bryan Burrough, "Banking on Failure," *Washington Post,* 5/9/1993; Brooks Jackson, *Honest Graft,* pp. 4, 178–79, 188, 194–95, 199.

18    Mayer, *The Greatest-Ever Bank Robbery,* Appendix B.

19    Benjamin Stein, *A License to Steal,* p. 205.

20    Hearings before the Subcommittee on Telecommunications and Finance of the Committee on Energy and Commerce, House of Representatives, One Hundred Second Congress, first session, "Financial services restructuring: Including H.R. 797, a bill to amend the federal securities laws to equalize the regulatory treatment of participants in the securities industry," April 11, June 20, July 10 and 31, August 1, and September 13, 1991, vol. 4, p. 98.

21    George A. Akerlof and Paul M. Romer, "Looting: The Economic Underworld of Bankruptcy for Profit," NBER Working Paper No. R1869, pp. 43–44, 46–47, 50–51, For a discussion of confidence in Milken, see the discussion of "highly confident" letters in Bruck, *Predator's Ball,* p. 166.

22    Bruck, *The Predators' Ball,* p. 100.

23    James B. Stewart, *Den of Thieves.*

24    Bruck, *The Predators' Ball,* p. 245.

25    Zey, *Banking on Fraud,* p. 161.

26    Stewart, *Den of Thieves.*

27    Zey, *Banking on Fraud,* p. 20.

28    Nathaniel Nash, "Panel Gets No Answers From Milken," *New York Times,* 4/28/1988.

29    Stein, *License to Steal,* pp. 152–53.

30    Landon Thomas, "Cold Call," *New York,* 2/18/2002.

31    "The Secret World of Mike Milken," *Manhattan, Inc.,* September 1987, http://www.edwardjayepstein.com/archived/milken_print.htm.

32    Stewart, *Den of Thieves,* p. 468; Bruck, *The Predators' Ball,* p. 259.

33    Bruck, *The Predators' Ball,* p. 259.

34    Donald Barlett and James Steele, *America: What Went Wrong?,* p. 190.

35    Glenn Bunting, "Drexel Develops Strong Ties to Political Powers: Bradley Is Among Prominent Figures Who Are Part of Aggressive Lobbying by Junk Bond Firm," *Los Angeles Times,* 5/7/1989.

36    Ibid.

37    Donald L. Barlett and James B. Steele, "How special-interest groups have their way with Congress," *Philadelphia Inquirer,* 10/28/1991; Donald L.

Barlett and James B. Steele, "Tax favors seem to follow cash flow in Congress," Knight-Ridder News Service, 4/28/1988. Rostenkowski ran the committee tasked with tax policy. For the importance of tax policy to junk bonds, see Zey, *Banking on Fraud*, p. 196–97.

38  "Robert Strauss Had Key Dual Role in MCA Acquisition," *Los Angeles Times*, 12/1/1990.

39  Glenn Bunting, "Drexel Develops Strong Ties to Political Powers: Bradley Is Among Prominent Figures Who Are Part of Aggressive Lobbying by Junk Bond Firm."

40  Ruth Shalit, "The Undertaker," *New Republic*, Vol. 212 Issue 1, January 2, 1995; Brooks Jackson, *Honest Graft*, pp. 96–98, 303, 317.

41  Harry Bernstein, "How Unions Might Revive Under Clinton," *Los Angeles Times*, 12/22/1992.

42  Stewart, *Den of Thieves*, p. 137.

43  Zey, *Banking on Fraud*, p. 163.

44  Bruck, *Predator's Ball*, p. 299.

45  Hearing before the Subcommittee on Economic Stabilization of the Committee on Banking, Finance, and Urban Affairs, "Oversight Hearing on Mergers and Acquisitions," May 12, 1987, testimony of Dennis Rich, Director of Business Planning for the Goodyear Tire & Rubber Company, p. 83.

46  Ibid., pp. 165–66.

47  Hearing before the Subcommittee on Economic Stabilization of the Committee on Banking, Finance, and Urban Affairs, "Oversight Hearing on Mergers and Acquisitions," May 12, 1987, testimony of Dennis Rich, Director of Business Planning for the Goodyear Tire & Rubber Company, pp. 83–84.

48  Michael Lev, "U.S. Seizes Columbia Savings," *New York Times*, 1/26/1991; Stein, *License to Steal*, p. 18.

49  Hearing before the Subcommittee on Economic Stabilization of the Committee on Banking, Finance, and Urban Affairs, "Oversight Hearing on Mergers and Acquisitions," May 12, 1987, testimony of Dennis Rich, Director of Business Planning for the Goodyear Tire & Rubber Company, p. 88.bid., pp. 84–86.

50  For a good review of the private equity business mode, see Eileen Applebaum's *Private Equity at Work: When Wall Street Manages Main Street*.

## CHAPTER EIGHTEEN
### Tech Goliaths and Too Big to Fail

1  Charles Ferguson and Charles Morris, *Computer Wars: How the West Can Win in a Post-IBM World*, p. 67.

2  Bill Sing, "1985—A Year of Easy Money in Stock Market: Dow Surges to Its Best Annual Gain Since 1975," *Los Angeles Times*.

3   Vartanig G. Vartan, "Wall Street In 1986; Top Performers Are a Diverse Lot," *New York Times*, 1/2/1987, p. D5.

4   Jesse Kornbluth, *Highly Confident: The Crime and Punishment of Michael Milken*, p. 132.

5   Michael Lewis, *The Big Short: Inside the Doomsday Machine*, p. xv.

6   Robert Reinhold, "Housing Woes Lessen Allure of the Crowded Silicon Valley," *New York Times*, 12/23/1983, p. 1.

7   Suzanne Deffree, "Apple IPO Makes Instant Millionaires," *EDN Moments*, December 12, 2017, https://www.edn.com/electronics-blogs/edn-moments/4403276/Apple-IPO-makes-instant-millionaires--December-12--1980.

8   *History of the Eighties: Lessons for the Future, Vol. 1, An Examination of the Banking Crises of the 1980s and Early 1990s* (Washington, DC: FDIC, 1997), chapter eight.

9   Ed McBride, "Broken Heartland," *Nation*, February 8, 1986, p. 132.

10  Credit Deregulation and Availability Act of 1981, Hearings before the Subcommittee on Financial Institutions of the Committee on Banking, Housing, and Urban Affairs, U.S. Senate, July 9, 15, and 20.

11  See Gary Hart, *A New Democracy: A Democratic Vision for the 1980s and Beyond*. In this 1983 book, Hart is framing the policies he will use in running for president. In his short discussion of farming, he focused almost entirely on helping agricultural exports, and little on family farming.

12  "Iowa Layoffs Undermine Wisconsin Towns," *Wisconsin State Journal*, 9/20/1981, Section 3, p. 7; "Continued Layoffs Beleaguer General Electric's Birthplace," *Ithaca Journal*, 1/5/1987; "Eastern Air's Pay-Cut Plan," *New York Times*, 10/6/1987, p. 90; "New Layoffs by AT&T," *New York Times*, 1026/1985, p. 34; "As Economy Grew Since '83, Closings and Layoffs Took 9.7 Million Jobs," *New York Times*, 12/13/1988, p. 44. There were ten million layoffs between when the economic recovery started in 1983 and 1988, and 30 percent of those laid off took new jobs with pay cuts of at least 20 percent; Steven Greenhouse, "Former Steelworkers' Income Falls by Half," *New York Times*, 10/31/1984.

13  Studs Terkel, *Hard Times: An Oral History of the Great Depression*.

14  Freedom and Vigilance by Ronald Reagan, 1988 Francis Boyer Lecture on Public Policy, American Enterprise Institute, December 7, 1988.

15  Randall Rothenberg, "The Neoliberal Club," *Esquire*, February 1982, p. 37; Randall Rothenberg, "Six Governors in Search of an Answer," *New York Times*, 9/18/1988; Randall Rothenberg, *The Neoliberals: Creating the New American Politics* (New York: Simon & Schuster, 1984).

16  Paul Krugman, *Peddling Prosperity: Economic Sense and Nonsense in the Age of Diminished Expectations*, p. 251.

17  Rothenberg, *The Neoliberals*, p. 206.

18  Ibid., p. 207

19  Al From, *The New Democrats and the Return to Power* pp. 2–3; Peter Kilborne, "Democrats' Ideas on Economy Shift," *New York Times,* 8/12/1986.

20  Author interview with Tim Wirth. Wirth discusses the key intellectual influence of Lester Thurow, Alive Rivlin, and Charles Schultze over the Committee on Party Effectiveness. For a list of members of the Committee on Party Effectiveness, see this dissertation: Karl Gerard Brandt, "Deficit politics and democratic unity: the saga of Tip O'Neill, Jim Wright, and the conservative Democrats in the House of Representatives during the Reagand Era," 2003, LSU Doctoral Dissertations 2780, https://digitalcommons.lsu.edu/grad school_dissertations/2780, pp. 20–21.

21  Lester C. Thurow, *The Zero-Sum Society: Distribution and the Possibilities for Change,* p. 120.

22  Al From, *The New Democrats and the Return to Power,* p. 118.

23  "Democratic Party Platforms, 1984," Democratic Party Platform Online by Gerhard Peters and John T. Woolley, The American Presidency Project, https://www.presidency.ucsb.edu/node/273258.

24  Ibid., p. 71.

25  David Broder, "A Welcome Attack of Sanity Has Hit Washington," *Washington Post,* October 6, 1985.

26  See Brooks Jackson, *Honest Graft.*

27  Martin Mayer, *The Greatest-Ever Bank Robbery: The Collapse of the Savings and Loan Industry,* p. 237; "Report of the Special Outside Counsel in the Matter of Speaker James C. Wright, Jr.," Committee on Standards of Official Conduct, U.S. House of Representatives, 2/21/1989, p. 23.

28  Martin Tolchin, "Washington at Work; From Yale Days to Bank Lobbyist, a Friend and Adviser to the Bushes," *New York Times,* 7/19/1991, p. A12.

29  Jerry Knight and Susan Schmidt, "Bush, Clinton Reluctant to Discuss Coming Wave of Bank, Thrift Failures," *Washington Post,* October 4, 1992.

30  "George H. W. Bush Retrospective," December 1, 2018, Gallup, https://news .gallup.com/opinion/gallup/234971/george-bush-retrospective.aspx.

31  Knight and Schmidt, "Bush, Clinton Reluctant to Discuss Coming Wave of Bank, Thrift Failures."

32  Alan Abramowitz and Ruy Teixeira, "The Decline of the White Working Class and the Rise of a Mass Upper Middle Class," Brookings, April 8, 2008.

33  John Judis, "Why Democrats Must Be Populists," *American Prospect,* August 19, 2002.

34  Bethany Moreton, *To Serve God and Wal-Mart: The Making of Christian Free Enterprise*; "Democratic Party Platforms, 1992," Democratic Party Platform Online by Gerhard Peters and John T. Woolley, The American Presidency Project, https://www.presidency.ucsb.edu/node/273264.

35   Jeffrey Birnbaum, *The Lobbyists: How Influence Peddlers Get Their Way in Washington.*

36   Saule T. Omarova, "The Quiet Metamorphosis: How Derivatives Changed the 'Business of Banking,'" *University of Miami Law Review* 63 (2009): p. 1041; University of North Carolina Legal Studies Research Paper No. 1491767, https://ssrn.com/abstract=1491767.

37   Stephen Labaton, "U.S. Versus Microsoft: The Policy Makers; Despite a Tough Stance or Two, White House Is Still Consolidation Friendly," *New York Times*, 11/8/1999.

38   Dr. William Heffernan, "Consolidation in the Food and Agriculture System," *Report to the National Farmers Union,* February 5, 1999.

39   See opening statement of Hon. Conrad Burns, U.S. Senator from Montana, as well as Senate Joint Resolution No. 11, 56th Legislature, Montana, both included in "How Mergers in the Nation's Agricultural Industry Impact Consumers," Field Hearing before the Committee on Commerce, Science, and Transportation, United States Senate, 106th Congress, 1st Session, July 24, 1999.

40   Charles Fishman, *The Wal-Mart Effect: How the World's Most Powerful Company Really Works—and How It's Transforming the American Economy,* p. 80.

41   Antonia Juhasz, "What Wal-Mart Wants from the WTO," *AlterNet,* December 13, 2005. Chinese trade deficit statistics are from the Census Bureau's measurement of Foreign Trade, Trade in Goods with China, https://www.census.gov/foreign-trade/balance/c5700.html; United States Census Department, 1992: U.S. Trade in goods with China; United States Census Department, 2000: U.S. Trade in goods with China

42   "The Challenges of Success," remarks by Lawrence H. Summers, Deputy Secretary of the Treasury, Hambrecth & Quist Technology Conference, San Francisco, April 28, 1998, Clinton Presidential Library Online, https://clinton.presidentiallibraries.us/files/original/d60b4784f1b1715d14f432df9bde6e31.pdf.

43   John F. Lehman and Stephen L. Brooks, "Rapid Escalation: An Overview of Private Equity Investing in the Aerospace and Defense Industry," *The Journal of Private Equity* 3, no. 2 (2000): 7–11, www.jstor.org/stable/43503167; Marjorie Censer, "Defense companies brace for a different kind of consolidation this time around," *Washington Post,* 1/12/2014.

44   "Mergers, Concentration, and Market Power: Some Facts," Council of Economic Advisors, May 22, 1998, Clinton Presidential Library Online, https://clinton.presidentiallibraries.us/files/original/b2691b25ce685ae00d6883a27cf667c6.pdf.

45   Stephen Labaton, "U.S. Versus Microsoft: The Policy Makers; Despite a Tough Stance or Two, White House Is Still Consolidation Friendly" *New York Times*, 11/8/1999.

46    "Mergers, Concentration, and Market Power: Some Facts," Council of Economic Advisors.

47    "Vance Opperman's Donations Under Scrutiny," *Minneapolis Star Tribune,* 4/15/1997, p. 7.

48    *Verizon Communications Inc. v. Law Offices of Curtis V. Trinko, LLP,* 540 U.S. TK ___ (2003).

49    As quoted in Gary L. Reback, *Free the Market!: Why Only Government Can Keep the Marketplace Competitive,* p. 162.

50    Ibid.

51    Matthew Lasar, "The Unix revolution—thank you, Uncle Sam?" *Ars Technica,* 7/19/2011, https://arstechnica.com/tech-policy/2011/07/should-we-thank -for-feds-for-the-success-of-unix/.

52    For good background on these battles, see Reback, *Free the Market!*

53    Reinhold, "Housing Woes Lessen Allure of the Crowded Silicon Valley."

54    Ferguson and Morris, *Computer Wars,* p. 60–61, 66–71.

55    Reback, *Free the Market!,* p. 159.

56    Ferguson and Morris, *Computer Wars,* p. 66.

57    Matthew Lasar, "The Eternal Antitrust Case: Microsoft Versus the World," *Ars Technica,* September 26, 2010.

58    "An Energetic Trustbuster, but Not a Boat Rocker," *New York Times,* 7/25/1994, pp. D1, D3.

59    "Clinton and Technology: Some Policies Clash," *New York Times,* 4/11/1994, p. D2; "Economic Scene," *New York Times,* 7/21/1994, p. D2. Ironically, Fisher would serve as lead witness for the Department of Justice in its suit against Microsoft four years later.

60    Elizabeth Corcoran, "After Five Years of Talks, Gates Ends Fight with U.S.," *Pittsburgh Post-*Gazette, 7/19/1994; Reback, *Free the Market!,* p. 166."

61    Reback, *Free the Market!,* pp. 202–04.

62    Ibid., p. 252.

63    "The Clinton Presidency: A Historic Era of Progress and Prosperity," https:// clintonwhitehouse5.archives.gov/WH/Accomplishments/eightyears-01.html.

64    Quotes from Clinton White House Archives: THE CLINTON-GORE ADMINISTRATION: PAYING OFF THE DEBT BY 2012, fact sheet released June 26, 2000, https://clintonwhitehouse3.archives.gov/WH/New/00Budget Framework/appendix1.html; "Bush: 'Our Long National Nightmare Of Peace And Prosperity Is Finally Over,'" *Onion,* January 17, 2001.

65    Willard K. Tom, "The 1975 Xerox Consent Decree: Ancient Artifacts and Current Tensions," *Antitrust Law Journal* 68, no. 3 (2001).

66    Barack Obama, "Restoring America's Promise of Opportunity, Prosperity, and Growth," speech at the launch of the Brookings Institute Hamilton Project, Washington, D.C., Wednesday, April 5, 2006, http://www .hamiltonproject.org/assets/legacy/files/downloads_and_links/Restoring

_Americas_Promise_of_Opportunity_Prosperity_and_Growth_Transcript
.pdf.

67  Roc Armenter, "A bit of a miracle no more: the decline of the labor share,"
    *Business Review,* (Federal Reserve Bank of Philadelphia), issue Q3, 2015,
    pp. 1–9.

68  "Wal-Mart's Influence Grows," *USA Today,* 1/29/2003: "Anyone whose stocks
    rose in the late 1990s owes Wal-Mart, the world's biggest company. It alone
    accounted for as much as 25 percent of the U.S. productivity gains from 1995–
    99, says consultant McKinsey & Co."

69  Adam Tooze, *Crashed: How a Decade of Financial Crises Changed the World,* p. 2.

70  Matt Stoller, "The Housing Crash and the End of American Citizenship," *Ford-
    ham Urban Law Journal* 1183 (2012), vol. 39, issue 4, https://ir.lawnet.fordham
    .edu/ulj/vol39/iss4/8.

71  Andrew Clark and Jill Treanor, "Greenspan - I was wrong about the economy.
    Sort of," *Guardian,* 10/23/2008.

72  "Welch Condemns Share Price Focus," *Financial Times,* 3/12/2009.

73  Barack Obama, *The Audacity of Hope: Thoughts on Reclaiming the American Dream.*

74  Paul Kiel and Olga Pierce, "Dems: Obama Broke Pledge to Force Banks to
    Help Homeowners," *ProPublica,* February 4, 2011.

75  Leo Hindery, "Political Malpractice in the First Degree," *Huffington Post,* May 25,
    2011, https://www.huffingtonpost.com/leo-hindery-jr/political-malpractice
    -in_b_784108.html.

76  Timothy F. Geithner, *Stress Test: Reflections on Financial Crises.*

77  "What Timothy Geithner Really Thinks," *New York Times Magazine,* May 8,
    2014. Obama also lauded financiers. "I know both those guys," he said about
    Goldman Sachs CEO Lloyd Blankfein and JP Morgan CEO Jamie Dimon,
    both of whom became billionaires during the crisis, adding that "they are very
    savvy businessmen."

78  Ibid.

79  Phil Magness, "Alexander Hamilton's Exaggerated Abolitionism," *History News
    Network,* 7/27/2015: "In a passage that Hamilton's modern biographers usually
    tread lightly around, Hamilton's own grandson described this entry thusly: 'It
    has been stated that Hamilton never owned a negro slave, but this is untrue.
    We find that in his books there are entries showing that he purchased them
    for himself and for others.'" Also see historian William Hogeland, "Hamil-
    ton and the Tenner," personal blog entry, https://williamhogeland.wordpress
    .com/2015/06/21/hamilton-and-the-tenner/) 6/21/2015.

80  Anne Case and Angus Deaton, "Mortality and Morbidity in the 21st Century,"
    *Brookings Papers on Economic Activity,* Spring 2017; Brian Feldman, "The De-
    cline of Black Business," *Washington Monthly,* March/April/May 2017.

## CONCLUSION

1   "Address to be Delivered by Wright Patman, Before the National Conference of the 4-H Clubs, on Tuesday, June 24, 1941, at 10:30 A.M., in the Auditorium of the South Building, U.S. Department of Agriculture," Washington, D.C., Box 16A, WPP.

2   Matt Stoller, "How Democrats Killed Their Populist Soul," *Atlantic,* October 6, 2016, https://www.theatlantic.com/politics/archive/2016/10/how-demo crats-killed-their-populist-soul/504710/.

3   David Leonhardt, "The Monopolization of America," *New York Times,* 11/25/2018; "America's Concentration Crisis," Open Markets Institute, 2019, https://concentrationcrisis.openmarketsinstitute.org/.

4   Tweet by @TomGara, 3:23p.m., May 6, 2017, https://twitter.com/tomgara/status/860938163526799362?lang=en; "Senate Committee Vents About Hijacking of Big Tech for Information War," NPR, September 5, 2018, https://www.npr.org/2018/09/05/644607908/facebook-twitter-heavies-set-to-ap pear-at-senate-hearing-google-may-be-mia; Pranav Dixit, "Sri Lanka Has Blocked Most Major Social Networks After A Facebook Post Sparked Anti-Muslim Riots," *Buzzfeed,* 5/13/2019, https://www.buzzfeednews.com/article /pranavdixit/sri-lanka-has-blocked-most-major-social-networks-after-a.

5   Taylor Soper, "Report: Amazon takes more digital advertising market share from Google-Facebook duopoly," *Geekwire,* 2/20/2019, https://www.geek wire.com/2019/report-shows-amazon-taking-digital-advertising-mar ket-share-google-facebook-duopoly/; "Google embraces ad-blocking via Chrome," *Economist,* 2/17/2018; search engine market share data from Statcounter, accessed June 8, 2019 (http://gs.statcounter.com/search-engine -market-share); Steven Englehardt and Arvind Narayanan, "Online Tracking: A 1-million-site Measurement and Analysis," in *CCS '16: Proceedings of the 2016 ACM SIGSAC Conference on Computer Communications Security, Vienna, Austria— October 24–28, 2016,* pp. 1388–1401, Association for Computing Machinery, https://doi.org/10.1145/2976749.2978313; "Mobbo Reveals Which Ad Networks Perform Best for Mobile App Marketers," *PR Newswire,* 2/14/2017, https://www.prnewswire.com/news-releases/mobbo-reveals-which -ad-networks-perform-best-for-mobile-app-marketers-300413189.html; Jonathan Taplin, "Is It Time to Break Up Google?" *New York Times,* 4/22/2017; Elisa Shearer and Katerina Eva Matsa, "News Use Across Social Media Platforms 2018," Pew Research Center, 9/10/2018, https://www.journalism .org/2018/09/10/news-use-across-social-media-platforms-2018/pj_2018-09 -10_social-media-news_0-01/.

6   Nicholas Thompson and Fred Vogelstein, "Inside the Two Years that Shook Facebook—And the World," *Wired,* March 2018, https://www.wired.com/ story/inside-facebook-mark-zuckerberg-2-years-of-hell/.

7   Penelope Muse Abernathy, "The Expanding News Desert," UNC School of Media and Journalism, Center for Innovation and Sustainability in Local Media, link, https://www.poynter.org/news/about-1300-us-communities -have-totally-lost-news-coverage-unc-news-desert-study-finds.

8   "Hearing before the Joint Economic Committee of the Congress of the United States," in *The Future of Newspapers: The Impact on the Economy and Democracy*, September 24, 2009; see comments of Denise Rolark Barnes, Publisher, *The Washington Informer,* https://www.gpo.gov/fdsys/pkg/CHRG-111shrg55622 /html/CHRG-111shrg55622.htm.

9   Advocates for Independent Business, "Independent Retailers and the Changing Retail Landscape," November 2017 survey, https://ilsr.org/wp-content /uploads/2017/11/2017_SurveyFindings_ChangingRetailLandscape.pdf.

10  Brad Stone, *The Everything Store*, p. 25.

11  Ibid., p. 28.

12  See Lina M. Khan, Amazon's "Antitrust Paradox," *Yale Law Journal* 126 (2016), https://www.yalelawjournal.org/note/amazons-antitrust-paradox; Stacy Mitchell and Olivia Levecchia, "Report: How Amazon's Tightening Grip on the Economy Is Stifling Competition, Eroding Jobs, and Threatening Communities," Institute for Local Self-Reliance, November 29, 2016, https://ilsr.org/amazon -stranglehold/.

13  Jeffrey A. Trachtenberg, "'They Own the System': Amazon Rewrites Book Industry by Marching Into Publishing," *Wall Street Journal,* 1/16/2019; Joshua Brustein, "Amazon Turbocharged Audible's Domination of Audiobooks," *Bloomberg,* 3/13/2018.

14  Karen Weise, "Amazon Knows What You Buy. And It's Building a Big Ad Business From It," *New York Times,* 1/20/19, https://www.nytimes .com/2019/01/20/technology/amazon-ads-advertising.html; https://seeking alpha.com/article/4140036-much-amazon-web-services-worth-now.

15  Stone, *The Everything Store*, p. 84.

16  "Anticipating the 21st Century: Consumer Protection Policy in a New High-Tech, Global Marketplace," May 1996, Federal Trade Commission, Commission and Staff Reports, https://www.ftc.gov/reports/anticipating-21st-century -competition-consumer-protection-policy-new-high-tech-global.

17  Charles Duhigg, "The Case Against Google," *New York Times Magazine,* 2/20/2018, https://www.nytimes.com/2018/02/20/magazine/the-case-against -google.html.

18  Press release from Interactive Advertising Bureau on December 21, 2007, "Interactive Advertising Bureau Supports FTC's Embrace of Self-Regulation of Behavioral Advertising," https://www.iab.com/news/interactive-adver tising-bureau-supports-ftcs-embrace-self-regulation-behavioral-advertising/; "Online Behavioral Advertising: Moving the Discussion Forward to Possible Self-Regulatory Principles: Statement of the Bureau of Consumer Protection

Proposing Governing Principles For Online Behavioral Advertising and Requesting Comment," Federal Trade Commission statement, December 20, 2007, https://www.ftc.gov/public-statements/2007/12/online-behavioral-advertising-moving-discussion-forward-possible-self.

19  Australian Competition and Consumer Commission, "Digital Platforms Inquiry: Preliminary Report," December 2018, p. 27.

20  "Federal Trade Commission Closes Google/DoubleClick Investigation," Federal Trade Commission press release, December 20, 2007, https://www.ftc.gov/news-events/press-releases/2007/12/federal-trade-commission-closes-googledoubleclick-investigation.

21  "In the matter of Google/DoubleClick, F.T.C. File No. 071-0170, Dissenting Statement of Commissioner Pamela Jones Harbour," December 20, 2007, https://www.ftc.gov/sites/default/files/documents/public_statements/statement-matter-google/doubleclick/071220harbour_0.pdf.

22  Michael Grothaus, "Google Drive will surpass a billion users this week," *Fast Company*, 7/26/2018, https://www.fastcompany.com/90208580/google-drive-will-surpass-a-billion-users-this-week.

23  David Kirkpatrick, *The Facebook Effect: The Inside Story of the Company That Is Connecting the World* (New York: Simon & Schuster, 2010), p. 254.

24  Alexis de Tocqueville, *Democracy in America* (London : Saunders & Otley, 1835).

25  Oral history transcript, Wright Patman, interview 1 (I), 8/11/1972, by Joe B. Frantz; *LBJ Library Oral Histories*, LBJ Presidential Library, accessed June 08, 2019, p. 1-2, 45, 49, https://www.discoverlbj.org/item/oh-patmanw-19720811-1-74-97; Mark Stanley "The Death of Wright Patman: Mourning the End of an Era," *East Texas Historical Journal*:Vol. 42: Iss. 1, (2015), http://scholarworks.sfasu.edu/ethj/vol42/iss1/9.

# INDEX

# ABOUT THE AUTHOR

MATT STOLLER is a Fellow at the Open Markets Institute. Previously, he was a senior policy advisor and budget analyst to the Senate Budget Committee. He also worked in the U.S. House of Representatives on financial services policy, including Dodd-Frank, the Federal Reserve, and the foreclosure crisis. He has written for *The New York Times*, *The Washington Post*, *The New Republic*, *Vice*, and *Salon*. He lives in Washington, D.C.